Modern Economic Thought

The American Contribution

Modern Economic Thought

The American Contribution

By

ALLAN G. GRUCHY

PROFESSOR OF ECONOMICS
UNIVERSITY OF MARYLAND

REPRINTS OF ECONOMIC CLASSICS

AUGUSTUS M. KELLEY · PUBLISHERS
NEW YORK · 1967

FIRST EDITION 1947
(New York: Prentice-Hall, Inc., 1947)

Reprinted 1967 by
AUGUSTUS M. KELLEY · PUBLISHERS
BY ARRANGEMENT WITH ALLAN G. GRUCHY

LIBRARY OF CONGRESS CATALOGUE CARD NUMBER

66 - 22624

PRINTED IN THE UNITED STATES OF AMERICA
by SENTRY PRESS, NEW YORK, N. Y. 10019

To Florence

Preface

It is the purpose of this study to inquire into the nature and significance of the American movement to reconstruct economic science which had its beginnings in the work of Richard T. Ely, Simon N. Patten, and Thorstein Veblen, and which has in recent years undergone considerable modification at the hands of John R. Commons, Wesley C. Mitchell, John M. Clark, Rexford G. Tugwell, Gardiner C. Means, and other American economists with a similar approach to economic studies. It is now generally conceded by historians of the evolution of economic thought that this movement to revamp economics has turned out to be the most distinctive American contribution to the progress of economic science. Although by now the general pattern of the movement is fairly clear, as yet little has been done to explain in any detailed fashion the nature and scope of the scientific reconstruction envisioned by Veblen and other critics of economic orthodoxy. It is the general aim of this treatise to endeavor to remove this deficiency in the field of modern American economic thought.

In the first three decades of the current century the American movement to revamp economic science came to be known as "institutionalism," while the work of the economists concerned with this movement was described as "institutional economics." In the closing years of Veblen's career there appeared other American economists who were also greatly interested in the reconstruction of economics. Although their work has much in common with Veblen's economics, the younger exponents of economic heterodoxy do not describe their thought as "institutional economics." Such terms as "social," "experimental," and "collective" have been substituted for "institutional" in descriptions of the new economics. Since 1929, the year in which Veblen died, it has increasingly become the custom to use the term "institutional" to refer to Veblen's special accomplishments rather than to describe the efforts of post-Veblenian economists to carry on the work of reconstructing economics. It is not proposed in this study that any attempt should be made to alter the use of the term "institutional" which is now well established both in this country and abroad. The writer is of the opinion that no useful purpose would be served in running counter to the usage which keeps the term "institutional" intimately associated with the name and work of Thorstein Veblen. The suggestion is therefore made that some other term be adopted to describe the work of those American economists, including Veblen, who have been responsible for what the writer calls the distinctive American contribution to modern economic thought. Since none of the descriptive terms used by the heterodox economists who came on the scene after Veblen has become widely used, the term "holistic" has been adopted in this study to describe the twentieth-century version of economics which has been developed by Veblen, Commons, Mitchell, J. M. Clark, and other exponents of economic heterodoxy. The term "holistic" has been selected because it calls attention to what is most characteristic of the new economics: its interest in studying the economic system as an evolving, unified whole or synthesis, in the light of which the system's parts take on their full meaning.

The writer does not agree with those who believe that the new economics is a minor flank attack upon economic orthodoxy which will prove to be ephemeral; instead, it is his conviction that "holistic economics" is the product of a genuine reconstruction which will turn out to be of lasting significance. This twentieth-century version of economics reflects the many important changes which have occurred in the past half-century in both the material and intellectual foundations of American economic life. It came into being during that stage in the evolution of the American economy not only when this economy was undergoing many basic changes in both its structure and functioning, but also when new scientific and philosophical developments were playing havoc with inherited ways of thinking about human nature and the external world. As a product of the new age of mass production and monopolistic enterprise, the economics of Veblen, Commons, Mitchell, and other critics of economic orthodoxy stands in marked contrast to the equilibrium economics which originated in the era of small-scale, competitive capitalism. This contrast arises from the fact that the new economics introduces fundamental changes in philosophical orientation, methodological approach, and psychological interpretation.

What is particularly important about the work of the holistic economists is that it represents one of the most thoroughgoing attempts to close the gap between economic theory and practice. The bridging of this gap is one of the most urgent problems now demanding attention from those who are deeply concerned with the future progress of the science of economics.

The procedure followed in this study of the American contribution to modern economic thought has been to select six outstanding exponents of holistic economics for special consideration. These six economists have been chosen for special treatment for the reasons that they have all written fairly extensively about major economic problems, they have approached the problems of economic science from the viewpoints of substantially different specialized interests, and they all have also taken time to discuss the relations between their specialized economic studies and the broader problem of reconstructing economics. The procedure in each chapter has been to discuss first the economist's intellectual orientation, then to pass on to his views on scientific methodology, his theory of human behavior, and his analysis of the structure and functioning of the modern economy, and finally to analyze his views on the nature and scope of economic science as seen in the light of the prior discussion. In the concluding chapter the writer summarizes the contributions of Veblen, Commons, Mitchell, Clark, Tugwell, and Means, and then goes on to indicate how these contributions fit into the framework of a twentieth-century version of economic science.

Whatever repetition is involved in the above-mentioned procedure serves the useful purpose of emphasizing the point that the American exponents of economic heterodoxy comprise a distinct new school of economic thought. It has all too frequently been said that these economists have been united in their attack upon economic orthodoxy, but that they have shown no similar unity in handling the more difficult problem of reconstructing economics. A careful study of the work done by these heterodox economists since 1900 does not support this criticism of holistic economics. On the contrary, such a study reveals what may be to some students of economic thought a surprising degree of uniformity in the holistic economists' proposals for the building of a realistic twentieth-century version of economics.

The writer is exceedingly grateful to Wesley C. Mitchell, John M.

Clark, Rexford G. Tugwell, Gardiner C. Means, and the late John R. Commons for reading and criticizing the chapters dealing with their economic thought. While he has benefited very greatly from their constructive criticisms, the writer must nevertheless assume sole responsibility for whatever interpretations he has placed upon the work of these economists. Dr. Dudley Dillard of the Department of Economics of the University of Maryland and Mrs. Louisa Gardner Dillard read the entire manuscript and gave the writer the full benefit of their careful scrutiny of what he had to say. He is greatly indebted to them for their many constructive suggestions and their sympathetic handling of the entire study. Professor Martin G. Glaeser of the University of Wisconsin and Professor John S. Gambs of Hamilton College were kind enough to read various portions of the manuscript. The author also desires at this time to thank the Social Science Research Council for its financial assistance in the preparation of this study.

ALLAN G. GRUCHY

College Park, Maryland
April 3, 1947

Contents

CHAPTER   PAGE

1. INTRODUCTION: ECONOMICS IN TRANSITION   1

The Great Depression and the Growth of Economic Heterodoxy   5
The Philosophical Basis of Economic Orthodoxy . . .   10
The Philosophical Foundation of Economic Heterodoxy .   15
The School of Holistic Economists   18
Cultural vs. Formal Economics   21
Holistic Economics as a Cultural Science   23

2. THE INSTITUTIONAL ECONOMICS OF THORSTEIN VEBLEN . .   31

Veblen's Criticism of Marshall's Basic Assumptions . . .   35
Veblen's Criticism of Marshall's Methodological and Psychological Theory   45
The Concept of Process   50
Veblen's Social Psychology   58
Veblen's Theory of Institutions   68
The Interpretation of Modern Capitalism   80
Consequences of the Corporate Revolution   93
The Theory of Economic and Pecuniary Values   105
The Nature and Scope of Veblen's Institutional Economics   116
The Significance of Veblen's Institutional Economics . .   123

3. THE COLLECTIVE ECONOMICS OF JOHN R. COMMONS . . .   135

Commons' Background Influences   138
Commons' Pragmatic Approach   155
The Theory of the Labor Movement   168
The Theory of Banker Capitalism   189
Judicial Sovereignty and Reasonable Capitalism . . .   199
Commons' Framework of Interpretation   214
The Nature and Scope of Collective Economics   233

CHAPTER   PAGE

4. THE QUANTITATIVE ECONOMICS OF WESLEY C. MITCHELL . 247

Mitchell's Pragmatic Psychology 253
The Quantitative Method of Analysis 264
The Scope of Economics 273
The Theory of Economic Guidance 282
Mitchell's Theory of the Business Cycle 290
Economic Reform and National Planning 301
The Concept of Economic Welfare 314
Mitchell's Pragmatic Economics 323

5. THE SOCIAL ECONOMICS OF JOHN M. CLARK 337

Clark's Intellectual Background 340
Clark's Pragmatic Psychology 349
The Economics of Overhead Costs 357
Clark's Theory of Social Organization 370
The Social Control of Business 375
Clark's Social-Liberal Planning Program 383
The Nature and Scope of Social Economics 394

6. THE EXPERIMENTAL ECONOMICS OF REXFORD G. TUGWELL . 405

The Economics of Simon N. Patten 408
Tugwell's Psychological and Methodological Views . . . 416
The Theory of Economic Development 425
Tugwell's Social Management Program 436
The Nature and Scope of Experimental Economics . . . 452

7. THE ADMINISTRATIVE ECONOMICS OF GARDINER C. MEANS . 473

The Corporate Revolution 479
The Problem of Economic Stability 493
The Concept of a Managed Equilibrium 509
Means's National Planning Program 519
The Nature and Scope of Administrative Economics . . 527

8. THE EMERGENCE OF A 20TH-CENTURY POLITICAL ECONOMY . 541

Economic Theory and the Growth of Monopoly 543
The Definition of Holistic Economics 550
The Basic Assumptions of Holistic Economics 557
The Theory of the American Economic Order 565

PAGE

CHAPTER

8. THE EMERGENCE OF A 20TH-CENTURY POLITICAL ECONOMY
   (*Continued*)

The Price Theory of the Holistic Economists 581
The Distribution Theory of the Holistic Economists . . 588
Marginalism vs. Holistic Economics 594
The Contributions of the Holistic Economists 605
The Significance of Holistic Economic Thought . . . 612
BIBLIOGRAPHY 631
INDEX 657

Modern Economic Thought

The American Contribution

CHAPTER

1

Introduction: Economics in Transition

The western world is now passing through an era of widespread economic change which presents a serious challenge to the ability of the advanced capitalistic nations to manage their economic affairs successfully on some collective basis. It is also a challenge to orthodoxy in both scientific and philosophical thought. This orthodoxy has found it increasingly difficult in recent years to withstand the attacks of those who regard the current situation as a great opportunity in which to create a better social and economic order. This is as true in economics as it is in all other fields of human thought. Since 1929 heterodox economic views have come to enjoy a wide currency, especially in the realm of national policy making. It is not surprising, therefore, to find that recent economic and political developments in the United States have once more brought into prominence the work of those enterprising economists who, ever since the establishment of Richard T. Ely's "new school" in the final quarter of the nineteenth century, have been deeply interested not only in the reform of economic society but also in the reconstruction of economic science. These heterodox economists and their followers have had considerable influence in the shaping of national economic policies in the past fifteen years. They have had much to say in those situations in which economic theory has come face to face with the concrete facts of economic experience. It is without doubt the relevance of their economic thought to the problems of the era of the Great Depression which has given these forward-thinking American economists the "wide area of power" to which their critics have made reference.[1] While trying to close the gap between theory and practice, these economists who have thought along the lines laid down by Ely, Patten, Veblen, Commons, and Mitchell have

---

[1] Robbins, Lionel, *An Essay on the Nature and Significance of Economic Science*, Second Edition, page 114. London: Macmillan and Co., Limited, 1937.

come to the front with a significant challenge to what is ordinarily referred to as "economic orthodoxy."

The movement to reconstruct economics was well established in the United States long before 1929. By 1914 Thorstein Veblen had unfolded the major features of his "evolutionary" or "cultural" version of economics. In the years before the outbreak of World War I, Veblen's disciples, who then included Wesley C. Mitchell, Robert F. Hoxie, Walton H. Hamilton, and other less well-known economists, were enthusiastic in their defense of the new economics, which came to be known as "institutional economics." [2]   Academic interest in the new version of economics became so widespread by 1918 that one of the round table conferences of the annual meeting of the American Economic Association of that year was devoted to the topic of institutional economic theory.[3]   By 1921 Veblen's institutional economics appears to have reached the high-level mark of its popularity.   In the years of prosperity which followed the depression of 1920-21 the movement to reconstruct economics continued to add new members to its list of advocates, but it did not slavishly follow the lines drawn in earlier years by Thorstein Veblen. Younger exponents of economic heterodoxy, such as John M. Clark and Rexford G. Tugwell, brought new emphases to the work of revamping economic thought.   These new members of the group of economists who were interested in modernizing economic science were prone to be somewhat less speculative and more concerned with immediate economic and social issues than was Veblen.   They were more willing to envision economic reform within the limits of the existing private-enterprise system.   Furthermore, they began to find various parts of the Veblenian interpretation somewhat outmoded. This is not to say, however, that these younger revisionists of the postwar period had developed a basic approach to economic studies which was different from Veblen's approach.   On the contrary, their work was in its essentials within the Veblenian tradition. Like the pioneering leader of the movement to revamp economics,

[2] According to A. B. Wolfe it was Max S. Handman who first described Veblen's economics as "institutional economics." Wolfe makes this claim in his article entitled "Institutional Reasonableness and Value," *The Philosophical Review*, March, 1936, Vol. XLV, page 192 fn.

[3] The discussion of the round table conference revolved about Walton H. Hamilton's paper on "The Institutional Approach to Economic Theory." See *The American Economic Review*, March, 1919, Vol. IX, Supp., pages 309-318.

these later heterodox economists had an intellectual orientation which revolved about an evolutionary, dynamic world outlook. They followed Veblen in their tendency to emphasize the importance of studying the economic system as a whole rather than as a collection of many unrelated parts. They also made use of a social rather than an individualistic interpretation of human behavior. In addition, these younger critics of economic orthodoxy possessed Veblen's interest in the problem of creating some form of collective control or management for the changing economic system.

The proponents of economic heterodoxy who appeared after 1918 were not likely to be Veblen's own students, since he did little teaching after that year. Nor was it likely that after 1918 many young Veblenians would be indirectly nurtured by his writings, since few universities gave their students any opportunity of becoming familiar with Veblen's economics. Some economists like John M. Clark and Rexford G. Tugwell, who have much of Veblen's interest in the reconstruction of economics, have been influenced by Veblen only indirectly by virtue of the fact that a great deal of his economic thinking has become a part of the intellectual milieu of the twentieth century. It is not surprising, therefore, that some of the economists who have come in recent decades to hold views about the nature and scope of economics which are similar to Veblen's views should at the same time not label their version of economic science "institutional economics." Even Wesley C. Mitchell, who is a well-known disciple of Thorstein Veblen, has not done much to popularize the use of the term "institutional." He is himself much better known as an advocate of "quantitative" than of "institutional" economics. John R. Commons, a contemporary of Veblen, published his *Institutional Economics* in 1934 at the close of a long academic career. Although he used the term "institutional" in the title of his volume on the evolution of economic thought, Commons more frequently described his type of economics as "collective," "volitional," or "investigational." Other members of the group interested in the reconstruction of economics usually refer to Veblen's work as "institutional economics," but they do not apply the same term to their own economic thought. Thus John M. Clark describes his work as "social economics," while Rexford G. Tugwell refers to his as "experimental economics."

The situation has now developed in which the American exponents of economic heterodoxy have no term which is accepted by all of them as being descriptive of their economic thinking. Since the term "institutional" is now generally used by both Veblen's critics and his proponents to refer to his special contributions to economic thought, there is no point in altering the use of the term so as to make it refer to the work of Veblen and of those other American economists who have all approached the problem of reconstructing economics from the same general viewpoint. When it is realized that some of these economists have shown a very strong disinclination to apply the term "institutional" to their own type of economic thought, there appears to be all the more reason for finding some other term which will satisfactorily describe their work as well as Veblen's. Since no descriptive term which has been used by the economists, whose work is the center of interest in this study, has come into general acceptance, the term "holistic" has been adopted in this study to describe their economic thought. This term was coined by the eminent South African scholar and statesman, Jan Christiaan Smuts, from the Greek word *holos*, which means "whole." [4]   Smuts used the new term to describe the kind of scientific thinking which grew out of the researches of Charles Darwin (1859) in biological evolution, of Antoine Henri Becquerel (1895) in radioactivity, and of Albert Einstein (1915) in the theory of relativity. This type of scientific thought is evolutionary or dynamic rather than mechanistic or static in its emphasis. It runs contrary to the type of thinking which dominated the pre-Darwinian world, and which provided the intellectual matrix from which came nineteenth-century classical economic thought. The post-Darwinian type of scientific thought which Smuts describes as "holistic" takes the physical world to be an evolving, dynamic whole or synthesis, which is not only greater than the sum of its parts, but which also so relates the parts that their functioning is conditioned by their interrelations.

The holistic viewpoint which has proven so fruitful in the biological and physical sciences is precisely the viewpoint of the heterodox economists whose work is the primary interest of this study. These economists all have the same holistic orientation or intellec-

[4] For a discussion of the meaning of the concept of holism see J. C. Smuts' chapter on the "General Concept of Holism" in his *Holism and Evolution*, pages 85-117. New York: The Macmillan Company, 1926.

tual approach which Smuts finds to be so characteristic of modern scientific and philosophic thought. As we shall see, they take the American economic system to be an evolving process or going concern any one part of which is to be fully explained only in the light of its relations to the whole dynamic economic complex. Their ultimate scientific interest is an interpretation of the functioning of the total American economic system.

The Great Depression and the Growth of Economic Heterodoxy

Two conditions account for the increasing popularity in recent years of the type of economic thought which is here described as "holistic economics." The first condition relates to the types of economic problems that have confronted the American people since 1929. The period since the onset of the Great Depression has been one in which both cyclical and secular movements have combined to disrupt seriously the smooth functioning of the American economy. After 1875 both the structure and the functioning of the American economy underwent great changes. By 1929 that economy had become a mixed or hybrid system in which monopoly was no longer a minor feature of economic activity. On the contrary, there is much support for the opinion that by 1929 the tempo of American economic life was being determined more by those industries in which were to be found large monopoly elements than by whatever competitive economic activities had survived from the nineteenth century. After 1929 the differences between the sectors of the economy in which monopolistic conditions were basic and those in which competition continued to be a dominant force were made apparent even to the man on the street. In many important large-scale industries it was obvious that selling prices neither coincided with costs of production nor responded freely to changes in supply and demand conditions. It was also apparent in the case of the large-scale industries that surplus incomes were not a temporary deviation from competitive investment returns, and that inefficient firms were not always eliminated by pressures originating with the more efficient enterprises.

Looking at the functioning of the economy as a whole after 1929, one could observe that automatic adjustments were no longer very effective. The self-limiting forces of the formerly competitive economy had been in large part replaced by the self-reinforcing forces of the new hybrid economy. Unemployment, instead of leading to those conditions such as lower selling prices and lower wages which would tend to provide more work for the unemployed, was followed by economic conditions which resulted in more rather than less unemployment. The more widespread unemployment became after 1929, the more insistent were the demands for the maintenance of old wage and price levels. Furthermore, during the depression years low interest rates, instead of causing less money saving and more consumption as the traditional analysis predicted, were accompanied by the hoarding of money and decreased consumption. In addition, lowered interest rates failed to stimulate the flow of private investment funds. In many industries the falling off of demand did not lead to lowered selling prices and a maintenance of old production schedules. The decline in demand was followed instead by a curtailment of production along with a maintenance of old price arrangements. The net effect of these wage, interest, and price developments in the years after 1929 was to make it very difficult for the nation to rise above the low levels of economic activity to which the depression had reduced it.

The holistic economists have found their economic theorizing to be quite relevant to the problems of the American economy of the 1930's with its tendency to remain at low levels of employment for men and machines. This was to be expected in view of the development of heterodox economic thought from 1900 to 1930. In the three decades prior to 1929 Veblen had written about an economy in which "partial employment" of productive resources had been a usual rather than an abnormal condition. In *The Theory of Business Enterprise* (1904), and later in *Absentee Ownership* (1923), Veblen analyzed an economic system in which the center of gravity was to be found not in competitive industries but in those industries which later economists have described as "oligopolistic" or predominantly monopolistic. Ever since 1913 Wesley C. Mitchell has been interested in explaining an economic system which has rarely been in that normal condition of equilibrium described by the equilibrium economists. In the years before the first World War John M. Clark turned to an economics in which the center of interest was in those large-scale industries in which were to be found, even "in the long run," much excess productive capacity, profits in excess of competitive returns, and selling prices not closely tied to the total cost of production per unit.[5]   From 1912 to 1917 Robert F. Hoxie and Carleton H. Parker investigated an economic system in which Taussig's "general rate of wages" was not to be found.   These two pioneering labor economists dealt with an economic system in which organized labor, collective bargaining, inflexible wage rates, and wide wage differentials were common facts rather than exceptions to the rules previously worked out by the orthodox economists.[6]

The events of the World War period of 1914-18 and the following era of postwar adjustments stimulated an interest on the part of Walton H. Hamilton, Rexford G. Tugwell, John R. Commons, John M. Clark, and others of a similar intellectual bent in the problem of what Hamilton described in 1918 as the "larger and more comprehensive control of economic activity and development."[7] The legacy of the first World War to these unorthodox economists, some of whom had actually helped to plan the war economy of 1917-18, was an interest in the functioning of the total economy with an eye to its collective management in the future for the enlargement of general economic welfare.   All during the 1920's, even in the face of strong disagreement on the part of the entrenched orthodox economists and of little interest on the part of a population which had been lulled into a false feeling of security by a belief in permanent national prosperity, the exponents of economic heterodoxy continued to think along lines that were to prove of particular national interest after 1929.   In their 1924 "manifesto of the younger generation," published in *The Trend of Economics,* W. C. Mitchell, J. M. Clark, R. G. Tugwell, A. B. Wolfe, M. A. Copeland, and S. H. Slichter called for the construction of an economic science that would pay more attention to the theory of production and less to the mechanics of a competitive price system.   The older economics

[5] Clark, J. M., "A Contribution to the Theory of Competitive Price," *The Quarterly Journal of Economics,* Aug., 1914, Vol. XXVIII, pages 747-771.

[6] Hoxie's economic thought is presented in his collected essays and lecture notes under the title of *Trade Unionism in the United States.* New York: D. Appleton-Century Co., 1917. See also Hamilton, W. H., "The Development of Hoxie's Economics," *The Journal of Political Economy,* Nov., 1916, Vol. 24, pages 855-883. For Parker's views on labor problems see his essay entitled "Motives in Economic Life," *The American Economic Review,* March, 1918, Vol. VIII, Supp., pages 212-231, and also *The Casual Laborer and Other Essays,* 1920.

[7] Hamilton, W. H., "The Place of Value Theory in Economics," *The Journal of Political Economy,* March, 1918, Vol. 26, pages 345-407.

of the market place was to recede into the background as economists turned their attention to the problems of surplus incomes and inequalities of income distribution.   Prior to 1929 these critics of economic orthodoxy were well aware of the growing deficiencies of the free enterprise system.   They observed that the consumer had lost much of his power to direct the flow of productive activity, and that, in addition, the system of free capitalistic enterprise habitually underproduced.   These conditions had been revealed in a striking manner by The Federated American Engineering Societies' study on *Waste in Industry* (1921), and by the report of the President's Conference on Unemployment on *Business Cycles and Unemployment* (1923).   The heterodox authors of *The Trend of Economics* asserted that business management was concentrating its attention on securing markets rather than on improving industrial techniques and on eliminating waste.   They also found that labor was emulating business management by adopting restrictive policies, and that a deep-seated and extremely bitter conflict between capital and labor was being fostered.

The opponents of economic orthodoxy oriented their economic thinking about the central problem of how to control the working of the economic system.   Their economic theorizing had a strong pragmatic flavor which was fully appreciated only after the debacle of 1929.   As early as 1921 Veblen had provided the bare outlines of a planned economy in *The Engineers and the Price System*.   In 1926 John M. Clark made a plea in his *Social Control of Business* for more intervention by the federal government in the nation's economic affairs.   Wesley C. Mitchell found in his study, *Business Cycles: The Problem and Its Setting* (1927), that the American economy of the decade of the 1920's was one in which there was little effective coordination of its many activities.   As he put it in 1927, the economic system in the large had "neither general plan nor central direction."   In his treatise on *Industry's Coming of Age* (1927) Rexford G. Tugwell pointed out long before Alvin H. Hansen and other later exponents of the theory of a mature capitalism that the American economy was passing out of adolescence into industrial adulthood.   He explained that the mature industrial system called for new economic attitudes on the part of those who were most responsible for that system's direction.   There was also a need for new institutional arrangements which would provide for more centralized control of the economy. The same problem was analyzed by Horace Taylor in 1928 in his *Making Goods and Making Money*. Taylor stated that our economy would not make use of its great productive potentialities until there was a higher degree of correspondence between our social interests in making goods and our private interests in making money.

Although the types of economic problems of concern to the holistic economists and the theories created by them to deal with these problems were such as to make their economic thought of widespread interest in the years after 1929, there was a second important factor contributing to the popularity of their work. This second factor was the intellectual or philosophical orientation of the holistic economists, which proved to be quite attractive to many social science students in the post-1929 era of great economic and social change. It was an intellectual orientation that was appropriate to an era of widespread dissatisfaction with traditional modes of thought and action.

The intellectual orientation of an economist constitutes the general framework of interpretation into which he fits his thought on particular economic issues, and in the light of which he makes his suggestions for the improvement of economic society. This framework of interpretation is a "Weltanschauung," or world view of things. It is the economist's point of departure in his analysis of the realities of the economic world. It constitutes, in essence, a way of thinking about or of interpreting the world of reality. This intellectual orientation or way of looking at things is of great importance, since it determines the scope of scientific investigation. The scientist's Weltanschauung or general framework of interpretation establishes the borders within which his theorizing is carried on. It influences the manner in which the scientist goes about selecting and organizing his data, and determines how far he will go in abstracting from the facts of concrete experience.[8] This framework of interpretation or way of looking at things is the end product of the

---

[8] Social scientists are slowly beginning to realize the importance of the investigator's intellectual orientation with respect to the broad contours of his theorizing. In the field of history Charles A. Beard has pointed out that ". . . any selection and arrangement of facts pertaining to any large area of History, either local or world, is controlled inexorably by the frame of reference in the mind of the selector and arranger. This frame of reference includes things deemed necessary, things deemed possible and things deemed desirable . . . any written history involves the selection and organization of facts by the processes of thought.

scientist's personal make-up, his contacts with the flow of human events, with the work of illustrious thinkers, with great books, and with whatever is of significance in the molding of the human mind. It is not something that the scientist subjects to verification by any inductive procedure. Instead, it is a mental set with which the scientist, either consciously or unconsciously, begins his investigations.[9] All scientists have frameworks of interpretation or mental sets, but unfortunately for the progress of scientific thought they are not all fully aware of their own Weltanschauungen.

The Philosophical Basis of Economic Orthodoxy

The importance of the economist's intellectual orientation can best be explained by contrasting the intellectual orientation of the heterodox economists with that of the orthodox academic economists of the nineteenth century and their twentieth-century followers. The intellectual orientation of the academic economists who dominated American economic thought prior to 1929 was a static orientation in the light of which the world, as Allyn A. Young explained, was analyzed in terms of "some simple and stable mechanism." [10] The economic system was taken by the economists who possessed this static orientation to be a stable order of things, the functioning of which could be reduced to a highly refined "system of general relations." This mechanistic Weltanschauung or world view emphasized the fixed or persisting features of economic life to the neglect of the dynamic, changing aspects of economic activity. It assumed that beneath the fluctuations of daily economic activity there was an abiding structure or order which should be the main concern of the economist. An analysis of this underlying static order was supposed to provide a body of general economic principles of universal applicability.

This selection and organization—a single act—will be controlled by the historian's frame of reference composed of things deemed necessary and of things deemed desirable." See Beard's presidential address entitled "Written History as an Act of Faith," in *The American Historical Review*, Jan., 1934, Vol. XXXIX, pages 227-228.

[9] Thorndike, E. L., *Human Nature and the Social Order*, page 10. New York: The Macmillan Company, 1940.

[10] Young, A. A., "Economics," in *Research in the Social Sciences*, edited by Wilson Gee, page 60, New York: The Macmillan Company, 1929; and "Economics as a Field of Research," *The Quarterly Journal of Economics*, Nov. 1927, Vol. XLII, page 70.

This mechanistic or static intellectual orientation of the academic American economists of the 1920's had its origins in the English philosophic and scientific thought of the seventeenth and eighteenth centuries. It was Sir Isaac Newton who popularized the concept of a static universe among the physical scientists of the seventeenth century. For Newton, as for the later classical physicists of the eighteenth century, the universe was a closed, unchanging order or system whose operations could be reduced to a number of unchanging or universal propositions or laws. Newton was followed in the eighteenth century by John Locke and other deistic philosophers, and by the Scottish common-sense philosophers, who conceived the social and physical worlds to be parts of a divinely ordered cosmos. This cosmos of the eighteenth-century English and Scottish philosophers was like Newton's universe in that it was a block universe of a static nature. Since this block universe was held to be unchanging, change and development were regarded by these eighteenth-century thinkers as superficial phenomena of no basic significance.

This mechanistic interpretation of the physical and social worlds was imported into the United States during the eighteenth century. By 1800 it had become the accepted view of most of those individuals who taught the social and natural sciences in American universities.[11] This was especially true in the field of economics, where academic economic thought flourished as a mixture of the static philosophy of the Scottish common-sense philosophers, Thomas Reid and William Hamilton, and of the mechanistic social science of David Ricardo, James Mill, and William Nassau Senior. In the period from 1800 to 1850 the theorizing of such American economists as John McVickar, Henry Vethake, Francis Wayland, and Thomas Cooper followed the eighteenth-century design of an abstract science concerned with the universal principles of a mechanistic world of free competition. The main currents of academic economic thought in the United States followed the same general direction after 1850. Arthur L. Perry in his *Elements of Political Economy* (1866) and Francis Bowen in his *American Political Economy* (1870) continued well after the Civil War to regard the economic system as

---

[11] For a discussion of the influences shaping American scientific and philosophic thought at this time see Riley, Woodbridge, *American Thought*, 1915, especially Chapters III and IV, and Townsend, H. G., *Philosophical Ideas in the United States*, 1934, Ch. VIII, "The Academic Tradition," pages 96-115.

"God's handiwork," and its laws of operation as "the ordinances of Divine Providence." [12]   Both the economic system and the laws of its functioning were held by these mid-century economists to be of an immutable, static nature.   From 1875 to 1899 orthodox American economic thought had to contend with the claims of Richard T. Ely's "new school" of economists, who asserted that the older political economy was excessively abstract and unrealistic.[13]   For a quarter of a century economic orthodoxy in the United States was on the defensive.   It was rescued from this uncomfortable position in 1899 by John Bates Clark, who inaugurated that neo-classical revival in the United States which was to continue for the next thirty years.   In his *Distribution of Wealth* (1899) Clark injected new vigor into the study of "Static Social Phenomena" and into the search for what he called the "Universal Laws of Economics."   By 1900 academic American economics was back in the same intellectual groove in which it had been in 1800; that is to say, it was once more under the influence of the mechanistic intellectual orientation which had been so popular at the beginning of the nineteenth century.   Although a considerable refinement of the main body of orthodox economic thought had been achieved in the century after 1800, the spirit and essence of the science as it was taught in most university class rooms remained substantially unaltered all during the century.

Although the neo-classical revival in the United States reached its high water mark under the stimulus of the leadership of J. B. Clark, F. A. Fetter, Irving Fisher, and F. W. Taussig in the decade preceding the outbreak of the first World War, neo-classicism continued to have a considerable influence on the development of American economic thought long after 1914.   The mechanistic intellectual orientation, the interest in equilibrium analysis, and the search for the general principles of an abstract economic science continue even now to be the main interests of many academic econ-

---

[12] Perry, A. L., *Elements of Political Economy*, 1867, Second Edition, page 28. A short review of the development of economic thought in this period is given by Normano, J. F., in *The Spirit of American Economics*, pages 53-116.   New York: The John Day Company, 1943.

[13] For the views of Ely's "new school" see his essay on "The Past and the Present of Political Economy," in the *Johns Hopkins University Studies in Historical and Political Science*, Second Series, III, 1884, and the contributions of E. R. A. Seligman, E. J. James, and H. C. Adams in *Science-Economic Discussion*, 1886.

omists in spite of the growing dissatisfaction of many individuals with the established orthodox economics. Textbooks are still largely written in the pattern sanctioned by Alfred Marshall and John Bates Clark at the turn of the century.

Recent American economics textbook writers have for the most part not attempted to provide their readers with an interpretation of the dynamic American capitalistic economy. They have written instead in terms of a highly abstract universal science. Thus Albert L. Meyers, in his widely used *Elements of Modern Economics* (1937), defines economics in general terms as "the science that deals with human wants and their satisfaction." Meyers' volume on elementary economic principles gives the student what Frederic B. Garver and Alvin H. Hansen have described as a "whole arsenal" of analytical tools or heuristic devices which may be used to explain any economic system of any time and place.[14] His elementary treatise does not provide the student with anything that approaches being an explanation of the functioning of that total cultural complex known as modern capitalism. Other textbook writers who are even more formalistic than is Meyers seek to reduce economic science to the level of mere tool-making. The "fundamental tools of analysis" which are the object of these formalistic economists' attention are supposed to be applicable to any type of economic system. In his extremely formal textbook entitled *Economic Analysis* (1941) Kenneth E. Boulding takes economic analysis to consist of "a body of general principles and a discipline of logic which may be applied to the interpretation of all economic problems, past or present." Although the work of Meyers, Boulding, and other recent textbook writers is without doubt of considerable value as far as it goes, one notes a tendency on their part to direct their readers' attention more to "the discipline of logic" than to a realistic interpretation of twentieth-century capitalism.

Even in the case of those academic economists who have in recent years felt a need to revise the system of neo-classical economics so as to give more attention to the facts of monopoly behavior, the inherited intellectual orientation with its mechanistic bias continues to exert a powerful influence. This is quite evident in the case of Edward Chamberlin's study of monopolistic competition. Chamber-

[14] Garver, F. B., and Hansen, Alvin H., *Principles of Economics*, Revised Edition, page 5. New York: Ginn and Company, 1937.

lin's point of departure in *The Theory of Monopolistic Competition* (1932) is a competitive equilibrium into which he introduces various monopoly elements. As he explains it, "A complex system may be better understood by breaking it into its parts, and the problem of individual equilibrium will serve as a helpful introduction to the more complicated one of the adjustments over a wide field." [15] Instead of taking the monopoly problem to be an indication of a changed industrial order in which free competition is no longer the dominant way of doing business, Chamberlin studies monopoly as a deviation from the norm of pure competition. He fits the facts of monopoly activity into the mechanistic framework of interpretation which he took from his orthodox mentor Allyn A. Young. Chamberlin does not take the monopolistic aspects of modern industrialism to be evidence of changes at work which are carrying the modern economy far from the standard of pure competition envisioned by the nineteenth century equilibrium economists. Characteristically he is not concerned with any theory of economic development which would seek to explain the shift from competitive to monopolistic enterprise. Although he takes account of many facts that the earlier orthodox analysis ignored or omitted, and although he professes to wish to make his economic theorizing less "remote and unreal" than that of his orthodox predecessors, Chamberlin keeps his theorizing restricted to the same rigid analytical molds that served the generation of A. Marshall, J. B. Clark, and F. W. Taussig.

As long as the dominant national economic policies of the United States were those of nonintervention and official refusal to recognize the facts of economic change or to deal with its consequences, the intellectual orientation which took the world to be a "simple and stable mechanism" was not subjected to much critical analysis. Even in the era of illusory prosperity during the nineteen twenties, the established economics with its mechanistic orientation continued to monopolize both textbook writing and university instruction. When, however, the deficiencies of the private enterprise system could no longer be ignored, and national economic policy had shifted to a basis of collective management, as was the case after 1929, the established academic economics with its mechanistic intellectual orientation became less acceptable to many individuals. It

[15] Chamberlin, E., *The Theory of Monopolistic Competition,* Third Edition, page 74. Cambridge: Harvard University Press, 1938.

was found that the mechanistic outlook was not very helpful in a world where change was the order of the day. In a world where inherited economic arrangements were fast giving way to the sweep of institutional change, an economics that gave little attention to the factors transforming economic life could not help but suffer a deterioration of its intellectual supremacy. Orthodox textbook writers could continue to revise their outmoded publications, as F. W. Taussig did in 1939 with the statement that "the book remains in essentials such as it was when written thirty years ago," but those responsible for the determination of national economic policies were bound to turn to less orthodox sources for their inspiration and guidance.[16]

The Philosophical Foundation of Economic Heterodoxy

The intellectual orientation of the American exponents of economic heterodoxy stands in marked contrast to the orientation of orthodox economists. The Weltanschauung of the former group of economists is a product of the nineteenth century, and especially of the progress in human thought which occurred in the second half of that century. This heterodox orientation combines both European and indigenous American influences. It is a product of the thinking of Hegel, Marx, Darwin, and Spencer in Europe, and of Peirce, James, and Dewey in the United States. Early in the nineteenth century Georg Hegel attacked the mechanistic world view of Isaac Newton and later Anglo-Saxon thinkers. He substituted the concept of "becoming" for the idea of "being" as the keystone of his framework of interpretation. In place of Newton's concept of a closed, unchanging universe Hegel put an evolutionary view of the universe. Taking Hegel's concept of "becoming" and applying it to the realm of economic affairs, Karl Marx in 1848 presented in his *Communist Manifesto* a theory of the development of capitalistic economic organization. The evolutionary thought of Hegel and Marx was given a firm scientific foundation in 1859 with the publication of Charles Darwin's *The Origin of Species*. The philosophic concept of process or of becoming was now combined with the biological concepts of change and development. The effect of the penetration of the idea of becoming into the biological sciences

[16] Taussig, F. W., *Principles of Economics*, Fourth Edition, Vol. I, page vii New York: The Macmillan Company, 1939.

was to give the evolutionary outlook a more widespread public acceptance. It was Herbert Spencer who first popularized the evolutionary outlook among social scientists by showing the applications of Darwinian thinking to the field of social science. In the fourth quarter of the nineteenth century Spencer spread the principles of "social Darwinism" throughout England and the United States.

The new anti-mechanistic way of looking at the world order was not merely a borrowed intellectual product as far as American thinkers were concerned. A unique movement in the intellectual history of the United States was begun in 1868 by Charles S. Peirce with the publication of a number of essays on the nature and logic of scientific thought. In order to explain his scientific views Peirce had to work out an explanation of the nature of the universe. In doing so he started with the fundamental proposition that the basic features of reality are not its uniformity and its capacity to remain unaltered, but its diversity and its capacity to change and develop. As Peirce explained it, our universe began with an original "germinal nothing" which consisted of an "undefined and unlimited possibility—boundless possibility . . . freedom." [17] According to Peirce's interpretation the universe developed out of an original spontaneity which has in time, merely as the result of chance happenings, come to exhibit certain uniformities of behavior. Even now, he explained, a great deal of spontaneity and diversity remains in the world order of things. In making spontaneity and diversity primary, and uniformity and stability secondary aspects of reality, Peirce reversed the traditional way of looking at things which had come down from Isaac Newton, John Locke, Thomas Reid, and other seventeenth- and eighteenth-century British thinkers. This inversion by Peirce of the traditional way of looking at things was in effect an intellectual revolution. With one penetrating insight he had cast doubt upon the whole thought pattern or framework of interpretation of those individuals who clung to the inherited mechanistic Weltanschauung. Peirce made the point of departure for philosophic and scientific thought not a closed or block universe but an open universe filled with potentiality for

---

[17] Peirce, Charles S., "The Origin of the Universe," in the *Collected Papers of Charles Sanders Peirce*, 1935, Vol. VI, page 148, edited by C. Hartshorne and Paul Weiss. See also Muirhead, J. H., "Peirce's Place in American Philosophy," *The Philosophical Review*, Sept. 1928, Vol. XXXVII, pages 473-474.

change and development. He thus substituted a world of probabilities for the orthodox thinker's world of absolutes. Probabilities,
especially in the field of social science, leave the doors open to the
possibility of change or novelty, whereas universals or absolutes
close those doors by making change imaginary or superficial. In
this manner Peirce provided American scientists and philosophers
with a new framework of interpretation in which the physical and
social worlds could be taken to be dynamic rather than static, emergent rather than immutable. In the final analysis Peirce may be
said to have restored life and growth to a universe which had been
almost stilled by the absolutist convictions of those who clung to a
mechanistic intellectual orientation.[18]

Peirce's views on a universe filled with spontaneity, diversity, and
chance development were accepted by William James and John
Dewey, who came to regard Peirce as the founder of American pragmatism. James and Dewey, following Peirce, take the world order
to be not a stable mechanism but a continuum or an emergent process. This emergent process is a pluralistic scheme of things marked
by change, fluidity, and variety. It is dynamic and pluralistic
rather than static and monistic. The world order is composed of
many parts which are undergoing change at different rates, and
which consequently do not fit into any well-integrated or balanced
system. This order can be viewed from both the structural and
functional aspects, but it is the functional aspect that is most significant for the pragmatists. The functional aspect is held to be
basic, because a thing is defined in terms of how it functions or behaves. This view of the world order calls attention to the dynamic,
changing features of social relationships. It does not assume that
beneath the daily fluctuations of human activity there is an abiding
social order whose functioning may be reduced to a system of general
relations or a set of immutable, universal principles.

It is in the climate of intellectual opinion created by Hegel, Marx,
Darwin, Spencer, Peirce, James, and Dewey that the American
holistic economists have fashioned their intellectual orientation.
This orientation is based on a world view in which the economic
order is taken to be an open system subject to change and growth.
It is an orientation or framework of interpretation that is particu-

[18] See Morris I. Cohen's "Introduction" to Peirce's collected essays entitled
Chance, Love and Logic, 1921, page xiii.

larly useful in an era of great economic change and dislocation. It gives the student of economics a way of thinking about economic realities which fits in with the kinds of economic problems that are encountered in a period of great economic disorganization and widespread institutional change. Such an orientation focuses the attention of the individual on the factors that lead to new economic developments, on the consequences that flow from those developments, on the need to alter economic attitudes and institutional arrangements, and on the need to control the forces which lead to the disruption of old ways of making a living.

The School of Holistic Economists

The intellectual orientation of the holistic economists is not only a factor making for the favorable reception of their type of economic thought in recent years. It is also a factor that makes it possible to regard these economists as members of a distinct school. By a "school" of economists is meant a group of scientists whose work reflects a common intellectual orientation.[19] Their common orientation or world view is a fountainhead from which flows the unity that is to be found running through their economic thought. This unity which binds the members of a school of economists shows up in their framework of analysis, their psychological theory, and their scientific methodology. All three aspects of the school's work exhibit an underlying intellectual compatibility. This is well illustrated in the case of the neo-classical school of Alfred Marshall and John Bates Clark. The static framework of analysis of the neo-classicists was united with a static rationalistic psychology which pictured individuals as contemplative, calculating beings living and working in what Marshall described as the "stationary state." The psychological theory of the neo-classicists was no more dynamic or exploratory than was their mechanistic view of the economic order. Furthermore, the method of analysis employed by the neo-classicists was particularly well suited to the study of the economic system

---

[19] This is not the only way in which to define what is meant by a school of economists. Such a definition may be made in the light of other criteria such as the particular economic theories to be attributed to a group of economists, or the special concrete economic problems with which they are concerned. For the purposes of this study the separation of schools of economists from one another on philosophical grounds has been found to be the most useful way of proceeding with the analysis.

when it was taken to be a "simple and stable mechanism." Their methodological approach involved moving from the simple to the complex. It paid little attention to the economy as a dynamic functioning whole, since interest was centered on the separate parts that composed the mechanistic whole.[20] As is quite evident, the mechanistic framework of analysis, the static individualistic psychological theory, and the atomistic methodological approach of the neo-classical school all lend support to the same intellectual orientation. Individual members of the neo-classical school have varied in the extent to which they have fitted into a common intellectual mold, but the intellectual unity of the school is apparent. Even today those who work in the orthodox or neo-classical tradition are found to conform to the same general intellectual pattern that shaped the thinking of Alfred Marshall and John Bates Clark.

Just as with the school of neo-classical economists, the holistic economists have an intellectual unity running through their work. This unity finds expression in a framework of interpretation, a psychological theory, and in methodological views which are strikingly different from those of the neo-classicists. As we have seen, the intellectual orientation of the holistic economists leads them to view the economic order as an evolving scheme of things or cultural process. Associated with this organismal point of departure or framework of analysis is a collective or social psychological theory. This modern psychological theory takes the individual to be a participating member of the economy as a going concern or system. This going system conditions the behavior of the individual by setting up certain collective standards or norms of conduct. The individual is therefore treated as a social being whose behavior is largely collective and habitual. Likewise, when they come to examine the economic system, the holistic economists substitute an overall approach for the particularistic or atomistic approach of the neo-classicists. They pay special attention to the functioning of the economy as a whole, since much of the meaning of parts of the economy is de-

[20] As Talcott Parsons has so well pointed out in his analysis of Marshall's economics, this anti-organismal or atomistic approach has continued to dominate English, and it might be added American, economic and social thought since the time of Thomas Hobbes (1588-1679) and John Locke (1632-1704). See Parsons' essay on "Economics and Sociology: Marshall in Relation to the Thought of His Time," in *The Quarterly Journal of Economics*, Feb., 1932, Vol. XLVI, pages 321-330.

rived from the nature of the whole economy. The organismal framework of interpretation, the social psychology, and the holistic or overall methodological approach are all related features of one intellectual "gestalt" or pattern. It is these basic features of their way of thinking about economic problems which condition the theorizing of the American exponents of economic heterodoxy. Behind all their different scientific interests and their special economic doctrines is a common intellectual orientation which not only distinguishes these economists from their orthodox predecessors, but which also establishes them as a separate and distinct school of American economists.

In the opinion of the holistic economists the substitution of their post-Darwinian intellectual orientation for the mechanistic orientation of the neo-classicists constitutes the first step in the reconstruction of economic science. They mean by the reconstruction of economic science a general overhauling of its intellectual underpinnings or a reworking of its philosophical foundations, and the working out of the full significance for economic science of this change in philosophical foundation or intellectual approach.[21] This reconstruction of economic science has not meant a complete wiping out of all the work of earlier economists and a starting off with a clean slate. As we shall see at a later point in this study of the reconstruction of American economic science, some of its critics have mistakenly thought that holistic economics is a denial of what was accomplished by the nineteenth-century classical and neo-classical economists. The heterodox American economists of the past half century, including Thorstein Veblen, have all been aware of their great indebtedness to the long line of illustrious economists that began with Adam Smith. They realize that much of the theorizing of these earlier economists is a permanent deposit of worth-while scientific thought. No reconstruction of a science ever amounts to a

[21] Since 1875 English and American neo-classical economists have attempted to incorporate something of the Darwinian outlook into their general way of looking at the world. Thus Alfred Marshall writes of "progress" but it is progress towards the realization of some fixed goal such as maximum satisfaction. In Marshall's concept of progress there is no place for random variations or blind economic changes such as we actually find in cultural evolution. Marshall makes room for the idea of evolution without abandoning his essentially static outlook. For a further discussion of this point see Talcott Parsons, *op. cit.*, pp. 316-347.

complete break with the past.   Instead, such a reconstruction is a cumulative process which periodically breaks forth to find expression in the establishment of some new school of scientists.   In the thinking of any such new school there is much that is inherited as well as much that is novel.   The reconstruction of American economic science can be likened to the construction of a building along new architectural lines but with the aid of both old and new materials.   In the new building many remnants of old structures may be found; and also the new architectural lines are reminiscent of something from the past.   But throughout the building the general atmosphere is new and fresh, and remains so until the next epoch in man's unending quest for novel ways of self-expression.

Cultural vs. Formal Economics

In reconstructing their science the holistic economists have not sought to duplicate the formalistic science of their orthodox predecessors and contemporaries.   Instead they have endeavored to create an economics that is a "cultural" rather than a "formal" science. According to their interpretation, formal economics is a type of scientific thought which gives too much attention to the shape or form of its theorizing, and not enough consideration to the content of that theorizing and its relation to the real facts of economic life. To be sure, all science is formal to some extent, since it is the purpose of scientific thought to uncover order or pattern in the maze of daily happenings.   The scientist takes a heterogeneous mass of data, analyzes it, and extracts from this mass of data whatever regularities, uniformities, or patterns he can discover.   If he analyzes a body of data and finds no order, shape, or pattern of things in it, then the scientist finds nothing "scientific" about that body of data.   To a certain extent, therefore, all established sciences are formal, since they are concerned with bodies of knowledge that exhibit form, shape, or pattern.   However, if the scientist is to remain close to reality, he must put no more order in the facts of life than there is scientific ground for so doing.   Sometimes scientists find more form, order, or pattern in things than actually exists.   They do this by ignoring certain groups of facts, or by refusing to give adequate weight to such data.   Obsessed with the desire to make their science "exact," or to find support for their preconceived ideas, these scientists narrow their investigations, ignore large bodies of data, and fill in the gaps of their thought systems with the aid of hypothetical or fictional data in order to arrive at a position where they have a logically constructed thought system. Such a thought system may have much more form or shape, but it usually lacks content or connection with reality.

The holistic economists assert that this greater interest in "form" than in "content" dominated the development of academic economics in both England and the United States from the time of William Nassau Senior to the close of the nineteenth century. It was Senior who, in 1836, introduced the formalism in English academic economics which soon found widespread acceptance in American university circles. In *An Outline of Political Economy* (1836) Senior laid the foundation for a formalistic economics by constructing his economic thought system on the foundation of four general postulates. By limiting himself to a consideration of these four basic postulates Senior was able to contain the dynamic English economic life of the mid-nineteenth century within the limited categories of equilibrium economics. Those economic data that did not lend support to Senior's chosen postulates were either ignored or held to be unimportant. In this manner he found a deceptive amount of form or logical pattern in the data relating to the expanding capitalism of nineteenth-century England.

Senior's abstract economics was made even more formalistic by the subsequent work of J. E. Cairnes, J. N. Keynes, and W. S. Jevons. Cairnes in *The Character and Logical Method of Political Economy* (1857), and later Keynes in *The Scope and Method of Political Economy* (1890), reduced economics to the level of an abstract science made up of a number of general, universal principles. It was the master logician, William Stanley Jevons, the author of several volumes on formal logic, however, who gave the finishing touch to what he described in 1874 as the "comparatively formal science" of political economy. Jevons explained in his treatise on logic and scientific method, *The Principles of Science* (1874), that "in human affairs the real application of scientific method is out of the question," since controlled experimentation was impossible on any large scale. All that the economist could do in this situation, according to Jevons, was to retreat from reality by making economics "a mathematical science . . . comparatively abstract and general, treating mankind from simple points of view." [22]   Jevons' simple point of view turned out to be no more than a reproduction of Senior's formalistic viewpoint from which the economic system was taken to be a simple, competitive order.[23]   His formalized version of economic science took the form of a highly abstract analysis of a competitive economy in which there was nothing to prevent the establishment of a general equilibrium of all supply and demand forces in the long run.   This highly abstract view of English economic society was only a first approximation to the realities of economic experience. But the hard shell of this first approximation was such as to prevent attention being given in later stages of analysis to many of the dynamic features of economic life.   The effort to keep economic analysis within the rigid confines of static equilibrium analysis led Jevons and later neo-classical economists to oversimplify their interpretation of economic behavior.   They reduced the highly complicated, evolving industrial system of Western European nations to the form of a simple competitive economy in which economic change played no important role, and in which economic behavior was largely a simple matter of rational calculation.   In fashioning this simplified, formal version of economic science, these nineteenth-century orthodox economists largely ignored the contributions of the more recent sciences of social psychology, sociology, and cultural anthropology.   Consequently there is to be found in their type of economic thought little of the modern cultural approach.

Holistic Economics as a Cultural Science

When the economist makes his science a cultural rather than a formal science, he seeks to provide for his science a larger setting than that provided by more formal economists.   This means that the economist as a cultural scientist is prepared to abandon the restrictive conceptual schemes or thought systems of the formal econ-

[22] Jevons, W. S., *The Principles of Science*, Second Edition, pages 759-761.   London: Macmillan and Co., Limited, 1924.

[23] It is to the credit of Jevons and other formalistic economists that in actual practice they did not always follow the dictates of their extremely formal science. On occasion they turned to real economic issues and wrote significant monographs, which, however, had no place in their general scheme of reasoning.   It is the contention of the holistic economists that with a more "cultural" and less "formal" view of economic science the nineteenth-century English economists and their American contemporaries would have produced a much more socially significant version of economic science than they did.

omists. The cultural scientist seeks to achieve the aim of a broader and more realistic science by systematizing his thought within a new conceptual scheme which is broad enough to make room for the recent contributions of cultural anthropology, sociology, and social psychology.[24] The new holistic or overall conceptual scheme of the cultural economist centers in the concept of the economy as a going system or process rather than a stable mechanism. Economic society as a "connected system" is a cultural pattern or complex with a past, present, and future. It is like an historical event which mirrors within itself something of the past and the future. As a going concern the economic system has what Alfred N. Whitehead has described as an "essential unity."[25] It is not a mere assemblage of parts or elements. Instead it is a structurally interrelated whole whose many parts are functionally interdependent. Although the concept of the economic system as a cultural whole or entity implies that all its parts are functionally interrelated, this does not mean that all parts of the whole have a necessary harmony between them. Cultural harmony or balance is quite different from the equilibrium of the formalistic economists' stable mechanism. It is a balance that is brought about by a number of factors which include habitual behavior, inertia, individual self-interest, and collective action. Being open to the forces of economic and social change, this cultural balance is at best only precariously established.

In analyzing the structure and functioning of the economy, the cultural economist makes use of the principle of interrelatedness. According to this principle no part of the economic system can be adequately explained until its relations to the rest of the system have been fully explored. Each aspect of the economy must therefore be analyzed within the context of the cultural whole in which it functions. The economy as a going system may be likened to the modern physicist's concept of a "field" of force or energy. In the physicist's gravitational field the meaning of any one item or element

[24] Cf. Löwe, Adolf, Economics and Sociology, 1935. Werner Sombart has made some contributions to the framework of a new conceptual scheme. See his article entitled "Economic Theory and Economic History" in The Economic History Review, Jan. 1929, Vol. II, and also his essay on "Capitalism" in Vol. III of the Encyclopaedia of the Social Sciences.

[25] Whitehead, Alfred N., Science and the Modern World, pages 106-107. New York: The Macmillan Company, 1925.

can be grasped only by relating it to the structure and functioning of the entire field. In other words what happens at any one point within a gravitational field is the outcome of the functioning of the whole field.[26] The fields of the economist and the physicist have no precise boundaries, since a field is an area which is comprehensive enough to include all the forces or factors that have a bearing upon the problem being investigated.

The analysis of the total "economic field" leads the cultural economist to broaden his investigations, and to include within the scope of his analysis many facts ignored by more formal investigators. This explains why the cultural economist disregards the traditional boundaries of the social sciences, and why he borrows so much from the related social science disciplines. Whether he is a political scientist, a sociologist, or an economist, in each case the cultural scientist considers any data which throw light upon the functioning of the segment of the cultural complex in which he is interested.

Besides the principle of interrelatedness the cultural economist makes use of a theory of cultural development. Since the economic system has a past, present, and future, the cultural economist finds it essential to inquire into the reasons for economic change and growth, and to consider the pattern or logic of that growth. He analyzes the factors that alter the structure and functioning of the economy; and he also inquires into the consequences that flow from the alteration of that structure. Where the cultural economist has a pragmatic bias, as in the case of the members of the holistic school, his scientific analysis will be tilted towards the future. It will be concerned with the trends of economic development and with the possible outcomes of this development. Although the cultural economist cannot predict in a scientific fashion what the future course of economic development will actually be, he is in a position to draw attention to the alternative courses of development. Furthermore, he can emphasize the point that it is possible to make some useful generalizations about the nature and direction of eco-

[26] For a further discussion of the field concept see Eddington, A. S., *The Nature of the Physical World*, 1929, and Cassirer, E., *Substance and Function, and Einstein's Theory of Relativity*, 1923, translated by W. C. and M. C. Swabey. An application of field theory in the realm of historical investigation is found in Morris Zucker's *The Philosophy of American History, The Historical Field Theory*, 1945.

nomic evolution. As we have seen, this futuristic aspect of the thought of the cultural economists is not to be found in the work of the formalistic economists.

Like the German cultural scientists Max Weber and Werner Sombart, the members of the holistic school look upon social science as a study of human culture.[27] Each of the specialized social sciences like political science, jurisprudence, and economics deals with particular cultural systems or spheres. Thus political science is concerned with the political sphere of human culture, while economics deals with the economic segment of that culture. As Wesley C. Mitchell has explained, the field of economic science is "the field of human culture . . . Anthropology, history, sociology, economics, political science, social psychology, all deal with culture."[28] According to the holistic economists, economic science seeks to explain the functioning of that segment of the total cultural complex which is concerned with the provision of mankind's material needs. As Veblen once put it, economics deals with the "scheme of material life." In all historical epochs mankind has been confronted with the problem of using scarce resources or means for the satisfaction of a large number of wants. Since at any time all wants could not be fully satisfied, an "economic" problem in the form of arriving at decisions as to how to distribute a limited quantity of resources among many alternative uses arose in every cultural era. In meeting this economic or "material" problem, mankind in various times and places has created different economico-cultural systems or patterns. Thus there are today in the world such strikingly different economico-cultural systems or complexes as the American capitalistic economy, the socialistic economy of the Soviet Republics, and the rural-communal economies of India and China.

The kind of economico-cultural pattern that is investigated by an economist depends upon his special interests. The holistic economists, whose contributions to economic theory are analyzed in subsequent chapters, are primarily concerned with the latest phase in

[27] Sombart's views on the nature of economic science are outlined by M. J. Plotnik in *Werner Sombart and His Type of Economics*, 1937. See also Sombart's *Weltanschauung Science and Economy*, 1939, translated by Philip Johnson. Max Weber's views on the nature of social science are discussed by Talcott Parsons in *The Structure of Social Action*, 1937.

[28] Mitchell, W. C., "Thorstein Veblen," in *The Backward Art of Spending Money*, page 289. New York: McGraw-Hill Book Company, Inc., 1937.

the development of the American capitalistic economy; that is to say, with what Veblen described in *Absentee Ownership* as an inquiry into "the economic situation as it has taken shape during this (twentieth) century, particularly as exemplified in the case of America." From this viewpoint economic science is a study of the disposal of scarce means among various alternative ends as determined by the conditions of a mature capitalism.   In short, the economics of the holistic school turns out to be a study of the structure and functioning of twentieth-century American capitalism.   As Wesley C. Mitchell explained in one of his early essays, it is a proper aim of economists to seek to create a "theory of the capitalistic organization of business enterprise."   As he saw it, they should be less concerned with a science of formal abstractions and more interested in working out an interpretation or "theory of the current economic regime."[29]

In the final analysis the differences between the holistic and orthodox economists can be summarized as a disagreement as to how far economists should go in abstracting from real economic experience. The evolutionary intellectual orientation and the pragmatic bias of the holistic economists dispose them to search for a realistic, cultural economics.   The situation is different with the more orthodox economists.   Following the dictates of their static intellectual orientation with its anti-pragmatic bias, the economists who work in the orthodox tradition inherited from the past century are satisfied with an abstract universal type of economics.   These advocates of the formalistic viewpoint in economic analysis assert that by applying their formal principles to concrete historical situations, they can qualify or amend their formalistic economics into a more realistic type of social science.[30]   The members of the holistic school assert, in reply, that no amount of qualification or amendment of formal principles can ever convert static, formalistic economic theory into a realistic interpretation of the dynamic capitalistic economy of the twentieth century.   They state that where the economist sets out to make the core of his science a body of universal, formal principles, he later finds it impossible to clothe the logical structure of his thought system with the flesh of reality.   The heterodox American economists adhere to this position because they find that formal

[29] Mitchell, W. C., "The Rationality of Economic Activity," *The Journal of Political Economy*, Feb., 1910, Vol. 18, page 215.
[30] See Robbins, Lionel, *op. cit.*, pages 38-39.

economics is more than a mere body of economic theories. It is, more importantly, an inherited way of analyzing economic data, which in their opinion precludes the possibility of adequately comprehending the realities of twentieth-century economic experience.[31]

The arguments put forth by the school of holistic economists to support their attack on formalism in the field of economic science are discussed in considerable detail in the following chapters, which analyze the economic thought of six outstanding members of this school. These six economists, who are of primary importance for this study of the reconstruction of American economic science, are Thorstein B. Veblen, John R. Commons, Wesley C. Mitchell, John M. Clark, Rexford G. Tugwell, and Gardiner C. Means. The criticisms levelled against economic orthodoxy by these economists, and discussions of their efforts to reconstruct economic science can be found only in many scattered essays and treatises. None of these economists has taken up the task of working out a detailed statement of just what it is that constitutes the nature and scope of the field described in this study as holistic economics. The only important effort in this direction was made by John R. Commons in his volume *Institutional Economics,* but this otherwise worthwhile study fell short of presenting a well-rounded statement of the nature and scope of the new economics as it has been developed by Veblen and later critics of economic orthodoxy. There now exists a great need for a general statement of what it is that has been accomplished by those economists who have lent their support to the movement to reconstruct economic science. It is the aim of the following six chapters to lay a foundation for the general statement of the nature and scope of holistic economics which is the special topic of interest in the concluding chapter.

[31] For a recent statement of this position see Ayres, C. E., *The Theory of Economic Progress,* pages 4-7. Chapel Hill: The University of North Carolina Press, 1944.

In so far as it is a science in the current sense of the term, any sci-ence, such as economics, which has to do with human conduct, be-comes a genetic inquiry into the human scheme of life; and where, as in economics, the subject of inquiry is the conduct of man in his dealings with the material means of life, the science is necessarily an inquiry into the life-history of material civilization, on a more or less extended or restricted plan.

THORSTEIN VEBLEN: *The Place of Science in*
Modern Civilisation

The Institutional Economics of Thorstein Veblen

Among those American economists who were deeply interested in the reconstruction of economic science in the closing years of the last century was one who was destined to become known as the founder of institutionalism. The economist chosen for this important intellectual role was Thorstein B. Veblen. Other economists like R. T. Ely and S. N. Patten had turned to the problem of reconstructing economics long before Veblen, but they did not go very far beyond destructive criticism to the further achievement of providing a solid foundation for the progress of the new economics. It was Veblen's lot to become the spiritual leader of a renascence in American economic thought which was to offer a serious challenge to the economic orthodoxy of the nineteenth century. It was Veblen who emerged as the spearhead of the new movement in American economic thought, who provided this movement with the necessary philosophical inspiration, and who charted in broad outline the course that the new economics was to take in the first half of the twentieth century.

In the economics textbooks of the last quarter of the nineteenth century was summarized a body of economic doctrines which displayed all the refinement of thought and symmetry of logical construction that several generations of economists had been able to provide. It would have been much less exacting for Veblen to have accepted the contributions of these generations of orthodox economists and to have gone on to further achievements within the general framework of their equilibrium analysis, as did Herbert Davenport, John Bates Clark, Frank W. Taussig, and many other economists. Veblen, it seemed, had no choice but to contradict and refute these doctrines; everything conspired to give him a critical attitude toward the academic economics of his time. His personal make-up, his cultural origins, his social environment, and his scientific training gave him a strong predisposition for the unorthodox in human thought in general and in economics in particular.[1]

Veblen lived in an era of growing intellectual ferment. In the last quarter of the nineteenth century a new American outlook was being fashioned on the basis of fresh scientific and philosophical insights. This new American outlook was more realistic and more critical than the naive, romantic outlook which it was displacing. It heralded the development of a philosophical sophistication that had long been lacking among thinking people in the United States.[2]

While Veblen was a student at The Johns Hopkins University in 1881, Charles S. Peirce, the founder of American pragmatism, was lecturing there on the logic of science and the philosophy of scientific methodology. Peirce called attention to the deep philosophical problems that underlay scientific thought: what is meant by scientific truth, and how does the scientist go about revealing that type of truth? [3] Above all, Peirce insisted that scientific truth is derived from two sources, namely, the observed data and the general outlook or orientation of the scientist. Prior to 1880 many scientists had been unaware of the influence of their own general outlook upon the scientific truths which they uncovered. This lack of critical self-awareness led to the acceptance of extremely naive theories of the nature of scientific understanding. Peirce helped put an end to this widespread scientific naivete, and made scientists more critical of their own work. Veblen learned from Peirce and others of a similar intellectual bent, such as William James and John Dewey, to be as critical about the work of scientists as he was about the work of outmoded, speculative philosophers. He made much use of Peirce's keen observation that scientists develop relatively perma-

---

[1] Since the details of Veblen's academic career are now well known, there is no need to recount them here. Those who are not familiar with the course of Veblen's career should consult Joseph Dorfman's *Thorstein Veblen and His America*, 1934. See also Hobson, J. A., *Veblen*, 1937, and Teggart, Richard V., *Thorstein Veblen, A Chapter in American Economic Thought*, Publications in Economics, University of California Press, Vol. II, No. 1, 1932.

[2] See Parrington, V. L., *The Beginnings of Critical Realism in America*, 1860-1920, Part Two: "New Patterns of Thought," published in 1930 and edited by E. H. Eby.

[3] For a brief discussion of Peirce's views on logic and philosophy see Eugene Freeman's *The Categories of Charles Peirce*, 1934.

nent habits of thinking which serve as guiding principles in their analyses of the facts of the objective, external world.

When to the naturally skeptical outlook of Veblen is added the critical element of Peirce's pragmatic thought, the result is a searching, probing type of mind that takes little time to cut through to the essentials of a problem. This combination of personal and environmental forces was sufficient to make Veblen a mordant critic of the inherited American outlook in science and philosophy which was shot through with a naive romanticism and a blind optimism. It became one of Veblen's principal intellectual interests to expose the inadequacies of early American, pre-Darwinian scientific and philosophic thought. This he did by the simple device of questioning the basic preconceptions upon which American thought had been erected prior to 1880. Once these preconceptional foundations were revealed to have fundamental defects, it was an easy task for Veblen to proceed with the demolition of the superstructure of thought in whatever field of scientific interest he chose to concentrate his deadly attention.

If Veblen learned from Charles Peirce, William James, and others to question the substructure of inherited, scientific thought, it was from other pioneer thinkers that he learned what to substitute for those portions of inherited social science and social philosophy which he thought it necessary to discard. Veblen found much in the writings of Karl Marx that was both novel and worth while. But Marx had drawn the major outlines of his socio-economic thought without the benefit of such social sciences as cultural anthropology, sociology, and social psychology. Veblen was able to find some scientific support in the newer social sciences for what he took from Marx. These social sciences also provided him with new viewpoints from which the Marxian analysis of society could be critically examined. Of all the new social sciences the one that was most influential in shaping Veblen's thought was cultural anthropology, the study of the cultural complexes of the various races of mankind and of their influence on human behavior. It was this new branch of social science, first introduced to the American public by the publication in 1877 of Lewis H. Morgan's *Ancient Society*, that laid the foundation of much of the advanced thinking in the related fields of sociology and social psychology.

Veblen always displayed a deep interest in human culture and the study of cultural anthropology. When he was a graduate student at Yale University during the 1880's William G. Sumner was lecturing on the subject of human culture. Sumner explained how folkways and mores shaped the thinking and behaving of mankind, and how man's ideas and attitudes were largely social or cultural products.[4] This understanding of the socio-economic origin of the individual's thinking and acting proved to be a remarkable advance on mankind's intellectual front. It prepared the way for the development of a "social" as opposed to an "individual" psychology. In the work of James Baldwin, G. Stanley Hall, and Charles H. Cooley the individual became a "social self" whose behavior was largely culturally conditioned. Absorbing this new cultural approach to the interpretation of the behavior of the individual, Veblen became extremely impatient with the strongly individualistic psychology that was widely accepted by the late nineteenth-century academic economists.

The developing study of cultural anthropology also introduced a new way of comprehending socio-economic phenomena. To the cultural anthropologist culture was an evolving process and not a static mechanism. As social organization was usually undergoing change and development it was taken to be an emergent process subject to the special dynamics of cultural change. In his analysis of the emergent process the investigator came to place more emphasis on the whole process and less upon its many parts. He learned to uncover the meaning of isolated data by referring them to the larger cultural whole of which they were but minor parts. When social scientists in general absorbed this new interest in the whole rather than the part, they worked out a concept of process which became a new framework of interpretation for analyzing the data of the rapidly changing social system.

As a student of philosophy and economics Veblen had close contact with the writings of Georg Hegel and Karl Marx, who had

[4] For an example of Sumner's use of the concept of the folkway see *Essays of William Graham Sumner*, 1934, Vol. I, pages 55-58, edited by A. G. Keller and M. R. Davie. At the time that Sumner was investigating human culture there was a flourishing school of German cultural anthropologists with whose writings Veblen was undoubtedly familiar. In England Herbert Spencer and E. B. Tylor were doing similar work. For an outline of the development of the science of cultural anthropology see Alexander Goldenweiser's chapter on "Cultural Anthropology" in *The History and Prospects of the Social Sciences*, 1925, edited by Harry Elmer Barnes.

both preceded the nineteenth-century investigators of human culture in emphasizing the importance of the concepts of "process," "emergence," and "wholeness." [5]   But neither Hegel nor Marx (in his earlier writings) had had the advantage of the discoveries of the cultural anthropologists in supporting their views about the nature of human society.   Veblen was in a position to support whatever he borrowed from Hegel and Marx with a much larger fund of scientific evidence than had been available to either of his famous predecessors.   Being familiar with the new cultural anthropology, sociology, and social psychology, Veblen was in a unique position to strike out in novel directions in the field of economics.   Reaching intellectual maturity at the dawn of a new era in American social thought, it was Veblen's general aim to show how the inherited social sciences of his time, and especially the orthodox economics, were too closely wedded to outmoded ways of thinking and investigating.   But his criticisms of orthodox economics were not merely destructive.   Except for his major critical essays Veblen's economic writings are primarily devoted to an exposition of his "evolutionary economics."

Veblen's Criticism of Marshall's Basic Assumptions

The major questions which Veblen raised when he first turned to an analysis of the problems of economic science were the following: what determines the views of economists with respect to the nature and scope of economics, and how do they go about making their economic analyses? [6]   Veblen's answers to these important questions can be best explained by turning to his analysis of the work of Alfred Marshall, whose economics may be taken as the best example of the kind of economics that dominated the academic scene when

[5] Hegel and Marx had been preceded by a number of eighteenth-century French thinkers in the application of the concept of evolution to human society.   See Grossman, Henryk, "Evolutionist Revolt Against Classical Economics," The Journal of Political Economy, Oct.-Dec., 1943, Vol. 51, pages 381-96, and 506-22.

[6] Veblen realized at an early date that orthodox economists were largely unaware of these scientific questions.   A generation later Joan Robinson was to write (in An Essay on Marxian Economics, 1942, page 2) that "Marx was conscious of his purposes.   The economists were in general unconscious.   They wrote as they did because it seemed to them the only possible way to write, and they believed themselves to be endowed with scientific impartiality.   Their preconceptions emerge rather in the problems which they chose to study and the assumptions on which they worked than in overt political doctrine."

Veblen first made his critical observations on the nature and scope of economic science.[7]   In studying the economics of Alfred Marshall and of other late nineteenth-century orthodox economists, Veblen observed that the writings of these economists could be adequately understood only by inquiring into the philosophical orientation, the method of analysis, and the theory of human nature associated with their work.   It was because he could not accept their philosophical orientation, their methodological procedure, and their psychological theories that Veblen found himself unable to accept the work of the late nineteenth-century economists.

Veblen describes Alfred Marshall's economics as "systematic" for the reason that Marshall strove to build up a logically consistent thought scheme for the interpretation of the economic system.   In Marshall's *Principles of Economics,* which first appeared in 1890, there is to be found a body of economic thought dealing with the central problems of value and distribution.   These theories constitute what Marshall calls the "economic foundations" or first principles of his science.   Running through these basic economic concepts is one fundamental idea which provides a framework of reference for all of Marshall's theoretical analysis.   He explains in the preface to the first edition of his volume on the principles of economics that "As, in spite of the great differences in form between birds and quadrupeds, there is one Fundamental Idea running through all their frames, so the general theory of the equilibrium of demand and supply is a Fundamental Idea running through the frames of all the various parts of the central problem of Distribution and Exchange."[8]   Marshall makes use of this basic concept of an

---

[7] It must be kept in mind that Veblen's criticism of Marshall's economics relates to Marshall's position at the close of the nineteenth century.   As the years of the new century rolled by, Marshall modified many of his earlier views; and, in general, he came to possess a much more tentative attitude towards his economic science than he displayed in the first edition of his *Principles of Economics.* It is not surprising therefore that late in life he should observe that "A thousand years hence 1920-1970 will, I expect, be *the* time for historians.   It drives me wild to think of it.   I believe it will make my poor *Principles,* with a lot of poor comrades, into waste paper.   The more I think of it, the less I can guess what the world will be like fifty years hence."   Quoted from the *Memorials of Alfred Marshall,* edited by A. C. Pigou, page 490.   London: Macmillan and Co., Limited, 1925.

[8] "Preface to the First Edition," reprinted in Marshall, A., *Principles of Economics,* Eighth Edition, page viii.   London: Macmillan and Co., Limited, 1920. Hereafter, unless otherwise indicated, all references to the prefaces of the *Prin-*

equilibrium between demand and supply by first studying supply and demand in relation to particular commodities. He explains how values are determined in the market by the operations of the forces of supply and demand over various periods of time. He then passes from a study of market values to an analysis of the distribution of incomes. The same "scheme of general reasoning," which consists of an account of the relations between supply and demand, is applied to the earnings of labor, the interest on capital, and the earnings of management. As was the case with market values, so also wages, interest, and profits are found in the long run to reach certain equilibrium levels where they are held in balance or at rest by the equally potent forces of supply and demand.

Marshall carries out his analysis of the economic system on the assumption that beneath the phenomena of actual economic experience there is at work a set of demand and supply forces moving the economic system toward some sort of balance. This condition of equilibrium is described as a normal condition in the sense that it would be the condition found if enough time were allowed to elapse so as to eliminate all disruptive forces that interfere with the smooth functioning of the forces of demand and supply. Marshall explains that in his *Principles of Economics* "predominant attention" is paid to "the normal conditions of life in the modern age." Consequently, his economics deals with normal prices or values, with the normal willingness to save, and with the normal alertness to seek the best markets in which to buy and sell.

Marshall's principles of economics were thus woven around a normalized concept of the economic system tending toward a condition of balance or equilibrium. That the economic system tended in this direction was something to be taken for granted, not something that remained to be proved. This fundamental idea of the economy in equilibrium was a point of reference or center around which his equilibrium thought scheme was built up. Marshall was aware that in actual economic life change was constantly going on, and that there were many forces that impeded the movement of economic society towards a state of rest or balance. In the preface to the eighth edition (1920) of his treatise on the principles of economics he made reference to many non-competitive forces which

ciples of Economics and to this volume itself will be taken from the last, or eighth, edition of Marshall's work.

did not fit into his equilibrium view of the economic system.[9]   But he felt that, as these disruptive forces played only a secondary role, they did not materially alter the general trend of the economic system toward a normal condition of equilibrium.   So secondary were these forces, he believed, that there was no need to discuss them in a volume on general economic principles or "economic foundations."   In his opinion the study of these non-competitive, disruptive forces belonged "to a volume dealing with some part of the Superstructure" of the science of economics but not with its first principles.

It was Marshall's general plan to lay the foundations of his economics by first analyzing the normal conditions of a competitive economy, and then to pass on to other studies which would bring his introductory analysis somewhat closer to economic reality.   Accordingly, the first volume of his *Principles* dealt with an abstract and hypothetical model of the actual economic system to be found in highly industrialized countries at the end of the nineteenth century.   It was concerned with the "fiction" or "hypothesis of a stationary state" in which only normal, thoroughly competitive conditions prevailed.[10]   The second volume, which he projected in 1890, was intended to bridge the gap between his hypothetical or fictional view of the economic system and the actual economic system.   Whereas the first volume of the *Principles* dealt with the theoretical side of economic activity, the second volume was to be concerned with "the realistic side," with the "Industrial Revolution of the present generation, which has far outdone the changes of a century ago, in both rapidity and breadth of movement."[11]   So clearly did Marshall have this plan in mind that the early editions of his *Principles of Economics* were labelled "Volume I."   Although he gave an implicit promise in 1890 that Volume II would soon make its appearance, thirty years were to elapse before the projected work was completed.[12]

Marshall's failure to follow up the volume on introductory principles with a second volume of more realistic studies opened him to

[9] "Preface to the Eighth Edition," page xiv.
[10] *Principles of Economics*, pages 366-369.
[11] "Preface to the Eighth Edition," page xii.
[12] Marshall followed up his *Principles of Economics* of 1890 not with one but with two volumes. *Industry and Trade* appeared in 1919, and *Money, Credit, and Commerce* in 1923.

the charge that his equilibrium economics did not provide the key to a realistic interpretation of economic activity. After 1890 doubts arose as to whether or not the realities of economic life could be adequately explained by Marshall's plan of first studying the so-called normal conditions of economic life and then trying to qualify or modify the theories dealing with normal conditions so that they would somehow fit actual economic experience. In the preface to the last edition (1920) of his *Principles,* Marshall attempted to explain his failure to write a second volume "within a reasonable time" after 1890. He attributed the thirty-year delay in writing the companion volume of his *Principles* to the difficulty of making a realistic study of the rapidly changing economic system. Significantly he did not raise the question as to whether or not his *Principles of Economics,* which did not include a theory of economic change, was a suitable introduction to the study of a rapidly changing economic system. This was the fundamental question that always remained uppermost in Veblen's mind. If the basic assumptions and the point of departure of Marshall's *Principles* were inadequate for a comprehensive interpretation of economic reality, then no amount of qualification or modification of his original position or viewpoint could ever make his systematic, equilibrium economics a satisfactory introduction to the explanation of concrete economic activity. This was the conclusion to which Veblen came when he studied Marshall's treatise at the turn of the century. After 1895 Veblen's time and energy were devoted to an explanation of how he arrived at this important conclusion relating to Marshall's economics, and how he proposed to create an economics that would throw more light on the realities of twentieth-century economic experience than did Marshall's analytical economics.

In trying to show why Marshall's equilibrium economics could not lead to an adequate interpretation of concrete economic experience Veblen cut through as rapidly as possible to certain basic problems. He criticized Marshall's equilibrium economics from three different viewpoints, the philosophical, the methodological, and the psychological. An analysis of each of these critical approaches to the academic economics of Veblen's time will serve as an illuminating introduction to an inquiry into the nature and scope of his own "evolutionary economics."

Veblen attributes Marshall's choice of a static view of the economic system to Marshall's general outlook or philosophical orientation. Every economist's orientation centers in a system of beliefs which provides the ultimate or final terms for scientific analysis. "This ultimate term or ground of knowledge," said Veblen "is always of a metaphysical character. It is something in the way of a preconception accepted uncritically, but applied in criticism and demonstration of all else with which the science is concerned." [13] This philosophical orientation is of fundamental importance to the economist, since it determines how he looks at the external world around him. It influences the framework of analysis that he constructs for the guidance of his investigations, and it provides the fundamental unity which gives order and direction to the flow of his scientific thought. In addition, the philosophical orientation has a profound influence on the way the economist goes about making his investigations, and how he selects his data for analysis. The general outlook or metaphysical position permeates every part of his work, and leaves an indelible imprint on all his doctrines, hypotheses, and generalizations.

Marshall's philosophical orientation, said Veblen, was centered in a "preconception of normality," [14] one that assumed that behind the changing features of day-to-day economic life there were certain all-important, persistent, and unchanging features or aspects. In Marshall's view the economic system was similar to the external physical world, which preserves its main features in spite of the many minor changes that take place. Marshall explains his concept of "normality" in very clear language: "In the same way every use of the term normal implies the predominance of certain tendencies which appear likely to be more or less steadfast and persistent in their action over those which are relatively exceptional and intermittent." [15] The aspect of economic activity which most deeply impressed Marshall was its fixity or unchangeability. It should be recalled that his basic assumption was made in the fourth quarter of the nineteenth century, when it seemed likely that the competitive economic system would continue substantially unaltered. Indeed, the competitive tendencies of the economic order of

[13] Veblen, Thorstein, "Preconceptions of Economic Science, III," reprinted in *The Place of Science in Modern Civilisation*, page 149. New York: B. W. Huebsch, Inc., 1919.

[14] *Ibid.*, pages 173-179.

[15] *Principles of Economics*, page 34.

1875 were taken to be of a "steadfast and persistent" nature. These competitive conditions were labelled "normal conditions"; and the course of action that could be expected from individuals in these circumstances was one of "normal action." The essence of Marshall's preconception of normality was found in the assumption that the core of economic activity was of a static or fixed nature; and it was this fundamental premise that provided the ultimate terms for Marshall's economic theory.[16]

Veblen explains that the preconception of normality and the related static view of the economic system would not have come to dominate nineteenth-century economic thought had there not been powerful cultural forces making for this intellectual outcome. Marshall accepted the preconception of normality as the fundamental organizing concept of his economic theorizing because this unifying concept fitted in with the requirements of his cultural experience. It was "a reverberation of the scheme of life" to which Marshall was accustomed.[17] This is the usual experience, Veblen said, of most thinkers. Every scheme of life or culture has a great influence upon the manner in which scholars express their thoughts and make their scientific generalizations. Their culture shapes their general outlook, and provides the terms in which their thoughts are expressed.[18] This is plainly to be seen in the case of Alfred Marshall, whose economic theorizing reflects the scheme of life that was dominant in England in the first three quarters of the

---

[16] There is some evidence that Marshall was not completely satisfied with this mechanistic, rigid view of economic life. In the early editions of his *Principles* he pointed out that "It must be admitted however that the theory of stable equilibrium of normal demand and supply in its most abstract form assumes a certain rigidity in the conditions of demand and supply which really does not exist. It helps indeed to give definiteness to our ideas; and in its elementary stages it does not diverge from the actual facts of life so far as to prevent its giving a fairly trustworthy picture of the chief methods of action of the strongest and most persistent group of economic forces. But when pushed to its more remote and intricate logical consequences, especially those connected with multiple positions of equilibrium, it slips away from the real conditions of life, and soon ceases to be of much service in dealing with practical problems." Quoted from the second edition of the *Principles of Economics*, 1891, page 493.

[17] "Preconceptions of Economic Science, I," page 105.

[18] In making this investigation of the relations between cultural values and intellectual activities Veblen was a pioneer in the development of what was to be known later as the "sociology of knowledge." For a recognition of Veblen's contribution in this connection see Louis Wirth's preface (pages xvii-xix) to Karl Mannheim's *Ideology and Utopia*, published in 1940.

last century, a period when English culture was conditioned by a small-scale competitive business system in which the forces of demand and supply operated to keep the economic system reasonably close to Marshall's "normal economic conditions." Marshall's "scheme of general reasoning," based as it was on the idea of an equilibrium between the forces of demand and supply, reveals a very close connection with the competitive scheme of economic life to which he had been accustomed in the formative years of his academic career.[19]

As long as industry remained small-scale and competitive, Marshall's scheme of general reasoning, based on the preconception of normality and a mechanistic view of a competitive economic society, served as a useful point of departure for economic analysis. His equilibrium economics was close enough to the realities of nineteenth-century cultural experience in England to provide a worthwhile explanation of the operation of the economic system. But industry and business had not ever been wholly competitive, and did not remain as essentially competitive as they had been. Progress in science brought about important changes in industrial technology which were soon followed by major alterations in the shape and function of the business superstructure. As the nineteenth century wore on, the joint stock company displaced the partnership, and the public company superseded the private company; meantime the independent factory became but one link in a long chain of industrial organization, and the operations of demand and supply became progressively more complex. As a consequence of these fundamental changes in the structure and functioning of the economic system at the turn of the century, Marshall's "scheme of general reasoning" based on the preconception of normality was seriously impaired as a point of departure for an analysis of the emerging large-scale twentieth-century economy.

Marshall's faulty point of departure for the analysis of modern capitalism resulted from what Veblen describes as a cultural lag. Marshall's scheme of general reasoning was a cultural product the

---

[19] Although Marshall's *Principles of Economics* did not appear until 1890, the general shape of his economic thought was already fixed by 1879 when, in collaboration with his wife, he published his first economic treatise entitled *The Economics of Industry*. See especially the prefaces to the first two editions of this volume for a brief discussion of Marshall's scheme of general reasoning.

validity of which depended upon the continuance of the cultural conditions which had given it birth. When these cultural conditions changed, new modes of thought and new points of departure were required for a grasping of the changed economic realities. In Veblen's opinion Marshall failed to cope with this intellectual problem of the cultural lag, with the result that his economics became as outmoded as his scheme of general reasoning.

There were reasons, of course, why the preconception of normality and the related mechanistic view of economic society continued to hold economic science in their grasp after 1875. In the first place, academic economists continued to pattern their science after the science of physics, whose principles and theories were subject to verification through experimentation. Writing in 1881, Marshall was moved to observe that "Social sciences have made slower progress than physical sciences. One reason of this is that men have only recently begun to apply to social sciences those methods of classification, and that systematic study of each class of truths, which have been so useful in the physical sciences." [20] In an effort to make their science as exact as possible, and not being in a position to carry on laboratory experimentation, the academic economists resorted to the exactness of mathematico-logical analysis. Thus William Stanley Jevons asserted that "If a science at all, it (political economy) must be a mathematical science because it deals with quantities of commodities." [21] Since mathematical analysis could more readily be applied to a static rather than to a dynamic type of social situation, an economics oriented about a view of the economic system as a static mechanism continued to hold the interest of those investigators like Marshall who were skilled in mathematico-logical manipulation. "The function of a pure theory," Marshall said, "is to deduce definite conclusions from definite hypothetical premises. The premises should approximate as closely as possible to the facts with which the corresponding applied theory has to deal.

[20] *The Economics of Industry,* page 4.
[21] Jevons, W. S., *The Principles of Science,* page 759. It should be pointed out in fairness to Marshall that he was less enamored with the mathematico-logical approach to economic studies than was Jevons. Marshall appears to have been more aware of the limitations of mathematico-economic analysis than was his famous predecessor. In this connection see Marshall's Appendix D on "Uses of Abstract Reasoning in Economics," in his *Principles of Economics,* pages 781-784.

But the terms used in pure theory must be capable of exact interpretation, and the hypotheses on which it is based must be simple and easily handled." [22]   Exact interpretation was taken to mean interpretation that could be thrown into some form of mathematical expression in which the emphasis was placed upon a logically precise analysis rather than upon a realistic analysis which was close to the world of concrete realities.[23]   The outcome of this union between economic science and mathematico-logical analysis was a type of systematic or analytical economics that continued to revolve about a static competitive view of the economic system long after this view of the economic system had lost much of its conformity with reality.

A further reason for the continued vogue after 1875 of an economics that was oriented about a static, competitive view of the economic system was the imperviousness of academic economics in England and the United States to new trends in scientific thought. In the less advanced fields of social science such as sociology, cultural anthropology, and social psychology, new types of thinking met with much less resistance than was the case with economics.   After the appearance of Charles Darwin's *Origin of Species* in 1859, the social sciences other than economics experienced a period of great intellectual ferment.   The new Darwinism was added to the intellectual force of Marxian thought, which, especially in Germany, continued for many decades to fructify the thinking of social scientists.   When Veblen turned to the study of economics in 1891 there was little evidence that the main stream of Anglo-American economic thought had been appreciably affected by either Darwinian or Marxian analysis.   John N. Keynes' definitive and classic study of *The Scope and Method of Political Economy* (1890) made no reference to the contributions of either Darwin or Marx.   As far as English and American academic economics was concerned, the general scientific

[22] Quoted from Marshall by J. N. Keynes in *The Scope and Method of Political Economy*, Fourth Edition, page 240. London: Macmillan and Co., Limited, 1930.

[23] In the second half of the nineteenth century the tendency of academic economists was to sacrifice concrete reality in the interests of a logically consistent body of economic doctrine. It is not surprising, therefore, that John Neville Keynes, whose treatise on *The Scope and Method of Political Economy* (1891) became a standard work for academic economists, should also be the author of the once widely read *Studies and Exercises in Formal Logic* (1884). In Keynes' work there was consummated a union of systematic economics and formal logic.

outlooks and methodologies of both Darwin and Marx were apparently of little or no consequence. If, at the close of the last century, Veblen had consulted Palgrave's *Dictionary of Political Economy* (first published in 1894) for a definition of what he was primarily interested in, modern capitalism, he would have found that this economic term had not even been listed.

Veblen's Criticism of Marshall's Methodological and Psychological Theory

Closely tied up with Marshall's preconception of normality and his static, competitive view of the economic system were his views on scientific methodology. His method of analyzing economic data is best described as the "additive" or "summative" method of analysis. In analyzing economic life Marshall and other late nineteenth-century academic economists moved from the simple to the complex. This procedure involved a breaking up of all large, complex problems into many smaller issues that could be handled one at a time. In Marshall's own words, "The element of time is a chief cause of those difficulties in economic investigations which make it necessary for man, with his limited powers, to go step by step; breaking up a complex question, studying one bit at a time, and at last combining his partial solutions into a more or less complete solution of the whole riddle. . . . Each exact and firm handling of a narrow issue, however, helps towards treating broader issues, in which that narrow issue is contained more exactly than would otherwise have been possible." [24] Thus the way to analyze a broad economic issue is to examine the many minor issues that make up one broad issue. According to this methodological view a whole is no more than the sum of its parts; any whole is a mere summation or assemblage of its many parts or elements. The meaning of such a whole is derived from the meaning of its various parts, and is to be grasped by inquiring into the meaning of the various elements comprising the whole. Since it is held that meaning flows from the parts to the whole, the additive method is alleged to be the proper method of economic analysis.

In Marshall's opinion the proper way to analyze a whole such as the economic system is to start with inquiries into the simple

[24] *Principles of Economics,* page 366.

problems of day-to-day prices in the market place. From this beginning the investigator passes on to more complex problems of market values, and then moves on to still more complicated questions relating to the distribution of incomes. When enough "partial studies" of value and distribution have been made to cover all matters taken to be worthy of scientific investigation, the study is then brought to a conclusion. By going through this procedure of adding together many partial studies, the economist is supposed to acquire an understanding of the nature and functioning of the entire economic system. Since there is no meaning of the whole apart from the meaning of its parts, there is no special need to consider the whole economic system as a distinct entity with meaning drawn from its own collective nature. Hence it was that when Veblen examined Marshall's *Principles of Economics* he found no chapters which purported to explain the nature of the economic system as a distinct entity or organized whole.

Veblen points out that Marshall employed the additive method of scientific analysis because it was appropriate to his preconception of normality and his mechanistic view of economic society. He was predisposed to employ the additive method of analysis by the normalizing tendency of his thought processes. Since this normalizing tendency led him to pay special attention to the static, unchanging features of economic activity, it is not surprising that he chose a method of scientific analysis which had been worked out by the late eighteenth- and early nineteenth-century physical scientists to investigate what they took to be a static, mechanistic physical universe. If he had been more concerned with problems of economic growth and change and less with an analysis of equilibrium or normal conditions, Marshall might have felt the need for something beyond his inherited, additive methodology.[25]   In patterning the body of his economic thought after the work of John Stuart Mill, Marshall borrowed the methodological theory that was widely

[25] Veblen fails to point out that Marshall was aware of some of the major deficiencies of his additive or taxonomic method of scientific analysis. In 1891 Marshall stated that "economic problems are imperfectly presented when they are treated as problems of statical equilibrium, and not of organic growth. For though the former treatment [what Marshall calls "the statical method" or what Veblen calls "the additive method"] alone can give us definiteness and precision of thought, and is therefore a necessary introduction to a more philosophic treatment of society as an organism; it is yet only an introduction." Quoted from the second edition of the *Principles of Economics*, 1891, page 496

accepted by the scientific world in the middle of the last century.[26] Although Marshall made some very considerable progress beyond Mill's position of 1848, it was Veblen's opinion that the methodological and philosophical foundations of Marshall's normalistic economics were largely intellectual products inherited from the first half of the nineteenth century.

Marshall's preconception of normality was also important as a factor in determining the kind of psychological theory that he used to explain economic behavior. According to his interpretation, economics is a science of human behavior. It studies "men as they live and move and think in the ordinary business of life." [27] Although Marshall opens his *Principles of Economics* with this very broad definition of economic science, he soon limits the scope of economic analysis to the study of normal business behavior, meaning by normal economic behavior that type of competitive behavior in which self-interest plays a dominant role. In the preface to the second edition of *The Economics of Industry* he explains that "in this world, as it is, the chief active principle in business is the desire of each man to promote the material interests of himself and his family." [28] Opposing this active principle of self-interest were such factors as custom, ignorance, and inertia, which were regarded by Marshall as being only "passive elements." He believed that in the long run the active principle of self-betterment would overcome the "passive resistance" of such retarding factors as custom, ignorance, and inertia. This long-run behavior was normal behavior. It was the kind of behavior that would result from the operation of the forces of demand and supply "persistently in the same direction" in a purely competitive society.

The normal economic activity that is of primary interest to Marshall thus centers in the hedonic calculus, in the universal propensity of human beings to weigh gains against the costs of securing them. Marshall's "normal action" is always a problem of a little more or a little less, of balancing the marginal increment of output

---

[26] In the preface to *The Economics of Industry* (1879) Marshall says that he regards his work as an extension of the work already done by John Stuart Mill with provision made for important contributions made by economists after 1848.

[27] *Principles of Economics,* page 14.

[28] Marshall, Alfred, and Mary P., *The Economics of Industry,* Second Edition, page vi. London: Macmillan and Co., Limited, 1881. See also the "Preface to the First Edition," *Principles of Economics.*

"against the corresponding increment of its cost of production" at the margin of application.[29] Such hedonic action is the very core of normal economic behavior. It is the standard form of economic action with which all other forms of economic behavior are to be compared and contrasted. This normal economic action is best represented by the behavior of what Marshall calls "city men," businessmen who occupy strategic positions in the economic system, and who base their business decisions on "deliberate and far-reaching calculations . . . executed with vigour and ability." [30] Surrounding this core of normal, hedonic economic behavior is the behavior of all those individuals who are not quite as "business-like" as "city men." Marshall was well aware that many people fail to conform to his standard of normal economic behavior. He understood that custom, ignorance, and inertia have a way of interfering with the functioning of the personal drive toward self-improvement. But he felt that in the long run such interferences would give way before the pressure of the active principle of self-betterment. As Marshall puts it, "Custom never holds its own in opposition to a strong active economic force working for many generations persistently in the same direction." For this reason he felt that normal economic action was the substantial basis of all economic activity, and that it was "applicable to the actions of the unbusiness-like classes in the same way, though not with the same precision of detail, as to those of the merchant or banker." [31]

In selecting for analysis mainly that portion of economic behavior which conformed with his preconception of normality, Marshall kept his theorizing close to his "Fundamental Idea" of an equilibrium of demand and supply. As a consequence his psychological theory fits in neatly with his general scientific outlook and with his methodological procedure. In concentrating his attention on that portion of human action which is based on "deliberate and far-reaching calculations" of self-advantage, Marshall was little concerned with problems of changing economic behavior. Unlike customary behavior which is subject to constant change, the behavior patterns that are dominated by calculation, choice, and self-seeking

---

[29] "Preface to the First Edition," *Principles of Economics*, page x.
[30] *Ibid.*, pages vi-vii.
[31] *Ibid.*, page vii.

do not raise problems of social and economic change. The pattern of behavior based on self-interest alone is as universally unchanging as is the physical and psychological make-up of mankind. It is not surprising, therefore, that Marshall's normal economic behavior is as unchanging as is his mechanistic view of the competitive economic system. It is the kind of action that can be expected to persist in a static competitive economy where the forces of demand and supply operate to keep the individual on the path toward material betterment. Furthermore, normal economic action, like the hypothesis of the competitive economy in equilibrium, can be broken down for investigation by the additive method of analysis. Such action is individual, not groupal or collective. It is action that can be easily isolated from the broad flow of human activity and studied at the margin of production, where the only important considerations are those of minimizing costs and maximizing gains. In addition, it is a type of behavior that readily lends itself to Marshall's "partial studies" which move from the simple to the complex.

This brief analysis of the philosophical, methodological, and psychological foundations of Marshall's systematic economics reveals how his preconception of normality functions as the fountainhead of his economic thought. It shows how this preconception conditions his general scientific outlook, influences his methodological procedure, and shapes his views relating to the nature of human behavior. Marshall's preconception of normality is the primal source from which is drawn the general bent of his scientific thought and the basic unity underlying his economic thought. It permeates every important department of his economic thinking. It determines his point of departure; it follows him throughout the breadth and length of his symmetrical thought scheme; and it remains with him until he draws his theoretical analysis to a conclusion. Times could change and new developments could occur in related social sciences, but as long as Marshall clung to his basic preconception of normality his systematic equilibrium economics remained impervious to significant intellectual innovations. Marshall did appreciate that important philosophical and scientific developments had occurred after the publication, in 1879, of his first volume on the elements of economic science. Yet he did not make a place in his economic theorizing for these new intellectual achievements, because, in Veblen's opinion, he was unable to free himself from the binding influence of his preconception of normality.

The Concept of Process

Veblen's criticism of late nineteenth-century academic economics took the form of a vigorous attack on the preconception of normality which played such a major role in the formulation of orthodox nineteenth-century economic thought.   He felt that if it could be shown that the preconception of normality was unsatisfactory as the basic premise of economic science, then doubt would necessarily be cast on the adequacy of the general outlook, the methodology, and the psychological assumptions of orthodox economics.   This would be the case since these three aspects of economic thought were very closely related to the preconception of normality.   Adopting this line of attack, Veblen denied the adequacy and validity of Marshall's preconception of normality.   He sought to undermine the whole structure of Marshall's equilibrium economics by pulling the preconception of normality from under it.   Since he had come to the conclusion that Marshall's preconception of normality was not a satisfactory instrument to be used in interpreting the course of economic development, Veblen substituted a new preconception for Marshall's outmoded one.   This substitution of preconceptions in turn called for fundamental alterations in the general outlook, the scientific methodology, and the psychological assumptions of economic science.

The preconception that he substitutes for Marshall's idea of normality is described by Veblen as the "preconception of process." [32] His major preconception is based on the view that the most significant features of economic life are not "steadfast and persistent," as Marshall had assumed, but dynamic and emergent.   In Veblen's opinion the fixity or steadfastness of economic life is largely an illusion that is created by taking a short-run view of things, and by failing to pay attention to the emergent aspects of economic activity. To Veblen the essence of economic life is emergence, growth, or development, and not permanence or persistence.   What appears to be fixed and unchanging at any one instant of time is really the product of a continuous process of emergence or development.   An economic

[32] Veblen, Thorstein, "Why Is Economics Not an Evolutionary Science?", reprinted in *The Place of Science in Modern Civilisation*, page 62.

system is like an historical event that has its roots in the past, but which also exists in the present, and carries within it much of future significance. For this reason Veblen finds that the economic system incorporates within itself something of the past, the present, and the future. Veblen was not the originator of this viewpoint. Thirty years before he published his views on this matter Karl Marx had outlined a similar viewpoint. In the preface to the first edition (1867) of the first volume of *Capital* Marx explained that the "standpoint" from which he made his study of capitalism was based on the concept of the economic system as an evolving process of natural history.[33] To Marx, as to Veblen, the economic system was more changeable than the physical universe in which it functioned.

The concept in which Veblen lodges his basic idea of emergence is the concept of "process," a concept that stands in marked contrast with the concept of mechanistic equilibrium in which Marshall had lodged his idea of permanence. By the term "process," Veblen means a "sequence, or complex, of consecutive change," or something in process of development.[34] He borrowed the concept of process from the biological sciences in which it had become customary to look upon living objects as processes, or objects undergoing a process of change or development.[35] In the biological organism each phase of growth merges into the succeeding phase, so that there is always a continuity of biological existence. The same thing is true of Veblen's view of the economic system as a process. Since each phase of economic evolution gives rise to a succeeding developmental phase, there is always a continuity of economic development. All phases or periods of economic growth are tied together by a relation of cause and effect; consequently, each new phase of development is to be explained with reference to the conditions existing in the prior developmental period.

In considering the economic system as an economic process, Veblen does not take it to be an actual biological process. Cultural processes have much in common with biological processes, since the

[33] Marx, Karl, *Capital*, Vol. I, pages 15, 23. Throughout this chapter all references are to the three-volume, Kerr edition of Marx's *Capital*.

[34] Veblen, Thorstein, "The Evolution of the Scientific Point of View," reprinted in *The Place of Science in Modern Civilisation*, page 32.

[35] Although the term "process" had been used long before the appearance of the modern biological sciences, it took on a new meaning with the development of these sciences.

essence of both types of process is change, growth, and emergence; but there are some very fundamental differences between the two types of processes.   Because they have some personal independence, the individuals who participate in the affairs of a cultural process are unlike cells functioning within a biological organism.   Unlike biological cells, individuals have the power to alter the shape of the cultural complex of which they are integral parts.   To what extent they can exert this influence is a point on which Veblen is not always clear.   Furthermore, the economic process has no social mind dominating it; hence the functioning of the economic process, unlike that of the biological process, does not consist of many responses to one nerve center.   Diverse factors hold the total pattern of economic relationships together.   These factors include custom, habit, biological drives, and conscious, purposive human action.   Although the economic process has close connections with the biological inheritance of mankind, it is primarily a cultural and not a biological product.   The economic process functions on levels of human action which are far above the merely biological levels of action.

A phrase which is more descriptive of Veblen's concept of the economic system than "economic process" is the phrase "going concern," because this expression emphasizes the cultural rather than the biological aspects of economic activity, and calls attention to the fact that economic activity is largely a cultural affair.   From the cultural viewpoint a going concern is a functioning complex of cultural relationships in which individuals are associated to achieve certain goals.   It is a pattern of things that derives its cohesion from the common habits and interests of the individuals who participate in its affairs.   In a few places throughout his writings Veblen drops the term "process" in favor of "going concern."   In referring to the industrial arts, for example, he states that "Technological knowledge is of the nature of a common stock, held and carried forward collectively by the community, which is in this relation to be conceived as a going concern." [36]   Unfortunately, however, Veblen does not make any thorough analysis or extensive use of the concept of the going concern.   Since the term "process" has such a definitely biological connotation, Veblen would have freed much of his analysis

[36] Veblen, Thorstein, *The Instinct of Workmanship and the State of the Industrial Arts*, page 103. New York: The Viking Press, 1937.

from an excessively biological bias or atmosphere if he had not relied so heavily on the terminology of the biological sciences.

Veblen's concept of the economic system as a process or going concern was worked out as a protest against the static theory of the academic economists of the last quarter of the nineteenth century. Their concept of a mechanistic economic equilibrium focussed attention on *structure* rather than on *function*.   In his economic analysis Marshall was concerned with the economic system as a final product with an unchanging structure.   His systematic economics investigated the movements of the various parts comprising the fixed structure of a competitive economic society.   His concept of structure carried with it the idea of movement or motion, but not the idea of change or development.   He explained that his volume on the foundations of economics was "concerned throughout with the forces that cause movement," and that in his equilibrium view society was "full of movement." [37]   The keynote of his treatise on economic principles was dynamics.   But it was a dynamics similar to the dynamics of physics, since it was concerned with economic motion or movement and not with economic change or development.

In contrast to the concept of mechanism of Marshall and other late nineteenth-century orthodox economists Veblen's concept of process emphasizes *function* rather than *structure*.   To Veblen the economic system as a process or going concern is not a final product with an unchanging structure.[38]   It is a "becoming" rather than a "being," a pattern of economic relationships "on the make" or emergent, rather than a pattern of relationships in a final, static condition.   The very terminology that Veblen uses is post-Darwinian rather than pre-Darwinian as was Alfred Marshall's terminology. Whereas Marshall's economic equilibrium has movement like the motion of a machine, Veblen's economic process "functions" in many ways like a biological organism.   For, whereas mechanistic motion or movement is repetitious and unchanging, cultural and biological functioning always carries with it the possibility of change or development.   Because it functions, Veblen's economic process

[37] *Principles of Economics,* pages xiv-xv and 367.
[38] Karl Marx had made the same criticism of the classical economists of his time. As he expressed it, "In so far as Political Economy remains within that bourgeois horizon . . . the capitalist regime is looked upon as the absolutely final form of social production, instead of as a passing historical phase of its evolution." See *Capital,* Vol. I, page 17.

has a cumulative rather than a static character.[39]   The whole process is in a fluid state with its structure being constantly modified by cumulative changes.

According to Veblen's interpretation the essence of things is to be found in their functioning or in their performance.   Hence, Veblen's attention centers in the relations between functioning or changing parts of the emerging economy, and in the interrelations between these parts and the whole economy.   His economic theory is dynamic, not because it deals with the laws of mechanistic movement or motion, but because it deals with the interpretation of economic functioning or development.   For the dynamics of physics, which Marshall found so appealing, Veblen substitutes the dynamics of cultural science.

The concept or idea of emergence, which is the fountainhead of Veblen's economic thought, carries with it a different emphasis than does Marshall's idea of permanence or duration.   Whereas Marshall's idea of permanence emphasizes the particular rather than the general, or the parts rather than the whole, Veblen's idea of emergence focusses attention on the whole instead of the parts.   In the field of philosophical thought where the concept of emergence was first extensively used, as in the work of Georg Hegel, the concept of emergence was laid out on a broad canvas.   For the earlier logic of "being" Hegel substituted a logic of "becoming," and in applying his logic of becoming he converted the universe into a gigantic process whose main characteristic was emergence.   Hegel's general procedure was always to think in terms of large units or wholes into which minor or subsidiary parts or elements were fitted.   When this concept of emergence was taken up and applied by Darwin in the field of biology, the same emphasis on "wholeness" was made.   In Darwin's view a biological organism was not a structure composed of many parts or elements that could be isolated from the whole environment for investigation; an organism was a functioning whole which was to be explained in terms of the entire environment or total situation in which it functioned.

In the social sciences the introduction of the concept of emergence was followed by the same consequences as were to be found in the fields of biological and philosophical thought.   When Marx, Sombart, Hobson, Veblen and other economists applied the concept of

[39] "Why Is Economics Not an Evolutionary Science?", page 61.

emergence to economic life, they worked out their economic theory with reference to the whole emerging economic system. They took as their general outlook an overall view in which each functioning part of the economic system was interpreted ultimately with relation to the whole functioning economy.

Veblen does not spend much time on an analysis of what he means by a "whole." In other scientific fields the concept of the "whole" has been given more precise meaning through the addition of the concept of the "field." [40] The whole operates or functions in a field which is so interrelated with the whole that it can logically be regarded as an extension of it. From this viewpoint the field is merely a continuation of the whole. Although this concept of the "field" has been used with some success by biologists, sociologists, and social psychologists to give more meaning to their concept of the whole and to render the term "environment" less vague, Veblen did not bestir himself to keep in touch with this new intellectual development. Nowhere in his writings does he attempt to inquire fully into the meaning of the concept of an economic or social whole. Had he done so, it would have materially strengthened his theoretical position. There was a great need for a clarification of the point, since Veblen was introducing into American economics some very novel ways of looking at the data of economic life. But as was all too frequently the case, Veblen felt no compulsion to cultivate intensively ideas that were apparently clear to him, albeit startlingly new and somewhat turbid to many of his readers.

Nonetheless, Veblen's concept of wholeness greatly influenced his views on scientific methodology. He calls his method the "evolutionary method" of economic analysis.[41] The essence of his methodological approach is that economic data are to be selected, abstracted, and interpreted in the light of the fact that they are integral parts of a larger, evolving whole. All parts of the economic system are to be investigated with the realization that they are but "items in the scheme of life" known as modern capitalism, and that they draw much of their meaning from the scheme of things of which they are constituent parts.[42] The phenomena relating to the economic system as a cultural process are not "neatly isolable"

[40] Cf. Smuts, Jan Christiaan, *Holism and Evolution*, page 111 ff.
[41] "Why Is Economics Not an Evolutionary Science?", page 81.
[42] *Ibid.*, page 71.

phenomena. Yet Veblen was aware that for some purposes the various parts of the economic system may be investigated in isolation from the whole system. This was especially the case in the early stages of the development of the science when economists were assembling the first principles of their science. But Veblen felt that in the more mature stages of the development of economics a methodological approach was needed which would look for economic meaning in the relations existing between the whole of the economy and its many subsidiary parts.

Veblen's discussion of his "evolutionary method" remains very unsatisfactory. Although he criticizes the additive methodology of the orthodox economists at considerable length, he makes no exhaustive study of his own method of analysis. His explanations of the nature of his "evolutionary method" remain quite fragmentary. No considerable portion of his essays or treatises is devoted to an analysis of the kind of scientific method that would be most appropriate to his evolutionary economics. It would have been much more enlightening to his readers if Veblen had chosen some other term than "evolutionary" to describe his scientific method. It is true that he was concerned with interpreting changing economic data, but he was also concerned with explaining the part-whole relations existing between data. Many investigators before Veblen's time had inquired into the nature of social science data from an evolutionary viewpoint. But these early investigators had not made much use of the concept of the part-whole relation. Their method of analysis was not centered in the idea of discovering the meaning that flows from the whole to the part as was the case with Veblen's methodological approach.

Two terms appear to be more descriptive of Veblen's methodology than is his own term "evolutionary." These terms are "synoptic" and "holistic." The term "synopsis" refers to a viewing of things together.[43] It emphasizes the togetherness or interrelatedness of phenomena, but it is not always associated with the idea of emergence. The term "holism" refers to an interpretation of the universe in which it is recognized that the universe is made up of a number of

[43] For a discussion of the synoptic method on the philosophical level see Beck, Lewis W., "The Synoptic Method," *The Journal of Philosophy*, June 22, 1939, Vol. XXXVI, No. 13, pages 337-345.

evolving wholes. These wholes are not reducible to more elementary parts except by a process of scientific abstraction, which leaves out of account much of the real nature of the wholes comprising the universe. The "parts" of each whole are nothing more than "abstract analytical distinctions" created by the scientist for various analytical purposes.[44] They are scientific abstractions which, even when brought together, do not cover the whole of reality. In the holistic method of scientific analysis the meaning of the parts is therefore supplemented or enlarged by relating the parts to the whole. Since Veblen's methodological procedure follows similar lines, it is fitting to describe his method of scientific analysis as "holistic."

The nature of the holistic method of analysis can be readily explained by noting that there are different levels on which scientific data may be analyzed. In analyzing an economic datum such as a price, for example, the economist may push his investigation in two different directions, one reaching up into complex levels of analysis and the other leading down into less intricate levels of analysis. Moving in one direction, the economist may analyze situations where price merely equates supply and demand in a given market. In this case price analysis is abstracted, simplified, and ultimately confined within the narrow limits of an hypothetically pure or fictional situation. When the investigation moves in the opposite direction price analysis passes into more complex analytical levels, where prices are investigated in the light of their connections with the whole functioning economic system. On these levels of more intricate analysis the economist fits individual prices into "price systems" which are, in turn, related to the total economy. He finds that the influences of prices ramify throughout the whole economy in such a manner as to affect the distribution of national income, the investment of savings, the volume of employment, and many other important economic activities. By making his investigations of prices in these two different directions the economist achieves a well-rounded interpretation of the phenomena of price.

In Veblen's economic analysis the tendency is always for his interpretation to reach out into the more realistic and more complex

[44] Smuts, Jan Christiaan, *op. cit.*, Chapter V, "General Concept of Holism," pages 85-117.

levels of analysis. He pays little attention to interpretation in the opposite direction. This is not to say that he regards such interpretation as unnecessary or ill-founded. In spite of his sometimes sardonic criticism of those economists who devoted almost all of their energy to inquiries on the less complex levels of economic analysis, Veblen had to admit that their work was both useful and necessary.[45] Furthermore, it would certainly have strengthened Veblen's own economic thought if he had shown more interest in pushing his scientific inquiries into the less intricate levels of economic analysis. But Veblen does not seem to have possessed either the patience or the interest to steer his economic investigations into the less complex levels of scientific analysis. Perhaps it is asking too much of any economist to show capabilities in both directions. However, it is not asking too much to have proper credit given to both types of analysis, and to work toward their fusion. Although it was never Veblen's intention to divorce the two aspects of holistic analysis, his writings sometimes had this effect.

Veblen's Social Psychology

Besides influencing his views on scientific methodology, Veblen's basic concepts of emergence and wholeness were instrumental in shaping the psychological theory which underlies his "evolutionary economics." In his economic analysis the separate acts of the individual are interpreted with respect to the whole changing behavior which the individual develops as a member of a particular economico-cultural complex such as modern capitalism. Veblen does not analyze the economic behavior of the individual on the assumption that his choices are unrelated to the existing economico-cultural scheme of things. Instead, he regards the individual as a functioning whole who reflects the essence of the capitalistic culture in which he participates. In order to understand the economic behavior of the individual, Veblen finds it necessary to investigate the many forces at work shaping the individual's behavior patterns. It is this concept of a framework of reference or a general pattern of cultural arrangements which is the new tool of psychological analysis that

---

[45] In his less critical moments, Veblen felt constrained to say that "Of the achievements of the classical economists, recent and living, the science may justly be proud. . . ." Quoted from "Why Is Economics Not an Evolutionary Science?", page 59.

Veblen brought to his task of explaining economic behavior.[46] This shift of interest from the part to the whole, from a portion of the individual's behavior to his whole behavior pattern, results in dropping the individualistic psychology in favor of a social psychology.

Veblen's explanation of human behavior runs in terms that were being worked out by the experimental and social psychologists at the turn of the century. One of the most fundamental advances made by these late nineteenth-century and early twentieth-century psychologists was a recognition of the fact that human behavior is a social or cultural product. Through much of the nineteenth century the most widely accepted psychology had been nothing more than an introspective psychology. Those who adhered to the basic tenets of the introspective psychology failed to grasp the intimate interlinking between individuals and their cultural life. The introspective psychologists made an unrealistic separation between instincts and reason; they overemphasized the role of reason or intelligence in human conduct; and they ignored or neglected the social or cultural framework of reference to which individual behavior should be related for its proper and full interpretation. In place of this individualistic, introspective psychology of the nineteenth century, which was deeply embedded in economics and other social sciences, Veblen substitutes a psychology that is collective rather than individualistic, objective rather than introspective.

The cultural psychology which underlies Veblen's evolutionary economics originated in the second half of the last century. A German school of cultural anthropologists laid the foundations for what was then called "folk psychology," the chief contribution of which was to point out that among primitive peoples individual behavior was very greatly influenced by inherited ways of behaving and thinking.[47] In the hands of Wilhelm Wundt and those who followed

[46] This concept of the cultural pattern or total framework of reference appears to be the forerunner of the Gestalt concept which has figured so prominently in recent developments in the field of psychology. See Köhler, Wolfgang, *Gestalt Psychology*, 1929, Ch. VI, "The Properties of Organized Wholes." Alexander Goldenweiser in his essay on "Anthropology and Psychology" (page 85 fn.), which appears in *The Social Sciences and Their Interrelations* (1927), observes that "Unless we are badly misguided, a concept of the general type of *pattern* or *Gestalt* may yet come to mark an epochal advance in our conceptual exploration."

[47] See Wundt, Wilhelm, *Elements of Folk Psychology*, 1916, translated by E. L. Schaub.

him, the new folk psychology tended to give attention more to cultural than to psychological factors.[48] It remained for later social psychologists such as William James, James M. Baldwin, Charles H. Cooley, and others in the United States to take up the original suggestions of Wundt and his cultural-anthropological school, and to work out a social psychology which combined the two levels of individual and cultural psychological processes into one functional whole. Like the German folk psychologists, Veblen had a deep interest in the study of primitive and advanced human cultures, but unlike them he was free from the Hegelian mysticism which was so prominent a feature of early German cultural studies. Owing to this freedom from Hegelian mysticism he was in a good position to combine the best elements of both German and American sociopsychological thought.

In working out the details of his social psychology Veblen first turns to a study of tropisms and instincts. He defines tropisms as automatic responses of the individual to external stimuli. They are hereditary traits that are deeply embedded in the physiological and neurological make-up of the living organism. Their prime characteristic is action of a reflex nature that does not call into play the higher rational faculties. Tropismatic action is a matter of motor responses rather than intelligent responses guided by the rational faculties. It is a basic level of activity common to all biological organisms, human and otherwise.

Above the level of tropismatic action are to be found the various proclivities or instincts, which are distinguished from tropisms by the fact that they call intelligence into play when they function. Veblen explains that instinct, "as contra-distinguished from tropismatic action, involves consciousness and adaptation to an end aimed at." Impulsive action which "is in no degree intelligent . . . is not properly to be called instinctive; it is rather to be classed as tropismatic." [49] Veblen does not imply that there is any clear-cut division between tropisms and instincts. On the contrary, since the tropisms shade into the instincts, some of the lower instincts, such as the hunger and sex drives, may be classified as "quasi-tropismatic

---

[48] For an outline of Wilhelm Wundt's psychological work and the contributions of his contemporaries see F. B. Karpf's *American Social Psychology*, 1932, First Edition, Ch. II, "The Development of Social-Psychological Thought in Germany."

[49] *The Instinct of Workmanship*, pages 4, 38.

or half-instinctive." They are on the border line between tropisms and instincts. On the opposite end of the scale from the quasi-tropismatic, half-instinctive proclivities are the higher instincts such as the parental bent, the self-regarding impulse, and the instinct of workmanship, all of which have a highly intellectual content.

For the purpose of explaining behavior at the level of human culture Veblen finds the instincts to be all important. "For mankind, as for the other higher animals," he said, "the life of the species is conditioned by the complement of instinctive proclivities and tropismatic aptitudes with which the species is typically endowed. Not only is the continued life of the race dependent on the adequacy of its instinctive proclivities in this way, but the routine and details of its life are also, in the last resort, determined by these instincts._ These are the prime movers in human behavior. . . . Human activity, in so far as it can be spoken of as conduct, can never exceed the scope of these instinctive dispositions. . . . Nothing falls within the human scheme of things desirable to be done except what answers to these native proclivities of man." [50] It should be clear from this excerpt that Veblen thought that as prime movers the instincts determine the general scope of human behavior. They set the ultimate goals of human conduct, and prompt the individual to seek the attainment of these goals. While each instinct involves the conscious pursuit of some one particular, objective end, the whole complex of instincts provides the general range of objectives for human endeavor.

In explaining the nature of instincts Veblen adopts an operational definition. An instinct is not to be defined in terms of a concrete something of a physical nature which may be uncovered by laboratory experimentation, but rather in terms of those fixed behavior patterns which reveal how people function or operate. When he wrote *The Instinct of Workmanship and the State of the Industrial Arts* in 1914, the controversy as to the nature of instincts was very heated. Veblen asserts that the opponents of the concept of instinct err in assuming that instincts are isolable elements whose existence can be proved or disproved by some experimental procedure. Not finding any such "discrete and specific elements" in human nature, some psychologists conclude that instincts have no real existence. Veblen counters this argument by saying that instincts

[50] *Ibid.*, page 1.

are not discrete things or elements located somewhere in the individual's physiological system; instead they represent a fixed inheritable tendency toward a special mode of behavior. In his view an instinct is not a fixed element tucked away somewhere in man's biological make-up. It must rather be defined in terms of what the individual does or how he behaves as a matter of ingrained habit. "The distinctive feature by the mark of which any given instinct is identified is to be found in the particular character of the purpose to which it drives." [51] Thus the instinct to acquire is not to be discovered in any particular part of man's physiological or neurological make-up. Such a search will end nowhere. The existence of an instinct to acquire can only be ascertained by observing the behavior of individuals to see if it reveals a fixed tendency to act in an acquisitive manner. When it is established that human behavior reveals a fixed acquisitive tendency, Veblen feels that one is justified in speaking of this behavior tendency as an instinctive drive or proclivity.

Having established to his own satisfaction that the concept of the instinct is a useful one for the explanation of behavior at the level of human culture, Veblen passes on to a discussion of the role of the instincts. He explains that each instinct has its own particular end toward which it stimulates the individual to act. Each instinctive end or purpose is without reference to the existence of other instincts with different aims or objectives. It is thus possible to have instinctive drives which are operating at cross-purposes to one another. It is at this point in his analysis that Veblen introduces the factor of human reason or intelligence. "The ends of life," he said, ". . . are assigned by man's instinctive proclivities; but the ways and means of accomplishing those things which the instinctive proclivities so make worth while are a matter of intelligence." [52] Intelligence in-

---

[51] On this point Veblen follows William James. Cf. James, William, *The Principles of Psychology*, 1890, Vol. II, page 391 fn.: "The minuter study of recent years has . . . decided that what is called an instinct is usually only a tendency to act in a way of which the *average* is pretty constant, but which need not be mathematically 'true.' "

[52] *The Instinct of Workmanship*, pages 5-6. William James had given a similar explanation of the role of intelligence twenty-five years earlier in *Principles of Psychology*, 1890, Vol. II, page 393, where he states that "In other words, there is no material antagonism between instinct and reason. Reason, *per se*, can inhibit no impulses; the only thing that can neutralize an impulse is an impulse the other way. Reason may, however, make an *inference which will excite the*

tervenes to provide guidance for the various instincts, and, in addition, to mediate between them. Its role is of a selective nature: reason selects those instinctive drives which are to be given the fullest expression in any given cultural situation. The net result of the use of human reason is a somewhat harmonious adjustment of the various instincts to one another so that the use of intelligence brings about a "concessive adjustment" of the many instincts possessed by man.

The relations between instincts and intelligence worked out by Veblen permit him to assume that the instincts are not all absolutely rigid and unrelenting in their demands for satisfaction. The simpler instincts, such as fear, pugnacity, and gregariousness, act imperiously and somewhat independently of the individual's intelligence. But the less specific and vaguer instincts, such as the parental, workmanship, and acquisitive bents, are much more pliable; they can be made to fit into a "scheme of co-ordination" set up by the individual with the aid of his intelligence. Veblen is careful to point out that in instinctive action the individual acts as a whole; indeed the many instinctive proclivities are so fused as to create a "web of correlation and inter-dependence." "In instinctive action," explained Veblen, "the individual acts as a whole, and in the conduct which emerges under the driving force of these instinctive dispositions the part which each several instinct plays is a matter of more or less, not of exclusive direction. They must therefore incontinently touch, blend, overlap and interfere, and cannot be conceived as acting each and several in sheer isolation and independence of one another." [53] It is always a matter of give-and-take between the many instinctive proclivities, with the intelligence acting as a selective agent. Without this pliability of the instincts under direction of the human intelligence race survival would be extremely difficult under the changing conditions of climate, geography, and human culture.

Veblen does not attempt to draw up a complete list of instincts in his economic analysis. He makes special use of only four instincts, the parental, the acquisitive, the workmanship instinct, and the in-

imagination so as to set loose the impulse the other way; and thus, though the animal richest in reason might be also the animal richest in instinctive impulses too, he would never seem the fatal automaton which a merely instinctive animal would be."

[53] _The Instinct of Workmanship,_ page 11.

stinct of idle curiosity. The parental instinct is that predisposition which leads the individual to take thought of others than himself. It is the drive that leads to a "parental solicitude for the common good." Starting with a regard for the welfare of human offspring, the parental instinct widens to include concern over the well-being of family, tribe, class, nation, and even mankind in general. It is the opposite of the self-regarding bent or acquisitive instinct, which leads the individual to take thought of his own personal welfare as contrasted with the welfare of others. This self-regarding instinct predisposes the individual to acquire property, to deprive others of their rightful possessions, and in general to consider one's self rather than the community. It results in self-aggrandizement at the expense of others, in the attempt to get something without giving anything in return.

The third instinct that interested Veblen is the workmanship proclivity, or what William James once called the "proclivity to construction." [54] This is the instinct that is of the greatest importance in Veblen's economic analysis. He designates it as "Chief among those instinctive dispositions that conduce directly to the material well-being of the race, and therefore to its biological success." Indeed its importance is so great that "The only other instinctive factor of human nature that could with any likelihood dispute this primacy would be the parental bent." [55] The instinct of workmanship leads the individual to manipulate materials, to create useful products, and to concern himself with "devices and contrivances of efficiency and economy." It shows up best in the technological efficiency of the worker and in the accumulated technological proficiency of the general population. Most simply explained, it is a general desire to do a job in as workmanlike a fashion as possible.

The jobs that are to be done or the ends that are to be served are not themselves determined by the proclivity to construction; this is because "The position of the instinct of workmanship . . . is somewhat peculiar, in that its functional content is serviceability

[54] See *The Principles of Psychology*, Vol. II, pages 426-427. Occasionally Veblen refers to the "proclivity to construction" (*The Instinct of Workmanship*, page 11), but he usually substitutes "workmanship" for "construction," thereby giving his work an air of originality.

[55] *The Instinct of Workmanship*, pages 25, 27. Veblen does not regard the workmanship instinct as a simple, single drive. Instead he finds that it is a "concurrence of several instinctive aptitudes."

for the ends of life, whatever these ends may be; whereas these ends to be subserved are at least in the main appointed and made worth while by the various other instinctive dispositions." [56] For this reason the workmanship instinct is an ancillary instinct concerned more with the ways and means of achieving life's ends than with any specific end or goal of human existence. It is concerned with an efficient use of available resources to the end that the purposes of life may be easily accomplished. Supplementing the workmanship bent is the parental bent, an instinct that reenforces the desire of the worker to be efficient and economical, since it ties up the welfare of the community with an economical use of its available human and material resources. So closely are the workmanship and parental bents associated in their drive to establish "economy and efficiency," that Veblen makes no effort to draw a clear line of distinction between these two instinctive predispositions.

The fourth instinctive drive that interested Veblen is the "instinct of idle curiosity," that propensity which drives men to inquire into the nature of things, to work out explanations of the world's events in mythological and, later, in scientific terms. Veblen finds the instinct of idle curiosity very closely related to the aptitude for play, since both aptitudes are sources of spontaneous action. He goes on to explain that idle curiosity has two aspects, the irrelevant and the pragmatic.[57] On the one hand idle curiosity leads to "idle learning," which is the type of learning best exemplified by mythologies and folk legends in which the thinker makes an anthropomorphic or animistic explanation of the external world. The other type of learning to which the instinct of idle curiosity leads is "pragmatic knowledge" or worldly wisdom.[58] This is the type of learning that is useful or expedient, since it leads to a larger output of useful, material goods. It is a knowledge of skills, technological expedients, practices, and devices which may be employed for the improvement of the material basis of human existence.

The instinct of idle curiosity plays an important role in Veblen's scientific thought. Idle curiosity leavens cultural activity by providing the spark of human originality, which leads to innovations of

[56] *Ibid.*, page 31.
[57] Veblen, Thorstein, "The Place of Science in Modern Civilisation," reprinted in *The Place of Science in Modern Civilisation and Other Essays*, pages 8-9.
[58] *Ibid.*, pages 7-9 fn.

many kinds. Without this constant stream of innovations the complex of social custom would rest very heavily upon mankind. Fortunately, man is a self-active being whose instinct of idle curiosity provides him with an escape from the heavy weight of ancient customs. He does not have to wait for changes in the physical environment, which are slow and irregular, to bring about changes in cultural organization. His own probing, questioning "idle curiosity" is a disruptive factor that, largely by accident and seldom by design, softens the rigid "discipline of habituation" inherent in the culture complex.

What is significant about Veblen's instinct analysis is that it provides a biological foundation for his theory of economic disharmony. He uncovers in the biological make-up of mankind a basic incompatibility which exists between the parental and the self-regarding or acquisitive drives. In every individual there is an ever-present incompatibility or conflict between the desire to acquire something for himself, without any personal sacrifice if possible, and the desire to contribute to the welfare of the family, tribe, or nation. These two drives lead to ends that are mutually exclusive. The complete satisfaction of either drive necessarily means the denial of the other drive. Both drives are essential since the group needs to be protected from the selfishness of the individual, and also the individual must be safeguarded from engulfment by the group. In actual life some sort of balance needs to be struck between the satisfactions of the two drives. This is the purpose of cultural organization which seeks to place limits on the extent to which the self-regarding impulse is given expression. But even though a culture succeeds in providing a balance between the parental and acquisitive drives, the incompatibility remains as an ever-present threat to the future stability of organized human existence. The incompatibility may be subdued, but it cannot ever be entirely eliminated. Consequently, human culture is erected on a very unstable foundation, which history records as frequently collapsing. This is a thought that is ever-present in Veblen's mind. It accounts for his denial of the assumption of basic social or cultural harmony that underlies English classical and neoclassical economic thought. It also helps to explain the very pessimistic atmosphere that surrounds Veblen's interpretation of the evolution of economic society.

Veblen disagrees with both the orthodox economists and Karl

Marx with respect to the psychological incompatibility inherent in mankind. The orthodox economists assumed that there was a basic social or cultural harmony underlying economic activities. To them there were no fundamental antagonisms or incompatibilities to be observed either in the external industrial system or in the individuals who carried on economic activities. They accepted the proposition that the unhampered self-regarding bent of competitive businessmen would lead to widespread economic welfare. Hence the optimistic attitude of these orthodox economists toward the course of economic events, and their failure to see the need for any substantial economic reform.

Karl Marx took an opposite view. He found in the capitalistic system such fundamental antagonisms that, in his opinion, it was destined to pass away. Moreover, the economic antagonisms or contradictions that Marx observed were conceived to be "inherent in the movement of capitalist society." [59] These antagonisms had an economic or technological and not a psychological origin; they were external to the businessmen, landlords, and workers who participated in the affairs of capitalist society. As contrasted with Veblen's, Marx's social contradictions were not correlated with any enduring psychological antagonisms which were inherent in mankind's biological make-up. In Veblen's analysis the contradictions within the economic system are found related to an abiding psychological antagonism existing between the parental and acquisitive drives. The capitalistic system merely gives cultural expression to this psychological antagonism that lies deep within the nature of mankind. Therefore, according to Veblen's interpretation, this psychological incompatibility will endure as a real or potential threat to the stability of all types of economic society—even to that of a socialistic society. It was for this reason that Veblen was always less optimistic about the future of the evolving economic system than was Karl Marx.

The four instincts which are of special interest to Veblen do not directly give rise to action. There is no simple, direct connection between the raw instincts and the purposes to which they lead. Instead, the factor of habit intervenes between the instincts and the ends or purposes toward which the instincts drive individuals. As the individual develops, the repeated promptings of his instinctive

[59] *Capital,* Vol. I, page 26.

drives take on the form of habitual responses. In setting up habitual behavior patterns for the expression of his instinctive impulses the individual borrows heavily from the group in which he lives. So much is this the case that Veblen states that his analysis is concerned with individuals who are "immersed in the community and exposed to the discipline of group life as it runs in the community, since all life is necessarily group life. The phenomena of human life occur only in this form . . . in both respects, both in his inherited and in his acquired traits, the individual is a product of group life." [60] The individual is born into a community which has already well-established standards of thought and behavior. This "complex of the habits of life and of thought prevalent among members of the community" constitutes the cultural scheme of the community. Veblen describes it as a legacy of habits of thought which have been accumulated through the experience of many generations.

Veblen's Theory of Institutions

The habitual ways of thinking and acting which are established by individuals to give expression to their instinctive drives eventually take on "an institutional character and force." Where a customary way of thinking or behaving becomes a persistent element in the culture of an organized social group, it takes on the concrete form of an institution, and hence Veblen defines an institution as a customary mode of thinking or as a "settled habit of thought common to the generality of men." [61] Institutions such as private property, credit, absentee ownership, or leisure become the dominant forces that determine the course of individual economic behavior. They provide the "proximate" or immediate ends that guide the behavior of the individual. In contrast, the ends set up by the instinctive drives are described by Veblen as "ultimate ends." As long as the proximate ends set up by the community's institutions coincide with the ultimate ends sought by the instinctive drives, the behavior of the individual satisfies the demands of his basic instinctive needs. In other words, cultural harmony is then established. But institutional arrangements may fail to change so as to meet the requirements of new physical or technological condi-

[60] *The Instinct of Workmanship*, pages 104, 138.
[61] Veblen, Thorstein, "The Limitations of Marginal Utility," reprinted in *The Place of Science in Modern Civilisation*, page 239.

tions. In this situation the proximate and the instinctive ends of human behavior no longer coincide. If a revision of its institutional arrangements is not made by the group or community, its existence may be dominated by "imbecile institutions." Individual behavior guided by these outmoded institutions may lead to a "desperately precarious institutional situation, such, for instance, as now faces the people of Christendom." [62]

When Veblen turns to the habitual basis of human behavior, he develops a theory of institutions. The growth or development of institutions is conditioned by two factors, the "material environment and the persistent propensities of human nature." By material environment Veblen means the economic conditions or methods of production which materialize in industrial technology. Since the basic drives of human nature do not change, it is the changing industrial technology which is largely responsible for changes in institutions. Man is pretty much what he does: "As he acts, so he feels and thinks." [63] His way of making a living has a profound influence upon his mental habits. As the technology underlying man's way of making a living changes, new mental habits are established which eventually harden into new institutional arrangements. In this fashion the whole institutional complex guiding human behavior is subject to the disruptive pressure of a changing technology.

Veblen's theory of institutions is not based upon a rigidly deterministic interpretation of institutional change. Indeed institutional change is not a mere function of a changing technology, as some of Veblen's critics would have us believe.[64] Veblen admits that factors other than technology, as, for example, changes in climate and physical environment, the mixing of races, population pressure, or mankind's idle curiosity, have some influence on the course of institutional development. He contends that institutional development is a matter of interaction and not merely a movement in one direction from technology to changing institutions. In the preface to *The Instinct of Workmanship* Veblen clearly states that although "It is assumed that in the growth of culture, as in its current main-

---

[62] *The Instinct of Workmanship*, page 25.
[63] *Ibid.*, page 192.
[64] See MacIver, R. M., *Society, a Textbook of Sociology*, pages 452-459. New York: Farrar and Rinehart, Inc., 1937. MacIver asserts that Veblen holds to a "strict" technological explanation of institutional change.

tenance, the facts of technological use and wont are fundamental and definitive, in the sense that they underlie and condition the scope and method of civilisation in other than the technological aspect," the assumption is not made in such a manner as to ignore the ways in which non-technological factors react on the state of the industrial arts.[65] Veblen gives full recognition to the action and reaction that occur in cultural or institutional change.   All that he asserts is that in some cultural eras the technological factor takes on special significance as a cultural determinant.   Especially in the case of a modern industrial community does Veblen find that the readjustment of institutions is "in the last analysis, almost entirely of an economic nature." [66]   He is much too sophisticated a student of human culture to adopt a purely deterministic theory of institutional development.   Although one may not accept the importance that Veblen attaches to technology as a factor influencing human behavior, he can hardly convict Veblen of being a naive student of human culture, or accuse him of clinging to a simple deterministic theory of institutional change.

In explaining the role of technological change in the development of human culture, Veblen points out that man is a self-active agent, who does not blindly respond to the stimuli of a changing material environment.   Veblen is careful to explain that "The changes that take place in the mechanical contrivances are an expression of changes in the human factor.   Changes in the material facts breed further change only through the human factor." [67]   Because men are endowed with selective intelligence and probing "idle curiosity," the individual necessarily makes adjustments to the changing industrial technology.   But much of this adjustment represents blind, instinctive responses of the individual to a changing economic environment.   Indeed, Veblen was not much impressed by mankind's capacity to make adjustments in a reasoned manner.   Veblen does not close the door on the possibility of more reasoned adjustments to the demands of a changing material environment; he simply remains skeptical about any improvement along this line.

[65] *The Instinct of Workmanship,* page vii.

[66] Veblen, Thorstein, *The Theory of the Leisure Class,* page 193.   New York: The Macmillan Company, 1912.

[67] "Why Is Economics Not an Evolutionary Science?", pages 71-72.

When Marshall and other late nineteenth-century economists reduced human behavior to little more than "rational response to the exigencies of the situation," they ignored, in Veblen's opinion, the fact that behavior is a social or cultural product, and that much of human behavior is habitual or institutional. Since they took economic behavior to be little more than the selecting of pleasurable rather than painful sensations, there was no need for any explanation of the cultural conditioning of the individual. In Veblen's judgment the orthodox, late nineteenth-century economists solved the problem of the influence of Western European culture upon individual behavior by adopting two devices. The first device was to take for granted (and thus to place beyond all inquiry) the whole capitalistic culture of which the economic system is but a part.[68] Thus the money institution was not fully interpreted because it was taken for granted by the simple device of assuming that money is an insignificant medium of transfer whose absence would have no disturbing effect upon an economy which was assumed to be no more than a refined system of barter. Yet when the money institution is recognized to be a vital part of our economic culture, it is soon discovered that this institution has a very appreciable effect upon the direction of individual economic behavior.[69]

A second device used by some orthodox economists of the eighteenth and nineteenth centuries in handling the cultural aspects of economic activity was to oversimplify the cultural setting of economic life. In those few cases where they inquired into the origins of economic culture they worked out their explanations in terms of an hypothetical anthropology which did great violence to the

[68] "The Limitations of Marginal Utility," page 233.

[69] Much recent monetary theory, such as the Keynesian analysis, has done precisely this. What is novel about Keynes' economic analysis is that he no longer takes money as something to be explained away as being a simple device for effecting the transfer of goods from seller to buyer. But even Keynes does not go as far as Veblen would have liked him to go in searching out the real significance of the money institution. Not having cut himself completely off from the orthodox English tradition in economic science, Keynes does not push his economic analysis very far into its institutional setting. Keynes explains that, in general, he takes as given factors psychological attitudes and economic institutions which "are unlikely to undergo a material change over a short period of time except in abnormal or revolutionary circumstances." See *The General Theory of Employment Interest and Money,* page 91. New York: Harcourt, Brace and Company, 1936.

actual findings of cultural anthropology. Adam Smith's "conjectural history" of the beginnings of barter in the transactions of primitive hunters, Nassau Senior's "natural state of man," and John Bates Clark's discussion of the "primitive life of the solitary hunter" are examples of twisting the cultural facts to meet the requirements of an inadequate introspective psychology. The nineteenth-century economists analyzed only those elements of the existing culture that fitted in with their normalized version of a competitive economic system. In the hands of these orthodox economists, said Veblen, the capitalistic system "disappears in a tissue of metaphors to reappear theoretically expurgated, sterilized, and simplified into a refined system of barter, culminating in a net aggregate maximum of pleasurable sensations of consumption." [70] This refined system of barter is a made-to-order cultural scheme that may be useful for those who accept a hedonistic view of human nature, but which is found by Veblen to be unsatisfactory as a point of departure for the study of the evolving capitalistic system.

In Veblen's opinion the orthodox nineteenth-century economists failed to work out an adequate theory of culture or of institutions. They made little use of the fact that the "wants and desires, the end and aim, the ways and means, the amplitude and drift of the individual's conduct" are greatly influenced by the cultural or institutional standards or norms that are adopted by individuals as the result of contacts with various groups in the community. In most of their psychological theorizing there was no cultural scheme intervening between the human mind and the sensations received by it from the external world. Human conduct was simply a matter of selecting pleasurable sensations over painful ones, and of reducing to a minimum all the pain-costs of securing pleasurable sensations. Not being students of the economic system as an evolving complex of institutional arrangements, the neo-classical economists paid little attention to the basic biological drives which find their expression in cultural or institutional arrangements. In addition, they made no place in their theory of human nature for a study of the cultural framework which gives unity to the separate acts of the individual. The only thing that united the several acts of the individual, according to the psychological interpretation of the neo-classical economists, was "a strong desire to think out a logical, consistent plan of

[70] "The Limitations of Marginal Utility," page 250.

life." [71] Such a view of human behavior Veblen considered an inadequate and unrealistic explanation of how individuals behave as participants in the affairs of the modern capitalistic system.

Veblen does not deny that human reason plays a very significant role in economic conduct. Indeed, he is quite explicit on this point. He agrees that "It is this element of discriminating forethought that distinguishes human conduct from brute behavior. And since the economist's subject of inquiry is this human conduct, that relation necessarily comes in for a large share of his attention in any theoretical formulation of economic phenomena, whether hedonistic or otherwise. . . . It is, of course, true that human conduct is distinguished from other natural phenomena by the human faculty for taking thought, and any science that has to do with human conduct must face the patent fact that the details of such conduct fall into the teleological form; but it is the peculiarity of the hedonistic economics that by force of its postulates its attention is confined to the teleological bearing of conduct alone. It deals with this conduct only in so far as it may be construed in rationalistic, teleological terms of calculation and choice." Veblen goes on to point out that "it is at the same time no less true that human conduct, economic or otherwise, is subject to the sequence of cause and effect, by force of such elements as habituation and conventional requirements." [72] He admits that a great amount of calculating and deliberate choosing are found in economic life, but he asserts that the orthodox economists failed to see that such calculation and choice operate only within a particular cultural milieu. Thus in the early nineteenth century the calculative and deliberative activities of businessmen were carried on in a cultural complex marked by private property, freedom of enterprise, and highly competitive business conditions. "Buying cheap and selling dear" became the habitual response of independent businessmen to the recurring stimuli of a thoroughly competitive economic system. Competing in an open market was the customary thing for businessmen to do. Individuals of the nineteenth century were brought up in an economic society that was controlled by competitive standards

    [71] Cf. Thorndike, E. L., *Human Nature and the Social Order*, 1940, page 160. Thorndike's concept of the "mental set" is similar to Veblen's idea of the institutional setting of the individual's behavior.
    [72] "The Limitations of Marginal Utility," pages 238-239.

or norms of behavior which found expression through the institutions of a competitive economy.   In this situation even the most competitive behavior had a firm foundation in habit or custom.

Veblen's explanation of human behavior is not completed by his analysis of the role of institutions.   He forges two more links in his chain of psychological interpretation.   These two additional links are the concepts of status and class organization.   From the individual's viewpoint status is a matter of enjoying the esteem of his fellow men; in the final analysis it is a matter of "regard for one's reputation" or "striving after a good name." [73]   Man always strives, works, thinks, and acts, with regard to the effects of his behavior upon his social or groupal status.   His constant concern is with what other people think of him, and with how he may improve their opinions of him so that he may thereby enhance his individual status.   Consciousness of self thus takes the form of an awareness of the interest of others in one's status.   From this viewpoint the self or ego of the individual is largely a matter of cultural status or standing.

Individual status is a matter of achieving and maintaining a certain ego-level.   Just as our bodies are anchored in space, so our individualities have an anchoring in the surrounding culture.[74]   This cultural anchoring, which is called status, is always a relative matter involving comparisons with other people and their attainments.   In the realm of human affairs there is a constant striving not only to equal the achievements of one's associates, but, if possible, to excel them.   For this reason status has a decidedly "emulative" quality.   Just how the emulation will find expression depends upon the kind of culture in which the individual lives and moves.   Veblen shows how emulation and the enhancing of one's status found expression in the peaceful, stone-age culture of early mankind through a striving to be serviceable to the community or nation.   "During that primitive phase of social development," he said, "when the community is still habitually peaceable, perhaps sedentary, and without a developed system of individual ownership, the efficiency of the in-

[73] Veblen, Thorstein, "The Theory of Socialism," reprinted in *The Place of Science in Modern Civilisation*, page 392.

[74] For a more recent statement of Veblen's psychological position see Sherif, Muzafer, *The Psychology of Social Norms*, pages 187, 196.   New York: Harper and Brothers, 1936.   Although Sherif's basic psychological theory is similar to Veblen's, it is much less speculative and much more experimental.

dividual can be shown chiefly and most consistently in some employment that goes to further the life of the group. What emulation of an economic kind there is between the members of such a group will be chiefly emulation in industrial serviceability." [75] In the stone-age culture status was acquired by giving full expression to the instinct of workmanship. The individual felt most "at home" in his cultural milieu when he was producing the community's material requirements in as efficient a manner as was possible.

Each culture has its own version of social status for the individuals who participate in its affairs. The stone-age culture was associated with an efficiency or serviceability type of personal status. In the predatory or barbaric stages of cultural evolution which followed the stone age, there occurred great changes in what was considered to be a desirable status for the individual. Veblen observes that in the era of barbaric culture the individual's standing was judged with reference to his capacity to be disserviceable to the community, to avoid effort that was productive, and to consume wealth wastefully and conspicuously. [76] Here the end of personal endeavor came to be the "differential advantage" of the individual rather than the "undifferentiated advantage" of the community. Economic conduct took on an emulative form with the individual seeking to outdo his fellow men in being disserviceable to the community. As the very core of the individual's cultural existence, this predatory view of social status has exerted a powerful influence on the course of individual conduct in all recent stages of cultural development.

With respect to the future, Veblen sees a struggle for dominance between those who favor the serviceable view of status and those who approve the predatory view. A culture that gives vent to the workmanship bent will tend to foster the development of a serviceability status. This will be a type of culture that will foster the improvement of industrial technology and the use of that technology to raise the standard of living of the masses. A different type of culture will be one that gives vent not to the proclivity to construction but to the self-regarding impulse or the proclivity to acquisition.

---

[75] *The Theory of the Leisure Class*, page 16.
[76] This is the general thesis of Veblen's *The Theory of the Leisure Class*. See especially Chapters II and III on "Conspicuous Leisure" and "Conspicuous Consumption."

This kind of culture will, to use the terminology of present-day social psychologists, "interiorize" its own special cultural standards or norms in the individuals who participate in its affairs.[77]   It will foster the development of a disserviceability concept of social status, which will create barriers to the improvement of industrial technology, and will cause individuals in strategic positions to divert the community's surplus production to their own, personal, anti-social purposes.   In the first half of the present century new cultural standards made their appearance.   New views on social status arose to conflict with the inherited predatory concept of status of the pecuniary culture of the nineteenth century.   From Veblen's viewpoint the economic conflict of the twentieth century can be summarized as a struggle for supremacy between two incompatible types of individual status, the serviceable and the predatory types.   In his opinion the victory of either status outlook will be largely a matter of historical accident.

Veblen goes on to explain that people with the same status will belong to the same general class, to a group of people bound together by a common outlook on life and by common ways of thinking and acting.   Each member of a class has the same frame of reference to which he refers all the problems that he meets in the course of his daily living.   Thus Veblen's "leisure class" is a group of people who possess similar attitudes toward the role of work and leisure in everyday activity.[78]   They all pursue a behavior pattern which involves avoiding activity that is serviceable or "productive"; they seek to outdo one another in being disserviceable to the community.

Just as there are only two basically different types of social status, so also, in Veblen's analysis, are there only two basic classes, the non-industrial and the industrial classes.   There may be many sub-classes within each of the two major classes, but all such sub-classes display the significant features of the major class to which they belong.   These two major classes are drawn by Veblen on vocational or occupational lines.   In the first class there are those who are engaged in "useful" activity or productive work.   Here are to be found the factory workers and the farmers.   Since the most important sub-class is made up of the workers, those who are close to industry and who come in close contact with the large-scale technology

---

[77] See Sherif, Muzafer, *The Psychology of Social Norms*, page 48.
[78] *The Theory of the Leisure Class*, pages 1-2.

of modern industry Veblen calls the "industrial class," and their work he designates as "industrial employment." [79]   Close contact with the industrial system gives expression to the workmanship bent and lays a foundation for the development of an efficiency status. Thus Veblen finds a close connection between workmanship bent, efficiency status, and the industrial class.

The second major class is the "non-industrial" class.   This class includes all those who are remote from the industrial system: the non-workers, the members of the leisure class, or those who are engaged in "unproductive" activities.   The most important sub-class within the non-industrial class is made up of businessmen.   These individuals are concerned with "getting something for nothing." Since they seek to amass pecuniary assets, Veblen describes their work as "pecuniary employment."   This activity stimulates the acquisitive impulse, and predisposes the individual to accept a predatory or disserviceability view of personal status.

In explaining the behavior of the non-industrial and industrial classes and their sub-classes, Veblen turns to a biological or instinctive interpretation.   He applies the same basic psychological interpretation to both individual and class behavior.   What directs the actions of individuals who are members of a class is not their reason so much as their instinctive drives and their acquired habits.   Veblen admits that human reason may influence class structure and class functioning, but he asserts that it does so only in a minor or secondary way.   In his opinion class solidarity is more a matter of habit and instinctive propensity than of "calculated material interest." [80]

This understanding of the importance of instinct and habit in class behavior leads Veblen to be less optimistic than Marx about the directing of class action toward given social goals.   He feels that Marx clung to a much too simple interpretation of class behavior, one drawn from a view of human nature which overemphasized the role of human reason, and paid too little attention to the significance of instinct and habit.   As Veblen sees it, Marx, following the lead of the classical English economists, stressed too much the rationality

[79] Veblen, Thorstein, "Industrial and Pecuniary Employments," reprinted in *The Place of Science in Modern Civilisation*, pages 279-323.
[80] Veblen, Thorstein, "The Socialist Economics of Karl Marx and His Followers," reprinted in *The Place of Science in Modern Civilisation*, page 441.

of human behavior.[81]   This difference between Marx and Veblen with respect to the interpretation of class behavior is very significant. Veblen feels that those who accept Marx's position rely too heavily upon class consciousness and reasoned class interest for the achievement of the goals they have in view.   They tend to be excessively optimistic about the possibility of appealing to class reason for the attainment of their goals.   Veblen asserts that such optimism has no foundation in fact.

In working out his concept of class organization, Veblen introduces the concepts of the cultural lag and class conflict.   According to his theory of culture the most important single factor that alters institutions, and hence human behavior, is technological change. However, all people and all classes are not equally exposed to changing technological conditions.   That portion or class of society that is less exposed to the forces of technological change adapts its views and scheme of life to the altered technological conditions more slowly than the class which is more directly exposed to the changing technology.[82]   There are thus set up different rates of mental adjustment to the new economic conditions.   As a consequence of these different rates of psychological adjustment, cultural lags make their appearance.   These cultural lags take the form of differences in the cultural standards that provide guidance to individual behavior. Thus, the wealthy leisure class, which is sheltered from the changing technology of the modern industrial system, finds that its institutional norms or standards of behavior are quite dissimilar to the institutional behavior norms of the industrial class.

Out of cultural lags, said Veblen, there arises class conflict. Where classes have different institutional standards and mental habits, their members find themselves acting at cross-purposes. Members of the non-industrial class are busy amassing pecuniary

---

[81] Although it is true that Marx took a great deal from the classical economists, he usually modified what he borrowed.   In criticizing Marx's rationalistic psychology Veblen overlooks the extent to which Marx went in working out a social psychology.   He makes little reference to the relations between Marx's economic interpretation of history and his theory of human behavior.   Veblen ignores the whole discussion by Marx of the social or environmental influences that shape human behavior.   While it is true that Marx makes much of human reason and little of human instinct, it is hardly justifiable to confine him to the simple rationalistic psychology accepted by the classical English economists.   In this connection Veblen's criticism appears to be more sweeping than correct.

[82] *The Theory of the Leisure Class*, page 193.

assets, whereas the industrial class is creating useful commodities. This clash between class interests and class behavior is largely the product of a blind drift of circumstances, which causes the industrial class to make mental adjustments to altered technological conditions ahead of the non-industrial class. Veblen asserts that classes do not reason themselves into conflict; they merely drift into class conflict. And because classes drift into conflict, they are not very conscious of the reasons for such conflict. Neither are they very clear about the aims or purposes of their conflicts. It was for this reason that Veblen, unlike Marx, did not look forward to any early breakdown of capitalism. There is no warrant, he said, "for asserting *a priori* that the class interest of the working class will bring them to take a stand against the propertied class. It may as well be that their training in subservience to their employers will bring them again to realize the equity and excellence of the established system of subjection and unequal distribution of wealth. Again, no one, for instance, can tell today what will be the outcome of the present situation in Europe and America. . . . It is quite impossible on Darwinian ground to foretell whether the 'proletariat' will go on to establish the socialistic revolution or turn aside again, and sink their force in the broad sands of patriotism." [83]

Veblen's psychology is in essence a collective psychology, based on the cardinal principle that "all life is necessarily group life." Since all human behavior has a collective aspect, the individual in isolation is a scientific abstraction that has no foundation in fact. Even though an individual is formally associated with no group, or with but few groups, he lives a collective or a "shared" existence. "Conduct," as John Dewey has said, "is always shared; this is the difference between it and a physiological process. It is not an ethical 'ought' that conduct *should* be social. It *is* social, whether bad or good." [84] In Veblen's analysis there is no such thing as individualistic behavior—behavior that is individualistic in the sense of being free from the influence of group activity. Even the most apparently independent individual acts and thinks in the deep shadow of his community's cultural norms or standards. In this sense human behavior is always, and only, collective behavior; and in the field of

[83] "The Socialist Economics of Karl Marx and His Followers," pages 441-442.
[84] Dewey, John, *Human Nature and Conduct,* page 17. New York: H. Holt and Company, 1922.

social science psychology is necessarily collective or social psychology. From Veblen's point of view an individualistic psychology has no meaning.

Now that an analysis of Veblen's general scientific outlook, his methodological procedure, and his psychological theory has been made, one can grasp the fundamental unity running through these three approaches to his economic thought. All three approaches draw their inspiration from Veblen's fundamental preconception of process. His concept of process with its related ideas of emergence and wholeness has nurtured the view of economic society as a going concern; it has given significance to the holistic method of analyzing scientific data; and it has provided a favorable setting for the creation of a collective psychology. It remains to be seen how Veblen works out his idea of an "evolutionary economics" in the light of his preconception of process. This will involve an analysis of how he uses his concept of the economic system as a going concern, his holistic method of analysis, and his social psychology in interpreting the modern economic system.

The Interpretation of Modern Capitalism

The preceding introductory remarks relating to Veblen's interest in philosophy, social psychology, and scientific methodology should not blind us to the fact that Veblen was primarily an economist, and that his major interest was in an analysis of the modern capitalistic system. In the preface to his last volume, *Absentee Ownership and Business Enterprise in Recent Times* (1923), he explains that his work is "an inquiry into the economic situation as it has taken shape during this (twentieth) century, particularly as exemplified in the case of America." Although Veblen displays a great deal of interest in the origins and early development of the modern economic system, the ultimate objective of his scientific endeavors is to explain the functioning of the modern economic system. His concern is with economic conduct in the most recent phase of the evolution of Western European industrialism. It is the conduct of men, groups, and classes which are participating in the affairs of twentieth-century capitalism that is analyzed by Veblen with special enthusiasm.

In making his investigation of the development of twentieth-century capitalism Veblen does not find it necessary to carry his analysis any further back than the era of handicraft industry. He explains that this handicraft industry originated in the cracks and crevices of the feudal order. In the course of time there were sufficient numbers of masterless craftsmen to establish centers of handicraft industry throughout Western Europe. The technology of the handicraft system was such that the masterless craftsman owned his own tools, and used only his own labor to turn out useful products. When a man saved a portion of his income, he invested it in the instruments of production and in the inventories that he used in his own business enterprise. In the early form of handicraft industry the masterless craftsmen used no hired labor, found it unnecessary to be in debt to any lender, and exchanged the product of his labor for the products of other craftsmen. The only trade at this time was "petty trade" in which craftsmen exchanged their products without the use of middlemen.

What Veblen finds significant about the early handicraft system is that it was an economy in which there was always a close relation between effort put forth and remuneration received. All incomes received by the handicraftsmen were "earned" incomes. The craftsman was not a landlord, a lender of funds, an exploiter of hired labor, or a middleman. The real income of the handicraftsman was obtained only through the expenditure of human effort. Personal wealth was measured in terms of useful, tangible goods; and ownership meant the possession and control of these useful material products obtained through individual effort. It is true that the output of this early handicraft industry was exchanged with the help of a price system. However, this was no obstacle to the proper distribution of industrial output, since prices were rough but accurate measures of the individual efforts incorporated in handicraft products. Prices of handicraft products were only sufficient to cover the costs of production, and to leave what was considered to be an adequate return for the efforts put forth by the masterless craftsman. In this early form of handicraft industry it was difficult, if not impossible, for the masterless worker to obtain an "unearned" or "free" income, or, as Veblen would express it, to get something for nothing.

The close cooperation of the handicraftsmen in their guild activity, and the joint rules under which they operated, developed habits of thought and behavior which led to "a solidarity of economic interests." [85]   Any attempt to destroy this solidarity by giving vent to the self-regarding or acquisitive impulses was very quickly ended by the joint action of the handicraft guild.   In this situation the parental bent was allowed to triumph over the destructive, acquisitive urge.   Those handicraftsmen who stood up for the guild's interests, and who placed guild welfare above personal welfare, were the acknowledged leaders of the community.   Furthermore, the workmanship drive was called in to support the parental bent.   Each craftsman was given an opportunity to express his workmanship drive in his chosen vocation.   Since emphasis was placed by the community on excellence of workmanship and economy in the use of materials, making goods was elevated above making money.   With money or profit making placed in a subsidiary position, there were no major conflicts between the two processes of making goods and making money.   In these circumstances the solidarity of economic interests was accompanied by a balancing of man's cooperative and acquisitive urges.   For a brief period in the early handicraft economy of the medieval towns and cities mankind found relief from destructive economic conflicts and antagonisms.

As the handicraft system underwent further development, the close connection between efforts put forth and rewards received suffered some deterioration.   The institution of absentee ownership made its appearance in a variety of ways.   Veblen explains that absentee ownership is a claim to unearned or free income, and that the absentee owner or vested interest is an individual who gets something for nothing.   The receiver of unearned income is referred to as an "absentee," because he is absent from or not directly concerned with the actual processes of production.[86]   In addition, the absentee owner is one who enjoys "the ownership of material wealth in excess of what he can make use of by himself."   Veblen also refers to the absentee owners as the "vested interests."   These vested interests are composed of individuals possessing "prescriptive rights to get something for nothing."

[85] Veblen, Thorstein, *The Theory of Business Enterprise*, page 290.   New York: Charles Scribner's Sons, 1904.

[86] Veblen, Thorstein, *Absentee Ownership and Business Enterprise in Recent Times*, pages 12, 49.   New York: B. W. Huebsch, Inc., 1923.

Veblen points out that there was a number of sources of absentee ownership or claims to unearned income in the later handicraft era. Where the land was worked by persons other than the landlord, ownership of land and its resources enabled certain individuals to claim an income without putting forth individual effort. Veblen is careful to explain that not all ownership of natural resources is a form of absentee ownership. The small farmer who operates his own farm without the use of hired labor, and who thus mixes his labor with the resources of the land to produce various crops, is not an absentee owner. Only where a person lays claim to income without making an adequate contribution of useful tangible goods do we have the phenomenon of absentee ownership.

The lending of money was also a manifestation of absentee ownership. As the handicraft industry matured, those who saved portions of their annual incomes, especially from the exploitation of the land, did not invest this surplus income in their own industrial enterprises. Instead they made investments for profit in other people's enterprises. Veblen explains that in lending funds, creditors came to lay claim to a part of the useful goods produced by the working borrowers. Something was obtained for nothing, and thus a new source of absentee ownership was created. In addition, master craftsmen came to depend more and more upon hired labor for the operation of their establishments. These employers who hired laborers laid claim to a portion of the output created by the wage earners. The result was a further development of absentee ownership. Finally, the growth of large-scale trading enabled the merchant princes to get an income without adding to the supply of useful goods. In these ways the path was cleared for an expansion of the institution of absentee ownership in the late stages of the handicraft era.

Although the trend was increasingly away from the production of useful material goods toward the amassing of pecuniary assets or money values in the late stages of the handicraft era, absentee ownership did not become a dominant institution in this period. It did not become what Veblen calls a "master institution" until the handicraft technology had been converted into a machine technology. Consequently, all during the handicraft era, incomes were still mainly earned incomes, prices reflected real economic values, productivity of useful goods rather than pecuniary values continued to be the major guiding principle of economic activity, and full employment of labor and tools was closely approximated.

The cumulative technological changes of the handicraft era eventually led to the substitution of a machine technology for the less intricate handicraft technology. Along with the machine technology came the "Era of Free Competition," an era in which the factory replaced the handicraftsman's shop and the "captain of industry" became the dominant economic figure. Industry remained on a small scale, but it was of a mechanical nature involving considerable financial outlay. The workers were now separated from their tools, credit was widely used, and production was no longer primarily for local markets. The collective features of handicraft industry were gradually replaced by the individualistic features of the atomistic, competitive business system; and the old solidarity of interests among different groups of handicraftsmen disappeared in the midst of the struggles of individual captains of industry to enhance their private fortunes.

The era of free competition brought with it a number of new emphases. After 1800 emphasis was placed on self-aggrandizement or private acquisition to the neglect of the expansion of the community's welfare. The weakened parental bent bowed before the vigorous, newly released acquisitive drives, and the workmanship proclivity was driven into the background. In the routine of the factory system the skilled worker had little opportunity to give expression to his workmanship drive; furthermore the old serviceability status now lost its appeal. Individuals increasingly found prestige and esteem by amassing money values rather than by showing proficiency in the production of useful, material goods. Veblen explains that "Enhanced income from investments became the paramount incentive of civilised life; and the Captain of Industry— the substantial citizen who controlled much of the nation's workmanship and so came in for a largely enhanced income—became the paramount exponent of the community's aims and ideals as well as the standard container of all the civic virtues." [87]   A wedge was now driven between the producing of useful goods and the making of profits as the captain of industry strove to become a specialist in the acquisition of pecuniary assets. In this effort he sought to estab-

[87] *Absentee Ownership,* page 71.

lish a pecuniary status based on disserviceability to the community.

The era of free competition marked the beginning of new class alignments and new class antagonisms. The workers retained habits of thought and behavior that gave some expression to the parental and workmanship drives and to the concept of a serviceability status. Without pecuniary assets and closely tied to the machine, the workers felt little in common with the new business classes, especially with the captains of industry. The businessmen rapidly acquired new views on what was a desirable personal status, and new attitudes with respect to the ends and purposes of economic activity. They saw to it that disserviceability to the community displaced serviceability, and that acquisition was favored over workmanship. In this manner there were set up opposite psychological poles around which businessmen and workers clustered. Workmanship was set up against acquisition, private welfare against community welfare, and worker against employer. The psychological unity underlying the solidarity of economic interests found in the early handicraft era was soon dissipated, and was gradually replaced by psychological disunity. In the economic world solidarity in outlook was thus changed into an ever-widening antagonism.

Although the era of free competition marked the beginning of new class alignments and class conflicts, these developments were only in their early stages during the competitive era. It was not until the era of free competition merged into the era of corporate capitalism that these conflicts and antagonisms reached a high level of development. During the era of free competition the laboring population was largely unorganized and had little class consciousness. Workers were employed by thousands of scattered, small-scale business enterprises. Even the captains of industry were not entirely dissociated from the productive system. Most of them, having risen from the ranks, had some experience with the actual work of producing goods. For this reason Veblen describes them as "captains of industry" and not "captains of business." Although they were mainly concerned with the business or pecuniary ends of economic activities, they were not unfamiliar with the actual productive processes. This contact early in their lives with the productive system blurred their pecuniary aims, and to some extent mitigated the rigors of the acquisitive struggle.

During the era of free competition the institution of absentee own-

ership expanded very slowly. As long as active competition between businessmen prevailed, there were very definite limits placed
upon the opportunities of businessmen to lay unwarranted claims
upon the growing surplus products of the improving industrial technology. All during the competitive era there existed what Veblen
calls a "competitive production of goods." Competition was of such
a nature as to force businessmen to outdo one another in turning
out useful goods. Businessmen competed with one another by
striving for lower costs of production, and by continuously under-
selling less active competitors. Improvements in methods of production resulted in lower costs of production and lower selling prices
to the masses of consumers. For this reason many of the advantages
of the improving machine technology were passed on to the general
public. Since competing businessmen were unable to absorb a major portion of the expanding national income, they were unable to
augment their absentee ownership. The only classes in the community who were able, during the era of free competition, to augment their unearned income were the owners of land and other
natural resources. To some extent the expanding population and
the growing demands of the improving industrial system made possible higher land rents and enhanced prices for raw materials.
These higher rents and raw-material prices permitted a considerable
expansion of "free" income. Apart from this case the era of free
competition was not the era of a great increase in absentee ownership; that was to come in the following era of semi-monopoly and
large-scale production.

After 1850 in England, and somewhat later in the United States,
the era of free competition began to give way to new developments.
The decay of the "old-fashioned competitive system" was hastened
by the further development of the machine technology, by the reduction in the supply of new market areas, and by the introduction
of the corporate form of business enterprise with its related "corporation finance." Small firms were eliminated or gradually converted
into the links of larger industrial chains. The actual management
of the industrial system fell more and more into the hands of "un-
businesslike technicians" or technical experts, while the captains of
industry became less concerned with the production of goods and
more concerned with the pecuniary aspects of business enterprise.
The captain of industry developed into a captain of business, and

the separation of technicians from businessmen was now completed.

In the early stages of this new era in the development of modern capitalism, the expanding productive capacities of the improved industrial system resulted in a competitive struggle to dispose of large outputs. The efforts of large business enterprises to sell an expanding output brought on price wars and "cutthroat competition." The market situation was further complicated because progress in industrial technology led to the continuous organization of new firms with lower costs of production than firms already established. The older firms not only suffered from excessive productive capacity, but were also confronted with the problem of unduly high costs of production brought about by the use of outmoded capital equipment. With many large firms saddled with high fixed charges and burdened with industrial equipment that was rapidly becoming outmoded, the new business era degenerated into a period of surplus productive capacity, declining profits, and cutthroat competition. By the end of the nineteenth century the usual state of business was one of "chronic depression." Writing in 1904, Veblen was of the opinion that "depression is normal to the industrial situation under the consummate regime of the machine, so long as competition is unchecked and no *deus ex machina* interposes." [88]

According to Veblen's analysis there were two ways to check the business system's "untoward tendency to chronic depression." One way was to free the old firms from the devastating competition of new low-cost firms by having the energies of the new firms absorbed in government spending programs. The productivity of the new low-cost firms would be allowed to exhaust itself in the erection of public buildings or in large-scale preparations for war. This scheme of preventing chronic depression by widening the flow of public waste did not prove adequate to meet the problem in the final quarter of the last century. Consequently recourse was had after 1895 to a second expedient which Veblen describes as the "expedient of coalition." Since the business system was unable to balance the surplus productivity of an improving industry with wasteful private and public expenditures on a wide scale, businessmen sought to secure a balance between production and consumption by curtailing and regulating the output of goods. It was the successful recourse to this "expedient of coalition" that eventually

[88] *The Theory of Business Enterprise*, page 255.

led to the new era of business stabilization in the early years of the twentieth century.

The basic aim of the "expedient of coalition" was to pool the interests of former competitors so that output would be curbed, and prices would be adjusted in order to restore what were regarded as adequate profits. When enough of the productive capacity of an industry had been brought within the pooling arrangement, output and prices were so adjusted as to maximize the net profits received by the various firms participating in the pooling arrangement. Such an arrangement, to be successful, must not only provide for control of production and price policies, but it must also provide adequate control over the influx of new investments into the industry. When the pooling arrangement has been perfected so as to provide adequate control over new investment, production, and pricing, the goal of business stabilization may be said to have been achieved.

The informal coalition efforts of the latter part of the nineteenth century were soon followed by the introduction of a new type-form of business organization, the holding company. Along with the holding company came the investment banker who was an important factor in the working out of the new alignment of ownership and business enterprise. Prior to 1890 the large key industries had been unable to eliminate cutthroat competition among themselves. There was no third party or independent mediator who could provide a policy of united action which would lead away from the ruinous situation of "unguarded competitive production." At this critical juncture in the evolution of American capitalism the investment banker appeared with a kitful of such ingenious devices as the holding company, the interlocking directorate, and the voting trust. The usual procedure of the investment bankers was to unite a number of formerly competing companies into a holding company that would control enough of the productive capacity of the industry so as to make "unguarded competitive production" no longer possible. In carrying out this consolidation of business enterprises the investment bankers became the owners of large blocks of common stock, securities that represented, for the most part, the capitalized goodwill of the new holding company. After having acquired large amounts of common stock the investment bankers found it advantageous to merge their financial interests with the original large holders of the common stocks of the key industries.   In this manner a "community of interest" grew up between the original owners of the key industries and the newly arrived investment bankers.   This community of interest soon gave birth to what Veblen called the "One Big Union" of the vested interests or absentee owners.

Writing in 1923 Veblen was of the opinion that the "One Big Union" of industrialists and financiers had such an effective control of credit, production, and price policies that depressions and uncontrolled downward movements of prices were no longer possible, except when willed by the "custodians of administrative control." "There is in the current situation," he explained, "an element of sobriety and a factor of salutary reserve that were lacking in the nineteenth century.   Prosperity ran somewhat headlong in those days, and came, in the ordinary course, to a headlong liquidation, ending in panic, crisis and depression.   Under the surveillance of the Federal Reserve and the One Big Union of the Interests in the twentieth century the prosperity of business, that is to say the inflation of capital and prices—does not run riot.   It is an orderly advance, in the course of which the progressive creations of credit and capital are duly stabilized and 'digested,' distributed and consolidated under the aegis of the Interests, with such effect as to make them a secure ground on which to hypothecate further creations of the same character, in indefinite progression.   And no undesigned liquidation need be apprehended in this case, since the major debits and credits are pooled, in effect, by being drawn in under the custody of these major Interests that informally make up the One Big Union." [89]   By 1923, in Veblen's opinion, the substitution of administrative control for the former competitive control of the business system was almost completed.   The era of "Big Business" had reached a maturity which marked the successful completion of the efforts of businessmen to subdue an unruly industrial technology.   As Veblen saw it, by 1923 it could be said without much dissent that "workmanship" was required to wait on "business."

The "new order of business," whose development Veblen has traced, is significantly different in structure and functioning from

[89] *Absentee Ownership*, page 391 fn.   The course of events since 1929 has not supported Veblen's assertion that the One Big Union of vested interests has learned how to subdue the up-and-down movements of prices and business activity.

the competitive business system about which Alfred Marshall wrote in his *Principles of Economics*. The atomistic structure of the old competitive order is now replaced by a partly competitive, partly monopolistic structure; and the fluid competitive business system of the nineteenth century has hardened into a "new hierarchy of business." At the top of this hierarchical structure are the "key industries" which include the coal, steel, oil, and transportation industries. These are the activities in which the modern large-scale industrial technology has made the most progress. As they are at the "tactical center" of the industrial system, they "effectually govern the movements of the country's industrial system at large, as a comprehensive going concern." These key industries set the pace for the entire economy; they operate like an economic vortex into which all the rest of the economy is drawn.

Below the key industries in the industrial hierarchy are the other branches of production and trade which become less monopolistic and more competitive as the bottom of the hierarchy is approached. At the bottom of the industrial stratification are the remnants of the old competitive system: small-scale manufacturing, retailing, and farming. These activities continue to exist on the periphery of the new industrial order where they "wait on the movement of things" in the key industries.[90] Especially in the rural areas and country towns are the appearances of the former competitive era preserved, but even there local business comes under the domination of Big Business.

The functioning of Veblen's new order of business is dominated by the large corporate enterprises in the key industries whose price and production policies are quite different from the policies of the small-scale competitive firms. The competitive enterprises of the nineteenth century were constantly working under a pressure to enlarge output and to sell this expanding output at reduced prices. Veblen finds the reverse to be true of the modern economy. He observes that the tendency of the firms in the key industries is to restrict output and to raise prices in order to maximize net profits. Modern corporate enterprise finds the "need of a vigilant restraint on production." The administrative controls over business exercised by the managers of corporations bring about a substitution of

[90] *Absentee Ownership*, page 214. See especially the section of Chapter VII entitled "The Country Town."

the "closed market" for the formerly open, competitive market. In the closed market prices are set by corporate management at the level of "what the traffic will bear," which is the level providing the maximum net return on corporate investments. Output, costs, and prices are adjusted by the corporate administrators in order to maximize net profits on the inflated capitalizations of those few firms which are permitted to enter the key industries.

The substitution of closed, partially monopolistic markets for open, competitive markets does not mean the end of all competition, or the complete failure of supply and demand forces to operate. Veblen explains that the form of competition has changed, and that the forces of supply and demand now "move obscurely in the background of the market." In the new industrial order the forces of supply and demand have not been eliminated; instead, they have been driven underground where they continue to influence the course of economic activity, but not in the direct, overt fashion as seen in the nineteenth century. In the old system of open competitive markets individual firms within each industry competed with one another. The situation is changed in the modern economic system. Today, in the key industries, firms within each industry do not compete, but the various industries themselves compete with one another for the consumer's dollar. Instead of intra-industry competition, as of old, we now have mainly inter-industry competition. "The result," says Veblen, "is not that competition ceases or declines . . . but only that it takes a new turn, commonly with an increased vigor and persistence. . . . It becomes a competition not within the business but between this business as a whole and the rest of the community." [91] The oil, steel, transportation, coal, building, and other major industries vigorously compete with one another to secure as large a share as possible of the available consumer purchasing power.

The restrictive price and production policies of the large corporate enterprises call forth similar reactions on the part of the farmers and the workers. The new order of business induces not only businessmen but also workers and farmers to seek to "buy cheap and sell dear." The farmers feel the need to limit production and to raise the prices of agricultural products; but they have no "spirit of community interest" that binds them together in a collective

[91] *Absentee Ownership*, page 128.

enterprise. Consequently, they are unable to adopt successfully the price and production policies of the key industries. The result is that farmers are kept quite close to the minimum of subsistence, while the surplus or net product coming from agriculture is drained off by the large corporations, which buy raw materials at low prices from the farmers and in return sell their manufactured products at high prices. In effect farmers and their productive equipment are a natural resource the use of which is obtained on very favorable terms by the large corporate enterprises, but on terms that are exasperating to the farm population.

In the struggle to match the price and production policies of the key industries the workers do better than the farmers. Veblen refers to the large national trade unions, which are members of the American Federation of Labor, as "businesslike coalitions endeavoring to drive a bargain and establish a vested interest, governed by the standard aims and methods of the price-system." Following the practices of the large corporate enterprises, the national trade unions monopolize the supply of skilled laborers and thus create a "scarcity-price" for certain types of labor. These groups of skilled laborers are not class conscious. They are conscious only of their own special interests, and are prepared to augment their income at the expense of any groups that might fall in their way, even of other laboring groups and farmers as well as of businessmen. To the organized skilled workers, as to the businessmen, it is a struggle of their special group against all the rest of the community for as large a share as possible of the national income.

This struggle of each vested interest against the rest of the community results in an economy that operates with only "partial employment of equipment and man-power." Occasionally, as in boom periods, the economy approaches "full employment," but the usual condition is one in which men and machines are only partially employed. In the old competitive economy of the first half of the nineteenth century full employment of men and machines was enjoyed because competition forced businessmen to seek lower costs in an expanding output. But this was true only in the early stages of the factory system. After 1875 full employment of equipment and man power led to cutthroat competition and chronic depression. By 1923 there was an established system of partial employment. As Veblen sees the matter, we now have a business system which always has a reserve of unemployed equipment and man-power.   In the key industries of coal, steel, oil, and transport there is more investment than can be profitably used.   In the old com-petitive system equipment and man power could not continue for long to be unused because the forces of supply and demand would push them into those lines where they would find employment. But this is not true today in the sluggish modern economy where closed markets greatly impede the operations of the forces of supply and demand.

The modern economic system that Veblen describes is a hybrid or mixed economy.   It is no longer mainly competitive; instead, it combines both competitive and monopolistic features.   The mo-nopolistic portion of the economy is inflexible or rigid.   This in-flexibility comes from the administrative controls that are imposed by the corporation managers and owners.   In contrast, the com-petitive segment of the economic system is flexible and subject to many adjustments.   Here are to be found free prices, open markets, and competitive adjustments.   But the mechanisms of adjustment of this competitive portion of the economy are called upon to absorb the shocks of disturbances originating in the monopolistic part of the hybrid economy.   In this situation most of the burdens and costs of adjustment are thrown on the competitive segment of the dual economy.   This means that the major burdens fall upon the workers, the small businessmen, and the farmers, since the vested interests and their business representatives or "guardians," who con-trol the inflexible monopolistic part of the economy, are in a good position to insulate themselves from the recurring disturbances of a poorly integrated economy.

Consequences of the Corporate Revolution

The mixed or hybrid economy that Veblen analyzes is also one in which the pace is set by the large corporation.   The new tech-nological basis of industry has been matched by a "mutation of the scheme of things in business enterprise" which takes the form of the modern corporation.[92]   This master institution, the corpora-tion, has wrought some profound changes in the system of business enterprise.   Not only has it eliminated the personal contacts of em-

[92] Veblen, Thorstein, *The Vested Interests and the State of the Industrial Arts,* page 44.   New York: B. W. Huebsch, Inc., 1919.

ployers and employees, but more importantly, it has altered the very nature of the ownership of private property. The corporation has denatured and depersonalized ownership. Prior to 1875 ownership had meant the personal control of material means of production by the owner himself. The owner was personally responsible for the management and use of his own property. Besides receiving income from his property, the owner recognized the various duties and responsibilities associated with the ownership of private property. Under the new corporate regime ownership has lost a part of its older functions. Ownership now means not active control of material property but passive possession of intangible corporate assets or of "anonymous corporate capital." Veblen observes that the great majority of corporate owners are now reduced to the status of "anonymous pensioners" in the corporate enterprises. Even those who possess large blocks of corporate stock, and who therefore possess a great deal of economic power, are prone to place the actual management of their property in the hands of business representatives or "Guardians of the Vested Interests."

The changes in the functions of ownership have been accompanied by changes in the very nature of the thing owned. Prior to the advent of the modern corporation, ownership related to the control of tangible material assets or means of production. In recent times ownership has shifted to an intangible basis, and is now more concerned with the possession of intangible corporate assets. These intangible corporate assets revolve around certain values which the courts have recognized as business goodwill, and have assigned to the corporate owners. The essence of this business goodwill is some form of control over the industrial system which enables those who possess it to levy tribute on all who are embraced within the system of corporate controls. The most important source of intangible corporate wealth is control of the technological processes of the industrial system. In the handicraft era, and also very largely in the later era of free competition, industrial technology was the common property of all producers. No one producer could seize a portion of the community's technological knowledge and then use it to augment his free or unearned income. Technological knowledge was equally available to all industrious producers. Consequently, there was no ownership or private property in the intangible form of control over technological processes.

Veblen finds that the situation is quite different in the new industrial order of the twentieth century. Through the control of patents and other devices the owners of the key industries have placed themselves astride the modern industrial technology. They have placed themselves in strategic positions with reference to the control and use of this technology, and can now decide who shall use the modern technological processes and under what conditions. In this situation the surplus or net product made possible by the modern industrial technology is drained off by the large corporate owners. Technology thus ceases to be "common" property and becomes "private" property; and the communal interest is set aside in favor of the vested interests.

The device of corporate credit has aided the corporate owners of large means in cornering the community's technological knowledge and skills. By corporate credit Veblen means not only bonded indebtedness and short-term borrowing from banks but also stock ownership. Veblen breaks away from the traditional treatment of corporation finance by regarding corporate stock primarily as a form of credit.[93] He explains that large stock owners have frequently obtained much of their stock by making no investment of their own funds. The usual practice has been to issue additional stock on the basis of the expanding goodwill or earning capacity of the corporation. As industrial technology has improved and the earning capacities of corporations have increased, instead of lowering prices, as in the era of free competition and thus passing on the benefits of lowered costs of production to the consumers, the vested interests or large corporate owners have capitalized the increased earning power to their own advantage. They have done this by giving themselves newly issued common stock that is backed not by material assets but only by the increased earning power of the corporation. They have laid claim to the growing surpluses of the improving industrial technology by taking them in the form of dividends on stocks for which nothing was ever given. In Veblen's opinion these additional issues of common stock are indistinguishable from an increase of the liabilities of the corporation. Veblen regards the dividends on the new stock issues as additional overhead

---

[93] For a discussion of Veblen's theory of credit see Ch. V, "The Use of Loan Credit," in *The Theory of Business Enterprise.* See also Ch. XII, "The Larger Use of Credit," in *Absentee Ownership.*

charges. For this reason he places these stock issues in the same class as corporate debentures. In both cases the corporation is saddled with new liabilities; and the line between debt and property, credit and capital, or stock and bond becomes blurred.

Besides altering the functions and nature of private property the corporation has brought collective action to the forefront. Veblen observes that throughout the economy this collective action leads to the organization of classes. Thus by 1923 a discernible class situation was in a fluid process of development: the large stockholders and the corporate managers had formed a loose organization in the form of the One Big Union of vested interests; the skilled workers had their large national unions federated in the American Federation of Labor; the industrial union with its larger coverage of different types of labor was on the horizon; and the farmers were experimenting with the cooperative form of collective action. Increasingly it was becoming the case that policies were being formed and issues were being drawn on the level of class action. By 1923 the growth of classes had not yet gone very far; and class lines had not been clearly drawn. It was still a situation of each group or class against all the other groups in the community. But underneath this immature class situation Veblen professed to see certain trends that heralded the eventual split of economic society into two major classes: the absentee owners and the underlying working population.

Not only has the corporation given a stimulus to the development of collective action and class organization, but it has also sharpened the conflict between the absentee owners and the workers with respect to the proper goals of economic activity. The corporation, with its restrictive price and production policies and its emphasis on intangible pecuniary assets, has given a new emphasis to the acquisition of a pecuniary status. This new emphasis on the pecuniary gains to be derived from the manipulation of corporate affairs has thrown into deeper relief the contrast between the pecuniary status of the absentee owners and the serviceability status of the workers. The ground is being well prepared for the development of a sharp division between those who aspire to a serviceability status and those who seek a pecuniary status. Although the workers and technical experts are far from being a class-conscious group, Veblen feels that their views on the desirability of an efficiency or serviceability status are being rapidly crystallized.   And so he believes that the trends of the modern corporate economy are all designed to bring out still further than in the past the deep psychological antagonisms between absentee owners and workers.   Some trends are fostering self-aggrandizement and the pecuniary status, while others are nourishing workmanship and the serviceability status.   A continuation of these trends in the development of corporate enterprise can only mean the growth of a psychological conflict of large dimensions.

Along with corporate enterprise has come the problem of economic power.   Veblen explains that the era of free competition was a period when businessmen possessed little economic power. Since business activities were controlled by the general forces of supply and demand, no individual businessman had any appreciable amount of control over his production, prices, or competitors. Each businessman was free from domination by other businessmen, and at the same time he could exert no control over any other businessman.   The succeeding era of corporate enterprise is quite different from the era of free competition.   It is an era of coercion, retardation, restraint, of "collusive control of industry."   It is an era in which the issue is between those who have enough wealth to exert control over the economic system and those who do not have enough wealth to be in a strategic position.   The upshot is, says Veblen, "that the population of these civilized countries now falls into two main classes: those who own wealth invested in large holdings and who thereby control the conditions of life for the rest; and those who do not own wealth in sufficiently large holdings, and whose conditions of life are therefore controlled by these others. It is a division, not between those who have something and those who have nothing—as many socialists would be inclined to describe it—but between those who own wealth enough to make it count, and those who do not." [94]

Veblen means by the power of coercion the possession of the ability to interrupt the free functioning of the forces of supply and demand.   In the present era of corporate enterprise those in control of the affairs of the large corporations have a great deal of economic power.   On the negative side they can curb production, withhold supplies, and retard the improvement of industrial technology.   On the positive side they can manipulate prices, determine

[94] *The Vested Interests*, pages 160-161.

who shall enter the industry, fix the amount of employment, and set the tempo for the entire economy.   In the era of free competition ownership meant only the control of the material means of production; but in the new era of corporate enterprise ownership means the possession of intangible pecuniary assets that carry with them powers of coercion, intimidation, and retardation.   Property is sought not for its contribution to the nation's income stream but for its capacity to invest its owners with dictatorial powers over the destiny of the whole economic system.

The quest for economic power is not restricted to the owners of corporate stock.   Labor organizations have discovered a potent source of economic power in their control of the supply of skilled services.   They have the power to offset the influences of supply and demand, and to dictate to some extent the terms upon which labor may be hired and recompensed.   Through their organizations the workers have endeavored to match the economic power possessed by the absentee owners and their business representatives.   So eager have the skilled workers been to adopt the power-gathering tactics of the absentee owners that they have frequently sought economic power as a bargaining advantage and not as a means of eliminating the power position of the vested interests.   It is because of this short-sighted aim of the organized skilled workers that Veblen refers to their American Federation of Labor as a "quasi-vested interest."   In the growing struggle for economic power long-run goals have frequently been ignored, with the result that the conflict over economic power has at times fallen to the level of merely predatory action aimed at "a conscientious withdrawal of efficiency" by workers as well as by businessmen.

What of the future of this rapidly maturing capitalistic economy?   In the concluding chapter of his *Absentee Ownership and Business Enterprise in Recent Times* Veblen carries the secular trends of the business enterprise system into what he calls the "calculable future."   He looks forward to a deepening of the conflict between the absentee owners and the "underlying population."   Like Karl Marx, Veblen believes that the economic society of the future will fall into two major divisions.   A distinct line of cleavage will appear, but not between those who own something and those who own nothing, as Marx thought.   The cleavage will be between "those who own more than they personally can use and those who have urgent use

for more than they own." Veblen asserts that the socialistic interpretation, as it came from Marx, has been rendered obsolete by the
new alignment of economic forces. It is no longer a question of
ownership or of equity in the distribution of income; it is no longer
an issue between the "haves" and the "have nots." Veblen explains
that the issue is one of expediency rather than moral revulsion.
The underlying population is antagonistic to the vested interests or
absentee owners not on moral grounds, but because the former class
no longer finds it expedient to leave the vested interests in control
of the industrial system. The main problem is a question of getting
work done expeditiously, and is not one of distributing the national
income. Veblen feels that when the problem of producing abundantly is successfully handled, the question of dividing output will
be easily settled.

Out of the "progressively settled and malevolent hostility" between employers and workers, says Veblen, there will develop a "progressive deficit of industrial production." The efforts of both businessmen and workers to create artificial scarcities of services and
commodities will gradually whittle away the net product of industry.
As this process continues, the time will come when not only will
there be no net product from industry, but even the capital equipment of the nation will not be kept intact. The former annual industrial net product will then have been converted into an annual
deficit. With the nation failing to maintain its industrial equipment and the national output of commodities progressively declining, the underlying population will suffer a contraction of its standard of living. The industrial system will then be operated on the
basis of a "progressively diminishing return," until a point will be
reached where further reductions in real income will no longer
be tolerated by the working population. At this point an industrial
stalemate will make its appearance.

Veblen is not at all certain as to what will happen after this industrial stalemate has been reached. As he sees it, two developments
are possible. In order to preserve their privileged positions the absentee owners and their business representatives may appeal to the
national government for protection. Since the personnel of the national government is mainly drawn from those classes that have a
stake in the continuance of absentee ownership, Veblen believes it to
be quite possible that the employer-owners may be protected from

the advances of the workers on the ground that the national interests are in jeopardy. The state would then come to exercise a coercive administration over economic affairs which would put an end to the encroachments of the underlying population. Although such a development would preserve the rights and privileges of the absentee owners and their business representatives, it might prove to be transitory. In calling upon the national government to protect their rights and privileges, the absentee owners would be calling upon a power far greater than themselves. Should the government of the nation fall into the hands of a military class, there might be a reversion to a barbarian form of culture in which military power would curb not only the underlying population but also the vested interests or absentee owners.[95]

Veblen raises the question whether or not the underlying population would stand idly by while the absentee owners carried their plea for protection to the national government. Might not the underlying population, or a portion of it, seek to put an end to the existing business system? Veblen explains that "There is always the chance, more or less imminent, that in time, after due trial and error, or duly prolonged and intensified irritation, some sizable element of the underlying population, not intrinsically committed to absentee ownership, will forsake or forget their moral principles of business-as-usual, and will thereupon endeavor to take this business-like arrangement to pieces and put the works together again on some other plan for better or worse."[96] What would this shifting of the economic base involve, and what would be its general direction? These are questions that hold for Veblen only a "speculative interest," since he feels that the establishment of a new industrial order is only a remote possibility. There are many obstacles to be overcome before the working population will forsake the business system to which it is accustomed. The most serious obstacle is the deferential attitude of the workers toward the vested interests which control the industrial system. This "sentimental deference" of the working masses springs from a bent of self-abasement or subservience which leads the working population to accept the leadership of the

[95] For a discussion of this point see Ch. X, "The Natural Decay of Business Enterprise," in *The Theory of Business Enterprise*.
[96] *Absentee Ownership*, page 425.

vested interests.[97] So powerful is this deferential bent, that only a long-continued social crisis could sufficiently divert it to permit the revolutionary experiment of setting up a "regime of workmanship."

Fully aware of the speculative nature of his analysis, Veblen outlines the probable steps that would be taken by those who might attempt to set up a new industrial order. In setting up a regime of workmanship provision would have to be made for certain prerequisites. In the first place an extensive campaign of inquiry and publicity would have to be carried out in order to acquaint the underlying population with the general aims of the plan for industrial reconstruction. It would be the purpose of this campaign to show in a convincing manner what are the defects of the present control of industry by the business classes, and what could be expected from the management of industry by technicians. In the second place the establishment of a regime of workmanship would require the creation of a common understanding and a solidarity of feeling between the technical experts and the working forces of the key industries. The engineers, economists, and workers in the key industries would have to cultivate a spirit of teamwork. This spirit of teamwork would be an energizing force that would permeate the whole underlying population and unite the many rival labor organizations. Finally, a competent group of economists and engineers would have to come forth, by a process of "self-selection," to provide the necessary leadership for the movement to establish a new order of production.

Once the spirit of teamwork was in evidence and the underlying population was sympathetically aroused, the next step would be to call a general strike of as much of the country's staff of technicians as would bring the industrial system to a standstill. At the same time all absentee ownership would be disallowed. All legal instruments such as stocks, bonds, mortgages, and other evidences of debt would be voided. With one stroke the institution of absentee ownership and all vested interests would disappear. Veblen feels that, even though the absentee owners would reluctantly abdicate when faced by the fact that the industrial situation was beyond their

[97] For a further discussion of this bent and its relation to patriotism see Veblen's *An Inquiry Into the Nature of Peace and the Terms of its Perpetuation*, pages 41-46. New York: The Macmillan Company, 1917.

control, forcible dispossession of the vested interests could in all probability be avoided.

The incoming central directorate of engineers and economists would organize the industrial system on the basis of production for use rather than for profit. Economic activity would be broken down into the major activities concerned with the production, transportation, and distribution of commodities. Each industry would be organized on the basis of local, regional, and national councils. Over all of industry would be the central directorate or executive council. This central directorate would have three major goals which would include an efficient, balanced use of resources, man power, and equipment, an avoidance of waste and the duplication of productive facilities, and an equitable distribution of goods and services to consumers. These goals would be achieved through a program of fact-finding, overall analysis, and consultation with the spokesmen of the various industries. As a result of this reorganization of economic life the powerful productive forces of the modern industrial system would be released from the restrictive influences of business controls. The end result would be full employment of men and equipment and an abundance of goods and services for the underlying population.

The establishment of the socialized economy that Veblen has in mind would mark the return to an era something like that of the earlier stone age. The stone-age culture, as pictured by Veblen, was one in which the parental and workmanship bents had free play. At that early time men cooperated in the production of those services and goods which contributed to the preservation of the human race. Since the self-regarding impulses were effectively curbed, they were prevented from leading to individual action that would have been detrimental to social welfare. Although the technological foundation of the new socialized economy would be far removed from the simple, technological system of the stone-age culture, the psychological climates of the two cultural eras would have much in common. The new industrial order envisioned by Veblen would be of "a collective and cooperative nature" in which the individual would be led by the discipline of a new habituation to identify his personal interests with those of the world community. The workmanship bent would be free to stimulate industrial progress and to provide the community with an ever-expanding real income. The economic gains thus achieved would be safe-guarded and used to the best advantage under the guidance of mankind's urge to cooperate in the preservation and advancement of group welfare. In the end there would be established "neighborly fellowships of ungraded masterless men given over to 'life, liberty and the pursuit of happiness' under the ancient and altogether human rule of Live and Let Live."

The regime of workmanship that Veblen would like to see established in the future would be a democratic regime. He observes in modern society an upsurge of democratic tendencies. What is counting for more and more in the modern world is the frame of mind of the common man. Veblen points out that "The advice and consent of the common run has latterly come to be indispensable to the conduct of affairs among civilised men, somewhat in the same degree in which the community is to be accounted a civilised people." Those who are in positions of control in modern society are finding it increasingly necessary to secure at least the "permissive tolerance" of the common run in carrying out their plans. The frame of mind of the common man is a "conditioning circumstance" that cannot be successfully ignored. As the frame of mind of the common man becomes more alert and more matter-of-fact, Veblen believes that it will be a more effective force in the shaping of a democratic society. How this will be so he does not explain in any detail. Nor does he ever launch into a discussion of how the new industrial order that he envisions would be democratically operated. At no point in his analysis of modern economic society does Veblen come to grips with the impact of politics upon economic activity. He makes no mention of the political problems that would remain even if a "regime of workmanship" were established. The reader is left with the impression that the democratic economy of the future, if it were realized, would be plagued with few, if any, political issues. Past history gives little support to this view. Veblen's failure to inquire deeply into the political basis of his new industrial order may be explained on the ground that, since he had little hope for an early establishment of his regime of workmanship, he felt that the whole inquiry was remote and very speculative.

Veblen was much more pessimistic than was Karl Marx as to the outcome of the conflict between the vested interests and the workers. He was not much impressed by the abilities of individuals or groups to extricate themselves from social difficulties through the use of their reason.   He did not deny that "interested parties" have shrewdly turned popular movements to their own advantage, and that to this extent they "have exercised something of a selective guidance over the growth of institutions."   But in the long run human struggles on the social plane have been little different from animal struggles on the biological plane.   Both types of struggles have been largely blind reactions to uncontrolled and uncontrollable environmental stimuli.   On this point Veblen's final position was that "Whether any given people is to come through any given period of such enforced change alive and fit to live, appears to be a matter of chance in which human insight plays a minor part and human foresight no part at all." [98]

As a scientist Veblen was interested only in the "objective consequences" of institutional development.   He analyzed the capitalistic system as an economic process passing through various periods of development.   This evolution of capitalism was not a cultural movement involving only chance, accident, and fortuitous development. On the contrary, Veblen professed to see a certain logic in the process of capitalistic development.   He observed two great forces at work, "two lines of improvement in methods in business and in technology," which were converging in such a way as to disrupt the smooth functioning of the industrial system in a progressively serious manner.   He felt that this hostility or incompatibility between the business and the technological systems could "logically be counted on to rise in due course to that pitch of vivacity where it will stick at nothing."   This was to be the end result of the working out of the logic of economic development as determined by the nature and circumstances of modern capitalism.

The prediction of an industrial stalemate was as far as Veblen's logic of capitalistic evolution would scientifically carry him.   Such a logic could tell him that "it seems plain that there should be an eventual limit" to the continuance of the incompatibility between the business and industrial systems.   But this same logic would tell him little concerning the final result to which the breakdown of capitalism would lead.   Karl Marx's logic of capitalism permitted him to predict the final outcome of capitalistic decay to be a communistic society, but Veblen's logic of capitalistic evolution provided

[98] *Absentee Ownership*, pages 18, 20 fn.

no basis for any such clear-cut, definite prediction. Instead, Veblen came to the conclusion that the eventual outcome of the decay and breakdown of the capitalistic system could not be definitely predicted. It could lead either to a militaristic, barbaric society, or to a socialized, cooperative commonwealth. However, any statements about the final outcome of the decay of the system of business enterprise were at best only unscientific, blind guesses. As a social scientist Veblen was unwilling to push his logic of capitalistic development into the realm of blind guessing or wishful thinking. It is not surprising, therefore, that he refused to place much confidence in long-run predictions about the final outcome of the decay of the system of business enterprise. He did feel, however, that the economist could, with some scientific support, peer into the immediate future; and, in general, he felt pessimistic about the "calculable future." Writing in 1921, he said that "There is nothing in the situation that should reasonably flutter the sensibilities of the Guardians or of that massive body of well-to-do citizens' who make up the rank and file of absentee owners, just yet." In the final paragraph of his last volume, written in 1923, Veblen retained the same general outlook, concluding his observations on the course of capitalistic development with the remark that "For the immediate future the prospect appears to offer a fuller confirmation in the faith that business principles answer all things."

The Theory of Economic and Pecuniary Values

Veblen explains that the modern economic system is an organization which creates two types of values, namely, economic and pecuniary values, a division which corresponds with the basic dichotomy between industry and business. Industry is concerned with economic values, business with pecuniary values. At certain times in the evolution of the economic system the streams of economic and pecuniary value have run close together. There has then been such a high degree of coincidence between the two types of values that it could be said that they were harmoniously related. In such a situation pecuniary values reflect or are rough measures of economic values. At other times in the development of the economic system the streams of these two types of values have moved away from each other so that discrepancies between the two types of values have made their appearance. In this circumstance pecuniary values are no longer adequate measures of economic values. Out of this lack of coincidence between pecuniary and economic values have come the basic economic issues that now confront society. Veblen's economic analysis is directed toward an explanation of how the lack of coincidence between economic and pecuniary values has arisen and of how it may be eliminated.

According to Veblen's interpretation, economic values are the real or tangible values that are produced by the industrial system. These real or economic values are defined by Veblen to be useful physical products or commodities. They are the end products of the industrial processes which give effect to the modern large-scale technology. The "usefulness" or "serviceability" of these tangible commodities has both a private and a social aspect. From the private viewpoint a commodity is useful when it meets a personal need of any kind. A tangible commodity may be used by an individual to meet any one of a number of his personal needs. But what meets the personal need of an individual may not also meet a social need. Veblen points out that there are two types of needs or purposes: immediate and ultimate needs. These needs are not always in harmony as, for example, in a situation where the self-regarding individual satisfies his own needs at the expense of the community. In such a situation a good or economic value may meet the immediate needs of the individual but not the ultimate needs of the community. To be really useful in the Veblenian sense a tangible commodity must meet the needs of both the individual and the community at the same time. The usefulness or serviceability of economic values is thus both a private and a social matter.

When is a material product socially useful or serviceable? To have a social or "substantial" usefulness a product must be serviceable to the community. In Veblen's analysis a material product is serviceable to the community when it permits the biological drives of individuals to be satisfied and thus makes for race survival. A socially useful product must meet "the test of impersonal usefulness— usefulness as seen from the point of view of the generically human." The test is whether the product "serves directly to enhance human life on the whole—whether it furthers the life process taken impersonally." [99] If a ·product meets this test of impersonal usefulness,

[99] *The Theory of the Leisure Class,* pages 98-99.

then it possesses "social serviceability" or social utility. It contains within itself a "brute serviceability," [100] by which Veblen means a basic or elemental usefulness which is to be found in material products after they have been stripped of all the superfluities that have been added to them to meet the requirements of conspicuous or wasteful consumption. Brute serviceability is at bottom a matter of material serviceability, of usefulness derived from the material nature of the good. It has within it a core of reality which makes economic values much more "substantial" than the pecuniary values of the market place.

Who is to decide when a material product has social utility or brute serviceability, and how are these decisions to be made? Veblen answers these questions by stating that the court of final appeal in any question of "economic adequacy" or social serviceability is the instinct of workmanship. Individuals, since they possess the instinct of workmanship, are gifted with "a dispassionate common sense" which enables them to determine whether or not a material product is being used in such a way as to bring a "net gain in comfort or in the fullness of life." Those individuals in whom the workmanship drive has had the fullest development would therefore be the ones who are most qualified to decide when a product possesses social utility. This means that the technical experts would be the members of the community who are the most competent to decide when the industrial system is turning out economic values, and to determine how the stream of such values could be enlarged. From the viewpoint of these technical experts social utility or serviceability is a matter of mechanical or technological efficiency. It is a matter that can be objectified or made concrete according to the objective, scientific standards set up by industrial science. In so far as it is possible to secure agreement among technical experts as to the scientific measures of technological efficiency, it is possible to have a consensus of scientific opinion as to the nature and extent of the social utility or serviceability to be found in material products. Far from being an indefinable and unmanageable quantity, social utility when interpreted in terms of mechanical efficiency becomes an objective and manageable concept. In Veblen's own terminology

[100] Veblen, Thorstein, "On the Nature of Capital, II," reprinted in *The Place of Science in Modern Civilisation*, page 367.

social serviceability then has a "substantial" foundation in "material circumstances reducible to objective terms of mechanical, chemical, and psychological effect."

Serviceability or usefulness beyond mere "brute serviceability" presents a difficult problem to which Veblen does not address himself. The serviceability that he is concerned with relates primarily to the material needs of mankind. He is fully aware that there are other kinds of human needs beyond the material needs, and that therefore there are other kinds of serviceability beside economic or material serviceability which are of interest to the community. But Veblen has no special interest in the satisfaction of the non-material needs of mankind. He appears to adopt the position that economic serviceability is basic to all other kinds of serviceability, and that once the community was well supplied with economic values or useful material products the satisfaction of the non-economic needs of humanity would then be a relatively simple task. Veblen realizes that human survival is not merely a question of the production of economic or material serviceability. He would, however, be one of the first to point out the extent to which survival depends upon the supply of useful, material goods.

In contrast to real or economic values are exchange or pecuniary values. Whereas economic values are the end product of the industrial system, pecuniary or market values are the final product of the business system. Pecuniary values are exchange values which are determined by the various forces at work in the market place. At bottom these pecuniary values are "psychological" rather than "substantial," and consequently they have all the variability that goes with psychological phenomena. Unlike economic values which rest on "material circumstances reducible to objective terms of mechanical, chemical, and psychological effect," pecuniary values rest on the uncertain foundation of "vendibility." By vendibility Veblen means the capacity of an item to bring pecuniary gain to its owner. Vendibility is a matter of "pecuniary serviceability," that is to say, of usefulness for the purpose of accumulating pecuniary gains. This vendibility or pecuniary serviceability has an air of caprice about it. It fluctuates not in accordance with changes in material serviceability or social utility, but with changes in mass or crowd psychology which are so apparent in times of panic or speculative inflation. Since they are so responsive to the vagaries of panics and speculative periods, pecuniary values frequently bear little relation to the more substantial economic values; and consequently they fail to exhibit a high degree of coincidence with economic values.

In the early stage of handicraft industry pecuniary and economic values had a high degree of coincidence; they were, Veblen said, "constitutionally" in touch with each other. In this stage of industry the masterless craftsmen used no hired labor and borrowed no capital. They put into their products only their own direct labor plus a fraction of the labor which they had put into the simple tools with which they worked. The goods of these masterless craftsmen were exchanged on a competitive basis, with the result that the prices at which they were exchanged were rough measures of their labor costs or their "cost of workmanship." [101] Within the limits of the handicraft system only those who produced were remunerated. Remuneration was therefore a function of productivity; and productivity could be measured in terms of either economic or pecuniary values. Since the prices of commodities were kept close to their labor costs, there was no room for any discrepancies between economic and pecuniary values. Competition between equally skilled craftsmen left no room for monopolistic practices. There were few opportunities to limit output, raise prices, and thus divorce pecuniary values from their foundation in material circumstances.

In the development of the economic system since the early handicraft stage of industry Veblen finds a progressive decline in the coincidence of pecuniary and economic values. The decline in the coincidence of these two types of values was not serious, however, as long as the business system remained substantially competitive. The forces of competition tended to keep productivity and remuneration in close touch with each other, and to keep pecuniary values anchored in material circumstances. Pecuniary values continued to represent tangible assets in the form of commodities and industrial equipment. As long as free competition prevailed there was little opportunity through various monopolistic practices to divorce pecuniary values from their foundation in material serviceability. The one major exception to this general situation was to be found in the case of the landowners. As population grew and the demands of industry for raw materials increased, landowners came to enjoy a monopolistic position. In this circumstance the materials

[101] *The Vested Interests,* page 28.

extracted from the land came to command prices far "beyond the cost of workmanship that goes to bring out the supply."

The appearance of the new order of business at the turn of the century marks the beginning of the rapid decline in the coincidence of pecuniary and economic values. This separation of pecuniary and economic values is explained by Veblen as being the result of the rapid conversion of the business system from a competitive to a monopolistic basis. By the term monopoly Veblen does not mean the exclusive control of output by one producer. In his analysis monopoly refers to business conditions that are described by an early student of the problem as cases of "partial monopoly." [102] Veblen finds few cases of complete business control or of "strict monopoly" in the modern economic world. He observes that the major portion of business enterprise falls in between "free competition" and "strict monopoly." It is the price and production policies of the big semi-monopolistic key industries, made up of a small number of large firms, that are of major concern to Veblen. He is of the opinion that it is these large, partially monopolistic firms that are most responsible for putting pecuniary and economic values "constitutionally out of touch" with each other.

The prices placed upon their output by large corporate enterprises are determined not by the competitive principle of supply and demand but by the monopolistic principle of "charging what the traffic will bear." In determining what the traffic will bear the corporation must take into account the price and production policies of its large corporate associates as well as the reactions of the consuming public. If it can successfully offset the policies of its competitors and can win over a large section of the buying public through effective salesmanship and advertising, the corporation is then judged to be successful. In this situation the corporation's prices or charges may bear no relation to "costs or the use-value of the service rendered." To the economic value of its product the successful corporation now adds the "prestige value" of a trade-mark or brandname. This prestige value is not a matter of material serviceability or social utility. It adds nothing to the ability of the commodity to serve the material needs of the community. It is only a "substitution value" which arises from the fact that the corporation has suc-

[102] Ely, Richard T., *Monopolies and Trusts*, pages 31-32. New York: Grosset and Dunlap, 1900.

cessfully induced its customers to substitute its product for that of other producers. These substitution values are very important, for they drive a wedge between economic and pecuniary values. It is the aim of the large, semi-monopolistic corporations to inflate their pecuniary or market values by adding as much "substitution value" as possible to the basic costs of production. The discrepancy between economic and pecuniary values is then widened to the extent that prestige or substitution values are created by the salesmanship and advertising activities of the corporations, and are successfully incorporated in market prices.

In the modern business system it is not only the pecuniary and economic values of material commodities that no longer coincide or are "constitutionally out of touch."[103] The same condition is found with respect to both capital and labor. Industrial equipment is not valued for its capacity to turn out useful material products, but for its capacity to add to the pecuniary gains of its owner. Capital has two aspects, the pecuniary and the industrial. From the pecuniary viewpoint capital is a matter of market values or pecuniary efficiency, while from the industrial viewpoint it is a matter of economic values or mechanical efficiency. Veblen asserts that in the modern business system the industrial aspect of capital is being rapidly subordinated to its pecuniary aspect. The mechanical efficiency of industrial equipment is receiving less and less attention as competitive business arrangements give way to monopolistic developments. Increasingly, capital is being valued more for its pecuniary efficiency or serviceability than for its mechanical efficiency. As a consequence of this new development in business enterprise the discrepancy between pecuniary and industrial capital is rapidly enlarging.

The situation is the same with respect to the labor factor. Just as the forces of competition are no longer present in sufficient force to cause pecuniary and industrial capital to coincide, so also the competitive forces no longer keep the productivity and remuneration of labor "constitutionally" related. In the modern semi-monopolistic business world the basis for wage payments is not productivity but pecuniary serviceability. Labor is not remunerated for its efficiency in producing useful, material goods but for its pecuniary serviceability, that is to say, for its efficiency in adding to the pecuniary

[103] "Industrial and Pecuniary Employments," page 303.

gains of those who employ it. As with capital, labor has both pecuniary and industrial aspects which are getting constitutionally out of touch with each other as rapidly as monopoly supersedes free competition in the field of business enterprise.

The problem of the discrepancy between economic and pecuniary values introduces Veblen's theory of the surplus or net product of industry. He defines the net product of industry as that amount by which the community's annual output "exceeds its own cost, as counted in terms of subsistence, and including the cost of the necessary mechanical equipment." [104] This net product of industry is a surplus of material products and not of exchange or pecuniary values. Unlike Marx, Veblen is not concerned with a theory of surplus exchange value. To Marx the surplus of the capitalistic economy was a surplus of exchange value which the laborer created but which was taken away from him by the exploiting capitalist. Veblen substitutes his theory of "surplus product" for Marx's theory of "surplus value." What he is concerned with is a surplus net product of useful material goods created by the whole industrial system, not with a surplus allegedly created by the laborers. Veblen is interested in the surplus net product of industry as a mark of the efficiency of the whole system of production. He is not concerned with working out a theory of surplus exchange value which would be useful "as a campaign cry designed to stir the emotions of the working class." [105]

The size of the net surplus product of economic values or useful material products depends upon three factors: material resources, man power, and industrial technology. These three conditioning factors do not play equally important roles in the production of the surplus product of industry. In Veblen's opinion technology or workmanship is the "dominant creative force" in industry.[106] Industrial technology is regarded by Veblen as a living structure which performs an indispensably creative function. It converts the brute energy of mankind into highly efficient labor, and transmutes brute matter into "ways and means of productive industry." As the industrial arts improve, labor becomes more efficient and raw materials more useful. For this reason Veblen asserts that the efficiency

---

[104] *The Vested Interests,* page 55.
[105] "The Socialist Economics of Karl Marx and His Followers," page 445 fn.
[106] *Absentee Ownership,* page 62.

of labor and the availability or usefulness of raw materials are both functions of the state of the industrial arts. He concludes by observing that "The state of the industrial arts, therefore, is the indispensable conditioning circumstance which determines the productive capacity of any given community."

It must be understood that, although Veblen assigns a certain primacy to technology in the production of economic values, he does not say that technology alone creates these values. There is no one cause or determinant of economic values; instead, there are the three contributory factors of labor, raw materials, and technology. Each factor, however, is not equally significant in the creation of economic values. In the handicraft era it was labor that was the indispensable or creative factor, not in the sense of being the only creative factor but in the sense of being the decisive or the most vital factor of production. At that time the other two factors of production were also necessary or indispensable, but they were only "subsidiary" or "auxiliary factors" of production. In the new industrial order of the twentieth century the relations between these three productive factors have been radically altered. The community's common stock of technological knowledge is now the strategic creative factor, while labor has become only an auxiliary or subsidiary creative factor.

The only claims to the net product of industry, or to "the excess of serviceability over cost," that Veblen recognizes as being justified by the circumstances are the claims of those who make some contribution to this surplus product. Owners of pecuniary values are not entitled to any portion of this net surplus product, because "ownership does not of itself create a net product, and so it does not give rise to earnings, but only to the legal claim by force of which the earnings go to the owners of the capitalized wealth." Owning property is not a productive function; rather, it is a matter of taking surplus product away from those who help to create it. Veblen goes on to say that production is a matter of workmanship, whereas ownership of pecuniary values is merely a matter of "business" or market manipulation. He does not accept the opinion of the classical economists that ownership is a spur to increased production. He finds that production in the modern, highly complex machine economy is the result of the workmanship drive of the workers combining with an industrial technology that contains great productive powers. In general, the working population does not labor because of the prospect of enjoying the legal claims of ownership, but because of the human propensity to work, to manipulate materials, and to create a useful product. Far from aiding this workmanship bent, ownership of pecuniary assets frequently acts as a barrier to the full expression of the workmanship drive and to the free functioning of the industrial system. Instead of being a productive factor entitled to remuneration, ownership, in Veblen's analysis, is a totally unproductive factor.

The same line of reasoning is also applied to the risk-taking function of modern business enterprise. Veblen does not look upon risk taking as an economic function that is productive or as one that merits a return. Orthodox economists maintain that the rewards going to risk taking act as a spur to inventive activity. Veblen's reply to this assertion is that invention and technological progress come about as the result of the operations of the instincts of workmanship and of idle curiosity, and as a consequence of the accumulation of technological developments. To the extent that invention depends upon man's biological drives it is a spontaneous activity giving expression to these drives and requiring no special financial reward. Once industrial science has been firmly embedded in a nation's culture, technological progress develops freely out of the spontaneous behavior of those individuals who are concerned with the production of useful material goods. Veblen states, furthermore, that the risks involved in the accumulation of pecuniary values do not aid the creation of economic values. The risks of modern business enterprise are only risks that rival businessmen create as they seek to maximize pecuniary gains. They are not risks that are of any concern to technicians and workers. Nor do these business risks have any beneficial effect upon the size of the net product of industry. On the contrary, instead of being a creative or productive factor, risk taking, according to Veblen's analysis, places unnecessary restrictions upon the full employment of men and machines. It diverts materials and man power from the only truly productive function of goods making.

Veblen believes that most of the risks now associated with the production of economic values could very easily be eliminated with no harmful effect upon the size of the national income. All risks associated with the promotion of corporate consolidations and mergers, with sales and advertising campaigns, with the establishment of new brand names, with the exploitation of patents and franchises, and with the attempt to capitalize business goodwill should present no major difficulties with respect to their elimination.   Veblen goes on to point out that there are very few real risks involved in meeting the basic living requirements of the working population. The only risks that the technicians cannot overcome with a high degree of success are those that are the result of the vagaries of climate and weather and the occurrence of natural catastrophes. Since these risks are not a matter of individual responsibility, they could be provided for by the community out of the net surplus product of industry.   No private risk-taking function would then require remuneration.

As Veblen sees it, the only really functional claimants to the net surplus product of industry are the technicians and the workers; and, in the socialistic economy of the future that he envisions, the surplus product of industry would be distributed between these two groups.   Veblen, however, does not make any detailed inquiry into how a socialistic economy would remunerate only those who contribute to the national income of real goods or economic values.   All that he has to say on this important question is that there should be "an equitable distribution of the consumable output" among the workers and the engineers.[107]   What is an equitable distribution of the surplus net product of industry?   Would it be a distribution based on the estimated marginal contribution of the various classes of workers, or would it be based upon their estimated needs?   These are questions for which Veblen does not supply answers.   As in so many other instances, Veblen has introduced an important problem, but he has failed to examine it with any degree of thoroughness. When it comes to concrete suggestions for collective action, Veblen has nothing or, at the most, little to say.   He remains satisfied with having put his finger on what he believes to be the root of the problem.   Not having a vigorous urge to translate economic theorizing into actual practice, Veblen does not address himself to many practical issues amongst which would be the problem of how to distribute the national income of a socialistic economy.

[107] Veblen, Thorstein, *The Engineers and the Price System*, page 152. New York: B. W. Huebsch, Inc., 1921.

The Nature and Scope of Veblen's Institutional Economics

In Veblen's opinion economics is a science of human behavior rather than a study of prices or wealth. Although it is concerned with prices or wealth, its focus of attention is on the activities or conduct of individuals and groups as they go about the task of providing the material needs of life. "Economic action," said Veblen, "must be the subject matter of the science if the science is to fall into line as an evolutionary science"; for in economics "the subject of inquiry is the conduct of man in his dealings with the material means of life." [108] This emphasis upon the psychological basis of economics bulks large in Veblen's views on the nature of his science. It is important because it draws attention to the need of adequate psychological theories for the interpretation of economic phenomena. Where the economist keeps it in mind that he is explaining economic action or conduct, he will be more insistent upon utilizing the most recent contributions of the psychologists. He will attempt to keep abreast of the progress being achieved in the related social sciences, especially with those that throw light upon the nature of human behavior. It is this insistence that economics is a science of human behavior which explains why Veblen devoted so much of his attention to an analysis of psychological theory and its relation to economics. He felt that economists had lost sight of the fact that their science was primarily an explanation of a special type of human conduct. It was his firm conviction that the reconstruction of economics had to start with a reconstruction of the psychological theory underlying that science.

As a science of human behavior economics is primarily concerned with human relations and not with things or objects. Individuals function in a network of social relations. They carry on economic transactions that involve relations with many individuals, groups, and classes. These economic relations may take the simple form of bargaining transactions between independent producers and consumers, or they may be transactions between powerful groups representing diverse economic interests. In the more advanced stages of economic evolution economic relations have a tendency to coalesce in the shape of class organization. In making economics a

[108] "The Limitations of Marginal Utility," page 241.

study of human relations Veblen therefore calls special attention to the role of collective action in controlling individual action.

What is significant about human behavior is that it falls into patterns or schemes of organization. Whenever two or more individuals come together, they create habitual or routine ways of behaving toward one another which form the nucleus of their economic system. An economic system is defined as a systematic union of individuals developed for the common purpose of providing various commodities and services,—a "scheme of conduct whereby mankind deals with its material means of life." Such schemes vary all the way from the simply organized, rural-communal economies of India and China to the mature capitalistic economies of Western Europe and the United States.

The schemes or patterns of economic conduct that are of interest to the economist are concerned with the "material means of life." Every group, community, and nation is confronted with the problem of meeting the material needs of life from a limited supply of man power and material resources. The economic problem is therefore one of "adaptation of means to ends," or of "the ways and means of turning material objects and circumstances to account." Every community is faced with the problem of having more needs than can be satisfied with the available resources; it is confronted with what Veblen calls the "economic interest." This interest in the disposal of scarce resources can be examined from the individual, the class, or the communal viewpoint. Veblen combines all viewpoints, but gives special attention to the overall or communal approach to the fundamental problem of utilizing scarce resources. He wants to inquire into how men collectively act in coping with their economic problems. Whereas Alfred Marshall and his followers analyzed the economic interest of mankind primarily from the viewpoint of the individual entrepreneur, Veblen analyzes it mainly from the viewpoint of the community or nation as a cultural totality or collectivity. This overall approach gives to Veblen's economics a collective emphasis which is lacking in the orthodox economics of his time.

The communal scheme of conduct which gives expression to mankind's economic interest is a cultural product. It is a going concern or cultural process with a past, present, and future. Consequently

Veblen would have economic science deal with the "continuity and mutations of that scheme of conduct whereby mankind deals with its material means of life." "Economics," he said, "is occupied about questions of genesis and cumulative change, and it converges upon a theoretical formulation in the shape of a life-history drawn in causal terms.   In so far as it is a science in the current sense of the term, any science, such as economics, which has to do with human conduct, becomes a genetic inquiry into the human scheme of life; and where, as in economics, the subject of the inquiry is the conduct of man in his dealings with the material means of life, the science is necessarily an inquiry into the life-history of material civilization, on a more or less extended or restricted plan." [109]   In making economics a study of the continuity and mutations of the community's scheme of economic conduct Veblen abandons the cross-sectional or one-dimensional approach of the late nineteenth-century orthodox economists.   Ignoring the past and overlooking the future, these orthodox economists had limited their economics to a study of a cross section of the flow of economic life as they saw it prior to the final quarter of the century.   In contrast Veblen's evolutionary economics becomes, in the final analysis, an interpretation of the development and future prospects of modern capitalism.

In clothing the community's scheme of economic conduct with the features of a cultural process or going concern Veblen places economics among the cultural sciences.   He finds "that an evolutionary economics must be the theory of a process of cultural growth as determined by the economic interest, a theory of cumulative sequence of economic institutions stated in terms of the process itself." Mankind's economic interest is only one of a number of basic interests which shape human culture.   The economic interest, like other basic interests, finds expression through various cultural arrangements, but it does not act in isolation.   Material culture should therefore be investigated in order to show how it affects non-material culture, and how in turn it is affected by the other lines of cultural growth.   In all such cultural studies, however, mankind's economic interest remains the center of attention, and provides the necessary framework of reference for the work of the economist.   Veblen therefore concludes that "in so far as the inquiry is economic science, specifically, the attention will converge upon the scheme of material

[100] "The Limitations of Marginal Utility," pages 240-241.

life and will take in other phases of civilization only in their correlation with the scheme of material civilization."

When Veblen takes economics to be a study of the economic aspect of human culture he does not convert his science into a merely descriptive study which is devoid of a theoretical structure. To him economico-cultural analysis is a "close-knit body of theory," whose center of attention is still what has been of concern to economists of all times, namely, the disposal of scarce means in a cultural situation where all material needs cannot be fully satisfied. To Veblen economics is a study of "a cumulative process of adaptation of means to ends that cumulatively change as the process goes on, both the agent and his environment being at any point the outcome of the last process." [110] The orthodox economists took the cultural arrangements of their time as given data, and merely analyzed the problem of the disposal of scarce means within the given cultural setting. They did not investigate how that cultural setting affected the disposal of scarce means, or how the disposal of scarce means could influence the cultural setting. Veblen addresses himself to these important problems that were ignored by the orthodox economists. He asserts that the cultural framework of any society conditions all the economic activities carried on within that society. The very aims or goals for which the disposal of scarce means is carried on very appreciably affect that disposal. In other words, in the economic world the ends or the cultural goals to be achieved affect the means by which those ends or goals are sought. Veblen's cultural economics would therefore give a very prominent place to this means-end problem of which the late nineteenth-century orthodox economists were largely unaware.

There is for Veblen no abstract science of economics that has universal applicability. He does not deny that there are certain common elements or similar features of economic life at all stages in the evolution of human culture and in all existing societies. This is due to the fact that elemental human nature is the same in all types of communities, and that it has not changed perceptibly over the centuries. But the cultural or institutional arrangements at various stages in the evolution of economic society, and in the different existing societies, are unique arrangements. Veblen's special interest is in only one type of culture, namely, modern capital-

[110] "Why Is Economics Not an Evolutionary Science?", pages 74-75.

istic culture. Consequently, for Veblen economic science is the study of the evolving scheme of economic conduct to be found in all highly industrialized countries, with special reference to the United States and England. Like Karl Marx, Veblen has "more particularly devoted his efforts to an analysis and theoretical formulation of the present situation—the current phase of the process, the capitalistic system." [111]

Veblen's critics have alleged that in tearing down the symmetrical system of classical economic thought he fails to make an adequate substitution for what he eliminates, that his work is more destructive than constructive. If by "constructive" analysis is meant economic theorizing that leads to a symmetrical system similar to the one produced by the equilibrium economists of the past century, then Veblen's economic analysis cannot be said to be critically constructive. But Veblen had no intention of competing with the orthodox academic economists on the level of systematic equilibrium analysis. He explains that "The question now before the body of economists is not how things stabilise themselves in a 'static state,' but how they endlessly grow and change." [112] In shifting attention from static equilibrium analysis to the study of a dynamic process Veblen does not find the self-contained and balanced system of economic theory of the orthodox economists adequate for his purposes.

The body of economic thought which Veblen substitutes for the systematic theory of the orthodox nineteenth-century economists is not an amorphous, unsystematized body of economic doctrines. Indeed his theory is systematic in the sense that it has one fundamental colligating or unifying principle running through it. This basic unifying idea is the concept of dichotomy or polarity. When applying this principle of dichotomy Veblen finds in the human mind two conflicting types of mental traits, one concerned with pragmatic matters and another with irrelevant or non-pragmatic matters. Pursuing the same idea, he observes in mankind's instinctive make-up two opposing types of impulses or drives. One set of drives centers in the self-regarding or acquisitive proclivity; the

---

[111] "The Socialist Economics of Karl Marx and His Followers," page 418.

[112] Veblen, Thorstein, "Economic Theory in the Calculable Future," reprinted in *Essays in Our Changing Order*, edited by Leon Ardzrooni, page 8. New York: The Viking Press, 1934.

other complex of drives revolves about the cooperative or parental bent. This dichotomous condition of mind and biological make-up has its counterpart in human culture. Running through human culture are two incompatible sets of institutions, those that are serviceable and those that are disserviceable to mankind. The serviceable institutions are concerned with the preservation of human life and culture. They are the institutions which are favorable to the progress of science and the improvement of the state of the industrial arts. The disserviceable institutions are the institutions which make for cultural decay and race suicide. They are the institutions which elevate the welfare of the individual above that of the community, and which are inimical to the progress of science and technology.

Within the economic segment of human culture is to be found a further dichotomy. This is the division or polarity between the industrial and pecuniary employments. The industrial employment with its "mechanistic logic of technology" is concerned with the production of economic values, while the pecuniary employment with its "business logic of the price-system" deals with pecuniary values. Finally, when looking into the future of the economic system Veblen discerns a dichotomy or bifurcation of economic trends. Some cultural trends are carrying the most recent phase of capitalistic development in the direction of a militaristic dictatorship, while other trends are moving the economy towards a socialistic regime.

Each dichotomy or division to which Veblen draws attention is a source of conflict. The individual carries within himself throughout life both psychological and biological conflicts; similarly there are in the community never-ending cultural conflicts between various types of institutional arrangements. The essence of economic life is therefore not harmony, as the orthodox economists believed, but conflict. These conflicts may be subdued but never eliminated, since they have roots in the dichotomies to be found in the unchanging nature of mankind. It is this fact of conflict growing out of the various dichotomies that creates an impassable gulf between the economic thought of Veblen and that of his orthodox predecessors and contemporaries. Whereas the central fact of the equilibrium economists' view of the economic system is rest or balance, the main fact of Veblen's view of the economic system is conflict or antagonism. Because Veblen built his theory on a principle of dichotomy, he does not create a body of economic thought that displays anything like the symmetry and balance of the system of the equilibrium economists. His thought system is not a formalistic construction which draws special attention to the logical precision of its generalizations. It is, instead, a scheme of interpretation which is designed to elevate realism over formalism. Its main purpose is to capture the essence of those dynamic economic realities which together comprise the modern capitalistic scheme of things.

In working out his asymmetrical but realistic system of economic thought Veblen did not dispense entirely with orthodox nineteenth-century economic concepts. It is a common belief that Veblen would do away with the entire body of classical and neo-classical economic thought. This is a completely erroneous view which stems from Veblen's failure to indicate to what extent he borrowed from the body of orthodox economic theory. Although Veblen takes over neither the spirit nor the general outlines of orthodox economic thought, he does make use of many of the concepts that were developed by the equilibrium economists of the nineteenth century. He takes it for granted that his readers have a thorough knowledge of the mechanics of competitive price determination and of the general principles governing the distribution of income in a competitive economy. Where this is the case, Veblen's readers can easily see for themselves how useful he finds the economic concepts that have been worked out by the long line of orthodox economists from Adam Smith to Alfred Marshall. What Veblen does is to provide a new framework of analysis into which he pours whatever he finds to be of value in the work of his orthodox predecessors.[113] He reworks economic theory in the light of a new frame-

---

[113] Wesley C. Mitchell has explained this vividly: "Yet Veblen might have admitted that the quasi-mechanical economics, which takes existing institutions for granted and inquires how they work, has a certain value. . . . Now, a theory such as Veblen's warm admirer, Herbert J. Davenport, developed on the express assumption that all men are animated by the desire for gain throws light on our economic behavior just to the extent that men are perfect products of the countinghouse. . . . Veblen would be the last to deny the importance of pecuniary institutions in modern culture. He does not, in fact, hold that work such as Davenport has done is wrong, or wholly futile. Yet he inclines to take what is valuable in it for granted, much as Davenport takes for granted the existing scheme of institutions. For Veblen is impatient of the well known and eager to develop aspects of the modern situation about which more orthodox types of

work of interpretation erected on the foundation of philosophical, psychological, and methodological assumptions quite at variance with the assumptions underlying equilibrium economics. The final result is that in Veblen's analysis old terms like credit, capital, business, money, and private property are vested with new meanings which run counter to the interpretations made by the orthodox economists of the last century. "Credit" is no longer merely deferred payment, "capital" is not synonymous with productive equipment, "business" is not the helper of productive industry, "money" is not merely the great wheel of circulation employed in a refined system of barter, "salesmanship" is not a productive facility of the middleman, and "private property" is much more than the ownership of physical goods.[114]

The Significance of Veblen's Institutional Economics

What is the significance of Veblen's reconstruction of economic science? His evolutionary economics presents a body of economic theories which are more relevant to the problems and issues of the twentieth century than are the economic theories of the equilibrium economists. This greater relevancy of Veblen's institutional economics is derived from its central theories of economic conflict and change. Besides closing the gap between theory and practice, Veblen's evolutionary economics gives a futuristic slant to economic thought. Although Veblen was unwilling to make any long-run predictions, he was very greatly interested in the economic developments of the "calculable future." He felt that his analysis of the logic of capitalistic development would enable the economist to peer into the immediate future with a certain degree of scientific objectivity. For this reason his economic theorizing provides a basis for public policy-making. It draws attention to the possibilities of collective action for the control of economic trends. On this point Veblen's economic thought is significantly different from the thought of the orthodox equilibrium economists. These economists have little concern with the trends of economic life, and therefore offer no interpretation of these trends. It is this feature of

economic theory have little to say." See Mitchell, W. C., "Thorstein Veblen," *The Backward Art of Spending Money,* pages 295-296. New York: McGraw-Hill Book Company, Inc., 1937.

[114] *Absentee Ownership,* page 419 fn.

orthodox economic analysis which explains why Alfred Marshall's equilibrium economics makes no provision for a theory of economic development. For Marshall's untroubled interest in the competitive *status quo* Veblen substitutes a searching inquiry into the nature of those forces which are transforming the modern economic order.

Although Veblen's evolutionary economics has a futuristic bias, and although his economic theories have a special appeal to those who are interested in formulating public policies for the control of economic life, Veblen was not himself especially interested in problems of economic policy.[115] Actually there are interwoven in Veblen's scientific personality two contradictory strains, the skeptical and the utopian. The skeptical strain in his scientific thought comes out in his analysis of the roles of habit and reason in economic activity. In Veblen's opinion man is very much a creature of habit whose intelligence is not a very effective safeguard against the inroads of destructive social habits. Looking at the evolution of economic society from a matter-of-fact point of view, Veblen is much impressed with the ascendancy of "imbecile institutions" and the feebleness of those instinctive drives that make for the survival of human culture. Veblen's skeptical attitude and his scientific matter-of-factness conform with the pessimistic bias of his general outlook. It is this combination of extreme skepticism and deep pessimism that explains the frequent recourse by Veblen to sardonic attacks upon the middle-class virtues of his day. It also explains his lack of interest in the reformist movements of his time. In spite of his deep understanding of the economic movements from 1890 to 1925 Veblen felt no compulsion to aid any of these movements. For the most part he remained academically aloof from the struggle and strife whose interpretation was one of his major intellectual interests.

The optimistic or utopian strain in Veblen's economic thought appears in his treatment of the influence of the technological factor in human culture. Veblen points out that changes in industrial technology result in a decay of old-fashioned habits of thought based

[115] Max Lerner asserts that the greatest weakness of Veblen's economic analysis lies in its lack of a direction that would provide the basis for economic action. For further discussion of this point see Lerner's essay on Veblen in *Ideas Are Weapons*, 1939, pages 136-138.

on an animistic or anthropomorphic interpretation of the external world. Technology has a "corrosive touch" which destroys habits of thought based on romantic notions of the nature of the external world and on traditional acceptance of differences in human rank. Those who are in contact with this changing technology substitute for the old-fashioned habits of thought new mental habits which are supported by matter-of-fact knowledge of the external world. In this manner a changing technology alters the norms or habits of thought which give guidance to human thinking and behaving. A changing technology cannot, however, make the individual more rational in the sense of being more critically aware of himself or more able to grasp the interrelations of things or events in a given situation.[116] Veblen does not say that the reason or intelligence of the individual is improved through contact with a changing technology. He maintains this view because he believes that human reason, like the instinctive proclivities, is unchanging over the centuries, and is therefore not altered by contact with a developing technology.

What Veblen does say is that the habits of thought within whose framework reason or intelligence operates are more favorable to cultural progress and race survival when they are based on matter-of-fact knowledge than when they are based on romantic or animistic impressions of the external world. But no habits of thought, even those created by the new technological discipline, can automatically make for cultural progress and race survival. Mankind has to use its intelligence or reason in a creative fashion within the framework of its habitual modes of thinking in order to work out its own salvation. Veblen is fully aware that recent habits of thought provide no guarantee that they will push mankind to the achievement of cultural progress and race survival. As yet the discipline of the new industrial technology of the twentieth century is still too near its beginning for the social scientist to make any worth-while predictions concerning its final outcome. The growth

[116] For a conflicting interpretation of this point see Mannheim, Karl, *Man and Society in an Age of Reconstruction*, page 58 fn. New York: Harcourt, Brace and Co., 1940. Mannheim asserts that it is Veblen's general thesis that the influence of industrialization or of a changing industrial technology is to improve the individual's "substantial rationality" or "insight into the inter-relations of events in a given situation." This interpretation makes Veblen's analysis of the influence of the technological factor in cultural development extremely naive.

of the new habits of thought, says Veblen, "has not yet had time to work itself clear"; as a consequence, he maintains a very skeptical attitude toward the final outcome of the new technological discipline.

In closing the gap between economic theory and practice Veblen's evolutionary economics gives support to a functional view of economic science. Those who hold this view of economics assert that it is the duty of economists to use the knowledge at their disposal, or to see to it that their understanding gets into the hands of those who can use it to the advantage of the community. Veblen does not himself make as much of the functional view of economics as he would have done had he been more actively interested in reconstructing economic society. Actually the skepticism and pessimism running through his mind seem to have prevented him from emphasizing the social significance of economics as much as it has been stressed by a later generation of economists. It has so happened, therefore, that Veblen's evolutionary economics has received the greatest acclaim from those economists who have little of Veblen's pessimistic outlook, and who are much more zealous about the functional view of economic science.

No careful reader of Veblen's essays and treatises can lay them down without feeling that there are certain very grave deficiencies in his work. The elements of his system of economic thought for the interpretation of twentieth-century economic enterprise are scattered over many essays and volumes. It is only by the expenditure of a great deal of time and energy that one is able to put together the mosaic of Veblen's thought. If he had shown a greater willingness to organize his ideas within a shorter compass, the nature and significance of his institutional economics would have been made available to a wider public. It is not that Veblen's extensive writings lack unity; rather the fault is that he was never formally interested in displaying that unity within the limits of one general treatise.

Furthermore, Veblen displays a lamentable unwillingness to pursue new insights until they have been drained of their final unit of significance. Frequently he has come upon a new field of thought but has failed to explore it fully. This shortcoming is illustrated in his handling of the problems of scientific methodology and of monopoly price determination. His discussion of the "evolutionary method" of economics remains vague and fragmentary. A similar criticism may be levelled against Veblen's study of monopoly price behavior. His treatment of the problems of monopoly price is hardly more than an introduction to this important field of economic analysis. At the turn of the century he stood on the threshold of a vast new field of economic investigation, but he never felt the urge to cultivate this field intensively. Veblen left it to others to do the painstaking work of marshalling the facts and fitting them into intricate patterns of price behavior. Had he possessed a greater capacity for the statistical handling of economic data, Veblen could have done much to provide a firm inductive foundation for many of his broad generalizations. But he makes no use of the devices of statistical analysis, nor does he seem to have been interested in grappling with the kinds of problems that are subject to statistical measurement. He explains in the preface to his *Absentee Ownership and Business Enterprise in Recent Times* that his analysis of twentieth-century capitalistic enterprise "makes no use of recondite information and makes no attempt to penetrate beyond the workday facts which are already familiar to students of these matters." Twentieth-century social science is no longer satisfied with only workday facts. It makes use of all the facts that can be made available; and, furthermore, it is particularly interested in facts that lend themselves to statistical treatment.

Veblen's most important contributions to economic understanding are also the source of his greatest inadequacies. This fountainhead of so much strength and weakness in Veblen's economic analysis is his psychological theory. On the constructive side Veblen's social psychology introduces a new outlook on the problems of economic behavior. Without his social psychology Veblen could not have worked out his theory of capitalistic economic organization, since it is dependent upon a theory of collective economic behavior. It was his interest in collective or institutional behavior that enabled Veblen to push his analysis beyond the supply and demand phenomena of the market place into the whole communal pattern of economic organization.

Unfortunately for the development of his evolutionary economics Veblen seems to have limited his psychological analysis to the progress in psychology that had been achieved by 1914. He never get beyond the psychological theory set forth in *The Instinct of Work.*

manship (1914), which is grounded on the idea of instinct.[117] Since the concept of instinct remains vague and unmanageable, the recent practice of social psychologists has been to pass hurriedly over the instinctive basis of human behavior, and to turn to psychological data which are more amenable to scientific handling. If Veblen had devoted more of his time and energy to analyzing his concept of economic status and the economic attitudes which are associated with class behavior, he would have been spared much of the criticism that has been levelled at "instinct psychology." But Veblen makes no painstaking effort to locate economic attitudes, to determine their order of development, or to measure their respective significance for the explanation of human conduct. Although Veblen's psychological theory is modern in its inspiration and general outline, it cannot be said that he exhibits much of the modern experimental attitude in his psychological analysis. It is not surprising, therefore, that in his psychological analysis Veblen proves to be long on speculative generalization but short on inductive substantiation.

Since 1914 instinct psychology has been giving way to a more integrative type of psychology. Human motivation is now considered to be not so much a matter of response to instinctive urges as of response to various situations in a given cultural orientation or scheme of things. Although motivation is a matter of satisfying basic human drives, the particular way in which the individual seeks to satisfy his drives depends upon the various situations in which he finds himself, and upon the cultural integration by the aid of which he interprets these situations. Since these cultural situations can be handled more objectively than the human instincts, the interests of modern social psychologists center in them rather than in the instincts. Although Veblen had a grasp of many of the elements of the new integrative psychology, he was unable to divest himself of his deep interest in the role of instincts. Since he was not interested in statistical analysis, and since he had a strongly speculative bent, Veblen did not find it easy to keep up with the trends in the development of socio-psychological analysis after 1914.

[117] See Bernard, L. L., *Instinct; A Study in Social Psychology,* pages 79-80. New York: H. Holt and Company, 1924. Bernard finds Veblen's treatment of the instinctive basis of human behavior "vague and elusive" and not very applicable "in close and critical thinking." Cf. also Thorndike, E. L., *Human Nature and the Social Order,* 1940, page 160.

As a consequence much of the psychological emphasis underlying his evolutionary economics is both inadequate and outmoded.

There are two important issues which Veblen does not raise. Will the technical experts, whom he takes to be motivated by the instinct of workmanship, be the type of individuals who are capable of providing effective leadership for the underlying population in the reconstruction of society? What is the possibility that Veblen's regime of workmanship will be a democratic form of economic organization? With respect to the first problem the issue is whether technical experts are sufficiently expert in the field of human relations to assume the burden of reordering the whole system of economic life. There are more than reasonable doubts that technical experts have this unique capacity. Veblen himself explains that technical experts are manipulators of material things and not of human beings. They are specialists in the handling of tangible products and not in adjusting human affairs. In their training and experience problems of human adjustment do not have an important place. The shift from a capitalistic system of economic organization to a regime of workmanship would be much more than a technological problem. It would require a most delicate handling of the system of human relations if the cultural fabric is not to be destroyed in the process of reconstruction, and if various cultural values are not to be lost. Veblen makes no claim that his instinct of workmanship provides technical experts with capacities that would enable them to handle human material successfully in the stress and strain of social upheaval. Nor does he explain how the technical experts would acquire such important capacities from other sources. He merely leaves the problem unresolved. Since there are legitimate doubts concerning the expertness of technicians in the field of human relations, Veblen's considerations of their role in the reorganization of economic society are far from being complete.

Closely allied is the problem of insuring a democratic regime of workmanship. Veblen does not inquire very deeply into this question of how his socialistic economy would function as a democratic form of economic organization. It is true that he looks forward to a new industrial order that will serve the needs of the common man, but what he has to say has reference primarily to the provision of the material needs of mankind. His assumption of the spontaneous rise of self-appointed technical leaders in the transition from capitalism to the new industrial order is too reminiscent, for intellectual comfort, of the rise of leadership in the totalitarian nations of this century.   History has all too frequently recorded the totalitarian consequences of spontaneous, self-appointed leadership.   It is for this reason that some of Veblen's readers find a totalitarian strain in some of his writings.   Veblen speculates about a regime of workmanship in which the "self-selected" soviet of technicians would govern with the support of the industrial rank and file.   But this popular support may be nothing more than a blind allegiance given to the country's technical leaders in return for certain guarantees as to material welfare.   Veblen has little to say about the preservation of democratic values and procedures in the disposal of the community's scarce resources.   It is plain, however, that the discipline of the new industrial technology has no special power to cause men to function in a democratic manner, or to make them see democratic goals with a special mental clarity.   The machine can improve neither the human reason nor the democratic leanings of those who come in contact with the new technology.   All that the modern industrial technology can do is to draw men together in a vast network of industrial relations.   This close industrial association may then offer some stimulation to the cooperative impulses of mankind. But whether or not these cooperative impulses will find expression in a democratic way of life is a matter that depends not upon the state of the industrial arts but upon the creative intellectual capacities of mankind.   The achievement of a democratically functioning economic society is more a psychological than a technological problem.   If Veblen had been more interested in translating economic theory into public policy he might have paid more attention to this important problem of industrial technology and its relation to the democratic organization of economic society.   It must be said in Veblen's defense, however, that his thoughts about a future regime of workmanship were hardly more than a by-product of his major scientific interests.   The deficiencies in his analysis of a future economic state stem from his failure to follow up various problems; they are not the logical outcome of his scientific reasoning.

The value and significance of Veblen's institutional economics can be measured only by the extent to which he has influenced other economists, and by the relevance of his thought to the major economic issues of the day. His influence upon some outstanding American economists is analyzed in the following chapters. It is sufficient to point out here that Veblen has helped to create a new intellectual climate for American economists. This new intellectual climate incorporates elements from the stream of European scientific thought, especially from the economic thought of Karl Marx. It also draws upon the contributions of many American social scientists who, in the closing decades of the old century and in the early years of the new century, were busy with the reconstruction of social science. Veblen's special contribution has been to carry this reconstruction into the field of economics. In this field he has made use of many of the new developments that have occurred in philosophy, cultural anthropology, sociology, and social psychology since 1880. The final outcome of these borrowings from related scientific and philosophic disciplines has been to change the intellectual atmosphere in which economists have been working. To be sure, many economists have paid no attention to the new intellectual climate, and have gone on with their work in the shadow of the inherited orthodox approach to economic studies. A substantial minority, however, have welcomed the fresh air of the new intellectual climate. Some of this minority have been close students of Veblen's evolutionary economics, and have therefore drawn inspiration for their own work directly from his writings. Others, especially those of a later generation, have been influenced by Veblen only indirectly. But in both cases the influence of the intellectual climate that owes so much to Veblen's pioneering efforts is unmistakable.

The economists whose writings are analyzed in the following chapters have not slavishly followed in Veblen's footsteps. Changes in the course of economic events would be a sufficient guarantee against such an undesirable outcome. More than that, much of Veblen's economic analysis has already been outmoded by the flow of events. He made his economic investigations from 1890 to 1925 when the American economic system was enjoying a period of phenomenal expansion. Whereas this third of a century was a lush era in the economic development of the country, the course of events since 1929 has taken a new direction. The years since that date have not been years of "conspicuous consumption." Economic thought since 1929 has been attuned to a conjuncture of events in

Collective action, as well as individual action, has always been there; but from Smith to the Twentieth Century it has been excluded or ignored, except as attacks on trade unions or as postscripts on ethics or public policy. The problem now is not to create a different kind of economics—'institutional' economics—divorced from preceding schools, but how to give to collective action, in all its varieties, its due place throughout economic theory.

JOHN R. COMMONS: *Institutional Economics*

3

The Collective Economics of John R. Commons

The long period of chronic hard times from 1873 to 1897 which nourished the rebellious spirit of Thorstein Veblen was also the period in which John R. Commons reached his maturity. Like Veblen he had seen the price level undergo a secular decline after 1873. He had observed business struggle against the depressing effects of a long-continuing deflationary era; and he had also witnessed the desperate attempts of the agricultural areas of the country to provide for their growing burdens of fixed charges in the face of shrinking incomes. As was the case with Veblen, Commons came to doubt the validity of the analysis provided by the conventional economic theory of the times. Events quickened his appreciation of the economic disequilibrium which was so widespread, and which appeared to be more characteristic of economic life than was the static equilibrium referred to in the generally accepted economic treatises. Along with R. T. Ely, E. A. Ross, and Veblen, Commons was soon enrolled in that group of economists who, at the turn of the century, began to challenge the general body of orthodox economic doctrine. However, Commons' heterodoxy in economics has been coupled with a buoyancy of spirit and an optimistic, midwestern outlook which are quite alien to the whole Veblenian interpretation of the course of economic development. Whereas the events of the last quarter of the nineteenth century served to bring out Veblen's inherent pessimism and iconoclastic proclivities, for Commons the same events merely whetted a desire to make the existing economic system more "reasonable" and less destructive of human values.

To the student of American economic thought John R. Commons

appears to be a "bewildering person." [1] As a professor of economics in one of the nation's leading state universities, he followed little of the usual pattern of academic behavior. While the majority of teachers were confining their efforts to classroom instruction, and, in the cases of the more energetic ones, to some research which infrequently took them off the campus, Commons spent much of his time away from the classroom. He was most satisfied when working for some government commission, or when, accompanied by a few enterprising graduate students, he was engaged in some kind of industrial survey. Unlike most pedagogues Commons was moved by a restlessness that urged him on to close contacts with the realities to be found beyond college walls. He chafed under the restrictions of a fixed curriculum and a system of formal instruction. As an instructor he had no interest in trying to convert the social sciences into something that would be more palatable to the masses of students who were pouring into our institutions of higher learning after the turn of the century. His appeal has been mainly to those students for whom scientific investigation is an all-consuming pursuit.

Commons' unusual academic behavior was but a reflection of his deep, underlying penchant for the unorthodox. His roving mind saw no need to keep itself within the prescribed limits of any scientific discipline. He always felt free to inquire into other fields of scientific interest such as jurisprudence, sociology, social psychology, and political science, and to relate their newest findings to his particular work as an economist. In the search for economic truth he recognized no boundaries except those pragmatically established by the nature of his scientific interests. In his treatises on economic theory he perplexed his conventional readers with his incursions into a wide variety of non-economic fields of study. In his lectures he stubbornly refused to follow any systematic treatment of the material; instead he preferred to work out whatever topics appeared to be of immediate interest to himself and to his students. His own words best describe how he gave up his first attempts at systematic instruction: "I began simply to tell my classes personal stories of my mistakes, doubts and explorations, just as they happened to occur

---

[1] This is the description of Commons given by Wesley C. Mitchell, who has looked with great favor on Commons' work. See Mitchell's review of Commons' *Legal Foundations of Capitalism* in *The American Economic Review*, June, 1924, Vol. XIV, page 240.

to me, injecting my generalizations, comparisons, and all kinds of social philosophies. . . . I think my students were more interested in my telling these stories and my dubious interpretations than they were when I attempted to expound systematically the consistent theories of economics." [2]

In the thirty-five-year period from 1890 to 1924, Commons wrote a great deal about immediate economic problems and the need for some forms of economic and social experimentation, but very little concerning abstruse problems of economic theory. To those outside his graduate seminars he appeared to have had no special interest in refining inherited economic theory or in working out new ways in which the science of economics might progress. In the final decade of his academic activity, however, he produced two highly original treatises of great theoretical importance, which established him as one of the most vigorous exponents of the trend in American economic thought known as "institutionalism." In 1893 Commons had written his first volume on economics, *The Distribution of Wealth*, in which his theorizing was dominated by the conventional economic thinking of the final quarter of the nineteenth century.[3] Yet forty years later his *Institutional Economics, Its Place in Political Economy* (1934) placed him in the vanguard of those economists who were no longer satisfied with the neo-classical combination of Ricardo's mechanistic cost analysis and the psychological economics of the Austrian school.[4] The half-century in which Commons pursued his economic investigations was a period of kaleidoscopic change to which his intellectual nature was peculiarly sensitive. As he explained in his autobiography, he was a part of two revolutionary cycles: what he called the "American Revolution of 1861," and the war revolutions of the years after 1914. A familiarity with Commons' personal history and development is essential if one is to understand this "bewildering person," who was labelled a dangerous radical in the difficult years at the close of the last century, but who later found himself classed with exponents of the conservative social philosophy of Samuel Gompers.

[2] Commons, John R., *Myself*, page 2. New York: The Macmillan Company, 1934.

[3] Commons, John R., *The Distribution of Wealth*. New York: Macmillan and Co., 1893.

[4] Commons, John R., *Institutional Economics*. New York: The Macmillan Company, 1934.

Commons' Background Influences

Born in 1862 of a Quaker father and a Presbyterian mother in the village of Hollandsburg, Ohio, John R. Commons spent the first twenty-six years of his life in rural Ohio and Indiana.[5] A pair of intellectually alert parents seems to have made up for any lack of mental stimulation from which the young Commons might have suffered in his mid-western rural environment. The penury from which his father was unable to rescue his family brought Commons into contact with the realities of life at an early age, and also appears to have given him an early appreciation of the importance of constructive activity designed to overcome obstacles. This sense of the importance of doing things, of struggling to overcome economic and social difficulties, was coupled with a persistent desire to inquire into the nature of things. "I was always experimenting," wrote Commons in his autobiography, "always trying out theories on other people. There was no reason or logic in it—a child's curiosity that always got me into trouble or inconsistency."[6]

Upon graduation from Oberlin College in 1888, where he seems to have distinguished himself more for his intellectual curiosity and persistency than for his scholarship, Commons went as a graduate student to The Johns Hopkins University. There he looked forward to studying political economy, having abandoned journalism for economics during his earlier years at Oberlin. In Baltimore Commons became a student of Richard T. Ely, who was at that time one of a group of educators building up one of the finest graduate schools in the country. Ely was a combination of economist and social reformer, who regarded the competitive system as a beneficent order capable of lifting the living standards of the masses to much higher levels than then existed.[7] He gave added significance to his functional view of economic science by widening the scope of economics to include historical and legal studies not generally dealt

---

[5] Commons died at Raleigh, North Carolina, on May 11, 1945. For a brief biographical sketch, see Perlman, Selig, "John Rogers Commons, 1862-1945," *The American Economic Review*, Sept., 1945, Vol. XXV, pages 782-786.

[6] *Myself*, pages 1-2.

[7] For a review of Ely's early work and influence see his autobiography entitled *Ground Under Our Feet*. New York: The Macmillan Company, 1938. The influence of the German historical school was passed on to Commons by Ely, who was a student of Karl Knies.

with by economists at that time. Furthermore, he advocated an
inductive approach to the study of economic problems which was
quite alien to much of the work of the late nineteenth-century
American and English economists. The type of work that Ely was
doing had a deep appeal for Commons. Under Ely's tutelage he
turned with great enthusiasm to the "new" political economy which
bore little resemblance to the deductive science of his undergraduate
textbooks.

Before finishing his work for the doctoral degree Commons embarked upon a teaching career which took him to Wesleyan University in 1890, to Oberlin in 1891, and then to Indiana University
where he followed in the footsteps of E. A. Ross, who had been a
fellow student of Commons at The Johns Hopkins University.
While at Indiana University Commons published his first important
economic treatise, entitled *The Distribution of Wealth* (1893), an
exposition that did not significantly depart from the neo-classical
tradition.   As yet there was little indication of Commons' heterodox
views concerning the nature and scope of economic science.   If one
looks for the origins of his later economic thought, he will find them
in what Commons was doing rather than in what he was writing for
consumption in the university classroom.   While at Bloomington,
Indiana, Commons kept up his interest in the social and economic
problems of the day.   He displayed an interest in the Christian
Socialist and Populist movements of that period and in proportional
representation as a device for the betterment of government.[8]
While Veblen was brooding, in rural isolation, over America's trend
towards capitalistic decay, Commons was far removed from any such
lugubrious speculation.   Indeed at the very time when Veblen was
preparing the foundations for his prophecy of the eventual elimination of the business system, Commons was looking forward with
great enthusiasm to the reconstruction of society by the aid of a
revitalized Christianity and the adoption of such political and
economic reforms as proportional representation, civil service, and
municipally-owned public utilities.[9]

In 1895 Commons was called to Syracuse University to fill the

[8] Commons, John R., "Proportional Representation," *Annals of the American
Academy of Political and Social Science*, March, 1892, Vol. II, pages 124-131.
[9] Commons, John R., *Social Reform and the Church*. New York: T. Y.
Crowell and Company, 1894.

newly established chair of sociology, which he occupied until his dismissal from that institution in 1899. While at Syracuse University he taught a long list of subjects ranging from anthropology to political economy. For purposes of instruction in these subjects the whole outside world became his laboratory. A lengthy list of matters including prison reform, the improvement of municipal government, and the cooperative movement engaged his attention. At Syracuse Commons wrote a series of articles dealing with "A Sociological View of Sovereignty." [10] The theory of sovereignty which he was working out in these early years was more economic than sociological, for he observed that the growth of the state paralleled the development of the institution of private property. The significant fact about private property, in Commons' view, was its power to control and direct the activities of those who possessed little or no property. Furthermore, as property became concentrated in fewer and fewer hands the abuses of property ownership developed *pari passu*. In Commons' interpretation the state had expanded as an institution to curb the abuses of the economic power which flowed from the accumulations of private property. Generalizations of this nature were quite discomfiting to those individuals who were amassing wealth in the troubled years at the close of the century. It was not long before they began to express great dissatisfaction with the type of instruction that Commons was giving to his classes. In 1899 the business interests from which Syracuse University was drawing much of its financial support succeeded in depriving Commons of his position by abolishing the chair of sociology. At first this rebuff from the businessmen, whom he had begun to look upon as labor's partners, was quite overwhelming; and he was led to believe that his interests would be best served by a permanent withdrawal from academic life. From this time on Commons never again sought out an academic position. If it had not been for the invitation extended to him in 1904 by Richard T. Ely to join the faculty of the University of Wisconsin, he would in all probability never have returned to university life.

The years from 1899 to 1903 were called by Commons his "Five

[10] Commons, John R., "A Sociological View of Sovereignty, I-VII," *The American Journal of Sociology*, 1899-1900, Vol. V, pages 1-15, 155-171, 347-366, 544-552, 683-695, and 814-825. See also Vol. VI, pages 67-89.

Big Years." [11] During these years he worked at a variety of projects which brought him valuable experience and gave him new insights into the functioning of American capitalism. His most important work in this period was with the United States Industrial Commission and the National Civic Federation. For the Industrial Commission he prepared reports on the connections between immigration and labor unionism and on labor's policies with respect to the restriction of production.[12] The Industrial Commission, he felt, was the first "brain trust" engaged in the task of trying to make capitalism more workable. In his work for the Commission Commons travelled widely and met a variety of laborers and labor leaders. It was at this time that he appears to have made his first extensive contacts with revolutionary unionism and the economic doctrines of Karl Marx. In 1900 he attended the national joint conference of mine workers and operators. There he saw the beginnings of "constitutional government in industry" and the emerging pattern of employer-employee relations which was to become his life's major interest and also the basic principle of what he was later to describe as "reasonable capitalism." In his autobiography he tells us that "The essential point, as I learned in 1900 at the miners' joint conference, was the elimination, as far as possible, of a third party, the arbitrator—whether King, legislator, governor, or dictator, handing down rules and regulations from above—and the substitution of rules agreed upon collectively, by conciliation. It was to be, as I then learned in 1900, not Democracy in the historic meaning of a majority overruling the minority, but representation of organized voluntary but conflicting economic interests." One has here, in embryonic form, Commons' theory of industrial government.

In 1902 Commons went to work for the National Civic Federation, which was a private organization devoted to the reduction of indus-

---

[11] *Myself*, Ch. IV, pages 63-94.

[12] Commons, John R., "Immigration and Its Economic Effects," *Reports of the Industrial Commission on Immigration and on Education*, 1901, Vol. XV, Part III, pages 295-448. See also Commons' testimony dealing with labor problems in the *Report of the Industrial Commission on the Relations and Conditions of Capital and Labor*, 1901, Vol. XIV, pages 32-48, and his essay, "A New Way of Settling Labor Disputes," in *The American Monthly Review of Reviews*, March, 1901, Vol. XXIII, pages 328-333.

trial strife through the popularization of various conciliatory methods.[13] The general idea of the Federation was to have employers and employees adopt the principle of the trade agreement. It was hoped that conciliation and the use of the trade agreement would eliminate any need of arbitration by the government or any other third party. In working for the National Civic Federation Commons had occasion to see many clashes between employers and employees and to judge the relative merits of various methods of handling these conflicts. He came to approve of that type of labor unionism later described by Robert F. Hoxie as "business unionism."[14] In Commons' opinion revolutionary unionism was excessively visionary, since it failed to come to grips with historical realities. It usually fell into the hands of "intellectuals," who succeeded in doing no more than misguiding the labor movement. In these early experiences with the labor movement, Commons came to distrust "intellectuals" of all types, whether they represented capital or labor. He came around to the view that the success of a plan for the improvement of employer-employee relations required the leadership of those businessmen and laborers who had worked their way up, and who, consequently, had the requisite intimacy with the facts underlying industrial strife. The intellectual, whether he was an economist, government expert, politician, or sociologist, had a place only as an adviser. We see here the origins of Commons' view that our economic system can be saved from destruction only by those who are actively participating in its activities. There is to be no savior who will come from outside the economic system to impose a workable plan on capital and labor. Ultimately, the solution must be found by those who are nearest to the central issues.

Closely allied with Commons' view of the role of the intellectual is his view on the importance of activity. At this early stage in his career he exhibited that antipathy towards conceptualism which continued to be a distinguishing characteristic of his scientific work. The conceptualist is one whose mental efforts are primarily directed towards the construction and analysis of concepts, and who

[13] Commons' work with the Federation took him into other fields besides labor problems. See his article entitled "Some Taxation Problems and Reforms" in *The American Monthly Review of Reviews*, Feb., 1903, Vol. XXVII, pages 202-208.

[14] Hoxie, Robert F., *Trade Unionism in the United States*, Second Edition, pages 53-77. New York: D. Appleton and Company, 1923.

pays little attention to the relations between these concepts and the realities of the world of experience. In other words, the form of the concept becomes more important than its content. The end result of the conceptualist's intellectual activity is a logical formalism that bears little relation to the historical realities. In the hands of the nineteenth-century economists conceptualism had led eventually to a static equilibrium economics. The kind of economics that Commons was forging in the heat of his early experiences in the realm of industrial strife was a dynamic economics. Commons explains this in his autobiography: "Eventually I made activity, and not pleasure or pain, as did the older economists, the focus of my Institutional Economics." [15] Commons' economics was always to remain very close to those activities which were the primary object of his investigations. Since so much of economic activity partakes of the nature of conflict, it is not surprising that one who kept himself very close to the economic experiences of the past half-century should have come to doubt the adequacy of conventional nineteenth-century economic theory.

In the interim between his dismissal from Syracuse University and his return to academic life at the University of Wisconsin, Commons had an excellent opportunity to put in practice his characteristic views concerning the proper approach to the study of economic problems. During these years he was in a position to apply what his former teacher, Richard T. Ely, had called the "look-and-see" method of studying the behavior of the economic system.[16] In Commons' hands the "look-and-see" method became more than mere induction with an historical or descriptive bias, for he added to Ely's inductive approach a new technique of analysis, namely, the "case" method. It became his practice to select special cases for investigation and to prepare the ground for larger generalizations by first accumulating the necessary funds of information. In his investigational activities during the years 1899 to 1904 Commons made special studies of strikes in the coal-mining, steel, public utility, and building industries. While analyzing the problems of industrial strife at the end of the century, he was in a unique position to study the various types of labor organization that had devel-

[15] *Myself*, page 91.
[16] See Commons' review of Ely's *Ground Under Our Feet* in *The American Economic Review*, March, 1939, Vol. XXIX, pages 22-24.

oped in different industries. The focus of his attention moved from the building-trades unions to the coal-miners' unions, then to the steel-workers' organizations, and so on over the face of the whole industrial system. In place of a simple, orderly competitive market for homogeneous units of labor with great mobility, Commons found labor markets that were more conspicuous for their irregularities and lack of symmetry than for their regularity and smooth functioning. Special case studies brought to light the importance of such factors as race conflicts, immigration, the mechanization of industry, and the emergence of the large corporation in determining the nature and role of labor organizations.[17]   In addition, they provided the raw data out of which Commons was later to fashion his twentieth-century version of economics.

After the "Five Big Years" there ensued what Commons called the "Wisconsin Years," a period devoted to influential teaching, fruitful research, and great service to the State of Wisconsin. During his years in Wisconsin, Commons spent much of his time on leave of absence from the University for the purpose of making surveys of various industries, drafting social legislation, seeing it through the legislatures, and acting as an expert for various economic commissions and boards. His was not the usual life of the academic economist. An intense interest in fact gathering led him to carry on extensive research into a large variety of topics. His university classes, especially those on the graduate level, were conducted more like research laboratories than university lecture sections. Commons found the routine of established courses irksome, since it tended to suppress his instinct of curiosity. He was plagued with "the irritation of doubt," which could be removed only by actual observation and accumulation of the necessary facts.[18]   As a consequence, we find him organizing new courses but dropping them as soon as they were well established. He frequently left the

[17] The results of Commons' case studies frequently appeared in various journals. See his "The New York Building Trades," "Types of American Labor Organization—The Teamsters of Chicago," "Types of American Labor Unions: the Longshoremen of the Great Lakes," and "Types of American Labor Unions: the Musicians of St. Louis" in *The Quarterly Journal of Economics*, 1903-04, Vol. XVIII, pages 409-436; 1904-05, Vol. XIX, pages 400-433; 1905-06, Vol. XX, pages 59-85, and pages 419-442, respectively.

[18] *Myself*, page 129.

classroom to travel through the country where he could observe employers and employees at work, government officials carrying on the work of their departments, city officials improving municipal government, and labor leaders charting new courses of action for their unions. When he returned to his classes within the university gates, Commons would draw upon the vast accumulation of facts, with which he had temporarily satiated his intellectual curiosity, to explain his theories and to provide support for his own views.

The two fields of study which absorbed Commons' interests after his return to academic life at the University of Wisconsin were labor problems and public utility economics. Commons' pioneer work in the field of public utility economics was significant because of the increasingly important role that large corporations were to play after the end of the century.[19] The corporate revolution was to have the effect of narrowing the area in which competitive economics could operate. It also emphasized the importance of the distinction between wealth as physical assets and property as a fund of pecuniary values. With the emergence of the corporation, such terms as the "going concern," "going concern values," and "intangible property" came into common usage and had the effect of making older economic categories less useful in the study of current economic problems. In his tax work for the National Civic Federation during 1902 Commons was first introduced to the problems of the going concern and the taxation of intangible values. He explains in his autobiography that out of the problem of taxing railroads and other public utility corporations "I got my first idea of a 'going concern' existing wherever it does business, distinguished from a 'corporation' existing only in the state of its incorporation. In the course of the next thirty years I worked out the idea of going concerns as existing in their transactions of conflict, interdependence and order."[20] When he turned from tax problems to the new field of public utility regulation, Commons found that an economics of

---

[19] Commons describes some of this early work in his articles entitled "The Wisconsin Public-Utilities Law," and "How Wisconsin Regulates Her Public Utilities," which appeared in *The American Monthly Review of Reviews*, July-Dec., 1907, Vol. XXXVI, pages 221-224, and July-Dec. 1910, Vol. XLII, pages 215-217, respectively.

[20] *Myself*, pages 97-98.

the going concern was a prime requisite in coping with the new types of problems which were to be found in that area of economic activity.

The experience that Commons had in drafting the Wisconsin public utility law of 1907 bore fruit in a number of different ways. Very soon after the completion of this work he organized the first university course in municipal public utilities. More important was the fertilization of his thought resulting from the study of how to regulate utilities. It was not long before he observed that the collective action of such conflicting parties as the consumers of utility services and public utility investors was of more importance than that individual action which was so basic in the analysis of the equilibrium economists. Furthermore, the center of interest in public utility economics was not market value but public value, which was a kind of value quite different from that produced by the competitive forces of supply and demand. The utility valuations and rates accepted by the courts were the product of a complicated economico-legal process, which bore little resemblance to the simple pricing process of a purely competitive economy. Public value raised in Commons' mind the two important questions of reasonableness and futurity. Reasonableness turned out to be the pragmatic question of reducing economic conflict in such a way that all interested parties would accept the compromise as a reasonable solution of the problem of keeping the going concern in operation. In addition, reasonable values were values that looked to a future in which various conflicting interests would come to accept some orderly settlement of their differences. For this reason Commons came to the decision that future expectations were more important in economic analysis than past commitments or costs. In recounting his experiences with the Wisconsin public utilities he explained that from his legal advisers he "got the idea, thrilling to me at that time, of legal valuations in economics as always looking to the future. From this starting point I worked for many years in making Futurity the main principle of economics, distinguished from all the schools of economic thought which based their theories on past labor or present feelings. . . . futurity became my connecting link between law, ethics, psychology, and economics." [21]

As more of the field of private enterprise fell under the control of

[21] *Myself*, page 125.

corporate managers in the first quarter of the new century, Commons was to find that his economics of the going concern was applicable to expanding areas of the economy. Although he soon gave up his course in public utility economics to devote more of his time to problems of industrial strife, his theoretical interests continued along the lines that had been suggested to him by his early experiences with the control of public utilities. The economics of collective action, which flowered out of his later labor studies and his analysis of the evolution of the capitalistic system, has been fashioned in large part out of the concepts and generalizations which he developed in his pioneering investigations into the problems of taxation and public utility regulation.

In the field of labor economics Commons developed courses in trade unionism, labor legislation, industrial relations, and immigration. The study of labor problems eventually led him into an analysis of the whole industrial system, of which the situation in Wisconsin was but a limited reflection. Commons had gone to Wisconsin at a time when the progressive political element under the leadership of Robert M. La Follette had swept the conservatives out of office.[22] An era of experiment and social reform was then introduced. For the next thirty years Commons was to observe the political conflicts of three groups, the Progressives, the Conservatives, and the Socialists. The issues at stake, largely economic in character, included such matters as property taxation, railroad rates, civil service reform, regulation of public utilities, workmen's compensation, unemployment insurance, and the elimination of industrial strife. In the ensuing decades Wisconsin was to take first rank as a state seeking to reconstruct its economic system along lines that were really democratic. But every advance on the economic and social front was met with opposition from some vested interest. As a result, political, economic, and social conflict became the order of the day. It was in this environment that Commons erected the theoretical structure of his special type of economic science. It is not surprising, therefore, to have him say that "I made, during these thirty years, Conflict of Interests, not the Harmony of Interests of the classical and hedonistic economists, the starting point of Institu-

[22] Commons summarizes his views concerning La Follette in his article "Robert Marion La Follette" in *The North American Review*, May, 1908, Vol. CLXXXVII, pages 672-677.

tional Economics." [23]   To help in bringing about more harmonious relations between industrial groups, Commons plunged into the field of labor economics with an all-absorbing zeal.   In 1905 he published his first treatise on labor, entitled *Trade Unionism and Labor Problems,* and in 1907 there followed his *Races and Immigrants in America.*   In quick succession, and as a result of aid received from many quarters, Commons brought forth *A Documentary History of American Industrial Society* (1910), *Labor and Administration* (1913), *Principles of Labor Legislation* (1916), *History of Labour in the United States* (1918), *Industrial Goodwill* (1919), and *Industrial Government* (1921).

In spite of the demands of his research activities and classroom instruction Commons was able to find sufficient time to engage in legislative activity and to work for various state and federal government agencies and commissions.   In 1911 he cooperated in setting up the Wisconsin Industrial Commission.   He withdrew from university life for the next two years so that he might devote his entire energy to placing the Commission on a working basis.[24]   Three years later Commons was called to Washington, D. C., to serve on the Industrial Relations Commission, which had been organized by the federal government to inquire into the problem of growing labor unrest.   In his report to the Commission in 1915 Commons suggested the establishment of a national labor board which would have provided for conciliation through the collective bargaining process.   Such a board, like the Wisconsin Industrial Commission, would have sought to encourage the adoption of the best existing practices of employers and employees designed to eliminate industrial strife.   Just as the courts determined reasonable values, so would the national labor board have determined reasonable labor practices.

Looking forward to the time when a national labor board would be an actuality, Commons continued his investigations into employer-employee relations and methods of making them more satisfactory.   In 1919 he made a survey of thirty outstanding business enterprises to see what they were doing to improve their labor man-

[23] *Myself,* page 97.

[24] Commons, John R., "The Industrial Commission of Wisconsin," *The American Labor Legislation Review,* Dec., 1911, Vol. I, No. 4, pages 61-69, and "How the Wisconsin Industrial Commission Works," *ibid.,* Feb., 1913, Vol. III, pages 9-14.

agement policies. The results of this survey were summarized in his *Industrial Government* (1921), which reflected the widespread enthusiasm of that time for personnel management as a means of improving employer-employee relations. After the depression of 1921 Commons turned to unemployment insurance as a device to aid in the elimination of industrial strife.[25] He had observed how the large corporations provided security for their stockholders by building up profit surpluses to be disbursed in lean years. In his opinion industry had the same obligation to provide for its workers by building up unemployment reserves in prosperous years. Accepting the analysis worked out by J. M. Clark in his *Studies in the Economics of Overhead Costs* (1923), Commons maintained that the business system should recognize that labor was as much of an overhead cost as was industry's capital equipment. It was not long before he was fostering a movement in Wisconsin for the enactment of a state unemployment insurance scheme. In 1924 Commons, as chairman of the unemployment insurance board of the Chicago clothing industry, had the opportunity to observe a voluntary unemployment insurance scheme in successful operation. It was not until 1932, however, that the State of Wisconsin finally enacted its unemployment insurance law. In a few years Commons had the satisfaction of seeing unemployment insurance adopted on a national scale.

In Commons' general plan for economic reform, as developed prior to 1929, unemployment insurance schemes were to be coupled with devices for the reduction of the up-and-down movements of the business system. During the war and post-war years Commons had observed the effects of rapidly rising and falling prices on various economic classes. He had seen the working classes deprived of much of the benefits of their increased productivity by the rising cost of living during the years 1914 to 1919. He had observed how the business cycle struck telling blows at labor with its widespread unemployment and chaotic financial conditions. At length Commons came to the conclusion that the labor problem could not be divorced from such problems as the control of the business cycle and the stabilization of economic activity in general. He tells us in his

[25] Commons, John R., "Unemployment Prevention," *The American Labor Legislation Review*, March, 1922, Vol. XII, pages 15-24, and "The True Scope of Unemployment Insurance," *ibid.*, Vol. XV, pages 33-44.

autobiography that in the late twenties he "joined the labor problem with the money problem. The business cycle first demoralizes labor, then pauperizes labor, then coerces labor. The most important problem was the stabilization of the average of employers' wholesale prices." [26]

Like many other economists in the post-war years, Commons joined with those who held to a monetary interpretation of the business cycle. He came to regard the abuse of credit as the primary explanation of the major fluctuations of the business system. The remedy for this economic evil was therefore to be sought along the lines of a control of credit with special attention paid to the controls exercised by the central banking authorities. This control of the credit supply was to be coordinated with a manipulation of the monetary system, which was designed to achieve a stabilization of the general price level. After 1921 Commons threw himself with enthusiasm into a study of the monetary problem. He became president of the National Monetary Association, and worked for the popularization of its price stabilization program. He explored the literature on the subject of money and credit control, and became acquainted with the monetary proposals of Fisher, Wicksell, and others. During these years Commons kept in close touch with the regulatory activities of the Federal Reserve System from the first feeble attempts to manipulate rediscount rates to the more vigorous policy of open-market operations. Monetary and credit control, however, were but one expression of a new era of capitalism, the era of "banker capitalism." In this stage of capitalistic evolution, said Commons, the employers were being displaced by the high financiers as the directing force of the business system. In this new situation the economic system was being organized around a vast complex of financial interrelations which were dominated by the investment bankers. This new era in the development of capitalism was faced with a number of serious issues, since the bankers were primarily interested in stabilizing profits, and had an insufficient regard for the need to stabilize employment and the earnings of the working masses.[27]

In Commons' view the bankers held the key which would open

---

[26] *Myself,* page 190.

[27] *Stabilization Hearings,* House Committee on Banking and Currency, H.R. 7895 (1927), pages 1074-1121, and H.R. 11806 (1928), pages 56-104, 423-444.

the door to lasting prosperity, if they could be induced to place community interests above their private interests. For him the main problem was one of converting "banker capitalism" into "reasonable capitalism." Although many economists were of the opinion that considerable progress was being made in the direction of a more reasonable form of capitalism in the first post-war decade, the worldwide collapse of 1929 quickly put an end to such premature optimism. The depression of 1929 was not the kind of depression to which Commons and his generation had become accustomed. It developed into the "Great Depression," which was followed by governmental intervention on an unprecedented scale. Concerning measures and devices by which a managed recovery could be made to work successfully, Commons had little to say. He left to younger economists the difficult task of devising ways of securing full employment in what some economists have described as a "mature" economy. In the depths of the depression he published his *Institutional Economics, Its Place in Political Economy* (1934), a statement of his overall economic ideas, and not a book designed to provide answers to the immediate problems of the day. "In the midst of the kaleidoscopic changes every day," said Commons, "no *books* can come out rapidly enough to keep up with the turnover of civilizations. The matter is one for daily, hourly, weekly publications. A book can only develop general principles and methods of investigation. The author and all others must turn, guided as they choose to be by principles and methods, to the immediate urgent problems which crowd upon all of them more or less alike." [28] With many years devoted to extensive research and a great deal of economic experimentation behind him, Commons in 1934 felt that his greatest contribution to future generations would be to explain his views concerning the nature and function of economic science in a world which was still subject to the destructive shocks of severe depressions. Although the urgency of the situation after 1929 called for the application of specific measures for relief and reconstruction, Commons felt that such measures could not be really effective in the long run, unless they were the product of a scientific orientation which was significantly different from the orientation of the nineteenth-century orthodox economists.

In the busy years from 1890 to 1924 Commons appeared to be

[28] *Institutional Economics,* page 611.

primarily concerned with making the economic system a more effective producer of goods and services. To the outside observer experimentation and reform were his major interests. In this period he had never become a party to academic discussions concerning abstruse points of conventional economic theory. Nor did criticism of inherited economic doctrines appear to engage his attention, for, unlike Veblen, he wrote no essays pointing out the limitations of orthodox economics. In the thirty-five years from 1890 to 1924 Commons wrote many books and published a large number of articles, but they were for the most part concerned with immediate economic issues.

In 1924, however, Commons, the widely known expert investigator of labor problems, appeared in a new role. This was the role of the theoretician, which was brought to the attention of economists in general by the appearance of his *Legal Foundations of Capitalism,* a book that an eminent economist has described as a treatise which "bids fair to prove one of the largest contributions made in this generation toward the construction of an economic theory that really illuminates the behavior of men." [29] This volume summarized Commons' efforts up to 1924 to provide a general theory into which he could fit the observations and generalizations about the economic order which he had accumulated ever since his graduate studies under Richard T. Ely in the late eighteen eighties. The inspiration drawn from Ely's historico-legal work combined with thirty-five years of extensive research to produce an economic treatise of unusual significance for the future development of economic science.

The *Legal Foundations of Capitalism* was designed to come to grips with the realities of actual economic experience. It drew upon Commons' abundant experience in drafting social legislation, setting up economic commissions, and participating in various economic experiments which brought him into close contact with the law and the courts. Although his legal study started off as an analysis of the theory of "Reasonable Value," it eventually turned into a study of the functioning of the capitalistic system, which he defined as a system of "production for the use of others and acquisition

[29] Mitchell, Wesley C., "Commons on the Legal Foundations of Capitalism," *The American Economic Review,* June, 1924, Vol. XIV, page 253.

for the use of self." [30]   Commons' genetic study of the role of the courts and the law in determining the course of economic activity was intended to supply an interpretation of modern capitalism.   In Commons' view the classical economists, with their mechanistic bias, and the neo-classicists, with their subjectivistic bias, had overemphasized the significance of commodities and feelings, and had failed to provide the heuristic devices necessary for the study of concrete economic culture.   To avoid the unrealistic results of the orthodox economists' analyses, Commons took as his starting point the study of actual cultural relations, the "transactions" or "working rules" of the economic order.   It was his purpose to study the capitalistic system as a cultural complex or going concern with an intricate structure of transactions or working rules.   Among the many transactions which constitute the economic order, legal transactions are of special significance, and it is to them that Commons devotes his institutional analysis.

The appearance of the *Legal Foundations of Capitalism* placed Commons in the category of economists known as the "institutionalists."   In his review of Commons' legal study Wesley C. Mitchell found that the study was a contribution which belonged to "the institutional type of economics," and was to be classed with the type of work represented by Sombart in Germany, the Webbs in England, and Veblen in the United States.[31]   Although he was familiar with the writings of these exponents of institutionalism, Commons does not appear to have borrowed very heavily from them.   His early association with Richard T. Ely doubtlessly stimulated his interest in the historical and legal aspects of economic problems.   After 1895 his acquaintance with Veblen's writings may have had some influence in molding his own thinking, for soon after 1893 Commons turned away from the orthodox analysis which dominated his first economic treatise, *The Distribution of Wealth*.   The fact that he was as much a sociologist as an economist in the early years of his academic career goes far in explaining his cultural or institutional approach to the study of economic phenomena.   As professor of economic and social science at Indiana University, and as professor

---

[30] Commons, John R., *Legal Foundations of Capitalism*, page 21.   New York: The Macmillan Company, 1924.

[31] Mitchell, W. C., *op. cit.*, page 253.

of sociology at Syracuse University, Commons was greatly interested in the problems of an evolving culture. When he later confined his interests to economic studies, the broad approach of the student of culture was kept intact.

Although Commons and Veblen were both students of Western European culture, their special interests followed different lines. Veblen displayed a special interest in cultural anthropology and its significance for the study of the modern scheme of economic organization. Much of his analysis is concerned with the significance of customary or institutional behavior in the life of primitive tribes as well as of highly industrialized nations. Commons was also interested in habitual modes of human behavior, but his approach was through the decisions of courts stretching over several hundred years. He substituted an intense interest in legal analysis for the cultural anthropology of the Veblenian investigations. Associated with these two different approaches to the study of economic culture have been certain methodological differences. Veblen's propensity for broad generalizations brought it about that much of his economic analysis was designed to support generalizations already arrived at rather than to open the way to new generalizations. We do not find in the Veblenian analysis anything like the applications of Commons' case method. Commons' interest in particular cases in the field of law as well as labor has given expression to a strong inductive bias that is not duplicated in Veblen's work, but Commons' analysis of the capitalistic system seldom reaches the lofty heights of cultural speculation to which Veblen introduces his readers. To some this will appear as a virtue on the part of Commons, whereas others will be inclined to the view that Commons' interest in the case method merely covers up a lack of ability to compete with Veblen on the higher levels of scientific insight.

In the decade after the publication of his *Legal Foundations of Capitalism* Commons devoted much of his energy to a rounding out of his analysis of Western European economic culture. In 1934, the year in which he retired from academic activity at the University of Wisconsin, Commons published his *Institutional Economics,* which not only extended the analysis of his earlier study of the capitalistic system, but also inquired into the methodological, psychological, and philosophical foundations of that type of economic analysis. Unlike other critics of economic orthodoxy who gave the impression that their work was to displace the product of earlier economic theorizing, Commons felt that his particular type of economic theory could very easily be reconciled "with the individualistic and collectivistic theories of the past two hundred years." [32] He was too much of a pragmatist, however, to be satisfied with a mere review of the development of economic thought and the relation of his own thinking to that development. Besides reviewing the theories of economists from Quesnay to Cassel, his study of institutional economics looked beyond theoretical analysis to "practical applications of a theory of Reasonable Value to current problems." His instrumentalistic drive kept uppermost in his mind the thought that his revamping of the older economics would make it a more effective tool for the proper guidance of economic activity in the twentieth century.

Commons' Pragmatic Approach

The half century during which Commons developed his "collective economics" was also the period in which John Dewey's instrumental pragmatism flourished. Dewey had preceded Commons at The Johns Hopkins University by only six years, having gone there for graduate work in philosophy in 1882. In 1903, the year before Commons went to the University of Wisconsin, Dewey started a long list of publications with his *Studies in Logical Theory*. Between Dewey and Commons there is a great deal of similarity, so much so that they both appear to have been nurtured by the same intellectual soil. In their philosophy of method, their psychological preconceptions, and their theory of society they have much in common. Dewey is interested in taking philosophy out of its academic environment and bringing it into the arena of human activity where it can be squared with the hard facts of everyday existence. He is opposed to the excessively rationalistic philosophical tendencies which have been inherited from older European philosophical schools. Dewey's primary interest has been in what he has termed "philosophical reconstruction." [33] To this end Dewey adopts the

---

[32] *Institutional Economics*, page 1.
[33] For Dewey's views on this matter consult his *Reconstruction in Philosophy*. New York: Henry Holt and Company, 1920. As Dewey puts it (pages 26-27), when philosophy surrenders its "barren monopoly" of "metaphysical distinctions," "it will be seen that the task of future philosophy is to clarify men's ideas as to

pragmatic approach, which is based on a functional view of intellectual activity. Philosophy is to be reconstructed by not permitting it to stray too far from our experience of the world about us, in which it is to serve as an agent or instrument for the reduction of strife and conflict. Out of this insistence that philosophy be carefully weighted down with experiential evidence came Dewey's interest in fact-gathering and experimental activity. From this same source came his abhorrence of vague generalizations masquerading as scientific and philosophical principles.

Like his famous contemporary, Commons is essentially a pragmatist in his approach to economic problems. He does not belong to the long line of classical and neo-classical economists, who were primarily interested in deductive analysis and the logical consistency of their scientific thought. The orthodox economists of the nineteenth century sought to make economics more "scientific" by the process of abstracting the irrational and non-uniform elements from economic phenomena, and then pouring the remaining data into the rigid molds of mathematico-logical analysis. The net result of the orthodox approach in economic science was a highly abstract set of economic principles, which became increasingly less applicable to economic phenomena as the evolution of modern capitalism moved further and further away from the small-scale, competitive economic system of the last century. Unlike the orthodox nineteenth-century economists, Commons displays little interest in universal principles or refinements of deductive analysis. In his scientific approach he has more in common with the historical school of Gustav Schmoller and Karl Bücher. The historical economists stressed fact-gathering rather than deductive analysis, and substituted an evolutionary theory of economic stages for the static theoretical system of the classical economists. The two dominant characteristics of the economic analysis of the historical school were its historicity and its relativity. Economic science was to be nurtured by historical rather than by logical analysis; and, in addition, economic principles were always conceived to be relative to particular historical epochs. Thus, there was little of the universal or the logically formal about the economic speculations of the historical school.

The historicity and relativity of the work of the historical eco·

the social and moral strifes of·their own day. Its aim is to become so far as is humanly possible an organ for dealing with these conflicts."

nomists are duplicated in the work of Commons. He has their intense enthusiasm for fact-gathering and their abiding disdain for mere conceptualism. Also duplicated in Commons' analysis is the historical school's evolutionary approach and their arrangement of economic phenomena according to a system of staging. But at this point the similarities between Commons and the historical school end. The historical economists' interest in concrete, historical facts relating to the economic system was more academic than pragmatic. They were not infused with an instrumentalistic bias which would lead them to orientate their fact-gathering around mankind's efforts to overcome the economic obstacles in its social and political environment. It was the lack of a central theme or purpose, such as the classicists' goal of creating an analytical science or the pragmatists' aim of forging a scientific tool which would be of some aid in coping with economic problems, that accounts for the eventual decline of *Historismus*. In contrast Commons made his historical research and his inductive analysis subservient to a larger purpose. He sought to make economics a functional science, just as Dewey has attempted to give a functional bias to philosophical speculation. Nor was Commons' fact-gathering merely a response to the instinct of idle curiosity. His insistence on keeping economic speculation grounded in experience stemmed from a persistent desire to reconstruct capitalism so that it might more adequately meet the needs of the masses.

In order to understand Commons' views on scientific methodology it is necessary to see how he relates progress in his science to the changes in investigational procedure adopted by economists. In the early period of the development of economics "academic research" came first. This was research designed to establish the first principles of the science. Commons finds that in this early period economists tended to be "pure theorists" who sought economic truth for its own sake. Since pure theory was the primary concern, it is not surprising that deductive techniques of investigation were given more attention than were inductive techniques involving observation and experimentation. Now that the first principles of the science have been worked out, Commons would substitute his "constructive research" for the earlier academic research.[34] This in-

[34] Commons, John R., *Labor and Administration*, pages 7-13. New York: The Macmillan Company, 1913.

volves shifting from pure to pragmatic theory which stresses the importance of inductive rather than deductive analysis. No longer is economic truth to be sought for its own sake but instead "for the sake of utility." Commons explains that pragmatic economists are those who "have an eye on the worthfulness of their reasoning for understanding, experimentation, taking chances, and guiding themselves and other participants in the future." [35]

What Commons finds to be unique about the methodology of the pragmatic economists is not that they have discovered a new organon of thought, or a new technique of investigation not formerly possessed by economists. The real novelty of the pragmatic method is found in the intellectual or philosophical outlook associated with this method, which determines the kinds of problems that economists select for investigation, and the investigational techniques that they use. If the pragmatic economist emphasizes the importance of observation and experimentation, it is not because he believes that induction *per se* is more useful or significant than deduction. In Commons' methodological outlook no one technique of investigation is superior to any other technique. The choice of methods of investigation, and the emphasis placed upon some methods as opposed to others, are matters that reflect the attitudes, aptitudes, and interests of the inquiring scientists and not the relative merits of the various methodological approaches. For this reason Commons regards all quarrels about the relative merits of different methods of scientific investigation as being entirely futile. Genuine disagreement can only arise in connection with discussions about the basic philosophical attitudes that should guide the scientist in his investigations and in his theorizing. It is Commons' general position that economists should in the future be less "pure" and more "functional" in their approach to economic studies.

The significance of the pragmatic approach to science can only be appreciated, Commons asserts, when a distinction is made between ultimate truth and pragmatic truths. With ultimate truth, whatever it may be, the pragmatist has no concern. Pragmatic truths depend upon the existing state of knowledge within a scientific field; and as the boundaries of the science are pushed back and the state of knowledge improved, pragmatic truths are altered, improved, and expanded. As a consequence, the truths which are

[35] *Institutional Economics*, page 102.

the object of the pragmatist's concern are relative rather than absolute. What these truths are at any one time depends upon the consensus of scientific opinion; and what they will be in the future depends upon the changes in man's physical and social environment. This concept of scientific truth brings up the whole question of the nature of scientific knowledge and how it is arrived at by the process of scientific analysis. For an explanation of Commons' views on the nature of scientific truth we must turn to this psychological theory.

The empirical psychology of the pragmatists is largely a reaction against the atomistic psychology which was introduced into English scientific thinking by John Locke and Bishop Berkeley.[36] According to Locke's subjectivistic theory of the mind, ideas are merely copies or reflections of the countless, independent objects existing in the world outside. By associating these ideas, the mind develops the concept of relations between objects. In this psychological view the mind is a mere mechanism, "a passive receptacle of ideas," as Commons has expressed it.[37] For when the mind is taken to be a passive recipient of ideas, one easily acquires a contemplative rather than a creative attitude towards the problem of explaining the meaning of experience. One is led to adopt an attitude of philosophical quietism in which he tends to accept readily the cultural status quo. This mechanistic and quietistic theory of mind is found by Commons to have dominated economic thought from the time of Locke down to the end of the nineteenth century. Following the psychological theories of John Dewey, Commons would eliminate this dualism between the mind and the external world by substituting a theory of the functional interrelatedness of the mind and the external world. In Commons' psychological view, the mind is regarded as a creative agency which does much more than reflect the external world of experience.

For Commons, as for other pragmatists, the external world is an immense flow of experience. It is the purpose of mental activity to reduce this flow of experience to some manageable order. Thinking is "an active mental construction of ideas selected and transformed internally in order to investigate and understand the otherwise unmanageable complexity of external activities." [38]   In analyzing experience the mind is active in the sense that it subjects the raw data of human experience to a process of elimination, selection, and refinement.   Thinking is not an arbitrary process, since it is directed by the purposes, aims, and wishes of the thinker. Thinking is not carried on *in vacuo* as the subjectivistic psychologists and philosophers would have us believe; instead it functions in relation to an individual who becomes habituated, socially and historically, to a specific environment.[39]   As the whole thinking process is carried on in the light of human aims or purposes, our ideas become tools or instruments which aid us in the struggle to live and to adjust ourselves more adequately to our environment. According to Commons' empirical theory of the mind ideas are "the intellectual tools with which we investigate" the conditions and situations to be found in the experiential world of hard and fast facts.

In place of the older mechanistic and atomistic view of the mind, Commons would substitute his "volitional psychology," which emphasizes two very significant aspects of the thinking process.   The first is the manipulative aspect of human thinking.   The mind is regarded as a creative agency which manipulates the external world and the people who inhabit it with the view to achieving certain desired consequences.   It is on the basis of this manipulative characteristic of human thought that Commons develops the theory of willingness which is so basic to his "volitional economics": an economics concerned with the human will in action.   The second important characteristic of the thinking process is its emphasis upon the future.   The mind as a creative agency necessarily looks towards the future in which expected consequences are to be enjoyed. Human thought is not only manipulative, but it is also futuristic. In Commons' empirical theory of the mind, ideas become plans of action, and thought bears a definite relation to future action. Thought without action is sterile, and action without thought is blind.

The subjectivistic psychology of Locke is conducive to static, de-

---

[38] *Ibid.*, page· 17.

[39] Commons' theory of the mind is strikingly similar to Dewey's theory.   See Hook, Sidney, *John Dewey, An Intellectual Portrait*, Ch. IV, "Body, Mind, and Behavior," pages 106-126.   New York: The John Day Company, 1939.

ductive analysis, because the mind's chief task is to place order among the many ideas reflected from the outside world. Consequently, logic becomes highly important, and deductive analysis is the primary concern of the thinker. In Commons' pragmatic psychology the main concern of the mind is not with the subjection of ideas to logical treatment. Instead the mind's primary concern is with the creation of useful knowledge, which results from the mind coming in contact with the continuous flux of the world of experience. Whereas Locke's theory of the mind leads to the primacy of deductive analysis, Commons' epistemological theory places more emphasis upon inductive analysis and close contact with external realities. His theory stresses action, conflict, purpose, and achievement, whereas Locke's theory emphasizes inaction, contemplation, and the endless juggling of static concepts. As a result of this basic disagreement Commons departs from the subjective, deductive bias of the orthodox, nineteenth-century economists. Although he does not dispense with the general body of orthodox economic doctrine, he does free himself from what he takes to be the contemplative attitude and the extreme subjectivism of the inherited economics.

Commons' pragmatic psychology is of importance not only in relation to his method of scientific investigation but also in relation to his theory of human motivation. He points out that from the earliest times men have been surrounded by a wall of custom and habits which has effectively limited the direction of their activities. Patterns of customary behavior have given them the things which they prize above everything else: security and the expectancy that the future will not be so very different from the present. For the masses of men customary behavior provides a retreat from a harsh world that is threatening to disrupt their petty schemes, and to force them to make some new and laborious adjustments to ever-changing circumstances. In Commons' view human beings do not start life as isolated individuals like the highly rational beings who were supposed to inhabit Locke's "original state of nature." On the contrary, modern man like his primordial ancestor is born into a world of "discipline and obedience." In this environment of socially sanctioned habits "we continue as members of concerns already going, so that conformity to repeated and duplicated practices—which is all that is meant by going concerns—is the only way to obtain life, liberty, and property with ease, safety, and consent.

. . . We start and continue by repetition, routine, monotony—in short by custom." [40] Hence the most significant characteristic of human conduct, and the one which should interest social scientists who would properly interpret human behavior, is its tendency to take on the form of habitual action.

Commons does not dispense with self-interest in human motivation, but he assigns to it an entirely different role from that given to it by his nineteenth-century predecessors. He attributes primary importance to collective action; in his view individual action has been subordinated and directed by various forms of collective action from the earliest social habit or custom of the prehistoric period down to the great social institutions of today. Here he takes sharp issue with his predecessors. They had alleged that what held competitive society together was individual self-interest. It was the gravitational force which drew everything to the market place, where the self-interest of many individuals blossomed into the social interest of the entire community. Commons insists that what holds economic society together is a binding force other than individual self-interest, a binding force of customary collective action which unites individual to individual and industry to industry. Even the competitive system of the nineteenth century was, in his opinion, a system based upon customary behavior. There were in that period customary ways of conducting business, which, if ignored by the businessman, meant loss of profit and possible economic ruin. As he interprets it, the shift from the handicrafts of the Middle Ages to the factory system of the competitive era of the nineteenth century was not a shift from status to contract, as Sir Henry Maine tried to show, but a shift from feudal custom to business custom. In all cultural eras "custom and habitual assumptions are the underlying principle of all human relations. Each may be named a 'law,' not in the sense of a 'law of nature,' but in the sense of a law of human nature. . . . They are a law of human nature in that they go to a fundamental and ultimate principle without which man cannot live in society—the principle of Security of Expectations. It is not justice, nor even happiness, that is fundamental—it is security, even the security of injustice and poverty." [41]

Another fundamental premise underlying Commons' theory of

[40] *Institutional Economics,* page 45.
[41] *Ibid.,* page 705.

human motivation is that behavior is basically a social and not an individual or personal phenomenon. As John Dewey would express it, the individual is a bundle of instinctive and habitual responses which are developed only in a social situation. Individual habits are largely reflections of the all-pervasive, dominating social patterns of conduct. Yet, even though the bulk of human action is of a customary nature, it must not be assumed that the individual is a mere pawn of the pre-established community patterns of conduct which have been imposed on him from birth. The individual is not a simple mechanism moved about by a complex of external stimuli. Since the human mind has creative powers, at times it selects the stimuli to which the individual will respond. Furthermore, since transactions and practices are seldom repeated in exactly the same form for very long, every custom or social habit has the potentiality of varying in accordance with changes in human choice.

Unfortunately man is not able to enjoy his refuge in customary ways of behavior for any great length of time. There are forces at work which tend to disrupt his life, to alter his customary patterns of behavior, and to compel him to develop new ways of behaving. From earliest times a variety of disruptive factors has always been changing the course of human behavior. In the primitive and early historical eras there were such factors at work as climatic changes, the growth of population, and the pressure of numbers upon limited natural resources. In more recent centuries technological changes of many kinds have torn men away from the protection of pre-established modes of customary behavior. These disturbances of customary ways of living elicit independent thinking on the part of individuals. When men are sufficiently prodded by external events, they turn to intellectual inquiry for a solution of their distressing troubles. In this situation, mental activity has a dynamic, instrumentalistic role. But once the necessary adjustments have been made and new social habits have been firmly established, the role of thinking again becomes minor in the life of the general population.

Under the pressure of never-ending change the potentialities of customs to vary tend to be actualized. New customs emerge as alternatives to existing customs. The prime mover in this evolution of customary modes of behavior, in Commons' opinion, is "changing economic conditions." They bring into being new customs, and give intensity to the competitive struggle for survival among social patterns of behavior. But this struggle for existence among customary modes of behaving is not a blind struggle. Commons avoids a simple materialistic interpretation of changes in human conduct by introducing the principle of willingness, according to which the human will injects itself into the evolutionary process by means of which new customs are established. Economic change merely provides the setting for the development of new customs, any one of which may be selected by the human will to suit changing social conditions. Commons explains that "If customs change, or conditions change, then a choice must be made between customs, and it is a conflict of reason and self-interest that determines the choice. Good customs should be selected, and bad ones rejected." [42] Thus, within certain limits prescribed by material factors, there is room for the exercise of that human volition without which there could be no economic progress. By combining social voluntarism with economic determinism, Commons saves himself from the deficiencies of an excessively deterministic interpretation of human conduct, which would be a denial of the basic tenets of his pragmatic philosophy.

As soon as customs change, conflicts of interest necessarily make their appearance. Customs originate as devices to provide and to preserve order in human relations. Patterns of customary behavior are the cement which effectively binds together individuals and groups, and provides coherence in society. Every custom, however, brings benefits to some individuals and lack of benefits to those who are precluded from taking advantage of the consequences that follow from customary action. Every change in custom is the source of much conflict, since a new customary arrangement of life means a different disposition of personal benefits. Men employ the great economic changes at work in their environment as a lever with which to pry open the gates of customary behavior so as to enlarge the world of personal opportunity. Commons introduces the concept of conflict at this point in his analysis, because he wishes to provide man with an escape from the deadening effects of a rigid world of customary behavior. It is through the agency of conflict, generated by the struggles of individuals and classes, that customs can be developed, altered, and improved. Conflict is thus the leavening agent which will eventually convert the crude, and in many ways

[42] *Institutional Economics,* page 47.

unjust, customs of "banker capitalism" into the selected, just, and salutary customs of "reasonable capitalism."

Man's early state was largely one of custom and a lack of self-consciousness, one in which private property was relatively unimportant because the means of satisfying bodily wants were still fairly abundant. With the growth of population and the intensification of the struggle for existence there developed a self-consciousness on the part of men which was associated with an increasing scarcity of the means of want satisfaction. As soon as private property emerges, the problem of coercion also emerges, because "Private property is but another name for that coercive relation existing between human beings through which the proprietor commands the services of others." [43] All institutions such as the family, the church, and the corporation have a material basis in the form of property which enables them to exercise coercion. The state emerges to meet this problem of coercion which is the source of so much insecurity, capriciousness, disregard of others' rights, and ignoring of the community welfare. Above all other things, men prize security of life, and this can be abundant only where the state is powerful enough to substitute public for private coercion. And so Commons comes to the conclusion that the germ of sovereignty was nourished by the growth of the "primitive all-pervasive principle" of private property. Sovereignty itself, however, is no "ultimate repository," but instead is a flow of "psychic influence." It is a dynamic, evolutionary process which can be adequately investigated only by making the necessary inductive and historical observations.

The state, like other institutions, has been subject to an evolutionary development. Its base has been broadened through the course of the centuries by the admittance of new groups into the circle of those who determine the nature and direction of community welfare. In this way the state has undergone a socialization which has enabled democracy to develop out of ancient forms of state absolutism. Since the state has a tremendous power by virtue of its ability to coerce individuals and groups, and since it continues to increase its coercive power as it develops, coercion by the state becomes a very important public problem. The purpose of admitting as many groups or classes as possible to a share in government is to

[43] Commons, John R., "A Sociological View of Sovereignty," *The American Journal of Sociology*, July, 1900–May, 1901, Vol. VI, page 88.

provide the necessary checks on the use of public coercion and to guarantee its use in the interests of community welfare.   Since the state is a reservoir of public coercion, it becomes the object of a great deal of attention on the part of various classes within the community.   This is because control of the state means control of the distribution of social privileges and burdens.   As soon as organized interests emerge in the form of distinct classes, there then develops a conflict between classes to exercise as much control as possible over the functions of government.   There emerges a harmony of interests between those groups that are organized as contrasted with those portions of the community that remain unorganized.   As new economic classes make their appearance, they seek to influence the state in the direction of their own interests.   Farmers come into conflict with businessmen over the problem of the tariff; debtors are set off against the creditor classes; small business organizes its numbers to cope with the activities of large-scale corporate enterprise; and organized labor pits its strength against capital in the struggle over the distribution of industry's income.

In the Marxian theory of social organization the property-owning classes not only come to possess control of the state, but they also continue to keep this control in the form of a governmental monopoly.   The capital-owning classes may come to wield more power than the land-owning classes, but at all times it is the property-owning classes in general that control the state and exploit the subordinate, propertyless strata of society.   In the Marxian interpretation the state as an instrument of exploitation would never be wrenched from the hands of the propertied classes until the capitalistic system had itself come to an end.   Contrast Commons' theory of social organization!   It is quite non-Marxian in its interpretation of economic conflict.   In place of the dualism set up by Marx between the "haves" and "have nots" Commons adopts a pluralistic view.   He converts the dualistic class conflict of Marx into a plurality of conflicts between labor and capital, buyers and sellers, farmers and wholesalers, borrowers and lenders, and various other opposing classes.[44]   He explains the situation in this manner: "No class can be trusted to decide for itself.   No class, either aristocrats, capitalists, educators, or workers, can see the needs, or rights, or duties, of

[44] *Institutional Economics,* page 718.

others as vividly as their own." Each class will endeavor to put pressure on the state with the view of increasing its own welfare; and in the past there have been too many occasions when a few classes have set the state against the general welfare of the community. In Commons' opinion the state is now undergoing a socialization process in which previously underprivileged classes are slowly being admitted to the round tables of government. In the course of history businessmen first gained a place in the government along with the landed interests; and in more recent times labor has been admitted to government councils in a number of countries. Commons looks forward to an extension of this socialization of the state, so that under a proper form of proportional representation all economic interests of any importance whatsoever will have a seat in the governmental chambers. He believes that when there is adequate representation of all important economic interests, government by "mutual concession" will then take the place of government by class domination.[45]

On some points, however, Commons does find himself in full agreement with Marx. He agrees that class conflict is irrepressible, and that the assumption of a preordained harmony made by many nineteenth-century economists should be challenged. But Commons is much more tentative about the outcome of class conflict than was Karl Marx. According to Commons' theory of society, economic classes are historical categories which by virtue of their "temporary and shifting" nature are constantly giving way to ever-new class alignments. A dualistic view of class conflict is much too simple an interpretation which does not do justice to the facts relating to the capitalistic system of the United States. The pragmatist's view of social organization is woven about no such simple pattern as the struggle between the propertied and propertyless classes. In Commons' theory of society we find the pluralistic view of John Dewey given its full economic application. Marx had envisioned the end of the class struggle as a situation in which a classless society would emerge, but for Commons class conflict has no end. It is a ceaseless process of progressive compromise, moving from conflict to conflict

---

[45] See Commons' discussion of the presidential address given at the 12th annual meeting of the American Economic Association, *The American Economic Review*, Third Series, 1900, Vol. I, pages 62-80.

but usually generating a higher level of social organization.[46]   Although there is no pre-established harmony of interests between classes, there is a solidarity of interests which finds expression in the desire of all classes to keep the going concern called society in continuous operation.   Every class has a stake in the continued operation of the whole social system.   If any one class or group should stop the social process, loss and deprivation would fall on all classes.

The Theory of the Labor Movement

In giving substance to his interpretation of the economic culture which had developed in the United States after the Civil War, Commons first chose the field of labor problems for special attention. At the time that he was being introduced to the study of the capital-labor issue by Richard T. Ely at The Johns Hopkins University, the American labor movement was entering a new phase of its development.[47]   The Knights of Labor had made their last futile effort to organize the working classes into one large union, and after 1885 the American Federation of Labor was to take possession of the field. Under the direction of Adolph Strasser and Samuel Gompers, organized labor substituted job consciousness for class consciousness. Strasser and Gompers had come to the United States as Marxist revolutionaries who were filled with enthusiasm for the class struggle.   After witnessing the failure of American labor to make progress along the lines of class organization during the years 1865 to 1885, and after becoming familiar with the unique conditions of the American labor movement, these two early labor leaders sloughed their revolutionary unionism for the "new unionism" with its trade-agreement philosophy.   It was soon after 1885 that the trade agreement made its appearance and heralded the establishment of a new era of union-management cooperation.   The trade agreement was to become the basis of a *modus operandi* which, Commons felt at the turn of the century, would' result in a "higher form of industrial peace." [48]   It was during the four decades after the organi-

[46] Commons, John R., "Organized Labor's Attitude Toward Industrial Efficiency," *The American Economic Review*, Fourth Series, Sept., 1911, Vol. I, No. 3, page 457.

[47] Richard T. Ely, as a pioneer student of labor problems in the United States, had written his *Labor Movement in America* in 1886.

[48] Commons, John R., "A New Way of Settling Labor Disputes," *The American Monthly Review of Reviews*, Jan.-June, 1901, Vol. XXIII, page 328.

zation of the American Federation of Labor, in which Gomperism became the widely accepted outlook of organized labor, that Commons studied labor problems and worked out his labor theories. His views on the labor-capital issue are therefore largely an intellectual product of the half-century preceding the Great Depression of 1929.

The social philosophy underlying Commons' theory of the American labor movement is gradualistic rather than revolutionary.[49] It stands in direct contrast to the social philosophy of those revolutionary labor organizations that seek to overthrow the capitalistic system. It allies itself with "business unionism" represented by the American Federation of Labor, with trade unionists who seek to preserve the capitalistic system, who accept the trends towards big business, and abandon all anti-monopoly alliances with farmers or small businessmen. While accepting big business as a desirable form of economic organization, the members of the American Federation of Labor look upon trade unionism as a necessary check upon business enterprise. This check is exercised by asserting control over working conditions and wage bargains. The trade unionist realizes, however, that there are very definite limits to the extent to which unionism can shackle business enterprise. In most circumstances the ownership and direction of business enterprise are to remain in the hands of the employers. Thus union-management cooperation is never interpreted by the trade unionists to imply cooperation in accepting the risks associated with the management function.

This "business unionism" of Samuel Gompers, with its emphasis upon the day-by-day improvement of labor's position and its abhorrence of sweeping revolutionary programs, had a great attraction for Commons. It coincided with his bent for piecemeal progress, close observation, and the desire never to get too far from the basic facts of economic or social situations. Commons explained that "The problems of depression, of unemployment, of wages, hours of labor, conditions of work, efficiency, competition, are problems of adjustment and accommodation which must be met every day. It is not a 'program' or a 'platform' or a schedule of 'inalienable rights' that

[49] For a statement of this trade-unionist philosophy by one of Commons' outstanding students see Selig Perlman's *A Theory of the Labor Movement*, Ch. V, pages 154-219. New York: The Macmillan Company, 1928.

bridges over the periods of hardship and depression, but it is the spirit of true democracy, which investigates, takes into account all the facts, gives due weight to each, and works out, not an ideal, but a reasonable solution day by day." [50]   Such a method of procedure elevates observation and experiment above class warfare and subversive attacks upon the business system.   In line with this pragmatic outlook, labor's interests are strictly limited to the area of economic activity.   Incursions into the field of politics are frowned upon, since they drain away the trade-union resources which should be reserved for the prime task of job control.   Where political action of some sort is found to be necessary to cope with adverse court decisions or to provide some needed piece of labor legislation, labor votes can be delivered to the political party which is willing to accept labor's terms in exchange for political support.

The position of the trade unionist, as of Commons also, is basically conservative.   In his autobiography Commons sums up his labor philosophy with the statement that "I concede to my radical friends that my trade-union philosophy always made me conservative.   It is not revolutions and strikes that we want, but collective bargaining on something like an organized equilibrium of equality.   This, I take it, was the social philosophy of Samuel Gompers.   It seems to me the only way to save us from Communism, Fascism, or Nazism." [51]   There is none of the militancy or impatience of the revolutionary in Commons; nor would he in any way seek to force the evolution of economic society.   Thoroughly familiar though he was with the unsatisfactory working conditions of the large, unorganized masses of immigrants, Negroes, children, and women, he would never permit himself to be stampeded by revolutionary zeal into what he thought to be ill-considered demands for the elimination of the capitalistic system.

According to Commons' interpretation of the American labor movement there has been a constant striving since 1860 to preserve the equilibrium or balance between the employing and working classes which has been upset by the crumbling of the competitive system.   In place of Adam Smith's "simple scheme of normal competition," there developed after 1860 a new economy of large over-

[50] Commons, John R., *Industrial Goodwill*, page 185.   New York: McGraw-Hill Book Company, Inc., 1919.
[51] *Myself*, page 73.

head costs, business cycles, and organized labor.[52] The old competitive economy had been able to bring about a rather full use of resources through the adjustment mechanisms provided by the competitive price system. In the modern economy Commons finds that the forces of supply and demand are no longer able to bring about anything like a full use of resources. Whatever elasticity modern capitalism still has is due to the existence of large reserves of men and machines; and the most usual condition of business is now one of disequilibrium and lack of full use of economic resources.[53]

Out of the economic disequilibrium created by the corporate revolution there has emerged not a class struggle but a struggle of what Selig Perlman has called "protectionist interests." [54] Both businessmen and laborers are divided into many different groups, each of which has a distinct property interest to protect. Businessmen are interested in particular corporate enterprises, and laborers in particular trade unions. Labor organizations hope to gain more by protecting their special property interests than by undermining the entire capitalistic system. Disagreement and friction, which are the products of a changing economic order, are reduced or eliminated through the bargaining activities of representatives of the business interests and trade-union leaders. As the result of collective bargaining a new balance is temporarily established. When bargaining powers are altered, the point of balance between the opposing forces may be shifted to a new position. But in spite of many difficulties and bitter conflicts, a *modus operandi* is somehow worked out to the satisfaction of both employers and employees. Beneath the day-to-day struggles of capital and labor there is a solidarity of interests which is strong enough to establish a moving balance of conflicting interests. Like a ship that continues along its course in spite of stormy weather, the economy continues to maintain some sort of balance all through the disorganization produced by industrial strife. This is because both capital and labor have enough interest in the economic system to wish to preserve it as a going concern so that they may continue to derive their livelihood from it.

[52] Commons, John R., "The True Scope of Unemployment Insurance," *The American Labor Legislation Review*, March, 1925, Vol. XV, pages 33-34.
[53] Commons, John R., "Unemployment Prevention," *The American Labor Legislation Review*, March, 1922, Vol. XII, pages 15-16.
[54] Perlman, Selig, *op. cit.*, page 185.

The preservation of the economy as a going concern, however, is not automatic. The success with which it is done depends upon the willingness of the interested parties to cooperate in the work of discovering devices by which employer-employee relations may be improved. Like other pragmatists, Commons is an activist who stresses the importance of voluntary effort in dealing with the problem of improving industrial relations. If the economy is to be kept in operation as a going concern, it will be kept so only because there are businessmen and labor leaders who are willing to work to that end. As an impartial observer of American industrial conditions, Commons devoted much of his time to a consideration of the means by which progressive businessmen and labor officials could lift industrial conflict to more reasonable levels. As an outsider, as an intellectual, he felt that his role should be that of an adviser rather than a leader. He believed that only those who actually participated in industrial affairs could provide effective leadership.[55]

The theory of labor which Commons worked out has been described by him as a "public-utility" theory of labor. In classical economic analysis labor was taken to be a commodity; and the relation of laborer to employer was held to be primarily a private affair. According to this view the laborer entered a market where the sale of his services came under the domination of the forces of supply and demand. He came out with a remuneration that was supposed to bear a proper relation to his specific contribution. This is what Commons calls the "commodity theory of labor."[56] In recent decades the scientific management movement has introduced the "machinery theory of labor," according to which the laborer is looked upon as a machine whose value is determined by the quantity of its physical output. In Commons' opinion both the commodity and machinery theories of labor have some validity, but only incomplete or partial validity. To round out the theory and to grasp a fuller understanding of labor, he believes that the earlier theories of labor should be supplemented by his public-utility theory of labor.

[55] Commons has been very severe in his condemnation of "intellectuals" as leaders in the labor movement. He has felt that, since these intellectuals are more "class conscious" than "wage conscious," they have all too frequently led labor down a blind alley. For his views on this matter see his *Myself*, pages 87-88.

[56] *Industrial Goodwill*, page 5.

According to Commons' public-utility theory of labor the competitive standards of ordinary business can no longer be freely applied to wage bargains. He puts it thus: "You cannot, it is true, overcome the law of supply and demand. But you can modify it, if you know how, within limits." He was likewise aware of the limitations of scientific management: "You cannot permanently withstand those improvements which, by enlarging output, reduce costs, but you can limit the improvement itself at the point beyond which, if carried too far, it increases costs elsewhere more than it continues to reduce them." [57] The laborer, being more than a commodity or a machine, has certain rights and liberties which, if they are not respected, are the source of conflict and disunity. The rights to healthy working conditions, to security of employment, to organize freely, and to enjoy something of economic justice, are now matters of public concern. Since 1850 both public and judicial opinion have undergone considerable change, and new notions of ethics and justice have made their appearance. Step by step the public has moved forward with its demands that certain protections be thrown around the working classes. As scientific investigations of the labor problem have made progress, public opinion has become more informed. The public-utility principle has then been extended to an increasingly large number of the needs and interests of the working classes.

Commons' public-utility theory of labor bears a close resemblance to the doctrine of solidarism which was popularized in France by Léon Bourgeois at the turn of the century.[58] According to Bourgeois' doctrine, solidarity is becoming an increasingly important factor in economic and social relations. The growth of this solidarism calls for additional intervention by the public authorities to insure social justice among all individuals and groups. In Commons' theory of the labor movement the growing solidarity of the employing and working classes finds expression in new forms of governmental intervention, which set the limits within which the capital-labor struggle is permitted to continue. These new forms of intervention by public authority accomplish, Commons said, "what, in France, is called solidarism, . . . a correction of individualism.

[57] *Ibid.,* page 17.
[58] Cf. Léon Bourgeois, "International Organization of Social Policies," *The American Labor Legislation Review,* March, 1914, Vol. IV, pages 186-202. Bourgeois worked out his philosophy of solidarism in his *Solidarité* (1896), and his *Essai d'une philosophie de solidarité* (1902).

The health and welfare of every wage earner are 'affected by a public interest' when the industry or the community is required to make good the loss. Each laborer then becomes a 'public utility.' " [59] In this way the doctrine of solidarism emphasizes the joint responsibilities of employers, employees, and the community in the securing of economic justice for all individuals.

The central principle of Commons' public-utility theory of labor is concerned with the nature and significance of industrial goodwill. When the commodity and machinery theories of labor are supplemented by the public-utility theory, the goodwill of labor then becomes a major concern. Industrial goodwill "is a beneficial reciprocity of wills . . . a matter of opinion and mutual good feeling as much as a matter of science. . . . It is that unknown factor pervading the business as a whole, which cannot be broken up and measured off in motions and parts of motions, for it is not a living being which dies when dissected. And it is not even the personality of a single individual, it is that still more evasive personality to which the responsive French give the name, *l'esprit de corps,* the spirit of brotherhood, the solidarity of free personalities." [60] What is so important about this industrial goodwill is that it is an intangible agent of production without which the other factors of production would be unable to operate effectively. For this reason it is a matter of great importance to the public. Without it there is disunity and industrial strife; with it there is a harmony of interests which permits the enjoyment of a high standard of living.

Commons states that the history of the American labor movement has been an account of the growing recognition of the need to foster industrial goodwill, and to create the devices by which this need might be met. One of these devices has been labor legislation,

[59] Commons, John R., and Andrews, John B., *Principles of Labor Legislation,* 4th edition, page 499. New York: Harper and Brothers, 1936. This analysis of labor laws is more significant for its evolutionary treatment of labor legislation than for the principles which it presents. As Lindley D. Clark points out in his review of the first edition (*Journal of Political Economy,* Vol. XXIV, 1916, page 903), the work "not only presents comparative studies, but also gives considerable space to the subject of historical development and the conditions under which laws come into being. Furthermore, the social and economic effects produced or desired are presented with a degree of fulness. Indeed, it is this developmental aspect that differentiates the work as a whole from any other that has attempted anything like it in scope."

[60] *Industrial Goodwill,* pages 19-20.

which has sought to bring the majority of businessmen nearer to the level of the most progressive employers by establishing certain minimum requirements with respect to working conditions. According to Commons' interpretation, it was not until labor, capital, and the public recognized the solidarity of interests existing among all classes that labor legislation became an important instrument of social control. The goal of labor legislation is a solidarity of interests between labor and capital; "On the side of a broader social philosophy it is the recognition both of class struggle and common interest as permanent facts, and then the adjustment of laws and administration so as to equalize the struggle and utilize the common interest for a public benefit." [61]

The type of labor legislation that Commons admired is one which enlists the support of both employers and employees in the effort to reduce the dangers, risks, and losses involved in the provision of labor service. Labor legislation should be less an expression of the will of a third party (such as the government or the public), which is imposed from without, than of the spontaneous willingness of those actually engaged in industry to cooperate in safeguarding the health and welfare of the working masses. In the first few decades of the twentieth century Commons observed the development of a new attitude towards labor legislation. Whereas liability laws and factory acts had formerly coerced the employer into accepting his responsibility towards labor and the public, the more recent type of labor legislation has secured the employer's cooperation in providing the necessary insurance against labor's industrial risks. The fear of criminal penalties has been replaced by the provision of financial inducements to the employer to reduce the losses and risks of the working population. Accident prevention, unemployment insurance schemes, and other industrial arrangements have been established in such a way that progressive employers have found it financially worth while to reduce industrial hazards. In this fashion intervention by third parties is reduced to a minimum, and private enterprise is left free to justify itself.

Closely associated with labor legislation as a device for building up industrial goodwill has been the industrial commission or labor department. In his report to the United States Commission on Industrial Relations in 1915 Commons pointed out that the federal

---

[61] *Principles of Labor Legislation*, Fourth Edition, page 501.

and state governments could not remedy the evils of industrial strife by relying primarily on their coercive powers, for the exercise of such powers merely begets a struggle on the part of employers and employees to gain control of the government. The police power of the state then becomes a weapon that is used by one economic group or class against other classes. Instead of seeking to eliminate industrial strife through the use of force, governments should seek to stimulate the willingness of the parties in industry to indulge in "progressive cooperation" which will lead to higher levels of industrial harmony. Commons believed that this could be done by establishing industrial commissions in the states and a federal industrial commission for interstate industry.

The industrial commission favored by Commons as a device for creating industrial goodwill should be a non-partisan body entrusted with the special task of enforcing labor laws and providing a machinery for the settlement of industrial disputes. Each industrial commission should have associated with it an advisory council composed of labor, business, and government representatives.[62] The purpose of the advisory council should be to discuss the proposed orders of the industrial commission before they are acted upon. In this fashion ample publicity would be given to the administrative rules and regulations of the commission. The work of the commission would be administrative and not policy-determining, since the state and federal governments would be the only policy-making bodies. After the government has decided upon a labor policy and has embodied it in legislation, the non-partisan industrial commission should then see to it that the government's policy is carried out. Since the industrial commission is so close to the day-to-day developments relating to the capital-labor struggle and comes into possession of significant facts through its investigational activities, it is in a position to influence not only legislative but also judicial opinion.[63] For this reason the industrial commis-

---

[62] Commons, John R., "Representative Advisory Committees in Labor Law Administration," *The American Labor Legislation Review*, Dec., 1929, Vol. XIX, pages 331-335.

[63] As Frank J. Goodnow, a pioneering student of the development of public administration in the United States has put it, "Authorities mainly political control administration, and authorities mainly administrative influence politics." See Goodnow, F. J., *The Principles of the Administrative Law of the United States*, page 15. New York: G. P. Putnam's Sons, 1905.

sion is in a good position to contribute a great deal towards the reduction of industrial strife.

The development of the state industrial commission has given expression to a new branch of government, the administrative branch.[64] In the complex conditions of the modern industrial system legislatures, executives, and judiciaries have found themselves unable to inquire into all the consequential facts presented by a multitude of economic and social problems. To meet this situation railroad commissions, public-utility commissions, and later industrial commissions were set up with the primary function of investigation. Commons explains that "Modern industrial conditions have become so complex, and the laws deal with such a variety of facts, that a fourth department of government is emerging whose purpose is primarily investigation. This is administration. If administration is legislation in action, it is because administration is investigation. It unites in one department the investigating activities of all departments." [65]

Administration, however, is more than a matter of investigation. It is investigation looking forward to the exercise not only of rule-making powers but also of quasi-judicial powers to determine who, in the first place, is responsible for those conditions which call for the enforcement of the regulatory legislation. In working out the rules and regulations which give effect to the legislature's standards of industrial welfare, the industrial commission performs both legislative and judicial functions.[66] Since reasonable standards of industrial welfare are difficult to describe in detail, legislatures have been prone to make only general statements of policy which apply to a large variety of circumstances. It is then left to the industrial commissions to define the contents of the legislative enactments in the light of concrete experiences with industrial strife. In recent years the courts have been loath to interfere or meddle with the rule-mak-

[64] See White, Leonard D., "Administration," and Freund, Ernst, "Administrative Law," in the *Encyclopaedia of the Social Sciences*, Vol. I, pages 440-449 and 452-455, respectively. Starting with F. J. Goodnow's *Comparative Administrative Law* (1893) the literature relating to public administration and administrative law in the United States has grown steadily. A recent treatment of this problem is to be found in J. M. Landis' *The Administrative Process*, 1938.

[65] *Principles of Labor Legislation*, page 449.

[66] See Andrews, John B., *Administrative Labor Legislation, A Study of American Experience in the Delegation of Legislative Power*, 1936, and also his *Labor Laws in Action*, 1938.

ing activities of the industrial commissions, unless there is strong evidence that the commissions are ignoring individual or public welfare. Since the legislatures and the courts are not in a position to make the same exhaustive investigations of all the pertinent facts as are made by the industrial commissions, they have come to accept the findings of the commissions as prima-facie evidence. In this way the industrial commissions have obtained a measure of freedom from both legislative and judicial control.

The extent to which the labor department may go in making the wage bargain a reasonable working arrangement between capital and labor by enforcing labor legislation is a matter which is determined by the demands of the public as expressed through legislative enactments, and by the decisions of the courts relating to the constitutional limits of legislative powers. Public opinion concerning what is a reasonable wage bargain has undergone many changes since the era of small-scale industry in the early decades of the nineteenth century. The content of the term "public benefit" has been continuously altered and enlarged, with the result that the rights and duties of employers and employees have been viewed from new standpoints. In response to the demands of a changing public opinion, legislatures have extended governmental regulation to cover wages, safety, health, hours of labor, and compensation for accidents.

The extent to which the legislatures may go in altering the terms of the wage contract through the use of such public powers as the taxing power, the power to regulate commerce, or the police power is not only a matter of legislative decision. It is also a matter for consideration by the courts, which are in a position to determine whether or not the use of public powers to alter the conditions of the wage bargain conforms with constitutional requirements relating to the protection and preservation of individual rights and liberties. In determining these circumstances the courts in effect determine the rights and liberties of both employers and employees. Since these rights and liberties affect the powers of employers and employees to obtain exchange values, they are forms of intangible property. "The wage-earner's 'property,'" said Commons, "becomes his right to seek an employer and to acquire property in the form of wages; his property in the sense of liberty is his right to refuse work or to quit work if the conditions are not satisfactory. The employer's 'property' is, in part, his right to seek laborers and acquire their services; his property, in the sense of 'liberty,' is his right to run his business in his own way, that is, in part, to withhold employment or to discharge the laborer if the bargain is unsatisfactory. . . . These definitions of property rights are evidently quite different from the older ideas of property in physical things, such as lands, buildings, machinery, or slaves. They signify rights of buying and selling, of access to a market. They are 'intangible' property, and not tangible. They are like the 'goodwill' of a business. They are defined as 'property' because they are necessary to give things and services that value in exchange which in modern industry depends as much on selling them as it does on 'producing' them." [67]

Accepting the view of Wesley C. Mitchell that modern industry is mainly a matter of buying and selling, Commons observes that the worker is interested in making the process by which he sells his labor as financially lucrative as possible. Not only is the laborer interested in producing a labor service, but he is also interested in selling his services on as favorable terms as he can secure. What he gets for his services depends upon a multitude of market conditions, many of which have been altered by the courts. As the courts enlarge the rights of labor, they add value to labor's service. Conversely, as they enlarge the rights of employers, they reduce the pecuniary value of labor's services. For these reasons, the courts after 1860 became "the first authoritative faculty of political economy in the world's history," which imposed its theories of property, liberty, and value upon both employers and employees.[68] In recent decades the courts have altered the meaning of equality in bargaining relations as well as the meaning of property and liberty. Aware of the fact that "where bargaining power on the one side is power to withhold access to physical property and the necessaries of life, and on the other side is only power to withhold labor by doing without those necessaries," the courts have come to understand that the equality of rights inherited from earlier economic eras has now degenerated into inequality of bargaining power. By altering inherited legal rights which were more appropriate to an era of small-scale, competitive industry, the courts have aided in the establishment of a new "equilibrium of equality." It is an equilibrium between two well-organized forces, capital and labor, which has

[67] *Principles of Labor Legislation*, page 508.
[68] *Legal Foundations of Capitalism*, page 7.

taken the place of the competitive equilibrium of the early nineteenth century.

The growth of labor legislation and the establishment of industrial commissions have been accompanied by significant improvements in collective bargaining arrangements.   Since the acceptance of the trade agreement in the closing years of the last century as a means of settling industrial disputes, collective bargaining has been developing both extensively and intensively.   On the extensive front Commons observes a tendency for labor organizations to duplicate in size and power the large corporate enterprises.   To further this tendency he has advocated the complete acceptance on the part of businessmen of labor's right to organize freely.   He believes that labor will have frequent recourse to political action as long as it is poorly organized and unable to compete on an equal basis with employers' organizations.   And, unfortunately, when labor unions enter politics, Commons finds that the door is opened to "the party politician, the intellectual, the lawyer, the lobbyist who succeed only in widening the gap between labor and capital."   Commons does not think in terms of organized labor emerging as a strong, independent political force, which might in the course of time come to dominate the political scene as it has in England.   On this matter he appears to have allowed the behavior of the skilled craft unions, rather than that of the large industrial unions, to dominate his thinking.

In accounting for the centripetal tendencies of the American labor movement Commons lays emphasis upon the development of nation-wide markets.   He asserts that it is "the historical extension of markets over this broad expanse of the United States from colonial times to the present that has changed the character of competition, intensified its pressure, separated manufactures from agriculture, introduced the middleman, produced new alignments of social classes, and obliterated the futile lines that distinguish the jurisdiction of states.   . . . it is not so much the mechanical inventions and the growth of industrial technique, which more properly belongs to the physical and engineering sciences, that have given character to American industrial movements, as it is the development and concentration of bargaining power over immense areas, whether in the hands of the merchant, the banker, the employer or the employee." [69]   Commons does not theorize to any great length about the causal connections between the course of technological change and the progress of the American labor movement.   Throughout his discussion of the labor movement he shows little interest in any technological interpretation of the course of economic evolution. It was not long after the appearance of Commons' interpretation of the American labor movement in the introductory chapter of the monumental *History of Labour in the United States* that other labor experts challenged his views on this matter.[70]   Frank T. Carlton found that Commons, in overemphasizing the expanding market as a factor leading to the growth of labor organizations, had worked out much too simple an interpretation.[71]   Carlton asserted that no explanation of the expansion of the American labor movement could properly overlook the "influence of changing machinery." Furthermore, according to his view, labor organizations had developed as the consequence of "very different combinations and balances of social forces."   It was therefore desirable to avoid all single-track explanations of labor movements, even though some primacy might be attached to changing technology as a factor in the evolution of labor organizations.

Commons never answered his critics on this issue, nor did he modify or develop further his own interpretation of the basic factors at work in the evolution of the American labor movement.   He has always been unwilling to allow himself to be drawn into the whirlpool of speculative analysis that frequently goes with a technological interpretation of the course of industrial evolution.   In contrast to Veblen, who has been positive and dogmatic in his handling of technological interpretations, Commons has perhaps gone to the other extreme in refusing to give ample consideration to technological factors in his theories relating to the American labor movement. As a contemporary of Veblen he may have provided a desirable

[69] Commons, John R., and associates, *History of Labour in the United States*, Vol. I, *Introduction*, page 6.   New York: The Macmillan Company, 1918.

[70] Commons had first worked out this explanation of the spread of the American labor movement in 1910 in an article entitled "American Shoemakers, 1648-1895, A Sketch of Industrial Evolution," which appeared in *The Quarterly Journal of Economics*, 1909-10, Vol. XXIV, pages 39-84.

[71] See F. T. Carlton's review of Volumes I and II of the *History of Labour in the United States* in *The Journal of Political Economy*, 1918, Vol. XXVI, pages 981-983.

antidote for the excessively dogmatic Veblenian analysis, but at the same time he appears to have gone too far in refusing to take from the Veblenian interpretation that part which may be regarded as scientifically acceptable.

Commons seeks to avoid what he believes to be the excessively deterministic interpretations of the "productionists," Marx and Veblen, who, he believes, overemphasize the significance of tools and industrial arrangements. He has been more prone to direct his theorizing along the lines of the work of Carleton H. Parker and Robert F. Hoxie, who paid special attention to the psychological basis of unionism.[72] Parker's psychological studies of the working classes led him to a study of industrial psychoses and their role in industrial conflict, while Hoxie paid special attention to the psychological basis of unionism with its manifestations in the varying temperaments of different labor groups. Commons has a very high regard not only for Hoxie's brilliant handling of the psychological aspects of labor problems, but also for his "dig-it-up method" which was all too rare when Hoxie was making his investigations in the early years of this century.

On the intensive front many important developments have in recent years indicated ways in which collective bargaining may be greatly improved. These developments are concerned with factory conditions and attitudes, which Commons takes to be the crux of the capital-labor problem. He explains that "The outlook is menacing for the worker, for industry, for the nation. The workers lose their interest in industry just at the time when they become more powerful than ever before in controlling industry through labor organization or politics. Without interest in their work they cannot be expected to pay attention or have a care for the economy, efficiency, or discipline, without which business goes bankrupt." [73] In the past fifty years Western European civilization has perfected a gigantic machine system of unlimited productive possibilities. But technological progress has not been accompanied by adequate changes in the psychological attitudes of employers and their workers. There has developed a cultural lag which poisons the reactions of the

[72] Cf. Parker, C. H., *The Casual Laborer*, 1920, and Hoxie, R. F., *Trade Unionism in the United States*, 1917. For Commons' opinion of Hoxie's work see his review of Hoxie's *Trade Unionism in the United States* in *The Quarterly Journal of Economics*, 1917-18, Vol. XXXII, pages 396-399.

[73] *Industrial Goodwill*, page 140.

participants in industry, and which is the source of much industrial strife. "The future of industry" says Commons, "is psychological. The inventors, engineers, businessmen of the future will be industrial psychologists." It should therefore be the major concern of employers and labor leaders to see to it that the industrial system does not continue to be a breeding ground for those industrial attitudes which must inevitably foster industrial ill-will.

Along with proper psychological attitudes should go a spirit of workmanship and loyalty to the industrial system. Commons does not believe, as do the romanticists, that the spirit of workmanship can be revived only by returning to medieval craft methods of production. Nor does he agree with the socialists that modern capitalism and a spirit of workmanship are of necessity incompatible. He agrees that a worker who is tied to some minute task in a large-scale enterprise will probably develop little of the spirit of workmanship, especially when he is unaware of his connection with the whole productive process. But if the worker is taught the importance of his own particular job and its significance in the entire productive process, he becomes a part of a "going concern" whose sociability and democratic functioning may give much stimulation to the spirit of workmanship. In this connection Commons distinguishes between "repetition" work and "automatic" work. Repetition work he considered as being merely the transitory stage between the older craft production and the automatic production of the twentieth century, which, under the proper conditions, should command the loyalties of workers as well as of businessmen. How to make automatic work interesting, and how to develop the workers' loyalty "is the big field of industrial psychology, which for the twentieth century opens up like the nineteenth for chemistry and physics."

Commons observes that improvements in shop attitudes and conditions have been brought about by progress in scientific management, in setting up personnel departments, and in establishing shop committees or councils. Of special significance for further progress in this connection, in his opinion, are personnel departments and factory committees. In his report to the United States Commission on Industrial Relations in 1915, Commons had argued that collective bargaining arrangements would not be successful until the absentee owners of the large corporations had been brought to an

adequate sense of their responsibility to their employees.   He therefore suggested the setting up of personnel departments which
would report their recommendations over the heads of corporation
managers to the boards of directors.   In the early postwar years he
became quite enthusiastic about the future possibilities of the personnel department.   It was to be more than an employment department; it would be "the department that deals with every human
relation within and without the establishment . . . the department
of industrial goodwill . . . the department that guides the entire
establishment in the administration of justice, industrial welfare,
and service to the nation."[74]   Subsequent events have shown that
Commons was unduly optimistic during the 1920's about the possibilities of the personnel department, but the device remains an
integral part of his general plan for the development of a form of
"reasonable capitalism."   If the personnel department, or some
similar agency, is unsuccessful in its work of socializing the modern
corporation and of developing the proper attitudes on the part of
corporate managers and absentee owners, such a condition would
seem to indicate that the private profit system is unable to achieve
that degree of reasonableness which Commons regards as essential
for its continued existence.   Commons is not unaware of this possibility, but he refuses to allow it to undermine his confidence in the
nation's ability to achieve some form of reasonable capitalism.

Commons' enthusiasm for the personnel department was matched
by his optimistic outlook with respect to the shop or factory committee.   He appears to have been very greatly impressed by the
success of the Whitley shop-committee movement in England during the World War of 1914-18, and for a time he looked forward
to the spread of the movement in the United States.   In his opinion the shop-committee plan marked the inauguration of a new
era of reconciliation between capital and labor.   At the time that
he wrote his *Industrial Goodwill* (1919), in which he presents his
views concerning this new development in the field of industrial
relations, Commons was engulfed by the tidal wave of optimism

---

[74] *Ibid.*, page 165.   In his review of Commons' *Industrial Government* (1921),
a survey of labor management policies which Commons published in collaboration with a number of his students, Paul H. Douglas found that the study reflected the excessive optimism concerning personnel work which was so prevalent
in the early postwar period.   For Douglas' review see *The Journal of Political
Economy*, 1921, Vol. XX, pages 844-845.

which swept through intellectual circles in the early postwar years. In those flushed years he felt that "now we and all the nations perceive, as never before, that the next stage in industrial progress is not that economic revolution which Karl Marx predicted, it is not even development in machinery and tools, but it is the increased production and the increased wealth of the world which are now dependent upon the health, intelligence, and goodwill of labor." [75] The whole world seemed to be turning away from material things to such spiritual matters as social solidarity and industrial goodwill. Technological progress after 1885 had brought not peace but strife, not plenty but want. After observing four years of destructive warfare, Commons felt that men would once more give their attention to improving the non-material basis of Western European culture. He believed, in 1919, that in the field of labor relations the emphasis would be placed upon improved industrial attitudes, which would help to eliminate the lag existing between progress in industrial efficiency and improvement in employer-employee relations. One of the means for the achievement of this end was to be the shop committee with its representation of both labor and capital. Unfortunately, with the passage of time Commons' enthusiasm in this matter has borne little fruit; indeed the widespread optimism of the postwar decade has turned to bitter disillusionment.

Commons asserts that no really successful nation-wide collective bargaining arrangements can ever be established, unless there is first an adequate foundation in the form of shop committees. He points out that "Organization, whether it begins with the workers or with the employers, must always begin at the bottom, in the shop, rather than at the top by legislation or national organizations of capital and labor." A spirit of reasonableness must grow up from the bottom. It cannot be injected into the capital-labor struggle from above. Unless they are fed by a spirit of reasonableness from below, national organizations of both capital and labor tend to become arbitrary and autocratic. These national organizations have a different role from that of the local shop committees or councils. With respect to national employers' associations Commons states that "Their new place is more professional and educational, and less executive and governmental. It is the place for comparing notes and statistics, sharing experiences, telling each

[75] *Industrial Goodwill*, page 192.

other of their successes and showing how it is done in dealing with labor. It is less and less the place for depriving the employer of his freedom to deal with his own employees in his own shop. Employers' associations will and must expand, but they should become great educational conferences on the methods, the purpose, and the spirit of shop organization, rather than lawmaking bodies for their members. . . . Likewise with national organizations of labor unions." [76] Employers and workers should not subject themselves so much to the control of national organizations that they are unable to use their ingenuity in working out new ways of increasing industrial goodwill.

When the local factory committee was being tried out as a device for the elimination of industrial strife in the 1920's, Commons had high hopes that this committee system would develop into the substructure of a system of industrial government. The industrial government that Commons had in mind would be a purely voluntary arrangement supported by employers and employees. It would spring up from the thousands of local shop committees in the many factories spread over the country. The local committees would be further organized on a district basis so that district industrial councils would determine the labor policies to be adopted for the various districts of the nation. Over the many district industrial councils would be a "National Joint Conference of Capital and Labor," which would be organized to deal with general policies affecting the two parties in industry. During the war years, 1917-1918, Commons had seen labor and capital come together for the peaceful settlement of their disputes under the guidance of the National War Labor Board with its equal representation from the American Federation of Labor and the National Industrial Conference Board. If the right motives could be substituted for patriotism, Commons felt that these war-time arrangements for the handling of industrial strife could very well be made a permanent feature of the modern capitalistic system.

In Commons' industrial scheme for the future there would be a separation of industrial and political government. The industrial government, composed of representatives from organized labor and from business, would function independently of the political government. The latter type of government would be concerned with

[76] *Ibid.*, pages 115-116.

the general interests of the public.   It would determine the limits within which labor and capital would be free to seek their own interests and to work out compromises whenever necessary.   The political government would act as a mediator whenever employers and employees were unable to reach an agreement about industrial matters.   In addition, it would provide the police power that would be necessary to enforce legislation and to bring recalcitrant employers and employees into line.   Thus far, collaboration of the government with organizations of employers and employees has been largely limited to the realm of state government.   Collaboration on a nation-wide basis has remained "the most difficult development in the past forty years." [77]   Only in extreme emergencies brought on by wars and serious depressions have labor and capital collaborated with the federal government to preserve the stability of the business system; and in these few cases the collaboration has been of a temporary nature.

Through the aid of such devices as labor legislation, industrial commissions, personnel departments, shop committees, collective bargaining arrangements, and favorable court decisions, "the public benefit period" of the American labor movement has taken on definite shape.   The aggressive labor movement which appeared after the Civil War, with its emphasis on the class struggle, has been tamed by court decisions, new legislative policies, and new methods of instilling reasonableness in employer-employee relations.   Since 1898, when the Supreme Court recognized in the *Holden v. Hardy* case that the wage bargain is clothed with a public interest, there has been less "class struggle" and more "class collaboration." [78] Socialist labor unions, such as the Amalgamated Clothing Workers of America, have sloughed their revolutionary aims, and have entered the conservative circles of the American Federation of Labor. By 1918 Commons could write that "Back and forth between the socialistic and anarchistic doctrines has the labour movement swung, according to periods, conditions, and leaders.   By a kind of natural selection a more 'pragmatic' or 'opportunistic' philosophy, based on the illogical variety of actual conditions and immediate necessities,

[77] Lescohier, Don D., and Brandeis, Elizabeth, *History of Labor in the United States, 1896-1932*, Vol. III, with an introduction by John R. Commons, page xxix.   New York: The Macmillan Company, 1935.

[78] *Ibid.*, page xix.

has taken form in the American Federation of Labor, the railway brotherhoods and industrial unionism, which is neither anarchism nor socialism but a species of protectionism combining both, and is analogous to the 'solidarisme' of recent movements in France, and the 'labourism' of England and Australasia." [79] In the welter of special conditions to be found in the United States, such as the presence of free land, the influx of millions of immigrants, and the spread of the market area over the entire nation, revolutionary class struggles dissolved into the milder conflicts of many protectionist groups. In the course of its evolution the American labor movement has drawn upon many diverse social and political philosophies. When these philosophies were added to the special economic conditions found in the United States, the outcome was an acceptance of the private profit system by labor and of the public-utility theory of labor by businessmen.

The development of the public-utility principle as it relates to the labor movement has not been without its difficulties, nor has the principle yet received full application. Conservative courts, uncooperative employers, and a slowly changing public opinion have served to delay the conversion of class struggle into class collaboration. "The evolution has," said Commons, "been a struggle of conflicting interests, as in all evolution, with its ups and downs, its strikes and blacklists, and we are yet in the midst of it." In the 1920's Commons' outlook on the American labor movement was extremely optimistic. By 1935 his post-war optimism had turned to deep pessimism, for by that time he was seeing "how this newly liberated and enfranchised [labor] class has become such a serious problem that it seems to bring on a reaction towards Fascism and Nazism." [80] Possessing all the doubts of the scientific pragmatist concerning the inevitability of economic and social progress, Commons was willing to concede in the 1930's that his public-utility theory of the American labor movement was a special product of the forty-year period from 1890 to 1929, and that there was considerable doubt concerning its applicability to the next forty-year period.

The depression of 1929 confirmed the view, which Commons had

[79] *History of Labour in the United States*, Vol. I, page 17.
[80] *Ibid.*, page xxv.

developed during the 1920's, concerning the necessity of shifting from a limited capital-labor viewpoint to a larger over-all view of the entire economy if there was to be a further development of his economic thought. This change in theoretical interest enabled Commons to round out his economic theory, and to convert his labor economics into a "collective economics." All the fundamentals of his interpretation of the labor movement reappear in his explanation of the development of modern capitalism. After 1929 Commons took the materials of his labor theory and applied them freely on a wider canvas. On this larger background he replaced the conflicts and struggles of employer and employee protectionist groups with the activities of a much larger circle of protectionist interests which included farmers, consumers, taxpayers, small businessmen, trade associations, large corporations, and many other organized economic interests. Instead of confining himself to an analysis of how the balance between labor and capital was maintained, Commons turned to a study of the managed equilibrium of the whole capitalist economy. His earlier theory of "class collaboration" became a broader theory of "reasonable capitalism." The piecemeal progress of the courts and industrial commissions in improving employer-employee relations turned out, in the larger analysis, to be a step-by-step progress in eliminating the exploitations of "banker capitalism." In this manner, the solidarism of the employer and employee groups was discovered to be but a reflection of that larger solidarity of interests which unites all the many protectionist interests to be found in the modern economy.

The Theory of Banker Capitalism

The organization of the American Federation of Labor in 1886 not only marked the first successful attempt of labor to federate on a national basis, but it also coincided with the appearance of big business or with what Commons calls "banker capitalism," an era of capitalistic development that is of special interest to him. Although his researches had taken him into the origins of the capitalistic system, as is to be seen in his study of the *Legal Foundations of Capitalism,* most of his attention after 1923 was directed to the most recent phase in the evolution of the capitalistic system. This is the period with which his labor theories were primarily concerned, a period which he found it necessary to comprehend, if his interpretation of the American labor movement was to be as well rounded as he wanted it to be.

In developing his analysis of the evolution of modern capitalism Commons has drawn considerable inspiration from such works as Karl Bücher's *Industrial Evolution* (1901) and Werner Sombart's *Der moderne Kapitalismus* (1928). Much of his data, however, relates to the evolution of capitalism in the United States, and was obtained at first hand while he was engaged in the researches which produced such monumental works as the *Documentary History of American Industrial Society* and the *History of Labour in the United States*.[81] Commons is not much concerned with how far American economic development has been paralleled in the other industrialized nations. Nor does he endeavor to work out an interpretation that would be applicable to all those nations that may be considered to be within the orbit of the capitalistic system. Actually there are in Commons' work few of those universalizing tendencies which are found in the studies of many continental European students relating to the origins and development of capitalism.

Commons breaks down his evolutionary concept of capitalism into three economic stages which he calls respectively merchant capitalism, employer capitalism, and banker capitalism. The first stage of capitalism developed out of the extension of markets in the seventeenth and eighteenth centuries. This first stage, mercantilism or merchant capitalism, was an era of scarcity in which economic activities were dominated by the rationing transactions of the central government. Bargaining transactions between individuals were relatively less important. Production was small-scale, technology was but little advanced, and economic activity was primarily concerned with the retailing activities of middlemen. During this epoch the legal control of goods was usually not separated from their physical control. The seller brought his goods to the market in person, and physically handed the commodities over to the buyers. Since both business custom and the common law made no distinction between the physical and legal transfers of commodities,

---

[81] Commons, John R., and associates, *A Documentary History of American Industrial Society*, Vols. I-X. Cleveland: The Arthur H. Clark Company, 1910-11, and Commons, John R., and associates, *History of Labour in the United States*, Vols. I-IV. The Macmillan Company, 1918-35.

ownership of a commodity and the physical commodity itself were taken to be one and the same thing. Commons finds that these views relating to commodities and their ownership later dominated the thinking of the classical economists, and were responsible for their failure to distinguish between wealth and assets, commodities and their ownership, or between corporeal and intangible property.

The development of industrial technology at the close of the eighteenth century, and in the early decades of the new century, gave rise to the second phase of capitalistic development known as the era of employer capitalism. In this era the factory operator takes the place of the travelling merchant, and the factory supplants the wholesale and retail establishments of the merchants as the dominant economic institution. In contrast to the era of merchant capitalism, this second era is one of "extreme abundance and pacifism." The fruitfulness of the factory methods of production soon makes itself apparent, with the result that the general population is freed from many of the strains and difficulties associated with the prior era of great economic scarcity. Abundance is accompanied by a relaxation of governmental control. The rationing activities of the state, so prominent in the prior period of mercantilism, are now replaced in large part by individual bargaining activities. A minimum of governmental control is accompanied by a maximum of individual liberty.

What is of greatest interest to Commons in the era of employer capitalism is the fact that in this period the legal control of commodities is separated from their physical control. The close association between the seller and his goods begins to disappear as factory operators become less interested in the production of goods and more interested in the legal aspects of commodities: in ownership which carries with it the right to legal control and transfer. In the early decades of the industrial revolution, while enterprise is still small-scale and the emphasis is upon production rather than the marketing of goods, this separation of legal control from the physical control of commodities makes little headway. Businessmen, factory operators, or employers are still closely wedded to the production of use-values or commodities. Since the credit system and large international markets have not yet become firmly established, there is still little incentive for the employer or businessman to see how he can subordinate the production of use-values or commodities to the production of pecuniary values or assets; therefore, the correlation between the physical and legal control of material goods remains fairly close. The early factory system, however, has the effect of driving a wedge between the physical and legal control of material goods. It only remains for new economic circumstances to drive the wedge in still further, and to split asunder the production of use-values and pecuniary values.

As the stage of abundance initiated by the industrial revolution advances, it merges into a new era of stabilization which Commons calls the era of banker capitalism. This is the era of the assembly line, of a highly complicated and extensive credit system, and of modern corporate enterprise. In this stage of "corporate capitalism" the businessman or employer-capitalist finds that he is deprived of his dominant position by the financier, who emerges as the major directing force of business activity. The entry of the banker as a dominating figure in the realm of economic activity heralds a time when the separation of the legal control from the physical control of commodities is a matter of great importance. Businessmen now become even more interested in the production of pecuniary rather than use-values. Indeed they become specialists in the accumulation of pecuniary values by withholding productive capacities and marketable commodities, and by thus restricting the production of use-values in the form of material goods. For this reason the era of banker capitalism becomes an epoch of stabilized scarcity.

In this era of stabilized scarcity, which appeared in the United States after the Civil War and which was well on its way by the turn of the century, there is a reversion to collective economic action reminiscent of the mercantilistic era. Commons observes that once more the dominant form of economic behavior is collective rather than individual. Again the pendulum swings back towards an age of extensive governmental control over economic life. But the new age of governmental regulation differs from the period of mercantilism, for the reason that restraints on individual behavior are not enforced from above as was the case in the seventeenth and eighteenth centuries. Nor is government the primary source of control of individual economic conduct. Restrictions on individual liberty are now enforced through the concerted action of corporations, labor unions, employers' associations, and numerous other groups. Individuals are mobilized behind leaders who assert that collective action is their only salvation. But as soon as one group is organized, it becomes necessary for other individuals to organize themselves in self-defense. As soon as businessmen set up collective arrangements looking to the preservation of their position, laborers feel a need to pursue the same policy. Presently the farmers come to realize the advantages of collective action for the preservation of their status; and, belatedly, the consumers enter the conflict as an organized group to defend their interests as against all other pressure groups. The final result is that the whole economy passes through a cartelization process.

The economic groups or organizations which have resulted from the cartelization of the American economy are described by Commons as going concerns. The going concern "may exist as a partnership, a union, an association, a corporation, a cooperative. The essential thing is the visible, tangible going concern of persons, with its invisible, intangible behavior of the immediate and remote future stabilized by working rules." [82] The going concern is an association of individuals motivated by common purposes, whose collective behavior is called by Commons a "going business." The going concern, such as an industrial union or corporation, when considered apart from the individuals who participate in its affairs, is not a metaphysical entity. Instead it is a form of collective behavior, a "flow of transactions along lines indicated by its own working rules." All going concerns have a composite or collective will which is not a metaphysical entity existing independently of the wills of the individuals who are associated in the going concern. The will of the going concern is composite or collective only to the extent that individuals participate in the affairs of the concern, and thus exert an influence upon the direction of the concern's collective behavior. Commons explains that this collective will "is the organized symposium of all the discretionary acts of all the participants as they go along from day to day, according to the rules of the organization. It is an organized mass movement." [83] Where discretion is limited to a small number of the individuals comprising the going concern, the composite will then reflects the purposes of a minority group. For example, in many large corporations the composite will of the corporation as a going concern is in reality only

[82] *Legal Foundations of Capitalism*, page 145.
[83] *Ibid.*, pages 146-147.

the will of a minority which happens to be in control of corporate affairs.

The collective behavior of the going concern is guided by more than its composite will. It is also guided by a set of "customs, practices, habits, precedents, and methods of work," which have been developed over time and which are passed on as "working rules." These rules are built up in accordance with the requirements of the statutory and common law, the decisions of courts, and all the rules and regulations imposed by the government. In the case of a corporation, the working rules are developed in the light of the requirements of the articles of incorporation, resolutions of stockholders, informal agreements, and binding contracts as well as of the common and statutory law. These working rules are important because they bring about unity of action by providing a pattern of behavior for the entire group of participating individuals: "They say what each member of the concern may, can, cannot, and must or must not do, in so far as the combined power of the concern is deemed to cover his conduct." In general, the working rules prescribe the boundaries within which members of the going concern must operate as they seek to further their individual purposes or those of the whole concern.

Of all the going concerns found in the modern economy the corporation is the most important one; and hence it is the corporate managers who are most responsible for the general functioning of "corporate capitalism." The corporation may be considered as either a "going plant" or a "going business." As a going plant it is a producing organization whose aim is technological efficiency. The problems of the going plant are engineering or technological problems. For this reason it may be said that the going plant of a corporation operates in an "engineering" or "technological economy," the aim of which is the production of a maximum of use-values with a minimum input of human labor and natural resources. This aim of technological efficiency is achieved by a proper proportioning of the various factors of production. All factors of production are divided by Commons into "limiting" and "complementary" factors. A limiting factor he defines as "one whose control, in the right form, at the right place and time, will set the complementary factors at work to bring about the results intended." [84]   All other factors of production are "routine" or "complementary" factors which have the potentiality of becoming "strategic" at some time in the future. Engineering or technological efficiency is at its maximum when strategic and complementary factors are most effectively combined to form the going plant.

In contrast to the "going plant" of the corporation is the corporation's "going business," the aim of which is efficiency in accumulating pecuniary values. Commons explains that "The going plant is a producing organization furnishing a service to the public, but the going business is a bargaining organization obtaining prices from the public." [85] Whereas the going plant is concerned with man's relation to nature and produces commodities and services, the going business is concerned with the relation of man to man and with the production of money-values rather than use-values. Unlike the going plant, which operates in an engineering economy, the going business functions in what Commons calls a "proprietary economy."   In this economy, bargaining transactions do not add to the supply of use-values or wealth; they merely redistribute the supply of ownership or pecuniary values. Efficiency in the engineering economy multiplies the output of wealth and services, but scarcity in the proprietary economy merely transfers ownership and adds to the pecuniary assets of some individuals at the expense of others.

Even though the going plant and the going business are unrelated in their aims, nevertheless they are both parts of the going concern. Every corporate enterprise is a combination of these two subordinate processes. As in the case of the going plant and the going business, the corporation as a going concern is faced with the problem of securing the most satisfactory proportioning of productive factors. But in the case of the going concern it is not a problem of maximizing either technological efficiency or proprietary scarcity; instead it is a problem of combining efficiency with scarcity, or technology with business. If production were carried on for use only, and there were no question of profit making, then there would be only a technological economy with its going plants. But since production for use is necessarily combined with production for

[84] *Institutional Economics*, page 628.
[85] *Legal Foundations of Capitalism*, page 182.

profits under the capitalistic system, the technological economy has somehow to be merged with the proprietary economy. Going plants must in some way be tied up with going businesses to form smoothly functioning corporate enterprises. Since, under capitalism, there can be no technology without business, in every economic enterprise the relations of technology to business are a matter of prime importance to all those who draw their livelihood from going concerns.

According to Commons the relation of efficiency to scarcity, or of the technological economy to the proprietary economy, constitutes the basic problem of the present era of banker capitalism. As long as economic enterprise was subject to the very effective checks provided by the competition of small-scale business, there was little difficulty in merging the technological and proprietary economies. The danger of a conflict between these two economies was always present, but, until the era of corporate capitalism, economic circumstances kept friction in check. Even though the aim of business activity is the augmentation of pecuniary rather than use-values, the interests of technology and engineering efficiency could not be widely subordinated to those of business efficiency until large-scale business came under the control of financial interests. Since 1880 various business and financial interests have increasingly sought to sacrifice technology to business. Working in the opposite direction, other forces have endeavored to bring about a satisfactory correlation of technology and business within each going concern or corporate enterprise. These constructive forces have had as their goal "the best going concern." In Commons' opinion, "The best going plant is one where the technological factors are rightly proportioned by managerial transactions, the best going business is one where the purchases and sales are rightly proportioned by bargaining transactions, the best going concern is one where technology and business are rightly proportioned." [86] As he sees it, there has been a tendency to make the ideal of the best going concern more of a reality since 1880; indeed this has been one of the distinguishing features of recent capitalistic development.

In the current stage of capitalistic evolution Commons observes a tendency on the part of large corporate enterprises to seek to preserve their best interests by stabilizing the operations of the econ-

[86] *Institutional Economics*, page 634.

omy. At first, stabilization efforts were directed towards the control of the production processes. These efforts finally flowered into the modern holding company which brought both vertical and horizontal integration to the basic industries of the nation. In more recent years the stabilization program has been extended from the production processes to the realm of finance and monetary arrangements. In the hope of stabilizing profit margins steps have been taken to eliminate large fluctuations of the general price level. The "amazingly narrow profit margins" on which the modern capitalistic system is conducted make the economy very sensitive to small changes in cost of production or wholesale prices. Slight changes in costs or prices can result in either deep financial distress or abundant success. When both prices and costs are stabilized, the corporation is then insulated against the disruptive effects of price-cost changes that arise from conditions beyond its control.

Commons finds that the stabilization programs of the era of banker capitalism have been deficient in three important respects. In the first place, the stabilization efforts have been directed towards the stabilization of "scarcity profits" rather than "efficiency profits." Where a monopolistic or semi-monopolistic corporation obtains its profits from non-competitive advantages which do not require the enterprise to improve its efficiency, Commons labels the gains "scarcity profits." But where a corporation increases its profit margin by improving its efficiency, the profits are said to be "efficiency profits." Because so much of modern industry is not purely competitive in nature, Commons finds that a great deal of modern profit-making is based on scarcity rather than efficiency. Many stabilization programs have therefore sacrificed efficiency to scarcity, and have perpetuated a number of conditions conducive to profit-making that warrant careful scrutiny, if the general welfare is not to be sacrificed.

The second respect in which the stabilization programs of modern business enterprise have shown unsatisfactory tendencies relates to fluctuations in the output of goods and services. While business has been cementing its position with respect to profit-making, there have been signs of a growing deterioration of the economic system as indicated by recurring periods of universal overproduction. This overproduction was presumed to be impossible according to the analysis of the orthodox nineteenth-century economists, but this conclusion was based on the assumption of a competitive economy in which the institution of money was assigned a minor role, and a stable price level was taken for granted. In the economy of today, in which we have imperfect competition and an oscillating price level, overproduction means production of more goods than can be sold at a satisfactory profit. Such overproduction occurs in periods of declining prices, and directly or indirectly affects all industries and nations. In spite of the stabilization policies of big business the interruptions visited upon the production processes by the vagaries of the business cycle continue to plague the modern economy and to strike at the very vitals of capitalistic enterprise.

The third outstanding defect of the stabilization schemes of banker capitalism is the failure to stabilize employment. Commons feels that this is the major failure of the present era of capitalistic development. He believes that unemployment is more of a menace to banker capitalism than is periodic overproduction, since lack of employment strikes at those persons whose reserves against want and misery are very slender. A type of economic control which cannot meet the issue of unemployment is doomed to failure from the beginning. One of the basic appeals to the masses of recent fascistic experiments derives from the fact that these totalitarian programs do at least temporarily provide work, and some degree of economic security. The work may be arduous and the security tenuous, but these conditions do not destroy the fundamental appeal to the masses that is to be found in politico-economic schemes which promise work for everyone. It makes no difference if the fascistic experiments break down in the long run, because they contain the seeds of their own ultimate destruction. What is most significant about these economic experiments is their immediate appeal to depressed masses of people. Workers value economic security, here and now, over peace and liberty without any guarantee of employment. And so we have Commons asserting that "In general, the most serious problem of capitalistic civilization is unemployment. The paradox of doubling, trebling, and even quadrupling efficiency, while perpetrating great alterations of employment and unemployment, makes it probable that war or communism or fascism may be preferable to peace and liberty. Consequently, with the great majority of people becoming a proletariat, the most important of all guides to stabilization is that of maintaining full and steady employment." [87]

Judicial Sovereignty and Reasonable Capitalism

Since the corporate capitalism which has grown up since 1885 has failed to elevate efficiency profits over scarcity profits, and has been unable to maintain a steady flow of national output, or to provide continuous employment for the masses, it has aroused the antipathy of various interests in the nation. In the early decades of the growth of banker capitalism, opposition came not so much from the government as from the law courts. In the shift from a small-scale, laissez-faire economy to a large-scale, imperfectly competitive economy a political lag developed. Owing to this lag, governments failed to alter their policies and programs to meet the demands of rapidly changing economic circumstances. Consequently the courts took upon themselves the difficult task of eliminating the harsh features of the capitalistic system, endeavoring as best they could to keep private welfare closely associated with general welfare. As the result of a series of well-known cases growing out of the enforcement of the antitrust laws after 1890, a pattern of legal restraints was created for the emerging corporate capitalism. While developing this pattern of legal control, the Supreme Court established "the American brand of dictatorship." The sovereignty of the state and federal legislatures was temporarily set aside in favor of judicial sovereignty. In exercising its judicial sovereignty the Supreme Court of the United States has significantly influenced the whole development of corporate capitalism. According to Commons' interpretation, this judicial sovereignty has had as its primary aim the elimination of the destructive tendencies of banker capitalism.

In exercising their judicial sovereignty the courts acted more as conservators than as innovators. The general principle that guided them in their work of interpreting the federal constitution, of defining economic terms, and of determining reasonable business practices and reasonable values was that at all times and in all circumstances the whole economic system, like other going concerns, must be kept in operation. The general welfare required the continued

[87] *Institutional Economics,* pages 804-805.

and smooth operation of the economic system. Every new economic device or business arrangement which was a source of economic conflict was examined in the light of its consequences with respect to the general functioning of the whole economy. Those devices and arrangements which were the source of a great deal of friction were subject to judicial disfavor, while those which contributed to a better functioning of the economy were soon sanctioned by the courts. In making decisions about economic changes that were acceptable to them, the courts did not pursue a policy based on highly speculative or logically precise distinctions. This was so, as Commons indicates, because the solutions that the courts sought were determined by the very pragmatic necessity of finding ways out of economic conflicts which would satisfy many contending parties. In dealing with these several parties, the courts found that the pragmatic necessities called for "reasonable" rather than "logical" solutions. Consequently, when the courts turned to logic in their work, it was more to justify their decisions than to determine them in the first place.

In their efforts to make banker capitalism a more reasonable form of capitalism the courts have pursued a "muddling-through" policy. They have refrained from making clear-cut distinctions, from giving precise definitions to terms, and from phrasing general principles, lest they prove too binding at some future time. Each case of economic conflict has been considered in the light of the special conditions out of which it has come. In moving from case to case the courts have left no well-defined trail behind them. Legal decisions have emphasized the value of making compromises between conflicting principles or interests rather than completely sacrificing one principle or interest to others. In this manner the courts' muddling-through policy has resulted in a middle-of-the-way program, which involves no drastic decisions and no wide deviations from those economic and social arrangements that already exist. At times, the courts have favored the small businessman, who has been threatened with extinction by the tactics of more powerful rivals. At other times, by a "rule of reason," the courts' policy has been to protect large semi-monopolistic and monopolistic enterprises from destruction at the hands of those who wanted to bolster the crumbling laissez-faire economy.

Since 1890 the courts have observed many changes in the ways of carrying on business, of handling employees, and of dealing with consumers. Especially in the field of employer-employee relations have new practices been of great social consequence, for it was at this point in the economy that the undesirable consequences of economic change first made their appearance on a large scale. It was not long before the practices of employers in dealing with their workers came under the scrutiny of the nation's courts. The courts then developed the concept of a "reasonable practice," which is one that conforms with the best practices that the industry can reasonably be expected to observe. In Commons' words a reasonable practice is one that meets the requirements of "the *highest* degree of safety, health, well-being of employees, and so forth, that the nature of the industry or employment would *reasonably* permit." [88] The practices an industry or firm can reasonably be expected to adopt is not a purely subjective matter to be determined by the courts in an arbitrary fashion. Commons asserts that the standard of reasonableness by which a practice is to be judged has a basis in objectivity. Reasonableness is "capable of investigation and testimony." It is in the light of this investigation and testimony that the courts sanction certain practices as being reasonable, practices that should be required of all businesses in an industry. "Reasonableness," said Commons, "is idealism limited by practicability," and "practicability is a matter that can be investigated and ascertained." [89]

Commons calls attention to the fact that reasonable practices are not static modes of behavior; what is reasonable at one time may cease to be reasonable at some future time. Progressive employers are always experimenting with new ways of dealing with employees, raw-material producers, and consumers. At first these progressive practices are carried on only by a minority. For some time the courts may be unwilling to require the majority of employers to raise their practices up to the level of the more progressive employers. Eventually, however, the courts come to the conclusion that changing circumstances warrant requiring the whole industry to adopt what were once the progressive practices of a small minority. Reasonable practices then become "just the ordinary, average, customs and practices" of all the businessmen in the industry. The

[88] *Myself,* page 155.
[89] *Ibid.,* page 156.

extent to which standards of reasonableness are raised in this manner depends upon the progress of the minority employers in improving their business practices, and upon the willingness of the courts to universalize the progressive practices of minority employers when they have been demonstrated to be both workable and reasonable.

After 1890 the courts came to sanction many business practices as being reasonable: collective bargaining arrangements, safety and health rules, and regulations governing hours of labor, child labor, and minimum wages were eventually established and applied to the conduct of all businessmen. In addition, new standards of market behavior were worked out and sanctioned by the courts. In more recent years business practices relating to consumers have come under the scrutiny of the courts, and are now being subjected to new standards of reasonableness. During the past half-century numerous changing business practices have been subjected to a sifting process which has succeeded in eliminating many undesirable ways of doing business, and which has gradually built up new patterns of behavior on a solid foundation of reasonableness.

In addition to reasonable practices, the courts have been interested in reasonable values. With the advent of large-scale business and the elimination of competition from large segments of the economy, the market has failed to determine values as adequately as it did in the past. Where the automatic processes of value determination failed to function, disagreements as to values soon arose. Conflicts appeared in connection with public utility and tax problems in which the necessity of determining rate or tax bases required the valuation of properties for which there were no competitive markets. With competitive standards of valuation no longer available, contending parties found themselves unable to agree on what were proper values for the properties under consideration. In accordance with its particular interest each economic group worked for the establishment of a value that favored its own particular point of view. In these situations the courts have endeavored to arrive at property values which would be "reasonable values." In determining reasonable values the courts have sought to make reasonable settlements of the disputes brought before them. Their primary aim has been to arrive at valuations of property for rate-making, taxation, or other purposes which would be accepted by all the conflicting parties as being reasonable.   In settling a dispute about property values the courts have taken all facts into consideration, and have given each its "due weight." Thus, in the case of *Smyth v. Ames* (1898), where many conflicting theories of valuation were advanced by the contending parties, the Supreme Court ruled that each value theory was to be given its "due weight" in arriving at a fair or reasonable value.[90]

The reasonable value which is of such interest to the courts is not determined by an appeal to pure reason or logic.   Instead, it reflects all the inconsistencies and irrationality that is to be found in actual economic behavior.   For this reason Commons states that "Reason differs from Reasonableness.   Man is not a rational being, as the Eighteenth Century thought; he is a being of stupidity, passion, and ignorance, as Malthus thought.   Hence Reasonable Value contains a large amount of stupidity, passion, and mistake."[91]   The reasonable values established by the courts have been worked out in response to the demands for solutions of conflicts and not as exercises in the use of pure reason or impeccable logic.   If the courts have used logic in connection with the determination of reasonable values, it is only to justify their determinations of values and not to make the determinations in the first place.   As Commons sees it, the courts' problem is the very pragmatic one of settling disputes over property values so that the economic system may be kept in continuous and smooth operation, simply because the stability of the economic system must not be jeopardized by long-continued disputes over property values.   In the face of immediate problems there is not enough time for broad speculations or very refined theoretical analyses; for this reason Commons finds that reasonable value "is pragmatic, not logical; it is action, not truth; justification, not justice."[92]

The concept of value developed by the courts is quite unlike the value concept of the nineteenth-century economists, which is, in Commons' words, "individualistic, subjective, intellectual and static."   The orthodox concept of market value is rationalistic and unhistorical, and relates to the valuation processes to be found only

[90] *Smyth v. Ames*, 169 U. S. 466; 18 Sup. Ct. 418.
[91] *Institutional Economics*, page 682.
[92] Commons, John R., "Evaluating Institutions as a Factor in Economic Change," *Special Lectures on Economics*, delivered before the Graduate School of the United States Department of Agriculture, Feb.-March, 1930, page 18.

in the static equilibrium of a purely competitive society. But the legal concept of reasonable value is an institutional concept, full of historicity and relativity. Commons explains that "Reasonable Value is the evolutionary collective determination of what is reasonable in view of all the changing political, moral, and economic circumstances and the personalities that arise therefrom to the Supreme bench. Natural rights lose their inflexibility and even begin to disappear in the determination of reasonable values. We can offer only a broad outline of the institutional and other changes which lie behind the historically changing concepts of reasonable value." [93] Like the common law, reasonable values are historical products which reflect all the diversity of cumulative historical change. Because of its flexibility and relativity, the concept of reasonable value has proven to be a powerful weapon in the hands of the jurists in their work of making capitalism a more reasonable economic system.

The nation's courts have accepted the responsibility of providing some direction for the changing capitalistic economy. They have functioned as a kind of funnel or bottleneck through which the developing economy has been forced to go. At times the courts have hindered the progress of economic evolution by rendering decisions which have been dictated more by narrow class interests than by considerations of the general welfare. Commons has never been blind to this fact. However, he believes that, in general, the courts have performed a valuable social function in harnessing the forces of economic change, and in making them more serviceable to the public. The courts have been an institution through which a changing public opinion has been able to express its demands for more enlightened views relating to the nature of public purpose. In this manner, improvements in public opinion have resulted in the further development of legal opinion. As to what originally changes public opinion Commons is quite explicit; it is "the change from free land to closed land, the changes in transportation and mobility of labor, the development of large-scale industry, all of them throwing large masses of labor together into active competition." [94] When the courts have been slow to respond to the demands of these basic economic changes, a changing public opinion has exerted its pressure in the direction of a more adequate legal control of economic activity.

By the second decade of the twentieth century judicial control of the direction of economic activity had reached its zenith. After 1910 a new factor of great significance for the development of the capitalistic system made its appearance, and eventually came to challenge the supremacy of the nation's judiciary. This new factor was administrative government, which found expression in the activities of the growing number of state and federal commissions and agencies. Commons finds that the rapid growth of administrative government dates from the year 1908 when the powers of the Interstate Commerce Commission were greatly extended. Since that year many commissions have been set up in various states to deal with such problems as fair competition, reasonable discriminations, reasonable values, and reasonable industrial relations. As the economic system has grown increasingly complex, there has developed a need for more scientific investigations which would provide a firm foundation for determinations of reasonable values and practices. Since the courts have not had the facilities required for making these investigations, this work has been passed on to the administrative agencies of state and federal governments.

In Commons' interpretation of the development of administrative control of economic activity, the commission is a device created for the purpose of meeting the problem of the traditional separation of legislative, executive, and judicial powers out of which had emerged judicial supremacy. This separation of powers is no longer a satisfactory working arrangement in an economy of large-scale industry and corporate enterprise. The problems which have developed in the modern economy require for their solution the administration of economic affairs by agencies or commissions that combine legislative, judicial, and executive functions. These governmental commissions "are the American discovery, during the past three decades, of a practical method of correlating law, economics, and ethics. . . ." [95] Commons explains that the theory underlying the work of these administrative commissions is "the legal theory of due process of law carried forward into the investigation of facts." Accordingly, orders issued by administrative commissions are held to be reasonable, if all parties affected by the orders have been given

[95] *Institutional Economics*, pages 718-719.

ample opportunity to confer with the commissions through their recognized spokesmen. Findings of fact on which all the interested parties reach agreement are accepted by the courts as reasonable findings. In the case of disputes over administrative orders the courts will not inquire into any findings of fact. For this reason the activities of the state and federal supreme courts are limited to the functions of a "trial court," which accepts as final the findings of administrative agencies. Obviously such a development restricts judicial sovereignty, and contributes to the advancing "twilight of the supreme court." [96]

Since the early years of the twentieth century the administrative commission has shown a growing capacity to eliminate economic conflicts. Railroad, public utility, industrial, tax, corporation, and market commissions have settled disputes between employers and employees, buyers and sellers, farmers and wholesalers, different classes of taxpayers, large and small businesses, and railroads and shippers. Commons asserts that the commissions have successfully tackled Marx's problem of class conflict by breaking down economic conflict into a number of less formidable struggles between many contending parties. There has been no frontal attack on the problem of economic conflict, but instead a whittling away of the mass of economic strife by a succession of minor attacks on restricted areas of friction. Every such successful attack on the problem of economic conflict by an administrative commission results in the further reduction of that exploitation which Commons takes to be the starting point of Veblen's economic analysis. Administrative commissions have cooperated with the nation's courts in the work of recasting modern capitalism in a more reasonable mold. In Commons' opinion both the commissions and the courts have been aided in this work by the development of scientific management, which made its appearance about the time that administrative government began its rapid development.[97]

According to Commons' analysis one important source of ex-

[96] Cf. Corwin, E. S., *The Twilight of the Supreme Court*. New Haven: Yale University Press, 1934.

[97] F. W. Taylor, the pioneer worker in the field of scientific management, published *The Principles of Scientific Management* in 1911. It would appear that Commons was overly enthusiastic about the contributions of scientific management to the creation of a more "reasonable capitalism."

ploitation remains to keep the modern capitalistic system from being a highly reasonable form of economic organization. This remaining cause of exploitation is the never-ending fluctuations of the price level, which arbitrarily determine the economic destinies of the many groups participating in the affairs of the modern economy. In Commons' opinion price fluctuations constitute "the most important of all problems of public policy and reasonable value, for they are a world-wide aspect of the ethical question, arising out of conflicts of interests: whether individuals and classes should get rich by their own improvements in efficiency or by taking advantage of changes in the value of the unit that measures scarcity." [98] This problem of price fluctuation is especially important because such fluctuations have a share in determining who is to get the fruits of expanding technological efficiency. Thus, if prices are stable and there are no increases in wages, the businessman receives the benefits of improving technological efficiency in the form of a wider profit margin. If profit margins and prices remain the same, the workers may secure the advantages of increased efficiency in the form of higher wages. But if prices to consumers are reduced, then the gains from a more efficient operation of the industrial system tend to be passed on to the consumers. The problem is one of protecting the individuals who are mainly responsible for improvements in industrial efficiency by guaranteeing that the results of greater efficiency will be passed on to the right parties.

The unusual progress in economic efficiency which came after 1900 has been the source of a great deal of conflict. Various economic interests have endeavored to secure for themselves as much as possible of the outcome of technological progress. Labor groups have sought wage increases; consumers have called for lower prices; and businessmen have endeavored to stabilize prices in such a fashion as to enjoy the wider profit margins which have accompanied stationary selling prices and falling costs. In the decade after World War I a new administrative agency, the Federal Reserve Board, began to experiment with price stabilization as a device by which the most recent phase of capitalism could be made more reasonable. Private efforts to stabilize prices had not met with

[98] *Institutional Economics*, page 789.

much success from the public point of view, because price stabilization by businessmen and private bankers in control of business corporations looked to a stabilization of scarcity rather than abundance.

At the time that Commons presented his analysis of the evolution of capitalism in his *Institutional Economics* (1934), the problem of price stabilization was far from being successfully handled. The Federal Reserve Board, "with low salaries and insecurity of tenure in dealing with men of fabulous salaries and the shrewdest of ability . . . ," had been unable to mark out a path of independent action. After 1919 it became evident that the Federal Reserve Board was unable to do much to weaken the "alliance of banking and industry." Later the depression of 1929 revealed that the Federal Reserve Board had been unable to purge banker capitalism of those maladjustments which resulted in great fluctuations in production and employment. Although the Board had in the late nineteen twenties indicated a willingness to adopt monetary measures that would run counter to the wishes of the business community, no effective monetary and credit control program was worked out in time to avoid the disastrous deflationary movements of the early thirties. By 1932 it was evident that no administrative agency of the federal government was yet able to cope with the problem of price fluctuations.

The failure of the Federal Reserve System to eliminate the exploitation that results from fluctuations in the price level has divided economists into what Commons calls the "bargaining" and "managerial" schools of economists. The economists of the managerial school hope to overcome our major economic difficulties by setting up a national economic planning council, which would look forward to the establishment of a system of quotas and rationing. The national economic plan would regulate prices and provide for the allocation of capital and labor among the various industries. The planners would seek to replace the automatic equilibrium of the nineteenth-century economists with a "regulated balancing" of the modern economy. This regulated balancing of the economic system would be the final outcome of the scientific management movement which was begun early in the present century. In order to secure this "managerial goal" of a planned economy, a national economic planning council would place its ultimate reliance on "the executive dictatorship of the state." If such a plan were effected, Commons believes that it would indicate a movement towards communism or fascism rather than reasonable capitalism. He asserts that the managerial philosophy can never be the basic principle of a democratic economy. The managerial point of view is essentially undemocratic, since it is based on the relation of superior to inferior, or of manager to worker. While this principle of superior and inferior has some valid applications in our economic system, Commons asserts that it can never become the basic principle of any truly democratic economic system. The kind of capitalism which he hopes to see established could never draw its nurture from the economic compulsion which he takes to be so central a feature of the point of view of the economists of the managerial school.

In contrast with the managerial school of economists, the bargaining school would avoid the direct rationing program of a national planning council backed by the executive power of the state. The advocates of the bargaining school would seek to achieve the elimination of price fluctuations, overproduction, and unemployment by a policy of indirection. Their attack on economic maladjustment would be made indirectly through domestic and international monetary and banking arrangements. No attempt would be made to elevate the managerial expert or engineer above the businessman, or to alter the basic institutional arrangements of banker capitalism. "The managerial school," said Commons, "looks to a great Economic Planning Council which shall prevent overproduction and unemployment by rationing. The bargaining school looks to a concerted international money and banking policy, something like the Bank for International Payments, and control of the world's gold and silver reserves, designed to prevent recurrence of overproduction and unemployment by stabilizing prices. The ultimate difference between the schools is that the bargaining school endeavors to retain, under new conditions, the older principles of equality and liberty in all bargaining transactions that determine prices, while the managerial school rests on the still older principle of superior and inferior in all managerial and rationing transactions which determine output and efficiency. The one looks towards equality of Bargaining Power, the other towards rationing of Producing Power. The one looks towards Reasonable Capitalism, the other towards Communism or Fascism." [99]

The voluntary or reasonable capitalism, which Commons takes to be the goal of the bargaining school, frankly accepts two things as fixed and necessary in the future. With respect to economic matters reasonable capitalism accepts as a probable part of the future economic system the bulk of those arrangements which Commons sums up under the term "banker capitalism." Banker capitalism, he points out, is accepted by the Supreme Court as long as it is willing to tolerate the presence of small businesses, and as long as it leaves the doors open to the introduction of more efficient methods and new products by small enterprises. Banker capitalism, as accepted by the courts and as taken by Commons to be a necessary part of future economic arrangements, is a form of "voluntary follow-your-leader capitalism." The large firms will be permitted to hold the umbrella over the small competitors as long as the public interests are kept paramount to all other interests. On the political side, reasonable capitalism accepts as a necessary part of future arrangements some degree of sovereignty exercised by the Supreme Court. This judicial sovereignty will be especially concerned with the preservation of the democratic features of any future capitalistic organization. Such a safeguarding of the democratic basis of the economy will be effected by insisting upon a recognition of the due process clause of the federal constitution, which provides for the orderly settlement of all problems of conflicting economic interests.

The two things in Commons' view of the future capitalistic system which remain unfixed and uncertain are legislatures and voluntary associations of laborers, farmers, and small businessmen. In other great economic experiments, such as Russian Communism and Italian Fascism, both democratic legislatures and voluntary associations have been abolished. Since Commons finds that legislatures and voluntary associations are getting progressively weaker in the

[99] *Institutional Economics*, page 891. Commons is to be criticized for making too sharp a division between reasonable capitalism on the one hand and totalitarian planning on the other. He appears to underemphasize the fact that it is possible to have many degrees of planning between his reasonable capitalism and totalitarian planning. For a similar criticism see Copeland, Morris A., "Commons's Institutionalism in Relation to Problems of Social Evolution and Economic Planning," *The Quarterly Journal of Economics*, Feb., 1936, Vol. L, pages 345-346.

United States, he believes that the future of democratic capitalism depends upon the successful regeneration of legislative bodies and the protection of voluntary associations of all types. The level of legislative activity has fallen very low in the great nations of the world at the very time that the burdens imposed on the legislative machinery have become considerably greater. He asserts that "legislatures are undoubtedly discredited in the modern world of universal suffrage and conflict of interests. In a sense the lobby is more representative than the legislative. It represents economic interests, the legislators represent miscellaneous individuals." [100] Instead of a legislature representing all the many important economic groups of the nation, we have a legislature based on geographical representation. The individuals sent to our legislatures have frequently been incompetent and easily taken in by lobbying influences, because the two-party system with its election by plurality or majority votes has brought to high office men who represent no particular economic interests. Commons believes that more competent men, truly representing all major economic interests, could be elected to fill our legislatures if a system of proportional or minority representation were to be adopted. If such a system were adopted, our national congress would then become more economic and less geographical in its representation.

It is important to have a revitalized legislature truly representative of all important economic interests, because the federal legislature could then secure legislators of sufficient ability and experience to hold the leaders of banker capitalism in check. Since big business has revealed its inability adequately to meet the demands of public welfare, Commons would have the state and federal legislatures, in cooperation with the courts, provide the necessary public checks upon private economic activity. In his view control over the economic system by the legislature does not mean centralized national economic planning by legislative edict. The growing complexity of economic life with its many conflicts is coming to place an intolerable burden on legislative machinery. Legislatures are discovering how to relieve themselves of a large portion of the burden of government by setting up administrative commissions to deal with the various conflicts between economic interests. The railroad, public utility, tax, industrial, and market commissions are semi-legislative

[100] *Institutional Economics*, page 898.

bodies which work along with voluntary advisory committees of the various conflicting interests in the effort to discover workable solutions to ever-changing economic problems.   In this manner a new form of government, namely, administrative government, has been developed to implement the work of the legislature.

What, then, is the proper field for legislative activity?   Commons answers with the statement that ". . . the modern legislature is learning to restrict itself to the field where it may be effective, notwithstanding and even because it represents conflicting interests. Its effective field is general laws and general standards of administration.   These general rules are matters of compromise between conflicting economic interests, and a deadlock merely postpones the compromise, while the semi-legislative administration goes on with details and execution of policies as before." [101]   It is the primary duty of the state and federal legislatures to provide the general policies which keep the economic system on an even keel in the turbulent waters of party strife and economic conflict.   In addition, the improved legislature which Commons has in mind would preserve the basis of democracy and democratic institutions by providing protection for all voluntary associations of laborers, farmers, businessmen, and consumers.   Since banker capitalism has a tendency to suppress the individual and his voluntary associations, Commons looks forward to a zealous effort on the part of the government to protect individuals and their right of free association.   In his opinion trade unions, farmers' cooperatives, and all similar voluntary associations of individuals are the "refuge of modern Liberalism and Democracy from Communism, Fascism, or Banker Capitalism."   Every generation must renew its bill of rights.   Today the bill of rights must go beyond the rights of free speech, free press, and free investigation to the currently most important of all rights, namely, the right of free association.   With voluntary associations active and zealous in their efforts to preserve the democratic way in economic life, and with the state and federal governments ably guided by the nation's most experienced and most competent leaders representing all important economic interests, Commons feels that banker capitalism would have a fair chance of flowering into "voluntary and reasonable capitalism."

[101] *Ibid.*, page 901.

With respect to the future of capitalism Commons does not have the blind optimism of the nineteenth-century liberal. Indeed, if he is to be classed as a liberal, he must be regarded only as a reconstructed liberal whose optimism has been shot through with a heavy charge of realism. Commons' pragmatic leanings prevent him from adopting the complacent attitudes of his nineteenth-century liberal predecessors. Throughout his life he has been too close to the daily conflicts of farmers, businessmen, laborers, and consumers to regard economic progress as slow but inevitable. His social philosophy is really a kind of "tentativism," which prevents him from assuming that banker capitalism necessarily has a long lease on life. He frankly writes that anything may happen in the future and that all predictions about the future have a very flimsy basis. In short, he believes that our capitalistic system could be molded into a reasonable form of capitalism, if people were filled with a faith in the future that would lead them to cooperate in the work of creating a more reasonable economic order. The future is therefore more a matter of abundant faith than scientific prediction. But faith in a democratic ordering of economic activity should be grounded in scientific analysis and interpretation. Faith unallied with observation and interpretation of the facts degenerates into wishful thinking or mysticism, whereas faith supported by adequate analysis and interpretation becomes an important factor in the search for greater human contentment. For these reasons Commons feels that economists have a great contribution to make in providing a firm, scientific foundation for that popular faith which is essential to the development of reasonable capitalism. In the closing sentence of his *Institutional Economics* he wrote: ". . . economists have, for the time being, a new equipment of experimental laboratories on three grand scales, in Russia, Italy, and America, for a rough and tumble testing of their classical, hedonistic, and institutional theories." [102] Since economists are scientists and not statesmen, it is not their primary duty to reconstruct the economic world. But Commons would be very unhappy, if, in the future, economists should prove to be unprepared to meet the requests of statesmen for that information and understanding without which a successful resolution of our economic difficulties is hardly possible.

[102] *Institutional Economics*, page 903.

Commons' Framework of Interpretation

This analysis of Commons' economic thought of the four decades from 1895 to 1934 shows that he went far beyond the deductive political economy which was taught in his undergraduate days at Oberlin College. When he left his graduate studies at The Johns Hopkins University in 1890, Commons felt little more than a general dissatisfaction with economics as a science purporting to explain the functioning of the economic order. It was out of his subsequent study of public utility and labor problems, of the legal foundations of the economic system, and later of the evolution of the capitalistic system that he fashioned new concepts and principles which have become the basis of a more realistic, rounded-out political economy. It has not been Commons' aim to clothe the framework of nineteenth-century economics with descriptive studies that would strengthen the interpretations of traditional economics. His excursions away from deductive economic analysis into the problems of our evolving capitalistic economy helped him lay the basis for a more dynamic economics. He felt that economics needs to be less of a deductive science and more of a cultural science, if it is to give us a more adequate grasp of the economic realities of the twentieth century. For this purpose mere description is not enough; inquiries must be made into the philosophical, psychological, and methodological bases of economic science. New frameworks of reference, into which the concrete data of economic experience may be poured, need to be developed; and in addition, new explanatory principles quite different from those of the equilibrium economists have to be fashioned. After forty years of a life rich in economic experience and dedicated to the close observation of the functioning of the economic system, Commons felt prepared to indicate the outlines of what he calls "twentieth-century economics."

In explaining his views on the nature and scope of economics Commons begins with an examination of the nature of the data of the social and natural sciences. He divides this data into three general categories.[103] There is, first, the data of the physical sciences which have as their unifying principle the concept of mechanism. Commons defines a mechanism as a system or entity which functions in accordance with the "natural movement of atoms,

[103] *Ibid.*, page 732.

waves, or vortexes," and which is acted upon by the blind forces of nature. Although these natural forces act without "cause, effect, or purpose, like the waves of the ocean," all mechanisms tend towards some form of equilibrium. As a consequence of this equilibrating tendency of natural science data, the analysis of the subject matter of the natural sciences has a frame of reference which is woven about the concept of a mechanistic equilibrium. Turning to the biological sciences, one finds a different situation, for the subject matter of these sciences displays the characteristics of an organism instead of a mechanism. An organism is a structure or organization which, unlike a mechanism, exhibits the property of life or activity, and whose activities are carried on with the aid of a number of mutually dependent parts. Whereas a mechanism functions as an equilibrium, an organism operates as a process. The concept of mechanism emphasizes the notion of repetitivity, but the organism concept draws special attention to the phenomena of change. As soon as the notion of change is introduced into a field of scientific data, attention is drawn to the problem of a series of changes over a period of time. The investigator is then brought to a consideration of the concept of evolution. Commons is careful to point out, however, that the evolution to be observed in the realm of biological data is the result of "unintended or accidental changes." The biological process contains nothing of the nature of human purpose; and, in this respect, it is not fundamentally different from the mechanical movements which result in an automatic equilibrium.

The data of the social sciences differ from those of the natural and biological sciences, because they contain the element of human purpose. Commons points out that "The subject matter with which an economist deals is not a mechanism or organism whose notions the investigator cannot *understand*—it is human beings whose activities he can fairly well understand by putting himself 'in their place' and thus constructing the 'reasons,' in the sense of motives or purposes, or values, of their activity under all the variable conditions of time and place." [104] Although the concepts of equilibrium and process, which are borrowed from the natural and

[104] *Ibid.*, page 723. Max Weber held a similar view of the nature of social-science data. Cf. Diehl, Carl, "The Life and Work of Max Weber," *The Quarterly Journal of Economics*, Nov., 1923, Vol. XXXVIII, pages 93-100.

biological sciences, are used by the social scientist in arriving at an understanding of human behavior, these concepts are modified in important respects. Instead of "unintended or accidental changes," the social scientist in his analysis of social-science data finds "intended or purposeful changes," while in place of the automatic equilibrium of the physical sciences he discovers what Commons calls a cultural equilibrium. The social process, under the direction of human wills, moves from one cultural equilibrium to another down through the course of historical change. In the course of this evolution the natural selection of Darwin's biological evolution becomes the artificial selection of purposeful social control.[105] The subject matter of the social sciences is thus something more than a mechanical equilibrium or biological process, for it incorporates the unique element of human purpose which Commons calls "willingness." Since social-science data are impregnated with human purpose or "willingness," Commons declares that this quality of voluntariness in social-science data places the social sciences in a category which is quite distinct from that of the physical or biological sciences. Furthermore, he feels that it is because of this unique characteristic or quality of voluntarity that social-science data require a special treatment not accorded to the data of the non-social sciences. For this reason he shifts his analysis from the concepts of mechanism and organism to the concept of going concern, which reflects the voluntarity of economic data. The going concern, whether it be the whole economic system or a single economic institution, is essentially purposive in its nature, is directed by the human will, and is always looking to the future.

Commons finds that the data of the social sciences, which have the concept of the going concern as their unifying principle, reveal another fundamental quality not to be found in the case of the data of the natural and organic sciences. Besides the quality of voluntarity, he finds that social-science data exhibit the quality of historicity. This is so because the investigations of the social scientist

[105] For an analysis of this view of economic society see Gruchy, Allan G., "The Concept of National Planning in Institutional Economics," *The Southern Economic Journal,* Oct., 1939, Vol. VI, pages 121-144. According to some interpretations, Commons is asserted to have overemphasized the extent to which natural selection of economic customs, habits, and institutions has been replaced by an artificial or purposive selection of economic goals. Cf. Copeland, M., "Commons's Institutionalism in Relation to Problems of Social Evolution and Economic Planning," pages 333-346.

deal with a reality which is part of a historical process. He therefore declares that "The method of investigation must . . . be different from that of the exact sciences because its outcome is the concerted but conflicting action of human wills in an historical evolution of determining what is workable within the changing economic, political, and ethical sequence." [106] Economic science deals with a system which is passing through a historical evolution. If the data of the economist are to be of any real help in interpreting the historical realities of the economic order, they cannot, in the ultimate analysis, be deprived of their quality of historicity. In the handling of economic data abstraction should, therefore, not be carried to the point where all or most of the historical significance is lost. Commons asserts that for some purposes economic analysis may properly be more deductive than empirical, but that abstraction and the desire for logical consistency should never be carried so far as to reduce economics to the status of a non-historico-cultural science.

As soon as Commons satisfies himself that social-science data have such special characteristics or qualities that the social and non-social sciences are to be regarded as essentially different scientific disciplines, he is immediately confronted by a very important methodological problem. This problem arises because he has the difficult task of constructing a science on the basis of what may appear to some economists as highly subjective or unique economico-cultural data. It is usual for scientists to declare that their investigations are scientific because they deal with data which may be objectively investigated, and which exhibit certain definite uniformities of behavior. Unless data can be objectively handled, and unless they are found to recur with some degree of regularity, it is said that there can be no basis for creating useful scientific generalizations of any kind. This matter did not escape Commons' notice; indeed he was acutely aware of the methodological difficulties involved in broadening the scope of his science. "We recognize," he said, "that there can be no science of political economy if the will is free, in the sense of being wholly capricious and undetermined. This requires us to look for uniformities in the operation of the will, if we would have an economic science." He was quick to agree that an economic analysis which is based upon the mere subjectivity of

[106] *Institutional Economics*, page 719.

human volition or the uniqueness of historical events could hardly be described as scientific. He asserted that his own economic analysis had a sound scientific foundation, because it was concerned with observations relating to the behavior patterns of twentieth-century economic enterprise.

The nineteenth-century economists met the problem of the voluntarity and historicity of economic data by subjecting their studies to a great deal of abstraction. Economic data were selected and refined until they related primarily to the behavior of purely rational beings. In this situation, individuals made their personal valuations and pursued personal ends with a uniformity of behavior which was amenable to a limited form of scientific treatment, simply because all valuations and realizations of human purpose were only those of thoroughly rational individuals. The neo-classicists thus created a theoretical system in which the economic order was taken to be a highly individualistic and competitive economy. Commons asserts that the defect in the theoretical position of the nineteenth-century economists was that they carried their abstractions too far in an effort to refine economic data so as to make them more amenable to mathematico-logical analysis. As a consequence, their economic analysis came to lack the essential quality of historicity.

In place of the neo-classicists' conceptual scheme based on the concept of a competitive equilibrium, Commons substitutes a conceptual schema oriented about a view of the economic system as a going concern. His theoretical scheme is a "moving, changing process . . . a formula for expressing the uncertain expectations of the future which dominate the activity of human beings in the ever-moving present . . . an adequate and therefore complex formula of transactions whose expected repetition, concurrence, and variability is a going concern." [107] Commons' "complex formula of

---

[107] *Institutional Economics*, page 733. Commons' "formula" bears a great resemblance to Max Weber's "ideal type." In developing his formula or conceptual scheme, in the light of which he makes his analysis of the capitalistic economy, Commons found Weber's study of scientific methodology very helpful. He does not, however, slavishly follow Weber in the matter of scientific methodology, nor is his formula a mere duplication of Weber's ideal type. See *Institutional Economics*, Ch. X, Section VI, "Ideal Types," pages 719-748. For criticisms of Werner Sombart's and R. H. Tawney's conceptual schemata see Commons' reviews of *Der moderne Kapitalismus* and *Religion and the Rise of Capitalism* in *The American Economic Review*, March, 1929, Vol. XIX, pages 78-88, and March, 1927, Vol. XVII, pages 63-68.

transactions" is oriented around the idea of economic power rather than the concept of economic rationality, which is the foundation of the theoretical system of the orthodox nineteenth-century economists. The supply-and-demand schema of the nineteenth-century economists had no place for the concept of economic power, since in a competitive economic system opportunities are not restricted, industry is small-scale, national income is widely distributed, and wealth is accumulated for its usefulness rather than for its power to withhold from others what they need but do not have. "The premises of the individualistic economists," explained. Commons, "did not include that of concerted bargaining power. Adam Smith, in basing his economic theory on the legal rights of the individual to liberty, equality, and property, strongly opposed both corporate and regulative forms of concerted action. As against them he set up an impersonal, quasi-mechanical competition which controlled individuals in their bargaining." [108] As long as economic analysis is kept at the level of economic behavior where the equilibrium conceptual scheme is applicable, economic power and coercion are of no importance. However, as soon as the economist turns to the analysis of a more complex level of economic action, such as is presented by the modern economies of highly industrialized nations, Commons finds that the economist's conceptual scheme needs to be revised to take account not only of the fact of economic rationality but also of the highly significant fact of economic power.

Commons orients his theoretical system around the concept of economic power, because he finds that property in the twentieth century has come to mean "economic power" rather than "economic utility." Owing to the basic economic changes of the past three-quarters of a century, economic opportunities have been seriously restricted, business has become centralized in the hands of a small controlling group, and property is now accumulated as a means of withholding from others what they need until they are prepared to accept

[108] Commons, John R., "Bargaining Power," *Encyclopaedia of the Social Sciences*, Vol. II, page 459. Commons' conceptual scheme has a strong resemblance to the framework of interpretation of John A. Hobson which is oriented about what the latter calls "economic force." See Hobson, J. A., *Confessions of an Economic Heretic*, page 48. London: G. Allen and Unwin, Ltd., 1938. Bertrand Russell has also drawn attention to the role of economic power in social affairs in his *Power, A New Social Analysis*, page 12. New York: W. W. Norton and Company, 1938.

the terms imposed by property owners.   It is this power aspect of property ownership that is the fact of central importance in the modern economy.   Since the coercion that accompanies the use of economic power can only be employed by some individuals or groups against others, a whole new set of problems not considered by the equilibrium economists makes its appearance.   There is, first, the problem of the power relations between individuals and groups; and, second, the over-all problem of economic instability resulting from the power relations of individuals.   The nineteenth-century equilibrium economists assumed that a stable economic order or basic harmony underlay social organization, but Commons finds that such an assumption is not applicable to an economy in which the power relations of individuals is a basic fact of economic experience.

Commons asserts that his dynamic concept of the economic system as a going concern or "complex formula of transactions" is thoroughly objective and amenable to scientific treatment.   Unlike the early classical economists and the later hedonistic economists, who used commodities or feelings of pleasure and pain as their starting points, Commons takes as his basic unit of analysis a legal-economic transaction between two or more persons looking towards the future. According to his definition, "The transaction is two or more wills giving, taking, persuading, coercing, defrauding, commanding, obeying, competing, governing, in a world of scarcity, mechanism and rules of conduct."   The ultimate investigational unit of economic science is "not an atom but an electron, always in motion—not an individual but two or more individuals in action.   It never catches them except in motion.   Their motion is a transaction." [109]   What Commons finds to be so important about transactions is that they are legal-economic relations between individuals and groups which reflect all the human problems associated with "rights, duties, liberties, private property, governments and associations."   It is in these transactions that he finds the meeting place of economics, physics, psychology, ethics, jurisprudence, and politics.

Economic transactions are not isolated human relations.   Each transaction occurs at a point in time, but all transactions together constitute a flow or process in which they merge into one another and become collective or institutional in nature.   The transactions which are thus brought together create patterns of economic behav-

[109] *Legal Foundations of Capitalism*, page 7.

ior in the form of institutions. The three types of transactions, namely, bargaining, rationing, and managerial transactions "are brought together in a larger unit of investigation, which . . . is named a Going Concern. It is these going concerns, with the working rules that keep them agoing, all the way from the family, the corporation, the trade union, the trade association, up to the state itself, that we name Institutions. . . . If we endeavor to find a universal principle, common to all behavior known as institutional, we may define an institution as Collective Action in Control of Individual Action." [110] The institutions which develop out of the flow of transactions may take the form of unorganized customs or of organized going concerns. No matter what forms the congealments of transactions take, the significant fact is that when transactions come together to create institutions they subordinate individual behavior to some kind of collective behavior. It is for this reason that the economist who makes the transaction his basic investigational unit develops an economics which is not only transactional but also collective and institutional.

In setting up the transaction as his primary unit of investigation Commons does not dispense with the commodities and feelings which were the primary units of investigation of earlier economists. Commodities and feelings are still important matters for scientific investigation, but they are to be considered only in relation to those transactions which together constitute economic activity. As economic theory has developed, there has been a shift of interest away from commodities and feelings, for they are "but the preliminaries, the accompaniments, or the effects of transactions." For this reason Commons states that economics has within recent decades become more transactional. It is more transactional because its primary interest is now in those many "economic bonds" such as bargaining transactions, debts, and property relations which bind individuals and groups, and thus provide coherence in the modern economy. It is this "transactional economics" which fits into Commons' special formula or thought scheme for the interpretation of twentieth-century capitalism, enabling him to describe his framework of interpretation as elastic, objective, and transactional.

Commons' study of economic transactions is carried on with the aid of five "principles of explanation." These five fundamental

[110] *Institutional Economics,* page 69.

principles, which condition, limit, and direct the complex of transactions comprising the capitalistic system, are the principles of "efficiency," "scarcity," "working rules," "sovereignty," and "futurity."
It is in the light of these principles of investigation that Commons
analyzes the economic aspect of "the total of all human acting and
transacting."

The principle of "efficiency" relates to the field of "engineering
economics," which is concerned with man's relations to his material
environment. In the realm of engineering economics efficiency is
a matter of maximizing wealth or use-values with the least expenditure of man-hours of labor; "By efficiency is meant, in terms of managerial transactions, the *rate of output per unit of input, the man-
hour,* thus increasing the power over nature but regardless of the
total quantity produced." [111] All the human relations of this engineering economy fall into a pattern of command and obedience.
For this reason the transactions to be found on the technological
side of the business economy are described as "managerial transactions." These managerial transactions know nothing about restricting output, improving scarcity values by withholding supply,
or performing services by refusing to produce. The only service
that is recognized by the engineer as he manages his plant is one
of increasing the abundance of material goods. Ownership and
the transfer of goods by the marketing process are of no concern to
him.

Commons' second explanatory principle, the principle of "scarcity," carries the economist out of the field of "engineering economics" into the realm of "proprietary economics." Here "production" and "wealth" take on different meanings; in fact they now
have double meanings. Whereas in the engineering economy production was the creation of wealth or use-values, in the business
or proprietary economy production becomes the creation of scarcity-
values or assets. In the business economy scarcity takes the place of
efficiency, ownership is more important than production, and restriction of output is more significant than abundance of output.
The bargaining transactions of the business economy are concerned
with the problem of scarcity rather than efficiency. Commons explains that "By scarcity is meant, in terms of bargaining transactions,

[111] *Ibid.,* page 259. See also Ch. VIII, "Efficiency and Scarcity," in the same
volume.

the *rate of proprietary income* from other persons relative to the *rate of proprietary outgo,* measured by the dollar." In the proprietary economy a new system of measurement is used, since the businessman's measure of the dollar is substituted for the engineer's measure of the man-hour. Also, scarcity involves the relation of man to man, whereas the efficiency of the engineering economy is a problem of the relation of man to nature. It is this change in human relations that leads Commons to shift his interest from managerial to bargaining transactions as he moves from an economy of use-values to one of scarcity-values.

Commons is careful to point out, however, that this separation of the engineering and business economies is purely a scientific abstraction. In reality the two economies are "socially inseparable." They both stem from the same human ability, which is the source of both producing and bargaining power. At times these two types of power are in conflict, and when this is so, they bring many economic problems into being. Commons points out that it was Marx who was the first to make a clear distinction between the two types of economic power, and to draw attention to the double meaning of production and wealth. At a later date Veblen accepted the distinction between producing use-values and bargaining for scarcity-values, and out of it he developed his theory of business enterprise.[112] But Commons, unlike his two predecessors, emphasizes the possibility of bringing about a coordination of producing and bargaining power through some form of collective action which would result in a reasonable form of capitalism.

The originality of Commons' economic theorizing does not relate to the two explanatory principles of efficiency and scarcity. These principles had already received considerable attention from both the orthodox and heterodox economists of the nineteenth century before Commons began his own economic studies. It is when he turns to the three remaining principles of "working rules," "sovereignty," and "futurity" that Commons' contributions to the science of economics are more apparent.

One of the most significant facts about economic transactions is their tendency to become customary modes of behavior. It is on

---

[112] Commons' distinction between engineering and proprietary economics is reminiscent of Veblen's separation of the industrial and pecuniary employments. Cf. Veblen, Thorstein, *The Place of Science in Modern Civilisation,* pages 279-323.

the basis of this fact that Commons develops his third explanatory principle, namely, the principle of "customary behavior" or "working rules." He explains that, "As a principle derived from a variety of facts, custom is similarity of compulsion. It is simply a working rule." [113] Every going concern such as a corporation, labor union, or trade association has its own set or complex of working rules or customary ways of carrying on economic activity. Individuals are compelled to learn how to adjust themselves to the large variety of these working rules or customs of the many going concerns comprising the economic system. If they fail to do so, it is only at the price of being unable to make a living in any of the generally accepted ways. The penalties for failure to learn how to adjust one's life to the demands of the working rules of the modern economy are so serious that most individuals offer little objection to the rule of custom. They are born into a world of customary transactions, and find little reason to resent the compulsions inherent in these customary modes of behavior.

Commons' principle of working rules applies to all types of economic systems, even the most highly competitive. In his view competition is a device by means of which individuals are required to observe customary modes of economic behavior without the intervention of the state. As he sees it, "enforcement need not be the authoritative enforcement by the constituted authorities of a concern. It may be enforcement by competition. The modern custom of purchasing commodities and paying debts by means of checks on solvent banks is compulsory on individuals, for whoever persistently refuses to accept and issue such checks, although they are not legal tender, cannot continue in business or even get into business. Checking accounts are a custom, and custom is not contradictory to competition. Competition is a means of enforcing custom. Those who enforce the custom are all individuals acting alike. . . . Hence, modern economic society has not passed from custom to contract— it has passed from primitive customs to business customs." [114] The traditional interpretation of competitive economic behavior, which takes its inspiration from the work of Jeremy Bentham and the early nineteenth-century economists, stresses the rationality of economic conduct to the exclusion of any habitual or customary fea-

[113] *Institutional Economics*, page 702.
[114] *Ibid.*, page 706.

tures which that conduct might have. Commons' principle of working rules seeks to correct this traditional explanation by bringing
to the fore the basic customary aspect of all bargaining and managerial transactions. On this issue Commons follows, not Bentham
and Ricardo, but Malthus, who drew attention to the irrationality
of human behavior and the role of custom in compelling men to
observe the customary transactions which enable them to exist together in some tolerable fashion.[115]

The principle of working rules has a most important place in
Commons' economic analysis because it is the foundation upon which
he erects the structure of his realistic analysis of the modern capitalistic system. It leads him to inquire into concrete patterns of
production, exchange, and consumption behavior, and to avoid excessively abstract interpretations of human conduct. The assumption that patterns of behavior are imposed from without by a divine
reason or an "invisible hand," or the assumption that such patterns
are the natural outcome of the interplay of many well-informed,
rational buyers and sellers, is displaced in Commons' economic
analysis by more realistic inquiries into actual cultural patterns of
human behavior. Commons' early interest in sociology and related
studies, his close contacts with actual economic experience in a
variety of circumstances, and his extensive research into the relations
between law and economics gave him an appreciation of the importance of custom and habit in economic affairs which was denied
to those economists who kept close to the paths of traditional, nineteenth-century economic thinking. Like Veblen, Commons was
quick to catch the significance of customary behavior in economic
life and to realize that, whenever economic activity is looked at from
the realistic or cultural viewpoint, the fact of prime importance
appears to be the tendency for economic affairs to fall into patterns
of customary behavior.

The principle of working rules is closely associated with Commons' fourth basic explanatory principle of "futurity." According
to this principle economic activity is not a repetitive process such as
would be found in a static world, but a flow of events that is based

[115] Commons joins Wesley C. Mitchell in condemning the intellectualist fallacy
of ignoring the habitual basis of man's behavior. He refers with approval to
Mitchell's article entitled "Bentham's Felicific Calculus" (*Political Science Quarterly*, June, 1918, Vol. XXXIII, pages 161-183), in which Mitchell analyzes the excessively rationalistic psychological basis of English utilitarianism.

upon certain occurrences expected in the future. Commodities, property, capital, and other values are significant in a proprietary economy only because of the benefits which their possession bestows upon their owners at some future time. Transactions involving the transfer of commodities, the rights to services, the use of capital, and so on, are carried on in an economy in which buyers, sellers, creditors, and debtors expect people to conform to certain patterns of behavior. If these expectations are not realized, then the value of commodities, capital, and property diminishes or disappears. It is this fact of futurity that makes the economy dynamic rather than static. Because the future is uncertain, there is always present the possibility of change. But where change is possible and economic activity is not merely a repetitive process, the door is open to both success and failure, to economic betterment or to serious maladjustment. It is this fact of futurity which keeps the economy from being a closed system in which economic activity gravitates towards some equilibrium level.

In developing his principle of futurity Commons returns to the economic transaction as his starting point. Every bargaining transaction has an element of futurity in it, for the transaction creates certain rights and duties. It gives rise to the expectation that the seller will fulfill a duty of performance, that is to say, that he will deliver the article sold. Likewise it is expected that the buyer will recognize a duty of payment, that he will pay for the article which is being transferred from seller to buyer. In this manner each bargaining transaction results in the debt of the seller to deliver and his right to receive payment, and in the debt of the buyer to pay and his right to have delivery of the article purchased. In economic analysis these rights to require future delivery or payment and these duties to make delivery or payment become debts and credits, which are intangible but which nevertheless have value in exchange.

The rights and duties or credits and debts arising from transactions are "economic quantities." Each transaction involves the transfer not of material "things" but of immaterial "economic quantities," which are rights or claims to the future use of things. What are exchanged in transactions are not things but the rights to things, not commodities but the rights to their ownership. For this reason Commons states that his primary concern is with "the proprietary economics of transferable rights and liberties," and that "Economics deals with legal rights over things." [116] Since legal rights are based upon expectations of future behavior on the part of buyers and sellers, economics becomes a science of futurity. This futurity embodies itself in the "economic quantities" or credits and debts which arise from the ceaseless flow of bargaining transactions, and which objectify themselves in the money or debt markets of the nation where future claims are bought and sold.

In explaining further how the principle of futurity applies to the modern capitalistic system, Commons turns from the futuristic nature of the bargaining transaction to a consideration of the relation of futurity to twentieth-century corporate enterprise. In his view the meaning of a corporation is "the expectation that both debtors will pay their debts and 'all the world' will pay profitable prices for materials or services . . . it is a going process over an expected flow of time . . . the going concern is a succession of incorporeal and intangible properties repeatedly created, continuing and lapsing." [117] The corporation as a going concern is a joint enterprise in which employers, managers, investors, bankers, and suppliers of materials are willing to participate as long as they have the expectation that the going concern will be able to pay the necessary rewards out of its joint income. Every individual who participates in the affairs of a corporate enterprise, who enters into a transaction to buy or sell a service or a commodity, acquires the status of creditor or debtor in relation to the going concern. Thus workers have a debt or duty to deliver their services to the corporation, and they also have a credit or right to receive wages in return for their services. Bondholders expect debt income in the form of bond interest, and investors look forward to the receipt of sales income as a return on their intangible property or corporate equity. In this way of viewing modern business enterprise the corporation becomes a complex of many transactions involving waiting, risking, forecasting, and planning, all of which look to the future.

Commons' futuristic view of the functioning of the modern corporation draws particular attention to the businessman or corporate manager, who shoulders the major responsibility for the success-

[116] *Institutional Economics*, page 400. Commons regards the Scottish economist Henry Dunning MacLeod (1821-1902), who first used the term "economic quantity," as the originator of institutional economics. See *Institutional Economics*, page 399.

[117] *Ibid.*, pages 421-423.

ful operation of the corporate enterprise. It is the prime responsibility of the businessman to see to it that the expectations of those who participate in corporate affairs are adequately fulfilled. Closely associated with businessmen are the bankers whom Commons describes as "specialists in futurity." As he succinctly phrases it, "while the engineer is the specialist in efficiency, and the business man is the specialist in scarcity, the banker is the specialist in futurity." [118] The banker aids the businessman by making loans in anticipation of profits to be made in the future. Modern capitalism has developed a "forecast system of money" in the form of bank deposits subject to checking. This forecast system of money enables businessmen to draw upon the available supplies of the factors of production with the expectation that consumers will in the future pay prices for commodities and services which will adequately reward all the working, waiting, risking, forecasting, and planning to be observed in the modern economy.

The fact that futurity is so important a characteristic of the bargaining relations of the modern economy raises the question of how successful people are in realizing their expectations of future uses of commodities and services or future receipts of money incomes of various types. When an economy is based upon credits and debts or rights and duties, which depend upon a flow of time before all duties are performed and all rights are exercised, there is a great deal of room for errors of judgment and conflicts of interest. A highly dynamic economy, such as the modern capitalistic economy, suffers from much friction, destruction of private individuals' rights or claims, imposition of intolerable debts or duties, and other maladjustments. Fortunately, these maladjustments that derive from the futuristic nature of bargaining transactions tend to be curbed by society through the exercise of its sovereign powers. Sovereignty, as expressed in the acts of legislatures, law courts, and administrative agencies, functions as a device by means of which the dislocations, interferences, and clashes of interest to be found in our dynamic, futuristic economic society are reduced to tolerable proportions.

The problems of a dynamic, futuristic economy lead Commons to a consideration of his fifth explanatory principle, namely, the principle of "sovereignty." In order to understand the capitalistic sys-

[118] *Ibid.*, page 512.

tem of the United States Commons finds it necessary to inquire into what he believes to be one of the fundamental social processes which condition economic activity. This basic process is sovereignty, "the changing process of authorizing, prohibiting, and regulating the use of physical force in human affairs." By the exercise of this sovereignty the state surrounds the bargaining and managerial transactions of economic society with a guarantee that force will be used, if necessary, to enforce the claims and to require the performance of the duties that arise from economic transactions. Contrary to the interpretations of the equilibrium economists, Commons finds no automatic settlement of the transactions between buyers and sellers, and especially has this been the case since the laissez-faire era has been replaced by an era of large-scale enterprise and corporate organization of business activity. In order to eliminate disputes and to give effect to expectations concerning future economic behavior, legislatures, courts, and, more recently, administrative agencies have drawn upon the sovereignty of the community. To bargaining and managerial transactions are thus added the rationing transactions of the state, which significantly alter the distribution of economic power among those who participate in the economic affairs of the nation. These rationing transactions result in a "proportioning of factors in a national economy," which is in addition to the proportioning carried out by private business enterprises.[119]

It is in the rationing activities of the state that Commons discovers the coordination of law and economics. He asserts that economists and jurists of the past century erred in isolating economic scarcity from the force or power of political sovereignty. "Analytic economics" he explains, "has to do solely with the function of scarcity, just as analytic jurisprudence has to do solely with the function of force. Its highest isolation has been that of the so-called 'economic man,' which is an abstraction of scarcity, just as the jurisprudential man is an abstraction of force. Each is abstracted, not only from the other, but from all functional relations to the other." [120] In his institutional economics Commons correlates law with economics. What enables him to do this is the presence of futurity in economic transactions. In their business transactions, in their competing and bargaining for scarce values,

---

[119] *Legal Foundations of Capitalism*, page 323.
[120] *Institutional Economics*, page 696.

individuals engage in activity looking towards an expected economic production or consumption. These expectations about future production or consumption are correlated in individuals' minds with expectations relating to the exercise of the community's sovereign powers which may or may not give effect to the anticipated production or consumption. A realistic interpretation of the modern economic scene cannot therefore divorce law from economics. Such an interpretation must consider the "functional intervening relationships" between economic and legal activity.[121]

Commons' five explanatory principles of efficiency, scarcity, working rules, sovereignty, and futurity have running through them a special unifying principle. This is the principle of "willingness" or volitiency. Problems of efficiency, scarcity, working rules, sovereignty, and futurity exist because there is at work in economic life a factor which seeks to control the environment for its own purposes. Commons calls this factor the "human-will-in-action." Individuals, living in a world of scarce human and natural resources, seek to manipulate these limited factors for whatever purposes they have in mind. For this reason, "the theory of political economy . . . is the whole of human will in its activity of seeking control of the environment, and is therefore an economic theory of the will."[122] In this very instrumentalistic outlook on the nature and scope of political economy Commons emphasizes the collective efforts of the community to make the best of a world of limited resources. Individual wills are congealed into a form of collective volitiency or will-to-action. Collective volitiency leads to collective action of many forms, which are designed to control individuals at their work of disposing of scarce human and natural resources. In view of these conditions economics becomes less a matter of "individual economy" and more a matter of "political economy."

So significant is the concept of futurity in his economic analysis that Commons makes "Future Time" or "Futurity" the most important single factor which distinguishes his collective economics from the traditional economics of the nineteenth-century economists.

---

[121] The legal structure must be considered along with the economic order which it houses. See Commons' review of C. B. Swisher's *Stephen J. Field: Craftsman of the Law* in *The Journal of Political Economy*, Dec., 1931, Vol. XXXIX, pages 828-831.

[122] *Institutional Economics*, page 634.

"The commodity economists of the classical school," he writes, "ignored Time as a factor in economic theory, because, for them, time was only a mental abstraction and therefore had no economic value. And they were correct from their standpoint, because their units of investigation were material things . . . and their method of investigation was an analogy to Newton's laws of motion of material bodies. . . . It required the whole of the Nineteenth Century, and even until the mathematical statistics of the Twentieth Century, for economists to find a place in economic theory for Time and its Measurement." [123] Time or futurity is significant because it is dynamic, institutional, volitional, and objective. Time is dynamic because it relates to actual, historical processes which reveal an ever-changing economic order. By keeping his analysis close to the changing realities of dynamic, historical, economic processes, Commons avoids the pitfalls of an excessively static or mechanistic approach to economic theory. In addition to the dynamic aspect of time, Commons is interested in its institutional aspect. Time becomes significant only in a cultural situation where the life of the individual, economic and otherwise, is bound up with many institutions, ranging all the way from the language of words and numbers to government. In order to comprehend the time or futurity dimension of economic activity the economist must acquaint himself with the whole institutional complex of laws, courts, governments, credit devices, banks, money markets, business arrangements, and so forth. It is through these many institutions that futurity or expectations about production and consumption are realized. "Man is more than organism," says Commons, "he is institutionalism, and it is only the institutional time-dimension of economic activity to which we give the name, Futurity. Futurity is institutional—the isolated infant and man, like an animal, would know little or nothing about it." Commons feels that it is man in his institutional setting who should be the concern of the economist, not some hypothetical individual in a world devoid of historical time.

Interest in the future dimension of economic activity also draws attention to the volitional features of economic life. Scientific attention is directed not so much to what has already occurred, as to the directions which economic activity may take in the future.

[123] *Ibid.*, page 406.

The psychology of buyers and sellers, employers and employees, and creditors and debtors becomes a negotiational and volitional psychology. The essence of ownership in a proprietary economy is a matter of future rather than present use. Market and capital values become present reflections of future expectations relating to the course of economic activity. Economic theory, therefore, must be "a volitional theory of economic activity directed towards purposes in the future." Commons' volitional economic theory has an emphasis quite different from the materialistic theory of commodities of the early nineteenth-century economists and from the subjective theory of sensations worked out by William Stanley Jevons and the Austrian school of economists. It stresses the dynamic and purposive qualities of an economic order based upon uncertain expectations relating to future production and consumption. It emphasizes the fact that a dynamic economy is open not only to the possibility of great risks and hardships for the many participating individuals, but also to the possibilities of continuously improving the living standards of the masses.

The final and most significant fact about Commons' concept of futurity is that it is thoroughly objective. Futurity or expectations concerning future production and consumption are continually being objectified in the present values that individuals attach to their expectations. There has been developed in the modern business system a highly intricate and sensitive money and credit structure, which enables individuals to agree on present values of future expectations. As economic conditions change, expectations concerning future production and consumption come to reflect these changing conditions. Future time is thus continuously revealing itself in market prices, capital values, and money or debt markets. Since futurity is continually objectifying itself in this manner it can be scientifically handled by the economist who deals with the objective realities of the whole economy. In place of Adam Smith's "Invisible Hand" or John Locke's "Divine Reason" as the unifying principle running through economic society, Commons would thus substitute Futurity. Since Divine Reason and the Invisible Hand are metaphysical concepts, which are not open to the scientific treatment to which Commons' concept of futurity lends itself, he concludes that "For metaphysics, we substitute Futurity." [124]

[124] *Institutional Economics*, page 96.

The Nature and Scope of Collective Economics

It may therefore be said that Commons' collective economics is an investigation and analysis of the capitalistic system in the light of five explanatory principles. These five principles are interdependent, and, although for purposes of scientific analysis they may be handled separately, together they constitute an interpretation of a total cultural situation described as the modern business system. Commons' collective economics deals then with "the expected repetition, with variability, of the total of all human acting and transacting within the limiting and complementary interdependence of the principles of scarcity, efficiency, working rules, sovereignty, and futurity." [125] The five different dimensions of the economy, scarcity, efficiency, working rules, sovereignty, and futurity, are functionally interrelated so that a change in any one of them alters all the others, and also the whole economy. Thus, if efficiency increases, scarcity diminishes, and there take place related changes or variations in working rules, the exercise of sovereignty, and expectations of the future. A technological change or invention which makes industry more efficient not only reduces the scarcity of goods or services, but it also results in far-reaching changes throughout the whole economy. Frequently a technological improvement will bring about changes in the customary working rules and regulations governing industrial and business life, in the ways in which the community's sovereignty is expressed through the acts and decisions of legislatures, courts, and administrative agencies, and also in individuals' expectations relating to future production and consumption.

In working out his five-dimensional interpretation of the modern economy Commons is careful to point out that he seeks to avoid the errors of both the formalistic economics of the classical and neoclassical economists and the descriptive economics of the historical economists. He seeks a union of the two types of analysis which will not overemphasize either the logicality or the historicity of economic behavior. He observes that an overemphasis of the logical character of economic behavior results in scientific tool-making and system-building with little regard for economic reality, while overemphasis of the historical relativity of the flow of economic events leads to the

[125] *Ibid.*, page 738.

accumulation of economic data as an end in itself.   It is Commons' belief that these two types of economic analysis can be successfully fused with advantage to both of them.   It is his purpose not to create a "collective economics" which will be divorced from preceding types of economics, but to develop "the whole of a rounded-out theory of Political Economy" which will incorporate elements of both the orthodox and historical types of economic analysis.

What, precisely, does Commons mean by a rounding out of political economy?   He means an analysis of economic behavior that will employ a new theoretical system in addition to the system developed by the laissez-faire, equilibrium economists.   It is a cardinal principle of Commons' economic theorizing that the understanding of economic behavior involves the use of more than one theoretical system or frame of reference.[126]   The viewpoint of the static equilibrium economists as embodied in their mechanistic theoretical system is helpful in arriving at a partial understanding of economic behavior, but it falls far short of providing a full, rounded-out explanation of economic activity.   Commons therefore finds it necessary to add his own theoretical system to that of the equilibrium economists.   His system is not a mere extension of the theoretical system of the earlier economists, because some of the basic assumptions of the equilibrium economists are at variance with Commons' assumptions.   In order to break through the closed system of the classical and neo-classical economists, Commons has had to alter the basic assumptions of the nineteenth-century economists in favor of more realistic assumptions about human nature and social organization.   It is on the basis of these revamped assumptions that he erects the special framework of reference required by his collective economics.

An illustration of how Commons would round out the science of economics by making use of his special theoretical system with its five explanatory principles may be found in his treatment of the value-cost problem.   According to his explanation, both the value and cost principles underlying economic activity are "eminently psychological," but not in the same sense that value and cost were found to be psychological by the English and Austrian psychological

---

[126] This view is similar to that held by Max Weber.   Cf. Parsons, Talcott, *The Structure of Social Action*, page 730.   New York: McGraw-Hill Book Company, Inc., 1937.

economists. According to these hedonistic economists, value was basically a matter of satisfaction or pleasure, and cost was a matter of discomfort or pain. Both value and cost were thus interpreted from the standpoint of individual feelings. In Commons' value-cost analysis the "feelings" of the psychological economists of the last century are replaced by anticipations and inducements, and by resistance and caution. Value becomes a matter of anticipations and inducements, whereas cost becomes a matter of resistance to inducements and of caution on the part of individuals in giving up their supply of scarce resources. Commons explains that, from the individual standpoint, value is anticipation of the control of commodities or services in the future. In an economy managed by engineers values are physical commodities, while in a consumption economy, the field of home economics, values are satisfactions derived from the use of commodities. But in a "proprietary economy" values become anticipations of future control or use of commodities and services for the purpose of personal pecuniary gain.

From the social standpoint Commons finds that the value or price system is a means of inducing people to devote their supplies of scarce economic resources to various social purposes.[127] Individuals are prone to withhold their services and commodities until adequate rewards in the form of satisfactory prices are offered. To the community or society these resistances to inducements or cautions on the part of individuals and groups are costs which must be met or covered if the commodities that the community wishes to have are to be produced. It is for this reason that Commons states that the value system has a communal or social function. Its function is to combine individual anticipations of personal value gains with social purposes involving the use of various supplies of commodities and services. Insofar as communal ends are poorly defined and are greatly influenced by pressure groups, the subservience of the value or price system to society's economic welfare is not fully achieved. In this situation individual and social values tend to diverge from each other, and the price system fails to be a reasonable price system. In Commons' opinion, "A reasonable system of prices can be judged to be such only as it conforms in some way to the psychological or ultimate goal of welfare and the physical or intermediate goal of production of wealth."

[127] *Legal Foundations of Capitalism*, page 379.

When value and cost are analyzed in terms of inducement, anticipation, resistance to inducements, and caution, it is necessary to push one's analysis beyond the market place where the supply-and-demand forces of a competitive economy operate.   The price system of the modern economy, being composed of competitive, semi-monopoly and monopoly prices which are influenced by private, judicial, and administrative agencies, reflects more than the simple supply-and-demand conditions of a competitive economy.   Commons observes that the terms and definitions of value-cost theories should therefore be fashioned out of more than commodities and feelings. They should be fashioned "in terms of persuasion, coercion, command and obedience"—in terms "of habits and customs operating within their legal limits of rights, duties, liberties and exposures"—and, finally, in terms of "the unseen psychological system of purposes" of the whole nation.   While fashioning his value-cost theory along these lines, Commons accepts the meanings of value and cost worked out by the nineteenth-century economists, but, since they are insufficient to explain fully the creation of values in the modern capitalistic system, he finds it necessary to round out value-cost theory by fusing the price system, the commodity system, and the system of purposes of the whole society.   As he puts it, he has taken the elements of the older value-cost theories and added to them so as to construct a "volitional theory of value."

The development of the equilibrium economics of the nineteenth century was accompanied by the working out of a set of principles or laws which exhibit a high degree of logicality and theoretical refinement.   This was made possible only by the choice of assumptions that lent themselves to a mechanistic equilibrium analysis.   Those who look for explanatory principles or laws in Commons' economics similar to the explanatory principles of competitive economics are necessarily disappointed.   Because of the nature of the basic assumptions upon which he builds the theoretical system or framework of analysis of his "collective economics," Commons must necessarily create principles of explanation that possess little of the logical neatness of the explanatory principles of equilibrium economics.   To those who object to the lack of symmetry in his theoretical system and to the broad generality of his five explanatory principles, he would reply that in the present stage of the development of economics no closer approximation to economic reality can be made.

All attempts to construct more logically precise categories, into which economic reality might be poured, merely result in sacrificing that reality to the demands of logical nicety and theoretical over-refinement.

Commons' rounding out of economics leads him to a definition of his science which incorporates some of the elements of older definitions, but which also introduces a number of new factors. According to his definition, economics is a study of the transactions relating to the disposal of scarce means by individuals and groups in the light of their individual and collective aims or ends with respect to private and public benefit. Political economy is "the proportioning, by means of the working rules of going concerns, of persuasive, coercive, corrupt, misleading, deceptive and violent inducements and their opposites, to willing, unwilling and indifferent persons, in a world of scarcity and mechanical forces, for purposes which the public and private participants deem to be, at the time, probably conducive to private, public or world benefit." [128] In this definition of economics the traditional mechanics of "production, exchange, distribution and consumption of wealth" are included, but they are given a secondary position. The emphasis is upon economics as a science of human transactions or cultural relations. What is of particular importance is the "set of relations of man to man." In order to understand the relations of man to man, and group to group, it is necessary to go beyond the abstract principles of equilibrium economics to inquire into the economic culture of the period under investigation. It is in this economic culture that are to be found the working rules of going concerns, the legal limits of economic behavior, and all those individual, group, and national aims or purposes which Commons unites with the principles of equilibrium economics. When these principles are immersed in their proper cultural milieu, the economist moves closer to the economic realities of the period which he is studying. In doing so he enlarges the scope of economics far beyond the limits set by nineteenth-century orthodox economists.[129]

Commons' definition of economics draws special attention to a

[128] *Ibid.*, pages 387-388.
[129] Commons, John R., "Twentieth Century Economics," *Journal of Social Philosophy*, 1939, Vol. V, page 29. Commons opens his article with the statement that "economics is a department of social philosophy."

type of human behavior, namely, collective economic behavior, which was largely ignored by the nineteenth-century systematic economists. He explains that "The economic theories of free competition and laissez faire, deductively worked out from the presuppositions of liberty, equality, self-interest, individual property and the mechanism of competition, give way to pragmatic theories of the reasonable use under all the circumstances of that bargaining power by concerted action which may be equally or unequally shared by individuals, classes or nations." [130] It is this "bargaining power by concerted action" that is of special interest to Commons. He goes on to point out that the disposal of scarce means is now largely a collective economic affair, with the result that the "relations of man to man" are becoming increasingly more collective and less individualistic. Commons observes that present-day economic transactions are carried on in a world of large-scale economic enterprise, of corporate activity, and of collective action by farmers, laborers, and consumers. Not only is the individual born into a world of customary economic and social arrangements, but also during his lifetime his efforts to plot an individual course of action are overshadowed by the larger, collective purposes of many special groups, and of the nation as a whole. The relations of man to man are thus essentially collective rather than individualistic. For this reason Commons' definition makes economics more a matter of "political economy" than of "individual economy."

In defining economics as a study of the disposal of scarce means in an economy dominated by collective action, Commons widens the scope of his science to include an analysis of the dominant socioeconomic purposes which give direction to collective economic action. Collective action in control of individual action becomes meaningful only when attention is directed towards the many purposes for the realization of which collective action is adopted. Commons therefore finds it necessary to inquire into the cultural aims or purposes embedded in institutions, customary modes of behavior, legislative acts, court decisions, and those larger socio-economic ideals which give direction to economic activity. He must inquire into the "purposes which the public and private participants [in industry] deem to be, at the time, probably conducive to private,

[130] "Bargaining Power," page 462.

public or world benefit." These collective and individual purposes may in some cases be harmonious, and in others conflicting. Whether these purposes are socially constructive or destructive does not alter the important fact that they have a very great influence on the direction and general level of the nation's economic activity. Consequently Commons finds that his grasp of economic reality is made more adequate when he has taken into account the relations between the disposal of scarce means and the major collective and individual aims guiding the flow of twentieth-century economic activity.

Commons' contributions to the building of a twentieth-century economics were limited by a number of unusual circumstances. If he had written his *Institutional Economics* early in his scientific career rather than at its close, he might have been in a better position during the most vigorous years of his academic life to bridge the gulf between traditional economics and a twentieth-century version of the science. But he did not arrive at his final conclusions about the nature and significance of economic science until he had had many years of experience in testing the applicability of the theories of conventional economics. The task before him, that of working out a new synthesis for economics, was a very formidable one; and as he tells us in his autobiography, he did not have that touch of genius which would have saved him from the long, arduous hours of digging and re-digging required by probing into new fields of scientific endeavor. "A genius can do in a few years," he wrote, "more than I could do in fifty years by intensive study. The genius can see through to the bottom of things without digging, but I must dig and re-dig." [131]   Personal qualities undoubtedly account for some of the delay in the development of Commons' theoretical position; but more important is the fact that he was a pioneer in the movement to revamp economic science. During his own lifetime psychological, philosophical, and sociological studies made tremendous advances. Unlike other economists of his own generation, who were content to ignore the new developments in related social-science disciplines, Commons imposed upon himself the obligation to become acquainted with the progress of social psychology, social philosophy, and jurisprudence. Every reader of the *Legal Founda-*

[131] *Myself,* page 3.

tions of Capitalism and *Institutional Economics* must be impressed by the evidence of Commons' wide reading in many related fields and of his deep understanding of numerous subjects other than economics. It was not until he had assimilated much of the social philosophy of William James, the pragmatic psychology of John Dewey, and the legal theories of the sociological jurists that Commons felt prepared to embark upon an exposition of the nature and significance of "collective economics."

In spite of his many years of graduate instruction, Commons failed to develop a following which has intensively cultivated the theoretical core of his new economics. This outcome can be explained on other grounds than the assertion of some of Commons' critics that his brand of economics is not a fertile soil for the development of a new school of economists. As already explained, Commons did not formulate the outlines of his collective economics until long after his arrival at the University of Wisconsin in 1904. If he had published his views on the nature of economics early in the century, he would at least have had a foundation upon which to erect a new type of graduate study. More serious is the fact that Commons was too prone to have his graduate students work on highly specialized aspects of economic activity rather than upon the broad theoretical foundations of economics.[132] He was more successful in stimulating his students' interest in labor and other specialized problems than in enticing them into the more intangible realms of philosophical and scientific thought which are of great importance to those who are concerned with the nature and significance of economic science. Without his background in modern philosophical thought, the logic of scientific method, and the various social sciences, Commons' students have, for the most part, been unwilling to take up where he left off. Finally, Commons' literary style is not one that attracts a large reading audience to either his *Legal Foundations of Capitalism* or his *Institutional Econom-*

---

[132] After reading this criticism Commons explained to the writer on June 28, 1942, that "I think my defects are in directing my students towards public affairs —you know I have a lot of them in the New Deal at Washington—but they have their own ideas—not mine—I have, indeed, a lot of trouble with my 'school,' they are gloriously independent." While Commons' students have sometimes differed with him on matters of economic policy, they have nevertheless accepted and worked within his general framework of economic interpretation. It is this framework of interpretation which his students have not done much to improve.

ics.[133] If Commons could have matched his erudition with an equal
capacity to convey in simple fashion to his less well-informed readers
the fundamentals of his scientific position, both his *Legal Foundations of Capitalism* and his *Institutional Economics,* and especially
the latter, would be much more widely read and appreciated than
they now are.

Commons' interest in a more realistic economics than the kind to
which he was introduced in the 1880's at Oberlin College grew out
of his varied experiences which covered not only America's era of
cultural awakening from 1890 to 1919, but also the subsequent era
of cultural disillusionment.[134] He found the inherited economics
of very limited use in grasping the realities of an era of rapid and
widespread economic change. The America which he first saw
critically in the closing years of the nineteenth century was a nation
which was comforting itself with a false idealism. This idealism
not only enabled the nation to ignore existing social, political, and
economic evils of an extremely serious nature, but it also put great
obstacles in the paths of inquisitive social scientists. In this atmosphere economics was rapidly becoming a sterile, formalistic scientific
discipline. What was necessary at the turn of the century was to
bring social philosophy down to earth, and to drive economic science
out into the welter of everyday experience.

In Commons is found a union of scientific curiosity and the reformist drive. The "irritation of doubt," which made its appearance early in his life, ceaselessly fed his deep curiosity about the
nature of economic activity. But the desire to grasp economic
realities more securely than had been done by earlier generations of
economists was accompanied by an urge to make social and economic
organization more reasonable and more conducive to better human
living. The search for economic reality was not spurred on by the
cold joy of merely contemplating economic truth in all its diversity.
The truth, when found, was to be made to serve the cause of a more
extensive human welfare. If there was to be a reconstruction of
economic science, it was to be carried out with the aim of making

[133] For criticism along this line from a well-known student of economico-legal
problems see Sharfman, I. L., "Commons' Legal Foundations of Capitalism,"
The Quarterly Journal of Economics, Feb., 1925, Vol. XXXIX, page 302.

[134] See Parrington, V. L., *The Beginnings of Critical Realism in America, 1860-
1920, Main Currents in American Thought,* Vol. III. New York: Harcourt,
Brace and Company, 1930.

economics a more useful science than it had hitherto been.   This instrumentalistic trend in Commons' economic thinking is nothing unique or special.   It is but a reflection of the reconstruction in all the fields of social science which pays heavy tribute to that larger "philosophical reconstruction" of which the pragmatist John Dewey is the ablest exponent.   John Dewey's pragmatic philosophy "has sprung from a clash of social ends and from a conflict of inherited institutions with incompatible contemporary tendencies," and in his opinion "it will be seen that the task of future philosophy is to clarify men's ideas as to the social and moral strifes of their own day.   Its aim is to become, so far as is humanly possible, an organ for dealing with these conflicts." [135]   The same conflicting cultural conditions nurtured Commons' collective economics; and it was for similar purposes that he devoted his life to the working out of a twentieth-century political economy.

In place of the misleading transcendental idealism of the fourth quarter of the last century, Commons substituted his more pragmatic "utilitarian idealism."   This type of idealism is one which combines idealism with utilitarianism, one that unites human aspirations with a recognition of the fact that there are certain very definite limits in actual experience to all such aspirations.   As Commons sees it, there is no divorce between social science and social philosophy. Social philosophy can be of the greatest value to the people only when it is solidly established on a basis of concrete fact and scientific understanding.   Commons' search for economic reality, and his efforts to improve the scientific devices used by economists in their work of uncovering this reality, seek to provide the necessary scientific guides for the nation's socio-economic aspirations.   The progressive Wisconsin to which Commons went in 1904, and in which he spent the remainder of his academic life, was a fertile field for the spread of his doctrine of "pragmatic idealism."   There were many people in that state who were misled by neither the outmoded Victorian philosophy of transcendental idealism nor the unrealistic doctrines of nineteenth-century, laissez-faire liberalism, and who were earnestly seeking to create a more reasonable socio-economic system.   At the University of Wisconsin—the "butter-fat" university

---

[135] Dewey, John, *Reconstruction in Philosophy*, 1920, page 26.   See also Wolfe, A. B., "Institutional Reasonableness and Value," *The Philosophical Review*, March, 1936, Vol. XLV, pages 202-205.

as he described it, Commons spent a lifetime working out a more realistic economics which would provide a firm scientific basis for the movement to set up a reasonable form of capitalism. In this work Commons has turned out to be what his early mentor, Richard T. Ely, described as "a symbol of aspiring America"—an America which is becoming more sophisticated about its socio-economic aspirations.

Economics is developing its old problems, attacking its new problems, improving its technique, and widening its alliances with vigor. If we do not reorganize the framework of our science as we move forward, it will be because the scheme excogitated by our predecessors proves more adaptable to changing needs than many of us now venture to believe.

WESLEY C. MITCHELL: *The Backward Art of
Spending Money*

4

The Quantitative Economics of Wesley C. Mitchell

The most outstanding exponent of "quantitative economics" in the United States is Wesley C. Mitchell, whose pioneering work in the field of business cycles has given much prominence to his broader theoretical views. Born at Rushville, Illinois, in 1874, three years after W. Stanley Jevons had announced his principle of final utility to the world, Mitchell graduated from the University of Chicago at a time when Veblen was striking at the foundations of orthodox economics. In the early nineties Mitchell discovered the University of Chicago to be "the most stimulating school of social science then to be found in any land." [1] President Harper had brought a number of illustrious professors and younger men of great promise to the new university of the Midwest, and there Mitchell came under the influence of doctrines that ranged from the most orthodox to the very heterodox. In economics he could pass from the lectures of J. Laurence Laughlin, with their deep reverence for economic theory as expounded by John Stuart Mill, to the unorthodox teachings of that "disturbing genius," Thorstein Veblen. Although many shades of opinion were represented by the social science faculty at Chicago, the balance was in favor of novel outlooks and new approaches to social problems. Even such a stalwart supporter of economic orthodoxy as Laughlin felt impelled for many years to give a course entitled "Unsettled Problems in Political Economy." Mitchell tells us that his student days at the University of Chicago were exciting, and that circumstances favored a great deal of intellectual cross-fertilization. John Dewey was there with his revolutionary views

[1] For Mitchell's tribute to the University of Chicago see his address delivered on the occasion of the dedication of the Social Science Research Building at the University of Chicago in *The New Social Science,* edited by Leonard D. White, pages 4-15. Chicago: The University of Chicago Press, 1930.

on the nature of human thought and the role of philosophy in human affairs. What he was teaching about the nature of human behavior fitted in very well with Veblen's views on the nature of economic processes. But what was most important for the coming generation of economists was that Dewey threw a flood of light upon the psychological assumptions of classical and neo-classical economics. Once doubt was cast upon the validity of the psychological basis of orthodox economics, the door was opened to new attacks upon the whole problem of economic behavior. The importance that Mitchell attaches to a proper understanding of the nature of human conduct undoubtedly dates from his contact with the pragmatic psychology of John Dewey.

Environment alone, however, is not the only important factor that is to be considered in explaining the origin and development of Mitchell's economic thought. There were many students subjected to the stimulating atmosphere of the University of Chicago who failed to develop a bent similar to that of Mitchell. Thus the same intellectual environment that nurtured Mitchell and Robert Hoxie also produced H. Parker Willis and Herbert Davenport. Such differences in environmental results can only be explained by reference to fundamental differences in personal make-up. Mitchell appears to have had the mental qualities which would make him particularly susceptible to the novel teachings of John Dewey and Thorstein Veblen. For this reason his reaction to orthodox economic theory was quite different from that of many of his student associates. Not only did he prefer to work on problems that did not greatly interest the orthodox economists, but he also reacted unfavorably to the methods employed by economic orthodoxy.

A casual acquaintance with Mitchell's economic studies might lead one to think that his preference for the statistical method determined the kind of problems he chose for investigation. According to Mitchell's own word, however, it was not really true that he approached the study of economics with a special predilection for the quantitative method of analysis. In a brief sketch of his intellectual development he tells us that he began studying economics and philosophy at the same time, and that he was struck by the similarity of the two disciplines.[2] Both the philosophy and the economics of the

[2] See the letter from Wesley C. Mitchell to J. M. Clark which appears in the latter's *Preface to Social Economics*, pages 410-416. New York: Farrar and Rinehart, Inc., 1936.

nineteenth century were found by the young Mitchell to be exces
sively deductive.   Both disciplines were inclined to build flimsy
thought structures on the foundation of very narrow premises.
What was excessively metaphysical did not appeal to Mitchell because he had learnt from Dewey to place little trust in finely spun
speculations which were far removed from any factual basis in human experience.   Applying to the work of economists what he had
learnt about the nature of the thinking process from Dewey, Mitchell found that he was more interested in explaining economic
theorists themselves than in interpreting their theories.   Very early
in his academic career he discovered that "The thing to do was to
find out how they [the economic theorists] came to attack certain
problems; why they took certain premises as a matter of course; why
they did not consider all the permutations and combinations of
those problems which were logically possible; why their contemporaries thought their conclusions were significant. . . .   Economic
theory became a fascinating subject—the orthodox types particularly
—when one began to take the mental operations of the theorists as
the problem, instead of taking their theories seriously." [3]   It was
John Dewey who helped stimulate Mitchell's critical faculties, who
caused him to drag out into the light the psychological theories hid-
den behind orthodox value and distribution theories, and who was
influential in turning him from deductive speculation to inductive
analysis.

Nineteenth-century economists had assumed that economic activities were basically rational.   Dewey kept bringing out in all his
courses at the University of Chicago the fact that men do not act rationally or turn to logical thinking except under stress of some sort.
It was most misleading to assert that consumers pursued a rational
course in their spending and consuming activities, for it was social
habit and not ratiocination that was their main guide.   Since men
do not have recourse to logical thought except in those infrequent
circumstances where they are under stress, it is not possible to deduce
what they will do by making the assumption that their actions are
fundamentally rational.   Mitchell applied this analysis of human
nature to economics.   "There is no way of deducing from certain
principles what people will do," he said, "because their behavior is
not itself rational.   One has to find out what they *will* do.   That is

[3] *Ibid.,* page 411.

a matter of observation, which the economic theorists had taken all too lightly."

From Dewey, Mitchell also learned a great deal about the role of logic in human conduct. He discovered that men were very prone to delude themselves with over-logical accounts of the world about them and to place their faith in "fabricated theories" that reached far beyond the realm of actual facts. From Plato to Alfred Marshall thinkers had created their logically consistent thought systems, and had been satisfied with logical consistency as the final test of truth. Speculation on the basis of certain premises, guided by the canons of logical thinking, had proved very fruitful in such fields as mathematics where one quite openly started off from hypothesis, not from observed fact; but such thinking when carried over into other fields of thought such as the social sciences was not so fruitful. In the field of economics it resulted in the theory of equilibrium, which Mitchell felt was incapable of providing an adequate interpretation of the course of contemporary economic events.

As a consequence of his early academic contacts Mitchell became familiar with the trends of scientific empiricism. Charles Peirce's early pragmatic views were passed on by William James and John Dewey to Mitchell at a time when the social sciences were groping for more adequate techniques of investigation. The broad sociological speculation of the second half of the nineteenth century was coming to a close. Instead of spending their time on system building, scholars were turning to "the patient processes of observation and testing—always critical testing—of the relations between the working hypotheses and the processes observed." What appeals to Mitchell about the natural sciences is that they are more successful in keeping their hypotheses and observations together than are the social sciences. He does not deplore deductive thinking as such, but what he does deplore is the tendency for rigorous thinking to get too far away from the realm of hard and fast facts. There is an acute need for thinking even more precise than that of David Ricardo, but, Mitchell points out, the place for such thinking is inside the investigation. Just as mathematics is used by the physicist to aid him in his observations and experiments, so should deductive analysis be an aid to the economist in his interpretation of economic reality. Deductive analysis must not be allowed to get out of bounds; problems in economics should be chosen for investigation in which deductive analysis can be controlled. Adequate control of economic speculation can be obtained only when "there is a great deal more passing back and forth between hypotheses and observation, each modifying and enriching the other." [4] In this manner there can be a synthesis of logical consistency and empirical verification which will be a fruitful source of economic truth.

Whereas Dewey was influential in molding Mitchell's psychological theory and social philosophy, it was Veblen and Laughlin who gave direction to his economic thinking. [5] Mitchell's interest in price analysis and monetary theory was first developed under the tutelage of J. Laurence Laughlin, but the framework of interpretation, into which his price and cycle analysis was fitted, was derived in large part from the work of Veblen. [6] Mitchell tells us that his early studies of the "greenbacks" and the history of prices failed to come to grips with fundamental issues because he had not yet worked out the general direction that his economic investigations were to take. It was not until he had become familiar with Veblen's highly important paper on "Industrial and Pecuniary Employments" (1901) that he came to see economic problems "in a larger way" which took him to the essentials lacking in his early work. With Veblen's theory of business enterprise as a point of departure, Mitchell proceeded to a study of the price system and its place in modern economic life. Working within the Veblenian view of the economic system, Mitchell came to regard his studies of price phenomena and the business cycle not as an extension of the work of the orthodox economists but as an introduction to a new type of economic theory. Early in his scientific work it came to be Mitchell's opinion that his work was not to be concerned with further refinements of the neo-classical thought structure handed down by Alfred Marshall, but with a reorganization of the general framework

[4] *Ibid.*, page 415.

[5] For Mitchell's commentary on Laughlin and his influence see "J. Laurence Laughlin," *The Journal of Political Economy*, Dec. 1941, Vol. XLIX, pages 875-881. Mitchell has explained to the writer that "Of course Mr. Laughlin knew nothing about business cycles. Nor did I until I had been several years in Berkeley and found the study of these cycles a necessary preliminary to a book I projected on the workings of the Money Economy."

[6] Mitchell's price and business cycle analysis was worked out in *A History of the Greenbacks*, Chicago: The University of Chicago Press, 1903. *Gold, Prices, and Wages under the Greenback Standard*, Berkeley: The University Press, 1908, and *Business Cycles*, Berkeley: University of California Press, 1913.

of economic science. It was for this reason that he felt compelled to write a chapter in his *Business Cycles* (1913) entitled "Modern Economic Organization," in which he elaborated upon the general view of the economic system which was to dominate his whole business cycle analysis.

It was Mitchell's early conviction that Veblen had progressed far beyond contemporary economists because he had a more adequate view of human nature and a broader understanding of cultural processes. Mitchell felt, however, that there was a deficiency in Veblen's analysis which did not make his "uncanny insights" as useful to economists as they might have been. What Veblen had done was to study the available data and to select certain facts as being worthy of particular attention. Although he had pushed his analysis beyond the borders set by his more orthodox contemporaries, and had introduced data that had been neglected by economists with classical leanings, nevertheless he was hampered by the lack of a technique that would enable him to handle masses of economic data. Like his more orthodox fellow-scientists Veblen was compelled to rely to a great extent upon speculations that were little controlled by empirical verification. What Veblen and his orthodox contemporaries lacked, namely, a technique for the measurement of the importance of the various factors at work within the economic system, was soon to be supplied by Mitchell. Mitchell acknowledges that Veblen drew in brilliant fashion the outlines of an arresting theory of modern business enterprise, but he also observes that Veblen was unable, with any degree of scientific precision, to assign importance to the various factors operating within the economic system. What were needed to make Veblen's work more valuable, in Mitchell's opinion, were "more intensive and tamer inquiries," and it was to these types of economic studies that Mitchell was to devote his energies. If Mitchell's economic analysis lacks some of the brilliance of Veblen's inquiries it is because he has preferred to spend his time on providing a firmer foundation for Veblen's pioneer work by carrying investigation into the somber details of the routine of business activities.

From the beginning of his scientific career Mitchell has exhibited a deep antipathy toward the building of "grand systems" of generalizations. Orthodox economists had worked out a deductive theory but had failed to meet the problem of verifying their system of economic generalizations. Mitchell prefers to take as his start-ing point a very rudimentary framework of analysis, and then pro-ceed to build up whatever theoretical system seems to be supported by the facts. Every hypothesis is to be subjected to "a process of attempted verification, modification, fresh observation, and so on." If it should be discovered that economic data did not warrant the creation of as neat and symmetrical a thought structure as the nine-teenth-century economists 'had constructed, it would be no reflection on economists and their work. Rather it would be a tribute to the desire of economists to keep their scientific interpretations as close as possible to an economic system which exhibits a great deal of conflict, confusion, and irrational action. So, wherever possible, Mitchell set out to check his speculations as far as he could by making use of the data of observation. Although not every bit of speculation can be subjected to the tests of empirical verification, be-cause there is a tendency for scientific speculation always to run ahead of the slower work of verification, Mitchell has always felt that it is the duty of the scientist to keep the work of speculation and verification as closely together as possible. From an early date he came to the realization that economics could make progress only on the basis of controlled speculation.

Mitchell's Pragmatic Psychology

Nothing is more essential for an understanding of Mitchell's eco-nomics than an appreciation of his views about the psychological basis of his science. Unlike the great majority of economists, he has a wide acquaintance with the literature of psychology, and has been in close contact with the new trends in psychological thinking since the opening of the century. In the early years of this century when economists like Herbert J. Davenport were advocating a policy of non-intercourse with the science of psychology as a means of meeting the attacks on the hedonistic psychology of neo-classical eco-nomics, Mitchell adopted a different policy.[7] His reaction to the criticisms of the psychological basis of traditional economics was not to say that we should divorce economics from psychology, but in-stead to assert that the relations between the two scientific disciplines should be more carefully investigated. He regarded the attacks on

[7] Davenport, Herbert J., *The Economics of Enterprise*, pages 99-101. New York: The Macmillan Company, 1913.

the hedonistic preconceptions of classical and neo-classical economic analysis as just so much more evidence of a need for a more adequate psychological basis for economics. In his opinion what was necessary was not less but more psychology in economic analysis. Out of his keen interest in a restatement of the relations between economics and psychology Mitchell has developed novel views regarding the nature and scope of economic science; indeed his economic heterodoxy is in large part a reflection of his uncommon views about the nature of human behavior. Just as it has been said of philosophers that their psychological theories have largely determined the kinds of philosophical systems that they have constructed, so it may also be said of economists that there is a direct connection between their theories of human nature and the kinds of economic systems which they build.[8] This important generalization with respect to the connections between psychological theorizing on the one hand and social philosophy and social science on the other is very well illustrated by the interrelations to be found between Mitchell's psychological thinking and his unconventional economics.

Like his illustrious teacher, Thorstein Veblen, Mitchell has been a critic of the psychological preconceptions of nineteenth-century English economics. Both attempted to modernize the psychological foundations of their science by introducing new developments from the field of psychology into economics, but there are considerable differences in their approaches to the study of economic behavior. Veblen based his notions of human nature on the scientific inquiries of Charles Darwin and William James and on available anthropological records.[9] During the early years of Veblen's creative work the foundations of modern psychology were only in the process of being laid. Psychology had begun to show promise, but it was still largely non-empirical and speculative. Too frequently it got bogged down in futile discussions about the nature and significance of such intangible and immeasurable factors as human drives or instincts. Statistical analysis was still in the early period of its development; consequently, like Darwin, who never made much use of statistical technique, Veblen and his great contemporary in the

[8] Edman, Irwin, *Four Ways of Philosophy*, pages 3-23. New York: H. Holt and Company, 1937.

[9] Mitchell, Wesley C., "What Veblen Taught," *The Backward Art of Spending Money*, pages 297-298. New York: McGraw-Hill Book Company, Inc., 1937.

field of psychology, William James, were inclined to be more speculative than experimental. Mitchell signalized this in his appraisal of Veblen's work: "What Veblen saw when he looked at man's activities differed from what other economists saw because his mind was equipped with later psychological notions. . . . Veblen adhered to the standard practice of the classical masters—he chose to reason out human behavior. But he sought to explain actual behavior, not what men will 'normally' do. . . ." But Mitchell saw the shortcomings in Veblen's approach: "Rarely does he undertake a factual survey. Many of his propositions are not of the type that can be tested objectively with the means now at our disposal. His work as a whole is like Darwin's—a speculative system uniting a vast range of observations in a highly organized whole, extraordinarily stimulating both to the layman and to the investigator, but waiting for its ultimate validation upon more intensive and tamer inquiries." [10]

As soon as experimental psychology had made some substantial progress, it was found that little could be done with the analysis of human instincts. Because instincts are not subject to scientific measurement, they have ceased to command the attention that they once did. It is precisely at this point that we note a difference between the psychological analyses of Veblen and Mitchell. Unlike Veblen, Mitchell is empirical rather than speculative in his analysis of human nature. He makes little use of Veblen's instinct psychology and prefers to adopt the more behavioristic outlook of John B. Watson's psychology, which was being developed at the same time that Mitchell was attempting to renovate the psychological basis of economic science.[11] Human nature can be analyzed, Mitchell said, from either outside or inside the human being. If one studies human nature from the outside, he enters the field of social psychology; and from this angle he can observe the many social patterns of conduct that govern individual behavior. Mitchell believes that economists should turn to this area of social behavior where psychological analysis can be objectified by the use of

[10] *Ibid.*, pages 299, 302.

[11] At the time that Mitchell wrote his article on "Human Behavior and Economics" (1914) the behavioristic trends in psychological thinking had come to a head in John B. Watson's work entitled *Behaviorism; an Introduction to Comparative Psychology*. New York: H. Holt and Company, 1914.

various statistical devices. The classical economists had chosen to examine economic behavior from inside the individual. In the early stages of the development of economics this method had some justification, but in relation to the present development of scientific thought Mitchell is of the opinion that the introspective approach in the study of economic behavior is "the most treacherous of all professedly scientific methods." The introspective method can never, it is true, be dispensed with, but certain safeguards must be employed if it is to be used without unfortunate consequences. In Mitchell's opinion these safeguards are the historical and statistical analyses of economic behavior.

What appeals to Mitchell about an historical and statistical examination of human conduct is its objectivity. As the meteorologist observes the weather and the geologist examines the earth's crust, so should the economist record the behavior of social groups. Mitchell believes that the observation of group behavior, as a new field of economic study, is one in which "the most rigorous standards can be applied, the most refined analysis developed, and the best-grounded hopes entertained for improvements in data and results." [12] Historical records and statistical surveys are not as intimate as the subjective operations of the human mind, and as a consequence, they provide a better basis for that consensus of opinion amongst scientists which is so essential for the progress of any science.

If Mitchell is to turn from the subjective analysis of the classical and neo-classical economists, what will be the object of his economic investigations? Following recent exponents of social psychology, Mitchell believes that further progress can be best achieved by investigating important social institutions, such as the legal and business systems, which influence economic conduct. Biological drives and human reason will always remain important factors influencing human behavior, but they work through social patterns of conduct. Mitchell's theory of motivation is neither biological nor individual but social; and it is in marked contrast to the motivation theory of the classical and neo-classical economists. In his view of the nature of human behavior, which closely parallels that of Edward Lee Thorndike, the individual begins life with a large number of

---

[12] Mitchell, Wesley C., "Wieser's Theory of Social Economics," *Political Science Quarterly*, March 1917, Vol. XXXII, pages 115-116.

inborn reflexes and instincts which vary from individual to individual but which are more or less fixed for the race. The behavior which results from man's inborn capacities is an unreasoning form of behavior, but fortunately for man he has a capacity to learn. He has "the capacity to form innumerable *combinations* among the innumerable original propensities." [13] What combinations of propensities will be made is very largely the result of the individual's relations with other human beings and his physical environment.[14] Since the capacity to learn is developed by intercourse with other human beings, Mitchell observes that intelligence is very largely a social product. Human intelligence stems from the original nature of man, but the "special character" of an individual's intelligence depends upon the community in which he develops to maturity.

In the development of the individual's intelligence Mitchell assigns special importance to the practical arts, writing, speech, and religion. These institutions provide "standard behavior habits— habits of feeling, acting, and thinking in the face of frequently recurring situations—that have approved themselves to the community," and that finally get embodied in the routine of a social institution.[15] Mitchell does not imply that all institutions have a predominantly rational basis. It does seem, however, that when intelligent action becomes sufficiently routinized, it takes the form of a social institution. For this reason Mitchell asserts that "the successful routine of today remains a triumph of yesterday's creative intelligence, and if today's hard thinking prove equally successful it may organize the routine of tomorrow. Of course, the growing individual must master the past achievements of intelligence before he can participate in work upon present problems. And these past achievements are embodied primarily in social institutions." [16] It is these social institutions that have a major role in the task of nurturing human intelligence and molding human behavior, for running throughout them are the abstract concepts of human intercourse, the tools for further thought, which are picked up by the individual and used when he finds that he needs them to resolve

---

[13] Mitchell, Wesley C., "The Role of Money in Economic Theory," *The Backward Art of Spending Money,* page 169.
[14] Cf. Thorndike, Edward L., *The Original Nature of Man,* Volume I in *Educational Psychology.* New York: Teachers College, Columbia University, 1913.
[15] "The Role of Money in Economic Theory," page 170.
[16] *Ibid.,* page 170 fn.

some difficulty in the social environment about him. These abstract concepts of scientific, philosophic, and theological speculation are important, for it is by them that the individual standardizes and rationalizes his own behavior. Of course the more adequately man's social institutions are adapted to "current social needs," the more will he get from the social habits of feeling, thinking, and acting inherited from the past, and the better prepared will he be to apply his creative intelligence to making life more worth while for generations yet unborn. But, whatever the state of the complex of social habits, it is within their enveloping limits that the individual exercises his capacity to form combinations among his many inherited reflexes and instincts.

Since social institutions are such powerful agents in the directing of human behavior, any adequate explanations of how individuals behave must be made in institutional terms. To the extent that these institutions are embodiments of past achievements of human intelligence, they provide a basis of rationality in the individual's behavior. "To find the basis of rationality," writes Mitchell, "we must not look inside the individual at his capacity to abstract from the totality of experience the feeling elements, to assess their pleasant or unpleasant characters, and to compare their magnitudes. Rather must we look outside the individual to the habits of behavior slowly evolved by society and painfully learned by himself." [17] At this point in his theory of human nature Mitchell climaxes his revolt from the psychological position of inherited economics. For nineteenth-century economists had assumed the action of men to be fundamentally rational; and they had then gone on to show how men would behave in a laissez-faire economy, and how they would there find expression for their rational faculties. Mitchell holds the opposite view that the institutions of a laissez-faire economy conditioned men and habituated them to a system in which, as a matter of habit and custom, they approached the position of thoroughly rational individuals. In other words, there were institutional pressures at work seeking to force plastic human nature into the rigorous molds of highly rational conduct. In the brief span of a few centuries mankind has been clamped into the straitjackets of commercial and industrial capitalism, and has been indoctrinated with an exaggerated respect for the standards of the

[17] *Ibid.,* page 170.

counting house. Since the development of commercial capitalism at the end of the Middle Ages, a particular economic institution has emerged to give shape and color to much of modern civilization. This is the great rationalizing habit known as the institution of money, which, more than anything else, has determined the tone or spirit of modern capitalism. The process of making and spending money has its own peculiar logic by the aid of which men weigh "the relative importance of dissimilar goods in varying quantities," and view the interests in terms of which they make their valuations. In this fashion, the influence of the money institution reaches out and affects other forms of institutionalized behavior. As a consequence, life today becomes standardized and rationalized not according to the requirements of any inherent principles of rationality existing in the human mind, nor according to any vague, extramundane standards of absolute reason, which are supposed to guide individual behavior from above, but according to the requirements of the use of money in an advanced capitalist society. Throughout the economic world a system of accountancy has grown up, and, wherever its influence has penetrated, men have been required to adjust their ways of getting a living in the light of highly commercialized standards of human conduct.

The effects of the use of money have been less important in the spending of money than in the making of it. This is because other social habits less standardized and rationalized than the making of money have prevailed in the operation of the household economy. If one is to explain why "Ignorance of qualities, uncertainty of taste, lack of accounting, carelessness about prices—faults that would ruin a merchant—prevail in our housekeeping," he must turn to the habitual ways of thinking and acting that canalize the life of the home. In 1912, long before the present interest in the consumer movement had developed, Mitchell wrote an essay, entitled "The Backward Art of Spending Money," to deplore the "notoriously extravagant" behavior observable in the economy of the household.[18] His solution for this lack of common sense in the handling of money, earned only at great effort by most people, was that the "citizens of a money economy" ought to plan the spending of money as carefully as they plan the making of it. The spending of money

[18] Mitchell, Wesley C., "The Backward Art of Spending Money," *The American Economic Review*, June, 1912, Vol. II, page 269.

should become more standardized and rationalized through the development of consuming habits appropriate to the demands of a twentieth-century civilization. Mitchell undoubtedly looks with much satisfaction on the recent progress of the consumer movement in the United States with its emphasis upon better buying and consuming practices. The progress of such a movement depends in the long run, however, not so much upon an appeal to the rational faculties of millions of prospective consumers as upon the development and spread of social habits that will bring the operations of the household economy within the range of the influence of the money institution. People, in general, may be induced to buy intelligently more as a matter of ingrained social habit than on the basis of an appeal to the rational faculty. It is only in this way that the masses of the population may come to have something of an adequate consumer psychology. Mitchell points out that most men and women will continue to accept, without critical thought, the scale of conventional values provided ready-made by their generation. If new values for the guidance of household economy could be developed by the exercise of man's creative intelligence, the habitual acceptance of these new values would provide the necessary solution to such problems as "conspicuous consumption" and careless spending of money.

This emphasis upon the prime importance of social habits in the shaping of human conduct and upon the minor role played by human reason has caused a number of Mitchell's critics to accuse him of clinging to an excessively behavioristic interpretation of human nature. Some of his critics allege that he pays too much attention to the studying of patterns of behavior, especially those which may be statistically treated, and that he makes too little inquiry into the more volitional aspects of economic activity. They call attention to his essay on "Quantitative Analysis in Economic Theory" (1925) in which he states that "If my forecast is valid, our whole apparatus of reasoning on the basis of utilities and disutilities, or motives, or choices in the individual economy, will drop out of sight in the work of the quantitative analysis, going the way of the static state." [19] It might have been more conducive to a wider

[19] Mitchell, Wesley C., "Quantitative Analysis in Economic Theory," *The American Economic Review*, March, 1925, Vol. XV, page 5. Mitchell continues with the statement that "The 'psychological' element in the work of these men

acceptance of his views if Mitchell had written about modifying the "whole apparatus of reasoning" of the nineteenth-century economists rather than about their apparatus of reasoning dropping out of sight as a consequence of the objective analysis of the newer psychology. For actually Mitchell's psychological analysis does not involve a complete abandonment of the reasoning of his orthodox precursors, but instead a revamping of their psychological theory. It is obvious that economic behavior is more than a matter of habitual responses, and that an adequate understanding of it involves inquiry into its volitional or teleological as well as its habitual aspects. Although Mitchell has never held any other view of human behavior, portions of his writings do not always reflect this tolerant viewpoint to which, in general, he adheres. Whatever lack of balance he has shown in his psychological analysis is to be attributed to the fact that he has been working in the forefront of new fields of economic study where devotion to new scientific procedures may quite easily be mistaken for a disregard for what has already been accomplished by earlier students of the subject.

Judging by Mitchell's interest in the broad areas of social psychology, one might expect his economic studies to range over wide areas of economic behavior. One is led to expect an analysis comparable in scope to the work of Thorstein Veblen, which extended from the productive processes to the field of consumption. That is not the case, however, for Mitchell has limited his analysis almost entirely to the business system. In the world of business, in spite

will consist mainly of objective analysis of the economic behavior of groups. Motives will not be disregarded, but they will be treated as problems requiring study, instead of being taken for granted as constituting explanations. . . . Psychologists are moving rapidly toward an objective conception and a quantitative treatment of their problems. Their emphasis upon stimulus and response sequences, upon conditioned reflexes; their eager efforts to develop performance tests, their attempts to build up a technique of experiment, favor . . . the quantitative analysis of behavior records, and a common aspiration—to devise ways of experimenting upon behavior." In his analysis of Mitchell's essays A. B. Wolfe states that "We have his reiterated conviction that economics is one of the sciences studying human behavior, but his positive thought on the psychology of motivation in relation to the task of economic analysis is somewhat obscure. . . . We are left in the dark as to what use the economist is permitted to make of motives even after he has discovered them through the statistical analysis of mass behavior." See Wolfe's article entitled "Thoughts on Perusal of Wesley Mitchell's Collected Essays," *The Journal of Political Economy*, Feb., 1939, Vol. XLVII, pages 9-10.

of a high degree of rationality, are to be found many customary modes of behavior. Indeed so habitual has the behavior of businessmen become, that a whole theory of the business cycle can be erected on the basis of customary business responses to recurring economic stimuli. Mitchell has not gone much beyond the investigation of the business system. He has left to others, Commons, Veblen, Tawney, Sombart, and Hobson, the task of investigating the broader fields of economic behavior not encompassed by the business system. For this reason Mitchell's interest in the psychological foundations of economics has been more a source of inspiration to later generations of economists than a basis for extensive research in psychologico-economic problems on his own part.

Mitchell's psychological views have been influential in shaping his attitude toward classical economics and the future of economic science. He has eschewed analysis lacking a firm inductive basis, and has had grave doubts about the claims of the exponents of "pure theory." [20] His interest in social institutions has coincided with an attachment for the statistical method which is so appropriate for the study of the mass phenomena of social behavior. Such studies have the virtue of directing the investigator to the past and to the future. As early as 1915 Mitchell was explaining to his readers that "A man who realizes that he is studying an institution keeps his work in historical perspective, even when he confines himself to analyzing the form that the institution has assumed at a particular stage of its evolution. By so doing he opens vistas enticing to future exploration, instead of suggesting a closed system of knowledge. He does not delude himself into believing that anyone's personal experience is an adequate basis for theorizing about how men behave; rather he is eager to profit by any light shed upon his problem by any branch of learning—history, statistics, ethnology, psychology." [21] If Mitchell has not made as many incursions into history, ethnology, and psychology as some of his institutionalist predecessors or contemporaries, it surely is not because of any narrowness of his interests, but because he has found a study of the business system to be a task which can very easily absorb more than a lifetime's energies.

[20] Mitchell, Wesley C., "Human Behavior and Economics," *The Quarterly Journal of Economics,* Nov., 1914, Vol. XXIX, page 46.

[21] "Wieser's Theory of Social Economics," page 117.

It should be noted that there is an important relation between Mitchell's psychological theory and his functional view of the nature of economic science. According to his psychological theory man is by nature an active creature, but his propensity for action encounters considerable interference. There is the whole institutional complex which surrounds the individual from birth, and continues to influence him as long as he retains any mental resilience. Fortunately social institutions may be altered to suit mankind's desires. Mitchell explains in his first essay on psychology and economics that his view of human nature provides "a firm psychological basis for optimism concerning the possibilities of social progress." The nurture of man's inherent capacities is a cumulative process, with the result that "Every increase of social wisdom may be applied in bettering the nurture given to the generation that follows, so that this generation in turn may give its successor training better than it received." [22]

It was not until after 1929 that Mitchell came to direct his scientific interests more and more toward the problems of economic reform and reconstruction. It appears that the latent reformist tendencies in Mitchell's economic thinking did not come to a head until the nation was confronted with a general breakdown of its economic system. Yet this apparently new interest in social reconstruction does not mark any real break with the earlier trends of Mitchell's thinking; the seeds had been deeply planted in the first three decades of the present century. In the early years of this century Mitchell had been very much intrigued with Graham Wallas' *The Great Society* (1914), which pointed out that a disharmony had grown up between the demands of the modern politico-social organization and the habitual ways of thinking and acting which had been handed down from prior generations. In looking at the economic system Mitchell observed a similar disharmony between the requirements of the modern economy and the stereotyped modes of behavior handed down by "generations of farmers, handicraftsmen, and petty shopkeepers." When a period of economic disorganization was ushered in after 1929, Mitchell was well prepared for such an emergency because his psychological theory laid the foundation for an explanation of economic instability.

As a student of psychologico-economic problems Mitchell does

[22] "Human Behavior and Economics," page 11.

not look upon economists as passive recipients of the discoveries made in the field of psychology. On the contrary, he feels that they may very well make contributions of their own to the developing science of psychology for the reason that no one should be more familiar with the economic aspects of human behavior than the economists themselves. Making one of his few references to the significance of economic factors in the shaping of human conduct, Mitchell states that "Human nature is in large measure a social product, and among the social activities that shape it the most fundamental is the particular set of activities with which the economists deal." [23] And that is why economists are in a most favorable position for cooperation with the psychologists in making progress with their scientific discipline. But in taking this opportunity to cooperate with the psychologists, economists will give a "new character" to their own science. Economics will "cease to be a system of pecuniary logic, a mechanical study of static equilibria under non-existent conditions, and [will] become a science of human behavior." Economics can then take its rightful place alongside the other social sciences which are all special branches of the larger science of human behavior. As a science of human behavior economics will focus more attention on the role played by institutional factors in behavior and less attention on the subjective operations of the human mind. Since Mitchell's economic analysis is concerned with objective mass behavior rather than subjective individual behavior, he labels his psychological approach the "behavioristic viewpoint" to distinguish it from the individualistic viewpoint of the neo-classical economists.[24]

The Quantitative Method of Analysis

There is a very close connection between Mitchell's psychological views and his philosophy of scientific method, for throughout his discussions his pragmatic bent is plainly visible. Like his social psychology with its strongly empirical leanings, his scientific methodology with its emphasis upon the importance of quantitative analysis in economic investigation reflects the pragmatic tendencies of recent American scientific thought.

[23] "Human Behavior and Economics," page 3.
[24] Mitchell, Wesley C., "The Prospects of Economics," *The Trend of Economics,*. edited by R. G. Tugwell, page 25. New York: A. A. Knopf, 1924.

In his essay on the role of quantitative analysis in economic theory Mitchell lays bare his attitude toward the qualitative and quantitative approaches in the study of economic phenomena. Quarrels over methodology hold no interest for him since he believes that they are by necessity sterile. "I see no need for controversy on the problem of how to work," he tells his fellow economists, assuring them that "no useful result [is] likely to come of discussions of method conducted in a controversial spirit." It is folly to quarrel about methods; "In economics we have tasks of many sorts to perform, and we have workers of many aptitudes. . . . But that we shall let our different predilections and opinions involve us in a controversy upon methods at large seems to me almost as improbable as it would be deplorable." [25]   Mitchell's attitude toward the problem of method is one of tolerance. Yet, although he is prepared to be tolerant of all approaches to the study of economic phenomena, he unconsciously shows his preference by being at his best when he is discussing the nature and significance of quantitative analysis. At the time that Mitchell produced his pioneering study on the business cycle, economic analysis was still of a very deductive and speculative nature. Even the critics of economic orthodoxy (Veblen, for example, who never tired of criticizing the excessively deductive nature of classical economics) were unable to free themselves from similar deductive tendencies. Veblen made excellent use of vast accumulations of historical data, but when it came to measuring the importance of various economic factors, or the testing of various hypotheses, he was hardly better off than his orthodox contemporaries. The historical method, whether in the hands of a Schmoller or a Veblen, had not proven to be as fruitful as some social thinkers had hoped, because, without refined statistical techniques, it was very difficult to extract much significance from accumulations of historical data. When Mitchell was first introduced to the study of economic phenomena in the early years of the present century he found that the historical school had failed to dislodge the analytical economists from their highly abstract position. In fact the historical school had never seriously threatened the formidable position of economic orthodoxy for the simple reason that it was unable to

[25] See Wesley C. Mitchell's round-table discussion at the annual meeting of the American Economic Association, December, 1927, *The American Economic Review*, March, 1929, Vol. XVIII, Supp., pages 39-41.

utilize effectively the vast supply of historical data which it had laboriously accumulated.

In his economic analysis Mitchell endeavors to supply the elements that were lacking in the work of the historical economists. In the preface to the first edition of his *Business Cycles* (1913), he explains that his treatise "offers an analytic description of the complicated process by which seasons of business prosperity, crisis, depression, and revival come about in the modern world." [26] It is this "analytic description" which is taken by Mitchell to be his contribution in the field of scientific methodology. He goes on to explain that "analytic" description is something more than "ordinary" or mere description, which is little more than an accumulation of historical or contemporary data. Ordinary description suffers from the lack of an adequate systematic basis, which would provide the necessary order and coherence for the accumulated data. Analytical description, in Mitchell's opinion, is superior to mere empiricism because it provides a systematic account of what is being inductively investigated. And so he points out that "A systematic account of cyclical fluctuations, taken seriously, becomes an analytic description of the processes by which a given phase of business activity presently turns into another phase." [27] This "systematic account" of cycles is obtained through the application of the quantitative methods of statistics to the description of business cycles. It goes beyond a consideration of the concrete events usually evaluated by the economic historian because it arrays the accumulated data in statistical categories, and constructs statistical patterns out of the welter of concrete, historical data.

With reference to his special problem of the business cycle, Mitchell points out that ordinary description deals with the actual cycles of historical records with all their diversity and irregularities, while cycle theory of the nineteenth-century type deals with "cycles of some speculative construction." His own analytical description rests on a middle ground between mere description and orthodox theory, and is concerned with what Mitchell calls cycles of an intermediate order. These are cycles which are neither historical nor speculative

[26] Mitchell, Wesley C., *Business Cycles*, Memoirs of the University of California, Vol. 3, page vii. Berkeley: University of California Press, 1913.

[27] Mitchell, Wesley C., "Business Cycles," *Encyclopaedia of the Social Sciences*, Vol. III, page 100.

but instead are typical or statistical cycles. By pouring his accumulated empirical data into the molds of various statistical patterns, Mitchell observes that he is in a position to do what economic historians of the past century had been unable to do. He finds it possible to measure the importance of various factors at work within the economic process. Statistical analysis of historical records results in the setting up of quantitative definitions for the preliminary treatment of raw data, the adoption of satisfactory units of measurement, and the arrangement of observations so that they may suggest certain explanations. New problems that were not open to attack through qualitative analysis are now laid bare. These problems are for the most part problems of measuring the relative importance of various factors operating within the economic system, and of determining the general trends in fluctuations of these various factors.

Mitchell's analytical description is quite different from the descriptive analysis of Sombart, Veblen, Commons, and others. Whereas these economists gather data relating to the origin and development of various economic institutions and then systematize the accumulated data as best they can to provide something in the nature of economic interpretation, Mitchell pays scant attention to similar data. Phenomena that do not fall into the statistical categories of measurable data are given but little notice. In 1913, when he wrote his *Business Cycles,* Mitchell appears to have felt that the descriptive analysis of other economists, with its emphasis upon historical, non-statistical data, while very important, had been carried out about as far as it profitably could be at that stage in the development of economic science. There was a great need for studies that would test scientifically the broad generalizations of such speculative economists as Sombart and Veblen. The brilliant work which these economists had begun could be carried further when a new technique for the handling of masses of economic data was developed. With this in view, Mitchell set about "to take great care in measuring the phenomena exhibited by business cycles." [28] It was not enough that cycle analysis should be empirical; it was essential that this analysis be quantitatively or statistically empirical.

The aim of Mitchell's scientific methodology is to provide a proper balance between deduction and induction, between theory and practice. In seeking this balance, however, Mitchell does not

[28] *Business Cycles,* 1913, page vii.

develop any new organon of thought for the improvement of his science. His quantitative analysis is only an improvement on the general inductive approach employed by social scientists since the turn of the century. What is important about his methodological position is that he represents a new attempt to offset the deductive bias of the classical and neo-classical economists. Orthodox economists thought out a deductive scheme, and then spoke about verifying it. Mitchell does not go to the other extreme of starting an inductive investigation with no framework of interpretation to guide his analytical description. After many years of reflection, he explains his methodological procedure in the following manner: "To me it seems that I try to follow through the interlacing processes involved in business expansion and contraction by the aid of everything I know, checking my speculations just as far as I can by the data of observation. . . . But this is not a simple matter which enables me to deduce certain results—or rather, to deduce results with certainty. There is much in the workings of business technique which I should never think of if I were not always turning back to observation. And I should not trust my reasoning about what businessmen will do if I could not check it up. Very likely what I try to do is merely carrying out the requirements of John Stuart Mill's 'complete method.' But there is a great deal more passing back and forth between hypothesis and observation, each modifying and enriching the other, than I seem to remember in Mill's version. Perhaps I do him injustice as a logician through default of memory; but I don't think I do classical economics injustice when I say that it erred sadly in trying to think out a deductive scheme and then talked of verifying *that*. Until a science has gotten to the stage of elaborating the details of an established body of theory—say finding a planet from the aberrations of orbits, or filling a gap in the table of elements—it is rash to suppose one can get an hypothesis which stands much chance of holding good except from a process of attempted verification, modification, fresh observation, and so on." [29]

Like the methodology of other pragmatists, Mitchell's methodology is extremely tentative and cautious. Starting with a few general ideas about the nature of the economic system, largely borrowed

[29] See the "Letter from Wesley C. Mitchell to John M. Clark," which appears in John M. Clark's *Preface to Social Economics*, page 411.

from Veblen and Sombart, Mitchell proceeds to build up economic generalizations with special attention paid to the movements of the business system. Essentially Mitchell reverses the methodological procedure of the orthodox economists who reasoned from a certain set of assumed motives and circumstances to hypothetically normal conduct, whereas Mitchell reasons from actual conduct and circumstances to general patterns of economic behavior.[30] In neo-classical analysis the economic norms, which are non-empirical and unhistorical, are abstract standards of economic conduct established by hypothesis, whereas Mitchell's norms of economic behavior are both empirical and historical. They are statistical norms in which the relative importance of the component factors has been quantitatively determined. In this fashion, by pouring the voluminous data of business cycle history through the narrow sieve of statistical analysis, Mitchell endeavors "to create order amidst the confused facts of observation." He points out that our instruments of scientific analysis are not capable of coping with the problem of "handling simultaneous variations among a large number of inter-related functions." He believes, however, that his statistical norms, which are based upon a limited number of variations of interrelated functions, are tools that will be found quite useful in the task of seeking an adequate understanding of economic activity. Adopting as far as possible the methodological procedures of the natural scientists, Mitchell patiently constructs his statistical patterns of business conduct. Although he is unable entirely to follow "the way of natural science," since he is unable to indulge in economic experimentation, he does endeavor to do as much observation and testing as is possible. As far as is possible, each forward movement in the improvement of economic theory is verified through observation in order to determine how adequately economic generalizations correspond with the facts of actual economic experience.

Many people find Mitchell's scientific method excessively inductive. They think that he is only paying lip service to non-inductive

[30] John M. Clark has explained that "The most obvious difference between Mitchell's method and that of traditional theory is that Mitchell reasons from conduct to conditioning motive and circumstance, while traditional theory, in appearance at least, reasons from motive and circumstance to 'normal' conduct." See Clark's essay on "Wesley C. Mitchell's Contribution to the Theory of Business Cycles," in *Methods in Social Science*, edited by Stuart A. Rice, pages 662-673. Chicago: The University of Chicago Press, 1931.

methodological procedures when he asserts that he is tolerant of all different approaches in scientific inquiry. Portions of his essays seem to lend support to this view. For example, in his essay on "The Prospects of Economics," written in 1924, Mitchell's enthusiasm for the statistical method seems momentarily to have carried him away. We find him saying that "The extension and improvement of statistical compilations is therefore a factor of the first consequence for the progress of economic theory. Gradually economics will become a quantitative science. It will be less concerned with puzzles about economic motives and more concerned about the objective validity of the account it gives of economic processes. . . . In proportion as economists face real problems they will strive to cast even their general theory into the quantitative mold." [31] And, again, in 1930 he wrote that "Economic theory of the speculative kind is as cheap and easy to produce as higher mathematics or poetry —provided one has the gift. And it has the same problematical relation to reality as do these products of the imagination." [32] From these statements it might appear that Mitchell would like to do for economics what the extremists of the behavioristic school have attempted to do for the science of psychology. Superficially it appears that Mitchell overvalues "objective validity" to the extent of ignoring qualitative considerations relating to the validity of economic doctrines. While some passages in his various writings appear to support such a view, a close examination of his methodology does not support this conclusion. If Mitchell has made little use of the deductive approach to economic studies it is not because he sees little value in such analysis, but because he has felt that the greatest opportunity for immediate improvement lay in an attack upon quantitative problems. As this was the field of inquiry which had been little cultivated at the time that Mitchell began his economic inquiries, it is not surprising that he has spent most of his time in carrying economic analysis "forward to the quantitative stage."

When he comes to consider the role of quantitative analysis in the future advancement of economic science, Mitchell's views on scientific method do seem open to some question. In 1929 he was

[31] Tugwell, R. G., editor, *The Trend of Economics*, 1924, pages 27-28.
[32] Mitchell, Wesley C., "Institutes for Research in the Social Sciences," *The Backward Art of Spending Money*, page 59.

predicting that "there is no doubt that the trend of current work sets strongly in the direction of dealing directly with the concrete and the actual rather than with the abstract and the imaginary. . . . There is a marked disposition to utilize quantitative analysis just as far as the necessary data are available; also, I think, a growing disposition to prefer problems that can be treated in quantitative terms." [33]   While it is quite true that there has been a very considerable increase in recent years in the output of inductive studies, there has been no decline in analytical studies.   The development of the economics of imperfect competition and the analysis of such questions as full employment and the optimum use of resources have given a new impetus to abstract and mathematical approaches in economics.   Cournot has been resurrected, and his mathematical economics has come to enjoy a widespread popularity.   Many economists may have ceased to label themselves as neo-classical, but they are still to be found carrying on the traditions of Marshallian thought as vigorously as ever.   The course of events has shown that Mitchell's expectations about the decline of deductive analysis in the field of economics have turned out to be largely wishful thinking.

In the minds of many economists quantitative analysis has as its prime purpose the statistical verification of the received body of neo-classical doctrine, but this is not Mitchell's view.   In his opinion many of the economic doctrines derived from the qualitative analysis of the nineteenth-century economists can not be verified by statistical analysis.   Instead, the quantitative analysis of the modern economic scene will in some cases call for a restatement of old theories and in other cases the substitution of new theories for old ones.   "Indeed," said Mitchell, "I incline to go further and say that there is slight prospect that quantitative analysis will ever be able to solve the problems that qualitative analysis has framed, in their present form.   What we must expect is a recasting of the old problems into new forms amenable to statistical attack.   In the course of this reformulation of its problems, economic theory will change not merely its complexion but also its content." [34]   Mitchell believes that the quantitative method, besides altering the content of economic theory, will help to bring a new unity into the field of

---

[33] Mitchell, Wesley C., "Economics, 1904-1929," *The Backward Art of Spending Money*, pages 400-401.

[34] "Quantitative Analysis in Economic Theory," page 3.

economic science. Like the other social sciences, economics will have a "common aim—the understanding of human behavior; a common method—the quantitative analysis of behavior records, and a common aspiration—to devise ways of experimenting upon behavior." Specialized quantitative studies will be integrated about an examination of the whole "dominant complex of institutions known as the money economy." Mitchell feels that if this is done, there will be little danger of statistical analysis degenerating into a number of specialized and unrelated economic studies.

Quantitative analysis, in Mitchell's opinion, promises to make other contributions in the field of economic investigation. The difficult problems of economic welfare, for example, may be deprived of some of their abstruseness if economists succeed in expanding the range of objective criteria in the light of which the content of welfare may be examined. For economic welfare has a scientific basis which can be explored, if only we are able to agree on objective measures of welfare. In the work of creating these objective indices of economic welfare Mitchell feels that the quantitative economist will play an increasingly important role in the future. Furthermore, as we make progress in discovering the objective basis of economic welfare, we should be placed in a better position to develop experimental policies and to plan for the future. As we expand our quantitative analysis of the economic system, we will have some scientific measurements of the costs and results of economic experimentation. In this manner, Mitchell believes, quantitative analysis will prove to be "indispensable to convert society's blind fumbling into an intelligent process of experimentation."

Although Mitchell looks forward to a considerable advance in economics as a result of the accumulation of statistical data, the development of statistical technique, and the spread of organized private and public research, he does not allow himself to be carried away by the potential fruitfulness of the quantitative approach. Every methodological approach has its advantages, but where too much reliance is placed upon any one method of analysis unfortunate results may ensue. Reality can be as easily distorted by quantitative analysis as by qualitative analysis. Indeed, statisticians who are not fully aware of the limitations of the quantitative method have distorted economic reality fully as much as those economists who have poured economic life into the rigid molds of mathematico-logical analysis. Mitchell emphatically states that "there is need of critical treatment of statistical procedure in economics . . . there is danger that the seductions of statistical technique may blind enthusiasts to the imperfections and inadequacies of the data. One who elaborates statistical series in ingenious ways may get as far out of touch with reality as one who excogitates a set of speculative assumptions." [35]

It is a tribute to Mitchell's grasp of the problems of methodology in economic science that he should acknowledge that the basic analysis of the economist is always more a matter of qualitative than quantitative considerations. The framework of interpretation into which the economist pours his quantitative or statistical studies is itself a matter of qualitative or deductive analysis. Statistical analysis cannot be applied to the general framework of interpretation that guides that analysis. For this reason we find Mitchell concluding his essay on "Quantitative Analysis in Economic Theory" with the acute observation that, in spite of the rapid advances of the statistical method in the work of economists, "Qualitative distinctions must remain basic in all their work." In spite of his deep admiration for the statistical method of conducting economic investigations, Mitchell never forgets that statistical analysis which is not nurtured by scientific intuition and deductive construction can never be more than a futile measurement of rather meaningless quantitative data. While it may become increasingly true that in economic investigations scientific judgments will be greatly aided by statistical observations, in the final analysis such judgments must rest on a broad basis of common sense which is the monopoly of no one methodological procedure.

The Scope of Economics

In Mitchell's opinion the boundaries of economic science should extend far beyond the limits set by the economists of the nineteenth century. The classical and neo-classical economists did an excellent service in working out their analytical economics. This economics was based on a cross-section of the competitive economy of the past century; and on this basis the older economists constructed a general theory exhibiting a high degree of theoretical refinement and logical consistency. On the basis of a simplified, rationalistic psychology,

[35] *Ibid.*, page 31.

on the assumption of a highly competitive business system, and by the elimination of cultural change, analytical economists perfected a deductive scheme of equilibrium economics which has been of great service to succeeding generations of economists. For some purposes this kind of economics has proven to be quite valuable; and Mitchell is careful to acknowledge its usefulness. This brand of economics has shed considerable light upon the valuation and distributional processes in a competitive economic system, but it has done so only by subjecting economic data to a process of refinement through abstraction and by assuming that the cultural processes were at a standstill. In actual fact, however, the cultural processes have moved on, and the economic world has undergone significant changes since analytical economics was developed and perfected. In order to explain what has happened to the economic system in the past one hundred years, Mitchell feels a need to push economic analysis beyond the boundaries of deductive economics to include a study of our changing economic system, the reasons for its changes, and the probable direction of future change. For this reason he would supplement equilibrium economics with a study of many problems not included by orthodox economists within the scope of their science.

In extending the scope of his science beyond the boundaries of the equilibrium economics of the nineteenth-century economists, Mitchell seeks "to explain at once the current working and the cumulative changing of economic processes." [36] The economists of the last century, having taken a cross-sectional view of the functioning of the economy, necessarily limited their analysis to a study of the current working of their economic system. Such studies of the workings of economic institutions will always, in Mitchell's opinion, remain a very important part of the work of the economist. But to this cross-sectional view of the operations of the economic system, he would add an analysis of the evolution of the economic system. In his view, the scope of economics should include a combination of cross-sectional and evolutionary analyses. There should be no differentiating of economic theory from the study of economic institutions. Mitchell observes that it was Karl Marx who first demonstrated "how the study of the evolution of institutions might be indissolubly joined with an analysis of their workings." Although

[36] "Human Behavior and Economics," page 37.

Mitchell disagrees with much of Marx's economic analysis, he finds in the latter's economics the prototype of the kind of science which he believes to be the proper concern of economists. Its scope would include three broad studies: an investigation of the evolution of economic institutions, an analysis of the current workings of these institutions, and a projection of the current processes of economic change into the future. Since the central problem running through these three types of studies is "the cumulative change of economic institutions," Mitchell describes this type of economics "that deals with a range of problems undreamt of in the philosophy of value and distribution" as "institutional" economics. In this type of economic investigation individual economic behavior is always analyzed with reference to a setting of collective or institutional behavior.

Karl Marx was the originator of institutional economics, for he was the first nineteenth-century economist to direct attention to the processes of institutional change within the economic system. But in Mitchell's judgment, Marx's institutional analysis suffered from two serious defects: he clung to the psychological views of the classical economists, and he permitted Hegelian metaphysics to dominate his views on institutional evolution. For these reasons Mitchell asserts that Veblen was really the first full-fledged exponent of institutional economics. He was the first economist to study institutional evolution in terms of a natural selection which freed his interpretation of cultural processes from any outmoded metaphysical bias. Economic processes are to be explained not by reference to any immanent principle, such as the working out of divine reason, as Adam Smith would have it, nor by reference to the necessary emergence of the socialist state, as Karl Marx would have it. Cultural change is very largely a response to "cumulative changes in the ways of making a living," and consequently existing economic institutions are to be explained objectively in terms of changes in the productive processes. Mitchell asserts that it is not the choice of institutions as an object for scientific analysis that differentiates institutional economics from orthodox economics of the deductive type. Did not Adam Smith devote many pages of his *Wealth of Nations* to a description of the economic institutions of eighteenth-century England? And did not John Stuart Mill and the Benthamites spend a great deal of time on speculations about desirable and undesirable institutions? Adam Smith, the philosophical radicals, and later economists all analyzed the working of their contemporary institutions, showed how the functioning of these institutions promoted or obstructed public welfare, and argued that bad institutions should be abolished to make way for good ones. But institutional change meant to them only a process of reform based upon rational insight into the functioning of social organization.[37] What distinguishes Veblen's institutional analysis from that of his predecessors is his way of investigating the evolution of institutions, and his application of a new conception of human nature to the problem of cultural evolution. This new conception of human nature emphasizes the importance of institutionalized habits in the directing of human behavior. Moreover, it turns the attention of the economic investigator to a consideration of the origins and development of social and economic institutions, because economic behavior is greatly influenced by cultural processes and their changes.

It was not only Veblen who molded Mitchell's views on the nature of economic science. Werner Sombart, who had been a close student of Karl Marx, had a deep influence on Mitchell. What Mitchell finds attractive about Sombart's monumental work on the evolution of the capitalistic system is that it deals with problems scarcely touched upon by books on "economic principles." Sombart has little to say about the problems of value and distribution; he is primarily concerned with the cultural situation described as modern capitalism. He is interested in modern capitalism as a form of economic organization which differs from all preceding forms of economic organization; and he tries to discover how it has come to be what it is, and what shape it will probably take in the future. What Mitchell would like to see is a fusion of the systematic economics of Alfred Marshall and the cultural science of Sombart and Veblen. There should be more linkage between the study of value and distribution and the analysis of the evolution of the capitalistic system. Mitchell points out that "if economics is to give us understanding of economic behavior, treatment of the one set of problems is as indispensable as treatment of the other set. The two approaches [analytical and evolutionary] complement each other, and

---

[37] Mitchell, Wesley C., "Commons on Institutional Economics," *The American Economic Review*, Dec., 1935, Vol. XXV, page 650.

an economist needs intimate acquaintance with both." [38]   The economic theorist needs to be something of an economic historian, just as an economic historian needs to have an understanding of economic theory if his fact gathering is to be really significant. Mitchell is careful to explain that there is no conflict between analytical and institutional economics.   Much of Veblen's writing creates the general impression that the two types of economics are mutually exclusive; indeed, he frequently gave the impression that nineteenth-century economics is entirely outmoded, and that it should be displaced by the newer type of economics of which he was an exponent.   Mitchell is of the opinion that Veblen never intended to give his readers this impression, and that he would have admitted the value of equilibrium economics if he had been pressed to do so.[39]   Veblen was too much inclined to take for granted what was really worth while in neo-classical economics.   If he had admitted a little of his indebtedness to his nineteenth-century predecessors, his own economics might have been more warmly received by his contemporaries.   Unlike Veblen, Mitchell has always been keenly aware of the debt of institutional economists to the economic theorizing of the classical and neo-classical economists; and he feels that economics of the evolutionary type should never be construed as a rival or substitute for orthodox economics.   The two types of economics should be merged to form a twentieth-century body of economic thought.

There is much in common between Mitchell and John R. Commons, who holds that "The problems treated by orthodox theory are genuine problems, and the two sets of discussions should be put into such form that everyone can see how they supplement each other." In explaining how systematic and evolutionary economics reinforce each other, Mitchell explains that economists should be concerned with four types of inquiries which make room for all kinds of contributions.   The first field of inquiry to be included within the scope of economics should be concerned with "the continuous process of providing and using commodities and services," with

[38] Mitchell, Wesley C., "Sombart's Hochkapitalismus," The Quarterly Journal of Economics, Feb., 1929, Vol. XLIII, pages 321-322.

[39] Mitchell, Wesley C., "Thorstein Veblen," The Backward Art of Spending Money, pages 295-296.

those operations which Veblen called the "making of goods." Herein are to be found the work of the farm, the mine, and the factory, all activities which are involved in the production of physical goods and related services. The second field of inquiry which is of interest to the economist is the process of making and spending money, which extends from the preparation of simple family budgets to the activities of high finance. Here physical equipment is of little importance, because capital is expressed in pecuniary form. These two "objective processes" of goods-making and money-making are the basic materials out of which the study of economics is to be made. At some points the two processes are quite distinct even to the point of being opposed to each other. For the most part, however, Mitchell finds that the two processes are usually found "running side by side, concerned with the same objects and supervised by the same men," so that at bottom there is nothing essentially antagonistic between the two phases of economic activity.

Mitchell goes on to explain that "we habitually interpret these two objective processes in terms of personal and social interest. These interpretations give us two other ways of looking at economics." [40] The field of personal interest, the third field of inquiry, is a "dim inner realm of consciousness" into which scientific technique has made few inroads. It is a realm of interest in which there are no technical experts and little is to be found that is really tangible. Consequently, this field of study is one in which Mitchell sees little hope of making much progress with our present limited psychological understanding. The fourth field of inquiry, the communal concern with the activities of goods-making and money-making, is more promising, because community welfare is to some extent more manageable by the scientist than is personal welfare. Here the major interest is in "serviceability to the community" rather than profit to the individual. The economist is especially concerned with the effective utilization of both private and public resources, with social rather than private efficiency. Technical experts in this new field of economic investigation are few in number, but there is a growing body of such people in public and private life. These experts have a difficult task before them, since they have shifted their interest from the concept of private capital to what

[40] "The Role of Money in Economic Theory," page 173.

Mitchell calls the broader concept of communal resources. These resources include "soil and climate, mines and forests, industrial equipment, public health, intelligence and general education, the sciences that confer control over nature, the sciences that aid in developing body and mind, and the sciences that bear upon social organization." All these resources constitute the foundation of that "commonweal" which is so frequently uppermost in Mitchell's mind.

How does Mitchell introduce order into this broad scope of economics which he has outlined? What is to be the center about which his economic analysis is to revolve? Mitchell's answer to these queries is that into "our conjoint attack" upon the four fields of economic interest outlined above "a clear recognition of the role played by money promises to bring more definite order and more effective cooperation. Among economic institutions the money institution is outstanding as a great rationalizing habit. About the use of money has grown up the whole business system which has given capitalism its characteristic qualities. The use of money gives society the technical machinery of exchange, the opportunity to combine personal freedom with orderly cooperation on a grand scale, and the basis of that system of accounting which Sombart appropriately calls 'economic rationalism.' It is the foundation of that complex system of prices to which the individual must adjust his behavior in getting a living. Since it molds his objective behavior, it becomes part of his subjective life, giving him a method and an instrument for the difficult task of assessing the relative importance of dissimilar goods in varying quantities, and affecting the interests in terms of which he makes his valuations." [41] Thus the money institution's influence penetrates all fields of economic activity. It dominates the activity of the farm, the mine, and the factory; and it also penetrates into the family household routine. It is not a mere counting device for the convenience of those who frequent the market place, but, on the contrary, it is a potent institution which colors life in many devious ways. What makes economic life rational is not some calculating faculty of the human mind but the whole institutional complex which is built up about the use of money. Man as an economic agent does not choose to

[41] *Ibid.*, pages 170-171.

be rational; instead, he is induced to follow the path of rational action by behavior habits which flow from the use of money in our daily routine.

Mitchell has devoted a great portion of his intellectual energies to an exposition of the role that money plays in contemporary civilization. Unlike Veblen, Tawney, the Webbs, Hobson, and Sombart, he has not allowed his intellectual curiosity to carry him over into a study of large cultural areas. Instead he has kept his interests tied to the combination of institutions known as the business system. He has done this because he has felt that economics would progress faster if more were known about the role of money in economic activity. An economics oriented about the institution of money will, in Mitchell's opinion, bring many advances in economic science. It will bridge the gap between economic theory and economic history by providing a unifying principle for studies of how economic organization has developed in the past, how it now functions, and how it will probably change in the future. This new economics will bring proper attention to the problem of the relations between business management and industrial efficiency. In addition, Mitchell believes that his economics will make economic theory "more useful," since it will direct attention to the actual problems confronting government in the work of social and economic reorganization. The analysis of economic activity from the monetary viewpoint will be more objective than much of the older economic thought, because it will be amenable to historical and statistical treatment. When economic analysis becomes increasingly objective, hypotheses will be stated in ways that will facilitate their "practical testing." Mitchell concludes with the observation that "Clear recognition of the role which money does play in economic life is more likely to broaden than to narrow the scope of economic theory. It should help us to design what we sorely need, a framework within which all sorts of contributions may find their proper places." [42]

The scope of Mitchell's economics may therefore be said to include investigations relating to the industrial process of making goods, the business process of making money, the way in which these two sets of economic activities are related to each other, the way they are related to the individual's inner life or personal wel-

[42] "The Role of Money in Economic Theory," page 172.

fare, and, finally, the way in which they are related to the "interests of social welfare." Such a framework of investigation differs considerably from that of the neo-classical economists, whose interests were largely limited to problems of value and distribution. Mitchell's economics would include price and distribution analysis, but it would also find a place for a consideration of the evolution of economic institutions and their relation to economic welfare. Mitchell observes that in the past century "the chief aim of economic investigation has been the understanding of how economic processes actually work. Hence analytical and genetic economics have been in the foreground." Since the turn of the century, however, economic interests have undergone considerable change, so that "Now our interest in economics centers in its bearing upon social welfare in the present and proximate future." Economists of the nineteenth century had always expressed an interest in social welfare, but they did not make it the ultimate subject of their theoretical interest. Without the pragmatic bias of the twentieth century, they were more interested in scientific explanation *per se* than an analysis of the implications of their scientific knowledge for the improvement of economic welfare. As a consequence of his pragmatic bent, Mitchell orients his "quantitative economics" about considerations relating to economic welfare. It is this instrumentalistic flavor which very definitely sets Mitchell's economics apart from the economics of his orthodox precursors.

This is not to say, however, that Mitchell devotes the major portion of his intellectual energies to a consideration of problems of economic welfare. It is obvious to anyone who is acquainted with his work that Mitchell has spent most of his time in the field of quantitative economics with special reference to the recent course of the business system. Very early he discovered that the "successful prosecution on a scientific basis" of studies in the field of economic welfare "presupposes considerable knowledge of how economic processes actually work at present," and since this requisite economic knowledge was not adequately available, he directed his early scientific efforts to the work of improving our understanding of the working of the economic system.[43] After several decades of close observation of the functioning of the business system, Mitchell is turning more and more to the neglected field of normative economics. He

[43] *Ibid.*, page 175.

appears to feel that economics has now made sufficient progress to warrant an application of our existing knowledge to the problem of augmenting economic welfare; consequently, in recent years a number of essays dealing with the nature of economic welfare and how it may be increased have come from his pen.[44]   Although he is still carrying on the work of scientific interpretation, especially in relation to the ups and downs of the business system, he believes that the time is now at hand for putting our scientific knowledge to work.   As he expresses it, economists should no longer "maintain a serene indifference to the fate of mankind."

The Theory of Economic Guidance

The view of the economic system which Mitchell held at the time that he wrote his *Business Cycles* (1913), and which appears in substantially the same form in the 1927 edition of his cycle study, is quite different from that of the orthodox economists.   The economic system which nineteenth-century economists were concerned about explaining was a competitive world exhibiting a high degree of economic balance.   Industry was small-scale, decentralized, and dominated by capitalist-employers who successfully combined the managerial and risk-taking functions.   By a process of abstraction orthodox economists arrived at a view of the economic system in which a state of equilibrium was the prevailing condition. Although equilibrium might not be achieved in complete detail, all the fundamental tendencies were supposed to operate in that direction.   The even processes of the market system were not upset by wide inequalities in the distribution of income; and business crises were regarded only as "sudden catastrophes which interrupt the normal" course of business.   Such interruptions were no more than a passing phase of the movement of the economic system toward a condition of general economic balance.

The view of the economic system that is basic in Mitchell's economic analysis differs from this orthodox view in many significant ways.   His "framework of economic culture" is built about a view of the economic system in which the large corporation plays a dominant role in finance, wholesale trade, transportation, manufacturing

---

[44] Indicative of recent trends in Mitchell's economic thought are such essays as "Social Science and National Planning" (1935) and "Intelligence and the Guidance of Economic Evolution" (1936).

and the extractive industries.   Mitchell draws attention to the un-even development of business enterprise in various fields.   No longer do we have the same general type of small-scale enterprise throughout the various areas of economic activity, for the homo-geneous world of orthodox economics has given place to the hetero-geneous economic system of today in which small-scale and large-scale enterprise exist side by side.   Although the "spirit of business enter-prise" has not yet made much progress among professional workers, farmers, small retailers and those who produce certain handicraft products, it has found a fertile field in those industries which have made the most rapid technological progress.   In Mitchell's hybrid picture, with its survivals of an earlier highly competitive system, the center of interest is the "typical corporate enterprises," for "it is within the circles of full-fledged business enterprise that the alter-nations of prosperity and depression appear most clearly, and pro-duce their most striking effects." [45]   What affects the large-scale corporate enterprises affects also the entire economic system, for there is a "thoroughgoing interdependence of business enterprises." It is this mutual interdependence which makes the business system a process and not a mere agglomeration of many separate producing units.   In Mitchell's view the economic system is like a living or-ganism which is a complex of many interconnected processes subject to all the vagaries of an ever-changing world.

In Mitchell's interpretation of the economic system there are three economic processes running side by side.   These are the "business" process of making money, the "industrial" process of manufacturing and transporting goods, and the "commercial" proc-ess of collecting and distributing goods.   The business system is primarily concerned with the making of profits, and so from "the business standpoint the useful goods produced or helpful services rendered are merely by-products of the process of earning divi-dends." [46]   The industrial and commercial processes are concerned with goods-making rather than money-making.   In orthodox theory the money-making and goods-making functions were supposed to operate in such harmony that there would be no conflict between

---

[45] Mitchell, Wesley C., *Business Cycles, The Problem and Its Setting*, page 87. New York: National Bureau of Economic Research, Inc., 1927.

[46] For his general view of the economic system Mitchell drew heavily from Veblen's *The Theory of Business Enterprise*, which was published in 1904.

the individual's profit-making activities and the national interest in the provision of an adequate supply of goods and services. In Mitchell's view of the economic system there is no such harmony to be found between the provision of money incomes and the production of commodities and services: "For the well-being of the community, efficient industry and commerce are vastly more important than successful money-making. . . . But the whip-hand among these three processes belongs none the less to business, since the very men who as manufacturers and merchants provide for the common welfare base their operations on the prospect of money profits. In practice, industry and commerce are thoroughly subordinated to business." [47] The control of the industrial system by businessmen would in itself be a problem of small importance were it not that the businessmen's control of economic life is accompanied by the evils of the business cycle. Since the industrial system is periodically convulsed by crises and depressions, which seriously restrict the material well-being of the community, the guidance of economic activity by businessmen becomes a highly important issue. While the industrial system is subordinate to the business system, the business system is in turn dominated by the factors which control present and prospective profits. At this point in his analysis Mitchell introduces his views on the nature and significance of the system of prices. He explains that economists of the past century went below "the money surface of things," because they felt that money and prices were phenomena quite secondary to the more ultimate factors of costs and utilities. In Mitchell's analysis the price system is itself an object of primary interest, for it has a very important function to perform "in the economic life of nations. It serves as a social mechanism for carrying on the process of providing goods. . . . Prices also render possible the rational direction of economic activity by accounting, for accounting is based upon the principle of representing all the heterogeneous commodities, services, and rights with which a business enterprise is concerned in terms of money price. Most important of all, the margins between different prices within the system hold out that hope of pecuniary profit, which is the motive power that drives our business world." [48]

[47] *Business Cycles,* 1913, page 25.
[48] *Ibid.,* pages 31-32.

In the classical view of the economic system the values which arose in the market place were reflections of both individual and community choices.[49] The competitive pricing process was highly efficient since it met all the requirements of the individual, and at the same time it provided for the most efficient utilization of society's natural and human resources. In Mitchell's analysis of the economic system individuals and society are frequently at odds because of the conflict between the private quest for profits and the public quest for general welfare. The goods that are sold are not always the ones that are most needed by the community, since goods are sold for a profit and not in response to the demands of social efficiency: "If the test of efficiency in the direction of economic activity be that of determining what needs are most important for the common welfare and then satisfying them in the most economical manner, the present system is subject to a further criticism."[50] In Mitchell's opinion price is a most unsatisfactory measure of human needs. It is possible that in a small-scale, competitive economic system with a fairly equal distribution of national income, market price might be a more satisfactory measure of human wants than it now is; but in the modern world of large-scale corporate enterprise price is becoming increasingly inadequate as a measure of human needs. And this is all the more so where we observe wide disparities in the incomes going to various social classes. For these reasons Mitchell observes that "in nations where a few have incomes sufficient to gratify trifling whims and where many cannot buy things required to maintain their own efficiency or to give proper training to their children, it can hardly be argued that the goods which pay best are the goods most needed."[51]

The theory of economic guidance provided by the nineteenth-century economists was quite simple. The entrepreneurs, as capitalist-employers, occupied the key positions in the economic system.

[49] John B. Clark pointed out in *The Distribution of Wealth*, 1927 (pp. 243-244), that "If we were here undertaking to present at length the theory of value, we should lay great stress on the fact that value is a social phenomenon. Things sell, indeed, according to their final utilities, but it is their final utilities *to society*." In Clark's analysis society as a whole, "the great composite consumer," is the appraiser of goods and the determiner of their relative utilities. The individual is supposed to fit neatly into this scheme of social valuations so that there is no conflict between the processes of individual and social valuation.

[50] *Business Cycles*, 1913, page 39.

[51] *Ibid.*

It was they who brought together land, labor, and capital, and combined them in the most efficient manner in response to the demands of the final consumers. Rational consumers and investors, guided by the principles of marginal utility and maximization of returns, called forth from businessmen the most efficient use of natural and human resources and the maximum satisfaction of consumer desires. The net result was the satisfaction of the most urgent economic needs of the community with a minimum of waste in either materials or human effort.

Mitchell's theory of guidance offers many striking contrasts to this orthodox theory of economic guidance. He argues that the introduction of corporate enterprise has resulted in a separation of ownership and management, which has led to a concentration of power in the hands of a limited number of active directors and high officials. Those who control the affairs of corporations are in a position to operate their enterprises in their own interest rather than in the interest of the stockholders and bondholders. Even small enterprises, though legally free to act as they wish, find themselves required to adopt a follow-the-leader policy which forces them into subjection to larger enterprises. Over the modern economic scene there hovers an influence which, in its power to direct economic activity, is superior to the few directors and high officials who dominate corporate policy. This is the financial power of lenders, of the banks and large capitalists, who act as a "higher court" in making important decisions with respect to the use of equipment and labor. Because of their power of review, the dominant financial interests are in a position to promote what appear to be desirable projects and to discourage those that do not find favor. The small individual investors now play a minor role, since they are unable to make intelligent decisions about how savings should be invested in the modern world of large-scale corporate activity. "The great mass of small investors," wrote Mitchell, "and not a few of the large, lack the experience or the ability to discriminate wisely between profitable and unprofitable schemes. . . . Not being able to obtain from impartial sources or personal examination the data necessary for forming an independent judgment, they cannot work out their problems along strictly rational lines. Hence they are peculiarly subject to the influence of feeling in matters where feeling is a dangerous guide. . . . Even those who are looked to for advice are not wholly immune from the contagion of emotional aberration. It follows that the guidance of economic activity by the investing class is not strictly comparable with the intelligent review of plans by competent experts." [52]   The investment process of today is far removed from the simple picture presented by nineteenth-century economists. To be sure, the large financial interests do provide some intelligent leadership, but there are many temptations to raise private welfare above that of the great masses of investors. For this reason the financial process directing the flow of investment funds and the industrial process concerned with the production of goods frequently fail to follow the parallel courses mapped out by the exponents of economic orthodoxy.

Mitchell also deviates very considerably from the traditional view of the role of the consumer in the guidance of economic activity. In the classical analysis consumers comprise a "court of last resort" that decides what goods will be produced. Producers are supposed to follow the leads supplied by the consumers themselves, so that not only do the original impulses toward consumption come from the consumers, but also the specific types of things wanted are determined by the consumers and not by the producers. Mitchell finds that the analysis of consumption presented by many of the current economic treatises is "an undeserved compliment to the mental energy of mankind." Buyers do not come into the market with their minds already settled about the kinds of goods they wish to purchase and about the prices that they are willing to pay for various amounts of these goods. The "average shopper" is possessed of neither the time nor the ability to make a satisfactory survey of the market's many diverse offerings. Since consumers are conscious only of the general outlines of their various needs, the specific goods which are actually purchased to meet these needs are offered by the producers rather than chosen by the consumers. It is a favorite theme of Mitchell that the spending of money is a "backward art" which does not place consumers in a very favorable light, and that the art of consumption has been a subject of more interest to the businessman and his advertising managers than to the general body of purchasing citizens. As a consequence of this backward state of the consumptive arts, consumers exert their in-

[52] *Ibid.,* page 35.

fluence upon the course of economic activity only in a very weak, indirect manner. They usually follow the path of least resistance in satisfying their various needs; they buy commodities in accordance with the dictates of long-standing customs or the success of advertising campaigns and high-pressure salesmanship. In place of "reflective choice" as a key to the understanding of consumer behavior, Mitchell finds that the "psychological categories important to the understanding of consumer demand are habit, imitation, and suggestion—not reflective choice." [53] Besides consumers' habits of spending the investigator would have to analyze the various factors controlling the distribution of income if he were to obtain an adequate explanation of consumer demand.[54]

Nevertheless, in spite of the rather passive reaction of consumers to the problem of guiding economic activity, the general body of consumers remains in a potentially very strong market position. Businessmen are constantly aware of this fact, and are ever alert in their efforts to "educate the public." There is always the possibility of consumers becoming that "final arbiter of production" about which the nineteenth-century economists hypothesized, but this can come about only after the arts of consumption have become much less backward than Mitchell found them in the early decades of the present century.

Writing in 1913 Mitchell found the role of government in the guidance of economic activity to be a very minor one.[55] In theory

[53] Not only is the practice of consumption backward, but also the theory of consumption has long been neglected by orthodox economists. While Mitchell was working on his analysis of the business cycle there were some indications of a growing interest in the theory and practice of consumption. Mitchell found evidence of this new interest in the economics of consumption in such works as Hazel Kyrk's *A Theory of Consumption,* 1923, and Henry Harap's *The Education of the Consumer,* 1924.

[54] *Business Cycles, The Problem and Its Setting,* 1927, page 167. It is interesting to note that Mitchell draws attention to "this fascinating line of analysis" as it relates to consumer demand, but that he does not himself follow it out. He feels that such analyses are certainly not irrelevant, but he does not allow them to direct his energies away from his major interest in the problem of the business cycle. Throughout his essays and treatises one finds many such interesting suggestions which are not followed up by further intensive analysis. Such analyses would have gone far in rounding out Mitchell's somewhat restricted economic studies.

[55] In the 1927 revision of his business cycle study Mitchell still found that government was only a "disturbing factor" in the flow of economic activity. It was not until after the depression of 1929 that Mitchell found government to be an

government aims at securing public welfare, while business aims at making money.   In practice, however, this difference in goals loses much of its significance, for there are tremendous obstacles to the pursuit of public welfare in modern industrialized nations.   The concept of public welfare is itself so vague that it is difficult to secure much agreement about various public policies affecting welfare.   But more important than the vagueness of the concept of public welfare is the habituation of a business economy, which leads individuals to apply pecuniary tests and standards to matters of public interest.   Mitchell finds that the citizens of a money economy have "a strong commercial flavor to their very statesmanship."   Yet, in spite of the many difficulties which surround its activities, the government manages to keep closer to "fundamental issues" than most businessmen.   In its own hesitant and indirect fashion it has managed to surround the pursuit of the "artificial" aim of pecuniary profit with a large number of restrictions and safeguards.   Unfortunately, most of these governmental regulations are negative in character so that they provide practically nothing in the nature of real direction for economic activity.   Lacking a clear understanding of the nature of public welfare, and not being free from the contamination of pecuniary standards and ideals, governments have been able to make little progress in providing guidance for the modern economic system.

As a consequence of the inability of the community to substitute adequate public guidance for the economic guidance provided by the businessman, there has arisen a conflict between individual efficiency in the making of profits and social efficiency in the augmenting of public welfare.   There has resulted a planlessness in the production of goods and services.   The business economy "provides for effective coordination of efforts within each business enterprise, but not for effective coordination of effort among independent enterprises. . . .   Coordination within an enterprise is the result of careful planning by experts; coordination among independent enterprises cannot be said to be planned at all; rather is it the unplanned result of natural selection in a struggle for business

active agent in the directing of economic activity.   From this date on Mitchell comes to have an interest in the large problem of national economic planning which presupposes government as an active force in the directing of the general trends of economic life.

survival. . . . As a result of these conditions, coordination within an enterprise is characterized by economy of effort; coordination among independent enterprises by waste." [56] What modern economic culture lacks is a "common programme." It has neither a general plan nor a central direction. Private initiative has made great strides in the recent past, but thus far social intelligence has not been organized to provide any systematic plan for meeting the economic needs of the masses. Private business enterprise has come up against a type of problem that is not to be solved by greater reliance on the managerial skill of business enterprises. Mitchell feels that for private-business skills and standards should be substituted different skills and standards which look beyond the quest for pecuniary gain to the raising of the general level of human living.

Mitchell's Theory of the Business Cycle

The economic activity which interests Mitchell does not display that balance and regularity of movement which are such prominent features of the economic activity described by orthodox economics. He asserts that ever since mankind has had any sort of trade or business it has been subjected to many kinds of crises and disturbances. The business systems of antiquity and of the Middle Ages suffered from such random disturbances as wars, population movements, and various "acts of God." After the emergence of commercial capitalism economic fluctuations took on a special significance, and it then became apparent that the business system was itself responsible in part for the uneven course of economic activity. To external factors leading to disturbance were now added internal factors which had their origins in the business system itself. In the course of time economists came to realize that business fluctuations exhibited something of a general pattern which could be summed up under the terms of expansion and contraction. During the nineteenth century the business cycle came to be recognized as a regularly recurring feature of the capitalistic

[56] *Business Cycles,* 1913, page 38. As the decades passed, Mitchell's opinion about the planlessness of the business system was strengthened and not weakened by the course of events. In writing the first annual report for the National Resources Planning Board in 1934 Mitchell incorporates this description of the business system which he had written twenty-one years earlier. See the *Final Report,* 1933-34, of the National Planning Board, page 21.

system that merited scientific attention. Business cycle analysis during the past century suffered, however, not only from a paucity of information relating to the general condition of business at various stages of the cyclical rhythm, but also from a lack of statistical techniques for the handling of large masses of economic data. Economic thought in general was highly speculative and deductive; and even where an attempt was made to inquire into historical facts, the investigator could not get very far beyond mere description. Attempts to indicate the importance of various economic factors or conditions were fruitless because the tools for scientific measurement were not yet available. It is not surprising, therefore, that nineteenth-century business cycle theory turned out to be as highly deductive and speculative as the general body of economic theorizing of the times. Cycle theorists were no special group of economists set off from the general community of social scientists by virtue of their superior methods or more realistic analyses. Not being in a position to handle the cycle problem successfully in an inductive fashion, the early cycle theorists were prone to seek out some special cause or causes as explanations of the cyclical behavior of the business system. Even where early cycle theorists paid particular attention to the historical data relating to business fluctuations, they were unable to penetrate the maze of economic data in order to measure the importance of the various factors at work. In this situation economic description was used merely to lend additional support to conclusions already arrived at in a deductive fashion.

Yet for the pioneers in cycle analysis Mitchell has nothing but deep admiration. Despite the limits of their scientific methodology and the difficulty of securing adequate information they had performed an admirable service in laying the foundation for future progress in cycle analysis. The twentieth century, however, was to bring to students of business fluctuations two aids which had been denied to the pioneers in this work: a changed theory of causation, and new statistical techniques for the handling of masses of economic data. Mitchell has relied very heavily upon both of these scientific aids in the work of advancing our understanding of the cyclical trends of the business system. In his pioneering study of the business cycle Mitchell informs his readers that he has shifted from a "causal theory" to "an analytic description" of the cycle.

He describes the cycle theory of the nineteenth-century economists as "causal" because they were primarily interested in discovering "the cause" of the cycle. Their usual procedure was to single out the recurrent fluctuations of some single economic process, and then to attach special causal importance to the chosen process. This procedure was in accordance with the theory of causation which dominated much of the social science of the past century. According to this theory it was deemed possible to uncover the cause or causes of particular results or effects to be observed in the world of social relations. Presently, however, as the complexity of social relations became better understood by social scientists, it was realized that such a simple theory of causation had little application to sociological, political, and economic problems.[57] It was discovered that there were many conditions which were responsible for particular effects in the social world, so that it was unscientific to label any one condition or a few conditions as "the cause" of a particular social or economic situation.

Adopting the new theory of causation, Mitchell transfers his attention from "the cause" of business cycles to "the conditions" which collectively produce the cyclical movements of the business system. He explains that "as our knowledge grows wider and more intimate, our attitude toward the discussion of causes undergoes a subtle change. When we have accounted in causal terms for each stage in a lengthy series of actions and reactions, we find that our analysis deals with many causes each one of which is logically indispensable to the theory we have elaborated. . . . All the conditions which are indispensable to produce a certain result stand on much the same footing from the viewpoint of science." [58] A cause is a factor which produces, or is especially responsible for, a certain effect or result, whereas a condition is anything that is essential or necessary for the bringing about of a certain result. A condition cannot be said to cause any result to come about, since only the totality of conditions may be said to be the cause that produces a

---

[57] The first abandonment of this simple theory of causation came in the field of the physical sciences where scientists became increasingly more interested in "how" various results came about and less interested in "why" they came about. Some scientists have sought to abandon the theory of causation in its entirety. Cf. Wolf, A., *Essentials of Scientific Method*, Second Edition, pages 106-112. London: G. Allen and Unwin, Ltd., 1928.

[58] *Business Cycles, The Problem and Its Setting*, 1927, pages 54-55.

certain result. In turning his attention to the many conditions that together bring about the result described as the business cycle, Mitchell does not attempt to point out any single cause or any few causes of the cyclical movement of the business system. He is not interested, however, in analyzing every condition that might conceivably contribute to the recurring fluctuations of the business system. His aim is not to provide a complete description of every aspect of the many-sided problem of the cycle. What Mitchell proposes to do is to provide an analytical description of the business cycle which would be a selective type of description designed to consider only the typical conditions that are indispensable to the production of the business cycle.

The questions may be asked: what does Mitchell mean by an "analytic description" of the business cycle, and how does it differ from ordinary description? His answer is that "A systematic account of cyclical fluctuations, taken seriously, becomes an analytic description of the processes by which a given phase of business activity presently turns into another phase." [59] This "systematic account" of cycles is obtained through the application of quantitative methods. Mitchell is ready to appraise concrete events such as are considered by the historian, but he goes further than the economic historian by arraying concrete events in statistical groups. Thus he extracts something of a statistical pattern out of the welter of historical, concrete data relating to business cycles; and analytical description then becomes a fusion of ordinary description and statistical analysis. It differs on the one hand from mere description, which lacks a systematic basis, and, on the other, from causal theory, which has an excessively deductive bias. Ordinary description deals with the actual cycles of historical records with all their diversity and irregularities, while causal theory of the nineteenth-century type dealt with "cycles of some speculative construction." Analytical description strikes a middle ground between mere description and causal theory of a deductive nature. It is concerned with what Mitchell calls cycles of an intermediate order which would be neither historical nor speculative but "typical" cycles. "We shall seek," he says, "to find what features have been characteristic of all or most cycles, and to concentrate attention upon them,

[59] See Mitchell's article on business cycles in the *Encyclopaedia of the Social Sciences*, Vol. III, page 100.

paying less attention to features which have been peculiar to one or a few cases."

Mitchell begins his analysis of the business cycle by refraining from making a definition of the general concept of the cycle. In both the first and second editions of his *Business Cycles* Mitchell does not undertake to formulate a definite conception of the cycle until he has reached the concluding portions of his work. He finds it more profitable to elaborate upon the facts first, and to defer consideration of a theory of the cycle until a later stage in the investigation. "An inquiry into business cycles," he writes, "cannot wisely begin by defining the general concept, and proceed systematically to take up one part of the whole after another. It should begin rather with the individual processes which can be studied objectively, seeking to find what these processes are, how they affect each other, and what sort of whole they make up." Of course, Mitchell realizes that no investigator can begin his study of facts without certain theoretical considerations to provide some sort of guidance. In his own case he begins his investigation of the cycle with pre-established views about the nature of modern economic organization and especially about the role played by the money institution.[60] These general theoretical considerations could hardly be said to constitute a theory of the business cycle. What Mitchell hopes to arrive at, eventually, is a theory of the cycle, but he regards his first two volumes on the cycle as being only preliminary work which provides a working definition. In the second edition of his *Business Cycles* (1927) Mitchell informs the reader that his "theory of business cycles" was deferred to Volume II which was soon to have been published. Since this proposed second volume, to be entitled *"The Rhythm of Business Activity,"* has not yet appeared, we must

---

[60] Whether one works from theory to facts or from facts to theory depends upon the kind of problem that is being investigated. In view of all the cycle theories that were current at the time that he worked on the cycle, Mitchell felt that the best procedure was to elaborate upon the facts rather than the theoretical considerations: "Whether it is better to begin a particular task by elaborating upon the theoretical conceptions employed, saying little about the facts for the moment; or to begin by elaborating upon the facts, saying little about theories for the moment, depends upon the problem in hand and upon the contribution which the investigator hopes to make toward its solution. In an investigation of moment, both the theory and the facts are elaborated at various stages of the proceedings, each by the aid of the other, and late workers start with a fact-theory blend improved by the new contribution." See *Business Cycles, The Problem and Its Setting,* 1927, pages 59-60 fn.

regard Mitchell's cycle analysis as an extensive introduction to the subject. In his 1927 volume on business cycles Mitchell did little more than "frame a working definition to use in trying to learn more—a definition which presumably will require modification as knowledge grows." [61] In the years since 1927 Mitchell has pushed his cycle analysis to more advanced levels where he has perfected various measures of cyclical behavior.[62] He has also been concerned with getting the information which is necessary to advance beyond his 1913 business cycle study.

When Mitchell begins his study of the business cycle by turning to facts rather than to general theoretical considerations, there immediately arises the problem of deciding what facts are to be studied. If analytical description is concerned with the various processes at work within the cycle, there is the question of deciding what processes are to be selected for analysis, since all economic processes are not related in time to the business cycle. Some economic activities have rhythms which originate in technical conditions not very closely related to the rhythm of general business. In searching out the economic processes operating within the business cycle, Mitchell proceeds in a very pragmatic fashion. He points out that "In working, we must be prepared to study any feature of modern life which appears to be intimately related to business fluctuations." Always keeping this pragmatic test in mind, he places special reliance upon three sources in determining what should be included within the boundaries of his investigation. These three sources are the cycle theories worked out by other investigators, the historical records of general business conditions in various industrialized countries, and the collections of economic statistics. It is the business annals that provide the general pattern of the cycle, "the recurrence of the prosperity-recession-depression-revival sequence." Not only do the business annals provide a general pattern of the cycle, but they also furnish the investigator with a set of "reference dates" or "bench marks" which mark off successive revivals and re-

---

[61] With reference to this statement Mitchell, in 1942, commented as follows: "Quite so in the 1927 volume. In the 1913 volume I did attempt more. What I am now attempting is to get the knowledge needed to do the 1913 job much better."

[62] Mitchell, along with Arthur F. Burns, has recently completed a statistical study entitled *Measuring Business Cycles.* New York: National Bureau of Economic Research, 1946.

cessions in general business. Such reference dates may then be used to determine whether the cycles in various time series are systematically related in time to the fluctuations of general business. From the numerous works of other theorists an insight is gained into the complexity of cyclical fluctuations, as attention is called to the many economic processes that have been made the basis of a large number of different cycle theories. In using the theories of his predecessors and contemporaries, however, Mitchell does not seek to present an "eclectic patchwork" of existing theories. The end result which he seeks to achieve is a "systematic account of all the relevant phenomena." The third source of information and guidance, the collections of economic statistics, is valuable because it provides a means of testing the elements of the general pattern of the business cycle derived from an analysis of business annals and various theories of the cycle. Furthermore, these economic statistics provide a means for studying the differences in the amplitude and timing of various economic processes; and they reveal the extent to which cyclical fluctuations in economic processes occur in combination with secular, seasonal, irregular, and other fluctuations. The collections of economic statistics also help to make clear that "a business cycle is a highly complex congeries of fluctuations in different processes."

As a result of his analysis of business annals, cycle theories, and collections of economic statistics, Mitchell has made "the recurrence of the prosperity-recession-depression-revival sequence" the basic element in his conception of the business cycle. He tentatively defines business cycles to be "a type of fluctuation characteristic of economic activities organized in the form of business economy or 'high capitalism,' to use the German term. They have a wavelike pattern—each cycle includes a phase of revival, expansion, recession, and contraction." [63] An analysis of this four-phase cycle could very well start at any point in the cycle which the investigator wishes to take as his point of departure. In Mitchell's analysis the starting point is the bottom of the depression phase of the cycle. After the depression has gone on for some time, it is only a question of time until an expansion of the physical volume of trade turns dullness

---

[63] "Business Cycles," *Encyclopaedia of the Social Sciences*, Vol. III, page 92. See also *Business Cycles, The Problem and Its Setting*, page 468, and *Measuring Business Cycles*, page 3.

into activity.   To be sure, some favorable events such as large governmental purchases or good harvests may hasten the process of recovery, but if these unusual events do not make their appearance,
Mitchell believes that it is only a question of time until the expansion of the physical volume of trade turns depression into recovery.
At this early stage of his analysis he introduces his theory of the
recurrence of the cycle.   The depression phase merges into the recovery phase with or without the aid of any "propitious events,"
since this period of the cycle contains within itself the seeds that
will inevitably germinate and flower into the following period of
recovery.   In turn, recovery merges into prosperity.   The prosperity period then breeds the stresses which ultimately alter the
very conditions upon which prosperity itself rests.   The two important stresses to which Mitchell calls attention are the increase
in supplementary costs and the growing tension in the investment
markets.   Although Mitchell did not go out of his way to stress the
importance of durable-goods industries in his first study of the
cycle, he did indicate that the industries which produce capital
equipment are especially sensitive to the fluctuations of the business
system.[64]   He explains in his first edition of *Business Cycles* (1913)
that "There is one important group of enterprises which suffers an
especially severe check from this cause, the accumulating tension in
the investment and money markets in conjunction with high prices
—the group which depends primarily upon the demand for industrial equipment.   In the earlier stages of prosperity, this group
usually enjoys a season of exceptionally intense activity.   But when
the market for bonds becomes stringent, and—what is often more
important—when the cost of construction becomes high, business
enterprises and individual capitalists alike defer the execution of
many plans for extending old and erecting new plants.   As a result, contracts for this kind of work become less numerous as the
climax of prosperity approaches." [65]   Strains of various kinds appear first in industries concerned with producers' goods and not
those dealing with consumers' goods, since decreases in consumer
purchasing power follow reductions in the payrolls of the producer-goods industries.

[64] Cf. Clark, John M., *Strategic Factors in Business Cycles*, pages 191-192.   New
York: National Bureau of Economic Research, 1934.

[65] *Business Cycles*, 1913, pages 501-502, and 574.

As depression merges into recovery, and recovery into prosperity, it is again only "a question of time" until the conditions of stress bred by prosperity require some radical readjustments. Prosperity then merges into a period of depression. During the early period of the depression phase of the cycle the contraction in physical volume of trade and the accompanying fall in prices reduce the margins of profit, but at the same time certain processes of readjustment are set in motion. It is through these processes of readjustment that the depression phase of the cycle is gradually overcome. Eventually the demand for commodities ceases to shrink, and after a time it begins to expand. At this point in his analysis Mitchell has returned to his original starting point. He explains the eventual conversion of depression into recovery by pointing to factors which cumulatively bring about recovery with or without the aid of external, propitious factors. Depression sooner or later turns into recovery because stocks of goods are wiped out and have to be replaced, population continues to increase, new tastes are developed and new methods of production are devised, and investment demand revives.

In developing his business cycle theory Mitchell has made special use of two organons of thought, namely, the theory of cultural cumulation and the theory of recurrence. According to the theory of cultural cumulation, economic activity in its larger aspects is a cumulative process. Superimposed on this slow, cumulative process may be such novel and irregular developments as wars, governmental programs, and innovations resulting from inventions and new popular tastes. But beneath these irregular and disturbing occurrences is the more basic cumulative movement of economic activity proceeding by small degrees and at a comparatively slow tempo. Cultural anthropologists and sociologists have employed a similar theory in their interpretation of cultural developments. They have pointed out that cultural activity is never at a standstill even in those periods when there is no rapid development of cultural patterns. In the absence of unusual causes of cultural disturbance such as population movements, wars, and inventions, cultural activity consists of a slow process of piling up or cumulation. In these circumstances change occurs very gradually, and it is usual to speak of a merging process in which one cultural situation slowly develops into another. Like the cultural anthropologists and sociologists, Mitchell writes about the "cumulative processes" of the business cycle and the "merging" of depression into recovery and recovery into prosperity.

In the work of the cultural anthropologists the theory of cultural cumulation is usually not associated with a theory of cultural recurrence.   Cultural cumulation, at least in its larger aspects, leads to new stages of cultural development but not to recurring cycles of cultural evolution.   Some cultural scientists have endeavored to show that the cultures of nations do move in cycles, but such analysis is still largely in the very speculative stage.   Thus far the theory of cultural cumulation has been more successfully applied to unilinear than to cyclical movements in culture.

In Mitchell's business cycle theory economic processes are held to be recurring as well as cumulative; each phase of the cycle merges into the next phase so that there is a continuous round of cycles. In each phase of the cycle the various movements of the business system tend to be self-reinforcing rather than self-limiting.   These movements carry on until they have gone so far that a reversal of some kind becomes inevitable.   In this situation each phase is a kind of incubatory period out of which the succeeding phase finally emerges.   Thus the responses of the business system to changes in prices and in profit margins comprise what J. M. Clark has described as "a closely-knit sequence of cause and effect in which a state of over-contraction appears to set in motion forces leading to over-expansion, and this in turn to over-contraction once more."

Mitchell's concept of the self-generating cycle has been the source of considerable scientific disagreement.   Some students of the cycle have argued that there is no natural tendency for the cycle to recur, and that the recovery phase could persist indefinitely in the absence of certain external economic factors.   According to this view business cycles are not continuous cycles, but rather each cycle is to be regarded as separate and distinct from the one preceding it.[66]   Mitchell cannot agree with this view since he believes that the evidence provided by the annals of business give sufficient support for the theory of the self-generating cycle.   He admits that each phase of

[66] Cf. Adams, Arthur B., *Economics of Business Cycles*, pages 195-197. New York: McGraw-Hill Book Company, Inc., 1925. For Mitchell's reply to the contentions of Adams see his *Business Cycles, The Problem and Its Setting*, 1927, pages 464-465.

the cycle does not always merge into a full-fledged specimen of the next phase, since special events frequently intervene to distort the usual course of the cycle. Still Mitchell feels that he is justified in saying that there is to be seen throughout the actual historical course of business cycles a regularly recurring pattern of the cycle with each phase generating the conditions which are necessary for the appearance of the next phase of the cycle.

With respect to Mitchell's theory of the self-generating business cycle it should be pointed out that the self-generation process does not go on *ad infinitum*. Mitchell is careful to explain that business cycles are a special feature of "a particular scheme of institutions," and that whenever the institutional scheme changes radically there is bound to be a related change in the performance of the cycle. Over and above the self-generating processes of the business cycle are the cumulative secular changes at work within the entire economic system which make for a change of the institutional framework within which the business system operates. For purposes of cycle analysis Mitchell has taken the larger institutional framework of the business system as a given datum. It is as if he had assumed that the capitalistic system of the latter part of the nineteenth century and the early decades of the present century had come to a standstill. Within this given framework he then develops his conception of a typical cycle and his theory of self-generation.[67] He is fully aware, however, that his cycle theory is relative to a particular historical epoch in the evolution of the capitalistic system. "The broader changes of economic organization," he explains, "are cumulative, like the lesser changes which make each phase of every business cycle evolve upon its successor. And, being cumulative, their dominating influence upon the phenomena of

[67] Paul T. Homan has observed that "In a certain definite sense, then, one may say that Mitchell's theory is of a 'static' sort. That is to say, he uses the ideas of 'process' and 'cumulative causation,' not to describe the evolution of the institutions through which economic activity takes place, as Veblen had done, but to describe the fluctuations which business undergoes within the confines of a given institutional situation. So far as his investigation is concerned, institutions are a relatively constant, not a highly variable, factor." See Homan's *Contemporary Economic Thought*, page 405. New York: Harper and Brothers, 1928. In the two decades since Homan made his critical study of Mitchell's economic thought the latter has come to pay more attention to the changing institutional framework within which the business system functions.

business cycles stands out clearly in the lapse of years. Hence it is probable that the economists of each generation will see reason to recast the theory of business cycles which they learned in their youth." [68] It would appear that the self-generating nature of the cycle derives, not from any permanent features of economic organization, but from the highly transitory characteristics of the present stage in the evolution of the capitalistic system. Conceivably there might come a time when business cycles would cease to be self-generating. This would be especially likely in an economic situation where collective economic intelligence had been organized so as to provide for a great deal of governmental control of economic activity. In a planned economy, if it should prove to be workable, the business system would cease to respond to changes in prices and profits in the cyclical manner characteristic of it since the dawn of the modern capitalistic system. In recent years Mitchell has come to display a growing interest in the possibility of an economy planned for the purpose of eliminating, or at least considerably reducing, the all-too-costly fluctuations of the business system. Indeed the powerful undercurrents of all his economic theorizing of the past four decades have been leading him to a consideration of the possibility of a planned economic system in which economic security and sufficiency would be associated with a high degree of economic liberty for the masses.

Economic Reform and National Planning

It is significant that the concluding sections of Mitchell's first study of *Business Cycles* (1913) are devoted to a discussion of the evil results that flow from cyclical disturbances in the business world as well as the possibilities of controlling such disturbances. Although Mitchell's primary interest at the time that he made his early study of business cycles was in a statistical analysis of cycle phenomena, he did not overlook the strictures levelled against the business system by Thorstein Veblen in *The Theory of Business Enterprise*. In these early years of the present century he was also absorbing the content of such thought-provoking studies as Anna Youngman's *The Economic Causes of Great Fortunes* (1909). In the final section of his *Business Cycles*, which is entitled "The

[68] *Business Cycles*, 1913, page 583.

Money Surface of Things and What Goes on Beneath," Mitchell directs his attention away from the price data which were the center of attention in prior sections of his cycle study.[69]   Like the classical and neo-classical economists he is interested in discovering what is going on beneath the pricing system, but unlike the orthodox economists Mitchell is not especially interested in the market behavior of purely rational individuals in a competitive economy. Instead he wants to know how business cycles react upon social well-being, how they create human suffering through extensive unemployment, how they waste the resources of the nation, and how they make for greater inequality in the distribution of wealth and income.   He wishes to inquire into the "double personality" of the citizens of the business economy whose ends of money-making for the individual and business prosperity for the entire nation are "artificial" ends foisted upon these citizens by pecuniary institutions.   Profit making and the securing of general business prosperity are not the "real" goals that cause men to direct their efforts toward the production of goods and services.   The ultimate motives that drive men to action are "the individual's impulsive activities" and "the vague ideals of social welfare fashioned by each generation."   But these ultimate motives have been blocked by the artificial ends imposed upon individuals by the business economy. Mitchell feels that men do not need to continue to have their personalities warped by the artificial goals of the business economy. And so he concludes his first edition of *Business Cycles* with a plea for a better utilization of organized social intelligence for the control of our economic system: "Subject as men are to the sway of pecuniary concepts and ideals they can still judge the workings of the money economy by more intimate and more vital standards. To make these latter standards clear, to show in what definite ways the quest of profits transgresses them, and to devise feasible methods of remedying these ill results, is a large part of the task of social reform.   Economic theory will not prove of much use in this work unless it grasps the relations between the pecuniary institutions which civilized man is perfecting, the human nature which he inherits from savage ancestors, and the new forces which science lends him.   To treat money as an empty symbol which 'makes no difference save one of convenience' is a habit exceeded in super-

[69] *Ibid.*, pages 596-599.

ficiality only by the habit against which it protests—that of treating money-making as the ultimate goal of effort." [70]

In the final section of the first edition of his *Business Cycles* Mitchell mentions the possibility of injecting some degree of social control into the recurring movements of the business system, which, if successful to any marked extent, would necessarily alter the self-generating powers of the business cycle. At the time that he wrote his first study of the business cycle he observed that the inventors of the "complicated machinery of the money economy" had not been able to control their own invention, although some progress in control had been achieved since the days of the Tulip Mania in Holland and the South Sea Bubble in England. When Mitchell first turned to the study of business cycles the injurious tendencies of business fluctuations had been overcome to some extent by means of laws against fraudulent promotion, by better control of security exchanges, more adequate information for investors, better bank policies, and the integration of industry. In spite of these improvements in the business system there were many very important aspects of business activity that were still beyond the control of businessmen. The inventors of the money economy were still unable to keep the construction of new industrial equipment on a steady basis, to control the market capitalization of business enterprises, or to keep stringency from accumulating in the money markets of the nation. In order to improve these conditions in the future Mitchell made certain proposals for the control of the business cycle. His suggestions of 1913 included the reorganization of the banking system, the development of government spending policies designed to concentrate public spending in depressions rather than in periods of prosperity, the stabilization of the dollar, and the democratizing of the knowledge of current business conditions possessed at that time by only a few of the more important business and financial leaders.

In the years following the publication of the first edition of his *Business Cycles* Mitchell devoted himself almost exclusively to an improvement of his knowledge of the cyclical movements of the business world. The prosperous period of World War I and the immediate post-war years drew attention away from the problem of the business cycle. There are tides in the thoughts of men, and

---

[70] *Business Cycles*, page 599.

until 1920 the movement was away from a public interest in the phenomena of the cycle. The crisis of 1920 and the depression of 1921, however, caused men's minds once more to turn to the problem of the business cycle. There was a new outlook associated with this renewed interest in the business cycle, because the World War had left a legacy in the form of public sentiment in favor of more economic control than had been exercised in the years prior to 1914. With this new interest in the control of the cycle Mitchell felt very much at home. At a round-table discussion of the annual meeting of the American Economic Association in December, 1921, he surveyed the possibilities of controlling the business cycle.[71] He drew special attention to the manipulation of rediscount rates by the Federal Reserve System, the establishment of unemployment insurance schemes, and the long-range planning of capital expenditures by private business enterprises as devices leading to a more effective control of the fluctuations of the business system. For Mitchell "economic control" still meant a piecemeal activity which involved the application of certain pressures or controls at different strategic points in the business economy. There was as yet no suggestion coming from him that the control of business cycles necessitated some overall scheme for the general planning of economic life. In 1921 Mitchell was still so engrossed in the work of improving his knowledge of business cycles that he does not appear to have been prepared to face the difficult task of deciding how to use his knowledge of business cycles. He was still calling for more economic data and for more quantitative analysis. "We must make an increasingly thorough use of quantitative analysis," he said; "we must be clear in our own minds about the role which institutions play in guiding our behavior. . . . Finally, I think we must adopt a courageously constructive attitude toward our problem." [72] At this time Mitchell had little to suggest beyond calling for the adoption of "a courageously constructive attitude."

The economists who discussed Mitchell's views at the 1921 round table appear to have been thinking along much the same lines of a piecemeal regulation of the business economy. There were indica-

---

[71] Mitchell, Wesley C., "The Crisis of 1920 and the Problem of Controlling Business Cycles," *The American Economic Review*, March, 1921, Vol. XII, Supp., pages 20-32.

[72] *Ibid.*, page 32.

tions, however, that concepts of economic control going beyond piecemeal regulation of the economic system were beginning to make some headway in the thoughts of the academic world. In his review of Mitchell's analysis of cycle control Walter W. Stewart raised the question whether private business enterprises could ever be relied upon to adopt those policies which would reduce the severities of the cyclical movements of business. He pointed out that in depressions each group in the community seeks to make its own position secure even at the expense of the other economic interests. In this scramble for economic security it is usually the business interest that succeeds in passing on the burdens of the depression to farmers, laborers, and consumers. Just as bankers could not be relied upon to raise public welfare above their private welfare without the presence of some extra-banking organization such as the Federal Reserve System, Stewart felt that private business could not be depended on to meet the problem of controlling the business cycle without direction and pressure from some extra-business agency dedicated to the preservation of the common interests. Businessmen needed to be protected from the business policies that they usually adopted in periods of depression. For these reasons an economic control agency or body, free from the competitive demands of the business world and ready to consider general welfare before business welfare, would be necessary to achieve any significant degree of control over the business cycle. Stewart did not specifically mention economic planning by a central agency representing businessmen, farmers, laborers, consumers, and the government, but the general trend of his thought was in that direction. He appears to have felt that controlling the business cycle was a large undertaking that could not be carried out by minor modifications in the existing system of business control. If similar doubts were harbored by Mitchell at this time, they did not get into his published remarks.

From 1921 to 1929 Mitchell was occupied with the work of directing the activities of the National Bureau of Economic Research. During these years he busied himself with an extension of knowledge relating to the phenomena of business cycles. With considerable resources and an adequate staff at his command Mitchell was now able to carry on with more success the project which was constantly uppermost in his mind. In 1927 he was in a position to digest the work of his associates and to publish the second edition of his cycle study under the title of *Business Cycles, The Problem and Its Setting*. During the 1920's, as director of research for the National Bureau, Mitchell retired into the quiet atmosphere of a private research organization where problems of the day were allowed to pass without much public comment. In a review of his research work for the National Bureau he tells us that "No doubt we might have been more prolific and attracted more attention had we pursued a different policy. We might have concentrated on questions of the day, endeavoring to enlighten public opinion upon this, that, or the other matter uppermost in men's minds for the moment . . . most of our energy has been spent upon fundamental processes that must go on in every society every day if men are to live—the production and distribution of goods." [73] After 1921 Mitchell would have preferred to continue with his work of improving our understanding of the "fundamental processes" of economic life, but, before long, events were to break rudely into his world of unhurried investigation. The break in the stock market in October, 1929, ushered in a new depression of such unusual duration and severity that Mitchell soon found himself compelled to do less work in the research laboratory, just as in 1918 when his appointment as chief of the Price Section of the Division of Planning and Statistics interrupted his academic work. [74]

In December, 1929, Mitchell was appointed chairman of the Research Committee on Social Trends created by President Herbert Hoover for the purpose of making a national survey of social trends in the United States. [75] As the chairman and the most outstanding economist on this Committee, Mitchell was in a position not only to disseminate his own views relating to the changing economy and its many problems but also to acquaint himself with recent trends in the other social science disciplines. The *point d'appui* of Mitchell and the other committee members in their analysis of recent economic trends was "the dynamic nature of this material culture, and

[73] Wesley C. Mitchell's report on "The National Bureau's Social Function," *Twentieth Annual Report of the Director of Research*, National Bureau of Economic Research, March, 1940, page 8.

[74] For a review of Mitchell's work during these war years see the *History of Prices During the War*, Price Bulletins Nos. 1-57 of the War Industries Board, Washington, 1919.

[75] For the report of the Committee see *Recent Social Trends in the United States, Report of the President's Research Committee on Social Trends*, published by the McGraw-Hill Book Company, Inc., New York, 1933.

the fact that the problems of society arising out of a changing technology are produced in large measure by this dynamic element." This dynamic element in material culture has in recent years found its highest expression in rapid changes in the means of communication, which have put an end to whatever remained of the pre-industrial-revolution culture of Western Europe. Added to the disruptive effects of improvements in the means of communication have been the many changes in the technology of industrial production which have brought about significant alterations in the economic structure of the nation, and have raised the question: "How can society improve its economic organization so as to make full use of the possibilities held out by the march of science, without victimizing many of its workers, and without incurring such general disasters as the depression of 1930-32?" [76] Mitchell and the other members of the Committee on Social Trends were unable to find any evidence which would show that society had the capacity automatically to absorb technological change without serious disturbance to its functioning. The complacent theory of nineteenth-century social scientists that each technological change would itself call into action the necessary adjustment mechanisms which would adequately distribute the costs and rewards of technological progress among the various economic classes found no acceptance in the Committee's final report. It was the general conviction of Mitchell and the other committee members that recent economic trends had cast much doubt on society's capacity to absorb technological change without serious losses to many individuals and classes.

Mitchell's analysis of recent economic trends in the United States indicated that society fell far short of making a full use of the productive possibilities inherent in modern technology. This under-utilization of productive capacities Mitchell held to be very largely the result of a lack of balance due in part to the impact of technological change upon the economic structure of the nation and in part to the "form of economic organization which the western world has evolved." From his observation of business cycles Mitchell was convinced that our laissez-faire society did not have the power to cope with the maladjustments arising from technological change and the recurrent fluctuations of the business system. It was his general conclusion, and that of the other members of the

[76] *Recent Social Trends in the United States,* page xxviii.

Committee, that organized social intelligence had to be applied to the problems of economic unbalance if they were to be handled satisfactorily. In some way collective management should be substituted for the former automaticity of the economic system, and hence the Committee concluded that "To maintain the balance of our economic mechanism is a challenge to all the imagination, the scientific insight, and the constructive ability which we and our children can muster. . . . To deal with the central problem of balance, or with any of its ramifications, economic planning is called for." [77] By 1933 Mitchell was thoroughly convinced that the system of private enterprise could preserve itself only by adopting some general economic plan for the regulation of economic activity which would take the place of the laissez-faire economic policies of the nineteenth century, whose continued acceptance as a guide to economic action would sooner or later sound the death knell of the capitalist system.

Soon after completing his work for President Hoover's Committee on Social Trends, Mitchell had an opportunity to continue the line of thought which he had developed for the Committee. On July 20, 1933, the Federal Emergency Administrator of Public Works appointed the National Planning Board, consisting of Frederic A. Delano, Charles E. Merriam, and Wesley C. Mitchell "to advise and assist the Administrator . . . through the preparation, development and maintenance of comprehensive plans . . . through surveys and research . . . and through the analysis of projects for coordination and correlation of effort among the agencies of the Federal, State, and local governments." [78] Starting as a modest movement to coordinate the public works programs of the various governmental jurisdictions, this planning board expanded its activities until its primary task became that of preparing the ground for a general economic planning program. In the two and one-half years during which he was a member of the

[77] *Ibid.*, page xxxi.

[78] *Progress Report*, National Resources Committee, Oct., 1937, page 1. For a summary of the work of the National Planning Board during the period in which Mitchell was a member of the Board see the *Final Report*, 1933-34, of the National Planning Board and *A Report on National Planning and Public Works in Relation to Natural Resources*, Dec. 1, 1934, issued by the National Resources Board. See also Gruchy, Allan G., "The Economics of the National Resources Committee," *The American Economic Review*, March, 1939, Vol. XXIX, pages 60-73.

National Planning Board Mitchell devoted his energies to the important work of creating a "plan for planning." During these years a planning organization was set up, a survey was made of the extent to which planning had already progressed, and a research program designed to make a thorough study of the possibilities of national economic planning was inaugurated. After the national planning effort had been placed on a sound basis, Mitchell then withdrew from active participation in the work of preparing for a planned economy. To a group of younger economists including Gardiner C. Means, Isador Lubin, Leon Henderson, Mordecai Ezekiel, Laughlin Currie, and others he passed on the difficult task of carrying to completion the program for a full, balanced, and efficient use of our human and natural resources, while he returned to his work of investigating the phenomena of business fluctuations.

Drawing upon his experiences and observations since 1929, Mitchell has written such essays as "The Social Sciences and National Planning" and "Intelligence and the Guidance of Economic Evolution," in which he discusses the relation of government to private enterprise and the need for national economic planning. He finds that, within an economic system ostensibly dedicated to laissez-faire, there are trends away from a situation in which the role of the government is minor. Ever since Adam Smith provided a philosophic foundation for the arguments of those who were opposed to the doctrines of mercantilism, there have been developments at work modifying his "obvious and simple system of natural liberty." The century and a half which have elapsed since Adam Smith gave scientific sanction to the attempts to remove the mercantilistic order have witnessed the appearance of two factors which Mitchell believes are responsible for the weakening of the doctrines of laissez-faire. The first important breach in the foundations of laissez-faire became evident as soon as man's irrationality was observed. During the nineteenth century it became increasingly evident that the level of rationality required for the working out of laissez-faire doctrines was not being achieved. The discoveries of psychologists served to bring out the basically instinctive nature of mankind; and, in addition, the work of sociologists demonstrated the extent to which men's actions are canalized by the important social institutions. As the nineteenth century wore on, it became clear that the human agents about which Adam Smith and Jeremy Bentham had philosophized were not basically the same as those people whom one meets on the street. It was the individual on the street who exposed the excessive rationalism underlying the theory of laissez-faire and its philosophical twin, the philosophy of utilitarianism.

As a consequence of the economic developments which have occurred during the past century, Mitchell believes that a new doctrine of the relation of government to private enterprise is now being developed. Ever since the establishment of the modern industrial system governments have been called upon to interfere with private business enterprises on a widening scale. After surveying the history of the relations between government and business in the past century and a half, Mitchell arrives at the conclusion "that we are in for more rather than less governmental planning in the calculable future." [79] He bases his opinion on the belief that technological progress will continue to press our economic system along the disruptive path of economic change. The growth of large-scale business will doubtlessly continue, and some attempt will have to be made to meet the consequences of this development. The mechanization of industry and the growing importance of overhead costs will feed the desires of corporate managers to suppress competition. The introduction of new products will threaten the stability of whole industries, and will throw the heavy burden of technological progress on all those with stakes in outmoded industries. Mitchell points out that the central government will have to extend its authority more and more into the area of local activities since the task of planning such matters as water supplies, power lines, highway systems, and sewage disposal can no longer be viewed as a local or state matter in our complex modern society. There will be natural resources to protect; and there will be social security required by those members of society who are the innocent victims of technological change. In this situation the trend will necessarily be toward an expansion of national economic planning.

As Mitchell finds himself in the realm of prophecy at this point in his analysis he proceeds cautiously. Will national economic planning enjoy an even, continuous growth, or will it meet many set-backs? Will the outcome of planning be a renovated capital-

[79] Mitchell, Wesley C., "Intelligence and the Guidance of Economic Evolution," *Scientific Monthly*, Nov., 1936, Vol. XLIII, page 460.

ism or some "as yet unchristened form of economic organization?" Mitchell feels that the course of national economic planning will be filled with many obstacles. There will undoubtedly be violent reactions in favor of laissez-faire, but he is emphatic in his assertion that "the indication seems to me fairly clear that in the long run men will try increasingly to use the power and resources of their governments to solve their economic problems even in those nations that escape social revolutions." [80] Whether it will be a matter of evolution or revolution in the United States Mitchell is not prepared to say. What will appeal to the people, whether it will be communism, fascism, or a form of regulated capitalism, only the future can tell. Of one thing Mitchell is certain, however, and that is that the choice does not lie between unregulated private enterprise and complete governmental regulation. The real choices include a number of possible mixtures of private enterprise and governmental regulation, but what mixture will be finally chosen will be a pragmatic affair determined by the forces of future circumstances.

Mitchell points out that planning is nothing new in the United States. "Piecemeal" planning has been in sporadic operation ever since federal aid was extended to the turnpike and canal companies of the early nineteenth century. We have planned in this same piecemeal fashion with respect to imports, silver output, railroad rates, liquor consumption, the preservation of competition, and many other matters. This type of planning is defective because it ignores the fact that economic and social processes are interrelated. An attempt to plan in one particular direction frequently brings injurious and unwanted results in other directions. The control of liquor consumption brings a wave of crime in its wake; high railroad rates stimulate motor and water transportation, thus bringing about an unwanted duplication of transport facilities. We have at times planned on a wider front in emergencies such as wars and business depressions.[81] In these circumstances the planning is not piecemeal but "emergency" planning, which suffers from the fact that there is usually insufficient time to work out a satisfactory overall planning program. A very good example of

[80] *Ibid.*, page 461.
[81] Mitchell, Wesley C., "The Social Sciences and National Planning," *The Backward Art of Spending Money*, 1937, page 99.

this type of planning is found in the case of the National Recovery Administration's planning activities which were hasty, ill-advised, and far from successful.

In addition to piecemeal and emergency planning, there is yet another form of planning in operation known as "business" planning. In this type of planning each group of business activities, dominated by a single financial interest or control, is coordinated according to some internal planning program. Mitchell finds that the most serious defect in this variety of planning is that it aims at the production of profits rather than goods and services. To the extent that it succeeds, this kind of planning does not subserve the higher social purposes. Its success is limited not only because it has the wrong aims, but also because planning *within* business enterprises has not been accompanied by planning *between* enterprises. The fundamental weakness of business planning is found to be in a lack of an overall coordination program. "Coordination within an enterprise," says Mitchell, "is maintained by a single authority possessed of power to carry its plan into effect; coordination among independent enterprises depends on so many different authorities which have no power to enforce a common program except so far as one can persuade or coerce others. As a result of these conditions, coordination within an enterprise is characterized by economy of effort, coordination among independent enterprises by waste." Business planning has been accompanied by additional unfortunate consequences. It has increased rather than decreased the existing inequalities of income distribution; it has placed the small businessmen at the mercies of the larger business units; and, furthermore, it has failed to rid the nation of those fluctuations in business which periodically demoralize economic life.

The conclusion to be drawn from Mitchell's survey of the private and public planning experiments which have been carried on in this country since 1800 is that planning has failed to make a great deal of progress because too little social intelligence has been devoted to the problem, a situation which Mitchell attributes to a cultural lag. The very considerable technological progress which we have enjoyed in the past century and a half has not been duplicated in our social and economic arrangements. Industrial science has greatly outstripped social science for two very important reasons.

The social sciences, which must provide the scientific basis for national economic planning, are much less exact and reliable than the natural sciences, and consequently social control is much more difficult than the control of natural forces. Furthermore, the difficulties of the social innovator are numerous. Unlike the industrial innovator, he rarely secures a personal profit from the innovations which he introduces. Furthermore, the opportunities for experimentation which are open to the social innovator are quite limited, and the obstacles presented by an uninformed and apathetic public opinion are difficult to overcome. If national planning is ever to succeed, it will do so only with great sacrifices on the part of the exponents of social control, and only after a widespread educational program has aroused a lethargic and frequently misdirected public to the need for social and economic planning.

Before national planning can succeed Mitchell thinks that two requirements must be met. First, there must be a recognition of the interrelations among social processes so that the full consequences of planning may be realized; and, secondly, there must be a willingness to come to grips with social and economic problems before they have created national emergencies. These requirements are basic for any systematic, long-range planning, and in order to achieve them it would be desirable to establish a national planning board with a competent technical staff and a wide circle of advisers. The work of such a board should be only informational and advisory. Among its tasks would be the problem of deciding where the line should be drawn between governmental and private activities. Its research activity would provide a scientific foundation for the planning pattern which would emerge. As the aims of the national planning board would not be to draw up any final plan for all future time, much of its work and its recommendations would be experimental. Mitchell explains that, "after doing its best to lay a scientific foundation for its plans, the board would often have to advise proceeding in an experimental fashion on the basis of probabilities. It would be doing pioneer work; for it would be trying to better the social organization of one of the most advanced countries in the world—to do things that have not yet been done." [82]

[82] *Ibid.*, pages 101-102.

Mitchell has no illusions about the future of national economic planning. He realizes that the nation may not succeed in overcoming the many barriers which keep it from enjoying the fruits of a well-ordered social existence. He believes, however, that there is some reason to hope for success, if social intelligence can be focussed on major social and economic problems through the device of a national planning board. The systematic long-range planning which Mitchell envisions would be a thoroughly democratic procedure. Since the national planning board would have only an advisory capacity, it would submit its recommendations to Congress. In the final analysis, the people would place their stamp of approval or rejection on the suggestions of the national planning board. The immediate problem, therefore, is to bring the people to a realization of the need for an examination of the possibilities which inhere in national economic planning. Without the proper educational program it would be quite possible, Mitchell believes, that the public would reject the plans for mobilizing the social intelligence of the nation. The danger in this situation is that the public, uneducated with respect to the need for long-range planning, may be stampeded into accepting remedies to meet grave national emergencies which may undermine the whole social structure. Mitchell points to the experience of European nations, which failed to prepare plans for handling large social problems, as a warning of what may happen in the United States. If we are to avoid either a fascistic or a communistic dictatorship with its undesirable regimentation of private lives, he feels that we must find the solution "in infusing a larger measure of intelligence into our public policy."

The Concept of Economic Welfare

The ends toward which national economic planning should be directed are not something that is given, but something that must be worked out in a pragmatic fashion. Unfortunately, the ends which the public seeks are not always clearly seen, nor are they always compatible with one another. Where planning is dominated by some definite aim such as the successful prosecution of a war, the problems of national planning are greatly simplified. But national planning in peace time is beset with many difficulties, since "the national scale of values" which provides guidance for economic activity reveals no simple pattern. Mitchell believes that in this situation, while national planning can never itself determine our social ends, it can make our ends more definite and can indicate whatever incompatibility they may possess. He makes it plain that "In a democratic country national planners would have to serve as an agency for accomplishing what the majority desired. But by throwing light upon the consequences that different lines of action would produce they could contribute much toward making social values more rational." [83]

In the service of the national economic planning agency would be a growing number of practicing economists who, as social engineers, would be concerned with the actual task of making provision for the enlargement of economic welfare. These practicing economists would put to use the scientific findings of the academic economists, who devote their time and energy to an analysis of the content of welfare and the various means which might be used for the achievement of an enlarged welfare. On only a few occasions has Mitchell himself joined the group of practicing economists; for example, in 1918 when he aided the federal government's war program, and in 1933 when he cooperated in the establishment of the National Resources Planning Board. Mitchell has preferred to leave the work of "scientific social engineering" to others, while he devotes himself to the important task of increasing, through further research, the supply of knowledge to be used by social engineers. Practicing economists are important because they subject to the tests of actual experience the ideas relating to the content of economic welfare which are developed by academic economists who do not very often go outside the classroom or the research laboratory. In writing about the growing profession of practicing economists Mitchell observes that "Among them are many of our most helpful collaborators and many eager consumers of our research products. They are perforce occupied with actual economic processes, and the prospects of turning economics into a realistic science are brightened by their daily labors." [84] According to the pragmatic interpretation of the nature of scientific truth, the validity of a scientific generalization is to be determined by the way in which it works when subjected to the tests of actual experience. It is this pragmatic test of scientific validity which Mitchell would like to see applied, by

[83] "Intelligence and the Guidance of Economic Evolution," page 465.
[84] "The National Bureau's Social Function," pages 20-21.

an ever-increasing number of practicing economists, to our generalizations about the content of economic welfare and the ways in which such welfare may be enlarged.

Mitchell's interest in problems of human welfare has been stimulated by the writings of a number of European and American economists. In England economists like A. C. Pigou and J. A. Hobson have shown how it is still possible to preserve one's scientific outlook when engaged in the analysis of such vague problems as the nature and significance of economic welfare. In the works of the German economists, with whom Mitchell is familiar, the "socio-ethical" element has been quite prominent. Mitchell's interest in social and economic welfare has been stimulated also by two streams of thought which have had their origins in the United States. The first intellectual influence has come from a familiarity with the speculations of those sociologists who inquired into the interrelations of sociology and economics.[85] The other influence has had its origins in the stimulating work dealing with the institutional setting of the valuation process which was done by economists like Veblen and Werner Sombart. With interest in social and economic welfare emanating from many different sources, it is not surprising that the socially minded Mitchell should feel the urge to relate his own particular economic analysis to the welfare problem. And so in 1916 we find him writing that "Now our interest in economics centers in its bearing upon social welfare in the present and proximate future." Economic science was shifting from a "counting house view" of economic life to one in which problems of general welfare were paramount. In his essay on the role of money in economic theory Mitchell shows how economic life may be regarded as a process of making and spending money, as a process of putting forth efforts in return for certain psychological satisfactions, or, more importantly, as "the process by which a community seeks its material welfare." In this third view of economic life every person's activity is scrutinized in the light of its effects on the commonweal; and the standard of judgment is service to the community rather than profit to the individual. Where account must be taken of the effects of various economic activities upon the "community's vitality," social accounting is substituted for the more usual business

---

[85] Cf. Charles H. Cooley's essay entitled, "The Progress of Pecuniary Valuation," *The Quarterly Journal of Economics*, Nov., 1915, Vol. XXX, pages 1-21.

accounting. At this point in his investigations Mitchell passes over into the realm of ethical analysis which has become so prominent a part of the social economics of John M. Clark.

According to Mitchell's analysis there are two important problems with respect to the question of economic welfare. The first problem is to determine the content of economic welfare, and the second is to analyze the means which may be employed to expand this welfare. The first problem, the discovery of the content of the welfare concept, is a matter of ends or aims. It is clear to Mitchell that the ends or goals of the community are based upon value-judgments which have their origins in the capricious preferences of individuals. These judgments with respect to what is good or valuable for the individual or community exhibit a great deal of whim or caprice, since emotional factors have an important role in the determination of individual and group aims. If ethical considerations were only matters of emotional bias and wishful thinking, the analysis of such considerations could hardly be called scientific. But this is not the case, for what is valuable or good to the individual or community is more than a matter of mere whim or caprice. In order to arrive at what is deemed ethically desirable, the individual must indulge in some deliberation. In all cases what is desirable involves some element of choice; and where the act of choosing is involved, the individual necessarily exercises his rational faculties. John Dewey has observed that "It takes *thought* to convert an impulse into a desire, centered on an object." The blind preferences of the animal, based on impulsive reactions, accidental circumstances, or habituation, differ from human selection, which adds the rational element to the determination of individual preferences. Since what is valuable or desirable is always to some extent a matter of preference determined with relation to some exercise of human reason, ethical analysis has some "genuine scientific standing." Mitchell believes that it is possible to set up some tentative, objective criteria for the measurement of economic welfare, concerning which there could be secured some consensus of scientific opinion. It would never be possible to objectify the entire content of human welfare, but the economic portion of this welfare appears to be amenable to some objectification.

Mitchell does not attempt to define the concept of economic welfare too rigidly, since he is aware that the "good life" can never be reduced to purely rational terms. The "good life" is not a matter of ethical absolutes which are handed down from above or which are arrived at through the processes of pure reason. What is deemed ethically desirable by a community is a reflection of its particular cultural development, and is relative to a particular historical epoch in the evolution of human culture. In order to understand the welfare concepts held by a nation one must familiarize himself with the cultural background and development of that nation. In all communities ethical ideals become embodied in habitual ways of doing things which canalize the activities and ethical life of individuals. Although the individual may blindly accept the ethical dictates of his cultural milieu, his ethical behavior will be rational to the extent that the social ethics of the community are themselves rationally determined. The less social intelligence there is reflected in the social ethics of the community, the less satisfactory will be the individual ethics of the various members of the community. But cultures change, and with them the social ethics embodied in these cultures also change. Economic progress would not be possible if the social ethics of the community were impervious to change.

Through a scientific exposition of the nature of contemporary social ethics and the ways in which they change, Mitchell hopes to indicate new fields for ethico-economic analysis; and by objectifying the content of economic welfare as far as is possible he hopes to show how far modern industrialism has fallen short in meeting the requirements of a civilized existence. Social ethics are thus taken to be the result of the interactions between man's psychological nature and the external social existence which together mold individual behavior. To the extent that we can understand these interactions and come to some agreement as to how they should be altered, we may lay the foundations for an expanded human welfare. In essence Mitchell's idea of economic progress is thus the rationalizing of our socio-economic ethics from which the individual draws his ideas of what is economically good or bad. For the individualistic and excessively rationalistic ethics of the nineteenth-century economists and other social scientists Mitchell has substituted the relativistic, social ethics of the pragmatists.

Mitchell has not written a great deal about the welfare problem, but his essays indicate that he is satisfied with the possibility of objectifying the concept of economic welfare. He believes that there are certain physical requirements for human welfare which majority opinion would sanction as being a necessary part of general human welfare. In his essay entitled "The Prospects of Economics" (1924) he writes that "In becoming consciously a science of human behavior economics will lay less stress on wealth and more stress on welfare. Welfare will mean not merely an abundant supply of serviceable goods, but also a satisfactory working life filled with interesting activities. At present welfare as thus conceived is rather vague, but it is capable of being made objective and definite in reference to such matters as food, clothing, shelter, sanitation, education, fatigue, leisure. And this realm of the definite in welfare will be expanded steadily by quantitative methods, so that we shall develop a criterion of welfare applicable to many lines of effort." [86] The application of the statistical technique to social psychology and other social sciences has provided a much firmer and wider scientific basis for the concept of human welfare. If Mitchell has preferred to spend his time on perfecting this new analytical technique rather than on the philosophical and ethical implications of the welfare concept, he should be excused in part on the ground that he has entered a realm where the signposts are as yet far from being adequate for the journey contemplated.

Mitchell's interest in national economic planning has necessarily turned his thoughts to an analysis of the social and economic aims of a reconstructed world. One such aim would be a more equitable distribution of national income. An economic system is not efficient when it successfully produces an abundance of goods, or has the power to do so, but yet fails to distribute the national output efficiently. Efficiency in distribution does not refer, in this connection, to the physical movement of goods but to the placing of goods where they meet what Mitchell calls "the most important needs." The modern economic system does not meet the requirements of efficiency, "if the ultimate test of efficiency is that of satisfying the most important needs in the most economical manner." Mitchell is unwilling to accept the pricing process of the market place as an adequate determinant of the social significance

[86] "The Prospects of Economics," page 31. Cf. Gruchy, Allan G., "The Concept of National Planning in Institutional Economics," pages 121-144.

or value of a good or service. A number of decades ago John Bates Clark pointed out that there was a close correspondence between social and market values in a purely competitive system. In such a system, where the least-cost principle was applied as extensively as possible, and where incomes did not vary much from individual to individual, one could expect natural and human resources to be devoted to the production of those goods most urgently needed by the community. But this is not so in the modern economy where competition no longer plays a dominant role. In the current economic situation where monopolistic enterprise gives rise to large unearned incomes and creates wide variations in the sizes of family incomes, market price is a poor measure of the social utility of a commodity or service.

In this part of his analysis Mitchell passes from the investigation of a fairly objective matter, such as a minimum standard of living, to an analysis of the division of the nation's income on the basis of justice to all classes. He has in mind a division of the national income which would maximize general human welfare. In this area of discussion it would probably be very difficult to secure much consensus of opinion. Mitchell's familiar tool, the statistical technique, cannot be of any help except to present a picture of the present distribution of national income. Yet, even though the problem is very difficult, Mitchell feels that it is capable of solution. In spite of the many difficulties to be overcome he has faith in the pragmatic possibility of working out a distribution of national income which will greatly enlarge the content of general economic welfare.

Other aspects of the problem of economic welfare are touched upon by Mitchell when he turns to a consideration of the problem of economic security. Welfare involves considerations of the future as well as the present, for not only must workers enjoy a sufficiency in the present but they must also have some assurance that the flow of goods and services which they are now enjoying will not be cut off or greatly reduced at some future time. With unemployment as a threat constantly facing the worker one of the essentials of economic welfare is lacking. "Cyclical unemployment," Mitchell explains, "is the labor side of the business-cycle hazard, and . . . that hazard is not shrinking. Technological unemployment is the labor side of industrial progress and that hazard is growing." [87] The extent to which unemployment, or the fear of unemployment, destroys incentive and lowers morale cannot be objectively determined, but the economist, as a social engineer, is required to take notice of the effect of unemployment on the ability of the economic system to meet the larger social needs.

In addition to economic security welfare includes the element of individual liberty. To Mitchell the problem of liberty within the economic system is a positive rather than negative matter. For individual liberty is less a matter of freedom from restraints and more a matter of what goods and services the individual is free to enjoy. In Mitchell's way of thinking a man is free when he is in a position to enjoy a wide variety of goods and services; "Indeed, it is only by preventing one group of citizens from exploiting other sets and by supplying those services which private enterprise cannot render that individual liberty can be secured." [88] This view of the nature of liberty has a different emphasis from the negative view of economic freedom held by the classical economists, who were much more interested in establishing the businessman's freedom from governmental interference than in analyzing the extent to which an individual's freedom could be actually enjoyed. The classicists assumed that once men were free from governmental interferences, the competitive system would bring to each individual whatever share of the national income his efforts warranted. For Mitchell individual liberty is a substantive matter, something firm and substantial, which modern industrialism has denied to a large section of the working population. Unfortunately, Mitchell does not carry his analysis of individual liberty any further than to point out some of the basic requirements of the concept. As is frequently the case, he makes only a passing reference to important problems such as economic security and freedom, and then he fails to work out the full implications of his thinking along these lines. He does not discuss, for example, the significance of collective action in relation to the problem of economic freedom. Is an individual free merely because he possesses an adequacy of goods and services? In a world which is daily growing more collective how does the individual

---

[87] "The Social Sciences and National Planning," page 93.
[88] *Ibid.*, page 101.

preserve his identity, and how does he exert an influence on his economic destiny? To these significant questions Mitchell does not address himself; he is apparently satisfied to leave the analysis of such problems to other socially minded investigators.

Mitchell is vitally interested in national economic planning, for in it he sees the possible realization of one of his fondest dreams, a situation in which specialists in the various scientific disciplines would cooperate in meeting our major social problems. He feels that the progress of the social sciences has been very greatly impeded by the lack of intercourse between the various sciences. Social scientists have been too hesitant to borrow from their fellow workers, with the result that new scientific developments have not been the source of as much change in scientific thought as they might have been had they been welcomed by scientists keenly alert to the significance of recent discoveries in related scientific disciplines. Cooperation between scientists in the tasks of national economic planning would not only break down the intellectual barriers between the various sciences, but it would also provide a source of recurring cross-fertilization of scientific thought. In addition, the dangers of scientific specialization would be very considerably reduced. It is when he is discussing the activities of a national planning board as a source of "the type of knowledge that the world most desperately needs—knowledge of human behavior," that Mitchell turns to his pragmatic conception of the nature of economic truth. In his view of things economists should expand the boundaries of economic truth by *doing* as well as by *thinking*. For Mitchell, as for John Dewey, the learning process is essentially a dynamic rather than a reflective process. As men endeavor to adjust themselves to their economic environment more satisfactorily through some form of national planning, they will come to learn more about the evolving economic system. Not only will the work of national economic planning extend the boundaries of economic understanding, but also economic science will become a more useful discipline. Economics has a social purpose to achieve, and in the realization of this end the cooperation of social scientists in national planning will prove to be most valuable. It is Mitchell's firm conviction that we should make "a fuller use of the social sciences," and that the search for scientific truth should always be subordinated to the tasks of human living. He is thoroughly convinced that if we would focus our collective intelligence on the problem of guiding our economic evolution and shaping our economic society more adequately to meet the requirements of general human welfare, economics would then perform the lofty function which he has envisioned for it.

Mitchell's Pragmatic Economics

This survey of the development of the economic thought of Wesley C. Mitchell reveals a considerable difference between the pioneering student of the business cycle of the first decade of this century and the exponent of national economic planning of three decades later. In spite of his abiding interest in the business cycle, Mitchell has rounded out his theoretical position, until today he is widely recognized as a leader in the movement to make economics a more realistic science. Although he has devoted most of his time and energy to an analysis of business cycles, he has always kept in mind the relation of that particular subject to the larger body of general economic theory. In fact, out of this interest in the relations of his business cycle studies to economic thought in general has come the real unity in his economics. Mitchell does not represent a minor deviation from the stream of economic thought which has come down to us from the nineteenth century. Nor has he taken on the role of an eclectic who endeavors to piece together all the best of both the old and the new. On the contrary, the unity that he seeks is a new scientific synthesis which will be more useful to future generations than the synthesis of economic thought created by the nineteenth-century orthodox economists.

In those early years during which Mitchell's economic ideas were taking shape in the stimulating atmosphere of the University of Chicago, economic science was undergoing a transformation. The symmetrical thought system, which Alfred Marshall has so patiently elaborated, was revealing a discomforting inability to explain the great changes that were at work in the early years of the new century. Marshall had presented a body of theory that was more appropriate to the years of his youth than to the early decades of the present century; and, like all other theoretical systems, his was giving way to a new system of a new generation. Mitchell has frequently pointed out that many major economic generalizations are but the reflections of some particular episode in the ever-changing career of mankind. Even his own generalizations, he feels, may soon come to be honored more for their place in the history of economic thought than for their applicability to the economic problems of the future. Meanwhile, he is faced with the problem of fashioning a framework of analysis which will be more useful than that of the nineteenth-century economists for the solution of our immediate economic difficulties. It was Wesley Mitchell's experience to have his attention directed to economic studies in one of those crucial periods in the history of economic science when established doctrines were on the decline, and new doctrines were not yet fully developed. Mitchell drew a great deal of his inspiration from the critical comments of Thorstein Veblen. But, although many of the general features of his framework of analysis were borrowed from the writings of that "disturbing genius," Mitchell has not been a passive recipient of Veblenian economics. The first effects of Veblen's critical treatment of the neo-classical economic thought of his day were to create disunity and dismay among economists and other social scientists. Perhaps this was inevitable, since it requires some very heavy blows to dislodge any well-established body of scientific doctrines. If that is the case, Veblen may have served his science very well in the sense that he was the one chosen by circumstances to assail the towers of economic orthodoxy. But the thinker who excels in destroying and eliminating is seldom one who is also deft in the art of rebuilding a dismantled thought structure. As a consequence Veblen passed on to less agitated personalities the task of shaping a new schema that would be more acceptable to twentieth-century economists than the theoretical system of the nineteenth-century economists. Mitchell was very well suited for the task of gaining adherents for the new movement in economic thought. Unlike Veblen he has always been mindful of his deep obligations to his nineteenth-century precursors, and he has been very careful to show respect for their work. Where Veblen enjoyed disturbing his readers and substituting dismay and doubt for their previously existing peace of mind, Mitchell appears to find no relish in substituting doubt where once there resided acceptance of the *status quo*. If Mitchell is to eliminate satisfaction with outmoded economic ideas, he will only do so when he can replace the outworn ideas with hopes for something that is more suitable for the interpretation of life as it is being lived in the twentieth century.   Undoubtedly much of this difference in the work of Mitchell and Veblen is to be explained by reference to the differences in the personalities of the two men.   One was vitriolic, hypercritical, and perhaps even sadistic, to such an extent that his fundamental respect for mankind was clouded over with much that should be regarded as being essentially superficial; whereas the other has the mental repose and genuine regard for the welfare of others which are indications of an inquiring mind at peace in the vision of a reconstructed society.

It is because the slow rebuilding of a body of integrated scientific doctrine is less spectacular than the routing out of the supporters of an outmoded thought system that Mitchell fails to shine as brilliantly as his illustrious precursor.   But this should not lead us to underestimate the contributions of Mitchell to the development of economic science.   Unlike Veblen's influence which has been largely centrifugal in effect, Mitchell's work has been more centripetal.   He has taken time off from his absorbing work of improving the understanding of business cycles to explain in a number of essays what is meant by the new unity in economic science that he is seeking to establish.   The unity which Mitchell is always expounding runs through three types of economics; that is to say, the systematic economics of his nineteenth-century, neo-classical predecessors; the historico-cultural economics introduced by Karl Marx and developed further by Veblen; and the normative economics which has always been present, in large or small measure, in all types of economic thinking.   Mitchell has enlarged the scope of economics to include the contributions of many different types of economists.   To some this may appear to be no more than an eclectic's attempt to incorporate many different viewpoints in one shapeless *omnium gatherum*.   But this is not the case, since Mitchell has a special colligating principle or tenet which unifies the three fields of economics.   This is the belief that economics, because it is a functional science, should have the "social value" of enabling mankind more easily to solve its various economic difficulties.   If work in the three fields of economics is to be worth while, it must be primarily motivated by the desire ultimately to improve the economic lot of mankind.   Mitchell writes that "In economics as in other sciences we desire knowledge mainly as an instrument of control.   Control means the alluring possibility of shaping the evolution of economic life to fit the developing purposes of our race. It is this possibility, of which we catch fleeting glimpses in our sanguine moments, that grips us. Always the center of our interest lies in the changes that have taken place in economic behavior, the changes that are now taking place, the changes that may take place in the future." [89] What distinguishes Mitchell's economic thought from more orthodox types of economics is this instrumentalistic turn of mind which shows up throughout his theorizing. The focus of his attention is always a consideration of the value of his work as a means of improving economic conditions; and, as a consequence, all his thoughts relating to the reconstruction of economics revolve about the main issue of using knowledge as an instrument of economic control.

Mitchell's views on the nature of economics reveal his pragmatic interest in the many problems of the rapidly changing economic world. From the viewpoint of the pragmatist the pluralistic world is always in a state of flux; everything is tentative and in a state of becoming. In this situation there are no clear-cut lines between the static and the dynamic, the changeless and the changing, or between what is cause and what is effect. Mental boundaries are not things that can be neatly laid out to mark off historical epochs, or to show the proper scope of various scientific disciplines. Life is a many-faceted thing, and likewise economics makes room for a number of different approaches to the study of economic phenomena. Mitchell combines these different approaches in his definition of economics as "a science of behavior." It is this view of economics, he contends, which "will give the valuable contributions of past theorists their proper setting and afford a framework within which the diverse contributions of the future will find their proper places. It will show that economic history, economic theory and applied economics have close organic relations, and it will dispel the darkness that has shrouded the relations between economics and the other sciences of behavior—psychology in particular." [90]

Mitchell admits that his definition of economics as a science of behavior is a very loose one which exhibits considerable vagueness. It lacks the precision of those views which take economics to be limited to "the study of the disposal of scarce commodities" in a

---

[89] "The Prospects of Economics," page 25.
[90] *Ibid.*, page 22.

situation in which human ends and the state of the industrial arts are taken as given data.[91] If the boundaries which Mitchell has laid down for economic analysis appear to be somewhat indefinite, it is because sociological, historical, and ethical data do not lend themselves to any neat categorizing. Mitchell is prepared to turn the bright light of scientific inquiry upon anything that will aid him in the work of explaining "social ways of thinking and acting" as they relate to the problem of getting a living. He feels that human "behavior is such a complicated affair that those who seek to understand it can ill dispense with any line of attack." [92] For this reason Mitchell does not consider it any disservice to his science to leave its boundaries in an unsettled state. Attempts to delimit the scope of economics in too rigorous a fashion serve merely to divide life into a series of air-tight compartments which distort the realities of human existence. What is more important than an attempt to make a precise statement of the limits of economic inquiry is an open mind that turns away from no avenue of inquiry revealing any promise of furthering our economic understanding.

Whether he is concerned with a study of the evolution of the economic system, of its current functioning, or of its probable future development, Mitchell throws his explanations into the molds of institutional interpretation. Like his more orthodox precursors Mitchell investigates the functioning of the entire economy, but, whereas the neo-classical economists eventually reduced their analysis to a consideration of individual utilities and disutilities, Mitchell pushes his analysis back to the basic institutional modes of behavior through which man's fundamental biological drives find expression. In his analysis the evolving economic system as an object of scientific investigation leads to a study of the changing economic institutions by means of which men have distributed scarce resources for the satisfaction of their fundamental needs. When Mitchell turns from a study of the emerging economy to a study of the current functioning of the economic system his investigation becomes an analysis of individual behavior as it is molded and guided by the dominant economic and social institutions which reflect the current ends or aims of the nation. Once more his explanation is

[91] Cf. Robbins, Lionel, *An Essay on the Nature and Significance of Economic Science*, 1935, page 38.

[92] "Economics, 1904-1929," page 413.

thrown into institutional terms. Finally, when he turns to a consideration of the trends of economic evolution, his ethical analysis is likewise concerned very largely with the institutional basis of social ethics. He sums the matter up in this manner: "As we work with the conception that economics is a science of behavior, we find our attention focusing upon the role played in behavior by institutional factors. . . . Accordingly, it is in these [social] habits that the student of economic behavior finds his chief problems when he studies the past or the present, and his chief hope when he thinks of the future. 'Institutions' is merely a convenient term for the more important among the widely prevalent, highly standardized social habits. And so it seems that the behavioristic viewpoint will make economic theory more and more a study of economic institutions." [93] It is this emphasis upon the institutional aspects of individual economic behavior which not only adds unity to Mitchell's economic studies, but which also distinguishes his economics from the work of the nineteenth-century economists of the neo-classical school. In essence Mitchell's "quantitative economics" is a form of collective economics which, although it owes much to the individualistic economics of the past century, presents a novel, collective approach to the study of economic problems.

The unity of Mitchell's economic theorizing finds further expression in his statement that "the systematically inclined among us are trying out various methods of conceiving the subject as a whole." Thus, what is of special interest to Mitchell is the working of the whole economy, and not the working of any one segment of it. For the emphasis of the nineteenth-century economist on the activities of the individual entrepreneur Mitchell would substitute an emphasis on the activities of the entire economy. Nineteenth-century economists did not ignore the general level of activity of the entire economy, as their interest in equilibrium economics testifies, but in their laissez-faire outlook there were no special problems relating to the economy's general functioning. In Mitchell's collective economics the operations of individual firms or industries have a place, but the center of attention is in the working of the whole economy. The general level of economic activity can no longer be taken for granted, or regarded as something that will be taken care of by the multitudinous activities of thousands of in-

[93] "The Prospects of Economics," page 25.

dividual firms. In Mitchell's economic analysis the general level of economic activity becomes a positive factor determining the level of activity in particular firms and industries. With the emergence of large-scale enterprise, businessmen have come to look upon the general level of business activity as a sort of economic barometer which indicates the future trends of the business system. These trends are then made the basis of vital industrial policies. But instead of the parts determining the functioning of the whole, the whole has come to determine the functioning of the parts. Rather than the general level of economic activity being a function of the level of entrepreneurial activities, the reverse is the case. As a consequence, the price and production policies of the large corporate business units, as Mitchell has shown in his analysis of the business cycle, are reflections of the general state of business, which, being the special concern of no particular group or interest, has been free to exert its powerful influence for good or evil according to the dictates of blind economic circumstances.

In taking "a fresh look at the total frame of economic activity" in which collective or institutional action in control of individual action has surged to the forefront, Mitchell seeks to unify his economic analysis about a consideration of the many important changes in the structure and operations of the modern economy.[94] When the economist centers his attention on the total functioning of the economy, he concerns himself primarily with the problems that have appeared because of basic changes in the structure and operations of the economic system. Mitchell's business cycle studies are very properly the core of any study that deals with the changing economy, since the problems which have come in the wake of fundamental changes in the structure of the economy are problems of economic instability and unbalance. But Mitchell has himself not gotten very far beyond these basic cycle studies. In devoting his energies very largely to an analysis of cycle phenomena he has been unable to make any very extensive investigation of the changing structure and behavior of the total economy. Such a study is a tremendous task requiring the combined efforts of many economic experts. Since the first decade of this century, when

[94] Taylor, Horace, "On the Current Skepticism Toward Systematic Economics," *Economic Essays in Honor of Wesley Clair Mitchell*, page 430. New York: Columbia University Press, 1935.

Mitchell started to investigate the business cycle, other economists have helped to fill in the gaps to be found in the analysis of the economy's changing structure and operations. But even so the investigation is far from being complete; and, to the extent that economic change continues, it will be a task that by necessity remains unfinished. Frederick C. Mills, one of Mitchell's many outstanding students, points out that this analysis of the operating characteristics of the modern economy is a difficult one, because these characteristics are not easily comprehended and are difficult to define.[95] Mitchell believes, however, that he has gone far enough in his study of the total functioning of the modern economy to point the way to a revitalized economics which may do for the twentieth century what Ricardian economics did for the nineteenth century.

In spite of much diversity there remains some similarity between the work of Mitchell and that of his neo-classical predecessors. The orthodox economics of the nineteenth-century economists was concerned with an automatic equilibrium established in an individualistic economy of pure competition. The consequences flowing from such an equilibrium were full utilization of natural and human resources and the maximization of output of goods and services. Like the neo-classicists, Mitchell also seeks an equilibrium in which there would be a maximum of output with a minimum of human sacrifice. But the economic equilibrium that Mitchell has in mind is not to be automatic in its coming about. Whatever equilibrium is to be achieved is to be a planned or managed equilibrium resulting from the application of organized social intelligence to the problem of marshalling economic resources for the production of whatever national income is set as a desirable goal. Many of the analytical tools employed by nineteenth-century economists will prove to be of great service in the task of working out the kind of economic equilibrium for which Mitchell would have our society make its plans. There is thus no complete break in the development of economics from the nineteenth century to the present. Mitchell has never entertained any thought of creating economic science anew. On the contrary, he has endeavored to keep in view the many connections between his own economics and that

[95] Mills, Frederick C., "On the Changing Structure of Economic Life," *Economic Essays in Honor of Wesley Clair Mitchell*, pages 357-391.

of his more orthodox predecessors. But the center of gravity in Mitchell's economic system is quite different from that of nineteenth-century economics. Whereas the equilibrium envisioned by the neo-classical economists was the equilibrium of an individualistic economy, Mitchell's concept of equilibrium relates instead to an economy largely dominated by collective action. Like other students of holistic economic thought, Mitchell is primarily concerned with a study of the disposal of scarce means in a cultural situation which is dominated by various forms of collective action in control of individual behavior.

Unlike Veblen, Sombart, Tawney, and others, Mitchell has displayed little interest in the genetic view of economics which leads the investigator into the origins and development of the major institutions comprising the capitalistic system. Although he has expressed much intellectual sympathy for the evolutionary view of economic science, he has himself done little with the full implications of such a view. His concern with business history does not go back much beyond 1860. We may say that his outlook has therefore been more contemporary than historical, since he is primarily interested in recent and contemporary economic culture. Although he refers quite frequently throughout his essays to "the cumulative change of economic behavior," his attention has been directed primarily toward behavior patterns of the recent past and the present. Furthermore, his interest in contemporary economic culture and current behavior patterns is limited largely to that portion of economic culture that has to do with the business system and the institution of money. What is lacking in Mitchell's economic analysis is a broad study of modern economic enterprise. Either he has not felt prepared to offer any such analysis, or he has believed that the time is not yet ripe for such a presentation. As a consequence, his economics remains quite fragmentary even though he has made considerable progress in drawing the outlines of a fresh view of economic science which may some day become the basis of a new economic synthesis.

What augurs well for the future of the reconstructive movement in economic thought, which Mitchell represents, is his lack of dogmatism. Throughout his years of research and economic analysis he has always preserved that modesty which is most appropriate for the social scientist in a situation where disagreement is rife. Before men can be brought together in agreement they must have the intellectual modesty and freedom from dogmatic assertion which will preserve their open minds, and prevent the creation of insurmountable mental barriers.   Mitchell is fortunate in that he possesses a great deal of this essential quality.   He appropriately closes his essay on "The Prospects of Economics" with the statement that "All this is full of promise.   But I must add that the task of the social sciences is supremely difficult, that progress will be checkered, that the particular changes I have prophesied in economic theory may not take place, that our generation may pass before men find a really fruitful way of attacking economic problems.   How all will go we cannot foresee.   Yet if we do the work of today and tomorrow according to our lights, we shall at least be helping on that long process of trial and error by which mankind is striving toward control over its own behavior.   A chance to share in this work with its exacting demands, its frequent disappointments, but its thrilling possibilities, is open to all who will." [96]

It is Mitchell's pragmatic bent that has colored all phases of his economic thought.   As is the case with most pragmatists, his theorizing lacks the symmetry and unity which are such prominent features of the thought systems worked out by the social scientists and philosophers of the nineteenth century.   Pragmatism, whether in philosophy or economics, places a premium on the tentative and the provisional as opposed to the certain and the axiomatic.   Mitchell's tentativism, however, does not leave him without philosophical and scientific direction.   Certainly he is not a mere dilettante who aimlessly follows his scientific curiosity wherever it may lead him. The pragmatist, as economist and social philosopher, is tentative and empirical in his scientific investigations primarily because he feels that one can acquire a better grasp of reality only by avoiding the speculative system-building of the past century.   But the explanation of reality is not the only concern of the pragmatist. Over Mitchell's economic analysis, as over pragmatic analysis in general, there hovers a certain sense of urgency which compels him to live in the present and to keep his thoughts on the future.   It is Mitchell's particular brand of social philosophy that very largely explains the course of his personal development from the pioneer-

[96] "The Prospects of Economics," pages 33-34.   See also Mitchell's "The Public Relations of Science," *Science*, Dec. 29, 1939, Vol. XC, pages 599-607.

ing student of the business cycle in 1913 to the exponent of national economic planning some thirty years later.   It is not surprising that a man who has spent his entire life on an investigation and analysis of economic instability should find the pragmatic philosophy of William James and John Dewey so suitable as a unifying principle for his entire intellectual outlook.   In those intellectual circles where classical philosophy, or some of its modern variants, reign supreme, the pragmatist remains *persona non grata*.   As is to be expected, therefore, much of the opposition to Mitchell's economic views stems from the anti-pragmatic philosophical outlook of his opponents, who are unable to agree with Mitchell since they cannot make the necessary philosophical adjustments.   This is especially true of those economists trained in the neo-classical tradition, who have unconsciously absorbed the narrow positivism of late nineteenth-century English economic thought.   Mitchell's greatest appeal is to economists who have similar philosophical leanings, and especially to those economists of the younger generation, who, though schooled in no particular philosophical tradition, have nevertheless unconsciously absorbed from their cultural milieu much of John Dewey's now widely accepted instrumental pragmatism.

The raw materials for a new synthesis lie temptingly about us; and the place it can fill, if successful, can hardly be overestimated. We face a need no less insistent and an opportunity no less commanding than that which was so greatly met by a certain absent-minded Scotch professor in the year 1776.

JOHN M. CLARK: *Preface to Social Economics*

The Social Economics of John M. Clark

Among American economists John Maurice Clark holds a unique position. Not only has he pushed beyond the boundaries of conventional economics to develop his own "social economics," but he has also been very intimately connected through family associations with the development of American economic thought since 1885. As one of the sons of John Bates Clark, who was America's leading exponent of the economics of marginalism in the closing years of the last century, John M. Clark has been in a position to draw inspiration from the thought and experience of two generations of economists. No economist has been better situated to absorb what was worth while in neo-classical thought, and to carry that type of economic thinking to still higher levels of scientific achievement. The younger Clark, however, has not taken advantage of his fortunate position to refine further the static economics inherited from his father. It is a tribute to the independent character of John M. Clark's economic thinking that he has not confined himself to the work of carrying on economic investigation from the point at which his father left it. Instead the younger Clark has struck out into new fields of scientific interest where much of the older systematic economics of his father's generation is of little aid, where a new scientific orientation and new conceptual tools are essential for the tasks at hand, and where the symmetrical body of theory of the nineteenth-century economists cannot be duplicated to any great advantage. If John M. Clark does not come to enjoy a fame equal to that of his illustrious father, it will not be because he has thought less rigorously or less deeply than his famous parent, for the field of dynamic economics is one which will certainly test the scientific mettle of the current generation of twentieth-century economists.

Born on November 30, 1884, in Northampton, Massachusetts,

John M. Clark went to his father's alma mater, Amherst College, in 1901 for his early academic training.   After completing his undergraduate work, he moved on to Columbia University for graduate study in the field of economics.   Clark began his teaching career in 1908 as an instructor in economics and sociology at Colorado College.   After two years at that institution he returned to Amherst College, where he was appointed associate professor of economics.   In 1915 Clark became a member of the economics faculty of the University of Chicago.   After doing brilliant work at that institution, he accepted the position of professor of economics in 1926 at Columbia University, where J. B. Clark was to have the great satisfaction of seeing his son fill the position from which he had retired.

When Clark completed his graduate work at Columbia University in 1910 his father had already rounded out his static economics in the *Essentials of Economic Theory* (1907).   In the hands of such a rigorously logical thinker as J. B. Clark, static economics had become a refined theoretical product which was then at the pinnacle of its development.   Starting off in the latter part of the eighteenth century as a body of generalizations relating to the emerging system of competitive business, static economics had by the early years of the twentieth century become a body of deductive analysis which was severely restricted by the hypothetical nature of its unrealistic premises.   In the early decades of the nineteenth century what later became the unrealistic premises of static economics had a fair degree of conformity with the facts of actual economic experience.   But a hundred years later this body of economic doctrine was so far removed from everyday economic experience that it was only "a methodological device for isolating and analyzing a highly important body of economic tendencies, an understanding of which is necessary for any realistic study of economic processes." [1]

The static economics of which Clark's father was America's most outstanding exponent was built around an analysis of the concept of economic equilibrium at high levels of abstraction.   A few basic assumptions were made the economist's point of departure.   These assumptions were that man is highly rational in his economic be-

[1] Anderson, B. M., "Static Economics and Business Forecasting," in *Economic Essays Contributed in Honor of John Bates Clark,* edited by Jacob H. Hollander, page 11 fn. New York: The Macmillan Company, 1927.

havior, that the economic system is composed of many small-scale, competitive enterprises, and that the institutional framework of society, the basic economic character of which remains unchanged, provides for an abundance of freedom with respect to the use of private property and the making of private contracts. In this fashion, the structure of the economic system was taken to be that of a purely competitive economy in which all elements of disturbance had been eliminated. The functioning of the economy was then described in terms of an equilibrium in which all economic factors were held to gravitate toward their normal levels. In this situation price and production relationships displayed a high degree of stability, for all deviations from economic norms were soon checked by the various adjustment mechanisms whose work it was to restore economic balance whenever temporary disturbances made their appearance. In short, a closed system was created in which impounded economic forces had to conform to the requirements of a static equilibrium. In such an economic world there was movement but no change, functioning but no development; and in the study of this type of economic system economics became an analysis of the disposal of scarce means in a highly individualistic economy where economic behavior was assumed to be highly rational.

In developing his static economics J. B. Clark apparently had no other intention than to reveal fully the nature of the basic assumptions of classical economic thought. He felt that economics could make progress only by moving from the simple to the complex. It was therefore necessary for the economist to understand thoroughly the working of an ideal, competitive economy before he could turn to an investigation of the actual economy. With this aim in view, J. B. Clark devoted many years of his life to the task of refining economic theory and making clear the nature and significance of the basic assumptions of equilibrium economics. It was his intention to pass from static or equilibrium economics to a more realistic and more complex economics which he labelled "dynamic." He explains in the closing chapter of *The Distribution of Wealth* that "Dynamic theory, if it were quite complete, would give results from which, in actual life, there would be no variation; for it is a part of the function of this division of the science to account for every element of friction, as well as for every change and movement that actual life shows. Among the lesser tasks that it will set for itself is that of reducing to clear formulas the principles which govern trusts, labor unions and other consolidations. . . . It will undertake a larger work, when it tries to reduce to law the growth of population and of capital, and a still larger one, when it shall try to determine the conditions that govern the rapidity with which methods of production change and become more fruitful." [2]   After the publication of *The Distribution of Wealth* in 1899 the elder Clark turned to the problem of bridging the gap between static and dynamic economics.   This new interest took the form of inquiries into the growing monopolization of economic activity and the problem of controlling trusts.   In 1901 Clark published his study on *The Control of Trusts,* which was followed in 1904 by *The Problem of Monopoly.*   Soon after the appearance of the *Essentials of Economic Theory* (1907), he became interested in the world peace movement.   As the years went by this movement came to absorb the bulk of Clark's intellectual energy, with the result that he never again returned to the problem of closing the gap between static and dynamic economics.   If he was perturbed by his failure to develop both kinds of economic analysis, the elder Clark must nevertheless have found great satisfaction in the work of his son, who was to become recognized as one of America's leading exponents of a realistic, dynamic economics.

Clark's Intellectual Background

Of the many influences shaping the career of John Maurice Clark the most important one was undoubtedly the close association with his father.   J. B. Clark passed on to his son two important contributions, the first of which was a completed body of static economic doctrine which was to serve as an excellent point of departure for future economic analysis.   The second contribution was an interest in improving economic science which has never ceased to be a source of great stimulation not only to the younger Clark but to all those who have followed his career and who have become acquainted with his writings.   In speaking of the first contribution made by his father, Clark states that he regards his own work as "that of one who wishes to carry forward the work of his greatest

[2] Clark, John B., *The Distribution of Wealth,* page 441. New York: The Macmillan Company, 1927.

THE SOCIAL ECONOMICS OF JOHN M. CLARK   341

teacher from the point at which that teacher left it. From this standpoint the main problem is how to proceed from static to dynamic economics. This problem will be viewed in the light of the fact that we possess a substantially complete static economics, while dynamics is in its infancy: of the further fact that statics is essentially provisional, a stepping stone to dynamics, simplifying the problem by attacking first those features which do not involve change; and of the final fact that dynamics must restore realism by putting in everything that statics leaves out, so far as possible within the limits of human understanding." [3] In carrying forward the work of his father Clark is faced with some very important problems. Will the shift from static to dynamic economics be merely a matter of starting with static conclusions and then adding the dynamic elements which have been omitted in the static analysis? Or will there be more fundamental changes involved in moving from the static to the dynamic position? In Clark's opinion the development of a dynamic economics is no simple problem. On the contrary, it involves radical changes in the thinking of the economist. It requires that the economist go back to the original premises of static economics and that he replace them with new, dynamic assumptions. In Clark's view, the introduction of the dynamic element into economic analysis involves some radical departures from orthodox, nineteenth-century economic theorizing.

Clark believes that, since a dynamic economics can be built only on the foundation of a new set of basic assumptions more in accord with the facts of actual economic experience, there is a great need for more inductive analysis. He explains that more induction is necessary to provide the factual basis for a new set of dynamic premises. Even after he has established his new premises, the economist will have a need for more induction, since conclusions can be drawn from the premises of dynamic economics only with the aid of further inductive studies. Clark asserts that the change from his father's static economics to the more realistic dynamic economics of the future is not just a mechanical change. It is not merely a question of converting static into dynamic conclusions by making quantitative allowances; instead, it is a question of making qualitative allowances, since dynamic conditions are basically different

[3] Clark, John M., "The Relation between Statics and Dynamics," *Economic Essays Contributed in Honor of John Bates Clark*, page 46.

from those which are static. New inductive studies must be carried out, new assumptions made, and an essentially different economics created. It is not a matter of pouring new wine into old bottles; rather it is a matter of making a distinctly new product. Of course, the materials with which the new economics is to be made will be taken in part from the corpus of traditional economics. Parts of the static assumptions and analysis will presumably always remain essential elements of economic science. No science, social or natural, grows by discarding all the accumulated knowledge and understanding of its pioneer workers. In the case of economics, however, the changes produced by the twentieth century are so fundamental that they appear to justify Clark and other exponents of dynamic economics in speaking of a reconstruction of their science.

The new assumptions of Clark's dynamic economics relate mainly to matters that are concerned with the nature of human behavior and the institutional setting of the economic system. In place of the static view of man associated with the concepts of marginal utility and the competitive equilibrium, J. M. Clark puts a "more realistic picture of human nature" with "its prevailingly dynamic character." He states that his dynamic economics cannot work successfully with the idea of the "economic man." Consequently his assumptions about human nature reveal less of the hedonistic psychology of the nineteenth-century utilitarians and more of the social psychology of William James, John Dewey, and Charles Horton Cooley. The elder Clark was the product of a generation to which the teachings of the early twentieth-century social psychologists were of little interest; and the psychological premises of his static economics were likewise a purely nineteenth-century product. The younger Clark prefers to abandon the static, inherited view of human nature, and to replace it with a view that is at once more realistic and much less susceptible to "definite and simple deduction." He wishes to start his economic analysis with an interpretation of human nature in which impulsive action plays an important part, in which habit and custom are seen to have a prominent role in controlling individual action, and in which self-interest is only one of a number of factors influencing human behavior. Clark asserts that "This means that to understand the [economic] system we must interpret it as containing a large admixture of non-individualistic action, both public and private, and action governed by incentives and motives other than material self-interest.   These cannot now be dismissed as non-economic, for they are necessary parts of the explanation of how the business system actually works, as well as of plans to make it work better." [4]

In substituting a dynamic view of human nature for the older static view Clark reverts to some of the earlier views of his father. In his earliest treatise on economics, which was published in 1885 before William James had introduced his pragmatic psychology and before Dewey, Cooley, and others had developed their social psychology, John Bates Clark had not yet started the task of perfecting his static, equilibrium economics.   Anyone who is acquainted only with the elder Clark's later writings is surprised to find him pleading in 1885 for a more realistic view of human nature than that to be found in classical economic thought.   In the preface to *The Philosophy of Wealth* J. B. Clark wrote that he "endeavored to contribute a share toward the reformulating of certain leading principles of economic science.   The traditional system was obviously defective in its premises.   These were assumptions rather than facts, and the conclusions deduced from them were, for that reason, uncertain. . . .   The better elements of human nature were a forgotten factor in certain economic calculations; the man of the scientific formula was more mechanical and more selfish than the man of the actual world.   A degraded conception of human nature vitiated the theory of the distribution of wealth." [5]   At this early date J. B. Clark was calling for a theory of human nature closer to "anthropological fact."   Unfortunately, at this time the science of psychology had not yet experienced that advance from which there later emerged more realistic interpretations of human behavior; and before long the elder Clark was absorbed in the task of working out the full significance of the doctrine of marginal utility, which he had developed independently of William Stanley Jevons and Carl Menger.   He never again returned to his early suggestions relating to the restatement of the basic premises of classical and neoclassical economic thought which pertain to the character of human nature.   This work he was to pass on to his son, who has profited

---

[4] "The Relation between Statics and Dynamics," page 58.
[5] Clark, John B., *The Philosophy of Wealth*, Second Edition, page 111.   Boston: Ginn and Company, 1894.

greatly from the development of modern psychology, and who has consequently prepared himself for the difficult task of creating a theory of human nature which is more appropriate to a realistic, dynamic economics. Since it is from the views relating to human nature that were presented in *The Philosophy of Wealth* (1886) and not from those found in *The Distribution of Wealth* (1899) and the *Essentials of Economic Theory* (1907) that the younger Clark has derived his greatest inspiration, he feels that he is only starting where his father left off in the closing decades of the last century when the social sciences were just beginning to feel the pulsations of a new era in psychological interpretation.

Besides introducing a dynamic approach to the study of human nature, J. M. Clark replaces the static view of economic institutions with a more dynamic view of the institutional framework through which human nature expresses itself. John Bates Clark and his contemporaries had not only eliminated all institutional change from their static analysis, but they had also taken as given data the institutional arrangements of an individualistic, laissez-faire economy. In this laissez-faire framework of interpretation, government interference was at a minimum; and, furthermore, there was no place in static theory for such forms of collective action as the labor union, the farmers' cooperative, and the trade association. With respect to the institutional setting of economic activity the dynamic economics of the younger Clark differs from static economics in two ways. In the first place it substitutes a twentieth-century institutional framework, with its many forms of collective action, for the nineteenth-century laissez-faire institutional framework. In the second place dynamic economics substitutes a genetic theory of institutional development for the static theory of institutions held by J. B. Clark and the other equilibrium economists. J. M. Clark points out that "The key to statics, as we have seen, is a problem: that of levels of equilibrium. This is an abstraction based on observation of the relative stability of economic values, and of oscillations whose behavior suggests a normal level toward which the economic forces of gravity exert their pull. The key to dynamics is a different problem: that of processes which do not visibly tend to any complete and definable static equilibrium. The importance of this shift from the search for levels to the study of processes can hardly be overemphasized; it is not less significant than the change from static to dynamic conditions." [6]   In essence, what J. M. Clark is seeking to do is to convert economics from a science of mechanistic equilibrium to a science of evolutionary process.

In his endeavor to make economics less mechanistic and more evolutionary, the younger Clark has drawn much inspiration from his father's early economic writings in which the outlines of a theory of economic development are plainly discernible.   In a chapter of *The Philosophy of Wealth* entitled "Non-Competitive Economics" J. B. Clark observed that "Individual competition, the basis of the traditional science, is, in extensive fields, a thing of the past.   It has been vitiated by combinations [in industry], leaving society without its former regulative principle." [7]   It was plain to the elder Clark by 1885 that economic theories which had been developed for the study of an economy midway in its evolution would not be equally useful for the investigation of an economy in which competition had been largely set aside.   What was necessary was a dynamic economics which would provide an understanding of a dynamic economy.   But in these early years J. B. Clark did not speak of economics as a science of process in contrast to a science of equilibrium.   As the Darwinian concept of process only slowly penetrated the field of economic thought, it was not until after 1895, when Veblen began to write in post-Darwinian terms, that J. B. Clark's early suggestions for the improvement of economics began to bear fruit.   By that time the elder Clark had turned from dynamic analysis to the more systematic field of static economics where

[6] "The Relation between Statics and Dynamics," page 51. In commenting upon this important problem of shifting from a mechanistic to an evolutionary economics Clark has pointed out to the writer that there are two aspects of the problem: "[1] adapting the science to the accepted fact of evolutionary processes; and [2] explaining how and why the basic evolutionary processes take place as they do. I suppose I was more interested in the first than the second, e.g., ready to take large-scale mass production for granted as a datum. I have never aspired to formulate 'laws of evolution.' "

[7] Clark, John B., *The Philosophy of Wealth*, Second Edition, page 189. This problem of the trustification of industry was further investigated by J. B. Clark in *The Control of Trusts*, 1901 (revised and enlarged in collaboration with J. M. Clark in 1912), and *The Problem of Monopoly* (1904). Late in his academic career the elder Clark wrote *Social Justice without Socialism* (1914), which J. M. Clark has described as "my father's valedictory to economics—a platform of moderate interventionism."

he could give free rein to his well-established bent for system building and highly deductive analysis.[8]

The younger Clark has also been influenced by the thinking of Charles Horton Cooley, one of America's outstanding sociologists. Throughout Clark's essays and treatises are to be found references to this early twentieth-century sociologist who did so much to free the study of sociology from the grappling chains of nineteenth-century metaphysical and theological thinking. By the time that Clark was an instructor in sociology at Colorado College (1908-1910), Cooley had made a name for himself with the publication of his *Human Nature and the Social Order* (1902) and his *Social Organization* (1909). His four significant contributions, which we find embedded in Clark's economic writings, were a pragmatic insistence upon more inductive studies, an emphasis on the social nature of human behavior, an interpretation of social organization as a complex of cultural processes, and a drawing of attention to the importance of collective action in control of individual action.

In a series of brilliant essays Cooley offered a number of pertinent suggestions to economists who, like Clark, were interested in carrying economics beyond the limits of static analysis.[9] He asserted that economics was "almost wholly a short-range study of mechanism, remarkable for elaborateness within a confined area, but not at all remarkable for breadth or for any light it throws on the wider economic and social significance of the mechanism of which it treats. To suggest the impression made upon one who takes up these studies after a long abstinence from them, I may say that the economic theorist appears like a man who should observe only the second hand of a watch: he counts the seconds with care, but is hardly in a position to tell what time it is."[10] Cooley suggested

[8] John M. Clark explains in *John Bates Clark, A Memorial* (1938) that his father had a unique propensity not only for simplifying problems but also for building systems. It could be argued that these special characteristics of J. B. Clark's mental make-up later proved to be barriers which prevented him from making equal progress in the field of dynamic economics.

[9] Cooley's essays included "The Institutional Character of Pecuniary Valuation" (1913), "The Sphere of Pecuniary Valuation" (1913), "The Progress of Pecuniary Valuation" (1913), and "Political Economy and Social Process" (1918).

[10] Cooley, Charles Horton, "Political Economy and Social Process," *The Journal of Political Economy*, April, 1918, Vol. XXVI, page 367. Although this article was not published until 1918 it was delivered as a paper before a group of students and instructors in 1910. See the selected papers of Cooley which appear in his *Sociological Theory and Social Research* (1930).

that an "adequate doctrine of process" should take the place of the mechanistic doctrines of orthodox economics. In spite of what might have appeared to have been a harsh criticism of systematic economics, Cooley did not support those who were asserting that received economic doctrine should be abandoned completely and that a fresh start should be made with a clean slate. He was equally critical of the historical school of economists which, he felt, had been much too empirical in its studies to provide the theoretical basis of a more realistic economics. The great need, as Cooley envisioned it, was for more economic theory, "but theory that without losing any of the substantial results of current economics shall so broaden them as to meet in some degree the requirements" of a dynamic economics of process. In reading Cooley's essays on the problems of economics Clark found no suggestion that the creating of a body of dynamic economic theory would be an easy task. Cooley was himself not certain how far one could go in infusing an adequate doctrine of process into the general body of economic theory, but he was convinced that the difficulties confronting the dynamic economist were not insuperable.

Cooley and Veblen were products of the same generation, and their influence upon social scientists has been quite similar in a number of respects. They were early students of the new social psychology, and both adopted the genetic approach in the analysis of social organization. Veblen, however, was inclined to be much more speculative and less empirical than Cooley. In 1923, summarizing a lifetime's observation of activity in the social sciences, Cooley outlined what he believed to be the major task of Clark's generation. He stated that "original work is likely to take the direction of more limited but thorough studies. This work will be theoretical—I for one am not interested in any work that is not—but the theory will spring from a more circumscribed and penetrating study of fact." [11] Throughout his economic studies Clark has revealed much more of Cooley's inductive bias than of Veblen's speculative bent.

There are additional ways in which Clark's economic thought is more reminiscent of Cooley than of Veblen. In Cooley's work there is much less of that deterministic flavor which is associated with

[11] Cooley, Charles Horton, "Now and Then," *Sociological Theory and Social Research*, page 285. New York: H. Holt and Company, 1930.

Veblen's technological interpretation of the course of economic evolution. Although Veblen was too keen a thinker to accept any purely materialistic interpretation of cultural phenomena, his economic writings appear at times to underrate the importance of what Cooley has called "collective rationality." The deep strain of pessimism running through Veblen's economic analysis led him to stress the impotency of mankind in the face of great technological changes, and caused him to give much less attention to the possibilities of economic control than did other critics of the capitalistic system. This pessimistic outlook on the economic future of mankind is not duplicated in the work of Cooley or Clark. Cooley broke away from the doctrine of the inevitability of social progress which was such an important feature of nineteenth-century social theorizing, but he did not go to the other extreme of looking upon the fate of mankind as a matter to be decided only by the unpredictable course of chance cultural developments. Cooley's optimistic attitude toward the future of economic society was grounded in a pragmatic awareness of the need to avoid wishful thinking and to seek progress only with the aid of scientific understanding. It is this optimistic outlook which has been duplicated in Clark's economic analysis.

Although Clark has had the advantage of contacts with the work of such pioneers as Veblen, Cooley, and Mitchell, all the basic elements of his thinking may be found at least in embryonic form in his father's writings. Undoubtedly many of the ideas borrowed by Clark have been improved through his contacts with the economic and sociological theories of other twentieth-century social scientists. But, as the younger Clark has explained, "Challenging fragments of the broader type of study" are to be found in J. B. Clark's economic treatises. These fragments include the suggestion that the basic premises of orthodox economics stand in need of a fundamental reconsideration, that economics should be modernized to meet the requirements of a rapidly changing economy, and that the ethical aspects of economic analysis should be thoroughly explored. The elder Clark, however, was too much a product of the second half of the last century to be able to follow these suggestions with constructive scientific analysis. It is probably true, as J. M. Clark has said of his father, that "Had he been born in the twentieth century, he would have had a different mental background, and would have faced an altered array of economic problems. Undoubtedly, his work would have been different; in what ways it is hardly fruitful to speculate." [12] The younger Clark has an essentially different mental background which goes far to explain why he has moved beyond his father's static economics to develop his own dynamic, realistic "social economics." Heeding Cooley's injunction to spend time on empirical rather than speculative studies, J. M. Clark has not only abstracted from the data of economic experience to a lesser extent than his father did, but he has also widened the scope of economic analysis.

Clark's Pragmatic Psychology

In overhauling the premises of orthodox economics, Clark has given special attention to the renovation of psychological theory.[13] When contrasting the psychology of Alfred Marshall and other orthodox economists with "modern psychology," he observes that there are two fundamental differences between the old and new psychologies. In the first place nineteenth-century psychology was excessively individualistic and introspective. It pictured man as living in "an age of self-reliant foresight beyond other ages," in which the environment was assumed to be a factor of negligible importance. Modern psychology, however, finds the individual surrounded by an environment which is capable of exerting a great deal of influence. And so, unlike the last century, "The twentieth century is an age which, beyond other ages, is aware how much man is molded by his environment, and is deliberately undertaking to control this molding process. This fact must be a dominant note in constructive contributions to theory in the immediate future, if the proper balance of emphasis is to be restored." [14]

The second way in which the old and new psychologies differ relates to the interpretation of consciousness. In the psychological theorizing which underlies nineteenth-century economics, consciousness is a purely static concept which emphasizes deliberation rather than action. For this static interpretation of the human mind Clark substitutes "a dynamic interpretation of consciousness," which elevates action above mere contemplation or deliberation. His

[12] *John Bates Clark, A Memorial*, privately printed by the children of J. B. Clark in 1938, page 18.

[13] Clark, John M., "Economics and Modern Psychology," *Preface to Social Economics*, pages 92-169. New York: Farrar and Rinehart, Inc., 1936. By permission of Rinehart and Company, Inc.

[14] *Ibid.*, page 98.

interpretation of human behavior takes on a new significance because it unites deliberation with action. It treats the individual
as a factor in a dynamic process of living, part of which may be
rational and part irrational. Clark's psychological theory takes the
individual to be a struggling being in a dynamic, historical process
rather than a contemplative, rational being who inhabits a world
of economic and social equilibrium.

It was assumed by nineteenth-century psychologists that after the
proper rational calculations had been made the individual would
seek only those things that he most desired. In the modern view of
psychology the explanation of mental activity is quite different.
Clark explains that whenever the mind directs its attention to an
object it also tends to desire it: "Every idea is in its nature dynamic
—an impulse to its own realization, which, if left alone, will act as a
motive force until some other idea takes its place." [15] A large part
of mental activity is therefore impulsive, and is under the direction
of "momentary interests." To make a man want something, all
that is necessary is to keep his attention focused on the idea of
getting what is wanted. There is no question here of the pleasure
to be derived from the possession of a good, or of the pain suffered
in giving up something in exchange for it. The mind is not a
calculating machine, but is instead a fluid complex of interests,
which is easily influenced by outside forces. One of these outside
forces to which Clark makes special reference is advertising. If the
human mind had functioned in the manner explained by the nineteenth-century psychologists, advertising could have made little
progress. Its progress is explained by the twentieth-century psy-
chologist who shows that advertising drills an idea into an individual's consciousness until it prevents "any critical weighing in the
light of all the possibilities and all the interests of a rationally
unified self."

Another deficiency in the psychological basis of nineteenth-century economics relates to the explanation of the nature of human
wants. The usual procedure of nineteenth-century economists was
to take human wants as given data which did not require any explanation. Although it was generally understood that human wants
had a biological basis, no attempt was made to explain how biological
tendencies of a very general nature develop into specific demands

[15] *Ibid.*, page 106.

for particular objects. According to Clark's theory of wants, a human want is not something with a static nature, but instead is a tendency to "action with a feeling-value attached." Since these tendencies to action are molded by the environment, the individual does not bring final or completed wants into the market place. "The fact remains," says Clark, "that what every man brings into the world of markets and trading is not wants but merely the raw material out of which wants are satisfied. The primitive instincts appear to be few in number, general in character, and attached to no one particular object. Economic wants for particular objects are manufactured out of this simple and elemental raw material just as truly as rubber heels, tennis balls, fountain pens, and automobile tires are manufactured out of the same crude rubber. The wheels of industry grind out both kinds of products. In a single business establishment one department furnishes the desires which the other departments are to satisfy." [16] From the viewpoint of the individual the industrial system is a potent environmental force which successfully canalizes the "underlying tendencies" of human nature, with the result that human wants are "manufactured" just as are the commodities used to satisfy these wants.

The two economic doctrines which Clark criticizes in the light of his twentieth-century psychology are the theory of marginal utility and the theory of production. He criticizes the marginal utility theory of orthodox economics on the ground that it is based upon an oversimplification of human nature. In place of the one abstract, pleasure motive, there are many motives which, although they are not subject to exact measurement, can be ranked in an order of preference so as to create a scale of motives or values. This scale of values reflects the influence of all the complex and varied cultural factors which condition an individual's behavior. It is not simple calculation or pure deliberation but these culturally determined values which tell us what we want, and whether we are willing to make the necessary sacrifices to satisfy these wants. Clark points out in his essay on "Economics and Modern Psychology" that "Calculation may tell a man just what it is he must sacrifice if he does a certain thing, but it cannot tell him whether he wants the thing badly enough to accept the sacrifice. . . . Calculation is necessary, but not final." What are more important than calculation of

[16] "Economics and Modern Psychology," pages 100-101.

gain or loss, of pleasure or pain, are the scale of values and the environment which so potently influence the individual. Marginal utility theory may explain how a rational being spends his income in a given environment, but it has little to say about the effects of the industrial system upon the ways in which men, in general, spend their incomes. According to marginal utility theory, rational individuals make the best of their given environment. Would they not be able to use their incomes more efficiently in a different environment? To this question Clark replies in the affirmative. He finds that the present industrial environment has many "grave shortcomings," and that it hinders the efficient use of income in a number of ways. Neo-classical economists made the error of taking marginal utility as something that was absolute, whereas in reality the significance of the marginal utility concept is purely relative. It is relative to what Clark calls the existing system of stimuli, many of which are an integral part of our industrial system.

At this point in his analysis Clark introduces the problem of individual versus social utility. The terms "individual utility" and "social utility" had both been introduced into economic science long before the younger Clark began his own economic investigations. John Bates Clark had taken up the problems of individual and social utility in *The Distribution of Wealth,* which was published in 1899.[17] In the elder Clark's static economics there was never any conflict or lack of harmony between the two types of utility, for the assumption was made that a perfectly competitive economic system would maximize not only individual but also social utilities. It was alleged that competitive market prices made possible that expenditure of an individual's income which brought to him the largest possible supply of utilities. Likewise these market prices indicated that society was maximizing its satisfactions.

John Bates Clark, like the other orthodox economists of his day, made little investigation of the extent to which actual market prices failed to maximize both individual and social utilities. His handling of the problem of individual and social utility is in direct contrast to J. M. Clark's analysis. Whatever might be true of a hypothetical, laissez-faire economy, the younger Clark is most em-

---

[17] J. M. Clark has explained to the writer that "It is probably true that the theory of 'inappropriables,' mentioned in the 'Philosophy of Wealth,' is the cornerstone of my thinking on 'social utility.'"

phatic in declaring that the economic system as it is known today is far from being a system in which market prices adequately measure both individual and social utilities, and in which there is a maximization of both types of utilities. In J. M. Clark's opinion the important problem of dynamic economics is to relate the concepts of individual and social utility to the evolving industrial system out of which all utilities emerge. His "social economics" endeavors to point out why individual and social utilities are not always maximized in the modern economy; and, in more tentative fashion, it suggests some ways in which a closer coincidence of the two types of utilities may be secured in the future.

Clark makes one further attack upon the validity of marginal utility theory. In the orthodox explanation of marginal utility, little attention was paid to the nature of the act of choosing or making a decision on the basis of various calculations. It was generally assumed that the making of choices was an effortless procedure, or even one that held supreme interest and enjoyment for a rational individual. Modern psychology has challenged this interpretation. Following William James and J. R. Angell, Clark asserts that the making of a decision involves such a psychological effort that there is a tendency for people to limit the areas in which they exercise their freedom to choose or to make decisions about alternative courses of action.[18] People in general do not permit themselves to be victimized by what Clark has described as the "irrationally rational passion for impassionate calculation." Instead, they turn to habitual ways of thinking and acting when they wish to avoid the psychological discomforts associated with the making of choices or decisions. Clark finds that "it is only by the aid of habit that the marginal utility principle is approximated in real life." This is true because the apparent, everyday calculations of most people are to a large extent based upon "routine choices" established in the past by conscious deliberation. Calculation goes on, as the orthodox economists maintained, but only within the boundaries of rather rigid patterns of human conduct. The explanation

[18] Clark quotes with approval the following explanation offered by C. H. Cooley in his *Human Nature and the Social Order*, page 34. "Indeed, to know where and how to narrow the activity of the will in order to preserve its tone and vigor for its most essential functions, is a great part of knowing how to live. An incontinent exercise of choice wears people out, so that many break down and yield even essentials to discipline and authority."

of economic behavior should therefore deal with these broad habit patterns, their origins, and their effects upon social efficiency, as well as with the calculations of the market place.

After having criticized the psychological theory underlying the orthodox doctrine of marginal utility, Clark turns to a consideration of the theory of production. In his opinion this theory should be made consistent with the dynamic interpretation of human nature which has become the foundation of the modern psychology of advertising. There should be a shift away from the static view of human nature toward that view which takes human nature to be a "series of attitudes toward the universe." This series of attitudes is subject to modification by many outside influences, of which the business system is a very important one. Since businessmen are very greatly concerned with human wants and expend much energy in "focusing general wants into the desire for particular objects," the theory of production should go beyond the explanation of how existing wants are gratified to include an explanation of the creation of wants by business enterprise. If businessmen do not exercise care in how they mold men's wants, they may seriously impair the whole productive system, because certain types of goods destroy the energy and efficiency of mankind. Undesirable wants may be stimulated at the expense of more desirable wants with the result that output may not be "in reasonably efficient proportion to the amount of human effort expended."

The final outcome of Clark's interest in the field of modern psychology has been a widening of the field of economic investigation. He shows no satisfaction with a mere criticism of orthodox doctrines; rather it has been his aim to expand his analysis of the psychological foundations of nineteenth-century economics to give it "the dignity" belonging to "an integral and working part of a broader theory." This theory is not to become another deductive thought structure comparable to that of Alfred Marshall.[19] The system which is built by Clark around his theory of the process of economic guidance has none of the perfection or logical precision of the formal, closed system of the neo-classical economists. This is so because his unwillingness to accept "the static view of human nature embodied in marginal utility, the independent demand schedule,

[19] "Economics and Modern Psychology," page 128.

and current definitions of production" necessarily results in a body of economic theory that is both tentative and unconventional.

When one turns from Clark's views on human nature to a study of his philosophy of scientific method, it soon becomes apparent that there is a very close connection between his pragmatic psychology and his theory of method. It is Clark's general position with respect to the problem of method that all methodological procedures merit some consideration; under no circumstance is any relevant fact to be neglected. For Clark, "the core of scientific method lies, not in induction nor in deduction, but in taking account of all relevant facts and excluding none." [20] Questions of method of analysis are to be settled not by *a priori* argument but by the test of doing—"by testing different theoretical methods in terms of their results." [21] Since he finds that the ultimate test of the validity of economic theory lies in an appeal to actual experience, Clark's economic analysis emphasizes the inductive rather than the deductive approach. He believes in "carrying theoretical study into the realm of those facts and forces with which business is consciously in contact . . . and generalizing upon that great wealth of inductive material which is accumulating at an ever increasing rate." [22] Clark appears never to tire of the search for more facts to substantiate an already developed theoretical approach. His economic researches are penetrated by a spirit of realism which is quite alien to much of the economic analysis of the closing years of the nineteenth century; and his general methodological aim is to develop an intimacy of contact with economic facts such that there will be an adequate "corrective for the over-abstract tendencies of the theorist."

As economic theory gets in closer touch with inductive investigations, its statements will tend to become more and more quantitative. Quantitative analysis alone, however, can never provide a complete understanding of the economic world. All that one can hope for are generalizations that are "significantly true." The goal of scientific method is the uncovering of economic truth; but, as

[20] Clark, John M., "The Socializing of Theoretical Economics," *The Trend of Economics*, edited by R. G. Tugwell, page 75.

[21] *Ibid.*, page 73.

[22] Clark, John M., *Studies in the Economics of Overhead Costs*, page x. Chicago: The University of Chicago Press, 1923.

Clark points out, what economic truth is depends in part upon what the investigator is seeking. Some economists are concerned with a description of the economic world, and they feel that, as they approach a more accurate description of the world, they are coming closer to economic truth. For this class of investigators economic truth partakes of the nature of "pure accuracy of description." The difficulty with this definition of economic truth is that it places no limit upon the gathering of facts, and provides no standards in the light of which the importance of various kinds of data may be determined. A complete description of the economic world is impossible, and any endeavor to realize such a description leaves the investigator with a mere catalogue of facts. In Clark's view description is valuable, but only as a device for making the task of evaluation and interpretation less difficult.

The search for economic truth through abstraction rather than description likewise has its limitations. It often leads to economic truisms which are logically consistent but of limited value, since they are too remote from the world of actuality. Deductive economics, if it yields to the temptation to seek statements that are true without exception, ends by becoming a series of tautological propositions which are distant from reality. "The disinterested search for pure truth" by the deductive method does not lead to the kind of economic truth that interests Clark, for he has a pragmatic view of the nature of truth according to which truth is more a matter of usefulness than of purity. What interests Clark is "useful truth," truth that is useful in coping with the community's major economic problems.

Each age has economic problems that are peculiar to itself, and in handling these problems certain generalizations are made by economists. During the nineteenth century, for example, the generalization that each individual was always the best judge of his own interests had some validity in England for that particular period; but this generalization, Clark points out, has no "absolute verity or eternal adequacy." The special circumstances of the nineteenth century gave rise to economic doctrines or generalizations the truth of which was only as permanent as was their environment. Each generation of economists is confronted by a new set of problems, the solution of which requires new economic doctrines.

New issues bring forth different selections of significant data which are embodied in new generalizations. In this manner each generation needs to discover anew for itself the essence of economic truth. If these generalizations prove to be useful in settling the issues of the time and place, then they are judged to be true by the test of consequences. This is the pragmatic test of truth according to which a generalization is true if the expected consequences follow upon the application of the doctrine to the issues calling for solution. Clark realizes that no body of economic doctrines ever settles all issues completely, and that economic truth can never be spoken of as being complete. At the best one can only expect an approximation to the successful handling of all trouble-giving issues and difficulties.

The Economics of Overhead Costs

Clark's position as one of America's ranking economists was established by the publication in 1923 of his well-known treatise entitled *Studies in the Economics of Overhead Costs,* which was dedicated to his father "as a very small contribution toward realizing his conception of a dynamic economics." In this study Clark adopts a number of assumptions relating to the structure and functions of the modern economy which run contrary to the underlying assumptions of traditional economic thought. His basic assumption is that the economic system is "a dynamic social organism, rather than a static mechanism with an endless uniformity of perpetual motion." [23] In effect, Clark alters the economist's framework of interpretation by substituting the concept of a dynamic process for that of a smoothly functioning mechanism. For the mechanistic interrelations of the competitive equilibrium he substitutes "organic interrelations," which are the source of a great deal of economic friction and instability. Although he does not fall a victim of the fallacy of likening society to a biological organism, Clark does observe that economic processes are in some ways quite similar to biological processes for the reason that both types of process have little of the uniformity of mechanical movements. Since the organic interrelations of the modern economy show many discrepancies that are of a very persistent nature, it is the

[23] *Studies in the Economics of Overhead Costs,* Preface, page ix.

purpose of Clark's study of overhead costs to come "to grips with the dynamic movements and resistances to movement" which are characteristic of the modern economy.

Another basic assumption underlying Clark's study of overhead costs relates to the immobility of capital. Nineteenth-century equilibrium economists had assumed that the productive capacity of industry was in the form of a highly elastic capital fund. Individual enterprises found it relatively easy to move into and out of various economic activities because they were not hampered by the presence of large investments in fixed capital equipment. In his dynamic analysis Clark dispenses with the assumptions of small-scale enterprise and highly mobile capital. He acknowledges the presence in industry of much large-scale enterprise with "a relatively inelastic fund of productive capacity." It is this great body of fixed capital investment which has outgrown "being a mere exception to the general laws of value and efficiency" and become "a large and important section of economic principles." Clark raises the question whether the analysis of overhead costs should be an "autonomous department of economics, or whether the whole body of economic thought must become an 'economics of overhead costs' in the sense of being integrally built upon this [overhead-cost analysis] as a part of its foundation." His answer to this question is that the whole body of inherited economic thought requires a general re-examination in the light of a new cost analysis so that economics may become a more useful tool for the handling of contemporary economic problems.

When classical economics took shape late in the eighteenth century, the businessman's primary investment was in labor and raw materials, with the result that most costs of production were directly charged to specific units of output. Overhead costs, the charges made by the businessman to his output in general, were of no great consequence. The cost theory developed by the classical economists reflects this early preponderance of variable costs. Although the classical economists recognized that some payments for overhead costs were unavoidable, the bulk of costs was assumed by them to be variable expenses directly traceable to each unit of output. As a consequence, economics was slow to assimilate the facts of overhead cost. J. S. Mill, Torrens, and Senior gave some attention to the theory of fixed costs, but the general body of classical thought failed to take much notice of the significance of this type of cost. For this reason Clark is "tempted to conclude that economics' prevalent ideas on expenses of production date back to the domestic system and are not really appropriate to any later stage of industrial development."

A number of developments in recent decades has focused attention on the problem of overhead costs: the maturing of the railroad industry, the growth of public utilities, improvements in the technique and theory of cost accounting, more adequate investigations into business cycle problems, and the recognition of labor as an overhead cost to society. With the passing of the railroads out of the pioneer stage of their development, the charging of uniform rates was displaced by a policy of discriminating between various classes of freight. It was soon discovered that a large part of a railroad's costs was fixed in the sense that they were independent of the amount of traffic hauled, and that, through a policy of rate discrimination, it was possible to cover the fixed costs of railroad service if competition between railroads was sufficiently restrained. It was also observed that other industries such as the public utilities had large fixed capital investments, and that their price policies had to give full recognition to the presence of both fixed and variable costs. The daily and seasonal variations in the output of various utilities drew attention to the need to use "idle overhead" in off peak periods. Those in charge of the utilities developed a program which had two major purposes, the improvement of plant utilization during off-peak periods and the allocation of cost burdens that did not vary with output.

The technique of cost accounting was greatly improved under the stimulus of the need to allocate such fixed costs as large interest charges on capital investments and increasing tax burdens. This was particularly true in the case of the railroads and public utilities. The growth of economic statistics made available the data with which the cost accountant could work. At the same time it came to be recognized by many economists that the business cycle was no mere aberration from an assumed competitive norm; instead it was discovered to be a regularly recurring phenomenon in which there were long periods of unused productive capacity. In depression years even the most efficient firms found themselves unable to use all their producing capacity, or to earn even a normal return upon their investment. "Cut-throat competition," for which there was supposed to be little room, if any, in a competitive economic system, became a widespread phenomenon which inevitably led to attempts to restrain competition. In these and other ways the attention of economists and businessmen was centered on the problem of overhead costs. Instead of continuing to be a minor consideration, as they were prior to 1880, overhead costs moved to the center of the stage after the emergence of large-scale production. It was not long before economists began to modify their doctrines in order to make more room for the concept of overhead cost. As time went by the modification of inherited doctrine was replaced with a demand by more heterodox economists for a new orientation in economic science.

After the appearance in industry of large overhead costs, the businessman continued to regard the costs of labor and raw materials as variable, because at any time he could reduce such costs by refusing to hire labor or to purchase additional raw materials. Clark, however, does not adopt the same point of view with respect to labor and raw material costs; in his analysis labor is an overhead cost just as is the fixed capital of industry. Once the community has brought a group of laborers into being, they are very similar to the productive capacity which results from investment in buildings and equipment. Both labor and fixed capital need to be maintained whether or not they are producing. The cost to society of supporting a group of laborers does not vary with their output, for this cost goes on even though the laborers produce nothing, as is the case in periods of enforced idleness which come in the depression phase of the business cycle. Ordinarily laborers are made responsible for their own maintenance, but where their wages are insufficient and the community does not make provision for the deficiency, there is a deterioration of the community's fixed investment in its labor force. The mere fact that in hiring labor by the day or by the week, and in adjusting his labor supply to his output, the businessman can regard labor as a variable expense and not as a part of his overhead costs, does not make labor less of an overhead cost to society. No matter what the businessman does, the cost of using labor remains an overhead cost to society. If businessmen were to agree to pay laborers an annual wage irrespective of the amount of work done, then labor would reveal its true nature as an overhead cost of business.[24]   It is only because of the kind of wage contracts now used that the cost of labor is a variable expense to the businessman.   Clark asserts that the businessman has in effect converted what really is an overhead cost into a variable expense, for under a different type of wage contract labor cost would become a fixed charge like interest, taxes, and rent.   Where the businessman makes the laborers responsible for their own maintenance, or where he throws this burden on the community, there occurs what Clark calls a "shifting and conversion of overhead costs."

It is conceivable that what is now generally recognized by businessmen and accountants as an overhead cost, the cost of using machinery, could be converted into a direct and variable cost. Clark cites the case of the United Shoe Machinery Company, which assumes much of the burden of the overhead costs of small shoe-manufacturing concerns by leasing machinery to them instead of selling it outright.[25]   In this fashion the cost of capital equipment is converted into a variable expense for the shoe-manufacturing enterprises, since the rental of the machines can be made to vary with the output of shoes.   The wage earner acts in the same way as does the United Shoe Machinery Company when he assumes the responsibility for his own overhead costs, but frequently he cannot bear the burden successfully, since he is unable to make a satisfactory wage bargain with the employer.   If laborers were able to get an adequate wage and a guarantee of continuous employment, or if they were fortunate enough to secure such high wages as to be able to make provision for their involuntary unemployment, they would then be in a position to take care of their own maintenance.

The concept of overhead costs is extended by Clark to include the cost of raw materials.   As an "ultimate fact" of human cost, the expense of producing raw materials is an overhead cost to society. The producer of raw materials invests funds in his enterprise; and, once his enterprise has been set up, the cost of maintaining it goes on whether or not there is any output.   A farmer or miner must be maintained by society in years of depression, unless society is wiiling to allow its farming and mining activities to deteriorate.

---

[24] The current movement in certain industries to provide labor with a guaranteed annual wage is a move in the direction of having labor cost recognized as a fixed charge by both private industry and society.

[25] *Studies in the Economics of Overhead Costs*, page 26.

The businessman does not assume the responsibility of providing for the maintenance of farmers and other raw material producers beyond purchasing their products whenever he finds it profitable to do so. He enters a contract for the delivery of farm produce and not for the maintenance of the farm population of the nation, with the result that the burden of providing for the welfare of agricultural enterprises falls primarily on the farmers, who may or may not be able to carry this burden successfully. In the depression phase of the business cycle farmers are frequently unable to carry the heavy burden of agricultural overhead. Unless society steps in to provide the necessary aid through relief programs, our farm enterprises deteriorate just as machinery deteriorates when it is not properly maintained.

After having demonstrated that from "the broadest social standpoint" the concept of overhead costs is as applicable to labor and raw materials as it is to industrial equipment, Clark goes on to show that the cost of keeping the industrial system a going concern is a social or collective overhead cost. In his view the industrial system has maintenance requirements just as does a piece of machinery. During the depression phase of the business cycle, the industrial system is like a huge factory only partly in operation; even though it is not functioning fully, many of the industrial system's costs go on just the same. If society does not take steps at such a time to assume the burden of industrial overhead, the economy inevitably suffers a serious deterioration. No businessman regards the good functioning of the whole industrial system as his special responsibility, nor are its general costs of maintenance assumed to be a part of his overhead costs. Consequently, he passes the burden of industry's overhead cost to the community. As soon as a depression begins, each private enterprise endeavors to protect its own profit margin by cutting down production and maintaining prices. The net result of this business policy is to create more unemployment, to reduce purchasing power further, and to bring on in more severe form the very evils which each businessman thought he was preparing to avoid. If all parties, including the workers, were willing to share cuts in profit margins, wages, interest, and rents, there would be more hope of avoiding the disastrous cumulative effects of meeting a depression by cutting down production and trying to preserve profit margins or high wage levels. There is here a conflict between private and social welfare, since the businessman wants to preserve his profit margin by reducing output, whereas the social interest calls for a continued output of goods and services.

The inevitable procedure of businessmen faced with a depression is to follow a course of action designed to prevent spoiling of the markets; and no single firm or industry is in a position to alter this private business policy. In 1923 Clark compared the existing business situation to the condition in which the national banks found themselves prior to the establishment of the Federal Reserve System in 1914. Prior to 1914 no one bank or group of banks could use their reserves to meet a financial panic. What was needed was cooperative action whereby scattered bank reserves could be used to prevent a financial panic from getting out of control. This concerted action was made possible by the Federal Reserve System, and since 1914 there has never been a repetition of the financial conditions that were witnessed in the latter part of 1907. Likewise, in the field of business individual action needs to be supplemented with coordinated action on the part of the businessmen, if the bad results of adhering to a private accounting view are to be eliminated. If the community's "reserves of productive power" are not to be wasted in years of depression, some form of cooperative action on the part of business needs to be worked out. Since business in the 1920's was shifting the burden of overhead costs upon shoulders unable to bear such a heavy load, Clark felt an obligation to bring the community to a full realization of this unsound business policy. As early as 1923 he saw a fundamental need for some form of national economic planning, but a whole decade was to pass before the destructive consequences of a world-wide depression were to bring economists to a full realization of the significance of Clark's early analysis of the economics of overhead costs.

In Clark's analysis of the modern economy, which has the problem of unused industrial capacity as its central theme, the general conclusions are in marked contrast to those arrived at by the equilibrium economists. Whereas in the older static economics high commodity prices meant general scarcity and much utility in terms of human need, in Clark's dynamic analysis high prices merely indicate the general prosperity which occurs in the upswing of the business cycle. In the modern economy of large-scale enterprise price no longer functions as a regulator of supply and demand, as was the

case in the small-scale economy of the nineteenth-century economists.   Furthermore, in a competitive economic system the production of a larger quantity of one commodity would be accompanied
by a reduced production of some other commodity, since, in a condition of full utilization of productive capacity, capital would have
to be shifted from one use to another.   In his study of the modern
economy Clark discovers that this generalization is no longer applicable.   Making more of one commodity does not involve making
less of some other commodity, because all too frequently there is
much idle productive capacity at hand.   In the economy of the
static economists the alternative to production in one line was production in some other line, but in Clark's dynamic economy it usually happens that the alternative to production is no productive
activity at all.   All during the depression phase of the business
cycle, and even during the recovery period, the alternative to production is only idleness for men and machines.

Carrying still further the contrast of an economy possessing a
large overhead investment with one that has little overhead, Clark
points out that the modern economy is one where there are persistent discrepancies between supply and demand; and when there
is unused capacity there is no apparent tendency for the various
productive factors to be rewarded at any one time according to their
immediate or short-run marginal contributions.   In summarizing
his *Studies in the Economics of Overhead Costs* Clark calls attention
to the fact that "we have a considerable body of economic generalization, bearing on the facts of overhead costs and decidedly at
variance with the assumptions and conclusions of that type of economics which searches for the conditions of a perfect equilibrium
of supply and demand."   In equilibrium economics demand was
taken as the starting point of analysis, with producers doing their
best to anticipate the requirements of this demand.   There were
no obligations on the part of producers or consumers to continue
supplying or demanding goods and services.   Any producer could
withdraw from the market without leaving a large part of the existing demand unsatisfied; and, likewise, any consumer could withdraw from the market without depriving producers of a considerable
portion of the demand for their products.   In a small-scale, competitive economy producers and consumers could be relied upon to
keep supply and demand in balance; but in Clark's dynamic econ-

omy the situation is quite different. "Another very noteworthy fact which has confronted us in the study of business cycles," says Clark, "is that the reduction of demand, which occasions unemployment of labor and capital, constitutes so serious and definite an injury that there is coming to be a sense of obligation for the maintenance of steady demand and of responsibility for the results of failing to maintain it. Producers come to have almost a rudimentary sort of right in the maintenance of demand for their products. They have responded to previous demands by investing their working lives and their capital to supply them, and have by that very fact made themselves to some extent dependent on the continuance of the demand for that general class of services and facilities. Their claim to continuance of demand may be called a natural right, in the rather elastic sense that too great disregard of it brings a natural punishment in the form of a general convulsion of the whole economic system." [26]   Industry must be kept in motion by supporting demand so that supply will also be maintained. Too frequently this responsibility for the maintenance of demand is ignored by those who purchase commodities and services, with the result that the modern economy seldom ever enjoys a situation in which supply and demand are equated, or in which industrial capacity is fully utilized.

The final conclusion that Clark draws from his study of the economics of overhead costs is that the presence of a large amount of fixed capital equipment in the modern industrial system has destroyed whatever tendency the system had to establish an equilibrium of the static sort. In place of equilibrium there now is persistent disequilibrium and the failure to produce those goods and services "which it is humanly worth while to produce." Since the equilibrium economists assumed that individual efficiency would lead to collective efficiency, they concentrated their attention upon the efficiency of the individual firm in its work of coordinating the various factors of production. Whereas in the orthodox interpretation collective efficiency is nothing more than the reflection of individual efficiencies, in Clark's dynamic economics "narrow commercial efficiency" does not lead to "economic efficiency in the large." Clark observes that the efforts of individual business enterprises to achieve efficient operation do not now result in the

[26] *Studies in the Economics of Overhead Costs,* page 466.

furtherance of collective or social efficiency, but instead their efforts bring about "the convulsions that sap the strength of business as a whole." The simple connection between individual and collective efficiency established by the economists of the last century has been destroyed by the new conditions of the twentieth-century economy, with the result that high efficiency in private profit-making is now correlated with a very low level of social efficiency.

The collective or social efficiency which is Clark's major concern differs from the technical efficiency of a machine and also from the business efficiency of a private enterprise. Technical efficiency is an engineering problem of determining the most efficient operation of a machine, whereas business efficiency is a matter of maximizing the net revenue to be obtained from a business enterprise. Social efficiency is a broader concept which deals with "human values and their organization." [27]   It is a matter of maximizing the social values to be derived from the industrial system with a minimum of social costs; in essence, social efficiency is a problem of measuring the performance of the entire economy.

Clark's theory of social values is based on the concept of "a truly organic social valuation." Social valuation, in contrast to market valuation, is a process of determining "what is the value to society of these utilities consumed by individuals, or the cost to society of these costs which individuals bear." [28]   Market valuation is deficient in two respects. It assumes that the prices placed on commodities in the market place are measures of value to the community as well as to individuals, and it ignores all those values which do not now command a price. Whatever cannot be measured in terms of market price has no place in the scheme of values which arises in the market place, but "The social value of the constitution, or rather, of the traditional interpretation of the bill of rights, has played a decisive part in determining many market prices. Here we have what may be called organic social values playing a part in the field of commerce." [29]   In explaining these organic social values Clark goes behind the competitive values of the market place to examine "higher and more elusive utilities." He recognizes that

[27] "The Socializing of Theoretical Economics," page 73.
[28] Clark, John M., "Toward a Concept of Social Value," *Preface to Social Economics*, page 49.
[29] *Ibid.*, page 56.

"The search for standards of social value in the economic realm is a baffling task, yet far from an unprofitable one. We shall presumably never discover a definite yardstick of social value comparable to the dollar yardstick of exchange values; but we may find standards by which those of the market may be revised or in some instances replaced." [30]   As economists enlarge their conception of what it is that constitutes an efficient way of living they will give more content to the category of social values. Social values will be further increased by improvement of the regulations which govern the exercise of property rights, by increased protection for uninformed consumers, and by the establishment of certain safeguards which prevent a lowering of the standards of living of the general population. Clark looks forward to developing a concept of social valuation which will be capable of scientific application to concrete cases. To be scientific a concept of valuation, whether it be social or individual, must be subject to some objectification. If economists cannot place social values on a firm foundation of scientific objectivity, there will be little hope of ever securing agreement about the nature and scope of these rather elusive values.

One very important aspect of the problem of social valuation is the emphasis that it places upon the various social and economic institutions which impinge on the institution of the market. In studying the nature and scope of social values it is no longer possible to take institutions for granted as if they were independent of the markets in which their effects are to be observed. This is illustrated in the case of the body of rules and regulations governing the transfer and control of private property. Decisions of the courts, which become embodied in the law, draw the lines between those values which may be appropriated by private economic interests and those which may not. In some situations a whole new realm of exchange values is created, as in those circumstances where the courts recognize intangible values not formerly accorded the protection of the law. At times "the scope of appropriable rights changes, by legislation or judicial evolution, and the meaning of a system of free exchange changes with it." [31]

Clark explains that it is very important to investigate the role of institutions as creators of social values. Because institutions

[30] "Toward a Concept of Social Value," page 44.
[31] *Ibid.*, page 46.

tend to become traditional, there is always the need to weigh them against other possible ways of doing things. If institutions are valued merely because they are the customary ways of achieving certain ends, there are tremendous possibilities of social waste. For this reason Clark insists that institutional valuations be distinguished from commodity valuations, and that the relations between these two types of valuation be clearly indicated. In this connection he writes about reversing the marginal method of valuation. In traditional economic analysis a commodity gets its price from the utility of the marginal unit of the supply; but in Clark's theory of social value the reverse is true. Each commodity gets its value from the whole complex of institutional relations of which it is a product. Clark points out that "The simplest exchange is not free from these complex [institutional] relationships which we have been discussing. Each one is a unit in a great social joint product. Thus the theory of social value is anti-marginal in the sense that the part—say the single commodity—takes its price from the value of the whole rather than the whole getting its price from the utility of the marginal part. In a similar way railway rates cannot be fixed by the marginal cost of separate services without running the whole road into bankruptcy." [32] When it becomes more widely understood that all market values are products of an institutional matrix, there will be more reason to hope that the discrepancies between market and social valuations may be reduced.

According to Clark's interpretation, those economists who operate in "the rarified atmosphere of technical discussions of the theory of value and distribution" have insulated themselves from the realities of actual experience. Most economists have either accepted the market value of a commodity as a true measure of the social value produced, or they have refused to meet the problem by ignoring the concept of social value. Clark asserts that in both cases these economists have only succeeded in detaching the theory of value and distribution from the real world. It is his conviction that the concept of social value will prove very useful not only in overcoming this detachment, but also in establishing a connection between the market process and those extra-market forces and institutions which are of great importance in the creation of economic values.

For the purpose of estimating the efficiency of the total economy

[32] *Ibid.*, page 59.

"financial accounting and cost-accounting on business principles" turn out to be quite inadequate, because private-business accounting falsifies the picture of the relative amounts of constant and variable costs. A new form of social accounting should be developed to show the discrepancies between commercial and community measures of efficiency, and to reveal the actual behavior of the "ultimate costs" of industry. What Clark would like to see established is " 'social cost-keeping'—a form of economic reckoning which cuts through the sophisms of private financial accountancy and calls social waste by its true name." [33] This social accounting would replace the costs and values of private accountancy with social costs and values. When one asks what are the standards by which society is to determine the costs of industry, he finds no such definite standards as are found in the market place. Clark is fully aware that society is faced with a very difficult task when it goes beyond the dollar standards of measurement provided by the market institution; but he thinks that the immense difficulty of the task should not be a reason for failure to cope with the problem. It is the duty of economists to reveal the hitherto neglected, unpaid costs of operating our industrial system, and to aid society in giving more meaning to the category of "social costs."

In developing his theory of "unpaid costs" Clark calls attention to those costs which are ignored by the "individualistic canons of responsibility to which business is accustomed." These unpaid costs include the costs of idle men and machines, the costs involved in the destruction of utilities through overemphasis upon the importance of fashion, the wastes resulting from competitive advertising and excessive private business secrecy, and many other wastes concerning which public opinion has not yet been fully crystallized. Communities, as Clark points out, have myopias which prevent them from fully appreciating the many unpaid costs of modern industry. This is true because too frequently economic institutions are looked upon by individuals as sources of private gain rather than as means to larger public ends. But the modern tendency, Clark believes, "is increasingly to view institutions as means to definite ends, and nothing can further this tendency more than a study of the particular economic gains and costs to society for which such institutions are responsible. This study the economist would seem to be espe-

[33] *Studies in the Economics of Overhead Costs*, page 485.

cially qualified to make." [34] When such studies have been made, social accounting will then become a more effective device for judging the efficiency of the modern economy as a creator of "human values."

Clark's Theory of Social Organization

In the concluding section of his *Studies in the Economics of Overhead Costs* Clark indicated the path along which his scientific interests were to go after 1923. The dynamic modern economy with its large overhead costs turns out to be a "New Leviathan" which has grown up without design. The unending string of inventions of the past two centuries has brought this "Leviathan" into being as the "unintended by-product" of man's cultural evolution. But Clark thinks that we now know enough about our economic institutions to have some prospect of successfully controlling them, and that economic control should not be shunned even though it means that we may have to remake our industrial system in the process.[35] It was with the intention of throwing some light on this problem of economic control that Clark published the first edition of his *Social Control of Business* in 1926. He realized that economic control was "at bottom the problem of adjusting conflicting interests and claims of 'rights,' and harnessing selfish interests to that mutual service which the division of labor has made one of the most fundamental and most commonplace features of industry." [36] It was Clark's purpose in his treatise on the control of the business system to analyze the many complementary parts of the whole process of adjusting conflicting economic interests, and to "present this process in its unity, as well as in its variety."

The view of society which underlies Clark's theory of social control is one of "an aggregate of individuals, interests, and groups which, however organically bound together, are still distinguishable." [37] It lies somewhere between the atomistic view of the nineteenth-century economists and the socio-biological view of the early sociologists which subordinated the individual to the larger social organization. Clark's theory of society is similar to C. H.

---

[34] "Toward a Concept of Social Value," page 65.
[35] *Studies in the Economics of Overhead Costs,* page 487.
[36] Clark, John M., *Social Control of Business,* First Edition, Preface, page xiii. Chicago: The University of Chicago Press, 1926.
[37] *Social Control of Business,* 1939, Second Edition, pages 7-8.

Cooley's theory in which the dualism between the individual and society is eliminated, and in which it is recognized that there is no such thing as a society which is completely independent of the individuals of which that society is composed. Unlike the early theories of society, which professed to see a fundamental harmony running through all social organization, Clark's theory takes conflict to be the fundamental fact about which social interests are organized. If there is harmony in social organization, it is incidental and largely the result of habitual modes of behavior. Unlike the equilibrium economists, who assumed that society was harmoniously organized because men were basically rational, Clark asserts that human reason is the source of a great deal of social conflict. If human conflicts are to be eliminated or reduced, social intelligence will have to be organized and injected into the social system. A harmoniously organized society is not a given datum, but rather it is something for which men must strive. In Clark's view the problem is one of securing more harmony and less conflict, the actual extent of harmonious social relations depending upon the amount of human effort put forth in that direction.

Clark's theory of society is unlike that of the socialists, which emphasizes the division of classes along purely economic lines. According to his pluralistic social interpretation there are many groups striving for various ends, but these groups do not follow the simple class divisions set up by the socialistic theorists. Like Commons, Clark stresses the importance of the larger entity called society which is composed of smaller groups with various degrees of consciousness of collective interests. The importance of this pluralistic view of social organization becomes evident when one turns to an analysis of the machinery by which society gets its work done. Clark points out in his study of the social control of business that society acts through its government, which may function for the furtherance of general human purposes, but which all too frequently acts in response to the demands of minority pressure groups. Society never attempts to satisfy all interests, but instead it endeavors to come to a decision as to what particular interests should be immediately served. Decisions about which group interests should be furthered and which should be restricted may be democratically or dictatorially made. For Clark the only type of society worth considering is the democratic type in which the decisions as to which group interests will be satisfied are made in a democratic, manner.

Clark's pluralistic view of social organization, with its emphasis on the clash of economic interests and the need for adjustments, fits in very well with his interpretation of the dynamic modern economy. In this economy there are many interests in conflict: laborers are pitted against corporations, small-scale business fights monopolistic enterprise, farmers are in conflict with industrial interests, outmoded industries deplore new types of enterprise which seek to eliminate the survivals from a past economic era, and public utilities argue against their customers, whose primary interest is not in investors' returns but in cheaper utility services.   And throughout the structure of the modern economy wanders the unorganized brotherhood of consumers which, cutting across many conflicting loyalties, seeks that elusive general economic welfare about which economists are becoming increasingly conscious.   It is the purpose of social control to resolve the conflicts of these many economic interests, so that the fruitfulness of our large industrial overhead may not be dissipated by a continuance of that socio-economic strife which has grown *pari passu* with the mechanization of industry.

Clark finds that the present era of economic control has come about as the result of the growth of democracy, the spread of large-scale organization in industry, and the development of science. The most important single factor responsible for the current need for social control has been the growth of science in the past hundred and fifty years, for it is science and the developing industrial technology which have created the machine process.   Unfortunately, the industrial system has evolved along lines which may be regarded more as adjustments to the requirements of the machine than as adjustments to the needs of decent human living.   The machines have not refused to gratify men's wishes, but they have gratified them only on the condition that this gratification is not secured at the price of their own welfare.   The price exacted by the machines has been their maintenance, or provision for their "overhead costs," which businessmen have been only too willing to meet.   Unfortunately, since human beings have not always made the same demand that their "racial" needs be met by the business system, their overhead costs have not been equally well provided for.   The machines "make a species of bargain with men, in which they are perfectly willing to give men anything that they may think they want, always provided that it is not inconsistent with the racial needs of the machines themselves. Human beings, be it noted, make no such reservation, for the very adequate reason that they do not know what their racial needs are, and for the further reason that even if they did know them, individuals could always be found willing to barter them away. And the machines take no pains to enlighten man's ignorance in this matter, so that the ultimate consequences of the bargain come upon man as a painful surprise, after he has committed himself too deeply to draw back." [38] Clark does not object to meeting the racial needs of the machine, for he is fully aware of the necessity of doing so; but he is greatly perturbed by any society which fails at the same time to take care of the many needs of its general population. It would be folly to ignore the maintenance requirements of our mechanized industrial system, but it may be "cultural suicide" to ignore much longer the maintenance requirements of large sections of our working population. In Clark's opinion there is no necessary contradiction between preserving the welfare of the machines and that of the community; all that is now necessary is that we awaken to a full realization of the economic needs of the community which the machine should serve. The problem is for the individual, through cooperation with other individuals, to take hold of the machine process and subject it to the necessary controls.

Clark observes that the machine process has had especially disastrous effects upon the well-being of the laboring classes. This is true because the machine has deprived the laborer of the opportunity of acting like a free and useful human being. He has failed to develop a proper sense of responsibility because he has felt that his job belongs to the machine rather than to himself. It is only within recent years that the laborer has come to a realization that he has a right to his job which gives him an interest in the machine comparable to the factory owner's interest. Besides feeling little responsibility for the results of his work, the laborer has little interest in his own economic destiny, since the making of the policies that dominate the machine process is restricted to the select few who own or control the machines. Power to interfere successfully with

---

[38] *Studies in the Economics of Overhead Costs,* page 487.

the operations of the machine process is still largely beyond the grasp of the laborers. As a consequence, they alternate between the slave morality of giving as little as possible and getting as much as they can, and the intermittent feeling of wanting to give expression to their potential power through strikes, sabotage, or some other obstructive program. Clark thinks that "racial equality" between men and machines cannot be secured as long as the working population is scarcely above the level of helots. The workers will be freed from this undesirable situation only when the machine process has been subjected to "the force of constructive human will, enlightened by collective intelligence."

Clark's interpretation of the operations of the machine process is clothed with an emphasis that is not found in Veblen's work. Although late in his career Veblen made the suggestion in *The Engineers and the Price System* (1921) that man might escape the domination of the machine process in a society directed by technicians, most of his analysis was concerned with revealing how men are unconsciously conditioned to meet the requirements of the machine age. As Clark's emphasis has been more on the ways in which men may subdue the mighty forces of industrialism, it is not surprising to find him devoting more attention than did Veblen to a future in which "collective intelligence," supported by "the force of constructive human will," may break the evil spell of the machine process. Along with improvements in scientific knowledge has come a new scientific attitude, which has altered men's views relating to the historico-cultural processes and the social institutions which function within these processes. It is no longer necessary to believe, as some social scientists once thought, that mankind is herded along the course of human living only by the blind forces of accidental cultural change. Man does not create the socio-economic alternatives among which he may choose, but he does have the freedom to choose that alternative which carries the greatest human appeal. In accepting this theory of cultural development Clark avoids the weaknesses of excessively deterministic or voluntaristic cultural interpretations. His cultural theory exhibits less determinism than is found in the work of Veblen, and also less of the idealistic optimism of the late nineteenth-century equilibrium economists. He has preserved something of the tradition of idealism, which has always emphasized the importance of the individual, but at the same time he has always kept his idealism within reasonable limits by blending it with the pragmatist's twentieth-century empiricism.

The Social Control of Business

When Clark published the first edition of his *Social Control of Business* in 1926 he made public utilities and trusts the central interest in the problem of economic control.   In the thirteen years which passed before the second edition of Clark's work appeared, social control entered a new era; after 1929 it was no longer "a matter of incidental abuses, but of an economic system failing in its main task, of energizing production."   Social control now "calls, not for piecemeal reforms, but for comprehensive treatment of an organic malady, ramifying throughout the economic system." [39] This organic malady, which takes the form of the business cycle, had been touched upon in some detail in Clark's earlier *Studies in the Economics of Overhead Costs,* but it received a much more extensive treatment in his *Strategic Factors in Business Cycles* which was published by the National Bureau of Economic Research in 1934.[40]   This latter treatise was published after many of the generalizations arrived at in the study of the economics of overhead costs had been given a firmer inductive basis by the work of research organizations like the National Bureau.   Clark's study of the strategic factors of the business cycle summarizes the findings of the National Bureau and of the Committee on Recent Economic Changes.   It also seeks to arrive at whatever conclusions seem tenable concerning the movements of the cycle and the causal factors which are strategically important in the light of the possibility of control.

The National Bureau of Economic Research had been making studies of various phases of the business cycle problem ever since its founding in 1920, and it had by 1934 accumulated a wealth of material relating to the fluctuations of business and industry.   Not only was Clark able to use all this statistical material in his work of drawing conclusions about the business cycle, but he also had access to the special studies of the Committee on Recent Economic

---

[39] *Social Control of Business,* Second Edition, Preface, page ix.
[40] For Clark's early analysis of the cycle problem see *Studies in the Economics of Overhead Costs,* Chapter XIX, "Overhead Costs and the Business Cycle," pages 386-415.

Changes, an organization especially interested in revealing the factors that throw our economic system out of balance. Up to 1930, the bulk of the work of the various research agencies throughout the country had been devoted to fact-gathering and the development of statistical techniques. By 1934 there appeared to be a need for some critical analysis of this preliminary research work. This was especially true in the years after 1930, when nations were experiencing the bitter consequences of a general breakdown of their business systems. The situation called for the immediate use of whatever facts about the business cycle had been already gathered and whatever analytical studies had been made of policies and programs by which the cyclical movements of business might be controlled.

As a close associate of Wesley C. Mitchell, Clark has drawn a great deal from the work of this outstanding business-cycle investigator. His cycle analysis, however, differs from that of Mitchell in two important ways. In the first place Clark has not concerned himself very much with an inductive study of the fluctuations of the business system. Nor has he spent years directing a research agency whose energies have been largely devoted to the refinement of statistical techniques and the detailed study of the history of business cycles in Western Europe and the United States. The interpretation of statistical data has always had a much greater appeal for Clark than the accumulation and preliminary handling of such data. As a result of this intellectual bias there is among Clark's economic writings nothing comparable to Mitchell's early *Business Cycles* (1913) or his later *Business Cycles, The Problem and Its Setting* (1927). Evidently Clark feels that the setting of the business cycle has now been so well explored that time can be more profitably devoted to an analysis of the existing supply of data relating to the fluctuations of the economic system. Early in his study of the strategic factors in business cycles Clark informs the reader that the task before him "is not primarily one of statistical description nor of statistical analysis in the usual sense. It is perhaps better described as an application of theoretical analysis to an unusually comprehensive array of concrete data. Thus, while the study deals with statistical materials, it makes no attempt to present a complete or voluminous statistical picture of the history of business cycles." [41]

[41] Clark, John M., *Strategic Factors in Business Cycles*, page 4. New York: The National Bureau of Economic Research, Inc., 1934.

In Clark's work one does not observe so much of that reluctance to grapple with large theoretical constructions which has delayed Mitchell in following his survey of the setting of the business cycle with an extensive theoretical treatment of the problem.

Clark's sense of urgency causes him to emphasize the importance of trying to use our present understanding of the cycle for purposes of social control. Whereas Mitchell has tended to work "from the standpoint of an objective diagnosis seeking to learn what brings about the conditions we observe," Clark has worked "with a more pragmatic eye to controlling these results." In his *Strategic Factors in Business Cycles* he has as his special objective the attempt to select those factors that are of strategic importance. Clark defines a "strategic factor" as one that "has real power to control other factors, and to determine the general character of the result; and it has peculiar strategic importance if, in addition, we have power to control it; if it is not, like the weather, beyond the reach of anything that we can now do." [42] When focusing his attention on economic control Clark makes two fundamental assumptions: that the independent action of businessmen will never be sufficient to eliminate the ups and downs of the business world, and that it is possible to control business fluctuations by manipulating certain strategic economic factors. Since Clark abandons all pretense that the economic system can automatically eliminate business fluctuations, he turns to the task of showing why the business cycle requires some form of collective economic action of a public or private nature if the cycle is to be satisfactorily handled.

The framework of Clark's theory of the business cycle incorporates a number of elements drawn from the theories of other cycle investigators. He pictures the business system as a pattern of responses to a number of external "originating forces." Outside forces such as wars, bumper crops, inventions, the discovery of new goods, secular changes in price levels, and changes in foreign trade are taken to be "originating causes," although Clark asserts that no such causes are "aboriginal" in the sense of not having causes themselves. In his cycle analysis causes are "originating" only for purposes of scientific analysis. When these outside causes impinge on the business system, certain responses such as rising or falling prices, changes in profit margins, and fluctuations in orders for

[42] *Ibid.*, pages 6-7.

capital equipment take place. Neither originating causes nor the responses of the business system, however, are sufficient in themselves to explain the cycle. "Some theories of business cycles," Clark explains, "run mainly in terms of originating forces, others in terms of the responses of the business system. It appears, however, that cycles cannot be regarded as results of one or the other of these groups of forces exclusively; they are joint results of the two groups and of their interaction." [43]

The responses of the business system "form a closely-knit sequence of cause and effect, in which a state of over-contraction appears to set in motion forces leading to over-expansion, and this in turn to over-contraction once more. In these swings, movements tend to be self-reinforcing rather than self-limiting, until they have gone so far that a marked reversal becomes inevitable." [44] Clark observes something of a general behavior pattern through which the responses of the business system operate. There is a great deal of variation in the behavior of such external forces as wars, climatic changes, and inventions; and where this variation is extreme, there is little regularity that may be taken as a basis for scientific generalizations or made the subject of a program of economic control. The responses of the business system, however, are quite unlike the external forces operating upon the business system. These responses, whether induced by a war or a new product, tend to follow the same course of action, and to produce "very similar symptoms" in the form of price movements, changes in employment, and developments in basic industries, retail and wholesale trade, and credit and security markets. From these observations Clark then draws the important conclusion that as far as the results of business fluctuations are concerned the responses of the business system are more important than the original outside disturbances. This is so because if one were to endeavor to control the outside disturbing forces, he would have to be prepared to control many highly variable factors. Where the control program seeks to control only the customary responses of the business system, it should be much simpler and much easier to put into effect.

Many of the responses of businessmen to the fluctuations of the economic system result in a "cumulative piling-up of impulses"

[43] *Ibid.*, page 14.
[44] *Ibid.*, page 18.

which inevitably brings on a period of excessive contraction. Clark explains that "Business men may simply regard the peak periods as their sources of greatest profits, and subordinate other things to the attempt to do as large a volume of business as possible at those times, living through the dull periods as best they can. This attitude tends to perpetuate instability." [45] What is necessary for the stabilization of business is a better recognition on the part of businessmen of their "long-run and collective interests" as opposed to their short-run, individual welfare. They should come to realize that their behavior in the upswing of the cycle results in a perversion of the profit function. Profits fail to operate as a regulator of general business expansion when businessmen fail to distinguish between profit-making which is the result of internal economies and that profit-making which develops out of a lack of harmony between selling prices, wage rates, and the cost of raw materials. What are necessary are new behavior patterns on the part of businessmen. Business policies relating to capital expansion, output, and employment should be adjusted to an outlook on the business system as a whole which does not fail to take account of the fact that there are many items of overhead cost which are not included in the accounting statement of the individual firm. If this desirable result is to be achieved, Clark believes that certain responses of the business system to external forces will have to undergo fundamental change.

Clark seeks to control the business system so that it will be in a position to minimize the effects of external disturbances. He has no hope of securing anything like complete insulation of the business world from the disrupting effects of wars, crop failures, and technological changes. Since complete stability or balance of the business system is an ideal that holds little interest for Clark, all that he hopes to establish is a "zone of tolerance." Somehow a line must be drawn between those disturbances of the business world that are to be tolerated and those that are not to be permitted to disrupt business activity. Clark believes that some such "zone of tolerance" can be established by selecting certain important responses of the business system for inclusion within a program of economic control. Once this is done, whatever disturbing factors remain would not be so serious in their economic effects that

[45] *Ibid.*, page 93.

they could not be accepted as necessary conditions of economic existence in a democratic society.

In order to explain how business responses should be controlled Clark outlines a "partial theory of business cycles," in which he takes as his starting point some impulse leading to an upturn of business, such as an increase in total consumers' demand which results from the offering of new goods, the depletion of stocks of consumers' goods, more selling effort, or a more optimistic mood.[46] Out of this original increase in consumer demand there arises a derived demand for producers' goods, which, however, involve a considerable amount of time in their production. The original upturn in consumer demand is then reinforced by the payment of increased wages by the producer-goods industries. Prices of both consumers' and producers' goods rise, speculative buying makes its appearance, and the rise in prices is intensified. "Guided by the rising prices rather than a statistical canvass of demand and supply," producers continue to expand their programs for the production of capital equipment and stocks of durable consumers' goods. The expansion of business is financed by an accompanying expansion of credit; and, as increases in prices become general, industry as a whole is stimulated. Eventually the supply of producers' equipment and the stocks of durable consumers' goods catch up with the demands of the market, which cannot expand indefinitely. The day of reckoning is hurried for the reason that not all of the increase in consumer income is spent. Some of this income is saved, while another portion is deflected from the markets for producers' and consumers' goods and is poured instead into the market for speculative securities. As soon as the markets reveal that a condition of oversupply is at hand, production of equipment and durable consumers' goods slows up; falling prices and the contraction of credit are soon followed by declining production and a reduction in consumer income. The pace of business activity slackens throughout industry in general, and the cycle is then reversed.

The central point of interest in this brief outline of the course of the business cycle is the relation between activity in the industrial-

---

[46] Clark is careful to point out that the original impulse may be any one of a large variety of impulses, or it may be a combination of more than one impulse. Also production may take an upturn without waiting for a change in consumer demand. See his *Strategic Factors in Business Cycles*, pages 174-175.

equipment and durable-goods industries and changes in general consumer demand.[47]   Clark shows that a decline in the rate of growth in the demand for consumer goods has a disproportionate effect upon the demand for industrial equipment.   When business-men realize that the rate of expansion of consumer demand has started to decline, they reduce their expenditures for new industrial equipment in anticipation of the need for less productive capacity. The net result is that a decline in the rate of general consumer-demand expansion is accompanied by a larger percentage of de-cline in the demand for new capital equipment.   Businessmen who were producing industrial equipment with the expectation of a continued expansion of consumer demand at an increasing rate of growth now find themselves faced with the possibility of an absolute decline in the demand for industrial equipment.   Should the situation become serious enough, even the replacement of exist-ing productive capacity might be indefinitely delayed.   When pro-ducers of industrial equipment find themselves in this predicament, they curtail production, decrease employment and wage payments, and thus bring about a further decline in the rate of growth of general consumer demand.   The dislocation and disorganization visited upon the producer-goods industries then spreads to busi-ness in general, and the cumulative deflationary movement con-tinues until the lowest levels of a depression phase of the business cycle are reached.

In the light of this partial theory of the cycle, Clark endeavors to pick out those factors which may be classed as peculiarly strategic in the sense that they are subject to considerable private or public control.   Originating causes such as abundant crops, wars, new goods, and new productive processes are less important than other factors in determining "the length, timing and specific features of business cycles and kindred movements."   More strategic are such factors as the derived demand for durable goods, price movements, changes in business confidence, fluctuations in profits, changes in consumer demand, and other related factors.   Of outstanding sig-

---

[47] Clark first inquired into changes in the ratio between the demand for finished goods and the demand for industrial equipment in his essay "Business Acceleration and the Law of Demand: a Technical Factor in Economic Cycles" which appeared in *The Journal of Political Economy*, March, 1917, Vol. XXV, pages 217-235.   He returned to this problem again in his *Studies in the Eco-nomics of Overhead Costs*, pages 389-396.

nificance in the control of the business cycle is the production of capital equipment and durable consumers' goods. In Clark's own words, "The tendency to intensified fluctuations of derived demand, including the demand for the work and the materials involved in producing durable consumers' goods, as well as producers' goods, is of basic importance, in the judgment of the writer. If it could be controlled in all its manifestations, the primary result would be a great stabilization of the average rate of productive activity by cutting off those fluctuations of production which exceed the fluctuations of consumers' current expenditures. As a secondary result, consumers' expenditures would themselves be made far more stable than they now are. Thus the effects of stabilization would be cumulative, and the back of the business cycle would be broken." [48]   To achieve this end Clark would apply a principle of regularization to the capital-equipment industries and to such durable consumer-goods industries as the housing and automobile industries.

The "primary method of procedure" advocated by Clark is the budgeting of capital outlays on a planned schedule which would prevent the overexpansion and overcontraction of capital equipment in response to the extreme ups and downs of the business cycle. No one industry could achieve much stabilization through its own efforts; what is necessary is a "more collective view" than the outlook which business has possessed up to the present. In the case of the steel industry, for example, the steel mills cannot stabilize their production and employment policies through their own efforts. Cooperative action on the part of the purchasers as well as the producers of steel products is essential if a high degree of regularization is to be secured. What is required is an extensive program of stabilization along lines of vertical integration in which the mutual interests of businessmen should somehow be given an opportunity to express themselves. Just what form of economic organization is necessary to provide capital budgeting for all the important equipment industries and related industrial activities is a question that raises many difficulties. It is Clark's suggestion that this organization should take the form of voluntary economic planning on a national basis. Whether or not such a planning proposal would be successful is a question that Clark does not fail to raise;

[48] *Strategic Factors in Business Cycles*, page 191.

he feels that the answer can only be supplied by "the process of experiment." Although Clark's suggested change from the existing system of unbudgeted capital outlays would be an evolutionary one, it would take us in the direction of a system of private enterprise quite different from the one with which we are now familiar. In addition, such a change would probably require at least a generation "for business to make the necessary mental and material adjustments." In Clark's opinion the path to be followed is clear, however, and all that is necessary for success is the will-to-action and a dogged perseverance.

Clark's Social-Liberal Planning Program

Clark's investigation of the nature and significance of overhead costs and his analysis of the strategic factors in business cycles raise the important question of what can be done with an economy which not only does not enjoy the full use of its productive capacity, but which also shows a persistent tendency away from the optimum use of its resources. He finds that there are three ways of meeting this problem. There is, first, the possibility of establishing the "completely fluid, freely-competitive system of individualistic theory." [49] In such a system Clark believes that booms and depressions would probably continue but not with the severity that they display under the present system. He is also of the opinion that the rate of long-run expansion would probably be faster than the rate of growth permitted by the present system, but there still is some doubt in his mind that the rate of long-run expansion would be as fast as the increase in our power to produce. In addition there would be almost insurmountable difficulties in the path of those who would seek to set up a laissez-faire economy. Corporate financial structures would have to be reorganized to eliminate fixed charges, wage rates would have to be made more elastic, and all rigid prices, including public-utility rates, would have to be softened until they approached the sensitive prices of a purely competitive economy. It is Clark's general conviction that "Moves in all these directions are desirable or even necessary to introduce much-needed elasticity into our system; but that they should go the full lengths required to achieve the free-competitive ideal is hardly thinkable; especially

[49] Clark, John M., "Productive Capacity and Effective Demand," in *Economic Reconstruction, Report of the Columbia University Commission*, 1934, page 122.

in the absence of more definite assurance than can be given that the net result would be to make us richer in the aggregate instead of poorer." [50]

The second possible course of action is the setting up of a "completely collectivist system" which would be at the opposite end of the scale from a purely individualistic economy. This collectivist system would have the advantage of being free from many of the limitations on production which are found in the existing economic system. There remain, however, so many unanswered questions with respect to the working of a purely collectivist economy, such as how managerial efficiency would be maintained, how capital would be accumulated, and how the evils of bureaucracy would be prevented, that Clark favors a third course of action which would be one of "smaller modifications" of the "present hybrid system." This third alternative would preserve the main features of the existing capitalistic economy, since it would endeavor to keep small-scale and large-scale enterprise operating side by side. It would call for a "social constitution for industry" which would organize all economic interests into one single group in harmony with the general interests of society.[51] This social constitution would be the basis for a program of national economic planning designed to "eliminate undesirable fluctuations of industrial activity and to make reasonably free use of our powers of production to support an adequate standard of living, on a sound and enduring basis." [52]

Types of economic planning are divided by Clark into the two major divisions of "limited" and "comprehensive" planning. Limited planning includes all types which are not designed to cover the entire economic system. Into this category would fall industrial planning based on the principles of scientific management, business planning on the basis of cartelization, and regional and local planning. Limited planning would also include recent agricultural-planning activity in the United States and the planning efforts of this country during the war periods, which were limited to the emergencies that called them into being. Under the heading of comprehensive planning would come some forms of business

[50] *Ibid.,* page 123.
[51] Clark, John M., "Economics and the National Recovery Administration," *The American Economic Review,* March, 1934, Vol. XXIV, page 23.
[52] *Social Control of Business,* Second Edition, page 455.

planning such as the Swope Plan, socialist and fascist planning, and what Clark calls "social-liberal" planning. As this last type of planning is the one which he believes would be most suitable for the United States, it is the kind of planning to which he devotes most of his analysis.

Clark has little patience with limited planning, but he does realize that it has contributed something to the development of an adequate theory of long-range planning. He points out that the wartime planning efforts of 1917-18 focused attention upon the need to work out some proper allocation of productive factors and to make a comprehensive statistical survey of resources and requirements. In addition, the endeavor to organize the labor market during the war years had some permanent influence on proposals for extending economic control in the postwar period. From regional planning there has developed a realization of the fundamental need to plan in advance so that a general planning program may be properly timed. In spite of their tendency to favor an "economy of scarcity," the various types of business planning have emphasized the importance of adjusting the supplies of various goods to the demands for them. In any adequate planning scheme there will always be a need for some form of restriction upon the sources of supply but the emphasis should not be in this direction. Business planning has tended to ignore the equally important problem of expanding demand until the population, in general, has an adequate standard of living. Intra-industrial planning, which centers in scientific management, has contributed the concept of "stabilized abundance" to planning theory. Planning within industrial units for greater efficiency has gradually directed the attention of observers to the aim of securing more efficient operation in larger spheres of economic activity than the factory or industry. This is the contribution of the engineer and not the businessman, whose efforts to plan have usually veered away from any such goal as "stabilized abundance." In addition, scientific management has contributed the idea of planning by a staff organization, which is different from planning by a line or administrative organization, whose purpose is to carry into effect the plans conceived by the staff organization.

No form of economic planning now in operation meets the requirements of the national planning program that Clark has in mind. Although much may be borrowed from previous experiments in economic planning, he is of the opinion that "we must set these [borrowed] elements in a new framework." In developing his concept of social-liberal planning Clark draws a distinction between "economic planning" and a "planned economy." According to his interpretation a planned economy is possible only in highly collectivistic economic circumstances such as are found in a socialistic or communistic society. Clark does not advocate the establishment of a planned economy of a thoroughgoing collectivistic nature. What he envisions is the planning of the existing private enterprise system in such a manner as to avoid any attempt by government to supervise the many details of private business activity. "Social-liberal planning," says Clark, "implies action on . . . a unified program via general controls that keep within the limits consistent with a healthy private enterprise, more complete controls being limited to certain strategic factors which condition private economic enterprise, these being such as a 'liberal' government may administer." [53]   Social-liberal planners would "plan" but would not "administer" the economy of the future, because Clark's type of national economic planning leaves the administration of production very largely in the hands of private entrepreneurs. Whatever the government would do to alter or plan the operations of the private enterprise economy, such actions would not include any considerable invasion of the field of intra-industrial activities.[54]

Clark's social-liberal planning has little in common with the proposals of other economists which have been described by their critics as "blueprint" planning.   Unlike Mordecai Ezekiel's planning program, which is outlined in *Jobs for All through Industrial Expansion* (1939), Clark's planning proposals set up no production quotas or extensive price-control schemes for the regulation of the private affairs of individual firms.[55]   Ezekiel's planning program calls for

[53] *Social Control of Business*, Second Edition, page 465.

[54] Clark explains that "One may hope that government need not assume the burden of doing something about every departure from the model of perfect competition."   See his article entitled "Toward a Concept of Workable Competition," *The American Economic Review*, June, 1940, Vol. XXX, pages 241-256.

[55] While Ezekiel's planning proposals are described by some of his critics as being of a "blueprint" nature, this is not to say that his national economic plan calls for an undemocratic regimentation of private enterprise. Ezekiel's plan, no matter how detailed it becomes, nevertheless remains a democratic plan

the voluntary surrender by businessmen in the key industries of their power to establish price and production policies without interference from the government. His attack upon business instability and fluctuations in national income is therefore much more direct than that of Clark.[56] Whereas Clark places his reliance for an effective regulation of economic activity mainly upon indirect governmental controls, Ezekiel finds it necessary to invade the inner recesses of the private enterprise system so as to alter the very nature of that system.

Clark's nonrevolutionary, social-liberal planning has both a quantitatively defined objective and a program designed to achieve this objective. His general planning objective takes the form of a "social budget of supply and demand" which would reveal the extent of the nation's productive powers, and both the actual and the potential consumer demands which these productive powers could satisfy in the right circumstances. Clark's national budget of supply and demand would not be like the budget of a socialistic state, which is designed to cover all the production and consumption details of a fully planned economy; instead, its purpose would be primarily to indicate "unused capacities for production and consumption." He is mainly concerned with the problem of fully utilizing productive resources so as to provide the entire population with the essentials of a health-and-decency standard of living. In Ezekiel's plan for "Industrial Expansion" the national budget of production and consumption turns out to be the starting point for a comprehensive control of the production and capital-expenditure schedules of individual firms in the key industries. The national budget would have no such important role in Clark's planning program.

The second major feature of Clark's social-liberal planning proposals relates to the means by which the goal of an enlarged national income would be achieved. The main organization responsible for achieving this objective would be a national economic

which has to be voluntarily accepted by businessmen if it is to be put into practice. For a comparative analysis of various planning proposals see Gruchy, Allan G., "The Concept of National Planning in Institutional Economics," *The Southern Economic Journal*, Oct., 1939, Vol. VI, pages 121-144.

[56] For the major features of Ezekiel's planning program see his *Jobs for All through Industrial Expansion*, pages 79-111. New York: A. A. Knopf, 1939.

council or planning board with fact-finding and advisory powers.[57] The success of this board would depend upon the support given to its recommendations by the executive and legislative branches of the government and by private business organizations. It would be necessary to have "a more formal organization within industry" which would give expression to the wishes of workers and consumers as well as of businessmen. There is a great need in the business world for "a scheme of voluntary working together," which would prevent any one economic interest from bringing about the partial use of men and machines in the interest of private profits but to the neglect of general economic welfare.[58]

After the national economic council outlines the broad aims of the planning program, which must be acceptable to both the government and private industry, it would then be the responsibility of the government to pursue those courses of action which would achieve the established planning goals. The government's planning activity would be "as now, mainly indirect, operating through strategic conditioning factors and through voluntary cooperation." Government controls would be carried out through monetary and fiscal policies, wage and price adjustments, credit restrictions, and many other economic measures. Clark hopes through such measures to remove enough of the fluctuation of business activity and of the obstacles to the full utilization of economic resources to secure

[57] A more extended discussion of Clark's views on the role of a national planning council is found in his testimony on a bill to establish a national economic council, which appears in the *Hearings Before a Subcommittee of the Committee on Manufactures*, S. 6215 (71st Congress), Oct. 22—Dec. 19, 1931, pages 210-220. See also the Report of the Subcommittee of the Committee on Unemployment and Industrial Stabilization of the National Progressive Conference which is reprinted in the *Preface to Social Economics* under the title of "Long-Range Planning for the Regularization of Industry," pages 229-269. Since this report is a joint product of four committee members who do not indicate their individual contributions to the report, it cannot be taken as representative of Clark's position with respect to the planning problem. In general the tone of this 1932 report on national economic planning is much more optimistic than Clark's chapter on "Economic Planning" in the 1939 edition of the *Social Control of Business*.

[58] Clark, John M., "Educational Functions of Economics after the War," *The American Economic Review*, March, 1944, Vol. XXXIV, Supp., pages 62-64. See also Clark's "General Aspects of Price Control and Rationing in the Transition Period," *The American Economic Review*, May, 1945, Vol. XXXV, page 162, and "How Not to Reconvert," *Political Science Quarterly*, June, 1944, Vol. LIX, pages 189-192.

a "breathing spell during which we may work out further evolutionary developments." He is not prepared to plunge into any comprehensive direct planning program for which the American economy is not yet fully prepared; instead, he prefers to proceed slowly in order to avoid mistakes which would possibly jeopardize all future planning within the framework of the mature, capitalistic economy. Clark wants to avoid pushing private enterprise to the breaking point by carrying out some ill-considered planning proposals. But at the same time he feels that the prospect of any such danger should not deter us from considering as yet untried proposals for the creation of "organs of guidance and control within the economic system itself." Giving expression to his solidaristic bent, Clark points out that "If a common interest exists, there is always a chance of action to promote it, if all the parties who have this common interest can be brought together. Industry has only begun to pay serious attention to this problem. When it realizes how much depends on it, we may see its best efforts spent in this direction. And labor must cooperate in the same spirit, if the effort is not to fail. The difficulties are great, and success is doubtful. But we cannot leave the problem alone, for it will not leave us alone." [59]

Clark's analysis of the problem of economic planning may be described as a search for the right balance between democracy on the one hand and social efficiency on the other. He is fully aware that the more a planning scheme opens the doors to democratic pressures, the greater will be the sacrifice in collective managerial efficiency. Some planning schemes such as totalitarian planning could conceivably provide the utmost in managerial efficiency, but only at the cost of the liberties which many men place far above economic efficiency in their scale of values. Even under a democratic socialistic planning scheme there would still be a cleavage between the wage earner and the salaried manager. If the socialist constitution gave the workers a great deal of control over their managers, one could expect much more inefficiency than in a situation where the managers were less responsible to their subordinate workers. The democratic process is by its nature slow and destruc-

[59] *Social Control of Business,* Second Edition, page 518. For a later statement of this problem see Clark, John M., "The Theoretical Issues," *The American Economic Review,* March, 1942, Vol. XXXII, Supp., pages 2-12.

tive of efficiency. Where expression of opinion on the part of the masses is called for, as in democratic-liberal planning of the kind advocated by Clark, there inevitably are time-consuming delays in getting things done. Furthermore, there is a dilemma of which Clark is fully aware: the public wants full employment and an expanding national output, but at the same time it wishes to be responsible for the general policies which dominate the productive processes. This difficulty has its roots in human nature and is therefore ineradicable. The suggestion is made by Clark that we should recognize this inherent difficulty and make the best of it. Much liberty and some efficiency is at all times to be preferred to great efficiency and little or no liberty. Man is a peculiar animal, and in the long run he prefers to sacrifice material welfare to things of the spirit such as liberty and freedom of conscience. Clark has done well to call attention to this problem of freedom versus efficiency which runs through all planning policies and programs.

The various tactics which may be adopted to achieve a desired end are placed by Clark in the two categories of gradual and revolutionary means of achievement. He is opposed to revolutionary ways of reorganizing economic life because the revolutionary process is usually a very destructive one resulting in much loss of life and property, and because the kind of spirit needed to make a revolution successful cannot at the same time be used for building a peaceful economic organization. Where revolutionary tactics are adopted, workers are taught to have a warlike spirit; and, as a consequence, they develop an attitude suitable only for destructive activity.[60] Such an attitude is not the kind upon which a democratic planned economy can feed, because "Organizations for irresponsible, warlike combat are not easily converted in a moment into organizations for peaceful cooperation. It is not easy to imagine a successful outcome unless, after a considerable period of chaos and suffering, a

---

[60] Cf. John Dewey: "The final argument in behalf of the use of intelligence is that as are the means so are the actual ends achieved—that is, the consequences. I know of no greater fallacy than the claim of those who hold to the dogma of the necessity of brute force that this use will be the method of calling genuine democracy into existence—of which they profess themselves the simon-pure adherents. It requires an unusually credulous faith in the Hegelian dialectic of opposites to think that all of a sudden the use of force by a class will be transmuted into a democratic classless society." See Dewey's *Liberalism and Social Action*, page 86. New York: G. P. Putnam's Sons, 1935.

different spirit is slowly developed under the pressure of hard neces-sity." [61]   After a revolution is successful, it is likely to fall into the hands of the "exponents of centralized coercion."   Revolutionary tactics are frequently associated with a revolutionist morality which makes the success of the revolution the overruling standard of right. This standard of what is right bows to neither objective truth nor humanitarian considerations; and, as in the case of Russia, the re-sult is "coercive dictatorship" which is inimical to personal liberty and freedom of thought and expression.

The tactics of economic control that appeal to Clark are those of "democratic gradualism."   He prefers a goal which does not neces-sitate a complete break with habitual ways of doing things.   If the controlled economy of the future is to enlist the support of the "trained and intelligent classes," and if it is to preserve valuable institutional relations, it must not require too much of an abandon-ment of cultural ties with the past.   There are limits to the whit-tling down of private enterprise through regulation and control.   If a planning program were to be pushed too far, a breaking point in the control of private enterprise would be reached beyond which further control would necessarily lead to the elimination of private enterprise and the substitution of state ownership and operation of the means of production.   It is Clark's aim to preserve the basic features of the present system, and to achieve this end "private enterprise must have some minimum adequate scope if it is to be successfully employed at all."   He turns to Sweden as an illustra-tion of a country which has succeeded in eliminating the more ex-treme vagaries of the industrial system while preserving at the same time enough of the basic features of private business enterprise to win the support of the technicians and the property owners. In the future industry must point the way to further possibilities of national economic guidance.   There is a common interest among employers, laborers, and consumers; and if this interest can be brought to the surface where it will be recognized and understood by all parties, one can expect a further development in the control of the modern economy.   But the development of common eco-nomic interests must be accompanied by the emergence of a coopera-tive spirit in mankind.   Planning efforts will never prove to be suc-

[61] *Social Control of Business*, Second Edition, page 511.

cessful until the necessary cooperative impulses in mankind have been released, and until cooperative habits and customs have been thoroughly established.

There is nothing utopian about Clark's planning proposals because economic activity, even though brought within the confines of a national planning program, is always to remain a somewhat irregular and highly adventurous field of behavior. He would be the last one to suggest that all the zest and interest be removed from the job of feeding, clothing, and sheltering the nation. But because this work appeals to men's creative desires is no reason why zest and adventure should be had only at the price of widespread economic insecurity and insufficiency for the masses. Economic activity, if properly planned, can be both daring and abundantly fruitful. Clark writes in his *Social Control of Business* that "In the end, we must never expect to be satisfied, for the simple reason that it is not in our natures. Man is the animal, which is 'adapted to maladaptation'; his aspirations outrun his performances, and his problem of adjusting himself to the results of his own inventions is as endless as the inventions themselves." Clark has no intention of keeping man's creative intelligence within the iron-bound limits of some excessively regimented planning scheme. Before this happens, he would much prefer to experiment with some other economic system which would make more use of mankind's natural enthusiasm for doing and living.

What if the planning scheme proposed by Clark should fail to achieve its objectives? Would there be a return to the old laissez-faire system of conducting business? Of one thing Clark appears to be convinced, and that is that there can be no return to old methods of carrying on business. Our economic destiny is wrapped up with an economic system of the future which will reproduce very little of the nineteenth-century laissez-faire economy. There are two alternatives if the voluntary planning scheme suggested by Clark should fail to win adequate support from the various groups participating in the business life of the nation. These alternatives are a more compulsory planning scheme, which would still attempt to preserve the essentials of the present economic system, and an entirely new economic system with a different legal and political framework. As economic planning becomes more compulsory, the importance of private enterprise is necessarily whittled away. In the opinion of some people it is possible to keep on restricting the field of private enterprise until we gradually move from a system of private enterprise to some form of socialism. According to this view there is a whole range of possible economic systems between a system of purely private enterprise and a system of government ownership and operation of the means of production; and public policy may choose to stop at any point between these two extremes of individualism and collectivism. Clark, however, does not agree that it is possible to go to great lengths in diluting private enterprise. He is of the opinion that compulsory planning would very soon meet insurmountable obstacles over which the spirit of private enterprise could hardly be expected to rise, because private production and compulsory regulation of economic life are basically antipathetic. Compulsory planning would very soon result in the demise of private enterprise and in the emergence of a collectivistic economic scheme devoid of the essentials of the present business system.[62]

The validity of Clark's assertion that social-democratic planning would in large measure reduce economic insecurity and insufficiency remains to be substantiated, in pragmatic fashion, by the test of consequences. His planning proposals are therefore an appeal to make that great economic experiment which would either substantiate or invalidate his statement about the feasibility of national economic planning. What is so disturbing to many people about the work of economists like Clark is not the kind of economic analysis that he has made; instead it is his suggestion that economic society should be converted into a gigantic laboratory in which democracy would experiment on a grand scale with the means by which it obtains its bread and butter. Such a proposal alarms many

---

[62] Clark explains that "To maintain the existing system, literally unchanged, is not one of the possibilities . . . the range of possible economic systems does not shade off from individualism to communism by continuous gradations . . . private enterprise must have some minimum adequate scope if it is to be successfully employed at all. . . . And the truth underlying the program of maintaining the existing system is the need of knowing what this minimum is and making sure not to encroach upon it, unless we are ready to accept some form of collectivism." See *Social Control of Business,* Second Edition, page 516, and "Our Economic Freedom," *The Annals of the American Academy of Political and Social Science,* March, 1942, Vol. 220, pages 181-185.

a vested economic interest; it also perturbs those individuals by whom social engineering is still classed with evangelism and various other alleged shortcuts to the promised land.

The Nature and Scope of Social Economics

The contributions which Clark has made to economic theory are not only important for an adequate understanding of the modern economy, but they are also significant as elements out of which he hopes to develop a twentieth-century version of economics. Running all through his special economic studies may be seen an interest in the development of a new framework of analysis which will provide a solid basis for his "social economics." This is an economics devoted to the interpretation of a pluralistic economy in which government enterprise, government-controlled industries, large private corporate enterprises, and small-scale businesses exist side by side. The modern pluralistic economy is one in which the tempo of economic activity is determined very largely by those dominant key industries in which heavy capital investments are found. It is also an economy of rigid as well as sensitive prices, of collective action as well as individual action, and one in which "it is quite possible for productive resources to be permanently expelled from the circle of active production and purchase, which becomes adjusted to the shrunken purchasing power resulting from their expulsion and cannot reabsorb them." [63]

Looking back over the growth of economic science in the United States since 1860, Clark sees a continuous stream of development which shows no sign of drying up.[64] First came the period of orientation between 1860 and 1883, in which the classical economics of John Stuart Mill and the teachings of the German historical school were combined to prepare the ground for the marginal economics which flowered at the end of the last century. No sooner had marginalism reached a high level of development than the third period in the growth of economics was inaugurated by Thor-

[63] "Productive Capacity and Effective Demand," page 375.
[64] Clark, John M., "Past Accomplishments and Present Prospects of American Economics," *The American Economic Review*, March, 1936, Vol. XXVI, pages 2-11. See also Clark's "Recent Developments in Economics," in *Recent Developments in the Social Sciences*, edited by E. C. Hayes, pages 213-306. Philadelphia: J. B. Lippincott Company, 1927.

stein Veblen's devastating attacks upon conventional economic theory. This third period, which became increasingly significant in the years before the outbreak of the first World War, was one in which "there was an increasing spirit of skepticism mixed with active iconoclasm, which before long came to seem the characteristic mood." In these years the critics of neo-classical economics were primarily concerned with pointing out the defects of that type of economic thought. They called attention to the inadequacies of the hedonistic psychology; they attacked the ethical implications of marginal economics; and they strenuously objected to the idea of pouring the fund of economic experience into the iron molds of static analysis. As a consequence of this emphasis on the negative aspects of critical analysis, it was easy for many economists to slip into an iconoclastic mood.

Since 1918 there has been a fourth period in the development of economic science during which a new synthesis appears to be working its way out. In the past three decades our understanding of the working of the modern economy has been greatly improved by the extensive quantitative analysis of economic behavior made by organized research in the United States and abroad. Along with these improvements in the statistical treatment of economic data has come a need for a new synthesis of the many specialized economic studies that have been made. This new unity has been supplied to some extent by what Clark calls "the rather elusive movement known as 'Institutionalism', which . . . may be more important as an underlying point of view orienting many different kinds of specific studies and lending changed significance to the day-to-day routine operations of the business system." [65] It has been Clark's purpose to clarify this underlying point of view, and to show how it can combine the many diverse studies of twentieth-century economists in a new type of economics which he describes as "social."

Clark's new economics is a synthesis of what he calls "Euclidean" and "non-Euclidean" economics. Euclidean economics is "the deductive, static economics of price, exchange value, and distribution" which was erected on the basis of the "assumptions of contentment"; non-Euclidean economics, as represented by the work of Veblen,

[65] *Ibid.*, page 7.

interprets the processes of economic change, and unlike the orthodox science is an economics of discontent.[66]   The two types of economics are quite antithetical.   Euclidean economics finds that there is an inherent tendency in the business system leading it to be of service to the community, while disservice, if there is any, is purely incidental.   Non-Euclidean or heterodox economics takes parasitism to be a fundamental characteristic of the modern business system, and if business renders any service to the community in general it does so only accidentally and not by design.   As Clark finds elements of truth in both types of economics, it is his aim to weld together what is best in both of them.   In this synthesis the underlying assumptions are that the business system is essentially sound, and that under the proper conditions its general drive would be in the direction of serving the basic needs of mankind.   Clark explains that "The synthesis which can unite them [Euclidean and non-Euclidean economics] lies largely in the realistic study of the social checks on private self-interest; their nature, adequacy and inadequacy, success and failure, actualities and potentialities."   While developing this synthesis, Clark takes his place among those economists who in the final analysis hold to a somewhat optimistic view of the future of the capitalistic system.

The new synthetical economics of which Clark is an ardent exponent is defined as "a description of the way economic forces work, and a study of the economic efficiency—or inefficiency—which results." [67]   It is the efficiency of the whole economic system rather than the efficiency of the individual entrepreneur that is of paramount interest to Clark.   He is concerned with the efficiency of the economic system not in relation to the maximization of business profits, but in relation to the achieving of the broader economic aims of society.   When the efficiency of the entire economy becomes the central problem, there is a need for new criteria other than market standards by means of which efficiency or the lack of it may be determined.   "The modern economist," says Clark, "is forced to use the yardstick of price for what it may be worth; but he is developing statistical data and techniques which enable him to study the physical quantities that lie behind the money measure and to supplement it in other ways.   Like Smith, we may recog-

[66] "The Socializing of Theoretical Economics," page 85.
[67] Ibid., page 73.

nize standards of welfare and of public policy independent of price." [68]   In the search for new criteria of collective efficiency old scientific boundaries are ignored and every possible source of information is tapped for enlightenment. It should not be surprising, therefore, if Clark turns up with some novel ideas about the nature and scope of economic science.

In order to understand Clark's concept of social economics it is necessary to realize that he takes the field of economic problems to be but one segment of the larger complex of social problems.   The "central problem" of all social science is that of society's scheme of values.   This problem "is of course more than economic, and yet it seems to be one problem and not many separate ones.   While its economic aspect is far from exhausted, the chief thing to be striven for is that this central problem shall have all the light that can be thrown on it from all angles, and that problems of exchange should be treated with this aim constantly in mind." [69]   In general, social science is concerned with how a community's scheme of values originates and develops, how the evolution of this scheme of values is affected by various social and economic factors, and, indirectly, how the value scheme may be altered. Economic science has its specific contribution to make to this problem from its own particular viewpoint, since it is concerned with the disposal of scarce means in relation to the community's general scheme of values.

Clark's definition of social economics, with its emphasis on the economic values which are ignored by the market place, brings up the question of the scope of economic science.   As is to be expected, he pushes the boundaries of his economics beyond the limits established by the equilibrium economists.   In discussing the proper boundaries of economics he asserts that, "Unless they have been finally and authoritatively established in some writing which has escaped my notice, I feel free to contend that it is less important to keep inside any traditional limits than to follow our natural questionings wherever they may lead, and do whatever work we are specially fitted for and find undone." [70]   Economics must not follow a policy of "Jeffersonian nonintercourse" with other fields of

---

[68] Clark, John M., "Adam Smith and the Currents of History," *Preface to Social Economics,* page 193.
[69] "Toward a Concept of Social Value," page 65.
[70] *Ibid.,* page 60.

knowledge; instead, it must feel free to accept the authoritative results of the other social sciences, and it must turn to every possible source of enlightenment that will aid economic understanding. Although Clark is unwilling to set any very precise limits to economic investigation, he does recognize three types of analysis as component parts of his social economics. First, the modern economist should be thoroughly familiar with the principle of free exchange, the validity of which has not been entirely destroyed but merely lessened by the course of economic evolution. Secondly, the modern economist should have an interest in economics as a form of cultural science; he should be acquainted with the cultural changes that have been so conspicuous in Western Europe and the United States in the past hundred years. He should be aware of the extent to which individual economic behavior is now controlled by the "new departmentalized government and the new integrated industry," which have fostered the development of such forms of collective action as trade associations, corporate enterprises, labor unions, and various cooperative organizations. This second field of economic investigation is very important because it provides an inductive basis for the new assumptions and the new framework of interpretation of a twentieth-century economics. When Clark writes about "socializing" theoretical economics, he does so in the light of the cultural analysis which bulks so large in this second field of economic inquiry.

The third type of study which Clark includes within the proper boundaries of economics is the analysis of those community aims which have a very important influence on the general level of economic activity. He does not take individual and social ends for granted, and then proceed to explain how the economic system meets or fails to meet the requirements of these given ends. Since the community's goals have a very definite bearing on the general level of economic activity, the economist should inquire into the relationship between community ends and economic efficiency. In Clark's economic analysis there is no artificial separation of means from ends; ends determine means, and in turn the means used help to determine the ends. The functioning of the economic system can therefore be fully understood only when the economist explains how social ends affect the course of economic activity, and how economic activity in turn is influential in shaping society's ends. Furthermore, the economic ends which society lists among its many goals are ever "on the make," because the cultural situations from which these ends emerge are themselves constantly changing. For Clark, as for other pragmatists, there are no such things as fixed or absolute national ends. Since the aims of a society are relative to the stage of cultural development in which it happens to find itself, the economist's study of community goals and their relation to the economic system is a never-ending task.

The three fields of economic investigation which Clark includes within the scope of his social economics have an underlying unity which stems from his view of the purpose of economic science. This view has as its keynote "the building of moralized economic communities." Clark points out that "The range of alternatives to which our economics must be relevant has increased. Between the 'thesis' of free exchange and the 'antithesis' of communism we are challenged to build up a working synthesis which may have a relation to the needs of our time similar in kind, if not in genius, to that achieved by Adam Smith. One may even conjecture what the keynote of the synthesis will be: the building of moralized economic communities, expressing and protecting by appropriate agencies all the essential interests concerned." [71] The economist should prove to be of special value in the work of building moralized communities, because he is an expert in the economic aspects of society's central problem, namely, its scheme of values. In times of extreme urgency men rightly demand that economics contribute to the solution of their pressing problems. For this reason Clark believes that the economics of the future will have an orientation quite different from that of much of the work of the late nineteenth-century economists, which was more contemplative than instrumentalistic in its bias.

The instrumentalistic bias of Clark's social economics stems from his basic pragmatic outlook. Like Commons, Mitchell, and Tugwell, Clark is keenly aware of the importance of avoiding the seductiveness of the contemplative mood of the academicians of the last century. In his opinion there is a burden placed upon the fraternity of economists to see that their thought is somehow translatable into appropriate economic action. He has, however, left to others the actual work of engaging in economic reconstruction. In social

[71] "Adam Smith and the Currents of History," page 195.

engineering it is necessary that some thinkers get above the work of the tacticians so that they may concern themselves with the broader scientific aspects of economic reconstruction. Such reconstruction can have a solid foundation only if it is carried out in the bright light of scientific understanding. For this reason Clark is careful not to allow his sense of the urgency of contemporary economic problems to blind him to the need for more economic understanding than we now possess before we embark upon the perilous journey to a land of planned abundance.

In his economic writings Clark has combined a broad intimacy with the facts of economic life and speculation on a high theoretical level. In this respect he has differed from his colleague, Wesley C. Mitchell, who has revealed an unwillingness to push his economics very far beyond the limits of statistical analysis. Clark is not similarly reluctant to plumb those depths of social philosophy into which economic issues inevitably lead anyone who is willing to follow far enough. It is precisely because he has been willing to make full use of the wider social implications of Mitchell's economics of instability that Clark has been able to secure an enviable position for himself in the field of contemporary economic thought. His excursions into the nebulous areas of social values and social costs, however, are not without their many difficulties. Many passages of his essays and treatises do no more than open up vistas which are highly stimulating; and of final answers there is no abundance in Clark's writings. Consequently his economic analysis is more provocative than definitive in nature. Especially is this true of his theory of social costs and values. Like other heterodox economists, Clark has as yet done little more than blaze a trail toward the world of a balanced, progressive economy in which a maximum of social value would be obtained at a minimum of social cost.

The realization of the introductory nature of much of his economic analysis has bred in Clark a modesty and a humility which are in marked contrast to the hypercritical attitudes of many of the critics of the orthodox tradition in economic thought. One does not find in Clark's work the devastating attacks of a Veblen or the somewhat dogmatic earnestness of a Tugwell. It may be the possession of either a peculiarly charitable spirit or of a unique quality of scientific balance which has led Clark to refrain from indulging in as destructively critical an attack upon the nature and scope of orthodox economics as has come from the vanguard of economic heterodoxy. In showing more interest in constructive than in negative criticism he has chosen the more difficult path, because constructive criticism is by nature tentative rather than dogmatic, elusive rather than definitive. He has also made economic heterodoxy less unpalatable to those economists who are still working within the tradition of economic orthodoxy. Clark's respect for the contributions of the neo-classicists and his skillful attempts to revamp their theoretical position have done much to bring new support for the type of economic thought of which Thorstein Veblen and Wesley C. Mitchell were early expositors. If the forces at work seeking to develop a synthesis of the economics of John Bates Clark and Thorstein Veblen should turn out to be successful, undoubtedly much of the credit for this achievement would have to be given to the younger Clark.

Within recent years the capacity of the business system to produce goods and services efficiently and abundantly has shown signs of serious deterioration. Now the main question relates to the possibility of reordering our economic life in such a way as to preserve the continuity of economic progress. Clark observes that there are already signs of a growing unanimity of opinion concerning the reasons why the economic system does not enjoy anything like a full utilization of its productive capacity. The major disagreements concern the measures to be adopted in order to draw unused capacity back into "the circle of active production and purchase." Since controlled experiments on a gigantic scale are not possible, economists will have to look forward to what Clark describes as "a world full of trial-and-error experimentation." Just as Veblen turned to "creative conjecture" in place of the experimental method in *The Engineers and the Price System,* so also must economists in the future rely upon their resource of constructive imagination. In Clark's world of trial-and-error experimentation there will not be found anything like the atmosphere of "relative stability and certainty" which Alfred Marshall's generation enjoyed. Economists will have to do without "the ease and beautiful simplicity" of the older generation's symmetrical thought structure as they turn to a struggle with "amorphous facts." [72] For the coming generation of

[72] "A Contribution to the Theory of Competitive Price," page 748.

If, however, I can furnish some clues to the rebuilding of a theoretical structure, I may have done something toward closing the gap between theory and reality. There will be sufficient ingenuity, and above all, adequate time for other minds to follow these directions."

REXFORD G. TUGWELL: *The Battle for Democracy*

6

The Experimental Economics of Rexford G. Tugwell

Among the many economists which the New Deal at various times drafted into its service none received wider public attention than Rexford G. Tugwell. When he went to serve the federal government in 1933, Tugwell had many novel ideas about economics and its applications to the serious economic problems which at that time confronted the national administration. For fifteen years prior to his going to the nation's capital Tugwell had been conducting university courses on American economic culture and had been writing about proposals for its reorganization. The programs for national economic reform and reconstruction which he advocated in the early years of the Great Depression can be understood only in the light of his views as developed in the years prior to 1933. On close inspection it will be found that Tugwell's heterodox economic thought is in striking contrast to the traditional economics which dominated the business world up to the eventful year of 1929.

Like Gardiner C. Means, Tugwell belongs to the second generation of exponents of economic heterodoxy. He was born on July 10, 1891, in Sinclairville, New York. Graduated from the Wharton School of Finance and Commerce of the University of Pennsylvania in 1915, Tugwell went out into a world which was being rudely shaken from its nineteenth-century complacency. He witnessed the great economic adjustments of the first World-War period, the succeeding era of international disorganization and false prosperity, and then, after 1929, the agonizing efforts of many nations to preserve their free enterprise economies and their democratic ways of living.[1] One should not be surprised to find little of the orthodox

[1] Tugwell explains that to him "The war was an experience of the massing of effort in common enterprise—though the enterprise was a destructive one—which

in the thought of an economist who in his own lifetime has seen little of economic balance and normalcy, and who has been gifted with the necessary mental equipment to penetrate the future with novel and challenging thoughts.

The teaching career upon which Tugwell embarked in 1915 drew its inspiration from an interest in the American economy as a "going system" in which public and private welfare were far from being one and the same thing. His doctoral thesis on *The Economic Basis of Public Interest,* presented to the University of Pennsylvania in 1922, was an inquiry into the nature of the public interest or welfare, which was taken for granted by traditional economics, but which was becoming a matter of greater scientific concern as the new century unfolded. When Tugwell joined the faculty of Columbia University in 1920, he went to an institution whose intellectual atmosphere was quite suited to the general disposition of an earnest disciple of Simon Nelson Patten.[2] Among the many outstanding faculty members at Columbia University there were two who had a special attraction for Tugwell: John Dewey, in the field of social philosophy and psychology, and Wesley C. Mitchell, who was "the bridge between classicism and instrumentalism in economics."

In the early post-war period Dewey was making much of the growing rift between formal education and social experience. Applying this approach to the teaching of economics, Tugwell came to believe that a new orientation was necessary if the teaching of economics was to be effective in the new century. The new orientation was to be built around the view that individuals should be educated for a world in which "social management" would have a significant

threw a flood of new light on potentialities we had not hitherto suspected. And we have had the experience since the war of tension so heightened as to be unique; of great prosperity and of vast disaster." See the chapter on "Economics" by Tugwell in *Roads to Knowledge,* edited by W. A. Neilson, page 93. New York: W. W. Norton and Company, 1937.

[2] Tugwell benefited very greatly from his academic contacts at Columbia University, which he describes as a "great influence." This influence, he explains, "was the contact I made at Columbia with the group which was laboring to integrate social science and philosophy and to reduce it to an order which would be understandable to students. This was a great intellectual adventure. Dewey influenced it greatly; but so did many others. I feel a deep debt to John J. Coss, Professor of Philosophy, for instance, who kept the group together and made each of us as individuals fertile for the others. I had new access to philosophy, history, psychology, and government as well as a change in economic influence in those years which was formative."

role. In addition to giving courses on "Phases of American Economic Life" and "Proposals for Economic Reorganization," Tugwell applied his idea of a new educational orientation in "the Columbia experiment," which was designed "to present a single course dealing with the problems of our industrial civilization." This course, entitled "Introduction to Contemporary Civilization," was created to eliminate the arbitrary boundaries between the social sciences, and to present a common approach in all the various social sciences which would mark a transition from scholasticism to instrumentalism. Education in the social sciences was to grapple with "the insistent problems of industrialism," and to assess "the worth of the contribution to human betterment which each discipline might make."

After serving as a member of the economics faculty of Columbia University during the years 1920 to 1933, Tugwell left academic work to accept the position of Assistant Secretary of Agriculture in the United States Department of Agriculture. During the difficult years from 1933 to 1937 he found himself a spokesman for the national administration when it was endeavoring to set up new institutional arrangements which would meet the pressing needs of a seriously dislocated business system. He wrote many articles and delivered numerous addresses with the aim of reorienting a disturbed and puzzled public so that it would be better prepared for the novel measures required for the elimination of the evils of depression. It was Tugwell's general message to the American public during these troubled years that the laissez-faire economy of the nineteenth century had matured into an economic system which would no longer respond to the automatic adjustment-mechanisms that had functioned with some success in the past. The situation at that time called for experimentation with new economic programs to determine the best way out of national chaos. Among the New Deal advisers none was more aware of the urgency of the situation and of the need for bold experimentation than was Tugwell, but as time went by it became apparent that the national administration was unwilling to carry out the full program that Tugwell had in mind. When the extreme urgency of the early years of the depression had given way to slow recovery, and devotion to economic and social reconstruction had become less zealous, the general interest in coping with basic issues died down. As a consequence of this turn in national affairs, Tugwell found that the task of social management was no longer congenial, and so in 1937 he withdrew from the service of the federal government.

After a brief period in private business Tugwell returned to the problem of social management on April 13, 1938, when he accepted the positions of Commissioner of the Planning Department and Chairman of the New York City Planning Commission. In this work he saw in smaller form many of the planning problems which he had observed on a national scale in the period from 1933 to 1937. On September 19, 1941, Tugwell dropped his city-planning activity to return to the service of the federal government as Governor of Puerto Rico. In this position he was confronted with the difficult task of planning the social and economic affairs of a people whose economy was severely shaken by the trends of international affairs after 1939. Tugwell left Puerto Rico in July, 1946, to resume his academic career at the University of Chicago.

The Economics of Simon N. Patten

The most important early influence in the development of Tugwell's economic thinking came from his teacher, Simon Nelson Patten (1852-1922), who became associated with the University of Pennsylvania in 1888.[3] Like many other social scientists of his time Patten had gone to Germany for advanced graduate study in economics, and had received from the German historical economists an outlook on economic matters which was very different from the viewpoint of the English classical economists. He found that "a new standpoint from which to view social affairs was introduced by the German economists. They saw that society, and not the individual, was the center of economic activity; and that productive power depends more largely upon the organization of society than upon the material environment. They began with an investigation of man and society, and not with nature."[4] It was this over-all, collective view borrowed from the German historical economists

---

[3] Tugwell has explained to the writer that Simon N. Patten's views "were the greatest single influence on my thought. Neither Veblen nor Dewey found their orientation to the future as completely and instinctively as did Patten. The magnificence of his conceptions and the basic rightness of his vision become clearer as time passes. I am eternally grateful to him."

[4] Patten, Simon N., "The Theory of Dynamic Economics," *Essays in Economic Theory*, edited by R. G. Tugwell, page 53. New York: A. A. Knopf, 1924.

that became the point of departure of Patten's dynamic economics, and that was later passed on to Tugwell. On returning to the United States with his organismic viewpoint Patten became a student of contemporary economic culture rather than a specialist in the handling of deductive economic analysis. Like his famous contemporary Thorstein Veblen, he soon found himself primarily interested in an interpretation of the evolving American economic culture rather than the less exciting task of refining the inherited economics of his time.[5]

Patten was a keen critic of the type of economics developed and passed on to later generations by David Ricardo and John Stuart Mill. He objected not only to some of the fundamental premises of classical economics, but also to the popular opinion of the significance of economic science that was current in the closing years of the nineteenth century. Patten refused to accept the general assumption of a niggardly and unyielding nature from which man was supposed to wrest a precarious existence. The Ricardian emphasis upon diminishing returns from an unsympathetic nature and the Malthusian view of a fecund humanity struggling over the limited supply of natural resources have no place in Patten's theoretical system. His whole system is erected on the assumption of a natural environment which is the source of an economic surplus rather than a deficit, and which is becoming increasingly productive as a result of the great improvements in experimental science and industrial technique. For Patten nature is not a material barrier to man's yearning for a better existence, but instead a great reservoir of potential abundance waiting to be tapped by the progress of industrial science. This view of the material environment came quite naturally to Patten, who had grown up in an atmosphere of great abundance in pioneering Illinois.

Not only did Patten question the classicists' assumption of the niggardliness of the material environment, but he also doubted the validity of the assumption of a basically competitive economy. In

[5] For a review of Patten's life and work see Tugwell, Rexford G., "Notes on the Life and Work of Simon Nelson Patten," *The Journal of Political Economy*, April, 1923, Vol. XXXI; "The Dr. Simon Nelson Patten Memorial," *The Annals of the American Academy of Political and Social Science*, May, 1923, No. 196, and the memorial addresses in the "Proceedings of the Thirty-Fifth Annual Meeting of the American Economic Association," *The American Economic Review*, March, 1923, Vol. XIII, Supp.

the years after he joined the economics faculty of the University of Pennsylvania (1888), Patten witnessed the emergence of large-scale corporate activity accompanied by a growing unionization of the forces of labor. The closing decades of the nineteenth century coincided with the expansion of a new industrial system which was in the process of altering many of the fundamentals of American culture. Patten observed the progress of experimental science, the improvement of industrial technology, and the urbanization of large sections of the population. Under the stimulus of specialists in agricultural science a new agriculture was making its appearance; and new products were being placed on the nation's markets, having been brought from distant places by the developing transportation system. "The young genius of the mechanical age" was coming into its own as it transformed the whole economic and social system. As a result of these many changes in the arts of production, the competitive struggle was giving way to new cooperative methods of meeting the economic problems of the day. The various economic interests, Patten believed, would be forced by the pressure of economic change "to accept the discipline of the new industrial regime." [6] Since the basic characteristics of the new machine age were cooperative rather than competitive, the individualistic competition of the early nineteenth century was being rapidly transformed into the cooperative activity of the new industrial age.

Patten was greatly disturbed by the erroneous views of large sections of the public with respect to the nature of the economic principles developed by the classical economists. Too frequently he found that the economic laws of "rent, profits and wages are treated . . . by the majority of people as the functioning of pure law emanating from a remote province of nature." The principles of economic science, as they are viewed by Patten, are not "supersocial" in origin but instead are derived from historical origins. He states that these principles should be related to "historical classifications," that is to say, to particular historico-cultural situations, when they are tested for their validity. In Patten's hands economics becomes an historico-cultural science which penetrates into the origins and development of the institutions and other customary modes of behavior comprising the economic culture of his time.

[6] Patten, Simon N., *The New Basis of Civilization*, page 77. New York: The Macmillan Company, 1912.

In this view of economics human motivation is taken to be more social than individual, since men are born into a social environment where much of their daily activity is determined by "social heredity" or "psychological environment." [7] Patten observes that this social heredity of mankind includes two sets of institutions. The first set is related to man's predatory habits, which seek to accumulate property and protect it from the claims of others less fortunately situated with respect to the enjoyment of wealth and income. The second set of institutions is connected with man's work habits, which are concerned with multiplying the supply of goods through co-operation with the forces of the material environment. These predatory and work habits have their origins in biological drives, but the extent to which they find expression depends upon those particular institutional arrangements and cultural conditions which are the main concern of Patten's scientific analysis.

Patten's special interest was not price determination in a free competitive market, nor was it the analysis of the distribution of national income in a purely competitive economy; instead, it was to explain the disposal of scarce means in the capitalistic system which developed in the United States after the Civil War. Like Veblen, who was at this time analyzing economic activity as a con-flict between the pecuniary and industrial employments of the new machine age, Patten approached the economic problems of his time in the light of the conflicts between the new industrialism with all its promise of a fuller, richer economic life and the mental attitudes that men had inherited from earlier generations. He explained that the economic difficulties of the day were in large part due to the fact that men were experiencing great difficulty in making the necessary psychological adjustments to the new industrial environ-ment. Mankind had its vision obscured by mental attitudes that were more appropriate to a vanishing age of small-scale, competitive industry. After 1860 America had undergone an "economic revolu-tion," but the necessary "intellectual revolution" was still to come.

Not only does Patten find that states of mind are difficult to change, but he also observes that mental attitudes which are in the process of crumbling actually appear to be most vigorous at the very time that they are about to disappear. Vested economic in-terests put forth their strongest arguments to explain away the

[7] *Ibid.*, pages 32-33.

inequalities of income distribution when the industrial system no longer provides a justification of these inequalities. The same is true of the military interests. Patten felt that the industrial state was slowly displacing the military state, but there was never a time when the military interests were more aggressive than when militarism was about to lose its role as a dominant cultural influence.

In explaining how men become adjusted to a new industrial system Patten adopted the position of the instrumental pragmatists who were coming into prominence in the early years of this century. Old cultural attitudes and modes of thought cannot be argued away into oblivion, because men's views are altered not by argument but by "new activity and an accumulating store of fresh experiences." When the foundations of civilization change there arise new problems for which old modes of thought are no longer appropriate. In meeting these new environmental difficulties men find that their cultural attitudes are changed by the heat and conflict of actual experience. The value of education in this situation is not that it can dictate the development of new modes of thought; education can only hasten the sloughing of old inappropriate mental habits and the acquiring of new ways of thinking which will enable mankind to tap the abundance inherent in the "new economic order."

Unlike Karl Marx, Patten did not divide society into the property-owning and the propertyless classes. According to his interpretation society is pluralistic rather than dualistic, since it is composed of a number of groups including farmers, workers, bankers, small businessmen, and large capitalists. These groups can be graded from the "decaying poor" up to the "decadent aristocracies," but there is no simple division between the capital owners and the workers. Capitalists and laborers "are not classes; they are fluid groups of men passing hastily through the temporary economic stages that replace the older social stratification." [8] Patten believed that there would be a levelling of the various income groups out of which would emerge socialized groups of workers, farmers, and businessmen whose aim would be cooperation rather than conflict. The end result of the evolution of economic society would not be a classless democracy but instead an "interclass democracy."

[8] *The New Basis of Civilization*, page 85.

In his various writings Patten did not discuss the details of the co-operative economic society of the future. He did state, however, that this new society was to control private property so that the social surplus, which was the inheritance of all, would be distributed more in accordance with a person's working capacity than with his social status. Income distribution would then be based upon personal capacity rather than class distinctions. When this economic democracy was established, the cooperative spirit which first moved primitive races would once more assert itself, and would be nourished most intensively by the city dwellers among whom the new industrialism would make its most rapid progress. Since city dwellers would be in close contact with the new industrial system, there would emerge a new "city industrial group" composed of those workers who tend the machines of the new economic order. Although the workers would not be the only group in society, Patten implies that they would comprise the most fundamental group. They would determine the tone of the new industrial society, because it would be through the workers that the new economic order would find its clearest expression. The competitive ethics of the nineteenth century would then be displaced by a new cooperative ethics; and all economic groups would come to possess such a social consciousness that the basic social instincts would find expression in a community no longer plagued by gross inequality of wealth and income distribution and by an appalling neglect of the many potentialities of human nature.

The basic ideas running through Patten's economic analysis may be summarized in the following manner. It is not by denying the basic trends of modern industrialism but by openly accepting them that man will find his economic and social salvation. Modern industrialism must be harnessed to the high social purpose of creating a society capable of providing adequate means for the expression of humanity's diverse capacities. The creation of a new economic order should be a co-adaptive process in the sense that as the industrial system undergoes change, man's social heredity should change *pari passu*. In this process of co-adaptation human nature proves to be the more stubborn factor. The economic environment readily submits to change and alteration under the impact of developments in the field of experimental science, but it is the human mind with its inflexibility that presents the major hindrance to economic and social progress. The major problem, therefore, is to get mankind to move in parallel fashion with the changing economic environment.

This brief résumé of Patten's economic views is sufficient to show the type of scientific thinking that nurtured Tugwell as an undergraduate and later as a graduate student. Patten's emphasis upon economics as a cultural science gave a realistic twist to his economic thought which was most congenial to Tugwell. In 1908 Patten wrote that "Economists can create systems, but it is only the trend of events that decides between them. . . . The road of the economist becomes the road of the people and the differences of economists are settled, not by their logic, but by the success or failure of the policy which each theory calls for." [9] This insistence that the final test to be applied in determining the validity of economic doctrines was the test of consequences, rather than the test of logical coherence, found a favorable response in Tugwell. Patten was himself more inclined to scientific generalizing than to economic experimentation, but in recognizing the need to keep theory close to the facts he passed on to his students what Tugwell has described as the "experimental attitude."

The approach to economic problems which Patten passed on to Tugwell was synthetical and emergent rather than analytical and additive. Like Veblen, Patten was responsive to those trends in social and philosophical thought which, at the turn of the century, were emphasizing the generalities rather than the particularities of things. His approach to economic analysis involved looking at the economic system as a synthesis which was more than the sum of its parts. He avoided the analytical, additive approach of the classical economists in which it was assumed that the whole was no more than the sum of its parts, and in which, therefore, attention was directed to the subsidiary parts rather than to the whole of the economic system. The classical view that community interest was no more than the summation of all individual interests found no place in Patten's analysis. According to his view, community welfare could not be adequately analyzed by investigating individual interests and then combining them with the expectation of arriving at the total communal interest. As Patten saw the matter, it was also necessary

[9] Patten, Simon N., "The Political Significance of Recent Economic Theories," *Essays in Economic Theory*, page 248.

to follow the reverse procedure in which the community interest was taken to be something more than the summation of individual interests, and was therefore to be analyzed separately from private welfare.

Patten's scientific approach stressed the fact that the economy is an emerging whole, the nature of which is being constantly unfolded by the course of human events. His attention was directed primarily toward the dynamic features of economic organization and to the relations between the various parts comprising the emerging economic whole. In explaining the emergent nature of economic life Patten made use of the economic interpretation of history. He explained that "As a follower of Professor [Thorold] Rogers . . . , I extended the thought so as to make the economic interpretation of history the means of getting at the dynamic laws of social change. . . . The economic interpretation of history, then, is the study of the prominent changes which take place in each epoch, and from a series of such studies one can create a general interpretation of genetic growth." [10] It was this "general interpretation of genetic growth" with its emphasis on the technological basis of economic culture that became the central doctrine of Patten's theoretical system.

Patten's concept of cultural emergence is associated with a second concept that has come to have a prominent place in the thinking not only of Tugwell but also of the other exponents of economic heterodoxy. This is the concept of the cultural lag. Cultural emergence is not a gradual, uninterrupted process; instead it is a spotty development in which certain cultural elements, such as institutions and social attitudes, fail to change as rapidly as other elements. This uneven cultural development creates cultural lags which are the source of many serious social and economic problems. In many cases these lags give rise to a great deal of cultural conflict. Mankind has at times, however, been able to cope with the problems arising from cultural lags by making more use of its cooperative impulses. In the final analysis the growth of economic culture is to be interpreted in terms of these two basic principles of conflict and cooperation.

It is not surprising that Patten's students should have come to hold a functional view of the role of economic science. In writing about the need for the reconstruction of economic theory in 1912 Patten pointed out that "In the past economists have striven to build a purely rational system that would be a monistic expression of progress. Their failures have created the present situation and awakened a demand for the reconstruction of economic theory. Economic thought should be based on industrial changes already made and on social reorganization plainly manifest. It will thus become pragmatic and incorporate in itself all the elements making for the improvement of mankind." [11] This espousal by Patten of a functional economics came at a time when the world was on the verge of a gigantic cultural upheaval. His instrumentalistic views on the role of economic theory were to find a fertile intellectual soil in the work of many economists belonging to Tugwell's generation whose personal experiences do not go much further back than the eventful year of 1914.

Tugwell's Psychological and Methodological Views

After the turn of the century the synthetical-emergent approach to scientific problems gained many new adherents in the physical and biological sciences, in philosophy, and in the social sciences, and by the second decade of the new century, when Tugwell was pursuing his graduate studies in economics, the new scientific viewpoint was well established. Especially in the field of psychology was progress made with the concept of the gestalt. This concept takes the individual to be a general pattern or configuration of behavior which is so integrated as to constitute a functional unit with properties that are not derivable from its parts. To understand human behavior from the gestalt viewpoint the investigator must analyze the individual as a living, developing whole. Human behavior then takes on meaning only as it is referred to some framework of interpretation in which the individual is regarded as a going system or pattern of conduct. In this manner a study of the individual as a gestalt or person-in-being reveals what cannot be understood by merely observing many isolated human acts or units of conduct.

In Tugwell's analysis whatever is to be investigated is thrown into a gestalt framework of interpretation. Whether he is studying

[11] *Ibid.*, pages 280-281.

the whole American economic system or some minor unit of it such as the City of New York, Tugwell assembles his data and develops his plan of analysis from the synthetical, gestalt viewpoint. He explains "that the behavior of a city is no more to be understood by analysis of its transport, traffic, water supply, police measures, public health devices, recreative facilities, and so on, than is the behavior of a person by analysis of his blood, nerves, and glands. There is a total, a whole, an 'emergent,' which has to be taken as such. And all the parts are to be understood in relation to that whole rather than the more customary reverse." [12] Like Patten, Tugwell is not satisfied with the additive approach of the neo-classical economists, because he observes that their approach derives from a mechanical concept of the economic order. His own approach has an entirely different metaphysical basis, since he substitutes the concept of emergence for the neo-classical concept of mechanism. Whereas the orthodox economist analyzes economic behavior from the viewpoint of the individual firm and then moves on from the separate firm to the whole economy, Tugwell reverses the procedure. He studies the economy as an over-all behavior pattern from which the individual firm derives its real significance. In analyzing twentieth-century economic problems he finds that there is needed a new method "which attempts to grasp the whole before it considers the parts, since these have only a derived, a contributory significance and none taken alone." [13] This is not to say that the additive, analytical approach of the nineteenth-century economists made no contribution. On the contrary economics like other sciences had to pass through early formative stages in which the "one-thing-at-a-time" viewpoint was quite fruitful, but when the science of economics was well established the need for a new scientific orientation was evident.[14] If the researches of early economic investigators are to bear abundant fruit, they must now be tied up with an over-all, emergent approach which will provide a new framework of interpretation.

Tugwell's new scientific viewpoint differs from that of the econo-

[12] Tugwell, Rexford G., "The Directive," *Journal of Social Philosophy and Jurisprudence*, Oct., 1941, Vol. 7, page 24.

[13] Tugwell, Rexford G., "Implementing the General Interest," *Public Administration Review*, Autumn, 1940, Vol. I, page 34.

[14] Tugwell, Rexford G., "Human Nature and Social Economy, I," *The Journal of Philosophy*, Aug. 14, 1930, Vol. XXVII, page 453.

mists of the past century because his metaphysical outlook is different. His metaphysical position is more than post-Darwinian, because it has been nurtured by the advances which have been made in scientific and philosophic thought during the past half-century. Tugwell owes much to Patten and the late nineteenth-century sociologists for making the shift from a mechanistic to an evolutionary metaphysics, but since 1900 much additional progress has been made in developing a new metaphysical position. The concepts of process, emergence, development, and change have been given more precise meanings; and, as a consequence, the crude evolutionism of the last century has been transformed into a highly refined, twentieth-century metaphysics of change. The new metaphysics has met considerable resistance, and has therefore been slow in uprooting the older mechanistic metaphysics of the nineteenth-century social scientists. Tugwell points out that "The persistence of the naive reasoning in which wholes are regarded as the simple sums of parts is more astonishing in social matters than elsewhere. . . . Why so simple and useful an idea has not been sufficiently used by social scientists it is difficult to understand. There must be some reason other than ignorance, although most reasoning devices are still, as they were when Veblen examined them several decades ago, pre-evolutionary. It seems not difficult to understand that the prosperity of society is something more than the total of individual prosperities: that social behavior is not to be predicted from knowledge of individual psychology. Yet there is a prevalent belief that the making prosperous of individuals is the way to make prosperous the nation. It is quite possible that the same persons who accept that view would take a different view in another field." [15]

Tugwell is also very much interested in rebuilding the psychological foundations of economics. The nineteenth-century economists were inclined to look upon human nature as a passive factor in a static society. In a world where change was alleged to be unimportant, the individual had no need for exploratory or experimental impulses. Consequently, the economists of the past century accepted an interpretation of human nature which emphasized caution, deliberation, and close calculation. When Tugwell substitutes his emergent view of the social order for the static view of the orthodox economists, he finds it necessary to make a change in

[15] "The Directive," page 22.

psychological interpretation.   Like John R. Commons, Wesley C. Mitchell, and John M. Clark, Tugwell discovers in human nature qualities and characteristics which would be of little value in a mechanistic world order of things.   Man is basically a self-active individual who is spurred to action by powerful biological drives. At times he may appear to have fallen into the deep ruts of customary behavior, but he never loses the capacity to bestir himself enough to break the bonds of antiquated behavior patterns.   Human nature has an exploratory, experimental aspect which derives not from rational faculties but from more fundamental biological impulses.   Reason is significant but "The part of reason in this whole process is much less important than the old common-sense view supposed.   It seems to be merely a selective part.   We do not act in response to reason; we only, through reasoning, decide upon the repression of certain undesirable modes of action and thus clear the way for acceptable responses, which, we perceive, will yield us in the long run the satisfactions we are driven to seek—those of instinct gratification." [16]

For his economic world of emerging institutions and a changing industrial technology, Tugwell requires a more "realistic account of human nature" than that handed down by orthodox economists. Following in the footsteps of Carleton H. Parker and Wesley C. Mitchell he calls for the substitution of a realistic psychology for the oversimplified, rationalistic psychology first formulated by the common-sense philosophers of the eighteenth century and later borrowed by the classical and neo-classical economists of the succeeding century.[17]   According to Tugwell's interpretation man has only recently in his evolution found himself transplanted from the world of the chase and the hunt to a cultural situation where purely instinctive reactions are unsatisfactory.   Fortunately, he is equipped with a proclivity which soon after birth initiates a process of learning.   This learning process enables man to alter outmoded habit patterns so that he may all the better meet the exigencies of civilized

[16] Tugwell, Rexford G., "Human Nature in Economic Theory," *Journal of Political Economy*, June, 1922, Vol. XXX, pages 318-319.
[17] Cf. Parker, Carleton H., "Motives in Economic Life," *The American Economic Review*, March, 1918, Vol. VIII, Supp., pages 212-231, and Mitchell, W. C., "The Rationality of Economic Activity," *Journal of Political Economy*, February, 1910, Vol. XVIII, pages 97-113.   See also Tugwell's "The Gipsy Strain," *The Pacific Review*, Sept., 1921, Vol. 2, pages 177-196.

living. Also, in the never-ending process of cultural adjustment the exploratory character of human nature is a great aid to mankind, since it leads to a constant testing of new ideas and new arrangements by means of which serious obstacles may be removed.

In addition to the exploratory aspect of human nature Tugwell calls attention to its cooperative aspect. He observes that "Men are, by impulse, predominantly coöperative. They have their competitive impulses, to be sure; but these are normally subordinate. Laissez faire exalted the competitive and maimed the coöperative impulses. Men were taught to believe that they were, paradoxically, advancing coöperation when they were defying it. That was a viciously false paradox . . . today . . . the coöperative impulse is asserting itself openly and forcibly, no longer content to achieve its ends obliquely and by stealth. We are openly and notoriously on the way to mutual endeavors." [18] Tugwell does not deny the existence of powerful acquisitive urges; on the contrary he is aware that the cultural-economic arrangements of the past hundred years have generally fostered "this rather unattractive human trait." But beneath the thin surface of our acquisitive society is the still more basic cooperative impulse of mankind. In other historical eras this cooperative impulse was given a much wider expression than that permitted by the organization of economic society in the nineteenth century. This eclipse of the associational tendencies of human nature, however, has been only temporary. The emergent social process is once more moving toward a situation in which the cooperative proclivity of mankind will again come into its own to provide a basis for that collective action which is necessary for a satisfactory functioning of our large-scale, twentieth-century economy. If collective action is required by the immensity of the problems of the modern economic world, such action will have a firm foundation in mankind's cooperative proclivity. It is this interpretation of human nature that enables Tugwell to be enthusiastic about the possibilities of social management. If his psychological interpretation is correct, then the cooperative, collective action required by a national planning program would conform with, rather than offend, the basic drives inherent in human nature.

Not only does Tugwell's theory of human nature give support to

[18] Tugwell, Rexford G., *The Battle for Democracy*, page 14. New York: Columbia University Press, 1935.

his metaphysical outlook, but his views on scientific methodology also harmonize with his general metaphysical position. Where the economist has an emergent metaphysics guiding his scientific investigations, he will be prone to have what Tugwell calls the "experimental attitude" toward scientific matters.[19] The economist will also be inclined to emphasize the need to square theory with fact and to test theory for its workability in actual practice, because he will realize that in the present century "There has been a drift toward the substitution of consequences for premises in the search for truth in all fields." [20] Many of the orthodox economists of the latter part of the last century were more interested in building a logically consistent theoretical system on the basis of a few given premises than in endeavoring to show how economic theories worked out in actual practice. Their scientific interest attached to what was ultimate or absolute rather than to what was relative or expedient; and their main reliance was upon the deductive method of analysis, since this method is designed to reveal the way in which the generality of things is woven about a few fundamentals or ultimates. Since the economic world was alleged to be basically unchanging, the nineteenth-century orthodox economists felt no great need for a constant checking of theories with the facts. To be sure, observation could not be entirely dispensed with, but it was hardly a vital, recurring need in a static universe. In addition, experimentation was not a pressing problem for the economist in an economic world where change and development were largely ignored.

In developing economic understanding the economist has three criteria or tests by means of which he may determine the validity of his scientific doctrines. He may ask the following questions: Are these doctrines logically consistent? Are they in correspondence or agreement with the actual facts? And, finally, do they work out in actual practice as predicted? To be scientifically adequate economic doctrines should conform with all three of these criteria, but unfortunately economists have not always rigorously applied the

[19] Tugwell, Rexford G., "Experimental Economics," in *The Trend of Economics*, 1924, page 394. See also Tugwell, Rexford G., Munro, Thomas, and Stryker, Roy E., *American Economic Life*, Chapter 36, "Toward an Experimental Economics," pages 587-596. New York: Harcourt, Brace and Company, 1925.

[20] Tugwell draws very heavily upon Patten for his views relating to scientific methodology. Cf. Patten, S. N., "Pragmatism and Social Science," in *Essays in Economic Theory*, pages 259-264.

three tests of validity.   The traditional economists have been prone to give too much attention to the first criterion of logical coherence and too little notice to the other two criteria.   Their metaphysical outlook has led them into the errors of a false intellectualism, which has resulted in overemphasizing the importance of system building. Tugwell finds that in the theorizing of the orthodox economist there is too much of the conceptualist and too little of the empiricist.   The orthodox economist has been too inclined to devote his energies to the construction of economic concepts which have more logical symmetry than experiential content.   Economic science has suffered unduly from the pernicious effects of this blind adherence to a narrow conceptualism.   "Conceptualism is the particular bugbear of the social sciences," Tugwell explains, "as, a century or two ago it was the bugbear of the natural sciences. . . .   Conceptualism still haunts the seminars of history, philosophy, political science, and sociology; but none of these suffers more severely than economics." [21]

The new metaphysics of twentieth-century economics strikes a heavy blow at the conceptualism of the last century, because it brings a distinctly fresh attitude toward the methodological problems in the field of economics.   Tugwell finds that in recent decades economics has evolved "toward matter-of-factness and away from abstruseness."   Economists have been sloughing their inherited rationalism in favor of a refreshing empiricism.   More and more the economist is adopting the position of the pragmatist whose primary concern is with determining the validity of doctrines by putting them to the decisive test of actual practice.   "The whole conception of science," says Tugwell "is experimentalism.   Scientists have learned to distrust premises and to depend upon consequences.   And in social science this is bound to involve social facts as they are to be observed in a going society.   These facts are the consequences.   Theory must have reference to them if it is to be useful." [22]   In recent times there has been at work within economists a new scientific spirit, a "restless, questing fever," which has driven them in business, in government, and in the research laboratory to manipulate and to experiment with industrial materials and forces.   There has been a strong impulse to isolate the forces of

[21] "Human Nature in Economic Theory," page 320.
[22] "Experimental Economics," page 395.

industry for investigation, to examine their operation, and to see how they may be brought together in new arrangements. Fortunately for the progress of economics economists have come down from their ivory towers in increasing numbers to cope with the difficult task of "replacing a foundation of outworn assumption with a foundation of ascertainable fact."

Tugwell's intellectual orientation emphasizes the exploratory and experimental approach to economic studies. Whether the economist is a researcher or a teacher he should preserve the experimental attitude toward the problems of economic science. It is not necessary, however, for every economist to be actually engaged in the work of economic experimentation. Many economists may devote their lives to less urgent tasks, but when they retire to the classroom or to the library, they should retain the mental outlook which abhors closed systems of thought, and which refuses to confuse reality with over-refined abstraction. It was the great weakness of the metaphysical position of the nineteenth-century orthodox economists that it eventually led them away from that economic reality which is the ultimate source of economic knowledge.

Tugwell has shown no inclination to be drawn into futile discussions concerning the relative values of the deductive and inductive methods of scientific analysis. Since he realizes that these methods have their own special advantages, he provides a place for both of them in his theory of scientific methodology.[23] What he takes exception to, however, is any abuse of either method of scientific analysis. Too much reliance on deduction can only lead to barren abstruseness, while too much emphasis on the inductive method is equally harmful to scientific work, because it leads to a pointless accumulation of data. The understanding economist refuses "to be confined to the unadorned and de-emphasized enumera-

[23] In his essay on "Experimental Economics" (page 396) Tugwell points out that "The experimentalists in economics have been rather frowned upon by those versed deeply in old theory; for one thing, because they were working in fields more or less unknown to the old theory, or at least fields that were so minor as hardly to be noticed in any text of *Principles;* and for another thing, because they have tended to remain more or less unaware of old theory and of its real value and so have seemed ignorant in an important respect to those who were versed in it. Mutual antagonism, sometimes serious, has resulted—serious because it led to closer adherence to old theory on the one hand and to a defiant repudiation of theory as impractical on the other."

tion of events, which, as a method for social science at least, must be almost wholly fruitless. Mere description becomes a dusty catalogue of nondescript happenings." [24]   The economist should never lower himself to the level of a mere data-chaser; he should realize that besides the accumulation of data there are the more important problems of selecting and interpreting data. This selection and interpretation must be carried on within a framework of reference which the economist brings ready-made to the analysis of the data at hand. His framework is built around certain basic premises which are arrived at very largely through an intuitive process. This does not mean that the economist obtains his scientific insight from the deep recesses of his subconscious mind; on the contrary his framework of reference and the premises on which it is based are derived from a life of contact with the external world. It is Tugwell's general position that there should be a union of generalized insight and inductive analysis which will keep scientific insight or intuition within the bounds of recognizable reality, and which at the same time will enable the economist to avoid an aimless wandering through a world of meaningless data.

Tugwell has observed a recent tendency among economists to place too much reliance on the quantitative method of scientific analysis. Being somewhat overwhelmed by the size of the problems to be tackled, some economists have too severely limited the area to which they apply their statistical analysis. This tendency to narrow the field of investigation is all too frequently assumed to be the proper way for the investigator to become "scientific." But in thus isolating certain economic relations for special study by the quantitative method, the economist frequently disregards many causes and consequences which are much more important than he takes them to be. This "contemporary preference for quantitative methods and for exactness in measurement" has serious shortcomings.[25]   It makes for the possibility of error in judgment by giving a concrete air only to those data that are subject to statistical treatment, while data that cannot be handled statistically suffer from being regarded as irregular or unmanageable. Limited statistical studies too effectively shut off that "ranging of the imagina-

---

[24] "Human Nature in Economic Theory," page 343.
[25] Tugwell, Rexford G., "The Theory of Occupational Obsolescence," *Political Science Quarterly*, June, 1931, Vol. XLVI, page 179.

tion" among the less obvious data which is frequently the source of genuinely fruitful economic thought.

The methods of scientific analysis used by the institutional economists have not escaped criticism by Tugwell, who finds that the "Institutionalists are apt to center attention on accounting for modern economic behavior by the sweeping use of anthropological material and consequently to build up categories which are over-inclusive." [26]   Broad generalizations are useful to express new insights and to prepare the foundations of new frameworks of analysis, but unaccompanied by analysis "in less heroic terms" such generalizations provide a flimsy basis for an interpretation of the realities of economic experience.   Tugwell observes that institutionalists like Veblen were prone to cover up the need for close, incisive analysis by using such broad and vague concepts as "pecuniary emulation," "the business order," and "the industrial employments."   If these terms are to have much conceptual value, they must be supported by a more detailed analysis of the factual basis of modern economic activity.   It is only when the broad generalizations and vague categories of the institutional economists have been grounded in more factual analyses that they will provide an adequate basis for the interpretation of the functioning of the modern economy. The intuitive capacities of economists like Veblen will then be held within proper bounds, and a fruitful cross-fertilization between broad generalization and factual analysis of current reality may then be set in motion.

The Theory of Economic Development

Before turning to Tugwell's analysis of the functioning of the modern economy, it is necessary to inquire into the philosophy of history or the interpretation of economic development which underlies his economic thought.   In Tugwell's analysis man is held to be a creature with an exploratory drive.   Although he may love peace and quietude, there is within man a force which relentlessly drives him to disrupt his own peaceful existence.   No sooner has he found one cultural haven of spiritual or philosophical rest than he is driven beyond its sheltering walls to seek the novel and the unexplained.   And the same is true of nature in the large; there is a peculiar dualism in nature which makes the historical process a

[26] *Ibid.*, page 190 fn.

movement from one cultural equilibrium to another. The historical process moves in a cyclical manner which is the counterpart of the individual's flight from peace to adventure, and then from adventure to peace.' At various intervals in the exfoliation of the historical process mankind has achieved a static state where culture appears to have blossomed forth within the limits of a recognizable pattern. For a time institutions and customs remain unchanged; men achieve something in a cultural way, and have time to marvel at and enjoy their cultural creations. But within every such static cultural state there have been forces at work which have eventually led to an upsetting of the cultural equilibrium. For this reason periods of cultural stability have been of relatively short duration, and have all been eventually swept away by the larger movement of the historical process.

Since the latter part of the eighteenth century mankind has passed through a period of widespread cultural change which, Tugwell believes, is now leading us to another epoch of cultural equilibrium in the not-too-distant future. We are moving "toward our apotheosis, the golden age of the machine. . . . The passivity of nature will have its way again for a time. There may be an interim, a period of comparative adjustment, and something like peace." [27] In the past century and a half, during which we have been working toward this golden age of the machine, our whole civilization has been transformed. This transformation is to be attributed in large part to the industrialism which has changed the social milieu from which comes art, literature, ethics, and other cultural manifestations. In his *Industry's Coming of Age* (1927) Tugwell inquires into the consequences which have followed the rapid spread of modern industrialism. He finds that we have developed a marvelously fruitful economic system, but that we have not yet made the necessary adjustments in the other areas of human behavior. We are, however, moving irresistibly in the direction of a new society in which industrial technology will be harnessed for the higher purposes of general economic welfare. This is coming about because modern technological arrangements are teaching us how to act cooperatively for the improvement of human welfare.

This technological interpretation of the course of cultural de-

---

[27] "Experimental Economics," page 375.

velopment bears a close resemblance to economic determinism. Our industrial technology is supposed to canalize our cultural exfoliation so that the social and political superstructure comes to fit the industrial scheme of things. The cultural superstructure is then but "an extension of industrial technique." [28] It should be pointed out that this technological interpretation does not make Tugwell a simon-pure economic determinist. He does not adopt the position of those social scientists who find in the technological interpretation a single key to the explanation of how the cultural complex changes. Tugwell is also enough of a voluntarist to see that, although culture is very greatly influenced by the machine process, there is still a place for the influence of non-technological factors. Mankind can in an independent fashion influence the cultural scheme of things; it can harness the machine process in order to make it serve the purposes of general human welfare. Until recently society has been inclined to allow the industrial system to shape human behavior and to influence social morality with but little interference from the human agent. Being very much of a realist Tugwell understands that our civilization must be accommodated to our industrial discipline, but at the same time he asserts that civilization need not do all the accommodating. The industrial discipline can and must be adjusted to our moral precepts— to our ideas of how such a discipline should contribute to a sound social system. Tugwell does not allow himself to slip into the fallacy of believing that everything is right merely because it happens to exist, and that things could not be otherwise. According to his interpretation of cultural development there is much room for human ingenuity in the task of improving civilization through the application of controls at strategic points in the industrial system.

Some economists of the nineteenth century assumed that there were immutable laws governing the development of economic society. Beneath the surface phenomena of everyday existence there were supposed to be natural laws of social development at work which could be exposed to popular view by the social scientist. This understanding of the nature of social development leads to two different cultural interpretations, the one idealistic and

[28] *Ibid.*, page 244.

the other materialistic. It leads to the idealistic view that, although these fundamental laws of social development are unaffected by man's intelligence, the whole cultural process is itself subject to control by some transcendental force or divine reason operating outside man's worldly order. In essence, this point of view is a form of idealism which rests on the basic assumptions that this is a pretty good world after all, and that it is moving inevitably toward a more progressive arrangement of things in spite of mankind's impotence with respect to the historical process and its general direction. There are two important consequences that arise from an adherence to this idealistic interpretation of cultural development. The first is that one tends to believe in the inevitability of social and economic progress, since transcendental powers could not do otherwise than provide for humanity in the long run. The second consequence is that there is a tendency to accept the *status quo*. This is so because the forces that are directing the evolution of society are held to be omniscient, and any endeavor on mankind's part to alter the course of things would be hardly more than an exhibition of effrontery in the face of cosmic reason.

The second type of interpretation to which the theory of the immutability of social laws leads is materialistic. The historical process moves on, not because of the intervention of transcendental reason, but because of some change in the material environment of mankind. Fundamental changes in material conditions, when once started, become cumulative and frequently end by transforming the whole cultural superstructure. This materialistic interpretation, like that of the idealist, also leads to a conception of inevitability, since the fundamental laws of economic change are supposed to operate independently of mankind. Economic change is regarded as the unthinking master of human destiny, which fashions the world to its own idle demands and plunges a helpless mankind into the great vortex of cultural development. The materialistic interpretation of the course of cultural evolution may also result in the adoption of a "do-nothing" social policy, because it assumes that man cannot expedite or alter the course of economic change through any effort of his own. According to this view of social development mankind would be very presumptuous to tamper with the dictates of blind economic change.

Tugwell has objections to both the idealistic and the materialistic interpretations of human culture. He points out that no one explanation is sufficient, and that both interpretations lead to a misunderstanding of the nature of the cultural process. By analyzing the half-truths buried deeply in both interpretations, he reaches the conclusion that an adequate understanding of the historical process converts both idealism and materialism into humanistic naturalism. This naturalism gives proper recognition to the collective intelligence of humanity as an independent force in the development of economic and social organization. Whatever "reason" is found in the historical process is the collective reason with which mankind has been endowed. Furthermore, the material factor in cultural development is no longer to be taken as all-embracing in its importance. Instead, it is to be regarded as something with which we must reckon and which may set limits to the application of collective human intelligence, but which is nevertheless subject to modification by the human will-in-action. It is Tugwell's firm conviction "that man can change society in very nearly any respect he cares to; he has only to will it persistently and strongly enough, to formulate his ideals distinctly enough, to go slow enough, and to keep close enough to present determinants in transforming his environment into the ideal." [29] Man is no mere pawn of the strange, uncontrollable forces of economic change. He is a creature of considerable dignity, who, although he cannot penetrate all of nature's secrets and so must ever be humble before her, has nevertheless been given the power to cooperate with nature as an independent partner in shaping his own economic and social destiny. Tugwell believes that mankind, being gifted with an exploratory nature and becoming increasingly aware of the value of the experimental method, should in the not-too-remote future arrive at a "really social system."

When he turns to an analysis of the functioning of the modern economy Tugwell combines his technological interpretation of cultural development with his theory of a mature capitalism. His general thesis as outlined in 1927 in *Industry's Coming of Age* is that the era of rapid economic growth, which began in the early part of the last century, is now reaching the highwater mark of its

[29] "Experimental Economics," page 391.

development.   The era of "economic development" is turning into an era of "economic maintenance." [30]   The technological changes of the past century and a half have contributed to the building of an intricate industrial society which will be more concerned in the future with the exploitation of the possibilities of an already highly mechanized industry than with further radical changes in economic organization.   The main problem today is to make the necessary changes so that the economic policies appropriate only to a rapidly expanding economy will be replaced by policies more useful in an economy which has reached a high level of industrial maturity. This will not be an easy task, because, although it may be said that "industry" has come of age, the same is not true of "business." Business continues to be guided by attitudes and policies which fail to recognize that industry has now very definitely reached a maturation point.

There has been a tremendous growth in national productivity since 1850.   The causes of this great improvement in national output are divided by Tugwell into technical and general causes.[31] Among the technical causes Tugwell lists such factors as directed industrial research, standardization of basic materials and processes, better accounting and budgetary controls, and better engineering practice in internal planning.   In addition, an improved organization of executive functions, an increasing scale of operations, better banking and marketing arrangements, personnel studies, and improved labor relations have made our industrial technique more efficient.   The onward surge toward greater efficiency in industry has derived further impetus from the general causes of increased productivity.   Among these general causes Tugwell places such factors as the increased mechanization of industrial processes, the additions to the accumulated store of technical skills and knowledge, the spread of general and technical education, a more efficient distribution of population, the absorption of women into the ranks of the employed, the combination movement among businesses, and

[30] This idea of economic maturity, while not widely accepted during the decade of the 1920's, has been more generally accepted since the advent of the Great Depression of 1929.   A more recent exponent of the doctrine of economic maturity is Alvin H. Hansen.   See his *Fiscal Policy and Business Cycles*, 1941, pages 400-410.

[31] Tugwell, Rexford G., *Industry's Coming of Age*, pages 65-203.   New York: Harcourt, Brace and Company, 1927.

the attempts on the part of businessmen to anticipate the vagaries of the business cycle. These various technical and general causes of increased national productivity have united in the past hundred years to create a gigantic and intricate economic system capable of eliminating any scarcities of production. As a consequence of the nation's technological advance since 1850, our production problems have been largely solved, and the basis for a health-and-decency standard of living for the population in general has been provided.

In less than a century the rapid advance of technological change has converted the United States into a highly industrialized nation. This shift from an agricultural to an industrial economy has altered social mores and customary modes of living. The development of cities has called for new adjustments and new types of education. Industry has required a growing number of technically trained hands, and, to the extent that it has provided a taxable surplus, we have turned to the construction of an educational system which will lead to still further economic surpluses. The preservation of our advances in technical knowledge and the passing on of them through formal education has not, however, been an uninterrupted process. Within recent years there have been increasing signs that the era of rapid expansion is coming to a close. Undeveloped territories have now been occupied, and in the industrialized nations population is becoming stationary or is actually on the decline. Small-scale industry has been largely replaced by large-scale enterprise; machinery has displaced much of the labor supply, and new and expanding markets have become progressively fewer. Basic structural changes have altered the contours of the nineteenth-century economy, with the result that a "mongrel economy" has replaced the predominantly competitive economy of the last century. In the mixed economy of today corporate enterprise has a leading role; large segments of the economy have fallen under monopolistic controls; and industrial autocracy has narrowed the field for freedom of enterprise. Structural changes have been accompanied by significant functional changes; and, as a consequence, the "market co-ordination" of the simple economy of the last century has been to a very considerable extent replaced by "corporate co-ordination." But the corporate coordination of the mixed economy has not been nearly so satisfactory as the older market coordination in keeping the economic system at a high level of activity.[32] This situation has developed because businessmen have failed to understand the requirements of the logic inherent in the technological advance of the past few decades.

Tugwell makes much of the idea that the technological progress of the past half-century has had a logic of its own. The changes in economic organization which this progress has brought about have required vast expenditures of investment funds, and have caused fixed costs to supersede variable costs in importance. This change in the cost structure of modern industry has made lower costs per unit of output possible. If the logic of technological advance is to work itself out completely, lower costs must be translated into lower selling prices which will clear the markets of expanding output. Unfortunately, the logic inherent in technological progress has not been free to work itself out. This outcome is explained by Tugwell on the ground that technological improvements have been injected into a business system which is unable to digest the consequences of technological advance. Businessmen have come to realize that, although lower costs resulting from technological improvements may seem promising, they are not always automatically obtained. There is no guarantee that technological improvements will work out as anticipated, or that there will be adequate demand for the enlarged output. The heavy investments in fixed capital made necessary by recent technological advances "constitute a commitment to full production schedules which is the nightmare of modern management." Full production schedules require a continuous market, but the modern mixed economy is unable to provide this continuity of operations under the direction of private business enterprise alone.[33]

In order to preserve its interests the large corporation turns to various defense mechanisms which only further deny the logic inherent in technological advance. Prominent among these defense mechanisms is the corporate surplus, which is regarded as insurance

[32] Tugwell, Rexford G., "The Responsibilities of Partnership," an address delivered before the Iowa Bankers Association, June 27, 1934 (mimeographed), page 4.

[33] "The Theory of Occupational Obsolescence," page 185. This is a problem which has recently engaged the attention of Thurman W. Arnold. See Arnold's *Democracy and Free Enterprise*, 1942, pages 12-22, and his *The Bottlenecks of Business*, 1940, pages 1-59.

against the time when markets will no longer absorb the expanding output. These liquid reserves "prevent the translation of improvements into lowered costs. For, if businesses are to be kept prepared for uncertainty by surpluses proportioned to all possible eventualities, prices cannot be lowered as costs are, but must be kept up. Thus funds which might be transmuted in lower prices—the equivalent of higher incomes for consumers—are used instead to increase costs of another sort. Even when sufficient time has elapsed to demonstrate the success of an innovation, the reluctance to reduce prices persists. Advertising expenditures are an illustration of these reluctance mechanisms. Undertaken at first to steady demand, such devices are frequently continued as a defense of prices." [34] Tugwell asserts that the liquid surpluses of modern corporations constitute "a major social problem," because they play a very disruptive role in the modern economy. These surpluses enable the individuals in control of corporate enterprises to expand or contract productive capacity as they see fit. If the corporate managers are reluctant to take the necessary steps, underinvestment may result; but if they are overoptimistic, their use of liquid reserves may result in overinvestment in plant and equipment. What is objectionable to Tugwell in this situation is that the functions of gathering and allocating capital are entrusted to the same individuals. He is convinced that "We have trusted the functions of gathering and allocation to the wrong individuals. We have too easily assumed that the power to make profits implies wisdom in the disposal of them. These are distinct functions and success at one of them may very well be a disqualification for the other. Some social control is needed here, perhaps, more than at any other point in our system."

The failure of the modern economy to maintain the continuity of its producing, selling, and consuming operations has made possible a growing separation of economic rights and responsibilities. In the competitive economy of the early nineteenth century there was a close connection between the possession of economic rights and privileges and the recognition of correlative responsibilities. The competitive economy was able, through its system of checks and balances, to vest economic rights and responsibilities in the same individuals. In the modern economy businessmen all too frequently

[34] "The Theory of Occupational Obsolescence," pages 186-187.

insist upon their economic rights, but fail to accept the responsibility of keeping the economic system a going concern. They take their profits, but they do not accept the obligation of maintaining a smooth functioning of the whole economy. What is necessary to correct this condition is a further development of the common law. The common law broadened its system of controls in the early years of the nineteenth century to protect the businessman from the landed interests. What is now required is a further adaptation of the common law to the new economic realities of the twentieth century. For a time, starting with the case of *Munn v. Illinois* (1876), it looked as though the extension of common-law controls to large integrated industries was going to provide a new basis for responsibility in economic affairs. But the movement to bring the major industries under public regulation lost its vigor in the second decade of this century. Tugwell believes that it is now desirable to set this evolution of common-law controls in motion once more, so that we may continue with the task of bringing about a closer correlation of economic rights and responsibilities. As this development makes further progress, the time may come when the planning and controlling of economic activity within the inherited legal framework of industry will appear as normal and regular characteristics of economic life.

Another disturbing development which has accompanied the failure of the modern hybrid economy to preserve its continuity of operations is the tendency for economic gains and costs to become separated. In the competitive economy of the last century the costs involved in turning out the national output were fairly well covered by the incomes paid out by business enterprises to the various agents of production. In the modern economy the situation is somewhat different. Owing to the rapid technological advances of the past half-century new costs have made their appearance for which corporate enterprise is unwilling to make adequate provision. One of the heaviest of these costs of industrial progress is "occupational obsolescence."[35] Technological advance has brought in its wake unemployment, a lessening of worker morale, and a need for new types of training for those who are preparing themselves for work in the mixed economy of today. The only

[35] For an extended discussion of this problem see Tugwell's essay entitled "The Theory of Occupational Obsolescence."

source of income with which to cover these social costs is the surplus created by the business system.   Since business enterprise is unwilling to dip into its surpluses voluntarily, it becomes the duty of the community to see to it that these surpluses are used in part to cover the necessary costs of industrial progress.   Just as there is a need to bring economic rights and responsibilities more closely together, so also is there a need to have the national income distributed in such a fashion that all the social and private costs of industry are met.   To bring this result about, consumer purchasing power should be enlarged through price reductions, education should be revised and enlarged, and adequate provision should be made for social insurance and employment exchanges.   Each step toward these goals narrows that separation of gains and costs which has been the source of so much economic conflict.

Tugwell summarizes his views with respect to the working of the modern economy with the statement that the fundamental difficulty in which we find ourselves arises from the fact that there is a basic conflict between "the logic of the economic system" and the ideology or system of beliefs of businessmen.   This ideology, which energizes businessmen and gives unity to their thinking, leads them to overemphasize the importance of technological progress.   As a consequence we have "industrial advance" which eliminates human effort in industry, but not enough "social advance" which would provide for a more satisfactory sharing of the results of technological improvement.   What is needed are "different ideological circumstances" which would open the eyes of businessmen to the necessity of a better strategy in meeting the serious problems of the hybrid economy.   "The conspicuous failure of industrialism," says Tugwell, "is not in what we ordinarily call technique, but in the wider field of strategy. . . .   Our technique is used not for its intended purpose but for quite another one: not to furnish us an efficiently functioning system, but to establish conditions in which businessmen shall dominate regardless of the costs to everyone else.   The strange thing is the genuine enthusiasm with which so many of us support the conspiracy."   The immediate problem before us is to extricate ourselves from the situation in which we have failed to recognize the logic inherent in modern industrialism.   We can do this only by coming to understand the logic of modern economic enterprise, and then taking appropriate action to permit it to work itself out. In Tugwell's opinion this means that we will have to turn to some form of national economic planning.

Tugwell's Social Management Program

When Tugwell turns to the problems of national economic planning he is once more concerning himself with an issue that has engrossed his attention ever since his undergraduate days at the University of Pennsylvania. The relations of government to economic activity are an issue over which he has never ceased to ponder, and it is when he is dealing with this particular issue that he is at his best. Since any economic planning program on a national scale rests upon the exercise of certain regulatory powers by the federal government, the type of planning program that one recommends will necessarily reflect his views upon the nature of government and its proper relations to the business system. Tugwell is no exception to this generalization.

Tugwell explains that the governmental pattern established in the United States in the late eighteenth century was appropriate to an age of small-scale business, but that the economic situation of today calls for a new pattern of government. He believes that we should abandon the "policeman doctrine of government," according to which governmental functions are "negative and arresting" rather than "positive and stimulating." The popular attitude toward the government in its relations with business has come down from a century when the government endeavored to keep the competitive processes of small-scale business activity free from interferences of any sort. Since 1870 the age of large-scale enterprise and industrial associationism has brought new responsibilities to those entrusted with the task of governing the nation, but there has been a lag in the adaptation of government policy to the new economic conditions. This lag has developed because it takes considerable time for technological changes to work their way up to the level of political activity. The time has now arrived, however, when the government should become more positive in the exercise of its powers, and should cooperate with businessmen in giving direction to economic life.[36] In the new epoch of "inextricable interdependence," when the point is reached that businessmen are

[36] For a more extended discussion of Tugwell's political theory see his essay on the "Design for Government," *The Battle for Democracy*, pages 3-16.

unable to create an adequate industrial program because they cannot agree on the necessary cooperative policies, the government should step in to provide the requisite unifying force.   It is now necessary to recapture "the vision of a government equipped to fight and overcome the forces of economic disintegration."   The check-and-balance theory of government based on Montesquieu's errone-ous analysis of the operations of the English government should be replaced by a political theory which will lead to a "vigorous gov-ernmental administration."

Tugwell recommends the establishment of a fourth branch within the governmental system which he describes as the "directive power."   Ever since the adoption of the Constitution in 1789 the legislative, executive, and judicial branches of government have been engaged in a continuous struggle for a position of dominance. Not only have the various governmental divisions themselves striven for advantage among themselves, but they have also responded to the demands of special minority interests rather than to the needs of the general public.   This has been especially true of the legisla-tive branch of government, because "Representative democracy always runs the risk that its legislatures will be filled with those who represent local and private intentions rather than general ones." [37]   Because of the breakdown of industry in recent years, the executive branch of government has asserted itself, and has en-deavored to protect the public from both the acquisitiveness of big business and the weaknesses of modern legislatures.   In this effort to protect the public welfare the executive has met the determined resistance of the judiciary, that "last champion of business, and the determined enemy of effectual government."

In its endeavor to elevate public welfare above the strife of party politics, the executive has sought to place further limitations upon the privileges and powers enjoyed by the other branches of the gov-ernment.   It has done so by fostering the development of adminis-trative law.   The executive branch of government has been strengthened in recent years through the creation of new adminis-trative agencies such as the Social Security and the National Labor Relations Boards, and through the revitalizing of the older govern-mental departments.   Unfortunately it has turned out that these

[37] Tugwell, Rexford G., "The Fourth Power," *Planning and Civic Comment,* April-June, 1939, Part II, page 10.

various administrative departments have championed special rather than general interests. Even though the development of administrative law has placed effective curbs upon both the legislature and the judiciary, and has thereby strengthened the executive arm of government, little success has been achieved in providing direction for the nation's economic activities. Since the executive branch of government has been unable to keep the various administrative departments in line with respect to the needs of general welfare, it has disqualified itself as an organ for the provision of national economic direction. All too frequently American presidents have not had the ability to give direction to the nation's economic activities; and, even when they have had the necessary qualifications, they have not always kept the public welfare uppermost in their minds. In the United States the chief executive is usually too responsible to party politics to give proper consideration to the requirements of national economic welfare; consequently, "A power is needed which is longer-run, wider-minded, differently allied, than a reformed executive would be."

The new directive branch of government should be independent of both the executive and the legislature. Its members should be chosen on the basis of very highly selective qualifications; and they should be given terms of appointment that are longer than those of all other government officials except the members of the judiciary. Aloof from party strife and the pressures of bloc interests, the directive branch of government would be well situated to cope with the many destructive economic conflicts which are gnawing at the vitals of contemporary economic society. In Tugwell's opinion what our democracy needs is some public agency which will protect it from itself; and he believes that the directive branch of government would be well chosen for this important function.

With respect to the questions of how and when a directive agency such as a national planning board should be established, Tugwell is quick to point out that there would probably be many difficulties encountered. The new branch of government may develop in an evolutionary fashion, or it may be fostered only sporadically. Tugwell is inclined to the view that it will take some national crisis to prepare the ground for the establishment of the directive, just as it required the constitutional crisis of the late eighteenth century to bring the executive into being.[38]   Although he cannot be certain just how the national directive will emerge, Tugwell believes that there is a logic in recent industrial development which impels us very forcibly in the direction of experiments in national economic planning and in the setting up of a directive branch of government.   Since we are only slowly becoming aware of this logic, the "new system may substitute itself for the old without clear recognition."   Once established, the directive branch of government would have a unique advantage not enjoyed by the other three branches of government, since it would have no traditional function to perform.   It would have an advantage over the executive in not being too closely associated with the daily operations of the government, and over the legislative in not having to represent a number of factions or regions.   Furthermore, it would be in a much more advantageous position than the judiciary, because it would be dealing with scientific facts rather than with inherited legal precedents.   The directive would also be orientated to the future; it would have "an interest in progress and modernization which is quite different from the traditional interests of the other three powers."   By adhering closely to the facts of the situation, the directive could establish a national policy for future economic guidance which would adequately subordinate the private purposes of minority interests to the larger human welfare.

One of the most frequent criticisms of the type of social management proposed by Tugwell is the assertion that national planning would be undesirable because of its regimentative nature.   The general argument is that social management would destroy the freedoms of the individual by pouring mankind into the arbitrary molds of regimentative planning.   Tugwell asserts that many of the opponents of national economic planning do not have a proper understanding of the meaning of "freedom" and "regimentation."

[38] Tugwell, Rexford G. and Keyserling, Leon H., *Redirecting Education*, Vol. I, page 56.   New York: Columbia University Press, 1934.   Tugwell states that "It is only some emergency which possesses the power to shake our wills into new energies and perceptions. . . .   It has been interesting to see, in these last years since 1929, how we have changed.   Interesting theories and proposals concerning social institutions suddenly began to develop about 1930. . . .   The thinking of men cannot be permanently tied to privilege; the merest jar will start it working on materials never before considered; and, once released, it can come to conclusions which are quite independent of wishes."

Reverting to Veblen's explanation of the effect of machine industry upon human conduct, he points out that modern industry requires men to abandon their former rule-of-thumb methods of production in favor of more precise methods. It is only by submitting to the discipline of the machine that man can become free to enjoy the fruits of the assembly line.[39] Such regimentation, far from being objectionable, is actually desirable because it guarantees an economic abundance to mankind. A maintenance of arbitrary, rule-of-thumb ways of doing things destroys the efficiency of the machine process, and subjects men to continued poverty. The regimentation which develops out of "measurement, exactitude, repetivity, and so on, all principles on which the machine process also rests," is the very foundation of national economic planning. One cannot with any show of reason object to this type of regimentation, since it is a requirement of the modern industrial system. The proper procedure is therefore to recognize this regimentation as inevitable and desirable, if one first agrees that the modern industrial system is worth preserving, and then not to attack regimentation *per se* but to distinguish between desirable and undesirable forms of regimentation. This procedure requires one to understand the industrial discipline under which future generations will have to work and live. It demands that we divest ourselves of notions of freedom from regimentation which might have been appropriate to the craft work of the Middle Ages, but which are not applicable to the machine work of the twentieth century.

To insure that the regulation of economic life would remain within the proper limits, Tugwell suggests that provision be made for "a rigorously fixed procedure of expert preparation, public hearings, agreed findings, and careful translation into law—which are in turn subject to legislative ratification."[40] The work of the directive should at all times be given the full light of publicity, and should proceed in a fashion calculated to inspire the confidence of the man in the street. It is only in this way that the regimentation required by the existing technology would be re-

---

[39] John Dewey has a similar attitude towards the problem of regimentation: "Regimentation of material and mechanical forces is the only way by which the mass of individuals can be released from regimentation and consequent suppression of their cultural possibilities." See his *Liberalism and Social Action*, 1935, page 90.

[40] "The Fourth Power," page 30.

stricted to the area to which it properly applies. On all matters of general policy final judgments would have to be made by the duly elected representatives of the people. Tugwell has no fear that in the long run the public would act contrary to the dictates of the modern industrial system, because an adequate educational system would enable the public to understand the nature of the machine process and its demands.

Since private business is unable to provide a satisfactory national economic planning program, it becomes the duty of the government to supply the necessary program. In Tugwell's proposed planning scheme the enterprises within each industry would organize an association whose purpose would be to establish a planning board for the entire industry. In all ordinary circumstances this industrial planning agency would depend for its success upon the voluntary cooperation of the various business enterprises within the industry. As far as possible it would be the aim to have the workers, consumers, and employers within each industry take care of their own planning requirements. Such a planning scheme would probably encounter various difficulties in connection with issues involving more than one industry, since producing groups have time and again demonstrated their inability to plan on an inter-industry basis. A central planning board, representing the affiliated industries and the government, would serve "as a mediating and integrating body, for the coördination of the several industries' plans and policies respecting production, prices, division of markets, working conditions, and the like." [41] The functions of the central planning board would be only investigational and coordinative. The board would have the preliminary task of carrying on the research which would provide the factual foundation of the national planning program; in addition it would have to combine the many local and regional industrial planning programs into one harmonious whole. The two major problems which this central planning board could not leave to the various subordinate industrial planning agencies are the allocation of capital and the control of prices. In order to prevent enterprises from burdening themselves with excessive equipment Tugwell suggests that corporations no longer be permitted to reinvest their surpluses at will.

[41] Tugwell, Rexford G., *The Industrial Discipline and the Governmental Arts,* page 212. New York: Columbia University Press, 1933.

If necessary, taxes on undistributed profits could be used to force these surplus funds into distribution. Enterprises would then have to have recourse to the regular investment markets to obtain funds for expansion purposes. Furthermore, Tugwell suggests that the device of federal incorporation might be adopted to give more control over new capital issues.[42] In this way a thorough check could be had on all funds invested in the fixed capital basis of industry. The allocation of capital, instead of being a haphazard industrial policy, would become a part of a larger, coordinated planning program designed to adjust industry's capital equipment to the various economic needs of the population.

Industrial price policy is the second major problem that would confront a central planning agency. The most important lesson which the 1929 depression has taught us, Tugwell feels, is that the price policies of the large corporations are among the factors leading to business recessions.[43] Where large corporations fail to pass on the advantages obtained from improvements in industrial technique, they accumulate large surpluses of undistributed profits. At the same time they do not provide the consuming public with enough purchasing power to clear the markets of their goods. Recession not only becomes inevitable, but, to make matters worse, when business shows signs of sagging the large corporations add to the difficulties by maintaining their prices and curtailing production. The result is unemployment, further losses of consumer purchasing power, and a further repression of business activity. Since these short-sighted price and production policies cannot be altered by industrialists acting alone, it becomes the duty of the central planning board to provide a way out of the difficulty.

Tugwell's social management proposals include more than an industrial control program. The general aim of his planning program is to achieve an economy in which a proper balance would be established between industry and agriculture. The national planning program should give special attention to agriculture because it is the real basis of our civilization. Tugwell maintains

[42] A similar recommendation was made to the Temporary National Economic Committee in 1941. See the final statement of the Committee's chairman, "The Preservation of Economic Freedom," Senate Document No. 39, 77th Congress, March 11, 1941, pages 11-14.

[43] See Tugwell's essay on "The Economics of the Recovery Program" in *The Battle for Democracy*, pages 78-96.

"that intelligent use of the land is the first criterion of any civilization. The fertility of the soil is the ultimate source of wealth. When that is gone, the civilization built upon it soon decays." [44] A nation which does not bend its efforts toward the preservation of its land and other natural resources cannot hope to preserve its culture for any considerable length of time. For the purpose of safeguarding our heritage of natural resources Tugwell has drawn the broad outlines of a national land-planning program which has two fundamental purposes: first, the preservation of land resources in general, and, second, the achievement of prosperity for those who utilize the land as the basis of their livelihood.[45] It would be the purpose of a land-planning program to preserve our natural resources for generations yet unborn, but at the same time we should bring prosperity to the present generation by placing agriculture upon a firm foundation.

The first aim of a national land program would be to convert into public land all those areas which are not now satisfactorily used under private ownership. Some of this land would be permanently withdrawn from cultivation and converted into forests and parks, whereas other acres which were suitable for cultivation would be withheld from private use until such time as it could be demonstrated that there was a need to cultivate them. More difficult problems arise in connection with the second part of the national land program, which deals with the areas to be kept under private cultivation. Production on these acres should be adjusted to the national demands for the various agricultural products. Tugwell's general aim is to have continuous production on whatever acres are cultivated without any piling up of unsalable surpluses. Control of the output of farm products may be secured in either of two ways. We can have less output from all the acres now under cultivation, or we can reduce the number of acres now

---

[44] Tugwell, Rexford G., "Economic Freedom and the Farmers," *The Battle for Democracy*, pages 238-239.

[45] Tugwell's agricultural proposals are summarized in his essays entitled "The Place of Government in a National Land Program" and "Economic Freedom and the Farmers" in *The Battle for Democracy*, pages 143-163 and 222-240. See also Tugwell, Rexford G., "The Agricultural Policy of France," *Political Science Quarterly*, Vol. XLV, pages 214-230, 405-428, and 527-547; "The Problem of Agriculture," December, 1924, Vol. XXXIX, pages 549-591; and "Farm Relief and a Permanent Agriculture," *The Annals of the American Academy of Political and Social Science*, March, 1929, Vol. 142, pages 271-282.

in use until we have only that amount of output for which there is an adequate demand. In the first method of controlling farm production it is necessary to control the amount of each important crop. This was the method adopted by the Agricultural Adjustment Administration as an emergency measure in 1933 to relieve the desperate farm situation. The second method, which involves reduction of the acreage under cultivation, is much more scientific, and is the one advocated by Tugwell as part of a desirable long-run agricultural control program. He would much prefer to see the poorest land withdrawn from cultivation so that only the more efficient farmers would be left on the better grades of land. If such a policy were adopted, there would be no further need for any special restrictions, since the land area under cultivation would create a supply of farm products just sufficient to meet the current national demands. All that would be necessary would be some guidance in the selection of crops such as is now provided by the United States Department of Agriculture. Any land areas withdrawn from cultivation would be held in reserve as public land to be used for crop purposes only when the demand for farm products had increased.

When one attempts to determine how many acres of land could be withdrawn from cultivation under an agricultural planning scheme, it is soon discovered that the solution of this problem is tied up with the future of foreign trade, the trends of population growth, and the possibility of raising the living standards of the entire population. The future of the foreign demand for farm products depends so much upon political complications both at home and abroad that no satisfactory prognostication can be made in this connection. One can make more satisfactory predictions about the probable domestic demand for farm products, because the trends of population growth are more open to scientific determination. It seems very likely that the population of the United States will soon be stationary or possibly declining. The future prosperity of American agriculture rests, therefore, not upon the demands of an increasing population, but upon a per-capita increase in the consumption of farm products. A better distribution of the national income would permit a large section of the population to use more poultry, dairy products, fresh fruits, and vegetables than they are now consuming. Studies on dietary standards made by various governmental agencies indicate that there is a great need for a per-capita increase in the consumption of farm produce. Furthermore, research in new industrial uses for agricultural products can also be relied upon to widen the markets for the output of our farms.

Raising the living standards of the nation and increasing the per-capita consumption of farm products do not depend upon the smooth functioning of agriculture alone. The problem is one which brings up for consideration the satisfactory functioning of the entire economic system. If agriculture is to be restored to lasting prosperity, there must be an increase in the purchasing power of the general public. Such an increase is in large part the responsibility of industry. At this point in his analysis Tugwell brings together the problems of national economic planning as they relate to both agriculture and industry. In the final analysis the successful working of a program for agricultural planning depends for its success upon the good functioning of some correlative plan for industry. There is a need to establish industrial activity upon a satisfactory and continuing basis not only to permit an increase in per-capita consumption of farm output, but also to absorb the farm workers who would be made superfluous by the agricultural planning program. Tugwell believes that the problem of absorbing these redundant farm workers would be a very difficult one, since it is estimated that one-half of the present number of farmers, using the best techniques of farm production, could produce all the farm products that we now require. There will probably be a continued decline in the number of people engaged in agricultural pursuits, not only because the population is growing less rapidly, but also because of the increased mechanization of agriculture. These changes in agriculture should be welcomed rather than deplored, since they mean that a larger portion of the population will be free to produce the goods and services made possible by the continued progress of industrial science.

What of the immediate prospects for the adoption of Tugwell's planning proposals?[46] There are a number of obstacles which may seriously impede our progress toward a reconstructed economic society. One important obstacle is the attitude of busi-

[46] Tugwell, Rexford G., "The Future of National Planning," *The New Republic*, Dec. 9, 1936, pages 162-164.

nessmen who in the past have behaved dictatorially within their own enterprises. Before social management can succeed, businessmen must have the necessary willingness to cooperate with the government and with other groups concerned with the national planning program. They must be willing to permit the democratic tradition to flow within their factory walls and to penetrate deeply into the inner workings of the industrial system, until intra-business as well as inter-business relations are conducted on a more democratic basis. Once this change in businessmen's attitudes has been made, the most fundamental difficulty will have been eliminated.

There would remain, however, a second source of trouble for those who anticipate an early adoption of some national planning scheme. This second difficulty would be the lack of knowledge concerning the industrial processes. In the period since the early 1920's a basis for agricultural planning has been developed by the various agricultural agencies of the state and federal governments. When the need for agricultural planning on a national scale arose after 1930, the United States Department of Agriculture already possessed the information and the personnel which were required to get the agricultural planning program under way within a relatively short period of time. But there is none of this preparedness on the industrial front. The smooth working of agricultural planning presents an impressive contrast to the clumsy efforts to control industry which were made by the National Recovery Administration. Since industry is the national "sore spot," a new form of "economic statesmanship" must be created if we are to succeed in planning our industrial activities. Of the three parties, the farmer, the businessman, and the laborer, only the farmer has thus far been forced by circumstances to cooperate with the federal government in its endeavor to achieve greater economic stability and security. Management has concentrated too greatly upon increasing profits, while at the same time labor has displayed a much too narrow interest in seeking to maximize its share of the national income. What is now needed is an economic society in which hatred will be replaced by "foresight and reason," and in which men will come to have "open and generous minds." Tugwell believes that it is possible to win over business and labor leaders to these new ideals of cooperative effort. He remains enthusiastic even though he realizes that "Perhaps in time the demand for economic statesmanship will sink in. Perhaps it will be approached with certain face-saving formalities and with appropriate indirection, slowly and awkwardly. As to this, I am not sufficiently gifted with prophecy to say." [47]

What will be the outcome of a national economic planning program? It should be pointed out that economic planning is not designed to give us an entirely new society; all that this planning can do is provide a sound foundation upon which a satisfactory social structure may be erected. In Tugwell's opinion "the protection of living standards is perhaps the most important single item in a generally reorganized system of social ideals." [48] The prime need of the twentieth century is to find some means of providing economic security and sufficiency for the masses. This can be achieved through the right kind of collective economic management, Tugwell is convinced, because such management would not only make the most efficient use of existing resources and productive technique, but it would also provide for an expanding national output.

Tugwell's primary concern has at all times been with the improvement of economic welfare. Although welfare is at bottom a psychological concept which varies from individual to individual, it is possible to arrive at some objective standards with respect to the nature of general economic welfare. There are certain essentials which the majority of people can be expected to agree upon as falling properly within the boundaries of the welfare concept. All will agree, for example, that the right to work should be a reality, that men should be secure in the knowledge that they will be able to find employment if they bend their efforts in the right direction. Furthermore, all will agree that a certain minimum level of family consumption is a proper part of the content of economic welfare. Tugwell calls attention to the fact that the United States Department of Agriculture has already determined the kind of diet that a family should have if it is to enjoy normal health. These are but a few of the welfare items upon which widespread agreement can be readily secured in giving content to the concept of economic welfare. It would be the aim

[47] *Ibid.*, page 164.
[48] *Industry's Coming of Age*, page 220.

of a national economic planning program to give the working masses these minimum essentials of a decent living standard. This program would "involve the social organization of the processes of production and distribution, taking advantage of ordinary and useful motives (with reduced stress on the monetary one, which seems to me to have been overemphasized) and existing machinery and methods, to achieve first a wider distribution and use of goods, and later (for this I think is likely to occupy our generation) whatever further aims seem desirable." [49] What should be aimed at beyond the provision of a health-and-decency standard of living is a most difficult problem to meet. It is a matter to which organized social intelligence will have to devote much time in the hope of satisfactorily expanding the content of the welfare concept. Also, it is a matter that the economist cannot settle alone, because "What is of value to the human spirit lies somewhere beyond the limits of a scheme for achieving generally greater incomes."

A national economic planning program should subserve the higher social purposes which the masses are seeking to actualize, and should therefore, in the end, be directed by the larger, non-economic aims of the general population. It is not the function of the economist to decide what should be our social aims, but once the public has indicated what its general aims are, then the economist should be prepared to show how the economic system may be harnessed for the realization of these aims. All that Tugwell expects from economic planning is the erection of certain bridges leading to an expanding welfare in the future. The economist may be unable to discern clearly all the future requirements of an expanding general welfare, but he can help us to be better masters of our economic destiny than we have been in the past. Tugwell indicates that he would be well satisfied with an economic planning program if it did nothing more, immediately, than to make working conditions more satisfactory, provide for technological progress, and achieve "something approximating justice in industrial affairs."

Unlike many other economists who are interested in national economic planning, Tugwell very penetratingly inquires into the implications of a planned economy for the future. Many of the economic planners state that national planning would make no

---

[49] "The Responsibilities of Partnership," page 3. See also *American Economic Life*, "The Remaking of Urban Life," pages 343-584.

complete break with the past, since this planning would be carried on within the existing institutional framework. Some suggest that old motives and attitudes which were satisfactory in a competitive economic order would have to be altered or supplemented in a planned economic society, but no effort is made to indicate how seriously economic motivation would have to be altered or how basically business arrangements would have to be changed. Tugwell faces these issues squarely. It is his belief that the logic of planning will require changes in institutional arrangements and economic attitudes of such a fundamental nature that one can speak of the end of the laissez-faire system of business enterprise. In referring to the need for discussion of the consequences of a planned economy he states that "It is my view that the prospective discussion ought to be carried out with a clear view of its philosophical implications and of its institutional requirements. If we accept the principle of planning we must accept its implied destruction of the structure of a laissez-faire industry. . . . To take away from business its freedom of venture and of expansion, and to limit the profits it may acquire, is to destroy it as business and to make of it something else. That something else has no name, we can only wonder what it may be like. . . . The traditional incentives, hope of money-making, and fear of money-loss, will be weakened; and a kind of civil-service loyalty and fervor will need to grow gradually into acceptance." [50] In the planned economy which Tugwell envisions there would be a reconsideration of the nature and role of private property and of the incentive to private profit making. This would be a recognition of the fact that property and profits have undergone considerable change since 1860, and will probably go through further changes in the future. The changes which have occurred in property-owning and profit-making have had the combined effect of creating new economic powers and of concentrating them in the hands of a few individuals or groups. One of the prominent features of a national economic planning program would be a relocation of these powers. In the modern economy of large-scale, corporate enterprise economic activity has frequently been guided more in the direction of power ac-

[50] Tugwell, Rexford G., "The Principle of Planning and the Institution of Laissez-Faire," *The American Economic Review*, March, 1932, Vol. XXII, Supp., pages 90, 92.

cumulation than of goods production. It should be clearly understood that social management would rigorously control all the surplus-creating activities which are the sources of large incomes and great economic power.

Because of his pragmatic outlook Tugwell is unwilling to draw the outlines of any final national economic plan for the future. He asserts that a program for social management should be as dynamic as the system that it is designed to control; and that those in charge of the program should always be prepared to alter it to meet the exigencies of our unpredictable economic evolution. There should be no "rigid theoretical commitment to a finished system"; instead there should be a special effort to avoid "blueprint" planning which endeavors to give direction to a nation's economic system in accordance with the view that a given economic scheme ought to work out. Tugwell's type of social management takes cognizance of the fluidity and complexity of economic affairs; and, furthermore, it fosters rather than curbs man's innate creativeness.[51] It is compounded of materials with which the American public is already quite familiar, materials such as mass production, scientific management, frequent invention, opportunity for individual initiative, democratic procedures, decentralized administration, and judgment by results or consequences.

Tugwell's planning proposals may be summarized as an attempt to carry scientific management to the still higher levels of social management where the problem is found to be primarily one of administration. It is not a matter of making a choice between oversimplified alternatives such as laissez-faire capitalism, fascism, or socialism.[52] Instead, the problem is one of finding those economic and political adjustments which would be in conformity with the development of productive techniques in the past half-century. It is apparent that businessmen have failed to meet this major administrative problem. Not catching the significance of the economic changes which have occurred in recent decades, they

[51] "The Responsibilities of Partnership," page 2.

[52] For Tugwell's criticism of the advocacy of such clear-cut alternatives see his review of G. D. H. Cole's *Guild Socialism*, "Guild Socialism and the Industrial Future," *The International Journal of Ethics*, April, 1922, Vol. XXXII, pages 282-288.

have turned out to be "ineffective administrators." [53]   What the future calls for is "constructive administration" which would provide the adjustments required by the new cooperative age.   This constructive administration, if successful, would result in the physical betterment of the nation through the rebuilding of its productive equipment, and in the establishment of more just and stable relations between producing groups.   It would once more create that continuity of operations which was found in the small-scale, competitive economy of the early nineteenth century, but which was interrupted by the corporate enterprise of more recent times, and without which a full functioning of the economy is not possible.

Tugwell's enthusiasm for his program of social management arises, in the final analysis, from his observation of the persistence of a deep "cultural faith" in the American people.   There is a powerful communal ethic which is pressing us to create a cultural organization in which there will be much more economic and social justice than now exists.   This communal ethic has thus far never been satisfactorily defined, but even in its undefined form it has been sufficiently powerful to overcome the clever calculations of "our business and political manipulators."   Tugwell is not able to give any precise description of this national ethic, but he finds that "Part of it is certainly a challenge to fate.   There is no passivity or fatalism in our national attitude.   There is rather a determination to create the sort of system in which privilege plays no part, in which a man is encouraged to do the best he can and is rewarded according to his efforts." [54]   The American society is striving to give further expression to this undefined social ethic by using the materials put at its disposal by the recent technological revolution in agriculture and industry.   Since 1890 there have been three movements at work to bring this national ethic closer to reality.   In the last decade of the nineteenth century, Grover Cleveland and William Jennings Bryan awakened the American conscience to the need for greater social justice.   During the early

[53] Address of Rexford G. Tugwell delivered before the International Institute of Agriculture at Rome, Oct. 24, 1934 (mimeographed), page 3.

[54] Tugwell, Rexford G., "The Progressive Tradition," an address delivered at Union College, Schenectady, New York, Jan. 25, 1935 (mimeographed), page 4, and later published in *The Atlantic Monthly*, January-June, 1935, Vol. CLV, pages 409-418.

years of the new century Theodore Roosevelt and Woodrow Wilson renewed the "battle for democracy"; and since 1929 a third battle has been under way. The great issue of the day now is whether or not the forces of democracy are sufficiently powerful and intelligent to reorder economic and social affairs in a manner that will be satisfactory to our "general ethical and moral sense." With faith in the concept of the good life, with modernized democratic procedures, and with enthusiasm for experimentalism as a technique of social investigation, the American people should go far in translating their ethical ideals into cultural realities by developing the proper program of social and economic management.[55] Tugwell thinks that it should not be so very difficult to indicate, at least in a general way, the directions which reform and reconstruction will have to take if we are to enjoy the inherent fruitfulness of the modern industrial system.

The Nature and Scope of Experimental Economics

An understanding of Tugwell's views relating to the nature of economic theory necessitates a preliminary inquiry into his explanation of the nature of scientific thought in general. Like John Dewey and other pragmatists, Tugwell accepts the view that human thought is largely the product of mankind's contact with the events of daily life. As these events take place, man's imagination is quickened or his reason is stirred by some new-found difficulty; and the consequences of this emotional and intellectual stimulation are the outpourings of poetry, art, religion, and science. Tugwell explains that human thought has relevancy to some interest in "doing," or to some problem to be solved.[56] Man is essentially a self-active creature, and his thoughts are designed to guide him as he pushes along the broad thoroughfares of life. At times human thought may fall into the ruts of tradition and inaction, science may become merely a formalized study, and social progress may be at a standstill. But after periods of stagnation or decay, the activistic quality of human thought usually reasserts itself, and

[55] Tugwell, Rexford G., "Where the New Deal Succeeds," an address delivered before the American Society of Newspaper Editors, New York Times, April 22, 1934.

[56] Tugwell, Rexford G., "Economics," in Roads to Knowledge, 1937, pages 95-96. For a similar view of the nature of human thought see Lerner, Max, Ideas Are Weapons, 1939.

once more humanity moves on toward higher levels of material and intellectual achievement.

Tugwell is primarily interested in that part of human thought which falls into the category of scientific interpretation or understanding. In this field the pragmatic nature of the thought processes is most evident, since the social scientist is being continually pressed to solve various human problems. The social scientist has what Tugwell describes as the "problem-approach" because he lives in a world in which scientific understanding is developed to meet the problems of daily existence. The purpose of scientific inquiry is not so much to uncover uniformities of social behavior as to discover "the efficient moving forces in an observable sequence of events." [57] Men are interested in these moving forces because they want to control the course of human affairs. They look upon social science as an instrument with which to probe the tissues of an unsettled world to the end that the sources of social friction and conflict may be revealed to those who propose to alter the organization of society.

Scientific thinking leads to the creation of various theories. The usual definition of a theory is that it is a scheme of explanation which offers a rational interpretation of the observed facts. But according to Tugwell's interpretation, theory goes beyond the explanation of phenomena. It is not a merely random mental activity; instead theory is explanation associated with an interest in resolving some human difficulty. Following this pragmatic line of analysis, Tugwell defines theory as "sustained thought about some difficulty of practice." [58] When he applies these ideas to contemporary or "current" economic theory, Tugwell observes that economic theories have their origins in the mental difficulties raised by the attempts to improve the material welfare of mankind. Current economic theory is sustained thought about economic phenomena which deal with immediate problems. It is to be distinguished on the one hand from "economic principles" which merely explain things as they are, and on the other hand from economic doctrines "which are economic principles that have passed into history." It is not surprising that Tugwell, having this view

[57] "The Theory of Occupational Obsolescence," page 182.
[58] Tugwell, Rexford G., "Economic Theory and Practice," *The American Economic Review*, March, 1923, Vol. XIII, Supp., pages 107-109.

of economic theory, should define economics as "the discovery and orderly stating of particular problems and the suggestion of solutions—the problems, being roughly, but not closely, defined as those having to do with our ways of getting and using a living."

Tugwell's problem-approach to economic studies and his pragmatic definition of economic theory lead him to a consideration of the causes of the many serious economic problems which beset the American people. All facts point to one main source of economic conflict, which is the changes that have occurred in industrial technology during the past century. These industrial changes have altered the structure and functioning of the American economy; they have modified its class structure, and have transformed the power relations between the various classes. Economic change has left individuals and groups stranded with outmoded ways of behaving and thinking; it has also nurtured new social attitudes and habits which are antipathetic to inherited canons of conduct. Tugwell has much to say about the industrial arts, the changes which have occurred in them, and the consequences that have followed these changes. So concerned is he with the developing industrial technology, that he states it is "the business of . . . [economics] to interpret the meaning and significance of the industrial arts." He believes that if economists would follow this special path of investigation, they would eventually have a body of economic theory which would be very useful in the task of finding solutions for our major economic problems. Like other economists Tugwell focuses his attention on "our ways of getting and using a living," but he does not approach this study from the viewpoint of the individual firm or the private market place. His point of departure is a consideration of the industrial arts and their relation to human living. This means that Tugwell's interpretation of our dynamic civilization is woven around the central problem of the rapidly changing industrial technology.

Having taken the meaning and significance of the industrial arts to be the primary concern of economics, Tugwell finds it necessary to explain the connections between economic life and the industrial arts. This problem introduces his theory of human culture or of social institutions, which makes use of a technological interpretation, a concept of cultural unbalance or lag, a crisis theory, and a concept of cultural equilibrium.[59]   These concepts are united by Tugwell to provide the following general theory of cultural development.   Man's creative genius combines with the sheer weight of accumulated technological change to undermine the structure of social organization.   A lack of cultural balance develops as soon as technological changes are made more rapidly than they can be absorbed by the existing social organization.   When the stresses of cultural unbalance have become sufficiently severe, a cultural crisis then develops.   This crisis is the liquidating device which prepares the way for the establishment of a new cultural equilibrium in which harmony is once more established between the pattern of social organization and the underlying economic conditions.   Applying this cultural theory to the early nineteenth century, Tugwell observes that the private market balance of that time was a reflection of the existing cultural balance.   Market and cultural equilibrium went hand in hand.   For a number of decades the competitive economy of that period was capable of adjusting itself quickly to the changes that were made in industrial technology.   As the century wore on industrial change became so widespread and so rapid, especially after 1875, that a cultural unbalance made its appearance.   The new collective ways of making a living were not accompanied by new ways of distributing and consuming the national output of material goods.   There has developed in recent decades what Robert S. Lynd has described as a "disproportionate structuring" of American society.[60]   The institutional structure relating to the getting of a living has been altered and developed in a fashion which has not been duplicated in the case of the other parts of the cultural complex.   The resulting cultural disequilibrium has left its imprint on the nation's economy in the form of a widespread economic disequilibrium.   The market system no longer equilibrates supply and demand sufficiently well so as to keep selling prices close to costs of production. Furthermore, it no longer eliminates the inefficient firms, or maintains a close relation between productivity and remuneration, or

[59] Cf. Mukerjee, Radhakamal, *The Institutional Theory of Economics,* Ch. VIII, "The Theory of Social Institutions," 1942, pages 192-212.

[60] Lynd, Robert S., *Knowledge for What?,* page 68.   Princeton: Princeton University Press, 1939.

provides abundant employment for men and machines. These serious market maladjustments are but reflections of the general cultural unbalance that is found in all modern, highly industrialized nations. There can be little hope for greater cultural stability until nations come to enjoy more economic stability.

Tugwell is not a specialist in cultural interpretation. He is interested in the analysis of human culture primarily because of the light which it throws on economic activity. His aim is to explain the structure and functioning of the total economic organization by means of which the American people obtain their living. The people have available to them a rich physical environment, a well-developed industrial technology, and a large supply of labor. In the course of three centuries they have built out of these three elements a complex, going system "for the provision of their material needs." In Tugwell's opinion it should be the aim of economics to explain the functioning of this large, going system known as the American economy. The economist should look at the total economy, not only from the viewpoint of the individual businessman or corporation executive, but also from the viewpoint of one who is interested in the general functioning of the whole economic system. The economist is necessarily concerned with business policies and the operations of the market place, but the individual firm and the market place are only two of the many economic institutions which make up the entire institutional complex known as the twentieth-century American economy. Any institution that directly or indirectly affects the flow of economic activity is worthy of investigation by the economist; but no one institution such as the individual proprietorship or corporation should provide the economist's point of departure. The entire going concern or economic complex is the primary consideration of economics as a cultural science. This going system should not only provide the economist's point of departure but it should also be the ultimate object of his scientific analysis.

In explaining the working of the twentieth-century American economic system, Tugwell uses a framework of interpretation that is quite different from the competitive framework of the equilibrium economists. He starts with the assumption that the economic system is a going concern or cultural process. This going concern is not a simple, monistic competitive order; it is a pluralistic system made up of different types of business enterprise. The modern "mongrel" economy breaks down into a number of different segments, one of which is occupied by a competitive agriculture which is always seeking to lessen the rigors of excessive competition. A second segment is made up of small-scale business enterprises whose numbers fluctuate widely with the various phases of the business cycle. A third segment of the economy is taken up by semi-monopolistic and monopolistic concerns which are important enough to influence the functioning of the entire economy. A fourth segment of the economy includes the various forms of government enterprise. These various segments together constitute a going system which displays all the irregularities and inconsistencies common to all cultural complexes. Within this intricate reality known as American capitalism there are forces making for harmony and equilibrium; at the same time other forces are very disruptive. Whatever equilibrium the economy possesses is a cultural and not a mechanistic product. By investigating the many parts that make up the whole of the modern hybrid economy and the relations of the whole economy to its various parts, Tugwell hopes to create a satisfactory explanation of the economic aspect of modern American culture.

In his various writings Tugwell has moved from broad cultural generalizations to problems of social management without stopping to devote much time to the systematization of a new body of economic doctrine. He has preferred to leave much of the reconstruction of economics to those who are gifted with more patience for theoretical refinement and the arduous systematization of economic analysis. Tugwell explains his position when he states that "If I can furnish some clues to the rebuilding of a theoretical structure, I may have done something toward closing the gap between theory and reality. There will be sufficient ingenuity, and above all, adequate time for other minds to follow these directions." [61] One finds many references throughout Tugwell's writings to such important topics as the shift from a simple, competitive economy to one dominated by large-scale, semi-monopolistic enterprises, the destruction of the free exchange relations that once existed between the various segments of the competitive economy, and the emergence of organized pressure groups with varying degrees of economic power. There is a very great need for the further investigation of

[61] "Design for Government," pages 4-5.

these problems of monopoly and the location of economic power, but ever since 1933, when he left the university campus to work for the federal government, Tugwell has been driven by the desire to make social management more of a cultural reality than it now is. The price of seeking to satisfy this strong personal urge has been that Tugwell has been forced to leave his "experimental economics" in a somewhat fragmentary and non-integrated condition.

Tugwell's "experimental economics" has no such fixed boundaries as are usually thought of in connection with those views of economics which limit the science to a study of the disposal of scarce means in a competitive equilibrium. Like Veblen, J. M. Clark, Hobson, and other critics of orthodox economics, Tugwell does not advocate rigid delimitations of the fields of the various social sciences.[62]   He asserts that the separation of the social sciences which is maintained by university curricula is largely a product of academic traditionalism.   Now that some of the natural sciences are no longer kept in isolation, Tugwell hopes that a similar development will take place among the social sciences.   The economist should not insist upon setting up arbitrary limits for his science.   Instead, he should be prepared to handle any data which will throw light on the problems associated with the disposal of scarce means in the particular cultural situation in which he finds himself. The emphasis should be upon furthering a broad understanding of the modern American economy rather than upon narrowing the field of economics to an arbitrarily delimited area of investigation which may suit some economist's predilection for a special technique of scientific analysis, but which is much too limited to provide a satisfactory interpretation of the modern capitalistic economy.

Tugwell's interpretation of the modern American economy is not merely an explanation of the working of a highly complicated economic society; it is also a plan of action or a basis for economic reconstruction.   He makes his analysis with the view of showing how it may be used to improve the lot of mankind.   According to Tugwell's way of thinking there should be no complete separation of economic investigation and ethical analysis.   There is a very close connection between economic and ethical analysis, because

[62] For similar views from an English standpoint see Hobson, John A., *Confessions of An Economic Heretic*, 1938, page 82, and Wootton, Barbara, *Lament for Economics*, 1938, page 261.

economic thought is bent toward the future, when it is to be used for the purpose of finding answers to various economic problems. When Tugwell states that his economics is ethical, "inescapably and rightly so," he is saying that economics and ethics have much to do with each other. He is not asserting, however, that they are one and the same thing, or that scientific and ethical analysis are so wedded that they cannot be distinguished from each other. In Tugwell's thinking there is no confusion of scientific and ethical analysis; instead there is a clear understanding of their important interrelations.

Tugwell explains that ethical goals are psychological values which reflect the wishes of the people. In a democratic community the people are free to set up whatever ethical goals they think are worthy of achievement. Although in any democratic society the final arbiter of what is socially desirable or good is the general public, the growing complexity of social organization makes it increasingly difficult for the public to arrive at satisfactory conclusions with respect to what should be proper communal goals. In this situation the social scientist may perform a very useful role. He should be prepared to bring to the search for proper social goals a wealth of technical knowledge not possessed by the general public. More than this, the social scientist, in the role of an informed citizen, should step forward and make recommendations concerning what would be the community's proper goals. The public should give very serious consideration to any consensus of opinion among its social science experts. "We should not . . . all of us," says Tugwell, "be concerned in matters of judgment any more than we are at present. We might veto the results, but democratic interference in a determination of communal goals would involve a dangerous substitution of vague desires for expertness." [63] The right to veto all suggestions made by social science experts should never be taken away from the public, if society is to continue to be democratic. But if the public at large insists upon determining in detail what its communal goals will be, the widespread lack of scientific understanding will result in a very unsatisfactory scale of social values. The new machine age with its technical complexity requires that much of the determination of social goals be delegated to those social science experts who are familiar with the intricacies of the issues

[63] *Redirecting Education*, page 75.

at stake.   This means that the public is to accept the social scientist as an expert who is prepared to give shape to the dimly perceived goals of the masses.

Tugwell calls attention to the fact that the community's economic goals are not fixed or absolute.   In an era of rapid economic change these goals undergo considerable modification about which the economist should have much to say.   When explaining his views on this point Tugwell introduces the concept of the means-end relation.   In making any communal economic goal a reality there is always the problem of finding the means by the aid of which the goal in view can be achieved.   The economist has much to say about the means by which the community's economic goals are to be secured.   But more than this, as he works on the problem of the various devices which may be employed to secure a given end, the economist sometimes discovers new aims to be achieved.   Communal goals are not created out of thin air; they are discovered in the daily routine of making a living.   Nor do they arise full blown. New goals are but vaguely comprehended at first, and are brought into clearer focus only as fresh observations are accumulated.   It is in the work of uncovering the means to achieve already established economic goals that new goals are given greater concreteness.   The economists' necessity of defining terms, making abstractions, and using quantitative tools results in a clearer understanding of what goals are to be achieved.   There is thus no complete separation of means and ends.   The ends condition the search for means, and in turn the search for means has much influence on the nature of the ends that are sought by the community.   It is because of these close relations between means and ends that our economic goals are tied up with what Tugwell calls a "logic of experimentation."   It is through experimentation that the means of achieving economic goals are tested, and at the same time this experimentation leads to new insights on desirable economic goals.   For this reason Tugwell describes the ethics which are so closely related to his economics as "experimental ethics."

Tugwell divides the work of the economist into four fields. There is, first, the work of the theorist who is gifted with the "intuitive habit of mind."   This mental habit gives rise to "that leaping deductive power" which enables the theoretical economist to make broad generalizations about the functioning of economic society. The theorists, in developing their intuitive insights, also draw attention to new ways of improving the economic organization of society. In addition to the intuitive habit there is the "verifying habit of mind," which is found in the research worker. Those economists who are researchers have as their special task the verification of the theorists' conclusions. They use all the available tools of inductive analysis in examining the suggestions of the theoretical economists and in assessing the value of their proposals. Still other economists may be of neither the intuitive nor the verifying habit of mind. Where this is the case, they.may be either teachers or historians. As a teacher the economist has a larger duty than merely to hand on to his students the accumulated knowledge about the economic system. In his teaching the economist should make his students aware of the problems that exist in the economic world, so that they may be intellectually prepared to bear some of the responsibility of creating a better future. Where the economist takes on the role of the historian, he should not merely attempt to introduce students to the history of economic doctrine. The specialist in the history of economic thought should present this history as the record of the efforts of mankind to come to grips with major economic problems. As Tugwell puts it, the history of economic doctrine should be the history of proposals for economic change.

The four fields of economics which comprise the work of the theorist, the researcher, the teacher, and the historian should have one thing in common. They should all give expression to what Tugwell calls the "experimental attitude." Even when the economist is not directly concerned with discovering ways of improving the economic system, he should keep in mind that the ultimate purpose of his work is to aid mankind in making provision for its material needs. In the classroom the teacher, though far removed from the actual work of economic reconstruction, should impress his students with the need to make bold suggestions for economic improvement. Economists in general should come to understand that "The intellectual atmosphere of the twentieth century is instinct with what might be called the experimental attitude." The major problem of the twentieth century is not to work out new economic goals, although that problem is in itself of great importance; instead the main problem is to find ways of reaching the goals which have already been established. There is now much agreement on such broad social ends as full employment, economic security, and economic abundance, but there is little agreement on how to attain these goals.   Tugwell's solution for this difficulty is to place less emphasis upon traditional thinking and established authority and to open the doors to more experimentalism.   He finds that the economics of the schoolroom has a bad metaphysical odor because it is still immersed in the Newtonian atmosphere of the eighteenth century.   This condition can be corrected, he asserts, only by a substitution of the experimentalism of the twentieth century for the outmoded intellectual orientation of the eighteenth century.   Such a substitution would be the first step in the rebuilding of economic science.

Further light is thrown on Tugwell's views relating to the nature and scope of economics by an analysis of his opinions concerning the contributions made by two outstanding predecessors, Thorstein Veblen and Wesley C. Mitchell.   In his essays on these two well-known exponents of institutionalism Tugwell. not only inquires into the essentials of their economics, but he also reveals his own intellectual ties with them.   Tugwell admires that scientific insight which enabled Veblen to reduce the complex economic phenomena of the late nineteenth and early twentieth centuries to the pattern of a theory of business enterprise.   He marvels at Veblen's ability to refashion the social scientists' framework of interpretation so as to direct them toward a new understanding of the complexities of their economic and social existence.   Vision and insight, however, are not enough.   Intuition, in order to be truly significant, must be brought down to earth and tested for its fruitfulness in the world of contemporary experience.   In other words, scientific intuition must be shown to be of value through the arduous inductive process of trial and error.   Veblen's economic thought is found by Tugwell to be unsatisfactory from this inductive viewpoint.   Veblen was not much interested in supporting his broad economic interpretations with any extensive quantitative analysis.   Tugwell explains that the argument in *The Theory of the Leisure Class* "rested upon an anthropological view for which no evidence was adduced, just as the opening argument of 'Business Enterprise' rested also upon a statement of the nature of business and of modern work which was unsupported.   Each of these generalizations carried a vast superstructure of theory; each must have been prepared with appalling labor and rigorous thought over many years.   Arrogance of simplification could scarcely have been carried further." [64] When Veblen was making his economic studies at the turn of the century, the science of economic statistics had not yet been carried very far in its development; nor did Veblen have any special interest in the task of improving the techniques of statistical analysis. Had he been so inclined, he might have passed beyond his daring intuitional pronouncements to cultivate the quantitative aspects of economic science.   According to Tugwell's interpretation the essence of Veblenian economics is to be found in "critical analysis" and not in "constructive understanding."   Veblen's economic analysis is more a protest against the predatory business activities of the time than a call to genuinely disturbed persons to reconstruct the faltering economic system.   Tugwell finds support for his interpretation of Veblen's economic thought in the peculiar psychological complex which made Veblen a "strange creature thirsting for intellectual revenge" against a civilization which was so much a denial of the thrifty existence of his Scandinavian forebears.

When Tugwell turns from the economics of Veblen to that of Mitchell, he turns from an example of keen, critical analysis which throws light largely on the offensive aspects of man's nature to an analysis which places more emphasis on the higher qualities of human nature, which may be temporarily submerged but which in the long run may very well prove to be triumphant over baser human qualities.   Instead of Veblen's deep irony and feeling of alienation there is Mitchell's critical understanding and faith in the ability of mankind to cope with the conflicts which arise between its preda-

[64] Tugwell, Rexford G., "Veblen and 'Business Enterprise,' " *The New Republic,* March 29, 1939, page 216.   For further criticism of Veblen see Tugwell's essay on "The Theory of Occupational Obsolescence" (page 190 fn.): "Institutionalists are apt to center attention on accounting for modern economic behavior by the sweeping use of anthropological material and consequently to build up categories which are over-inclusive.   If the four factors of production, and corresponding ones of distribution, which are so bitterly criticized as nonfunctional, are so wide as to have lost their conceptual value, so also, it seems to me, are 'pecuniary emulation,' 'the business order,' 'the industrial employments,' 'the ceremonial dependencies,' and others so familiar to students of Veblen.   They do not help in our essential task, which is to preside over growth and decay, to control in the light of experience and purpose.   For this we need analysis in less heroic terms, a delicate probing of complex industrial tissues."   As is obvious, Tugwell is somewhat irked by Veblen's superficial matter-of-factness, and by his unwillingness to reveal any great enthusiasm for economic and social reform.

cious and cooperative urges.   Mitchell is not the product of racial and cultural conflict that Veblen turned out to be.   Although he believes that much of Veblen's criticism of American economic life is well founded, Mitchell is too much of an instrumentalist to be entirely satisfied with Veblen's brand of institutionalism.   He has felt the urge to test Veblen's broad generalizations in the crucible of actual economic experience.   Since Veblen did not provide the necessary tools for this purpose, "all the constructive work remained to be done; and most of the tools for it were yet to be invented." [65] What impresses Tugwell is that Mitchell has improved the techniques of statistical investigation, and has used them to discover in the uniformities of group behavior a solid, inductive foundation for a twentieth-century version of economic science.   If we are to make progress toward a satisfactory understanding of the economic system, we must strengthen our scientific intuitions with an adequate underpinning of statistical evidence.   It is Tugwell's opinion that Mitchell has performed this task in a highly creditable manner.

The full-fledged experimental economist, as understood by Tugwell, is not satisfied with merely determining through observation and experimentation what economic interpretations are valid.   He wishes also to show how these interpretations may help mankind to make the necessary adjustments in a changing world.   The experimental economist possesses an attitude which leads him to test his hypotheses and proposals for the betterment of economic society by analyzing the consequences that would follow upon their adoption.   Such an attitude was quite alien to Veblen, who had little interest in discovering ways in which the economic system could be made to serve mankind more adequately; "An elaborate scientific pose was Veblen's answer to those who inquired concerning the future.   His was an analytical work, he replied, and he had no interest in prophecy." [66]   Tugwell observes that the same cannot be said of Mitchell because he is an exponent of "experimental economics."   Mitchell is a "bridge from classicism to instrumentalism"; he has paused in the midst of his investigations to point out how his information may be used to improve the economic organization of society.   Tugwell summarizes Mitchell's position by

---

[65] Tugwell, Rexford G., "Wesley Mitchell: An Evaluation," *The New Republic*, Oct. 6, 1937, page 239.

[66] "Veblen and 'Business Enterprise,'" page 217.

stating that "Your out-and-out experimental economist is exclusively interested in policy, in fact, and in the future. This means that change is his familiar ground. This suggests faith in social management and in the accommodativeness of individuals to circumstance, thus denying at once industrial laissez-faire, mechanistic human behavior and the closed system of Marx. And this is where, or very nearly where, Mr. Mitchell stands today." [67]

Tugwell has much in common with Mitchell, but at the same time his economic thought has a flavor which is distinctly its own. If he is to be compared to any other American economist, the comparison should be made with Simon N. Patten rather than with Veblen or Mitchell. Both Patten and Tugwell have a strong humanitarian bias which takes the form of a great interest in social and economic reform. Whereas it took Mitchell many years to arrive at the instrumentalistic position which he now occupies, Tugwell was from the very beginning of his academic career deeply stirred by "the economic basis of the public interest." [68] He is much more of the reformer than is Mitchell. It is difficult to rid one's self of the impression that Mitchell's primary interest is in analyzing the abundant statistical data of economic experience. Tugwell, on the contrary, is at his best when his thoughts are turned toward economic reconstruction. He is in his element when he is reconstructing a university curriculum in order to bring the economic world and the student closer together, or when he is formulating an economic program to bring prosperity to the laborer or to the farmer.

Like reformers in general, Tugwell exhibits certain characteristic weaknesses. His criticisms of the economists with whom he disagrees are inclined to be much too sweeping and exhibitive of intellectual impatience. No doubt many will think that his attacks upon orthodox economics and the way it is taught are overly harsh, and are not designed to bring opposing views together. He gives the impression to some of his readers that those economists who cling to the orthodox type of economic analysis are to be regarded as almost beyond redemption. In addition, his biting criticisms of neo-classical economics tend to create the false impression that he

[67] "Wesley Mitchell: An Evaluation," pages 239-240.
[68] This is the title of the doctoral dissertation which Tugwell wrote at the University of Pennsylvania and published in 1922.

finds little in this type of economics that is worth preserving. As is true of other heterodox economists, Tugwell does not take time to explain how much of economic orthodoxy should be incorporated in a reconstructed version of economics. Heterodox American economic thought did not gush forth as a pure intellectual stream from some Mosaic rock; like other intellectual movements it has borrowed a great deal from many different quarters. But, unfortunately, Tugwell leaves the casual reader with too much of the impression that his own brand of holistic economics draws mainly from intellectual sources which are largely unknown to those who now espouse economic orthodoxy. At times it appears as if he thinks in terms of a rather complete break between the economics of the neo-classicists and his own experimental economics. Such a break, however, would be a denial of Tugwell's evolutionary approach to the problem of reconstructing economics. Like the economic system which it investigates, the science of economics is evolving, but no matter how far it progresses it will continue to pay tribute to its early expositors.

Tugwell is also criticized on the ground that he wants to push social and economic reconstruction beyond mankind's present capacity for effective collective action. Those who are opposed to national economic planning think that Tugwell's planning proposals place too much of a burden upon our collective intelligence. They believe that he underestimates the limitations of human nature with the result that he is overoptimistic about the possibilities of social management. It seems, however, that a careful examination of Tugwell's views does not support this criticism. He is fully aware of "our British ineptitude for social, as contrasted with mechanical, thinking," and that "It is the genius of our people to arrive at social instruments by numerous slow and muddling approaches—rather by trial than by reason; rather by feeling than by logic. . . . We are suspicious of systems. These traits of ours are as much a condition to be faced by the advocate of change as are the other institutional conditions which have to be taken into account. We shall not get far in any advocacy of revolution. We shall have to work with an intimate knowledge of the historical spirit of the English institutions which we inherit . . . a massive conviction of rightness must be built up behind our proposals— that, even before they are put to the touch, our experiments shall,

as nearly as may be, have ceased to be experiments at all." [69]   From
the history of social and economic reform it appears that the only
way of settling disagreements about desirable reforms is by submitting the proposals for reform to the test of actual experience.
It would be Tugwell's position on this matter that the extent of
the gap between social needs and the human capacity to meet these
needs can only be determined by the trial-and-error method of
actual experimentation.

Prominent among Tugwell's contributions has been his insistence
upon the need for more philosophical sophistication on the part of
economists.   He finds that it is all too common for economists to
be unaware of the philosophical foundations of their science.   In
the past three quarters of a century American philosophical thought
has undergone revolutionary changes which have not been without
considerable influence on related fields of scientific interest.   The
net result of these developments in philosophical thought has been
that natural and social scientists have been introduced to new ways
of comprehending the realities of the external world.   Scientists no
longer approach these realities in the same manner in which their
nineteenth-century predecessors grasped the realities of their times.
Tugwell points out that all too frequently in the realm of the social
sciences outmoded philosophical views continue to dominate the
scientist's thought processes.   These outworn views have become
inherited intellectual traditions which confine scientific analysis to
obsolete thought patterns long after new intellectual frontiers have
been opened.   Further advance in scientific thought is then delayed
until the limitations of these old philosophical views have been
fully exposed.   This has been the situation for many decades in
the field of economics, where inherited eighteenth-century philosophical views have continued to exercise a strong influence over
the general pattern of economic inquiry.   In emphasizing the inadequacies of the philosophical substructure of inherited economic
thought, Tugwell has rendered his science a very worth-while service.   More than this, he has very considerably strengthened the
foundations of twentieth-century economic thought by substituting
a dynamic philosophy of becoming for the static, nineteenth-century philosophy of inertness.   As a consequence of Tugwell's inquiries into the philosophical basis of economic science and of his

[69] "The Theory of Occupational Obsolescence," pages 220-221.

efforts to modernize this basis, economists should in the future be much more philosophically sophisticated than they have been in the recent past.

Besides calling for a renovation of the philosophical underpinnings of economics, Tugwell has stressed the need for a fresh interpretation of economic behavior. He has introduced a new emphasis into the discussion of the nature of economic activity by drawing attention to the cooperative aspect of human behavior. Tugwell occupies a middle ground between the exponents of economic orthodoxy, who emphasize the role of reason in economic affairs, and economists like Veblen who draw attention to the importance of blind instinct and habit in relation to economic activity. He adopts no excessively optimistic or pessimistic position with regard to mankind's ability to direct its economic affairs. He asserts that there is a little-used resource in human nature which takes the form of man's capacity to cooperate in collective ventures for the reconstruction of society. Without this inherent ability on the part of mankind to cooperate, experiments in the collective management of economic activity would have little chance of succeeding. Tugwell explains that the economic changes of the past seventy-five years have given us a social organization which places a growing premium on cooperative activity. The freedom of the individual to act alone has been progressively narrowed by farmers' cooperatives, laborers' unions, and businessmen's trade associations; and it appears that the cultural trends are in favor of more and not less collective economic action in the future. Economics will have to make more use of a psychological theory which emphasizes the collective and cooperative aspects of human behavior if it is to become a realistic social science. What Tugwell is saying, in effect, is that not only should economists create a new, holistic way of comprehending the economic system, but they should also consider equally novel ways of understanding human nature.

Tugwell's third contribution relates to his treatment of economics as a cultural science. Like Veblen and Patten, he emphasizes the point that economics should be no mere study of formal or logical economic relations, but instead should be a study of the economic aspect of human culture. The economist should not be primarily interested in developing a body of formal economic principles with universal applicability. On the contrary, he should be more concerned with a body of doctrines which explain the modern American economy as an evolving system of economico-cultural relations dealing with the provision of the material means for the satisfaction of human wants. In order to understand the modern economy as a cultural product the economist needs to replace the antiquated cultural theory underlying nineteenth-century academic economics with an improved type of cultural theory. If economics is taken to be a cultural science, that is to say, a social science which is concerned with a particular aspect of human culture, the economist will make progress in explaining the modern economy only to the extent that he uses an adequate theory of human culture or institutions as his point of departure. He should do more thinking in terms of cultural processes, cultural accumulations, lags, and crises, if he wishes to arrive at a satisfactory interpretation of twentieth-century American economic life. In emphasizing the point that the economist should be a student of the economic aspect of human culture, Tugwell has given strong support to those economists who would make economic science less "pure" and more realistic.

Tugwell's final contribution is to emphasize the functional nature of economic science. He observes that the major economic issue of the twentieth-century is how to remove the disparities between the economic goals of individuals and special groups on the one hand and the economic ends of the community on the other hand. The problem now facing us is how a nation can use its collective intelligence so as to reduce to a satisfactory minimum the social costs of individual and group economic behavior. Tugwell asserts that those who determine economic policies should realize that individual and group behavior can never be completely freed from the retarding, pernicious influence of outmoded ways of thinking and acting. But if economic welfare is to be progressively enlarged, the influence of our collective intelligence, buttressed by scientific economic opinion, must somehow be injected into the stream of economic behavior. Economic policies need to be devised which will take account of the realities of a culture impregnated with socially irrational behavior, but at the same time these policies should focus attention upon the problem of giving more direction to our dynamic, irrepressible culture. Very little has been done as yet with this major problem, but Tugwell has much faith in the ability of

As the work of Adam Smith, 'the first great theorist of that stage of capitalistic enterprise which we call the domestic system,' had to be reconstructed during the nineteenth century to fit an economy dominated by the factory system, so must the modern economist redescribe economic relations in terms of an economy dominated by a relatively few huge enterprises in which both laborer and owner are separated from control. The individualism of Adam Smith's private enterprise has in large measure given way to the collective activity of the modern corporation, and economic theory must shift its emphasis from analysis in terms of competition to analysis in terms of control.

GARDINER C. MEANS: "The Separation of Ownership and Control in American Industry"

CHAPTER
7

The Administrative Economics
of Gardiner C. Means

In 1923 Thorstein Veblen published his final blast at a world too preoccupied with the post-war period of "economic normalcy" to pay much attention to this aging prophet of capitalistic doom. Veblen's *Absentee Ownership and Business Enterprise in Recent Times* summarized his critical analysis of the trends of large-scale corporate business which he had been elaborating ever since the turn of the century. As was the case with most of his earlier analyses, this last book of Veblen's was written for those few who endeavored to keep informed about the new developments in the evolving industrial system. The majority of people were too much concerned with the immense possibilities of the post-war era of prosperity to take note of the pronouncements of an unorthodox economist who professed to see not lasting prosperity but the inevitable decay of existing business arrangements.

If the rush of events proved to be unkind to Veblen, it was not similarly unsympathetic to Gardiner C. Means. Ten years after the appearance of Veblen's last volume, Means, in collaboration with Adolf A. Berle, Jr., published *The Modern Corporation and Private Property*. This analysis of modern corporate enterprise was so widely read and so well received that Means's reputation as a progressive young economist was soon established. Three years of a depression that revealed few tendencies to work itself out according to the usual pattern had created a public attitude which was very favorable to the reception of Berle and Means's study of the functioning of the modern corporation. What was of general interest was that their analysis went below the surface to the fundamental causes of a depression which threatened at any time to turn into an unprecedented social catastrophe. Having a message couched in terms more congenial than those Veblen was accustomed to use, Means soon found himself in the bright light of national affairs. In a few years after the appearance of his analysis of modern corporate enterprise he achieved a position of national significance as an economist in the service of the New Deal. While devoting himself to the planning activities of the federal government, Means continued to exercise a stimulating influence on the development of American economic thought with his unconventional views about the nature and significance of "administrative economics."

Gardiner C. Means was born on June 8, 1896, in Windham, Connecticut. As a student at Harvard University he found that his primary interest was in natural science, and so he prepared himself for a future in the field of chemistry. His contacts with the science of economics during his undergraduate years did not extend beyond Frank W. Taussig's course on the principles of economics. His early training in the field of the natural sciences has left an indelible imprint on Means's approach to economic problems and on his general economic theorizing. Unlike the armchair economists of the past century, he insists upon gathering the necessary facts for his economic generalizations; and, wherever it is possible, he turns to economic data that can be subjected to some form of statistical measurement. Because he seeks to be as precise as the natural scientist, Means is not given to generalizing or speculating on a slim foundation of factual information.

After securing his A.B. degree from Harvard University in 1918, Means served as a member of the staff of the Near East Relief in Turkey for the years 1919 and 1920. While in Turkey he came in contact with the operations of an economy still largely dominated by handicraft methods of production. The contrasts between the modern economy of the United States and the backward economy of Asia Minor were striking, and served to stimulate Means's latent interest in economic matters. Upon returning to the United States he enrolled as a student in the Lowell Textile School, and in 1922 he entered the textile manufacturing business. After two years of active business experience Means began to divide his time between business affairs and post-graduate study in economics at Harvard University. Although he received a thorough graduate training along the lines of orthodox economic analysis, he never lost contact with the realities of the contemporary economic situation. Courses under W. Z. Ripley, John Williams, and Allyn Young were sufficiently realistic to keep the problems of an ever-changing economic order always in view. In 1927 Means was engaged to carry on economic research for the Columbia University Law School. In close association with such well-known economic and legal experts as James C. Bonbright and Adolf A. Berle, Jr., he was in an excellent position to study the modern corporation as both an economic and a legal institution. While occupied with his economico-legal research, Means completed the requirements for his doctoral degree at Harvard University with a thesis on *The Corporate Revolution*.

In 1933 Means was raised to the position of associate-in-law in the law school of Columbia University, which he filled until he was called to act as an adviser on finance to the Secretary of Agriculture. In 1933 he also became a member of the Consumers Advisory Board of the National Recovery Administration. After a short time in governmental service Means gave up his academic position, and presently also his business connections, in order to devote himself entirely to government work. From 1935 to 1939 he was a member of the Industrial Section of the National Resources Committee; in this capacity he concerned himself almost exclusively with the problems of national economic planning. In the years 1940-1941 he continued to work along the same general lines but in the service of the Bureau of the Budget. Since 1943 Means has worked as a research economist for the Committee for Economic Development, a private organization established in August, 1942, to coordinate the postwar planning activities of businessmen. Although the demands of governmental and other research work have left little spare time for less urgent matters, Means has maintained his early interest in the problems of modern corporate enterprise, and has continued to inquire into the relations between this type of enterprise and the problems of national economic planning.

Very soon after engaging in research on problems lying in the borderland between economics and law, Means began to publish the results of his investigations. Papers appeared on such topics as "The Diffusion of Stock Ownership in the United States" (1930), "The Growth in the Relative Importance of the Large Corporation in American Economic Life" (1931), and "The Separation of Ownership and Control in American Industry" (1931). In 1932 Means collaborated with James C. Bonbright in publishing *The Holding Company, Its Public Significance and Its Regulation.* In the following year he summarized the results of his research for the period from 1927 to 1933 in the well-known work on *The Modern Corporation and Private Property.* After entering government service Means made two further contributions with the publication of *The Modern Economy in Action* in 1935 (with Caroline F. Ware as joint author) and *The Structure of the American Economy* in 1939.[1]

Of the above-mentioned writings Berle and Means's *The Modern Corporation and Private Property* enjoyed the widest circulation. Several years of continued depression had convinced many students of the business cycle that this most recent depression was deviating very significantly from past cycle patterns. Berle and Means's analysis of the role of the large corporation proved to be of great value in the search for novel explanations of the course of economic activity. Their general thesis is that the corporate enterprise of today is so fundamentally different from the economic enterprise of the last century that orthodox interpretations of prosperity and depression are now inadequate. It is their general contention that the corporation has so altered the pattern of property relationships and the logic of profit making that a general revision of the framework of economic interpretation is necessary. In addition, they find that many of the basic assumptions of nineteenth-century economics stand in need of a fundamental restatement. It was Berle and Means's general message to a befuddled world in 1933 that economic problems would probably not be solved in any satisfactory manner until the equilibrium economics of Alfred Marshall had made way for the new corporate economics of the twentieth century.

In developing his new economics Means makes no complete break with his nineteenth-century predecessors. Like the neo-classical economists, he recognizes the necessity of creating a systematic pattern of economic thought; without a basic theoretical pattern economic analysis would be little more than aimless description. But the thought pattern of the neo-classical economists was valid only for the interpretation of laissez-faire, nineteenth-century economic activ-

---

[1] As many of Means's publications are joint products, it is not always possible for the reader to disentangle easily his specific contributions. There is evident, however, in all these writings a clear progression of Means's economic theorizing. Wherever his thoughts are shared with other contributors, notice is taken of this fact throughout the chapter.

ity, so that in coping with the problems of the modern economy Means finds it necessary to repudiate this orthodox pattern of analysis. Since such a repudiation involves not only a change in the framework of interpretation, but also some changes in the basic assumptions upon which such a framework is erected, Means has given considerable thought to the new assumptions appropriate to an economy dominated by large corporations. His framework of interpretation acknowledges the presence in modern industry of a few large corporate units which have changed the nature of competition. Out of the factory system of the last century there has come a "reorientation of economic enterprise" which has greatly altered the freedom of enterprise, the freedom of contract, and the free exercise of private property rights which were so basic in the Marshallian interpretation of economic activity. The corporate enterprise of today does not merely provide new legal clothing for the private enterprise of the last century; instead it has transformed the whole nature of the profit-making system. This great change in the ways of doing business "presents a challenge. As the work of Adam Smith, 'the first great theorist of that stage of capitalistic enterprise which we call the domestic system,' had to be reconstructed during the nineteenth century to fit an economy dominated by the factory system, so must the modern economist redescribe economic relations in terms of an economy dominated by a relatively few huge enterprises in which both laborer and owner are separated from control. The individualism of Adam Smith's private enterprise has in large measure given way to the collective activity of the modern corporation, and economic theory must shift its emphasis from analysis in terms of competition to analysis in terms of control." [2]   This new collective economics emphasizes the extent to which the individualistic enterprise of the nineteenth century has receded into the background of the modern economic scene.

In order to give meaning to his new economics of control Means has to forge new tools of analysis. Economic categories that were useful for the development of nineteenth-century economic thought must now be altered or replaced by new concepts. Such concepts as wealth, price, property, and profit take on new meanings in an economy no longer dominated by small-scale, competitive business

---

[2] Means, Gardiner C., "The Separation of Ownership and Control in American Industry," *The Quarterly Journal of Economics*, Nov., 1931, Vol. XLVI, page 97.

units. Consequently Means's economic analysis runs in terms of multiple ownership, corporate interests, market controls, and administered prices—terms which call attention to the new pattern of economic behavior introduced by the technological advances of the past three-quarters of a century.

In putting together the pieces of a new pattern of economic thought Means is not especially interested in the cyclical approach to the study of economic problems. As industrial activity falls more and more into the pattern of large-scale corporate enterprise, and as the government finds it increasingly necessary to intervene in economic affairs, business fluctuations tend to conform less and less to previously established patterns of behavior. In place of an economy passing through the cyclical pattern outlined by Mitchell in his 1913 study of business fluctuations, Means finds an economic system which continues over a lengthy period of time to be unable to provide anything like a full use of human and material resources. It is a significant fact that he has done most of his constructive work since the beginning of the Great Depression of 1929, and during a period when there has been a great discrepancy between "economic potentials" and "economic performance." The major concern of economists is no longer with an economy that periodically goes far beyond some normal level of business activity only to be later plunged much below that level. It is for an economy that frequently is unable to reach the level of a full use of men and machines that Means develops a new framework of interpretation into which he pours the generalizations of his twentieth-century version of economics.

There is in Means's economic analysis a freshness of approach which distinguishes it from the work of Veblen, Commons, and Mitchell. In so far as the contributions of these older economists have become part of the scientific milieu of contemporary economists, Means, in common with other members of the younger generation, is greatly indebted to the pioneers of institutionalism. But changing times have brought with them new economic problems and different scientific interests. In many ways Means may be taken as representative of a new era in the development of American economic thought which had its beginnings in the years prior to 1929 but which became well established in the decade of the 1930's. He has done his economic theorizing in a period that has seen marked

departures from the principles of *laissez faire*. While national income has fallen to extremely low levels, and the checks of free competitive markets have been eliminated, individuals and enterprises
have worked out new means of self-preservation; but the result of
these efforts to preserve private economic interests has been to jeopardize further the smooth functioning of the entire economy. Corporate concentration, the resurgence of labor organization, the continued decline of agriculture, and the multiplication of international
trade restrictions have made the automatic functioning of the 'economy less and less possible. As a consequence of these developments,
the period in which Means formulated the principles of his administrative economics has been one "of ineffective use of national
resources, of uncertainty, of growing dissatisfaction with old policies,
of experimentation with new policies, some successful, some unsuccessful, of a prelude to the development and acceptance of a new
system of democratic national policies more able than those of laissez faire to bring about effective use of resources in an economy of
mass production and mass distribution."[3] Such a period could
hardly be without an important influence upon the development of
American economic thought.

The Corporate Revolution

The center of gravity of Means's economic analysis lies in the
study of the large corporation and its relations to the other factors
operating within the economic system. The corporation is more
than a legal device now widely used to overcome the deficiencies of
the individual proprietorship and the partnership as methods of
organizing business units; it is a legal device that has become the
center of attention of contemporary economic analysis. This is
true because the corporation has fallen into a strategic position from
which it dominates, and to some extent directs, the course of economic activity in the advanced industrialized nations of Western
Europe and North America. An understanding of Means's economics can be best obtained by examining his observations relating
to the role of the large corporation in the modern economy.

By 1930 the two hundred largest non-financial corporations, with
their two thousand directors, many of whom were inactive, con-

[3] Means, Gardiner C., "Economic Institutions," *The American Journal of Sociology*, May, 1942, Vol. XLVII, page 957.

trolled nearly one-half of the industry of the country. At that time there were 300,000 non-financial corporations, but only two hundred of them, or less than seven-eighths of one per cent, controlled 49.2 per cent of all the non-banking corporate wealth. Added to this was the impressive fact that these two hundred largest corporations received 43.2 per cent of the income of all non-banking corporations.[4] Means observes that in the modern economy there is at work a great centripetal force which has drawn together a vast amount of corporate wealth, and which is apparently going to intensify this concentration. As a result of the inroads of the large corporations upon the realm of business once dominated by the capitalist-employers, "These great companies form the very framework of American industry," and are no longer to be regarded merely as deviations from the competitive norms of business enterprise which are to be discussed only in the minor sections of economics textbooks devoted to the problems of monopoly.[5] It is therefore necessary for the economist to think "in terms of these huge units rather than in terms of the multitude of small competing elements of private enterprise. For most fields Marshall's representative firm has ceased to be a useful tool of thought, since the great companies that dominate one industry after another are in no sense 'representative.' The emphasis must be shifted to that very great proportion of industry in the hands of a relatively few units, units which can be studied individually and concretely. Such studies will reveal the operation of half of industry and what is more important, that half which is likely to be more typical of the industry of the future."

Quite as significant as the problem of the strategic importance of the large corporations is the question of the future trends in the development of corporate enterprise. After examining this question, Means arrives at the following major conclusions: the large corporations have been growing between two and three times as fast as the small non-financial corporations, and furthermore they are gaining control of industrial wealth at a still faster rate. In 1931 Means wrote that, if the rate of expansion of large corporations for

[4] Berle, Adolf A., Jr., and Means, Gardiner C., *The Modern Corporation and Private Property*, pages 28-29. New York: The Macmillan Company, 1933.

[5] Means, Gardiner C.. "The Growth in the Relative Importance of the Large Corporation in American Economic Life," *The American Economic Review*, March, 1931, Vol. XXI, page 36.

the period from 1905 to 1927 were to be maintained, by 1950 eighty per cent of all non-financial corporate wealth would be in the hands of the two hundred largest corporations. He explained that the corporate system had not yet reached the culmination of its development, and that, "Spectacular as its rise has been, every indication seems to be that the system will move forward to proportions which would stagger imagination today. . . . Only by remembering that men still living can recall a time when the present situation was hardly dreamed of, can we enforce the conclusion that the new order may easily become completely dominant during the lifetime of our children." [6]

The emergence of the corporation as a major factor in the modern economy raises a number of important questions for which answers must soon be found. Is the corporate organization of economic activity a permanent development, and will the movement toward concentration of corporate wealth become intensified or will it soon dwindle away? There is also the important question of the relations between these huge economic empires and the political organizations of the state. Will these large corporations dominate the state, or will the "positive state" endeavor to fit them into a general plan for the regulation of economic activity? In addition, there is the problem of how these large corporate enterprises will affect the interests of wage earners, consumers, and investors. There is in Berle and Means's analysis a note of deep concern for the interests of the general public in an economy no longer subject to the competitive checks of small-scale enterprise. No matter what the conditions of economic welfare in the future may be, Berle and Means are convinced that such welfare is inextricably interwoven with the future of the corporate economy, since "This system bids fair to be as all-embracing as was the feudal system in its time. It demands that we examine both its conditions and its trends, for an understanding of the structure upon which will rest the economic order of the future." [7]

There is a corporate revolution silently at work which will be fully as significant as the technological revolution of the late eighteenth and early nineteenth centuries. This corporate revolution

---

[6] *The Modern Corporation and Private Property*, page 1.

[7] *Ibid.*, page 9. See also Means, Gardiner C., "Democracy and Business," *The Virginia Quarterly Review*, 1941, Vol. XVII, pages 617-625.

has been accompanied by many changes which have seriously weakened the underpinnings of the competitive economy of the nineteenth century. One of these important changes relates to the concept of private property. According to the property concept handed down from the nineteenth century, ownership or property rights in wealth implied a coincidence of risk taking and the exercise of control over the management of wealth. The property owner was not only the one to invest his funds in an economic enterprise, but he was also the one who was responsible for the results of this investment because he exercised control over the management of his property. This concept of property is becoming increasingly less valid, because the corporate revolution is splitting the "atom of property" into two separate fragments, the ownership of property and its control. Corporate shareholders retain legal title to their property, but they have lost the right to exercise ultimate control over the use or management of this property.

There are two forces at work within the modern corporate system, the one a centrifugal force tending to spread the ownership of corporate wealth among more and more stockholders, and the other a centripetal force tending to centralize control over corporate wealth in fewer and fewer directors' hands. In the new logic of private property interest in an economic enterprise attaches to the stockholders who have risked their property in the corporate venture, but power over the enterprise resides in those who control the enterprise.[8] According to Means's interpretation control "may be said for practical purposes to lie in the hands of the individual or group who have the actual power to select the board of directors (or its majority), either by mobilizing the legal right to choose them . . . or by exerting pressure which influences their choice. Occasionally the major elements of control are made effective not through the selection of directors, but through dictation to the management, as where a bank determines the policy of a corporation seriously indebted to it. In most cases, however, if one can determine who does actually have the power to select the directors, one has located the group of individuals who for practical purposes may be regarded as 'the control.' "[9]

The history of corporate activity since 1880 has been a record of

[8] *Ibid.,* page 70.
[9] "The Separation of Ownership and Control in American Industry," page 72.

the introduction of new devices by means of which those in control of corporations have progressively weakened the position of the stockholders.[10]   The residual control of the shareholding group has been whittled away as rapidly as the ingenuity of corporate lawyers has been able to invent new devices for this purpose.   The introduction of the right to vote by proxy, the elimination of the right of stockholders to remove directors at will, the granting to corporations of the right to issue certain classes of stock without the right to vote, the issuance of stock for property as well as cash, the elimination of the stockholder's right to a fixed place in the capital structure of the corporation, and other statutory alterations of the common-law restrictions upon corporate activity have all served to convert the corporation from "a tight organization analogous to an overgrown partnership" into "a tremendous unit whose major preoccupation is distinctly not with the interests of its shareholders." [11] This shift in the stockholder's position from controlling importance to great weakness has been furthered as much by the increasing inability of the stockholder to manage his corporation as by the desire of those in control to manage corporate affairs in their own interests. The forces making for this divorce of the two fundamental attributes of property as they were understood in the nineteenth century are still at work modifying the property relations of the twentieth-century economic system.   Like all things that are "on the make," this new set of property relations has still to take on a much more definite shape before it can be easily understood and controlled. Although it remains ill-defined and elusive, this emerging type of property relations must be recognized as a "clearly distinguishable factor" of great importance in any explanation of modern economic activity.

With the emergence of large corporate enterprises not only has the property institution been transformed, but also the concept of private enterprise has undergone fundamental change.   Now that

[10] For an outline of this development see *The Modern Corporation and Private Property*, Ch. I, "The Evolution of the Modern Corporate Structure," pages 127-152.

[11] As stock ownership became more widely diffused, those who formerly owned a controlling interest in a corporation were induced to create devices by which they might retain control without actual ownership of the corporation. See Means, Gardiner C., "The Diffusion of Stock Ownership in the United States," *The Quarterly Journal of Economics*, Aug., 1930, Vol. XLIV, pages 561-600.

the ownership and control of corporate wealth have become separated, those who control this wealth are not the ones legally entitled to the fruits of such control; instead, the managers of corporations are expected to operate their enterprises in the interest of the stockholders. In this situation the whole basis of economic motivation has been altered, since the connection between efforts put forth and the fruits resulting from such efforts has been blurred. Where the ownership and control of wealth become separated, there arises the question as to whether or not those in control of a modern corporation will operate it in the best interests of the owners. Only if it is assumed that the interests of corporate managers run parallel with those of stockholders can it be said that corporate wealth will be managed to the advantage of the owners. Far too frequently corporate managers have sought to convert the formerly independent property owner into a mere recipient of the wages of capital, just as the independent craftsman was reduced by the factory system to the status of a mere recipient of the wages of labor. The whole history of corporate activity since 1880 is replete with examples of situations in which those who controlled corporations siphoned off much of the rewards to which the owners of corporate wealth were legally entitled. Although Berle and Means do not condone the efforts of those in control of corporations to direct the flow of benefits from the use of corporate wealth toward themselves, nevertheless they do see much logic in these activities. According to traditional theory, the profit reward had a two-fold function, to induce an individual to risk his wealth and to use it efficiently. In the modern corporate system this traditional logic of profits has been invalidated, since those who own wealth frequently do not control it, and those who control wealth are not legally permitted freely to garner the fruits of this control. This situation raises the important question: "Because an owner who also exercises control over his wealth is protected in full receipt of the advantages derived from it, must it *necessarily* follow that an owner who has surrendered control of his wealth should likewise be protected to the full?" [12] One cannot expect corporate managers to direct their enterprises in the "most socially beneficial manner," if the major portion of the results of efficient management go to the stockholders who perform the single function of risking their wealth in profit-seeking enterprises.

[12] *The Modern Corporation and Private Property,* pages 338-339.

The competitive economy of the nineteenth century could rely upon the profit reward as a spur to efficient enterprise, but now this reward does not always function in this manner. It is true that "The function of supplying capital and risking it in an enterprise requires some sort of reward, but today the reward of this function bears no relation to what is necessary to call forth such a function. But what if profits can be made more than sufficient to keep the security holders satisfied, more than sufficient to induce new capital to come into the enterprise? . . . The prospect of additional profits cannot act as a spur on the security holder to make him *operate* the enterprise with more vigor in a way to serve the wants of the community, since he is no longer in control. Such extra profits if given to the security holders would seem to perform no useful economic function." [13] If the traditional logic of profits is applied to the modern corporation, then only a return sufficient to induce the risking of wealth should go to the security owners, and the residual profits should go to those who are responsible for the control and direction of corporate affairs or to other interested parties. A portion of the profits could be paid to the employees of the corporation, or to those who supply the raw materials; or they could be returned to the consumers in the form of lower prices. Whatever the distribution of the profits of modern corporate enterprise, it must be recognized that the logic of profits found in conventional economics no longer fits the modern economy.

Modern corporate enterprise has greatly weakened another pillar of the competitive economy of the last century, because it has to a very great extent substituted "administered" markets for "free" markets. Means defines a free market as one "in which no one producer or organized group can influence price through expansion or contraction of its production to an extent sufficient to justify it in giving weight to this influence in developing its production policy." [14] Such a market is found in a small-scale, competitive economic system where competitive prices act as regulators of economic activity. Changes in price are followed by changes in production and by a redirection of investment; and the market mechanism

[13] *Ibid.*, pages 342-343.

[14] *The Structure of the American Economy*, Part I, "Basic Characteristics," page 109 fn. A report prepared by the industrial section of the National Resources Committee under the direction of Gardiner C. Means, and published by the Committee in June, 1939.

brings about a close approximation to a full utilization of human and material resources. A century ago when business was small-scale and government played a minor economic role, the free market was the major coordinating force, but during the past one hundred years large segments of the economy have been removed from its coordinating influence.

An "administered" market is one in which the free forces of supply and demand no longer provide the major coordination of economic activity; instead, whatever coordination there is comes in large part from the administrative decisions of the corporate managers. This type of market is identified by the presence of a limited number of producers, by the lack of price competition, and by considerable inflexibility of prices. Since each producer turns out a large portion of the total market supply, he always keeps in mind the effects of his price and production policies upon those of his rivals. In administered markets there is a tendency for competition, wherever it is found, to find expression through outlets other than prices, because price decreases when initiated by one producer are soon duplicated by other large producers. In recent decades the spread of administered markets has made so much progress that it may now be said that administrative enterprise has become the norm of economic activity in many important segments of the modern economy.

In the fields of government-operated enterprise, the railroads, and the various public utilities, administered prices have become commonplace. The situation is the same in manufacturing, where concentration has made great strides.[15] Many of the extractive industries have also fallen under the influence of administrative coordination; in the fields of retailing and consumer services the fixed-price schedule has become the norm of price policy. The only activity in which free markets have continued to function with some of their former vitality is agriculture. Means concludes that "it can be said that there is such a degree of concentration in relation to the market for the bulk of goods in the American economy that to a major extent the prices of goods are formed on an administered basis rather than on the basis of a free market. Only in the case of agricultural products and certain other products is price formed in

[15] *Ibid.,* Ch. VII, "The Organizational Structure," pages 96-121.

a free market." [16] Market coordination still remains a vital force in the modern economy, but habitual ways of thinking about economic matters lead many people to overestimate the importance of the free market as a coordinator of economic activity, and to ignore the growing importance of the administered market. So important has administrative coordination become that Means regards the "administration-dominated" prices of industry as much more characteristic of the modern economy than the "market-dominated" prices of agriculture.

The administrative coordination of economic life is fraught with many dangers. This coordination has provided order within the large "administrative units," but it has resulted in planlessness and a lack of coordination between large administrative units.[17] The main objection to the inflexible prices of administrative enterprise is that they do not permit the many economic adjustments which are required to keep the economy in balance with an approximation toward the full use of economic resources. The basic assumption of traditional economics that individual action leads to a smoothly functioning economy is no longer applicable to the modern economic system, because the activities of those in control of corporate enterprises inevitably lead to economic unbalance. Whatever economic balance we now achieve under administrative coordination is largely accidental, and it comes about only as we move from a state of unbalance in one direction to a new state of unbalance in a different direction.[18] The fact that administered prices do not result in "overall coordination" of the economic system does not mean that such prices are wrong, or that they are an unessential feature of the modern large-scale economy. "I want to make it clear," says Means, "that in pointing both to the fact and the importance of inflexible, administered prices, I am not saying that inflexible, administered prices are wrong. They seem to me inherent in modern technology. Nor am I saying that the inflexible prices should have come down during the depression. . . . I am only saying that inflexible, administered prices are incompatible with

[16] *Ibid.*, page 116.

[17] Means, Gardiner C., "The Distribution of Control and Responsibility in a Modern Economy," *Political Science Quarterly*, May, 1935, Vol. L, page 62.

[18] Means, Gardiner C., "Notes on Inflexible Prices," *The American Economic Review*, March, 1936, Vol. XXVI, No. 1, Supp., page 33.

automatic economic adjustment. Our economy has developed to the point where we simply cannot rely on the actions of individuals or enterprises acting independently to produce overall co-ordination and an effectively functioning economy. Unless we are willing to forego the benefits of modern technology, we are faced with the real task of figuring out how economic co-ordination can be achieved in the presence of inflexible, administered prices." [19]

Means's general economic aim is to obtain adequate over-all co-ordination without sacrificing the many advantages of large-scale production by resorting to a pulverization program which would break up large industrial concentrations. He has no quarrel with technological progress and economic concentration, but he is insistent that they be subordinated to general human welfare. Means feels that this general economic aim will be achieved only when administered prices are deprived of much of their disruptive influence. As long as we adopt policies appropriate only to a market-dominated price system, neither it nor the administration-dominated price system will function satisfactorily. More than this, the market place will tend to become a disorganizing rather than an organizing factor, since the maladjustments flowing from administrative coordination will be passed on by flexible prices to those portions of the economy which are unable to surround themselves with a wall of administrative defenses.

Much of Means's analysis has been devoted to a study of the effects of administered prices upon economic activity in depression periods. With the advent of a depression each major economic interest seeks to make its own position secure even at the expense of other important economic interests. Large corporate enterprises, faced with an inelastic demand for their products, adopt the policy of maintaining prices and curtailing production. Small-scale competitive enterprises, especially in agriculture, are unable to overcome the tendency of individuals to maintain production with the result that the prices for competitively produced products decline. From the point of view of price policy, "A depression can be described as a fall in prices at the flexible end of the price scale and a fall in production at the inflexible end." [20] The consequences of these price maladjustments are twofold. In the first place, the price and production

[19] *Ibid.*, page 35.
[20] *Ibid.*, page 28.

policies of large-scale, corporate enterprises place a disproportionately large share of the burdens of depression adjustments on the
agricultural and working classes.   Farmers, with their fixed charges
remaining what they were in more prosperous times, feed the nation
and produce raw materials at depression-level prices.   In addition,
laborers are forced to bear a large share of the brunt of the depression either through the unemployment created as a result of the curtailment of production by the large administrative business units or
through reductions in wage levels.   The second consequence of the
failure of administered prices to move in line with market-dominated prices is a more lengthy and more severe depression than
would otherwise be the case.   It is Means's conviction that if industry, after 1930, had maintained its production levels of 1928 and 1929
and had disposed of its output for whatever it would have returned,
as the farmers did, the depression would never have gone to the disastrous depths that were experienced.[21]   In a depression, if all manufacturers were to reduce their prices and maintain their production, maladjustments in the price-cost structure would be more
quickly eliminated and price-cost harmonies would be more easily
established.   How far such price and production policies would go
in bringing about these desirable results remains a matter of pure
conjecture, however, since no experiment along these lines has yet
been carried out.

Another bad consequence of the spread of administrative coordination in economic life has been the unsaddling of the consumer.
In the small-scale competitive economy of the nineteenth century
the consumer was in a position to exercise considerable control over
the course of production.   There were many sellers from whom to
buy, and also the simple, non-differentiated products of that time
did not present very great difficulties to the consumer in the act of
making decisions about what to purchase.   Although consumer
control of the productive processes was never a very well-developed
economic device for correlating production with general human
welfare even during the early part of the nineteenth century, the
economic development of the past one hundred years has reduced
consumer control to even lower levels of effectiveness.   The consumer has now only a few sellers among whom he may choose; fur-

[21] Means, Gardiner C., "The Consumer and the New Deal," *The Annals of the
American Academy of Political and Social Science*, May, 1934, Vol. 173, page 11.

thermore, consumer goods have become so complicated in their make-up that consumers are no longer able to make intelligent choices based on the relative merits of the goods offered for sale. As a consequence of the development of the arts of advertising, the consumer finds his patterns of consumption seriously warped by their contact with the forceful advertising and salesmanship activities of the great administrative units of the modern business system.[22] Far from enjoying the important role assigned to him by traditional economics, the consumer has become a helpless bystander watching, without much comprehension, the ordering of economic life by administrative enterprise engaged in a search for maximum net revenue rather than maximum human welfare.

In Means's view of the modern economy there are four major organizing influences which give cohesion to economic life.[23] There is, first, the market mechanism, which includes the interactions of individuals and groups as they buy and sell in free markets. A second important organizing influence is the administrative coordination supplied by large corporate enterprises, government bureaus, and public industries. In addition to market and administrative coordination are the laws, rules, and customs which canalize economic activity and narrow the scope of both market and administrative coordination. There is also "the organizing influence arising from the acceptance of the common goals which can bring about coordinated action of separate individuals without the presence of any common authority."[24] It is the combination of these four organizing influences which directs the flow of economic activity in the modern economy.

The roles which these organizing influences play in the guidance of economic life are today not equally significant. In recent decades administrative coordination has surged forward, narrowing the influence of the market mechanism, molding the framework of laws, rules, and customs to suit its own particular purposes, and shaping economic, social, and political community goals to conform with its narrow commercialized ends. In general it has favored the establishment of an economy of great instability and scarcity. The

[22] "The Distribution of Control and Responsibility in a Modern Economy," page 67.
[23] *The Structure of the American Economy*, Part I, Ch. VII, pages 96-121.
[24] *Ibid.*, page 97.

courts have not yet developed any adequate doctrines for the control of administrative coordination; and, to make matters worse, there was, up until 1930, "an abdication of the state" as a guiding factor in the affairs of modern corporations.[25] As a consequence, a form of economic absolutism has risen to challenge even the authority of the state to regulate its affairs. The problem, today, is to render this corporate absolutism innocuous, and to guarantee that corporate enterprise subserves the interests of the general public.

This analysis of Means's views on the nature and significance of corporate enterprise shows that much of his thought has paralleled the work of earlier investigators. But not all of his thought in this connection has been borrowed. Means has made use of new materials relating to corporate activities, and he has also stressed aspects of corporate behavior which are quite different from those emphasized by Veblen and other pioneering students of the corporation problem. In Means's study of the large-scale corporation there are three matters to which Veblen paid little attention: the role of the holding company, the significance of inflexible prices, and the separation of the ownership and control of corporate wealth. Veblen's study of corporate enterprise revolves around the concept of absentee ownership, which is different from Means's separation of interest in and control over corporate assets. In Veblen's analysis corporate management is still largely subservient to the absentee security owners, and not much notice is given the growing tendency for the absentee owners to be deprived of their dividends by those who actually control the corporations. Means's investigation of the operations of the large corporation emphasizes this new development in the corporate world which became prominent in the years after Veblen wrote his *Absentee Ownership* (1923).

Means improves upon Veblen's analysis of corporate enterprise by making a more thorough study of the price problem associated with large-scale economic activity. Veblen never got beyond very general statements about the price policies of the "key industries" which are developed around the basic "strategy of getting a larger net gain in dollars" by curtailing employment and output.[26] In addi-

[25] Berle, Adolf A., and Means, Gardiner C., "Corporations and the Public Investor," *The American Economic Review*, March, 1930, Vol. XX, page 68.
[26] Veblen, Thorstein, *Absentee Ownership and Business Enterprise in Recent Times*, 1923, page 217.

tion, Veblen did not make as much use of the actual records of price behavior as does Means. As he explained in the preface to *Absentee Ownership and Business Enterprise in Recent Times,* he was interested mainly in "an objective, theoretical analysis of the main drift" of business enterprise. His study made "no attempt to penetrate beyond the workday facts which are already familiar to students of these matters." Unlike Veblen, Means has been interested in gathering abundant statistical information as a factual basis for his broad generalizations about the industrial policies of large corporations. Since he prefers to rest his feet upon such solid economic data as are found in his study of "Industrial Prices and Their Relative Inflexibility" (1935), Means substitutes statistical investigation for that "summary description" which was so frequently the starting point of the Veblenian analysis.

The general orientations of the studies of business enterprise presented by Veblen and Means are basically quite different. Veblen asserted that he was making an impartial, objective analysis of the drift of American business enterprise. On those occasions when he veered from the position of an impartial critic, he thought in terms of an eventual decay of the business system and its replacement by a socialistic system which would give freer play to the expansionist tendencies of industrial technology. The orientation of Means's analysis reveals no such revolutionary outlook. He pursues his study of corporate enterprise in the belief that it is possible to preserve much of the contemporary business system. Veblen, on the contrary, displayed little interest in methods by which the private business system might be altered to make it more considerate of the common welfare; he viewed any such patching as a device to prolong temporarily the life of the present business system. With Means the situation is quite different, for he is ever on the alert to discover ways in which the modern economy may be made to function effectively without too much departure from current methods of conducting business. For this reason Means's study of modern business enterprise appeals to a much wider public than did the hypercritical, revolutionary analysis presented by Veblen.

Means's investigation of the nature of contemporary American business enterprise is of interest to him because he observes that it leads to considerations which are a fruitful source of stimulation for the further development of the science of economics. Economics is being revamped in a number of quarters to incorporate explanations relating to recent developments in the world of business enterprise; and various economic categories such as the concepts of wealth, private property, and market prices are taking on new meanings.[27] A new framework of analysis, centering about the large-scale enterprises that have become so prominent a feature of the modern economy, is being developed to replace the traditional framework handed down by nineteenth-century economists.   In addition, Means finds that the study of corporate enterprise is absorbing because it is an introduction to the highly important task of using economics as an instrument to obtain a better use of our economic resources. Means's basic drive is not that of an academician; instead he is a professional economist who is greatly stirred by the prospect of using economic science as an instrument for better human living. He is among the group of professional economists who, as Mitchell says, "are perforce occupied with actual economic processes, and the prospects of turning economics into a realistic science are brightened by their daily labors." [28]

The Problem of Economic Stability

In shifting his analysis from an examination of the operations of the modern economy to a study of how to make it function more effectively, Means makes further use, of the type of analysis which he found so helpful in his interpretation of the nature of administrative enterprise.   His framework of interpretation becomes the basis for a dynamic analysis which is quite different from the static analysis of traditional economics.   In the latter analysis conditions leading to changes in prices or output were supposed to be self-correcting in the sense that all original disturbances soon developed the necessary counteractive forces to restore economic balance without any serious

[27] Veblen would have looked with favor on Means's endeavor to alter the meanings of economic terms so that they will be more in accord with the facts of modern business enterprise.   It was Veblen's frequent complaint that "Then as always the theoretical discussions endeavored to formulate the new facts in terms derived from an earlier state of things.   Indeed, it has taken something like a hundred years for the formulas of the economists to adapt themselves to the new run of facts in business and industry which set in in the days of Adam Smith." See *Absentee Ownership and Business Enterprise in Recent Times,* pages 59-60 fn.

[28] "The National Bureau's Social Function," *Twentieth Annual Report of the Director of Research,* National Bureau of Economic Research, March, 1940, page 21.

declines in either production or consumption levels, and without changes in basic price and production relations. In Means's dynamic analysis of the developing corporate economy, which is similar to the analysis presented by John M. Clark in his *Studies in the Economics of Overhead Costs,* the self-correcting forces of equilibrium economics are replaced by a complex of self-reinforcing forces.[29] An initial increase in prices sets in motion forces which tend to aggravate the original price increase rather than to correct it; and, likewise, an initial increase in unemployment becomes cumulative, and is not corrected until widespread unemployment has reduced total economic activity to very low levels. In an economy of self-reinforcing forces there is no neutralizing of the effects of initial disturbances until there are wide departures from the full employment of men and machines. Of course, even in the corporate economy of today self-reinforcing disturbances must be eventually checked or neutralized at some point, if a complete breakdown of the economic system is to be avoided. The important point, however, is not that initial disturbances are eventually neutralized, but rather that they are checked only when the economy reaches very low levels of business activity where basic price and production relations are seriously disrupted.

An acceptance of the theory of self-reinforcing forces necessarily colors one's views about the means by which the economy should be controlled so that it may be kept near the level of a full functioning. It is not surprising, therefore, that Means's program for economic control is designed to neutralize price and production disturbances before they work out their ill effects through a lowering of the general level of economic activity. Since the uncontrolled economy does not any longer have the capacity quickly to neutralize self-reinforcing disturbances, Means believes that organized, collective management of some sort should be applied at various strategic points in the economy to do what the automatic functioning of the competitive system formerly did. Whatever neutralizing of economic dis-

[29] In John M. Clark's words, "The distinguishing characteristic of economic forces of the supply-and-demand variety, as usually analyzed in economic theory, is that they are self-limiting; the more they prevail the weaker they become, and the stronger grows the resistance. The business cycle shows unmistakably that the forces at work there are not self-limiting in the typical fashion but self-reinforcing throughout a great part of the swing of the pendulum." See *Studies in the Economics of Overhead Costs,* 1923, page 388.

turbances is done is to be a matter of economic design rather than the spontaneous operation of self-regulating mechanisms.

The problem of bringing about a full functioning of the economy presents itself to Means in two different ways.   There is, first, the problem of coping with economic unbalance and its disturbing effects in the present and immediate future.   This task is one of ferreting out those factors which are currently throwing the economy out of gear, and to apply short-run controls in such a fashion as to eliminate much of their influence; while the second task is to take a long-range view of our economic problems, and then to devise some general plan which will insure the continued good functioning of the economy.   Among Means's short-run suggestions for meeting our immediate economic difficulties are obtaining the right amount of money, balancing savings with the demand for new capital, determining satisfactory price and production policies for large-scale enterprises, preventing changes in foreign trade from 'causing maladjustments in the domestic economy, and providing means of enabling the growing classes of non-producers to maintain their expenditures for consumers' goods.[30]

With respect to the financial problem involved in the goal of a smoothly functioning economy, Means points out that "The main money problem is . . . to maintain an amount of money sufficient, and only just sufficient, to insure that money factors shall not interfere with the effective working of the economy." [31]   In the flexible-price economy of the nineteenth century there never arose any such problem of getting "the right amount of money," because too much or too little money in the hands of the public tended to work itself out through changes in the general level of prices.   These changes might increase or decrease prices, but they would not alter the fundamental relations existing between prices.   A decrease in the amount of money would be followed by a decreased demand for goods and services.   The smaller demand would be accompanied by a fall in prices and also by a decrease in the community's demand for money, since less money would be needed to move the existing supply of goods at the lower level of prices.   This readjustment would

[30] Ware, Caroline F., and Means, Gardiner C., *The Modern Economy in Action*, Part II, "The Problems of the New Economy," pages 65-180.   New York: Harcourt, Brace & Company, 1936.
[31] *Ibid.*, page 79.

work itself out until prices had fallen to the level where there was once more an equilibrium between the demand for and supply of money. As long as price relations remained undisturbed, production relations would also be unchanged; selling prices would be lower, but costs of production would also be lower. In this situation business would go on as before, and the only important change would be in the relations between debtors and creditors. Although this might be a serious matter for certain individuals, it would not seriously interfere with the smooth functioning of the economic system.

The situation is quite different in the corporate economy of today where changes in the supply of or demand for money do not work themselves out through changes in the general level of prices. Means finds that changes in the supply of money have "a seriously disorganizing influence." A decrease in the supply of money, instead of causing a decline in prices in general, brings about a drop in prices in the flexible-price section of the economy; in the inflexible-price section there occurs a drop in production instead of prices. This decrease in production is accompanied by a decline in the incomes of various classes in the community. Instead of being self-corrective, the original change in the money supply gives rise to a cumulative process which does not come to rest until the real income of the community is at a very low level. The final result is not a harmless change in the general price level, but a widespread dislocation of price and production relations accompanied by a disastrous decline in production in the inflexible-price areas of the economic system.

The prime monetary problem is to prevent this disturbance of price and production relations by keeping flexible and inflexible prices at the same general level. In this connection there are two possibilities: we may readjust the inflexible prices whenever there is a general change in flexible prices, or we may hold flexible prices in line with rigid prices by means of various monetary and fiscal controls. Means would follow the second suggestion, since he believes that the adjusting of inflexible prices to changes in flexible prices would be "a tremendous administrative task" with little chance of success. He looks upon "the group of inflexible prices as a table-land around which the price structure is to be built. If the level of flexible prices lifts above the level of inflexible prices, money restriction would be relied on to bring downward pressure on the flexible prices. If flexible prices fall seriously below the level of inflexible prices, an increase in the volume of money is called for to bring upward pressure on flexible prices. The actual amount of money change called for in any particular situation would depend on a wide variety of factors, some working to decrease and some to increase the amount of change required." [32] Although the price structure would pivot about the group of inflexible prices, this is not to say that inflexible prices would themselves be unchanging. Inflexible prices would be reduced whenever technological advances permitted a reduction in costs, and in the long run many such changes might bring about a general lowering of the level of inflexible prices. Such changes would be necessary in a dynamic economy where economic adjustments were being constantly made.

In Means's analysis the term "money" includes the supply of currency issued by the government, bank notes, and demand deposits. Since the most important single medium of transfer is the bank deposit, increases and decreases in the supply of money are to be obtained primarily through a change in the quantity of demand deposits. Changes in the volume of bank deposits have been made in the past by the commercial banking system not with the view of providing the "right amount of money" but for the purpose of increasing the profits of the private banks. Unfortunately, the profit policies of private banks, which have frequently called for larger supplies of bank deposits, have not always coincided with the monetary needs of the economy. Where private banking policy has called for larger money supplies but the requirements of the economy have pointed to a need for less money, the results have been disastrous. Means observes that the monetary requirements of the modern economy are likely to vary in the opposite direction from the changes in the quantity of bank deposits, since the nation is likely to need more money when depression sets in and less when business is enjoying a marked

[32] *Ibid.*, page 82. Means finds himself in disagreement with those who, like Lionel Robbins, maintain that all inflexibilities should be eliminated. It is Robbins' main contention that there is a "necessity for the elimination of all kinds of inflexibility. In order that recovery may be assured and future dislocations minimized, it is necessary not only that flexibility should be restored to the prices of different kinds of labour but that flexibility should also be restored in other markets. . . . If future fluctuations are to be avoided it is necessary that these things should disappear." See Robbins' *The Great Depression*, page 189. London: Macmillan and Co., Limited, 1934.

prosperity. Under present conditions the banks of the country are in a position to manipulate the supply of money but not the demand for it. The demand for money fluctuates with changes in beliefs about the safety of the nation's money supply, in the purchasing power of money, national income, the amount of business done and the ways of doing business, interest rates, and in the desire for liquidity. In the face of these changes in the demand for money, the commercial banking system, stimulated by the desire for private profits, frequently creates a money supply which is out of line with the needs of the community. If changes in the demand for and supply of money should happen to be made in conformity with monetary needs of the economy, such a result would be purely accidental; all too frequently community needs and commercial banking policies shift in opposite directions.

At present there are no private or public agencies in a position to keep the supply of and demand for money moving together so that the right amount of money is always available. The Federal Reserve System has certain indirect powers of control, but they are largely negative in their effects. In spite of all the extensions of its powers, the Board of Governors has been able to do little more than put curbs on expansionist tendencies at work in the banking system. For the most part, the initiative in the expansion or contraction of deposits remains with the individual member banks of the Federal Reserve System. Of course, the original stimulus making private member banks expand or contract their deposits comes from the business world, but in their reactions to the demands of businessmen member banks are still quite largely beyond the controls of the Federal Reserve System.

In Means's solution of the "money problem" the power of private banks to create money by expanding deposits would be taken away and placed in the hands of a central monetary authority. There would be a separation of the deposit and loan functions with the government controlling the deposit function and the private banks the loaning function. The government monetary authority would operate like a reservoir, increasing or decreasing the flow of money according to the dictates of a policy designed to provide the right amount of money. This money would be loaned by the monetary authority to the private banks, which in turn would lend their funds to private business concerns. The government would determine how much money there should be, but the private bankers would decide to whom the money should be made available. In this manner, the government would bring about no more financial centralization than was absolutely necessary. It would be in a position to control "the supply of money in relation to the demand in order that monetary changes will not work themselves out in distorted price relationships and over- or under-employment of men and machines in the concentrated industries." And there would then be that "positive control to insure the 'right amount of money' " which is "essential to the full use of resources to meet men's needs." [33]

Associated with the problem of providing the right amount of money is the task of balancing saving with the creation of new capital. Where saving and the formation of capital are in balance, saving cannot be a source of disturbance to the economy. Before the advent of large corporate enterprise, such a balance was much easier to achieve, because in the old, competitive economy there were flexible interest rates and market prices. There could be no problem of unbalanced saving, because excess saving was immediately followed by compensating adjustments in interest rates and market prices. If the supply became excessive in relation to the demand for savings, lower interest rates would tend to discourage further saving; and if the lower interest rates were not sufficient to discourage saving, continued saving would reduce current consumption and eventually bring about a general fall in the prices of consumers' goods. Furthermore, the attempt to convert savings into capital goods would cause the prices of these goods to rise. These changes in the prices of consumers' and producers' goods would reinforce the lowering of the interest rate in its tendency to reduce saving and to stimulate current consumption. In the modern economy no such adjustment between saving and capital creation can be brought about because of the distortions of the saving process introduced by corporate enterprise. Interest rates are no longer sufficiently flexible, and, in addition, the inflexibility of many prices prevents those changes in the prices of consumers' and producers' goods which would otherwise be an aid in the restoration of a balance between saving and investing.

The influence in favor of a balance between saving and the crea-

[33] *The Modern Economy in Action,* pages 111-112.

tion of new capital which the rate of return on investments continues to exercise is for the most part nullified by other more powerful influences. Changes in the market values of securities frequently have the effect of causing people to save less than they would if security prices were more stable. When security prices are rising and business is booming, people holding securities as investments feel free to spend more of their current earnings since their investments have an increasing market value. When security prices are declining, when business is depressed and corporate returns are greatly reduced, people observe that their savings invested in securities have fallen in value, and they are then prompted to try to save more of their current earnings. Declining security prices cause many people to save more from their annual money incomes at the very time that the demand for loanable funds is falling off. In some circumstances declining security prices and low capital returns, instead of discouraging saving, actually stimulate it. If savers were influenced more by rates of return and less by security prices, their behavior would be more conducive to the establishment of a balance between saving and investing.

Speculation is a second factor which tends to make saving vary independently of changes in the rate of return on investments. If excess saving causes security prices to go up and yields to decline, speculation may enter to magnify the maladjustment, and to prevent a drop in security yields from bringing about a decline in savings. Even more important than changes in security prices and stock-market speculation as factors in the disruption of the saving process are fluctuations in the desire for liquidity. During a period of business decline when interest rates are falling and returns on investments are declining, the demand for savings on the part of the business system falls off. At the same time, however, individuals who are fearful of the future refrain from consuming their incomes in order to accumulate savings in a liquid form. The community's decreased need for savings is thus correlated with a desire on the part of many people to add to their money savings. Once more the rate of return on investments fails to bring about a balance between savings and their investment.

A fourth factor which tends to distort the saving process of the modern economy is the corporate form of business enterprise, which has erected a barrier between the saving of money and the accumulation of real savings. The individual who wishes to save may invest accumulated money in corporate securities, but this investment of money savings may merely cause the prices of securities to go up. Unless corporations issue new securities and apply the proceeds to the purchase of new capital equipment, no real saving can result from the saving of money by individuals. Also, if individuals wish to consume their past savings, they cannot reduce the supply of real savings unless corporations are willing to retire some of their stock and reduce their capital assets. Ordinarily an individual will consume his money savings by selling his corporate shares and thus depressing the prices of securities. In this fashion efforts of individuals to consume or to increase their money savings frequently work themselves out through changes in security prices rather than through changes in the community's real savings.

More serious than the previously discussed causes of unbalance between saving and investing is the fact that an original lack of balance tends to magnify rather than to correct itself. In a purely competitive system where flexible prices are found, an increase in savings would mean that more would be spent upon capital goods, since the increased savings would have reduced interest rates and would have made it more profitable to invest in capital goods. Lower interest rates, however, would tend to discourage further saving. In addition, lower consumer-goods prices resulting from increased saving would tend to discourage new investments in capital goods, and would also induce savers to spend more of their incomes on the low-priced consumers' goods. In the modern economy, with its inflexible prices, increased savings do not set in motion forces which eventually put an end to the increased saving and thus restore the balance between savings and new investments. When there is a deficiency of consumer buying as a result of increased saving, businessmen do not find it profitable to invest funds in new capital goods even though such funds are abundant at low rates of interest, since with inflexible consumer goods prices there is no assurance of sufficient markets for the consumer goods that would be produced by the new capital equipment. The self-correcting movements of the purely competitive economy are now replaced by the self-reinforcing movements of the modern corporate economy. As a consequence, increased money savings and decreased consumer expenditures are now followed by a decreased demand for capital goods and by a general decline in national economic activity which continues until the restricted national income reduces the desire to save.[34]

After having analyzed the reasons for a lack of balance between money savings and the creation of capital goods, Means turns to the question of how an adequate balance could be achieved. The problem is one of controlling the volume of money savings accumulated by the community and the volume of capital goods created by the economic system. With respect to increasing or decreasing the money savings of individuals in accordance with the needs of the community, Means observes that the problem is a very difficult one. People save because of changes in stock-market prices, because of the influence of speculation, or as a result of the desire for high liquidity. If the stock market were stabilized and the forces of speculation very considerably subdued, and if personal security were made more widespread, the dislocating effects of fluctuating stock-market prices and periodic changes in the desire for liquidity could be somewhat reduced. Means believes, however, that at the most very little could be done directly to alter the propensities of individuals to save. In his opinion a balance between saving and the investing of savings could be more readily obtained by controlling the creation of new capital goods. Whenever savings reveal a tendency to become excessive, unbalance could be avoided by fostering a more rapid creation of new capital goods, or by increasing the expenditures of non-producing classes such as the unemployed, the incapacitated, and the aged. In times of uncertainty when stock-market prices are unattractive and the desire for high liquidity is widespread, the tendency for people to save too much of their money incomes could be offset through governmental borrowing for relief

[34] As Alvin H. Hansen has explained, the static economy analysis fails to take account of the dynamics of the problem. "An increase in thrift at any income level of necessity must cause a decline in consumption expenditures, and this decline would result in a fall in the demand for replacement investment and thus accelerate the decline in income. It is true that a low level of income would bring about a decline in the rate of interest. . . . Under these circumstances, the decline in the rate of interest will not stimulate investment sufficiently and therefore cannot bring the economy back to full employment." See Hansen's "Price Flexibility and Full Employment of Resources," *The Structure of the American Economy*, Part II, "Toward Full Use of Resources," page 33. A symposium by Gardiner C. Means, D. E. Montgomery, J. M. Clark, Alvin H. Hansen, and Mordecai Ezekiel, published by the National Resources Planning Board in June, 1940.

and public works programs. As private business cannot be relied upon to absorb the increasing money savings of the population at such times, it would be easier for the government to initiate a public works program than to endeavor to have the business system alter its investment program. In prosperous times when private industry seeks to carry capital-goods creation beyond the capacity of the community to save, it would be found necessary to place curbs upon the expansion of private industry. At times there would be a need for less saving and more capital creation, as during depressions, and at other times there would be the problem of more saving and less capital creation. Means explains that "the solution for saving in excess of capital creation is less saving or more capital creation. . . . The community's desire to save can be meshed with the community's need to spend savings only by making these two fluctuate together. Here again, as in the case of money, inflexible prices deflect the forces of adjustment and make of them forces for greater maladjustment. Only as savings and capital goods creation are maintained in balance can the full advantages of modern technology be realized." [35]

The problems of getting the right amount of money and an adequate balance between savings and investments are associated in Means's analysis with a third problem relating to "industrial policy." It is possible to have the right amount of money and a balance between savings and investments with the economic system operating at much less than full capacity. In this situation the level of economic activity at which the potentialities of our industrial technology would be more or less fully realized would not be reached. It is desirable, therefore, to correlate the control of the money flow and the saving process with industrial policies which are designed to take advantage of the fruitfulness of the modern economic system. In Means's analysis "industrial policy" refers to the price and production policies of the large corporations. These policies have in recent decades reversed the tendencies of the old, competitive economy toward an expanding industrial activity. They tend "on the whole, to exert a pressure toward contraction. . . . Instead of production being expanded until the added value produced just covers the wages of the last worker hired, production is stopped long before this point is reached. Nor are capital facili-

[35] *The Modern Economy in Action,* page 128.

ties expanded until the return on capital is reduced to the level at which new capital can be obtained. Not only is full economic activity not a reality; even the imaginative picture of such a condition, on which the old economist built his theory, has no longer. validity, for the forces pressing constantly away from the full use of resources are inherent in modern industrial conditions." [36]   The general aim of Means's program for the control of industrial policy would be to curb the restrictive tendencies of the price and production policies of the large corporations, so that an increasingly high level of economic activity could be obtained. Industrial policy should be designed to allow production to expand up to that point at which the laboring classes prefer to have leisure rather than more output, and at which it is decided to conserve natural resources rather than to consume them.

The industrial policies of large corporations have interrupted the smooth functioning of the economy by bringing about a maldistribution of national income, especially as between those who receive profits and those who receive wages. These policies, with their general aim of maximizing profits rather than output, have given investors "disproportionately high profits," and have limited the possibilities of mass markets by failing to provide the lower income groups with sufficient buying power. Excessive returns going to investors have raised the problem of oversaving at the very time that consumer expenditures are not proving adequate to maintain mass production. Unregulated industrial policy has contributed further to the disorganization of the economy because large corporations raise their administered prices in periods of prosperity just at the time that monetary policies are being pursued by the government for the purpose of bringing flexible prices closer to existing inflexible prices. [37]

Means points out that there are seven major ways of controlling industrial policies which can be employed without doing violence to accepted American methods of doing business. They include

[36] *Ibid.*, page 133.

[37] Alvin H. Hansen has explained that "Just as forced cyclical downward adjustments of administrative prices are to be avoided, so also an advance of administrative prices in the upswing is to be avoided. Such an advance similarly creates business expectations which tend to cause the accumulation of excessive inventories, leading to subsequent relapses." See *The Structure of the American Economy*, Part II, page 30.

control through government ownership, positive government control without ownership, negative government control through commission regulation, the payment of benefits for the acceptance of certain industrial policies, the setting up of price and production policies by industrial councils, and the influencing of industrial policies by labor unions and cooperative enterprises. Through a combination of these techniques of control it should be possible, in Means's opinion, to create satisfactory industrial policies.

Government ownership would prove useful in those cases where the services produced were so vital to the general welfare that there could be no thought of relying upon private enterprise to produce them. Such ownership would also prove desirable where initial costs are very high, maintenance is not a very important item, and low-cost government borrowing is a further advantage as in the case of low-cost housing and hydro-electric generation. The further advantage of government ownership is that it may be used as a "yardstick" to determine the efficiency of private enterprise. The most serious objection to government ownership is that it tends to be associated with inflexible prices which introduce a further element of rigidity into the economy. Government enterprise would prove to be desirable only if its price and production policies were adopted with the view of expanding production and obtaining a full use of resources. Government control without ownership, whether exercised through a public commission or some other device, avoids the expense of acquiring private property but suffers, as in the case of public utilities, from the tendency to adopt industrial policies which safeguard returns to investors at the cost of a less-than-full use of resources. Labor unions and cooperatives can be useful in offsetting the restrictive tendencies of large corporations because they can focus their attention on production rather than profits. They merit consideration in any program designed to overcome the inherent tendencies of the modern economy to favor scarcity rather than abundance.

Of special importance among the various techniques for controlling industrial policy is the establishment of price and production policies in key industries as the result of the deliberations of industrial councils representing all interested parties. This is the type of control that was used by the National Recovery Administration in its system of industrial codes. Although it was not successful, Means believes that something worth while can be developed out of this experiment. He would like to see each key industry create a framework of price and production policy within which individual firms could operate. In each key industry there would be a board representing the producers, the workers, the consumers, and the government. Prices and output would be determined with relation to the needs of the whole economy, and not with any special attention being directed toward returns to corporate investors. The type of key decisions would vary from industry to industry. In competitive industries industrial policy would not include much more than minimum wages and minimum standards of quality; in those industries where the conservation of natural resources was a major problem, the industrial policy would be built around the problem of providing the best use of a limited supply of resources. In all key industries decisions about industrial policy should seek to maximize production and to provide for an equitable distribution of goods and services. The two groups primarily interested in this expanding production are the consumers and the laborers. Means believes that any system of industrial code authorities or boards which gives adequate expression to these two groups as well as to businessmen would go a long way toward establishing a more fruitful economy. He is well aware that giving expression to the consumer and labor interests in the administration of industrial policy would not be a simple problem. Thus far the consumers have for the most part remained unorganized, since people are prone to regard themselves more as producers than as consumers.[38] There are now indications, however, of an expanding consumer interest, which, with some aid from the government, may be expected to show promise of being an effective force in the struggle to establish a well-functioning economy. This is especially true of such organizations as farmers' societies, labor unions, and women's leagues which have indirectly provided outlets for consumer opinion.

The labor interests have for some time been better organized than the consumers. They have proven effective in correcting one of the undesirable tendencies of the modern economy in so far as they have counteracted the tendency to give capital an excessively large share of the net value product of industry. But the situation is different with respect to the tendency to limit output, since organ-

[38] "The Consumer and the New Deal," page 16.

ized labor has often found its immediate interest to be in the restriction rather than the expansion of output. In this connection organized labor has failed to represent the whole body of workers. Means looks with favor upon the recent shift in labor interest from craft union to industrial union organization, because he thinks that when labor as a whole is organized it will be more interested in counteracting the restrictive tendencies of corporate enterprise. In addition, he believes that organized labor will be more insistent that it be given a place in the actual operation of industry.

In Means's general plan for the democratization of industry there would be no place for a system of governmental benevolence. According to some interpretations the government is supposed to represent the general interests of all the people; in other theories the government is taken to be the means by which the dominant economic group adds political control to its economic power. In contrast to these interpretations, Means asserts that actually "government in America comes closer to being an area of conflict among interest groups, responding to pressures from others besides the dominant economic group, and sometimes enabling those who are weak economically but stronger in voting strength to challenge the power of the dominant economic interests." The problem before us is to make our democracy more effective so that labor and consumer pressures may be more potent in their influence on governmental and industrial policy. The more genuine our democracy becomes the more effective will be organized laborers and consumers in neutralizing the "disastrous tendencies toward restriction and disproportionate profits."

The revamping of industrial policy contemplated by Means would redound to the benefit of many others besides consumers and laborers. If the restrictive propensities of corporate enterprise could be curbed, professional workers, small businessmen, farmers, and small investors would benefit greatly. The unbalanced economy created by large-scale corporate enterprise has been particularly injurious to small businessmen and farmers. Small businessmen, huddling precariously on the periphery of the business system, have been unable to make much of an imprint on the industrial system which encompasses them. Farmers have been particularly unfortunate since their incomes have varied directly with the incomes of the working population; industrial policies, which have at times seriously curtailed workers' income, have brought widespread misery to many farming communities. Even investors would benefit from more satisfactory price and production policies, since the earnings of corporations would be greater and more stabilized in a balanced economy. In the long run the benefits flowing from more effective price and production policies would be shared by all classes in the community.

Means's proposals for meeting our major economic difficulties in the immediate future are deficient in one important respect; they all fail to consider an over-all coordination of economic activity.[39] Each proposal is designed to provide an attack upon economic disorganization from some special viewpoint. No short-run proposal looks at the economy as a whole, and suggests a remedy which takes into consideration over-all adjustments covering the entire economic system. In general, the short-run proposals for coping with the immediate danger of an economic breakdown are not concerned with the larger issue of "steering the economy so as to make it yield to the American people the best living that is technically possible. The most desirable distribution of income would not be brought about simply by insuring that the total amount of money in circulation met the needs of the economy. The most effective use of resources would not be insured by price and production controls within each industry. Measures to balance savings with capital creation would not steer investment into one industry in preference to another." [40]

The failure of his short-run proposals to deal with the larger issues of giving positive direction to the modern economy leads Means to ask the question whether or not the economic system can ever function adequately without over-all coordination. What Means has in mind is some form of national economic planning which would coordinate the various short-run proposals for economic control which he has thought worthy of consideration. As he shifts his analysis from short-run to long-run considerations relating to economic readjustment and control, Means is firmly convinced that there is a great need for general economic planning. He observes

---

[39] For an analysis of Means's proposals relating to adjustments in foreign trade and the care of non-producing classes see *The Modern Economy in Action*, pages 162-195.

[40] *The Modern Economy in Action*, pages 196-197.

not only that the over-all coordination once supplied by the automatic forces of the competitive system is absent from the modern economy, but that there is no hope of restoring it. According to his interpretation, the only way out of our economic difficulties is therefore to supply the necessary coordination of economic activity by adopting some form of general economic planning.

The Concept of a Managed Equilibrium

Means's assertion that the long-run solution of our economic difficulties lies in some form of national economic planning is based upon his conclusion that we can no longer rely on traditional methods of achieving economic equilibrium. According to the inherited system of national policies for the direction of economic life, the government was supposed to limit its functions to the protection of property, the enforcing of contracts, the provision of a safe money medium, the regulation of business in those few cases where competition did not prove to be effective, and the provision of those services which private enterprise could not effectively supply. In such a view of national economic policy all other matters could be left in the hands of private enterprise, and the market mechanism could be relied upon to bring about a reasonably full use of resources.[41] The basic adjustment mechanism would be found in the sensitivity or flexibility of short-run prices, wage rates, and unit profits. For example, a deficiency in the employment of men and machines would be accompanied by less buying of goods and services. These reductions in buying and in the employment of men and machines would be followed by declines in the prices of goods, wage rates, and profit margins. The prices of goods would fall because of decreased demand and also because of lower labor costs; wages would fall as a consequence of the increased competition from unemployed workers, and the decline in unit profits would result from the increased competition of unused plant facilities. The general fall in goods prices, wage rates, and unit profits would result in such an increase in the purchasing power of the outstanding money supply that people would find their money supplies becoming redundant. They would then spend or invest this "redundant money," thus bringing about expenditures in excess of production. Eventually more men and machines would be employed to enable production

41 *The Structure of the American Economy*, Part II, page 10.

to keep up with the expanding sales. The increase in the purchas-
.ing power of money would have a pump-priming effect which would
eventually result in the elimination of the original deficiencies in
the employment of labor and capital. The series of automatic,
equilibrating adjustments would then be completed.

These automatic market adjustments had considerable effectiveness in the nineteenth century when the economic system was highly
flexible. Since 1885 new technologies, population movements, the
closing of the extensive frontier, the increased industrialization and
urbanization of the country, and fundamental shifts in the nation's
foreign trade have very greatly altered the structure of the American
economy. Especially significant have been the growth of large
corporate enterprises, the spread of collective action in the form of
trade associations, labor unions, farm cooperatives, and consumer
organizations, and the expanding role of the government as a regulatory agency. These major changes of the past fifty years have
greatly interfered with the functioning of the market as an adjustment mechanism, because they have substituted inflexible prices for
flexible prices.

Not only is there general agreement amongst economists that
there have been many departures from the inherited system of national economic policies, especially in the years since the first World
War, but it is also widely accepted that the structure of the American economy has changed significantly in the past half-century.
There is also general agreement that there has been a great deal
of unemployment of men and machines in recent years; but beyond these points there is not much agreement. Some economists assert that the inherited methods of dealing with unemployed
labor and unused capital are not inconsistent with the existing economic structure. In their opinion all that is necessary is to place
reliance on the initiative of individual enterprises, guided by the
market mechanism, to provide a reasonably full employment of resources.[42] Other economists hold the view that the former system of

[42] Means points out that "initiative of individual *enterprises*" (corporate enterprises) must be distinguished from the "initiative of individuals." Reliance
would not be placed on private individuals but on private enterprises. Those
who uphold this plan for securing full employment apparently believe that the
managers of large corporate enterprises may be relied upon somehow to insure
full employment of resources. See *The Structure of the American Economy*,
Part II, page 11 fn.

national economic policies, with its reliance upon the automatic adjustment of economic activity, is inconsistent with the present economic structure, and that the failure to meet the problem of the full use of resources is due to the failure to recognize this inconsistency.   These economists, however, do not agree on what should be done about this inconsistency.   One group would eliminate it by preserving the inherited system of national economic policies, and by recommending those changes in the modern economy which would restore the efficiency of the market as a mechanism for bringing about the full use of resources.   These changes in economic structure would call for the pulverization of big business and the elimination of many forms of collective action.   The other group of economists, which includes Means, would eliminate the inconsistency between inherited economic policy and the modern economic structure by changing this policy to meet the needs of the modern economy.   They advocate "some modification of the inherited system of [economic] policies as the remedy for unemployment," since they believe "that the market mechanism on which such a system of policies places responsibility for insuring reasonably full employment cannot be made to work effectively as a result of any structural changes that can be brought about in the reasonably near future.   They hold that the solution of the basic problem of unemployment should take the form of altering the inherited policy system by supplementing the market mechanism to the extent necessary to make the revised system more consistent with the existing economic structure.   This latter procedure would presumably also require some modification in economic structure to allow the modified system of policies to be effective and would not inhibit other structural changes undertaken to attain other ends, but it would not rely on structural changes as the main basis for insuring reasonably full employment." [43]

What Means is advocating is not a minor change in the inherited ways of providing for the necessary adjustments in economic life; instead he is advocating fundamental changes in the traditional methods of coping with an ineffective use of resources.   He sees no reason for relying on short-run adjustments in prices, wages, and interest rates as devices for insuring a reasonably full use of resources.   Short-run sensitivity of prices has largely disappeared and

[43] *The Structure of the American Economy*, Part II, page 12.

could only be recalled by pulverizing large-scale industry, and by sacrificing most of the benefits of technological progress.[44] Means distinguishes "depression and recovery sensitivity" from the longer-run or "secular sensitivity" of prices. Secular sensitivity, involving adjustments of price to such fundamental factors as technological change, the development of new resources, and alterations in consumer needs, could be obtained with relatively infrequent adjustments in price. Depression and recovery sensitivity, however, calls for frequent price changes all along the line comparable to the changes now observed in agricultural and security prices. In Means's opinion a large degree of short-run insensitivity of prices should be accepted and made the point of departure for any plan for the radical revision of the inherited system of national economic policies. Such a program should not overlook the possibility of structural change as a means of securing a more balanced and efficient use of resources, but at no time would Means rely on structural changes of the economic system as the principal way of securing a reasonably full use of resources. In the quarrel about structural versus policy changes Means has taken a very definite stand: what is necessary is a "major policy choice" designed to establish new ways of insuring the over-all coordination of the economic activity of the nation.

Major changes in national economic policy would involve the use of market and administrative controls. The market mechanism would be relied upon to bring about gradual or long-run adjustments in goods prices, wage rates, unit profits, and interest rates, but where it did not perform this necessary function adequately government regulation would be used. Administrative controls would play an especially important role in connection with short-run price adjustments which were made to insure a balance in international trade, to obtain a balance between savings and investment, and to reduce the underemployment of men and machines. If

---

[44] Means, Gardiner C., *Industrial Prices and Their Relative Inflexibility*, Senate Document 13, 74th Congress, First Session, Jan. 17, 1935, pages 1-38. For criticisms of Means's views on price inflexibility see Humphrey, Don D., "The Nature and Meaning of Rigid Prices," *The Journal of Political Economy*, Oct., 1937, Vol. XLV, pages 651-661; Tucker, Rufus S., "The Reasons for Price Rigidity," *The American Economic Review*, March, 1938, Vol. XXVIII, pages 41-54; and Backman, Jules, "Price Inflexibility and Changes in Production," *The American Economic Review*, Sept., 1939, Vol. XXIX, pages 480-486.

these market and administrative controls could be developed in such a way that national economic policies would "rely on the initiative of individual enterprises to carry the main responsibility for actual productive activity," and "if at the same time the new policies introduced were completely consistent with the country's democratic traditions, it seems highly probable that the final outcome of the whole policy controversy would be resolved in favor of such a system of policies." [45]

Means is fully aware that the acceptance of the existing short-run insensitivity of prices, wages, and interest rates as a necessary feature of the modern economy and the establishment of national economic policies consistent with this view of the economic system would require a new view of the relations between government and business.   Like Rexford G. Tugwell, Means believes that a fourth function of government in addition to the legislative, executive, and judicial functions should be recognized.   This fourth function would involve assuming the positive responsibility for giving direction to the economic activities of the nation so as to insure the realization of a high standard of living for the community.   This new responsibility of the government could find expression only through the adoption of some general economic plan which would be a substitute for the coordination once automatically provided by the competitive system.   The general goals of such a national economic plan are broken down by Means into three subsidiary goals.   There is, first, the goal of a full use of economic resources. If this goal could be reached, there would be no unemployment except that caused by seasonal factors and by temporary frictions involved in movement from one activity to another.   Any further effort to use labor or machinery for the purpose of increasing national income would not be worth the sacrifices and costs involved in such an endeavor.   Full use or employment, however, could be achieved even though natural resources were being wasted, or even though land, labor, and capital were not being combined as efficiently as possible.   Since a full use of our resources does not necessarily mean that they are being used in a balanced manner, a balanced use would be the second goal of a national economic planning program.   This end "would be met if resources were flowing into different channels of use in such proportions that the real national

[45] *The Structure of the American Economy*, Part II, page 16.

income could not have been raised through a shift of any *currently used* resources or group of resources from one use to another use." [46] If the real national income could be increased by shifting workers from cotton mills to rayon mills, then there would be an unbalanced condition with respect to the use of resources in these two industries. This balanced use has no direct relation to full use, since it is possible to have an economic system in balance which is operating at only a small per cent of its capacity. Since it is possible to have full employment with a lack of balance, or to have an approximation to complete balance without full employment of labor and machinery, what is necessary is both a full and a balanced use of men and machines.

The third subsidiary goal of a national planning program would be an efficient use of economic resources, which would be achieved when the minimum amount of resources was being consumed to get a given national income. There would be no further problem of moving labor or capital from one industry to another, but, given a certain amount of these resources in an industry, there would be the problem of using them as efficiently as possible. When this third goal was achieved, the larger goal of an "optimum use" of resources would be the final result. This optimum use of resources would be attained when "there would be no unemployment of men or machines. . . . The resources going into different uses would be in balance with each other and in relation to consumers' wants . . . and, finally, in doing any particular job, the minimum amount of resources would be used or consumed consistent with the job to be done." [47]

Among the three goals making up the "basic goal of optimum use" one is of special significance, namely, the goal of full employment of resources. The other two aims can usually be achieved by adopting some local or piecemeal policy. The problem of the efficient use of resources, for example, can be worked out by the factory manager. Of course, there are some problems of efficiency, such as the retardation of technological progress through the control of patents, which are of more than local significance, and which require for their proper solution some broader treatment than that provided by a factory manager. But even in relation

[46] *Ibid.*, page 5.
[47] *Ibid.*, page 4.

to these problems the national economy "as a single working whole" is not involved. The same is true of the problem of the balanced use of resources except in connection with such broad matters as the balance between industry and agriculture, or between various economic regions. For the problem of full employment, however, no such limited treatment is useful. It is Means's general conclusion that "It is primarily the problem of full employment which requires a system of policies developed in terms of the working of the national economy as a whole. In dealing with this latter problem the full gamut of economic institutions must be envisaged: money and banking, budget and taxation policies; goods prices, wage rates . . . consumer incomes . . . corporation finance and dividend policies. No amount of piecemeal adjustment, on the basis of piecemeal policies is likely to insure reasonably full employment. . . . Insuring reasonably full employment is thus the Nation's most basic economic problem." [48]

In the long run Means hopes to establish through national economic planning a general economic equilibrium very similar to the kind which Alfred Marshall regarded as the end-product of a smoothly functioning competitive economy. There is no disagreement between Marshall and Means with respect to their general economic goals; disagreement relates only to the ways in which such goals are to be achieved. In the purely competitive economy envisioned by Marshall there could be no overbuilt industries, no expansion of corporate enterprises merely to take business away from existing firms, and no "booming and sagging" of economic activity. Instead, the economic system would always be on an even keel, and even in the face of technological change there would be a progressive increase in efficiency without very serious wastes in the form of unemployed labor and unutilized capital. In Marshall's

[48] *The Structure of the American Economy*, Part II, pages 5-6. This line of reasoning is in agreement with the views of many of the economists who testified before the Temporary National Economic Committee. Isador Lubin explained in his testimony before the Committee that "If I might tie up that question with a general conclusion of what I am trying to bring out, I would say this: The problem that we must face is one of economic security, and by economic security I don't mean only for workers; we must have it for the investor and the farmer. I think that is the first problem we must face. . . . To get this economic security . . . we must have more and more production." See the *Hearings Before the Temporary National Economic Committee*, Dec. 1-3, 1938, Part I, "Economic Prologue," page 78.

view partial equilibrium would eventually flower into general equilibrium; but where his competitive equilibrium was automatic, and from the social point of view, unintentional or undesigned, Means's managed or planned equilibrium is volitional or optional. It is a matter of collective choice to be decided as a result of the deliberations of the entire community. There are no inherent principles or tendencies in the modern economic system that seek their full expression in some form of a planned economic equilibrium; a planned economic society, if it comes about, will do so only because organized social intelligence has translated human thought into action. We do not find in Means's economic analysis anything comparable to Marshall's theory of automaticity. Marshall's great regulatory forces, "the general relations of supply and demand," functioned independently of the human will; they were socially uncontrolled forces which were the spontaneous creations of a competitive system. In Marshall's view, although the forces of supply and demand were not directed by organized social intelligence, they nevertheless operated in the best interests of the community. With such views Means has nothing in common, because his theories are based on the observation that the competitive system has been seriously crippled by the structural changes of the past sixty years. As a result of these developments organized social intelligence is now called upon to take over that part of the regulatory functions having to do with the insuring of full employment, which were formerly exercised by the general relations of supply and demand.

General economic planning is itself a means and not an end, since it is but one phase of social planning the general aim of which is the maximization of human welfare. If an effective use of our economic resources cannot be achieved through a form of national economic planning that does not disturb the basic liberties of the individual, then Means is quite willing to place human freedom above the goal of an enlarged economic output. "The economic goal of reasonably full, balanced, and efficient use of our resources," he explains, "is in turn only one element in the larger goal of national welfare. Greater effectiveness in the use of resources is not an end in itself but is justified by its contribution to welfare. If welfare were to suffer through impairment of democratic institutions, greater economic effectiveness in the use of resources would

be bought at too great cost." [49]   Economic planning should therefore be adjusted to the requirements of a broader social planning.
It is necessary for the economist to be aware of the influence of the
whole complex of social institutions upon the problem of the effective use of economic resources as well as of the influence of the effective use of resources upon the social system itself.   For this reason Means argues that national economic planning is "a problem
of social organization."

There are many matters which are to be solved with reference
more to social policy than to the dictates of the market place.
Whether one resource will be used in place of another, whether
electric power will be used instead of coal, depends very largely on
the decision as to whether or not we wish to conserve our coal supplies.   There is always the question of deciding between the present
use of natural resources and their conservation for future generations.   Tied up with this matter of preserving our resources is the
further question of discovering at what point the working population would prefer leisure to a larger income from additional
employment.   Likewise, the question of income distribution is basically a social and political question.   Decisions about the distribution of income to be aimed at will have important effects upon
economic activity, because a reduction in the present income inequalities would turn production away from luxury goods toward
the "basic necessities for a high level of living for the masses."
Closely associated with the questions of how to preserve our natural
resources and what type of income distribution should be our goal
is the further question of how far we wish to go in closing the gap
between the existing economic system and an ideal one.   This
larger question becomes a problem of deciding how far we wish to
go in eliminating a wasteful and uneconomic use of natural resources and labor; in addition, we would have to decide how far
we wish to go in eliminating the cyclical fluctuations in the use of
labor and capital.   From the secular point of view there would be

[49] This general point of view is reflected in the work of the National Resources
Committee. "Planning is not only a useful tool of democracy, especially in dealing with modern complex social and economic conditions, but planning by a democracy must also be democratic. It must flow 'from the bottom up,' from the
roots of national life to coordinated public policy." See the *Progress Report*
of the National Resources Committee, 1938, page 1.

the problem of applying the law of comparative advantage to the entire nation so that the distribution of labor and capital would be in conformity with a policy of optimum national production.

National economic planning is basically a matter of the use and distribution of economic controls. Every interest or organized group in the nation is a potential source of control; interests and controls go together because no interest can function satisfactorily without adequate controls. The economic developments of the past seventy-five years have divorced interests from the controls which they formerly possessed, and have created new controls which do not operate to the advantage of all interests. The shift from competitive to administrative enterprise has deprived the stockholder of control over his property, the laborer of control over his work, and the consumer of control over the productive processes; and, furthermore, the small businessman has been pushed into the marginal and submarginal areas of an economy no longer predominantly competitive. The concentration of controls introduced by large-scale, administrative enterprise "leaves the security holders, the workers, and the consumers the forgotten men—with great and basic interests in industrial activity but with minimum controls over it. Controls without interests lead to irresponsible actions; interests without controls lead to social frustration.[50] The prime requirement of today is a new pattern of economic behavior which would have as its goal a reattachment of controls to the various interested parties such as consumers, workers, and small security holders. In developing such a pattern Means would be guided by the principle of securing the maximum decentralization of control consonant with a smooth functioning of the economy. As far as possible the bulk of the threads of control would be left in the hands of individuals or corporate enterprises. In some cases control would be carried up to intermediate bodies such as code authorities, while in other cases the threads of control might extend to the central seat of control in the government. What is to be avoided at any cost is a top-heavy, bureaucratic control structure which would lead to an overdeveloped centralization of control.

---

[50] "The Distribution of Control and Responsibility in a Modern Economy," page 67. See also Means, Gardiner C., "The Location of Economic Control of American Industry," *The American Economic Review*, March, 1939, Vol. XXIX, Supp., pages 110-115.

Wherever centralization of control is found to be necessary, those placed in control should at all times be responsible to the parties at interest. As Means puts it, the new economy should be so organized that ultimate interest and ultimate control go hand in hand.

The future economy that Means has in mind is a "regulated capitalism" which, although it retains some of the features of laissez-faire capitalism, is essentially a new pattern of economic life. It is an economy based upon neither private ownership as conceived in the nineteenth century nor upon government ownership as envisioned by the socialists. "For America, the immediate problem," says Means, "is to seek out a pattern or organization which is neither capitalism in the complete *laissez-faire* sense nor socialism in the sense of complete state ownership of the instruments of production. There are many who despair of any such intermediate ground and insist that it is necessary to choose between private property and government property." [51] In Means's opinion no such choice is imperative. Cultural evolution is not a matter of jumping from an old cultural situation to an entirely new one; instead cultural epochs merge into one another, and patterns of economic life only gradually take on new contours. Those who advocate a retention of the *status quo* are unaware of the fundamental changes affecting ownership of the instruments of production which have already taken place, while those who advocate the acceptance of an entirely new pattern of economic organization are unaware of the merits of other solutions. Means's intermediateness stems from his philosophy of gradualism, which is ever on guard against wishful thinking or doctrinaire suggestions about the reconstruction of economic society. His pragmatic attitude toward economic problems leads him to be suspicious of grandiose schemes for the reorientation of economic life, and keeps his "economics of control" very close to the hard and fast facts of everyday experience.

Means's National Planning Program

Means has not as yet worked out the details of a national economic planning program. It is quite in line with the general tenor of his economic thinking that he should refrain from attempting to fill in the details of a planning program until he has made a thorough analysis of the existing situation. His work as an economist

[51] *Ibid.*, pages 63-64.

for the National Resources Planning Board was devoted primarily to providing a broad study of the ·modern economy in action. Whenever he has shifted from the immediate task of gathering and analyzing statistical and other economic material, he has taken time out to consider strategic points in the economy at which planning efforts might be applied.[52]   Unlike Mordecai Ezekiel, who has also been a member of the industrial section of the National Resources Planning Board, Means has presented no comprehensive plan for the control of economic activity.   In *The Modern Economy in Action* are found some suggestions relating to the setting up of industrial code authorities for the fixing of price schedules and production quotas.[53]   There are also suggestions concerning the need to regulate the flow of capital into various industries, and to discriminate between efficient and inefficient firms.   Means believes that "One of the chief functions of general planning would be to direct new capital into industries and places where it was needed."[54]   He also agrees with Ezekiel that a general planning program should cover as few industries as possible.   Means's planning may be described as "strategic" because applications of the planning technique at a few strategic points are held to be sufficient to eliminate the major causes of the underutilization of men and machines.

The kind of general economic planning that intrigues Means "would be a continual process of formulation and reformulation. No absolute or static plan could be laid down for a dynamic industrial society.   Rather a developing pattern, as dynamic as the society itself, would be the only effective guide to a modern economy."[55]   There is nothing utopian about Means's planning proposals; he is well aware that general economic planning would be a difficult, complicated task.   Like those who were associated with him in his work for the National Resources Planning Board, Means wishes to avoid not only the evils of a planless economic anarchy but also the evils that would go with an over-regimented totalitarian state.   He

---

[52] *Final Report,* published by the National Planning Board in 1934, page 31.
[53] *The Modern Economy in Action,* pages 148-150.   Means is not unaware of the many difficulties that might arise in connection with attempts to set quotas for industrial products or to dispose of unsold supplies of these products.   He realizes that planning industrial production would be much more complicated than planning the production of homogeneous agricultural products.
[54] *Ibid.,* page 207.
[55] *Ibid.,* page 208.

is interested in "a kind of planning which is a peculiarly American custom, based on an enthusiastic belief in the ability of a democracy to utilize intelligence." [56]   What is now necessary is to develop the kind of economic statesmanship which will focus society's intelligence upon the basic problem of providing for an effective use of our resources.   The social frustration which has resulted from the public's growing awareness of the discrepancy between the potential and actual outputs of the modern economy makes the problem of finding some such workable national plan a very urgent one.   Too long a denial of satisfaction to the "instinct of workmanship," which rebels against a situation in which there is an inadequate "satisfaction of useful activity," may very well lead to a search for undemocratic solutions.   In a society where there is no effective use of natural resources and human skills men lose their self-reliance and soon dwindle in stature.   General economic planning is therefore more than a matter of raising the standard of living; it is also a matter of preserving human dignity in a situation where the swift currents of technological change are rapidly dissolving the foundations of the old laissez-faire economy.

Means's faith in economic planning as the way out of our widespread economic troubles is bolstered by the fact that planning is not entirely new to the United States.   Unheralded and almost unnoticed, there has been a movement on foot to inject more and more planning into American economic affairs ever since large-scale corporate enterprise became an important factor in the economic life of the nation.   For a number of years planning has been going on on three different fronts.   Large corporate enterprises have been perfecting a form of business planning in which all efforts are directed toward the primary goal of maximizing business profits. Since 1900 there has been a vigorous trend toward planning the use of our natural resources so that they might be conserved for future generations.   Also, much attention has been directed toward regional planning.   Cities and states have felt the need to build a wall around the private business system in order to prevent commercial standards from dominating the architecture of our towns

[56] *Progress Report*, National Resources Committee, 1937, page 2. For a discussion of the activities of the National Resources Committee see Gruchy, Allan G., "The Economics of the National Resources Committee," *The American Economic Review*, March, 1938, Vol. XXIX, pages 60-73.

and destroying the natural playgrounds of the people. These types of partial planning have been quite fruitful in their own limited way, but they have not been sufficient to solve the problem of unemployment. Partial planning has been useful as a means of introducing the American public to the idea of economic planning; in addition, it has guaranteed that any move to adopt general economic planning would not be a complete break with past economic experience.

The need of the present is an expansion of business, conservation, and regional planning into some form of national economic planning. This need does not arise only because general planning would be more useful in the attainment of our major economic and social aims; it also arises because there is a positive danger inherent in the various forms of partial planning. Taking a cue from Wesley C. Mitchell's analysis of business planning, Means observes that "In fact, it is the very extent of partial planning in America today which makes general planning appear to be necessary. Partial planning carried on without reference to an interrelated whole, is likely to make matters worse rather than better. When the corporation extended planning into areas which were formerly competitive it thereby destroyed the capacity of the economy to adjust itself, while at the same time increasing the need for adjustments. Business planning leads, as we have seen, to business decisions contrary to the interests of the economy as a whole. The rigidities introduced by partial planning have been major factors in making the economy break down." [57] This partial planning elevates a particular firm, industry, or region above the other factors comprising the economy, and the inevitable consequences are "a distortion of economic relationships" and a failure to plan the parts in relation to the whole.

The first step in the establishment of a general economic plan would be to develop production-consumption patterns which would show the major productive resources and the major consumption requirements of the nation. Some work has already been done along these lines by the National Resources Planning Board.[58] A

---

[57] *The Modern Economy in Action*, page 198.

[58] Studies conducted by various committees of the Board have been summarized in such monographs as *Technological Trends and National Policy* (June, 1937), *Patterns of Resource Use* (February, 1938), *Population* (May, 1938), *Con-*

great deal of information has been compiled with relation to existing resources, the industrial capacity on hand to convert these resources into goods, and the consumption requirements of the country. When a thorough understanding of the structural and functional aspects of the modern economy has been arrived at, it will then be possible to create a number of general economic plans. This will be true because there will be available production-consumption patterns showing the economy as it now is, as it would be under ideal conditions, and as it would be at any point between the actual and the ideal. These patterns will serve as guides by the aid of which various economic policies can be united in a general program to realize the goals for which society is planning.

Means is not impressed with the progress of recent economic planning in the United States. Especially unfortunate was our experience with industrial planning under the National Recovery Administration. Whatever may have been the general aim of this planning, the actual result was a planned scarcity rather than a planned abundance. No satisfactory cost-price relations were preserved, with the unfortunate consequence that prices increased much faster than costs. This cost-price disparity opened the door to an undue emphasis upon the maximization of profits at the expense of a planned abundance. Nor has agricultural planning proved to be much more satisfactory than industrial planning. Confronted with a lack of planning in the industrial segments of the economy, farming interests have endeavored to raise the prices for agricultural products by restricting output. In general, recovery efforts from 1933 to 1935 were heavily weighted in the direction of a stabilization of low production; what was particularly lacking in the early New Deal efforts to make a plan for the economy was a consideration of consumer welfare. A Consumers' Advisory Board was set up in the National Recovery Administration, but its establishment was little more than a gesture in recognition of the consumer. Means asserts that we must place a greater reliance on the consumer interest in the future, if we are to overcome the deficiencies in national economic planning revealed by experience with the planning movement since 1933.

sumer Incomes in the United States (August, 1938), Consumer Expenditures in the United States (November, 1939), The Structure of the American Economy, Part I, "Basic Characteristics" (June, 1939), and Capital Requirements, A Study in Methods as Applied to the Iron and Steel Industry (1940).

Only a strong consumer interest can in the long run overcome a scarcity economy and a possible "stabilization of the depression."

In any program for national economic planning a balance must be struck between the consumer and producer viewpoints. With an emphasis reminiscent of Veblen's general viewpoint, Means asserts that "Only as it is constantly kept in mind that the basic function of the economic process is the getting of goods and services to people, and the producing of values is only an incidental technique for accomplishing this end, will the necessary balance in administration be obtained." [59] In the creation of this balance between many interested groups the consumer has an important role. The mistake must not be made, however, of assuming that the government is a special protector of the consumer interest. The government reflects the pressure of all interests and usually acts in an intermediary manner in its relations with conflicting groups. It is necessary for consumers to stand on their own feet in the effort to work out economic justice for all important interests in a planned economy. Means does not recommend the organizing of consumers as such but rather the pooling of consumer interests drawn from women's organizations, farm groups, and labor unions. The government can do much to stimulate consumer leadership through such organizations as the Consumers' Counsel of the Agricultural Adjustment Administration, but it should not attempt to develop a consumer movement separate from other economic interests. The consumer interest should work from the bottom up; it should be a spontaneous reaction to economic difficulties on the part of the general public.

There is a further reason why Means's national economic planning program would be greatly concerned with the consumer. The bulk of consumer wants are related to such fundamental, easily standardized needs as food, clothing, and shelter. Means estimates that in 1935 sixty-five per cent of consumer expenditures were for these basic necessities.[60] It would be the first task of a national economic planning program to meet these elementary demands. Since these needs can be met with standardized products produced by large-scale corporate enterprises, it would be much easier to plan for an expansion of their production than for an increase in the

[59] "The Consumer and the New Deal," page 14.
[60] *The Structure of the American Economy,* Part I, page 21.

output of luxury goods. If we could provide for these basic needs through a planning program, a sound basis for a reconstructed society would be made available. Furthermore, experience gained in planning the production of staple commodities would later prove helpful in the more difficult task of planning the production of goods other than necessities.

In view of the fact that economic planning is but one aspect of general social planning, Means advocates more cooperation between social scientists. Economists, sociologists, jurists, and political scientists all have an interest in the reconstruction of society. Their knowledge, understanding, and experience should prove valuable in the work of planning a more suitable foundation for a democratic community. Means would agree with Wesley C. Mitchell when the latter says that "The economist who participates in planning policies finds that he must consider factors that are not commonly regarded as strictly economic. . . . The conclusion now drawn quite as frequently is that an economist should associate himself with men who can supply his deficiencies—engineers, accountants, business executives, lawyers, psychologists, and an indefinite list of other specialists. . . . While the need for a combined attack upon social problems may be clearest in practical affairs, it is dawning upon us that the several social sciences must cooperate all along the line." [61] Especially close should be the cooperation between economists and political scientists, because economics and politics are once more being drawn together to create a new, twentieth-century political economy.[62] Means sees a need to combine the two scientific disciplines because action by the state is once more becoming a very important factor in the economic life of society. Since political science is so much concerned with "problems of social associations and administrative organization," it has a great deal to offer which will aid the economist in working out a new political economy.

Associated with the new version of political economy would be a new theory of the relations between government and business. The economic changes of the past seventy-five years have very greatly

[61] Mitchell, Wesley C., "Economics, 1904-1929," *The Backward Art of Spending Money and Other Essays*, 1937, page 402.

[62] "The Distribution of Control and Responsibility in a Modern Economy," page 59.

weakened the old "government-out-of-business" tradition, and have forced the government to assume a more positive responsibility for directing the economic activity of the nation. The functions that a modern government is now called upon to perform are what Means calls "the genuinely impartial and the genuinely representative" functions. The impartial function relates to the gathering of information and the carrying on of technical research, while the representative function involves giving representation to all important interest groups in the community. The development of the modern economy has been accompanied by the appearance of many powerful economic interests. A government which is organized on the basis of an assumed "free and fluid economic situation" fails to take cognizance of the presence of these powerful interest groups. These groups have warped the nineteenth-century conception of political democracy, and have substituted a government which in theory represents "all the people" but which in fact is primarily responsive to the demands of various minority pressure groups.

What is now required is that we recognize that the disappearance of the laissez-faire economy requires a change in our conception of the nature of government. Fact and theory should be brought more closely together, and the extent to which a government representing "all the people" has been converted into one representing various interest groups should be acknowledged. Instead of trying to make government more representative of the "public interest," Means believes that we should accept the trend toward a government representing special interests. He approaches the position of political pluralists like Harold J. Laski and G. D. H. Cole, who advocate a system of group or "functional" representation to take the place of the present system of geographical representation.[63] The current form of government in the United States is "a dual system of representation, geographical in the legislative branch, functional in the administrative units." Since the various governmental departments have come to represent special economic interests more than the general public, their role in a governmental system which in theory represents "all the people" is not clearly defined. Without definite instructions to promote the welfare of special interests, governmental departments can follow no clear-cut policy. In order

---

[63] For a discussion of this proposal see Carpenter, William S., *Democracy and Representation*, pages 85-88. Princeton: Princeton University Press, 1925.

to remedy this situation, Means advocates the frank recognition of the presence of organized interest groups and the setting up of formal arrangements which would give adequate representation to all important interests.   Some interests, such as the consumers, are now poorly organized and have little representation in either the legislative or administrative branches of government.   What is necessary is that satisfactory channels be made through which all interests may express themselves.   When all interests are organized and given an opportunity to express themselves, there will then be the problem of creating an "even-handed balance" of interests.

Means's functional representation is a form of political centralism which, if carried too far, would be contrary to the anti-centralization sentiments of the American people.   To meet the demands of American habits of thinking which stress the importance of states and localities, Means's concept of political democracy "calls for taking over those functions, and only those, which are necessary to meet the problem, leaving the remaining functions untouched. While there is room for wide differences of opinion as to what the 'necessary' functions are, the essential method of only taking on the functions which the central agency should ultimately keep remains appropriate to the American system of government." [64]   No final statement of the role of the government in a modern economy is possible.   How far the government should go in adding to its functions is a question which only the future can answer.   It is certain, however, that the structure and functions of the government in a modern economy must be in conformity with the requirements of modern industrialism, and that the production relations of the modern industrial system require "a re-analysis and reconstruction of democracy on the basis of the new economy," if we are to avoid undemocratic attempts to solve our major economic problems.

The Nature and Scope of Administrative Economics

The kind of economics which Means is seeking to develop offers many striking contrasts to what he labels "traditional economics." The economics of the latter part of the nineteenth century was primarily concerned with an understanding of how economic activity is organized through the operations of a free competitive market. The nineteenth-century economist was aware of the fact that a part

[64] *The Modern Economy in Action*, page 220.

of economic life was organized through administrative activity, but he made little place for such activity in the general framework of his science. Means acknowledges that there was no particular harm in ignoring administrative activity in the early decades of the last century when economic enterprise was predominantly small-scale and competitive. But with the changes of the past half-century it is no longer possible to ignore the extent to which economic life is organized through administrative activity. Means believes that the refusal of traditional economists to shift the center of their attention from market to administrative control of economic activity isolates them from the major trends of the modern economy. The result has been that these economists have spent much of their time analyzing an area of economic enterprise which is constantly growing smaller. Pursuing this policy of regarding large-scale business enterprises as "special cases," orthodox economists have found themselves forced to abstract from the actual data of economic experience to an extent which threatens to make their science excessively unrealistic.[65]

In Means's economic analysis it is recognized that the older competitive way of organizing economic life has flowered into a variety of ways of carrying on business. In the pluralistic economy of the twentieth century, economic activity may take the form of small-scale competitive, monopolistic competitive, oligopolistic, or monopolistic enterprise. Alfred Marshall's economic norm of the "representative firm" is still applicable, in some measure, to that segment of our hybrid economy which is a remnant of the competitive order of the last century. But for the monopolistic portions of the modern economy Means finds it necessary to replace the Marshallian norm with a new economic norm in the form of the large-scale, corporate enterprise. It is this latter type of firm which sets the pace for the twentieth-century business system, and which also determines its general rules of conduct. In setting up a new corporate norm as the center of gravity of his economic analysis, Means has no intention of discarding the neo-classicist's competitive norm as a heuristic device for the interpretation of the modern business system. He is well aware that the economic theory revolving around the concept of the representative firm will always be of value to the

[65] "The Distribution of Control and Responsibility in a Modern Economy," page 60.

economic investigator, especially for the interpretation of that portion of the economy which is still organized on a highly competitive basis. Means's economic analysis is to be added to the competitive analysis of the earlier economists. It is designed to provide an interpretation of that segment of the economic order which deviates from competitive standards of behavior, and which is becoming increasingly important as time goes by. Means's economics is more than supplemental to the work of the nineteenth-century economists, because it has its own special orientation and a much broader scope than that of orthodox economics.

Means's concept of a corporate norm is much less precise than the neo-classicists' concept of the normal firm. One may ask whether his corporate norm can be usefully applied in contemporary economic analysis. The difficulty appears to lie not in Means's own handling of the concept of a corporate norm, but rather in the fact that the nature of modern large-scale corporate enterprise does not permit an easy development and application of the idea of a corporate norm. Each major industry has its unique characteristics, its special business customs, and its own methods of meeting its pricing and production problems. It is not surprising, therefore, "that a simple pattern does not present an inviting approach. As the world is not all black and white, so industry cannot be set down in terms of an antithesis between competition and monopoly. It holds far too much of detail and drama, of color and variety, to be crowded into a few simple molds. To set up a norm of 'perfect competition,' and to attempt to discover the principles that shape its imperfections, is as unpromising as a quest for the norms of abnormality. . . . Many of our most important industries . . . carry the marks of a half-planned growth in their structures, all have evolved their own distinctive usages. As creatures of society, these arrangements have divergent and changing patterns, and leave their distinctive marks upon the industrial activities which they govern." [66] In his economic analysis and suggestions for economic reconstruction Means constantly calls attention to the need to treat each industry as a special case. The day of easy generalizations, created to provide simple interpretations of our economic problems, is over now that the uniform, monistic world pictured in the com-

[66] Hamilton, Walton H., and others, *Price and Price Policies*, pages 22-23. New York: McGraw-Hill Book Company, Inc., 1938.

petitive economics of the neo-classicists has been transformed into a highly complex, pluralistic world.

If it were true that the modern economy contains so much diversity and uniqueness that each industry is a "special case" and nothing more, then economic science would be reduced to mere description. This is not the case, however, because there is enough of a uniform, repetitive character in the operations of large-scale corporate enterprises to provide a basis for many important economic generalizations and also to make the concept of a corporate norm very useful. If Means's scientific generalizations appear to be highly tentative, it is only because the changing economic world about which he is generalizing is similarly tentative. As it is always his aim to keep close to economic reality, he is unwilling to deprive his generalizations of their indefiniteness and tentativeness merely for the sake of greater abstraction and more theoretical refinement. He is unwilling to sacrifice economic reality on the high altar of theoretical refinement, since he takes it to be the primary duty of economists to grapple with reality rather than to enjoy the refinement of theory *in vacuo*.

In developing a new business norm for the monopolistic portions of the modern hybrid economy, Means has found it necessary to create a new set of basic assumptions to replace those that were applicable only to the small-scale, nineteenth-century competitive economy. He explains that the basic assumption out of which Marshall's economics of the representative firm was developed was the assumption of the existence of a "trading market." [67] In this type of market price is the outgrowth of trading between large numbers of sellers and buyers, and supply is equated to demand with the aid of highly flexible prices. Means substitutes for the nineteenth-century assumption of a trading market his new assumption of an administered market in which price is an outgrowth of administration rather than of competitive trading. He explains that "Earlier economists have abstracted from flexible prices and shown how an economy in which all prices were perfectly flexible would work. No one that I know of has assumed a high degree of inflexibility in prices

---

[67] Means, Gardiner C., "The Corporate Revolution," *Summaries of Theses Accepted in Partial Fulfillment of the Requirements for the Degree of Doctor of Philosophy, 1933*, page 251. Cambridge: Harvard University Press, 1934.

and shown how such an economy would work." [68]   When economists adopt the assumption of a market in which prices are highly inflexible, conclusions quite at variance with those of the neo-classical economists necessarily follow.

The traditional assumption of the determinateness of costs has also been found by Means to be unsatisfactory for an analysis of the non-competitive sections of the heterogeneous, twentieth-century economy.   In Marshallian economics the costs of the representative firm were taken to be largely of a determinate, variable nature.   Indeterminate, overhead costs played a very minor role, since the small-scale, competitive economy required very limited investment in industrial overhead.   But the cost conditions of business enterprise have changed very greatly in the past half-century because of the heavy investment in fixed capital; and, as a consequence, the assumption of indeterminateness of cost has come to have much more validity than that of determinateness of cost.   The large indeterminate costs of modern business have been one of the most significant factors leading to the deterioration of the older trading market and its replacement by the administered market.

The third assumption of conventional economics which Means finds it necessary to alter is the assumption of the unity of the process of saving and investing.   In the economy of the "representative firm" the saver was also assumed to be an investor who managed the industrial wealth into which his savings were poured.   In his analysis Means takes the process of saving to be a dual process in which the ownership of corporate capital and its actual control or management are separated.   He develops his interpretation of the modern process of saving on the assumptions that there are two independent groups of individuals concerned with the saving process, and that there are two separate markets, one for capital goods and one for claims to capital goods.   Where economic analysis proceeds on the assumption that the saver has little or no control over the flow of real savings, many of the conclusions of the orthodox, nineteenth-century economists are no longer admissible.

The fourth major assumption of nineteenth-century economics which has little validity in an economy dominated by Means's new

[68] Means, Gardiner C., "Business Combinations and Agriculture," *The Journal of Farm Economics,* Feb., 1938, Vol. XX, page 56.

corporate norm is the assumption that the profit motive can be relied upon to organize economic activity efficiently. Where the norm of business enterprise is the small-scale, competitive firm, profits are assumed to be effective in bringing about an efficient organization of economic activity. But this is not found by Means to be true in those areas of the economy where the large-scale, corporate enterprise is the norm of economic activity. He points out that corporation profits which go to stockholders do not necessarily give rise to the efficient management of corporate enterprises. In the corporate economy of today profits tend to have only the role of inducing the taking of risk by stockholders; efficient management, if it is achieved, is a result of corporate control and not of corporate ownership.

In developing new assumptions for his "administrative economics" Means has not thoroughly revised all the basic postulates of received economic theory. He has very little to say, for example, about the psychological assumptions that would be appropriate to an economy in which the collective action of corporate enterprise is superseding the individual action of small-scale competitive enterprise. Unlike Veblen, Mitchell, Commons, and J. M. Clark, Means has not written much about a theory of human nature which would be helpful in explaining twentieth-century economic behavior. There are indications throughout his writings that he is not satisfied with the psychological postulates of inherited economic theory, but he has done little to work out an interpretation of human behavior that would be appropriate to an economy in which collective action has in many ways come to control individual action. This failure to inquire in a comprehensive way into the psychological basis of modern economic life may be explained in part by calling attention to the fact that Means, like many other exponents of economic heterodoxy, has been more concerned with special economic problems than with a systematic revamping of orthodox economic theory. His criticisms of orthodox economics have been more a by-product of original research into pressing economic problems than the main concern of an economist primarily interested in the reconstruction of economic science. For this reason Means's economic thought is far from being well rounded.

Besides introducing a new business norm and a set of basic postulates applicable to that norm, Means enlarges the scope of economics beyond the limits fixed by traditional economists. The *point d'ap-pui* of Means's administrative economics is not the businessman at his task of combining the various productive agents in the most efficient manner, but instead it is the community or nation at its work of disposing of scarce economic means in accordance with existing individual and communal goals or ends. The center of analytical interest has thus been shifted by Means from the operations of the individual proprietorship to the functioning of the entire economic system as a going concern. "In order to be effective, an analysis of the economic structure," Means explains, "must treat the American economy as an integral whole—as a going concern. To treat only certain activities is to lose the essential unity of all the separate and interrelated activities which make up the whole." [69] Like Isador Lubin and Leon Henderson, who were associated with him on the Industrial Committee of the National Resources Planning Board, Means is vitally interested in the performance of the entire economic system as measured in terms of its ability to meet the economic needs of the total population. The American economy is a "vast and complex organic growth" composed of many industries each of which is likewise an organic growth.[70] It is a mixed economy in which the various subsidiary processes fail to work together in an harmonious way, with the result that a satisfactory over-all co-ordination is lacking. In order to understand the failure of the hybrid economy to operate with a full, balanced, and efficient use of economic resources, it is necessary to broaden the scope of economic analysis, and to inquire into the various factors which bring about whatever coordination in economic activity there actually is. Some light may then be thrown upon the causes for the failure of the modern economy to enjoy a more adequate over-all coordination.

Although Means has not discussed at any length his views relating to the scope of economics, he has very clearly indicated that no study of modern capitalism can be complete without a thorough understanding of the relations between law and economics. Since the growth of corporate enterprise has been very closely related to

[69] *The Structure of the American Economy*, Part I, page 4.

[70] For an introduction to the economic views of Isador Lubin and Leon Henderson see their testimony presented to the Temporary National Economic Committee, *Hearings Before the Temporary National Economic Committee*, Part I, pages 3-80 and 157-183.

the development of the legal system governing business activity, it is not surprising that Means should display a deep interest in the influence of the legal system upon the organization of economic affairs. He points out that "Studies have been made of the way laws came into being, the way government institutions develop, and the way individuals holding political positions acquire those positions or are displaced, but relatively little attention has been given to the organizing influence which laws have on economic activity. Until more extensive analyses have been made, it is not possible to indicate clearly the role played by canalizing rules. Yet such work as has already been done indicates clearly that laws, rules, and customs do play a major role in making the separate activities of millions of individuals mesh into the organized activity of the American economy." [71] Means looks upon John R. Commons's *Legal Foundations of Capitalism*, James C. Bonbright's *Valuation of Property*, and his own and Adolf A. Berle's *The Modern Corporation and Private Property* as significant efforts to broaden the scope of economics by inquiring into the legal basis of economic activity. How far the scope of economics is to be extended in this direction is a matter that can only be determined pragmatically by the needs of economic research. Means accepts the view that whatever renders economic interpretation more adequate should find a place within the new framework of economic analysis.

Means would enlarge the scope of economics to include more than the economic aspects of the "laws, rules, and customs" which constitute the legal framework of the modern economy. He would also examine communal or national goals as factors influencing the organization of economic life. In its broadest aspects economics is taken by Means to be a study of "the organization of the use of resources" in the light of the accepted goals of the community which help to bring about a meshing of the activities of many millions of people. He explains that "When two or more people agree to accomplish a certain objective it is often possible for their action to be coordinate simply because each one acts in terms of the logic implicit in the accepted goal. . . . In the complex life of every day, reliance is constantly being placed on the logic of accepted goals to guide individuals so that their separate activities fit together. . . . In situation after situation which could be analyzed,

[71] *The Structure of the American Economy*, Part I, page 121.

organization [of economic activity] is to a significant extent the result of the acceptance of some explicitly recognized goal though in more complex situations its influence is usually combined with that of the market mechanism, administration, and canalizing rules, the different influences in combination producing the organized result." [72]

How nations create their economic and social goals, and how they arrange them according to some scheme of communal valuation are still matters hardly touched upon by scientific investigation.   Means bemoans the fact that "so little study has been given to the part of the organizing influence of accepted goals in economic matters that it is not possible to set forth their role in the organizational structure of the whole economy.   It is well recognized that in times of war the national unity growing out of the widespread acceptance of the single war objective does act as an organizing influence.   In peace times there may be similar though less clearly discernible results growing out of the acceptance of national goals.   Until analyses along this line have been developed, the role of accepted goals which is so important to the organization of activity in lesser spheres cannot be set forth as it affects the organizational structure of the whole economy."   But, whether national goals merely reflect the heavy pressure of passing events or are the result of the application of organized social intelligence, they still remain potent forces which influence the general cultural drift and the existing level of economic activity.   If the economist is to grasp economic reality in the large, he must widen the scope of his investigations to include an analysis of the many ways in which accepted communal goals determine the use of scarce economic resources.

In the final analysis economic goals need to be fitted into a communal scheme of values which recognizes that food, clothing, shelter, and other economic desiderata are but means to larger social ends.   Of special importance in handling this problem will be the joint efforts of economists and political scientists.   The maintenance of democracy "is a problem so broad in its scope and so basic in its character that no simple solution is likely to be found, nor can a solution be found in a day or in a year.   If a democratic solution is to be worked out it will be the product of many minds working through a period of years.   It will require an increased understanding of the problem on the part of the leaders of business,

[72] *Ibid.*, page 121.

labor leaders, farm leaders, political leaders, and other leaders of public thinking. It will require continuing analysis by the technicians of different phases of the problem and a more detailed delineation of the characteristics of the national economy." [73] In the work of rationalizing the community's accepted goals Means thinks in terms of a new fusion of economics and politics reminiscent of that blending of economic and political thought which prevailed in the seventeenth and eighteenth centuries. Out of this fusion may emerge "the basic pattern of a new and distinctly American political economy." Like Wesley C. Mitchell and John M. Clark, Means hopes that there will not be too long a delay in the creation of this new political economy, because the social frustration resulting from the inability to take advantage of the great potentialities of the modern industrial system may soon cause individuals to turn to undemocratic ways out of our economic difficulties. Any plan for the future which did not make "the individual fulfillment in society the basic objective" would be a denial of the basic cultural trends set in motion by the rebirth of science and the spread of the doctrines of humanism since 1500.

When Means makes his administrative economics revolve about a consideration of the economic system as a going concern he joins company with Thorstein Veblen, Wesley C. Mitchell, John M. Clark, John R. Commons, Rexford G. Tugwell, and other economists with the holistic or systemic view of the nature of economic science. Veblen's economics of the "cumulative process," Mitchell's "science of human behavior," Clark's "social economics," Commons's "economics of the going concern," and Tugwell's "experimental economics" are all basically similar to Means's "administrative economics." These economists have in common a pragmatic philosophy and a social psychology from which their economics derives its realistic flavor and its functional bias. Since these economists are all interested in the economic system as a going concern, their primary interest is in the general level of economic activity which was largely taken for granted by the nineteenth-century economists. Furthermore, because the economic system as a going concern is made up of many forms of group or collective behavior in control of individual behavior, the economics of these heterodox thinkers is collective rather than individualistic. Collective action

[73] *The Structure of the American Economy,* Part I, page 171.

is institutionalized in many different ways with the result that a collective economics makes its explanations very largely in institutional terms. While it is true that much of Means's economic analysis is concerned with individual behavior, yet whenever attention is directed toward individual action it is done so only with frequent reference to a background of collective or institutional behavior.

Means's pluralistic view of the economic system is not a mere catchall into which he throws a disordered array of economic data. Like the theoretical system developed by the nineteenth-century economists, Means's thought schema has its special unifying principle. Whereas the body of traditional economic thought was colligated about the concept of individualistic, competitive enterprise, Means's economics derives its unity from the concept of collective corporate enterprise. It is corporate enterprise which sets the tempo and determines the whole atmosphere of the modern economy. The various segments of the economy function as dependent or subordinate divisions of a larger going system which draws its driving force from large administrative business units. Whether we turn from a consideration of the impact of technological change upon the whole economy to the basic problems of price and output, or whether we move from an analysis of the role of the capital-goods industries to a study of the insensitivity of the price system, the point of departure is an understanding of the nature and significance of administrative or corporate enterprise. Although the modern economy presents a picture of great economic diversity, Means observes a basic trend making for the continued expansion of administrative enterprise; and whatever coherence there is in his analysis of the economic system is derived from a consideration of this basic trend.

Means's administrative economics is important because it provides a new framework of interpretation for the study of economic phenomena. It is in the light of this new framework that such problems as unutilized resources, a lack of balance between saving and the creation of new capital, inflexible prices, and restrictive industrial policies are made to take on meaning; and it is because the traditional framework of analysis proved inadequate in the work of explaining these modern problems that Means felt a need for a new framework. This is the kind of framework that Wesley C. Mitchell has in mind when he speaks of "the future framework of economics"

that "is quietly developing out of our studies of specific problems.
. . . There are periods in which there is elaborated a system that embraces and accounts for all the known phenomena in so consistent and comprehensive a fashion that factual research seems for the time being a hunt for further decimal places. There are other periods in which new factual discoveries discredit the systematic notions in vogue and call for radical reconstruction. Various schemes of organizing the materials, old, and new, are tried; finally there emerges some system that serves the intellectual needs of the workers until they come upon more things in heaven and earth than are dreamed of in their philosophy—and so realize that they need a new system." [74]   Mitchell would look with great favor upon Means's work because he himself has not spent much time on the elaboration of a new framework of interpretation.   He regards the task of developing a new framework as a cooperative venture to be shared by many economists, who, like Means, have selected some special topic for analysis.   This task is so great that no one economist can hope to do much more than fill in a few gaps in the general scheme. It has been Means's particular contribution that he has specialized in an analysis of the nature and role of the large administrative business unit.   In doing so he has helped to round out our general view of the modern economy in action; and he has also hastened the day when economists with a flair for scientific synthesis will be able to unite the contributions of many of their predecessors in a new theoretical system which will be the special contribution of twentieth century economics.

In the light of his specialized interest in the modern corporation Means has revised economics so that it may be more useful to society in its task of domesticating the corporation and converting it into an instrument for better human living.   He has made it clear that one of the major economic problems of the twentieth century is to take account of the corporation's impact throughout the economic system; and he feels that when this has been accomplished he will have made an important step forward in providing a firm economic foundation for democracy.   The understanding and controlling of corporate enterprise may not be the open-sesame to a world of full use of economic resources and of a high standard of living for the

[74] Mitchell, Wesley C., "Economics, 1904-1929," *The Backward Art of Spending Money*, page 409.

masses, but they may very well be the keystone of a program designed to bring these goals much nearer to their realization.   In carrying out this program Means does not look forward to easy solutions of our many economic difficulties, because, like other pragmatists, he realizes that there is no way out but the hard way of painstaking, continuous effort to translate thought into action, and to convert ideals into realities in a highly intractable economic world.

The Emergence of a 20th-Century Political Economy

This survey of the economic thought of six outstanding members of the holistic school reveals that their scientific analyses fall into the mold of a common intellectual pattern. The general pattern of their economic theorizing is woven around a framework of interpretation which takes the American economy to be a dynamic, emergent going system or cultural concern. The holistic economists have all come to view the American economic system as an evolving, pluralistic complex of economic relations in which conflict of interests is the dominant cultural fact. Furthermore, they combine their new framework of interpretation with a fresh approach to the analysis of economic behavior. These heterodox economists agree on the need to replace the outmoded, individualistic psychology of the neo-classicists with a social or cultural psychology which gives proper attention to the importance in contemporary American economic life of collective action and of communal standards of conduct. They find their new psychological approach very useful in developing their theory of capitalistic enterprise. Although these economists have many specialized scientific interests, they all see the need to relate particular economic studies to a larger theory of the evolving total economic order. This theory of the total economic order is an interpretation of the structure and functioning of the economic segment of contemporary American culture. Having a strong pragmatic bias, the members of the holistic school pass on from their theory of the total economic system to the question of how this system might be improved. Since they are economic interventionists who think in terms of the necessity of controlling the flow of economic events to the end that a more fruitful economy may be created, the exponents of economic heterodoxy are as one in repudiating the principle of *laissez faire* as a criterion for the guidance of economic policy making.

It is not surprising that so much uniformity is found in the thought of Veblen and other heterodox economists. They are all products of the new era in the evolution of philosophic and scientific thought which opened with the publication of Charles Darwin's *Origin of Species* in 1859. This means that the holistic economists have in each case drawn inspiration from the evolutionary, holistic outlook which gives more attention to function than to structure, which emphasizes the relations between the parts and the totality of things, and which makes room in the scientist's theoretical system for an explanation of change and its consequences. When they unite their new post-Darwinian scientific outlook with their interest in the special problems of twentieth-century economic enterprise, these economists uniformly feel a need to broaden the scope of the inherited, nineteenth-century economics. They are all filled with a desire to go beyond the orthodox view which takes economics to be little more than a study of the highly refined, analytical principles dealing with the allocation of scarce means among various alternative uses. Veblen, Commons, Mitchell and the younger disciples of economic heterodoxy have the common goal of making economics a cultural science whose generalizations would cover much more than does the orthodox economics of Alfred Marshall and of those economists who continue to work in the neoclassical tradition.

No member of the holistic school has as yet presented a satisfactory synthesis of the school's contributions to the development of a cultural or institutional version of economic science. These contributions will be summarized in this concluding chapter so that one may see just what it is that comprises the content of holistic economics. It should be emphasized that we are here concerned with the contributions of all six members of the holistic school and not with the theorizing of any one member. In presenting this composite view one should keep in mind that these economists have not all covered the same ground in their analyses, and that where they have discussed the same points they have not always pushed their analyses the same distance.

Economic Theory and the Growth of Monopoly

This study of the work of several outstanding representatives of the new trend in American economic thought reveals that they are primarily interested in problems which were unimportant to the classical and neo-classical economists of the last century. These problems cluster around the central issue of the growing monopolization of economic life that has taken place in the United States since 1875. The evolution of the highly industrialized nations of Western Europe and North America has in recent decades carried these countries far away from their former simple, competitive economic systems. There have developed in these industrialized nations highly complicated economic systems which are capable of producing annual outputs far in excess of what is needed to maintain the working population and its industrial equipment. One of the main conditions fostering the growth of the intricate, highly productive economic systems of the western world has been the progress recorded by the industrial arts. Technological progress has not, however, been duplicated by similar progress in the field of social and economic relations. The expanding annual incomes of the advanced nations have been accompanied by a growing incapacity of the private markets to spread these incomes in an equitable manner over all classes. In the United States in the first half of the nineteenth century the competitive forces of the private market places could be relied upon to prevent any very great concentration of wealth and income in the hands of a few individuals. The competitive conditions found in agriculture, industry, and commerce were a guarantee that the various classes in the community would enjoy fairly adequate shares of the expanding national income. After 1875 the income-equalizing powers of the competitive markets were progressively weakened just at the time when the national output began to reflect a new era of progress in industrial science.

At the close of the last century when the advocates of the "new political economy" turned to the problems that grew out of the decline of competition, they found the inherited economics quite unsatisfactory for their purposes. The basic reason for this dissatisfaction was that orthodox economic theory was not especially concerned with the problems of monopoly and unearned income.

The economics of the classicists had been created for the purpose of explaining the disposal of national income in a simple, competitive situation. The only monopoly or unearned income that was given any considerable attention in the economic thought of Adam Smith, David Ricardo, and John Stuart Mill was the rent income going to landowners. Other incomes such as wages, interest, and profits were regarded as necessary payments for the contributions made by laborers, investors, and businessmen. These productive agents shared the national income that was not taken up by the landowners, but they shared only in proportion to their productivity or their contributions to the national income. In general, no surplus or unearned incomes were paid to these factors of production.

The late nineteenth-century economists were not especially concerned about the unearned incomes going to landowners. In England during the nineteenth century free trade introduced the competition of the more fertile lands of the rest of the world, and thus acted as a check upon the exploitation of the general public by the land-owning classes. In the United States a similar lack of interest in rent income was evinced by the academic economists. The presence of abundant, unused land until quite late in the century kept rent incomes within very restricted limits. Large fortunes might be made from speculating in the sale of land, but no great vested interests were established on the basis of the receipt of rent incomes. In the light of these circumstances in America and abroad it is not surprising that the classical economists and their followers paid little attention to the problems of monopoly and unearned income. In their scientific analyses these economists took as their model a purely competitive economy in which land was relatively abundant, in which rent incomes were kept within very limited bounds, and in which the national income went mainly to wage earners, investors, and businessmen as remuneration for services rendered to the community. As the classical economists understood the situation, not only were there few surplus or unearned incomes, but even at the best the incomes going to labor, capital, and business power or organizing ability were modest. The main economic problem was one of thinly spreading a limited national income over many recipients. It was always a matter of coping with scarcity, of great effort and little remuneration, of one factor of production getting more but only at the expense of other factors. Even late nineteenth-century, orthodox economic thought continued to be greatly concerned with "scarcity" and "earned incomes" and little interested in "surplus" and "unearned incomes."

There were two different reactions to the problem of the increasing inadequacy of nineteenth-century economic thought as an instrument for explaining the nature of economic activity in highly industrialized nations at the turn of the century.   One reaction took the form of admitting the limitations of classical economics, and of attempting to improve this type of economic thought by first raising it to new levels of deductive analysis.   The economists who followed this line with the hope of eliminating the deficiencies of orthodox economics no longer claimed that their theoretical system was a close approximation to reality.   Furthermore, they were frequently aware of the extent to which their basic assumptions failed to coincide with the realities of the economic world.   These economists believed, however, that it was best to proceed from a simple, unrealistic analysis of a purely competitive economy to an investigation of the functioning of the more complicated, real economic system found in the advanced nations of the twentieth century.   They were unwilling, and in some cases unprepared, to come to grips immediately with the complexities of the maturing capitalistic economy.   These economists were of the opinion that more could be achieved by first developing the pure theory of economic behavior and then supplementing it with an applied economics. The applied economics was to be integrated with the pure or abstract economics so that the net result would be a realistic interpretation of the actual economic world.

The second reaction to the growing deficiencies of the academic economics of the late nineteenth century was quite different from the reaction of those orthodox economists who endeavored to preserve the structure of classical economic thought by taking refuge in higher levels of analytical economics.   This second reaction, which is that of the holistic economists, led to the demand for a restatement of the basic assumptions of the science of economics and for a reconstruction of the economist's framework of interpretation.   It did not call for a further refinement of the core of economic theory which went under the label of "static economics"; instead the second approach to the problem of reconstructing academic economics resulted in a recapturing of the general purpose of economics at the close of the eighteenth century. At that time Adam Smith's aim had been to explain the structure and functioning of the emerging system of competitive capitalism. His primary purpose had not been to create "a box of tools for the analytical economist," but rather to offer an explanation of the economic organization of late eighteenth-century England, which was then sloughing the dry skin of mercantilism and exposing to view the vibrant new order of competitive capitalism. It was Smith's followers who turned economics away from the study of economic organization in particular cultural eras, and converted it into a formalistic analysis of abstract economic principles. The holistic economists have endeavored to make the central concern of economists once more the interpretation of the concrete economic systems from which people derive their livelihood. This does not mean that these heterodox economists believe that analytical or deductive economics is of no value. They concede that analytical economics has a function to perform which is of considerable scientific importance, but what these economists deny is that analytical economics includes within its scope the essentials of economic theory as it claims to do.

A good example of the first or orthodox type of reaction to the growing deficiencies of late nineteenth-century economic thought is found in the work of John Bates Clark. Upon returning to the United States from his postgraduate work in Germany, where he had come under the influence of the historical school, Clark expressed strong dissatisfaction with the orthodox academic economics of the time. His first reaction, as revealed in his *Philosophy of Wealth* (1885), was to call for a genuine reconstruction of economic science along the lines followed at a later date by Simon Nelson Patten and Thorstein Veblen. This original impulse soon faded away, however, and Clark turned in the opposite direction. In the late 1880's he conceived the plan of restoring academic economics to a place of high repute by first making further refinements in the general body of orthodox economic thought. Clark's procedure was to elevate the body of classical doctrine to the pure atmosphere of "Static Economics," and then later to convert this economics into a more realistic science by supplementing it with a "Dynamic Economics." About the turn of the century his plan for the reconstruction of economics was well established in neo-orthodox circles. Conventional economists sought, first of all, to establish definitely what Lionel Robbins was later to call the "ultimate nature" of economic science.[1] This was done by explaining the working of the "economic motive" in a fictional world of pure competition, or, as J. B. Clark put it, by proceeding "to isolate the phenomena of Economic Statics and to attain the laws which govern them."[2] The question was asked, how would a thoroughly rational person behave in a competitive world of scarce resources? The answers to this basic question were knitted together to make a body of static economic theory which was then taken to be the core of the science of economics. Everything else was subsidiary or supplemental, and "whatever movements the dynamic division of economic science may discover and explain, static laws will never cease to be dominant."[3] These static laws of economic science were held to be independent of cultural or social organization; they were "fundamental" or "universal," and operated in the "most advanced state, as well as in that of the most primitive."

An economist in any country, no matter how varied its cultural pattern might be, was supposed to be able to make use of Clark's hard and fast core of universal economic truths by making the necessary qualifications. This involved developing a subsidiary "applied economics" which would show how the science's core of abstract doctrines applied to all countries. How static economics was to be modified or converted into an interpretation of a concrete economic system, such as the maturing American economy, was a matter that was never really explained by the economists who accepted this method of reconstructing orthodox economics. It was assumed rather than demonstrated that one could shift from static to dynamic economics without great difficulty.

In spite of the fact that J. B. Clark was never able to follow up his studies on static economics with the supplemental dynamic economics which he promised, those who work in the spirit and tradition of Clark and Marshall are still very active. They continue to identify economics with a limited body of abstract economic principles. In England Lionel Robbins has argued in favor of a definition of economics which would make it the study of the formal or

---

[1] Robbins, Lionel, *An Essay on the Nature and Significance of Economic Science*, 1935, page 3.

[2] Clark, John Bates, *Essentials of Economic Theory*, 1907, Preface, page vii.

[3] Clark, John Bates, *The Distribution of Wealth*, 1899, page 442.

logical relations which arise from the disposal of scarce commodities among given ends. Taking human ends and the state of the industrial arts as given data, the economist is supposed to create what Robbins has himself so aptly described as a "shadowy abacus of forms and inevitable relationships" relating to the disposal of scarce resources.[4] With neater logic but with no more realism than Clark had exhibited forty years earlier, Robbins continues to find the essence or "ultimate nature" of economic science in a study of the universal, abstract laws of choice as they operate in any situation where scarcity exists. By some unexplained procedure the economist's "shadowy abacus" is to be clothed with the realities of the maturing twentieth-century capitalistic economy. How this is to be done is not explained by Robbins or any other contemporary exponent of economic orthodoxy. The problem is usually dismissed by stating that it will be met by another generation of students in the distant future. In 1899 John Bates Clark declared that "the task of developing this branch of science [dynamic economics] is so large that the execution of it will occupy generations of workers."[5] Twenty-five years later Joan Robinson wrote that "The reader who is interested in results immediately applicable to the real world has every right to complain that these tools of analytical economists are of little use to him. The knives are of bone and the hammers of wood, only capable of cutting paper and driving pins into cardboard." All that she can offer as solace to anyone who is interested in the functioning of the real economic world is the same advice given many years before by Clark and Marshall. As she has put it, those who want an economics that deals with the "real world" must wait until such time as the analytical or deductive economists catch up with the changing economic realities.

Joan Robinson explains that an "analytical economist" is one "who is prepared to work stage by stage towards the still far-distant ideal of constructing an analysis which will be capable of solving the problems presented by the real world."[6] Since there are questions in the minds of many economists both as to how this stage-by-stage modification of analytical economics can ever give rise to a

[4] *An Essay on the Nature and Significance of Economic Science,* page 39.

[5] *The Distribution of Wealth,* page 442.

[6] Robinson, Joan, *The Economics of Imperfect Competition,* page 327. London: Macmillan and Co., Ltd., 1933.

dynamic, realistic economics, and as to how long one can safely go on waiting for the birth of a new realistic economics, the method of revising economics which was adopted by orthodox academic circles late in the nineteenth century, and which continues to be widely accepted by orthodox economists in both England and the United States, has been very aptly described by some of its critics as the "optimistic" method.[7] This method of reconstructing economics is "optimistic" in the sense that it is grounded on faith rather than proof that analytical or deductive economics will somehow in the course of time turn out to be an economics which is capable of dealing with the economic problems of the real world of the twentieth century.

According to the holistic economists the solution of the problem of making economics more applicable to the issues of the real world of today does not lie in a gradual modification of the inherited equilibrium economics or of its later and more refined variants.[8] The position of these heterodox economists with respect to this problem is quite clear. They assert that the analytical economics of Clark, Marshall, and other exponents of economic orthodoxy cannot be taken as the starting point for a realistic interpretation of the twentieth-century American economy. They would agree with T. W. Hutchison that the "optimistic" procedure of the orthodox economists in endeavoring to modify or "extend" their deductive economics so that it might better meet the requirements of an interpretation of the real world has "come to a dead end," and that this orthodox procedure "may develop into an excuse for more or less useless deductive manipulation."[9] But the solution of the

[7] See T. W. Hutchison on "The 'Optimistic' Approach and the Present Position of Economics" in *The Significance and Basic Postulates of Economic Theory,* pages 73-76. London: Macmillan and Co., Limited, 1938.

[8] For a similar argument coming from a student of economic fluctuations, see Simon Kuznets, "Equilibrium Economics and Business Cycle Theory," *The Quarterly Journal of Economics,* May, 1930, Vol. XLIV, pages 381-415, and "Static and Dynamic Economics," *The American Economic Review,* Sept., 1930, Vol. XX, pages 426-441. Kuznets asserts that it is an intellectual impossibility to revise traditional or static economics so that it may be expanded into a new dynamic economics useful to the student of economic change. He summarizes his objections to traditional economics by explaining that static economic theory is a way of grasping economic reality which is unsuitable for handling what he describes as "the variegated stuff of changing reality."

[9] *The Significance and Basic Postulates of Economic Theory,* page 162. Cf. also Hansen, Alvin H., *Full Recovery or Stagnation?,* page 34. New York: W. W.

problem of how to make economics more realistic offered by Veblen and other members of the holistic school is not the same as that presented by Hutchison. He believes that this problem can be handled merely by making an "appeal to fact." The current difficulties with which economic science is faced are to be removed, if Hutchison is right, by "more tedious but necessary empirical investigation." [10] The American disciples of economic heterodoxy would agree with Hutchison that economics would be benefited by more consideration being given to the concrete facts of twentieth-century economic experience, but they do not believe that his appeal to the facts of economic life would be enough. They find it necessary to go beyond Hutchison's narrow positivism to explain that the progress of economics toward greater realism requires not only more use of the concrete data of contemporary economic life, but also a fundamental revision of the way in which these data are comprehended.[11] What this intellectual readjustment would involve can best be shown by inquiring into the views of the holistic economists relating to the nature and scope of economic science.

The Definition of Holistic Economics

From the viewpoint of the holistic school *economics is the study of the structure and functioning of the evolving field of human relations which is concerned with the provision of material goods and services for the satisfaction of human wants.* This definition indicates that the holistic economists have as their primary aim the interpretation of a particular "field of human relations," and that in their hands economics becomes a science of cultural or social relations. It endeavors to explain the total complex of economic relations into which the individual worker, consumer, or businessman fits himself. Since individuals and groups carry on their activities within an economic "field," they are subject to all the influences that run through this field, and to explain their behavior it is neces-

Norton and Company, Inc., 1938. Hansen states that "the danger of reasoning based on assumptions which no longer fit the facts of economic life" is a "sterile orthodoxy."

[10] *The Significance and Basic Postulates of Economic Theory,* pages 11, 74-75, and 162.

[11] For a criticism of Hutchison's position in regard to this problem of making economic science more realistic, see F. H. Knight's critical review entitled "What Is Truth in Economic Science?" *The Journal of Political Economy,* Feb., 1940, Vol. XLVIII, pages 1-32.

sary to view it as the product of the functioning of the total economic field. This field of economico-cultural relations does not have an independent existence, since it is but one part of a larger cultural whole. Although all cultural spheres or fields are but parts of one total cultural complex, it is possible for the purposes of scientific analysis to separate particular fields from their general cultural milieu. Like all other cultural spheres the field of economic relations has a past, present, and future. And just as no historical event can be properly interpreted without consideration being given to past developments and future trends, so also the field of economic relations is to be investigated as an evolving or developing area of cultural activity. This means that over a period of time both the structure and functioning of this sphere of human relations undergo basic changes.

The cultural relations that comprise the economic field are "concerned with the provision of material goods and services." All the social relations in this special area of human culture cluster around the problem of meeting a long list of pressing needs with a limited supply of material goods and services. This fundamental cultural problem has a twofold aspect. There is, first, the question of what limits the supply of material goods and services which is available for the satisfaction of human wants; and, secondly, there is the question of how any given supply of scarce commodities and services is allocated among various alternative uses. When the holistic economist turns to an investigation of any concrete field of economic relations, he wants to find out not only how the people dispose of a given supply of scarce means, but also what determines how great are the resources available for disposal. Orthodox economics has been much concerned with explaining how scarce resources are disposed of among alternative uses, but it has been little interested in explaining what it is that determines the size of the supply of scarce means. So strong has been this tendency of orthodox economic thought to emphasize only one aspect of the "economic problem" confronting mankind, that many exponents of economic orthodoxy accept the very limited definition of economics as the "study of the disposal of scarce commodities." [12] From the viewpoint of the holistic economists such a definition is totally inadequate.

[12] Cf. *An Essay on the Nature and Significance of Economic Science*, page 38. For a similar orthodox American view see Stigler, George J., *The Theory of Competitive Price*, page 12. New York: The Macmillan Company, 1942.

In order to explain what determines the size of the supply of material goods and services that is available to a people for allocation among its various needs, the holistic economist extends the scope of economics far beyond the limits established by the orthodox nineteenth-century economists and their latter-day followers. He discovers that it is necessary to inquire into the operations of all the important factors that condition the creation of the supply of material goods and services. These factors include both industrial technology and the scheme of human ends or goals which have a very great influence upon the general level of a country's economic activity. In some circumstances the state of the industrial arts and the scheme of human valuations have a very depressing effect upon the flow of economic goods and services, while in other circumstances they react very favorably upon the creation of material goods and services. Since this is true, the holistic economists, unlike the orthodox economists, do not take technology and human ends as given data which lie beyond the pale of economic analysis. They assert that economists should not divorce the flow of economic activity from changes in technology and human ends, but instead should give special attention to the many interrelations among the state of the industrial arts, the flow of scarce goods and services, and the scheme of human ends. In the opinion of the members of the holistic school, no adequate interpretation of the economic aspect of human culture can be made until these three groups of cultural phenomena are thoroughly investigated and their interrelations brought to light. When they take economics to be *the study of the changing patterns of cultural relations which deal with the creation and disposal of scarce material goods and services by individuals and groups in the light of their private and public aims,* the holistic economists seek to make provision for all the factors which are of importance in the shaping of economic behavior.

The evolving patterns of economic relations which are the major interest of the holistic economists are not of a uniform nature throughout the world. Since there is at present no single pattern of world culture, economic life breaks down into a variety of economico-cultural spheres which vary all the way from the simple rural-communal economies of India and China to the more complex economies of socialistic Russia and capitalistic America. These different fields of economic relations have some features in common, because they are all expressions of the same basic human nature. The structure and functioning of each field, however, are in many ways unique cultural products, with the result that generalizations about the structure and functioning of socialistic Russia would in many cases not be applicable to capitalistic America. When the holistic economist looks for scientific generalizations about economic activity, he does not seek generalizations that will be applicable to the economic spheres of all types of human cultures. O. H. Taylor has pointed out that "The only propositions that are valid and significant for all social economies that ever existed anywhere, or that can ever exist and remain economies, are a few extremely simple and broad or general propositions about the scarcity of resources, and its inevitable effects. But these few propositions do not constitute a scheme of economic theory." [13] In the hands of the holistic economists economics develops into a study of the organization of economic activity in particular cultural areas of the past and present. For every different cultural region there should be a theory of economic enterprise which explains the organization of economic life in that particular cultural area. Russian economists concern themselves with the theory of a socialistic economic order, while Indian economists are interested in developing a theory of an economic order which is neither socialistic nor capitalistic but "rural-communal" as Radhakamal Mukerjee has described it.[14] Since the American holistic economists are primarily interested in the economic sphere of twentieth-century American culture, from their viewpoint economics is the study of the structure and functioning of the maturing American economy.

The body of economic interpretation created by the holistic economists is not simply a "logically articulated statement of the laws which govern the fixing of economic values and control the distribution of income." [15] It is this much, but with a great deal more added to it. Their final product is a theory of a particular

[13] See Taylor's discussion at the 1931 round-table conference on "Institutionalism," *The American Economic Review*, March, 1931, Vol. XXI, Supp., page 139.

[14] Mukerjee, Radhakamal, *The Institutional Theory of Economics*, Ch. IX, "Typology of Contrasted Economic Systems," pages 213-232. London: Macmillan and Co., Limited, 1942.

[15] Homan, Paul T., *Contemporary Economic Thought*, 1928, page 442.

economic order or what Werner Sombart once called a theory of a "connected economic system." [16] What precisely is a theory of a total or "connected" economic system? Such a theory is a body of generalizations relating to the structure and functioning of the economic segment of some particular cultural area. The content of this theory can be best described by explaining how the economist goes about constructing such a theory. The first step is the development of some general notion of the nature of the economic order. In the case of the holistic economists this basic concept is the idea of the economy as a going concern which becomes a sort of intellectual bench-mark to which all other matters are in the final analysis referred. Any such fundamental notion of the economic order is eventually enlarged into a framework of interpretation within which is constructed the economist's theory of the economic order. This theory is the end-product of investigations relating to the structure and functioning of the economic system. If this system breaks down into a number of areas of different types of economic activity ranging from the purely competitive to the purely monopolistic, as is true of the contemporary American economic order, the economist formulates special generalizations for all different types of enterprise. More than this he seeks to uncover generalizations which explain the interrelations between the various segments of the total economy. There was no special problem in this connection for the early nineteenth-century economists, because the economies of the industrialized nations of the first half of the nineteenth century were predominantly competitive. The situation is quite different a century later when the modern mixed or hybrid economy engages the economist's attention.

The scientific generalizations which comprise the body of a theory of the economic order are primarily applicable to the special economic system which is the immediate object of investigation. The generalizations made by Veblen and other heterodox American economists have special application to the maturing American economy of the first half of the twentieth century. These economic generalizations have a special historical character in the sense that they are of value primarily in explaining the latest phase in the evolution of the American capitalistic system. If, in the coming

[16] Sombart, Werner, "Economic Theory and Economic History," *The Economic History Review*, Jan., 1929, Vol. II, pages 13-17.

half-century, the American economy passes into a new phase of its development in which its structure and functioning undergo profound change, much of the economic thought analyzed in earlier chapters of this study will become outmoded. This will mean that a new theory of the economic order will have to be created to take the place of the theory which has applicability to the current economic situation. Does this mean that economics becomes a matter of pure relativity since its generalizations have validity only at a particular point in historical time? The fixity of human nature would in itself be a sufficient guarantee against the possibility of any such rank relativism. It is obvious that much that was learned about economic behavior in the era of competitive capitalism has validity in the current era of monopoly capitalism. The principles of marginalism as they relate to both productive and consumptive activity are useful to the economist in his study of all historical manifestations of the human urge to engage in economic activity. But in the present advanced state of economic science the principles of marginal analysis are more a point of departure than an ultimate goal of economic investigation. The ultimate goal should be a theory of the contemporary economic order which makes use of the contributions of the marginalists but which goes far beyond their limited economic analysis. In going beyond the marginalists the holistic economists necessarily become less universalistic and much more relativistic in their economic theorizing. This is because their theory of the economic order is concerned with a particular epoch in the unending evolution of "that scheme of conduct whereby mankind deals with its material means of life." [17]

When weaving their generalizations about the structure and functioning of the economic order into the pattern of a general theory, the holistic economists discover that it is necessary to formulate a theory of economic development. This is true because all concrete economic systems, being historico-cultural products, necessarily incorporate within themselves something of the past, present, and future. Where an economist studies a concrete economic order such as the maturing capitalistic system of the United States, he cannot satisfactorily divorce the existing economic system from the cultural situation out of which it has developed, or from the trends which are carrying the economy to the next era in its evolution. When

[17] Veblen, Thorstein, "The Limitations of Marginal Utility," page 240.

formulating a theory of economic development the economist does not seek to establish any "laws" of economic change. In this field of analysis the search for laws similar in nature to the laws of the natural sciences or to the analytical principles of equilibrium economics has proved to be fruitless. There is nothing sufficiently regular or uniform about the behavior of the factors leading to economic change to permit the formulation of any laws which would have application to all eras in the evolution of economic society. However, the fact that no laws of economic development have thus far been discovered, and that there appears to be little likelihood that they will ever be discovered, does not mean that the phenomena of economic change are therefore beyond the limits of scientific treatment. There still remains the possibility of uncovering a logic of development which will throw some light on the role of economic change in the evolution of society. It is this possibility which is of great scientific interest to the holistic economists.

In looking over the evolution of the American economy in the past hundred years Veblen and the other holists come to the conclusion that this evolution follows a certain logic of development. Though controlled by no fixed "economic laws," this evolution is nevertheless subject to very definite restrictions, limitations, or compulsions in its unfolding which make it much more than a merely random affair. Just as a river is not a haphazard flow but is instead a movement of a body of water which shows the influence of the slope of the terrain and the forces of gravity, so likewise an evolving economic system is conditioned or guided in its development by the existing chain of natural and cultural circumstances. Where the network of circumstances includes a rapidly improving industrial technology, a region in which undeveloped geographical areas are few in number and in which the population is no longer rapidly expanding, and a society dominated by private enterprise and a laissez-faire social philosophy, the course of economic evolution necessarily reflects these given, hard and fast circumstances. All these circumstances act as "compulsives" which not only limit the field within which economic evolution can take place, but which also make it possible for the economist to uncover a pattern or logic in this evolution. The flow of economic events in the United States has, in recent decades, given rise to a great cultural lag, which is the product of the friction arising between a rapidly changing industrial technology and a slowly changing economico-political superstructure. Given a continuously improving industrial technology which is slowly closing the ranks of labor at the same time that it is enlarging the annual surplus of goods and services over what is required to maintain the population and its industrial equipment, and given a continuation of private enterprise bolstered by a legal system largely dominated by laissez-faire ideals and a political system which elevates pressure groups over the national welfare, the economist should not be surprised to find the logic or pattern of economic development pointing in the direction of a growing cultural lag.

Where the data of a science are subject to such rapid changes as are found in the realm of economic culture, one must be satisfied when analyzing these data with much less than the precision of the laws of natural science or the rules of mathematical analysis. It is only because the world of economic activity is not completely chaotic or disorderly that the holistic economist is able to create a theory of economic development. This theory does not stand apart from the general body of theorizing which relates to the current economic scene. A conjuncture of economic events is but one link in the long chain of economic evolution, and the full meaning of this link can be grasped only by relating it to the chain of which it is but a part. The analysis of any economic situation is therefore not complete until it has been tied in with the logic of economic development to which it is intimately related. When this is done the theory of the economic order can be regarded as complete or fully rounded, because the structure and functioning of the economic order are then properly associated with the unending flow of events which molds economic behavior.

The Basic Assumptions of Holistic Economics

The basic assumptions which underlie holistic economic thought may be divided into two general categories, one relating to the nature of the total economic system, and the other to the nature of human behavior. The basic assumption in the first category takes the economic system to be a cultural process or going concern rather than a mechanism or equilibrium of stable economic relations. The holistic economists abandon the mechanistic analogy and much that goes with it. When they write about the going economic system, these economists have in mind not the repetitive operations of an unchanging mechanism but the functioning of "one great, integrated, going-concern process." [18]   The economy, when viewed as a going system, is quite unlike the monistic, classical view of a static, competitive economy.   It is instead a pluralistic economico-cultural scheme of things which divides into a number of different types of economic activity ranging from the purely competitive to the purely monopolistic.   This pluralistic economy possesses a cultural rather than a mechanical balance or equilibrium, which is the result of the working of a number of factors such as social habit, self-interest, and communal controls of various sorts.   These various factors combine to give order to, and to provide a continuing basis for, the total complex of economic relations.   It should be pointed out, however, that there is nothing permanent about the balance which the going economic system possesses; at times this balance is quite precariously established, as in the recent half-century of great technological change.

Veblen and the other exponents of economic holism do not assume that there is a fundamental harmony of interests underlying the operations of the economy as a going concern.   They are unlike the classical economists of the nineteenth century who worked with the assumption that a basic harmony of interests ran through economic society.   The notion of a fundamental, pre-existing harmony of interests was perpetuated by the later neo-classical economists who clung to the fiction of a static, competitive economic society in which frictions were never so important as to be sources of major economic conflicts.   The holistic economists reject the assumption of a pre-existing harmony of economic interests, because they do not find anything in the operations of the going economic system to guarantee that harmony will prevail among the various economic interests.   At any period in the evolution of the economic system conflict or harmony of interests may be the dominant fact of the times.   In the early decades of the nineteenth century economic conflicts were not matters of great national concern in the United States.   But a century later the situation had greatly altered; and by this time conflict had replaced harmony of interests as the economic fact of major importance.   What will be the prevailing economic

[18] Wolfe, A. B., "Economy and Democracy," *The American Economic Review*, March, 1944, Vol. XXXIV, page 13.

condition a century from now is a matter of pure speculation.[19] The holistic economists hope that by that time mankind will have established an economic system from which many of the major causes of economic conflict will have been eliminated. They are convinced, furthermore, that their economic thought will prove very useful to anyone who seeks to bring about such a desirable economic situation. These heterodox economists, however, are not blind to the fact that in economic affairs nothing is preordained or guaranteed by extramundane or other forces. Whether conflict or harmony of economic interests prevails in the future will be a matter either of historical accident or of human design. Commons, Mitchell, and their followers hope to make order prevail over disorganization in economic affairs, but this does not mean that economic conflicts will be entirely eliminated. It means only that conflicts will then be kept within certain socially approved limits.

When the holistic economists say that the end-products of economic evolution are not predetermined, they do not argue that the development or "going" of the economic system is a merely random or haphazard happening. These economists work with the assumption that the functioning and growth of the American economy are to a very important extent controlled or conditioned by a logic inherent in that economy. John M. Clark has pointed out that there is in the economic world a "logic of events" or a "direction in which the forces of history appear to be driving us." [20] This logic of economic development reflects the influence of our changing industrial technology, which directs economic evolution only along those lines which are compatible with it.[21] If the evolution of the American

---

[19] Wesley C. Mitchell declares that "The future of a 'unified world' bids fair to be as full of social conflicts as the past has been, and just as interesting. I cannot forecast what will happen; but our successors will have at least as much sense as we possess and I doubt whether they will make a worse mess of affairs than our generation has made. Even we are managing to survive." See Mitchell's discussion of Herbert von Beckerath's paper on "Interrelations between Moral and Economic Factors in the Postwar World," *The American Economic Review*, March, 1944, Vol. XXXIV, Supp., page 49.

[20] Clark, John M., "The Relation of Government to the Economy of the Future," *The Journal of Political Economy*, Dec., 1941, Vol. XLIX, pages 805, 813-814.

[21] Cf. Heimann, E., "Industrial Society and Democracy," *Social Research*, Feb., 1945, Vol. XII, page 45. Heimann explains that, although the end-products of economic evolution are not predetermined, the basic presupposition of those who are "conscious of the social nature of man" is that the inherent technical tend-

economy continues without interruption, it is highly probable that the logic of economic development will continue to point in the direction of a greater collectivization of economic activity. There will thus be certain conditions of economic life which economic policy-makers will not only be able to count upon to continue to exist in the future, but which they will have to take account of if they are not to fly in the face of the hard and fast facts of the real world in their policy-making. If there was nothing predictable or highly probable about the evolution of the American economy, there would be little in this connection about which scientific generalizations could be made. The work of Veblen and other critics of economic orthodoxy could then not get much beyond the level of mere description. It is because they are convinced that economic evolution is more than a chance or accidental development that these heterodox economists think that worth-while generalizations can be made about the evolution of American economic life.

Along with the assumptions relating to the nature of the evolving economic system go equally important assumptions dealing with the nature of human behavior. The holistic economists make use of a psychological theory which fits in with their view of the modern economy as a cultural emergent.[22] This psychological theory, which is largely a product of the past seventy-five years, presents a view of human nature which is quite different from that found in the writings of the classical and neo-classical economists. These orthodox economists made use of a psychology which emphasized calculation and deliberation or the exercise of pure reason, since this interpretation of human nature was appropriate to their static view of economic society. In the orthodox economist's view of economic society activity was reduced to the reasoned procedures involved in making the best possible use of a scarce supply of resources wrested from a niggardly nature. In the economic world of the orthodox economists, where the structure and functioning of

encies of society have a "bearing" on its economic and political structure. Heimann pays tribute to the primacy of Thorstein Veblen's analysis in relation to this problem of the "technical necessities of industrial life."

[22] For a recent statement of a similar psychological theory and its relations to human culture when viewed as a going concern, see Kluckhohn, Clyde, and Kelly, W. H., "The Concept of Culture," in *The Science of Man in the World Crisis,* edited by Ralph Linton, pages 78-106. New York: Columbia University Press, 1945.

the economy were undergoing no basic modifications, there was no problem of making adjustments in basic ways of thinking and acting. There were no lags between unchanging ways of thinking and acting on the one hand and altered economic circumstances on the other hand. In the competitive world of Alfred Marshall everyone tended to behave like "city" men, who were absorbed in the business of getting the most economic gain from the smallest possible expenditure of pecuniary assets. In these static economic circumstances the primary psychological problem was one of calculation or deliberation and not one of adjustment to a world of ever-changing economic realities.

The situation is quite different when one turns to the thought of the holistic economists, who observe that the going economic system is a rapidly changing affair. In the altering circumstances of the twentieth-century American economy the individual finds himself undergoing a constant need to acquire new ways of organizing productive activity, of spending his income, and of protecting his economic interests. "For this generation," J. M. Clark explains, "there is to be no release from the stress of readjustment. Our best resource is to minimize the strain by a calm and matter-of-fact acceptance of this necessity." [23] In contemporary economic circumstances the human mind is less of a calculating machine and more of an exploratory device for making adjustments to ever-new economic arrangements. As he is swept into the vortex of economic change, the individual finds that old behavior patterns are no longer very useful. Alterations have to be made in inherited ways of thinking and acting, if the individual is not to be a victim of psychological lags. Many individuals, however, do not make the necessary adjustments. They go bankrupt, or they come into conflict with trade unions which have altered the thinking and acting patterns of their members, or they spend their money incomes in a wasteful manner. Since man is essentially a creature of habit whose reason plays only a secondary role, many individuals in the modern economy find themselves isolated from technological realities by a wall of outmoded habits of thinking and acting inherited from a past age.

Although the holistic economists find that man is largely a creature of habit, they also observe that he is gifted with a capacity to learn, to analyze situations, and to make adjustments in ways of

[23] "The Relation of Government to the Economy of the Future," page 816.

thinking and acting. Their pragmatic psychology takes the human mind to be an exploratory device which is useful for fitting the individual into the complexities of our twentieth-century culture. This exploratory or experimental intelligence enables the individual to replace outmoded behavior patterns with new patterns that are more in line with the necessities of the modern technological age. These new behavior patterns of businessmen, workers, and consumers do not develop in an entirely spontaneous manner; they require an understanding of the kinds of economic problems that are to be tackled, and a conscious effort to make the adjustments required for the solutions of these problems. The holistic economists point out that, up to the present, economic problems have accumulated at a rate which has far exceeded the rate of psychological adjustment on the part of the general population. In their opinion it should be one of the aims of economists to help in restoring a balance between the rate of economic change and the rate of psychological adjustment. Many forces interfere with the creation of this balance for the simple reason that various vested interests stand to gain from the continuance of the lack of such a balance. The preservation of outmoded ways of thinking and acting by small businessmen, by unorganized workers, and by uninformed consumers enables unscrupulous corporate enterprises to exploit these maladjusted groups. There is a great need for a freeing of the social adjustment processes from the hindrances created by tradition, inertia, and the activities of various minority economic interests. Man is by nature so much a creature of habit that he is all too easily induced to go on following behavior patterns which are out of touch with economic reality and to the advantage of only a small portion of the total population.

The problem of economico-psychological adjustment in the modern economy is largely one of having the individual fit into some form of group or collective organization where he can slough his inherited, individualistic behavior patterns in favor of the group's newer ways of thinking and acting. This aspect of the problem of economico-psychological adjustment explains why the holistic economists pay so much attention to collective economic action. They observe that in the contemporary American economy there is a trend toward more collective action in control of individual behavior. The corporate manager abandons inherited laissez-faire behavior patterns in favor of collective modes of behavior which meet the needs of small cliques of businessmen more effectively. The farmer submerges his intense individualism in the common front of the producers' cooperative; likewise the housewife seeks to replace her old-style consumer isolation with the well-informed collective atmosphere of the consumer cooperative. These are the trends of the modern economic world because the technological necessities of the machine age stimulate the cooperative bent of mankind. In contrast to the orthodox nineteenth-century economists, the heterodox economists assert that man is basically a cooperative and not a competitive animal. They point out that only for a very brief period in the history of Western European civilization, that is to say in the late eighteenth and early nineteenth centuries, were the competitive aspects of human behavior elevated to a position of primacy. At the close of the nineteenth century the maturing economies of the highly industrialized nations began once more to give free play to mankind's basic tendency to act in unison, to cooperate, and to meet the needs of the self through collective endeavor. The growing unionization of labor, the spread of the cooperative movement, and the ascendance of the corporate type of business enterprise, far from being contrary to man's inner drives, are really quite in line with the demands of his proclivities. Psychological adjustment in the complex modern economic system is aided by the possession by mankind of what Rexford G. Tugwell has described as the "coöperative urge." If this basic tendency did not exist in human nature, economico-psychological adjustment, which is today largely a matter of the immersion of the individual in collective or group existence, would hardly be possible. The presence of a strong cooperative urge in mankind makes it possible to look upon the adjustment of the individual to the requirements of the modern large-scale economy with a certain amount of restrained optimism.

The psychological views of the holistic economists may be summarized by pointing out that they take all economic behavior to be social or collective in the sense that all individual economic acts are carried on within the total gestalt or organizational complex known as the economic order. Individuals are born into an already functioning economic system which gives guidance to their economic behavior. In so far as the individual accepts the surrounding complex of economic rules, regulations, and institutions, he pursues his economic activities in an habitual manner. He calculates and deliberates with respect to the selection, transfer, and consumption of goods and services, but only within the limits of the complex of habit patterns known as the going economic system. In the United States and other industrialized nations economic behavior patterns are undergoing rapid changes, and the individual finds that old ways of doing things are no longer satisfactory. Inherited ways of buying, selling, producing, and consuming are no longer effective in a world of highly monopolistic business enterprise. In these circumstances the individual finds it necessary to alter the basic behavior patterns that guide his daily economic transactions. Under the guidance of an exploratory or experimental intelligence many individuals are weighting the scales in favor of basic drives that are more appropriate to an economic world in which a premium is placed upon collective economic action. This does not mean that the self-interest of the individual is no longer of great importance. It means that individuals who are living and working in the twentieth-century American economy find that their own special economic ends are frequently achieved more effectively through collective than through unorganized, individual action. Adam Smith's "higgling and bargaining" of the market place are still with us, but they are carried on today in a much more collective fashion than was the case a century and a half ago. Self-interest is an ineradicable feature of the human make-up, but its cultural expression is subject to extensive modification as time goes by. In the modern economic world self-interest is finding it increasingly difficult to rely upon purely individualistic modes of expression. Consequently, it is turning to outlets which are more collective than individualistic in nature.

When the holistic economists work with the assumptions that man is largely a creature of habit, that he is by nature essentially a cooperative being, and that his reason is basically of an exploratory rather than a contemplative nature, they are not offering an entirely new interpretation of human nature. What they are doing, in effect, is to lay emphasis upon aspects of human nature which were largely neglected by the orthodox economists of the last century. Their modern psychology involves a reworking of older views concerning human nature, with those alterations being made that seem to be of value in explaining human behavior in the complicated economic world of the current century. Just as every new age or epoch in the intellectual history of mankind is marked by a new philosophical orientation, so also each epoch has its own fresh psychological outlook. What this new psychological interpretation involves is a fresh interpretation of that original human nature which is itself so impervious to change.

The assumptions of the holistic economists relating to the nature of human behavior are in conformity with their view of the, economic system as an evolving cultural complex. Their psychology of adjustment and adaptation is useful in explaining human behavior in an economic world in which technological innovation has a very important role to play. A going economic system whose structure and functioning are being continuously altered by technological change requires for its successful operation the presence of individuals who are cooperative and adaptive, and who also possess the experimental outlook. Veblen and later holists work with the assumption that human beings are creatures who possess these necessary psychological capacities. They believe that mankind has enough psychological flexibility to be able to cope with the flood of new economic problems. Whether or not mankind will actually use this remarkable psychological adaptability to master the economico-cultural trends of the future is a question which only time can answer. In general the holistic economists believe that mankind will go on improving the edifice of human culture for a long time to come.

The Theory of the American Economic Order

When looking at the total economic organization of the United States, the holistic economists see a pattern of things quite different in shape and function from the pattern of competitive activity which engrossed the attention of the orthodox economists of the last century. The intricate pattern of twentieth-century American capitalistic enterprise has an inner core of monopolistic enterprise, which includes both private and public monopolies and also all those economic activities which are predominantly monopolistic.[24]

[24] In this discussion the term "monopolistic enterprise" includes, besides pure monopoly, any kind of business activity in which monopolistic elements are more important than the competitive elements. Enterprise is taken to be "monop-

In this central region of the modern capitalistic economy are found the public utility, transportation, iron and steel, oil, chemical, construction, and other key industries. This is the realm of what Gardiner C. Means has described as the "economic empires" of the business system with their interlocking directorates, their intricate holding company organizations, and their patent pools. This is the focal area of the economy in which are found, in their most workable form, all those production and selling arrangements such as price leadership, sharing the market, stabilization of prices, and price discrimination. Matching the key industries and the large governmental enterprises in size and importance in this inner core of monopolistic enterprise are the large national trade and industrial unions. In general the central area of the contemporary American economy is one in which competition is not technologically feasible, because there is room for only a few industrial units which cannot operate on a competitive basis. This central region of monopolistic activity may be described as an area of large-scale economic enterprise in which collective action in control of individual action is the rule rather than the exception.

Surrounding the modern economy's "heartland" of monopolistic enterprise are regions of economic activity which become less monopolistic and more competitive as one moves out toward the outer limits of the economy. These various regions are not differentiated from one another by clear-cut lines of demarcation; instead, like the colors of the spectrum, these outlying areas merge into one another only very gradually. Some industries are borderline cases, while others are clearly to be classed as monopolistic, imperfectly competitive, or competitive. In general the holistic economists have in mind a tripartite economy when they theorize about twentieth-century economic enterprise. They see surrounding the focal region of monopolistic enterprise, first, an area of "competing monopolies" or "imperfect markets," and secondly, an outer or

olistic" wherever the businessman behaves like a monopolist in spite of whatever competitive features or aspects his industry may possess. Unfortunately for our purposes, there is no word in the English language which covers that situation in which one finds both "pure" and "partial" monopoly existing side by side, as is the case in the inner core of the maturing American economy. Because of this language difficulty the term "monopolistic" will have to be used in this chapter wherever reference is made to an economic situation in which there are to be found both pure and partial monopolies operating together.

peripheral region of workable competition.[25] The area of imperfect competition is one in which are found the numerous, middle-sized enterprises with their highly differentiated products. Not being able to obtain a strong monopoly position through the control of a large portion of their industry's assets, these enterprises have a precarious monopolistic advantage resting on the uncertain foundation of what Veblen called "prestige values." In this region of competing monopolies are the food products, beverage, drug, and other manufactured-product industries. Each such industry is marked by the presence of a considerable number of sellers, an industrial technology much less advanced than that of the key industries, and an intensive differentiation of products.

Finally, there is the peripheral region of highly competitive enterprise in which are found the remnants of the old competitive economy of the nineteenth century. Here are all the small-scale manufacturing industries, much of the nation's retailing activity, farming, some of the extractive industries, and the personal and professional services. Clinging to the periphery of the modern capitalistic economy, these competitive activities are in marked contrast to the activities of the central region of the economy. Especially noticeable in the shrinking area of competitive enterprise is the lack of organized or collective economic activity. In this segment of the economy collective action in control of individual action is the exception rather than the rule, and for the most part the individual relies upon his own resources in the struggle to secure an income.

So much for the structure of the modern American economy as it is seen by the holistic economists. The next question is, how do they explain the working of this hybrid or mixed economy? In developing their explanation of the functioning of the American economy these economists do not ignore the fact that all sections of the economy are structurally and functionally interrelated. They do point out, however, that the inner region of monopolistic enterprise is of greater strategic importance than is any other area of economic activity. This inner core is the center of economic pulsation from which radiate the basic technological and business forces which account for the increasing centralization of American economic life. The American economy functions in a centripetal

[25] Copeland, Morris A., "Economic Theory and the Natural Science Point of View," *The American Economic Review*, March, 1931, Vol. XXI, pages 72-73.

manner which tends to draw economic activity into a close-knit scheme of things that is quite easily dominated by a limited number of people or groups in strategic positions. In effect, the inner core of monopolistic economic activity operates like a vortex or maelstrom which is drawing in toward its center more and more of the nation's economic life. Since at present the process of centralization is far from being completed, the holistic economists think in terms of a further expansion of the focal, monopolistic area of the economy at the expense of the competitive areas.

There are two causes for the increasing centralization of the modern American economy. The first cause is the flood of technological innovation. The assembly-line technology is flowing over from the realm of the heavy industries to engulf much of the formerly small-scale competitive enterprise. Not only have the key industries of the nation fallen under the control of a comparatively small number of corporate enterprises, but the trend is in the same direction in many other lines of economic enterprise. In the processing of foodstuffs and the making of beverages, in the provision of amusement by means of the radio and the motion picture, in the supplying of news services, and in the retailing of goods small-scale enterprises are rapidly giving way to the sweep of technological advance. This advance is concentrating the population of the nation in urban areas; it is centralizing industry in various geographical regions; and it is concentrating a major portion of the nation's industrial assets in the "heartland" of monopolistic enterprise where a small number of corporate organizations are in a position to make business decisions which vitally affect the working of the entire economy.

The second cause of the growing centralization of American economic life is the changing nature of business organization. Businessmen have found it profitable to "corporatize" economic activities. They have found it to their economic advantage to use the interlocking directorate, the multiple holding company, no-par and non-voting common stock, and many other corporate devices for centralizing the control of industrial assets. The profitability of these twentieth-century methods of organizing business enterprise has placed a large premium on the promotion of intricate corporate organization. And every step toward a more intricate corporate structure has meant a further decline in competition. This is true because the growing complexity of business organization has fostered both the horizontal and the vertical consolidation of industry. In much of the modern economy the corporate assets of various companies have been placed under centralized management, the entry of new firms has been made difficult, and technological innovation has become a matter of large-scale, corporate exploitation.[26]

Technological advance and progress in the methods of organizing business enterprise have not been unrelated developments. The shift toward mass production has favored the development of more centralized ways of organizing business enterprise. Willard L. Thorp explained to the Temporary National Economic Committee in 1938 that "I think over the long run the increase in size is definitely to be attributed to certain changes in the economic system, [in] the kind of products that we are producing. You can't produce automobiles with one or two employees; it has to be a fairly good-sized enterprise. The shift from household production over to producing in factories for many of our common necessities has been characterized by the growth of large-scale enterprises." [27] In turn, the large-scale corporate enterprises have stimulated technological advance by making financial provision for industrial research on a large-scale basis. A portion of the surplus money incomes going to corporate enterprises has been diverted to the further improvement of the technological basis of modern industry. With both technological innovations and innovations in the methods of carrying on business transactions pointing in the direction of a greater centralization of economic activity, it is not surprising that the holistic economists should find the modern economy's central area of highly monopolistic activity one of special scientific interest.

The centripetal tendencies of the twentieth-century American economy are accompanied by a polarization of the forces of technological and business innovation. This polarization arises from the fact that, although changes in both industrial technology and the organization of business enterprise have a centralizing effect, they

[26] Cf. Watkins, Myron W., "Trustification and Economic Theory," *The American Economic Review*, March, 1931, Vol. XXI, Supp., pages 54-76. Like Veblen and other heterodox economists, Watkins is greatly impressed by the extent to which "trustification" has altered the structure and functioning of the modern economy, and has therefore created a need for a restatement of economic theory in terms of an "economics of stewardship."

[27] *Hearings Before the Temporary National Economic Committee*, Seventy-Fifth Congress, P.R. No. 113, Part I, "Economic Prologue," page 111.

do not look to the same outcome. The trend of technological development is toward a more intricate, large-scale industrial system which is capable of enlarging the annual income of real goods and useful services. In contrast, the trend of developments in the field of business organization is toward a more intricate, large-scale business system which is capable of increasing the money incomes of the few individuals who manage or own the large corporate enterprises. The logic of the cumulative changes in industrial technology is explained in terms of vast aggregations of industrial equipment, the assembly-line technique of production, and an expanding output at a declining per-unit cost. But the logic of development in the field of business relations is explained in terms of a greater monopolization of business activity, and a removal of the competitive checks which tend to keep selling prices close to costs of production. The logic of business development moves in the direction of the restriction of output, the raising of prices, and the maximization of pecuniary income. With technological and business developments moving toward opposite poles, antagonisms and conflicts inevitably arise.

Technological and business forces do not currently play equally important parts in the polarization of the mature capitalistic economy, because businessmen occupy the key positions, and hence control the lines of economic power. The American economy is a "pecuniary" rather than an "industrial" economy in the sense that pecuniary considerations are more decisive with respect to the working of the economy than are technological considerations. The prime movers of the economy, the businessmen who are associated with large-scale corporate enterprise, direct the flow of economic activity for the purpose of maximizing pecuniary assets rather than the output of useful material goods and services. It so happens that the making of profits is at times accompanied by the production of a large supply of goods and services. But goods-making, or what John M. Clark describes as the creation of "service values," always remains in a secondary position in contemporary economic life.[28] Modern business enterprise does not give free rein to the potentially very fruitful industrial technology of the twentieth century. Furthermore, there is the additional problem of the distribution of the

[28] Clark, J. M., "Educational Functions of Economics After the War," *The American Economic Review*, March, 1944, Vol. XXXIV, Supp., page 58.

limited national output. Modern business organization not only restricts the free flow of economic production, but it also distributes the restricted national output on the basis of the possession of monopoly power rather than on the basis of actual effort put forth to maximize the production of useful material goods and services.

When the holistic economists make use of their concepts of the centripetancy and polarity of the American economy, they focus their attention on the operations of the price system. Coordination of economic activity is supplied from sources other than the price system, but the major device for uniting all parts of the economy and converting them into large going concerns is the price system. Like the orthodox economists, the exponents of economic holism have been very much interested in price phenomena. Much of Veblen's analysis is devoted to the pecuniary or price aspects of economic activity. His whole interpretation of the American economy is based upon a distinction between the "pecuniary" and "industrial" employments. Wesley C. Mitchell has spent a lifetime investigating the structure and functioning of the "money economy." Much of Commons' economic analysis revolves around a consideration of "reasonable values." John M. Clark's studies of overhead costs have emphasized the indeterminateness of market prices where fixed costs are a major consideration. Gardiner C. Means has built a whole system of economic thought around the concept of inflexible or "administered" prices. What these facts show is not that the heterodox economists have ignored the phenomena of the market place, but that they have emphasized the aspects of price behavior which have been given but scant attention by the inherited economics.

The orthodox economists of the late nineteenth and early twentieth centuries analyzed the price system of an economy which was assumed to be of a uniformly competitive nature. Using the technique of marginal analysis, these economists explained the pricing process so as to show that in the long run individual firms, entire industries, and the whole competitive economy would approach a condition of equilibrium. In the optimum circumstances of this competitive equilibrium the selling prices of each firm would do no more than cover all the necessary costs of production including a normal profit for business enterprise. Furthermore, in each industry there would be just that number of firms that would be required to meet the existing consumer demand, since all superfluous firms would be eliminated. Finally, from the point of view of the entire economy there would be an optimum allocation of resources, since each industry and each firm would be in an optimum position with respect to all other firms and industries. By making the necessary marginal adjustments, businessmen would bring not only their individual firms but also their entire industries into an optimum position. In following the principle that production should be expanded until marginal costs equal selling prices, businessmen, without expressly seeking it, would tend to bring about an efficient, balanced, and smooth working of the whole economic system.

Not only did the flexible, competitive price system of early nineteenth-century England and the United States work in the direction of an optimum allocation of resources, but it also tended to spread the national income over many income recipients. Labor, capital, and what Alfred Marshall described as "business power" or "organizing ability" received compensations which reflected the operations of the forces of supply and demand. Workers, savers, and businessmen carried on their bargaining activities in markets which were quite free from the inflexibilities later introduced by collective action. Since each agent of production competed with many other similar agents, the returns of all agents were reduced to the levels dictated by the prevailing supply and demand conditions. The returns that went to labor, capital, and business power were roughly measured by the marginal contributions of each competing agent of production. In small-scale competitive economies, such as the English and American economies of the first three quarters of the nineteenth century, the forces of supply and demand worked through the flexible price system to prevent any one agent of production from getting a share of the national income which was larger than its contribution justified. Competition acted as a great leveller of the incomes going to labor, capital, and business power; and where land was abundant, as in the United States, even rent incomes felt the levelling influence of the competitive forces of supply and demand.

When the holistic economists examine the price system of the modern hybrid economy, they find it is as hybrid as the economy itself. Prices range all the way from the purely competitive to the purely monopolistic, with prices in between these limits revealing various admixtures of both competitive and monopolistic elements. The price system is no longer the smoothly functioning, coordinating mechanism that the late nineteenth- and early twentieth-century orthodox economists took it to be. The capacity of the price system to allocate resources in a balanced, efficient manner, to distribute the national income widely over many classes in the community, and to maintain high levels of general economic activity has been seriously impaired by the changes which have occurred in recent decades in the structure and functioning of the maturing American economy. In the peripheral, competitive areas of the modern economy the price system continues to function as a fairly satisfactory adjustment mechanism. Were it not for the disturbing influences that emanate from the non-competitive areas of economic activity, the price system in the competitive segment of the modern economy would tend to make all the necessary adjustments without much difficulty. But the same cannot be said for other segments of the economy. In less competitive areas the price system fails to perform satisfactorily as a coordinating or adjusting mechanism. Furthermore, this failure becomes more apparent as one approaches the economy's inner core of monopolistic activity.

The failure of the monopolistic segment of the modern hybrid price system to make the adjustments which bring about a smooth functioning of the total economy shows up in three different ways. In the first place prices in the non-competitive areas of the economy show no tendency to fall to the level of costs of production. Nor are the discrepancies between selling prices and costs of production eliminated in the long run; instead they become permanent sources of incomes which are larger than necessary to induce businessmen to work or to risk their capital. In the second place, the modern price system does not function in such a manner as to allocate resources efficiently among the various lines of industry. In the lines where industrial concentration has made considerable progress the freedom of entry of new firms is greatly restricted; even though selling prices are well above costs of production in the long run, they are not free to attract new investments. Without the free movement of capital into highly monopolistic industries there can be no allocation of resources which conforms to the preferences of consumers. In circumstances where consumers prefer larger supplies at lower prices the managers of the monopolistic enterprises restrict output with the aim of maximizing profits. The third indictment levelled by the holistic economists against the hybrid price system of the mature capitalistic economy is that it tends to prevent a level of full employment for men and machines. In the monopolistic areas of the economic system the managers of corporate enterprise seek to establish selling prices which maximize net profits, but these prices do not provide for the optimum use of labor and capital. Instead they call for production schedules which are smaller than they would be if thoroughly competitive conditions were to prevail. The whole trend in the price policies of firms in those areas of the economy where monopoly factors are important is toward a restriction of output and a curtailment of employment for both men and machines.

The holistic economists explain that the modern hybrid price system functions in such a way as to combine the equilibrium of the individual firm with the disequilibrium of the whole economy. In the non-competitive areas of the mature American economy the individual firm may achieve a position in which it maximizes its net profits, but this is also a position which is associated with a poor allocation of the nation's resources, and with a less-than-full level of employment for labor and capital. In these circumstances the operations of the private markets cannot be relied upon to provide as large a national income as is possible, or to distribute this income in an equitable fashion. The failure of the hybrid price system to function adequately does not disturb the small number of individuals who manage or own corporate enterprises in the inner monopolistic area of the economy. In spite of the economy's poor over-all allocation of resources and the less-than-optimum level of general economic activity, these individuals are in a position to lay claim to large surplus or unearned money incomes. By various devices they draw to themselves enough of the nation's income flow to have an interest in preserving the economic *status quo*. This *status quo* is one in which the inner monopolistic area of the mature American economy exploits the outer competitive areas. Those who work in the competitive areas of the economic system are forced to sell their output of goods or services at competitively determined prices, while at the same time they must purchase the output of the large-scale firms in the inner monopolistic areas at non-competitively determined prices. In these circumstances, which are peculiar to the mature capitalistic economy, the old injunction to "buy cheap and sell dear" no longer redounds to the benefit of all parties, as was true to some extent in the highly competitive economy of the early nineteenth century.

The exploitation that develops out of the operations of the hybrid price system throws the final burdens of economic adjustment upon the competitive lines of economic activity. When cyclical or secular stagnation descends upon the business system, the firms enjoying monopolistic positions cut down their purchase of raw materials and their employment of workers. The monopolistic firms, which enjoy large net returns in prosperous years, assume little responsibility for the preservation of the agricultural and other competitive types of enterprise which supply the basic raw materials of industry. Nor do these monopolistic firms assume much responsibility for the well-being of their workers who are cut off the payrolls when prosperity vanishes. In general, as John M. Clark has shown in his *Studies in the Economics of Overhead Costs,* large-scale monopolistic enterprises show little regard for the need to keep the economy functioning as a going concern. If the incomes of farmers fall below what is considered necessary for ordinary living, the farmers turn to the state and federal governments for financial and other assistance. Likewise, the community is called upon to bear much of the burden of caring for unemployed workers who have been ejected from the areas of monopolistic enterprise in periods of business depression. Some of these unemployed workers who have been forced out of the inner region of monopolistic activity turn to farming, small-scale retailing, or some other highly competitive activity in search of work and income. The final outcome is a multiplication of the number of farms and small-scale business enterprises at the very time that these competitive activities are already overcrowded.

The surplus or unearned incomes received by the monopolistic industries at the core of the economy are not taken up entirely by corporate managers and owners. In these strategic industries various economic interests other than the corporate managers and owners have been in a position to lay claim to a portion of the industries' surplus income. In some instances individuals who are in possession of scarce natural resources used by the industries enjoying monopoly returns have been able to siphon off some of this surplus income through large royalties or high prices for raw materials. In other cases individuals owning patents have been able to drain off a part of an industry's surplus income flow. Organized labor has also enjoyed a strategic position. In the key industries of the monopolistic core of the mature American economy strong labor organizations have successfully laid claim to a share of the surplus incomes by demanding wages far in excess of competitive wage levels. In this manner raw-material producers, patent owners, organized labor, and corporate managers and owners have acted collectively, but usually informally, to exploit the less monopolistic areas of the economic system. John M. Clark explains that "This spirit of irresponsible self-seeking persisted into a new age in which the competitive checks are vanishing or being progressively weakened, and in which group organization is taking the place of the competing individual. These group organizations have power, for good or for harm, which the simple individual did not possess. As a result, irresponsible self-seeking can no longer be trusted (if it ever could be) to build a scheme of voluntary working together. But this system of group organizations is animated to altogether too great an extent by a spirit and philosophy suited to the individualistic era of one hundred years ago. This 'cultural lag' is one of the most threatening features of our whole situation." [29] A. B. Wolfe expresses the same opinion with respect to the dangers associated with the emergence in the modern economy of new power groups. "It is not to be expected," he explains, "that organized labor will invariably use its power with any more forbearance, fairness, and public spirit than big business formerly used its power, or than certain agricultural organizations have of late been using theirs." [30]

This union of corporate managers and related economic interests for the purpose of exploiting the outer, competitive areas of the modern economy has not always been a smooth-working affair. It has been dictated more by considerations of selfish group interests than by a regard for the general economic welfare. Such a union, however, accounts for the lack of a united front on the part of both labor and capital. Businessmen do not reveal any well-developed class consciousness; instead their numbers have broken down into a

[29] "Educational Functions of Economics After the War," page 64.
[30] "Economy and Democracy," page 12. For a similar view see Hansen, Alvin H., Fiscal Policy and Business Cycles, 1941, page 402.

variety of conflicting groups whose conflicts run along the lines of "small" versus "big" business, or of "rural" versus "urban" enterprise. The situation is the same with respect to the labor world, in which there is found not a well-developed class consciousness but a division of interests among the various classes of workers. In general, those workers who enjoy the shelter of monopolistic enterprise show little disposition to unite on common causes with the workers of the competitive sections of the economy. The front presented by the labor organizations is as disunited as the front shown by the business community. In both cases special group welfare takes precedence over class welfare except at those times when the interests of the entire class are seriously threatened.

The failure of the modern hybrid price system to allocate resources efficiently, to prevent the growth of unearned incomes, and to maintain general economic activity at a high level has not occurred without strenuous objections coming from various groups within the economic system. In seeking to achieve greater economic security and larger incomes these aggrieved groups have turned for aid from extra-market agencies or institutions. In the special circumstances of the maturing American economy only two other institutions could be called upon by aggrieved interests to mitigate the evils emanating from the private market places. These two institutions are the law courts and the government. In modern capitalism the family, the church, and other social institutions are powerless to interfere with the operations of the private markets. The situation, however, is quite different in the case of the law courts and the government, because both of these institutions are in a position to influence the flow of economic activity. They may give support to economic tendencies already in operation, or they may seek to deflect these tendencies in new directions which lead to greater general economic welfare. In the competitive capitalism of the first three quarters of the nineteenth century the extra-market operations of both the courts and the government were of little significance. They consisted primarily of giving encouragement to the competitive forces which were already well established. After 1875 the situation was radically altered; competitive capitalism soon succumbed to the deteriorating influence of the emerging monopolistic or corporate way of doing business. Before long both the courts and the government were actively engaged in domesticating the new monopoly capitalism with its imperfect markets and its hybrid price system. They endeavored to provide remedies for the poor working of the new hybrid price system by attacking two problems, monopoly and inequalities in income distribution. In attacking the monopoly problem the courts and the government sought to make the monopolists more responsive to the preferences of consumers. They tried to achieve this goal by removing some of the barriers which prevented the free entry of capital into the areas of the economy dominated by monopolistic enterprise. It was believed that this free entry, once established, would result in larger output, lower prices, and a better allocation of the nation's resources. By trying to clear the private-investment channels, the courts and the federal government sought to restore those marginal adjustments in the investment field which the former competitive price system had made possible, but which were becoming increasingly difficult in the new hybrid economy.

The courts and the government also attempted to interfere with the distribution of the national income, which after 1875 showed a tendency to concentrate in the hands of too few people. Since the hybrid price system could no longer guarantee a wide distribution of income, the courts and the government recognized an obligation to alter the emerging pattern of income distribution. This problem of growing income inequality was attacked from many angles. The regulatory devices created by the state and federal governments and sanctioned by the courts included price control, minimum wage regulations, progressive income taxation, unemployment insurance, and other forms of social insurance. Efforts were made not only to prevent the maldistribution of income, but also to correct the maldistribution which had already occurred. In general, the aim of the government and the law courts was to create a situation in which the community's most urgent economic wants would be satisfied first. Since the hybrid price system permitted the flow of excessive amounts of income to a few groups in the community, the least urgent economic needs of these select groups were being satisfied while many of the more urgent needs of less-favored groups in the community were going unmet. By transferring income from the high-income to the low-income groups the government and the law courts sought to restore something of that competitive situation in which a high price meant not only a high marginal but also a high social utility.

Prior to 1929 the courts and the government showed little concern with the third function of a satisfactory price system, the maintenance of a high level of economic activity. This is not surprising in view of the fact that the period from 1900 to 1929 was one of great national expansion and relatively full employment. Apart from short cyclical periods of depression there was during the first three decades of the twentieth century a high level of national economic activity. In the years from 1900 to 1929 total industrial production in the United States more than trebled, while per capita industrial production almost doubled. In these favorable circumstances, which were made possible by rapid technological and geographical expansion, although there was much inequality in the distribution of income, there were few years of mass unemployment. Surplus private incomes were used for either the establishment of new enterprises or the expansion of old firms, with the result that these unearned incomes were returned to the economy's income circuit-flow in the form of demands for labor, capital equipment, and raw materials. As a consequence the maintenance of full employment in this period of national expansion presented no major difficulty.

Since 1929 the problem of maintaining a high level of general economic activity has once more become a major concern of both economists and politicians, as it had been in the years from 1873 to 1898. According to the traditional economic analysis a period of deflation would not bring about mass unemployment for men and machines because many checks would operate to prevent such a development. Falling prices would stimulate less saving and more consuming until the proper balance was established between saving and consuming. Interest rates would decline, and in so doing they would stimulate more investment. In addition, wage rates would fall with the result that new and more profitable cost-price relationships would be established in the business world. In these and other ways the competitive price system was supposed to be able to withstand the shock of deflation without plunging the economy into a prolonged era of chronic stagnation. The holistic economists point out that these adjustments frequently do not take place in the mature American economy when depression sets in. All interests rates do not decline, and in the case of those that are lowered there may be little stimulation of private business enterprise. When prices fall consumption is not increased, nor is money saving decreased. Furthermore, in some segments of the modern economy prices and wage rates are inflexible or "sticky," with the result that adjustments are made through the curtailment of output and employment rather than through price and wage adjustments. It is the position of the holistic economists that there is nothing in the functioning of the modern hybrid price system to prevent a downward movement of business from being accompanied by mass unemployment for men and machines for an extended period of time. As they see it, the way in which the present, mixed price system actually operates is almost a guarantee that a deflationary price movement will be followed by a low level of general economic activity for a lengthy period of time.

The holistic economists who have been studied in prior chapters are in agreement with the view that the modern hybrid price system, if left uncontrolled, will not function so as to bring about, or to preserve, a high level of national economic activity. They all agree that some form of intervention is necessary if the price system is to perform in such a way as to allocate the nation's resources efficiently, prevent the accumulation of unearned income, and maintain a high level of economic activity. This agreement in the realm of economic diagnosis, however, is not duplicated with respect to what should be done to make the price system a more satisfactory adjustment mechanism. Veblen was of the opinion that the price system could not function properly as long as it was tied to a private enterprise system. From a much more conservative viewpoint Commons advocated the control of market operations by governmental agencies with additional checks upon the market mechanism being supplied by voluntary associations of small businessmen, farmers, workers, and consumers. Mitchell, Clark, Tugwell, and Means, while not recommending Veblen's radical program, go beyond Commons's limited suggestions to advocate some form of national economic planning which would seek to preserve the institutional framework of the mature capitalistic economy, but which would nevertheless interfere quite extensively with the operations of the private markets. In the planning schemes advocated by Mitchell, Clark, Tugwell, and Means the price and production policies of the key industries in the inner core of monopolistic enterprise would no longer remain purely private, corporate affairs. These economists do not agree on the extent to which price and production controls should go, but they do agree that the heart of a national planning program would be found in these two types of control.

The particular proposals of the holistic economists for making the hybrid price system a more satisfactory adjustment mechanism differ in many important ways, but the general purpose of their suggestions is the same in all cases. The price control schemes of these economists are all based on a recognition of the increasing centralization of twentieth-century economic activity. They accept the view that the competitive portion of the mixed price system will go on declining in importance in the future. This means that price control schemes will come to be more and more concerned with the inflexible prices of the expanding inner monopolistic core of the maturing economy. In the opinion of these heterodox economists all proposals for interfering with the operations of the private markets that do not take proper account of the centralizing trends in American economic life have no chance of being successful. The planning proposals of Veblen and other holistic economists have the further common aim of greatly reducing, if not entirely eliminating, the polarization of American economic life which has made such great strides since 1875. All these economists hope to reduce the conflict between money-making and goods-making which has become such a prominent feature of twentieth-century American economic life. They look forward to a future situation in which money-making and goods-making will be two harmonious aspects of a single, smoothly functioning economic process. This economic process would be one in which the price system allocated resources efficiently, prevented the receipt of unearned incomes, and maintained a high level of national economic activity.

The Price Theory of the Holistic Economists

In developing their theory of the American economic order the holistic economists have not had much to say about either competitive price theory or those refinements in price theory which have been the special interest of such revisionists as Edward H. Chamberlin and Joan Robinson. This does not mean that the heterodox economists have no place in their theoretical system for competitive or imperfectly competitive price theory.   If they had gone to the length of providing a thoroughly well-rounded explanation of the working of all the various segments of the hybrid American economy, the holistic economists would have found the price theory of the equilibrium economists very useful in their explanation of the functioning of those segments of the economy which lie outside the area of large-scale, oligopolistic and monopolistic enterprise.   But these economists have not been especially interested in the competitive and imperfectly competitive areas of the American economy; they have been much more concerned with the operations of the central core of highly monopolistic enterprise to which the price theorizing of the equilibrium economists has only a very limited application.

When Veblen first turned to economic analysis in the closing decade of the last century, price theory dealt with explanations of purely competitive and purely monopolistic prices, with the major attention of orthodox economists being directed toward the pricing processes of the competitive areas of the economy.   The orthodox economists of the late nineteenth century were little concerned with what lay in between the limiting cases of pure monopoly and pure competition, but the same cannot be said of Veblen.   His special concern was with what he described as "partial monopoly," or with what has in recent years become known as "oligopoly."   It was the large corporate enterprise, with its inflexible prices, its sometimes highly differentiated products, its large-scale technology, and its freedom from the pressure of many competitors, that absorbed Veblen's scientific interest.   The economists who followed Veblen continued to exhibit the same special interest in that area of the economy in which are found large partially monopolistic or oligopolistic enterprises.   In his 1913 study of the business cycle Wesley C. Mitchell drew special attention to the connection between large-scale corporate enterprise and the problem of business instability.   John M. Clark has always been interested in those industries which have large overhead costs, indeterminate prices, and excess productive capacity.   John R. Commons's concept of a "reasonable capitalism" is built around a view of the American economy in which "big business" plays a decisive role.   Gardiner C. Means's administrative economics takes special notice of the role in the modern economy of the large semi-monopolistic corporate enterprise with its administered prices and its restrictive production policies. It may be said that in general the holistic economists have centered their scientific interest in those lines of economic activity which, although preserving some of the features of purely competitive enterprise, have turned out to be in essence deviations from pure monopoly rather than from pure competition. These predominantly monopolistic lines of large-scale business enterprise have not been the lines of economic activity to which recent price-theory revisionists have primarily directed their attention.

In recent years price-theory revisionists like Edward H. Chamberlin and Joan Robinson, who have been "born and reared in a Marshallian environment," have followed Veblen and later exponents of economic heterodoxy in focusing their attention on market prices which are admixtures of both competitive and monopolistic elements.[31] But they have not been interested in that part of the middle ground between pure competition and pure monopoly which has claimed the attention of the holistic economists. This middle ground is a wide area in which there are market prices containing many different combinations of competitive and monopolistic elements. Where the monopolistic elements are dominant, market prices may be regarded as deviations from the norm of purely monopolistic price. Conversely, where the competitive elements are of major importance, market prices may be looked upon as deviations from the norm of purely competitive price. Chamberlin, Robinson, and other recent price theorists have limited their analysis primarily to those market prices which are deviations from the norm of pure competition. These economists have been especially interested in explaining price formation in the imperfectly competitive segment of the economy which lies between the highly competitive and the highly monopolistic segments. This is the area of the economy in which it is still possible to theorize, with a certain show of realism, within the limits of the same assumption that was made by the competitive price theorists of the late nine-

[31] Triffin, Robert, *Monopolistic Competition and General Equilibrium Theory,* page 188. Cambridge: Harvard University Press, 1940. Chamberlin acknowledges the early interest of Thorstein Veblen and John M. Clark in "the middle ground between competition and monopoly," but in 1932 he regarded this ground as being virtually unexplored. See Chamberlin's *The Theory of Monopolistic Competition,* 1938, pages 4-5.

teenth century, that is to say within the assumption that the "competing monopolists" or "imperfectly competitive" firms do not act collectively to limit production, fix prices, or restrict entry into the industry. Recent price-theory revisionists have restricted their analysis very largely to the imperfectly competitive segment of the economy, because they have found that their equilibrium approach, with its central doctrine of the determinate or equilibrium market price, is not so very fruitful in the more monopolistic areas of the economy. It is because the holistic economists are primarily interested in these more monopolistic areas of economic activity that they find it necessary to go beyond the recent thought of the equilibrium price theorists.

In their theorizing about the price and production policies of large-scale, semi-monopolistic or oligopolistic enterprises the holistic economists abandon the assumptions of equilibrium price theory. They work instead with the assumptions that concerted action to control price and production is the rule rather than the exception, that there is limited entry of new firms into the industry, and that ownership and control of the firm are not in the same hands. When theorizing within the limits of these assumptions which apply to the inner monopolistic core of the modern economy, the holistic economists find themselves in a world of economic indeterminateness. In this indeterminate world, as long as extra-market forces do not intervene, selling prices do not tend to cover only costs of production which include a normal profit for the entrepreneur; surplus profits are not wiped out; and inefficient firms are not driven into bankruptcy in the long run. The questions must then be raised, how far can the economist go in making generalizations about price and production policies in such an area of economic indeterminateness? How far can he get away from concrete cases in the direction of price theorizing on a high level of generality? After several decades of concern with the economy's central area of monopolistic enterprise, the holistic economists would say that theorizing about the price behavior of monopolistic enterprises cannot get very far from concrete cases and still remain relevant to the real economic world. As a recent critic of the theory of monopolistic competition has put it, in order to make progress in the field of oligopolistic enterprise, price theorizing will have to turn to "more pedestrian, but more fruitful methods." It will have to recognize the "richness and variety of all concrete cases, and tackle each problem with due respect for its individual aspects." In addition, less reliance should be placed "on a mere resort to the passkey of general theoretical assumptions." [32] It is the position of the holistic economists that as economic investigation is extended into the focal, monopolistic area of the modern economy, equilibrium price theory becomes progressively less useful as an interpretative device. As the economist moves in from the outer competitive areas of the economy the basic assumptions of equilibrium price theory become increasingly less relevant, and the analytical propositions based upon these assumptions become increasingly less applicable to the area of large-scale enterprise which is of such great interest to the holistic economists.

The position of Veblen and the later heterodox economists with respect to the work of the equilibrium price theorists is explained by Walton H. Hamilton in his volume on *Price and Price Policies*. He points out in this study that "To set up a norm of 'perfect competition,' and to attempt to discover the principles that shape its imperfections, is as unpromising as a quest for the norms of abnormality. To set cases down along a straight line that moves from monopoly through duopoly and oligopoly to competition pure and undefiled, and to measure competitive forces by the relative number and size of sellers and buyers, is to make hypothetical economic phenomena the subject of mathematical exercises. The tricks may be pulled off with neatness and intricacy; but the result is not a picture of the pragmatic reality called industry . . . although a sharp line can never be drawn, it is one thing to employ a set of hypotheses which defines the character of method and quite another to formulate patterns into which observed facts are to be cast. The line has been crossed when the results of inquiry bear a stronger resemblance to the tricks of the trade than to the phenomena brought under analysis. A generalization is exactly what the word implies—that which under careful observation is found to be general among a series of related instances. But when the general has its source in the method of attack, it is theology rather than science which is set down." [33] Of course it is not Hamilton's position that

---

[32] Triffin, Robert, *Monopolistic Competition and General Equilibrium Theory*, page 189.

[33] Hamilton, Walton H., and others, *Price and Price Policies*, 1938, pages 22-23.

no generalizations can be made about the price behavior of firms which operate in the non-competitive areas of the economy. He understands that it is the aim of the economist to reduce the complexity of modern economic activity to some sort of order or pattern. It is his scientific purpose to take the particulars of economic life and to draw from them whatever generality they possess. But Hamilton is unwilling to find order, pattern, or generality in the world of large-scale, oligopolistic enterprise by the procedure of starting off with oversimplified, arbitrary assumptions which place the real world of great economic complexity beyond the economist's framework of analysis.

Veblen, Commons, Mitchell, and their disciples find that the central area of the modern economy is always in a state of general disequilibrium, the bad effects of which are found working throughout the whole economy. It is the position of these heterodox economists that this condition of economic disequilibrium can be corrected only through the intervention of some extra-market agencies. Although they do not agree on what should be the form of economic intervention, these economists are in agreement that the deficiencies of the American economic system can be removed only through the abandonment of the laissez-faire principle as a guide in economic affairs. Since they are so much concerned with the problem of economic intervention, it would be reasonable to assume that the exponents of economic heterodoxy would devote considerable thought to the price and production problems which would develop out of a program of economic intervention. This would be especially true of those holistic economists who favor some form of general or over-all economic planning. Veblen, who advocated the establishment of a socialistic economy, said little about the price and production policies which would be followed by a socialist planning agency. He thought that under socialism there would be "a more competent management of the country's industrial system," which would call for a "due allocation of resources and a consequent full and reasonably proportioned employment of the available equipment and manpower." [34] This due allocation and reasonably proportioned employment of land, labor, and capital would be such as to maximize the want-satisfying powers of the available resources.

[34] Veblen, Thorstein, *The Engineers and the Price System*, 1921, pages 141-142.

Veblen did not, however, get beyond these very broad generalizations. He did not discuss the question as to whether or not a socialistic economy could function without a price system. If it was his position that a price system was as essential to a socialistic as to a capitalistic economy, Veblen left a fertile field of economic inquiry uncultivated. He did not compare and contrast the operations of unplanned capitalistic and planned socialistic markets with the intention of showing how much of equilibrium price theory would be applicable to both types of markets.[35]

The holistic economists who have thought in terms of general economic planning within a framework of private enterprise, have likewise not given much attention to the price and production problems which would confront a central planning agency. The goal of these economists is a planned or managed equilibrium in which the national planning agency would set forces in motion to bring about whatever desirable allocations of resources the private market mechanism failed to make. A. B. Wolfe has explained this goal with the statement that "The essential point is that under either ideal competition or ideal planning productive resources would be so organized, distributed, and proportioned that the production of consumption goods and services would be maximized and stabilized." [36] In pursuing this program of maximizing consumer benefits the central planning agency would meet its most serious difficulties in the highly monopolistic areas of the modern economy. Mitchell, Clark, Tugwell, and Means do not explain in any detailed manner how they would alter the price and production policies of the large-scale enterprises in the inner, monopolistic area of the American economy so as to bring about an optimum utilization of productive facilities. These economists have yet to broaden the scope of their economic analyses to include an explanation of the functioning of the price

[35] It was not until after the Great Depression of 1929, which brought a renewed interest in the reconstruction of economic society, that the price and production problems of a socialistic economy were subjected to an intensive theoretical scrutiny. For examples of this type of price theorizing, see Dickinson, H. D., "Price Formation in a Socialist Community," *Economic Journal*, June, 1933, Lerner, A. P., "Economic Theory and Socialist Economy," *Review of Economic Studies*, Oct., 1934, and Knight, F. H., "The Place of Marginal Economics in a Collectivist System," *The American Economic Review*, March, 1936.

[36] Wolfe, A. B., "Thoughts on Perusal of Wesley Mitchell's Collected Essays," *The Journal of Political Economy*, Feb., 1939, Vol. XLVII, page 25.

system in the novel economic situation in which the main responsibility for the guidance of economic activity would rest upon some central planning agency.

The Distribution Theory of the Holistic Economists

When Veblen criticized orthodox economic thought in the closing decade of the nineteenth century, the distribution theory of Alfred Marshall was widely accepted by academic economists in the United States. The general purpose of Marshall's distribution theory was to explain how national income was distributed in a highly competitive economic society in which monopoly activity and unearned incomes were conspicuous by their absence. The problem was primarily to explain the distribution of income in an economy where the forces of supply and demand were sufficiently powerful to prevent labor and capital from securing unearned incomes. Economic exploitation, or the getting of something for nothing as Veblen expressed it, was not a problem that interested Marshall very greatly. His main interest was in developing a theory of distribution which was applicable to an equilibrium condition in which a basic harmony of interests prevailed among all individuals and classes. In this equilibrium condition there were two basic functions, laboring and abstaining from consumption. The function of the laborer was to create various utilities by applying physical and mental efforts to the production of useful goods and services. The function of the saver was to increase the nation's supply of capital goods by diverting a part of the real-income flow away from consumption purposes. Being something of a realist, Marshall could not ignore the fact that the real economic world was far from being riskless. He was therefore compelled to regard risk-taking as a third essential function which required a remuneration for its being undertaken by businessmen. As one approached the theoretical limit of pure competition, however, the risk feature of economic society faded into the background to leave only the two functions of laboring and saving as essential functions requiring remuneration.

Having established to his own satisfaction that there were two basic economic functions, Marshall turned to his doctrines of "real costs" and "earned income." He explained that associated with the function of laboring was a real cost which took the form of the distastefulness or irksomeness involved in putting forth physical and mental efforts for the purpose of creating utilities. Likewise, there was connected with the saving function an "evil or discommodity" which resulted from the postponement of consumption by those who saved.[37] These two human sacrifices were psychological discommodities or inconveniences which had to be offset by economic rewards if they were to be borne by individuals. Marshall explained that in the market places of the competitive economy wages and interest rates were so adjusted by the forces of supply and demand that the sacrifices of the marginal workers and savers were offset by the returns received by these contributors to the national income. At the margin of business operations there was an equivalence between psychological sacrifices made and economic rewards received.

In Marshall's distribution theory not only did the forces of supply and demand make provision for covering the real costs of economic activity, but they also prevented the receipt by individuals of unearned or surplus incomes. Businessmen, laborers, and savers received rewards only in proportion to their contributions to the net product of industry. Real costs of efforts put forth, productivity of these efforts, and remuneration received were related to one another in such a manner by the forces of supply and demand that only those who contributed to the national income were in a position to draw upon that income. Money-making and goods-making usually went hand in hand; or, as Veblen would have put it, they were constitutionally related to each other. Whenever in the real economic world an agent of production found itself in a position to secure an "unnecessary profit" or "quasi-rent," this privileged position was soon eliminated by the ever-active forces of supply and demand.[38] Unearned incomes or quasi-rents were incongruous elements which were never allowed to become an integral part of Marshall's marginal productivity theory of distribution. This was so because his distribution theory was an extension of his equilibrium or normal price theory.

When contrasting the distribution theories of the late nineteenth-century neo-classicists and the twentieth-century holists, one must keep in mind that the two groups of economists are not concerned with explaining the distribution of income in the same type of eco-

[37] Marshall, Alfred, *Principles of Economics,* 1920, Eighth Edition, pages 140-142.
[38] *Ibid.,* page 424 fn.

nomic society. Marshall and other neo-classicists were mainly interested in an explanation of the distribution of income in a predominantly competitive society in which monopolistic activities of all types were relatively unimportant. The reverse is true of the holistic economists who are primarily concerned with an interpretation of income distribution in an economic society in which monopolistic activities are of such importance that the society can no longer be described as predominantly competitive. One may point out further that Veblen and later heterodox economists do not pay much attention to the distribution of income in the peripheral, competitive areas of the modern hybrid economic system. They are more interested in the ways in which incomes are earned and distributed in the inner areas of the American economy where monopolistic forces are of major importance. Since monopolistic situations are those in which some form of economic exploitation is usually found, the distribution theory of the heterodox American economists revolves around considerations of "unearned incomes" and discrepancies between money- and goods-making rather than the concepts of "earned income" and a fundamental harmony of economic interests.

In explaining the distribution of income among various individuals and classes the holistic economists observe that in the competitive areas of the hybrid economy there is a high degree of correspondence between goods- and money-making. The flexible prices of the free competitive markets are sufficient to guarantee that work done and remuneration received will be closely enough related to satisfy all those who contribute to the net product of industry. The situation changes, however, as one moves from the peripheral competitive areas toward the central monopolistic core of the economic system. When Veblen, Commons, Mitchell, and their followers turn their investigations in the direction of this central area, they discover that the money- and goods-making processes coincide less and less. The discrepancy between the two activities takes the form of an expanding unearned or surplus income. In the monopolistic areas of the economy the receipt of money incomes is less a reward for the function of producing useful material goods and services than a reward for restricting output, creating artificial scarcities, and otherwise securing a strategic position which provides protection from the levelling influences of the competitive forces of supply and demand. The holistic economists explain that in this central area of the economy there is a very wide discrepancy between the contributions to the nation's real income of those who specialize in accumulating pecuniary assets and those who specialize in the production of useful, material goods and services. The size of this discrepancy depends upon the extent to which those whose primary aim is to accumulate pecuniary assets have succeeded in establishing for themselves a strategic position based upon the control of corporate affairs. Where their strategic position is well established, the profit-makers have a strong bargaining power which enables them to draw toward themselves a large portion of the nation's money income. There is nothing determinate about these incomes going to the money- or profit-makers. They cannot be said to cover real costs of production or to equal contributions to the national income at some margin of production, because the competitive analysis does not apply to these incomes. Just like the selling prices which prevail in the inner monopolistic core of the modern economy, the share of the nation's income going to money-makers with strong bargaining powers varies from industry to industry, with its size depending upon the peculiar circumstances of each industry.

In Veblen's explanation of the distribution of income in a modern capitalistic economy goods-making was taken to be the primary function of individuals who labored, while money-making was taken to be the primary concern of those who saved or who underwent business risks. Individuals who saved did so only because they received unearned incomes far in excess of their consumption needs. They saved not because they abstained from consumption, but because they received incomes much in excess of what they could spend upon themselves. There was no question of any "real cost" or psychological discommodity with respect to the saving of income. The bulk of saving was done by those who took the usufruct or surplus product of industry from the workers, who had labored to produce this surplus product. Also, those who saved some of this usufruct did so only because they had more income than their consumption habits would permit them to consume. These savers of surplus income performed no useful function in the sense of contributing to the nation's supply of material goods and useful services. Likewise, the individuals who specialized in undertaking business risks performed no useful function, since risk-taking was designed to add to pecuniary assets rather than to the nation's real income. In the final analysis it was only the skilled and unskilled workers who, among the claimants to income in a capitalistic society, actually contributed to the community's social product or real income.

The heterodox economists who followed Veblen have not been as explicit as he was in his explanation of the distribution of income in the twentieth-century American economy. That their distribution theory remains the most incomplete portion of their economic thought is a fact which cannot be ignored. In spite of this failure of the latter-day exponents of economic heterodoxy to elaborate a theory of distribution which is applicable to the contemporary hybrid American economy, it is possible to indicate the general drift of their thought in relation to the problem of income distribution. Like Veblen, Mitchell and other holistic economists abandon Marshall's subjectivistic approach in their theorizing about the distribution of income. When they substitute their social or cultural psychology for the individualistic psychology underlying Marshallian economics, these economists shift their attention away from the real costs of production and their relation to the distribution of income. They turn instead to the more objective analysis of economic functions and their relation to the stream of social production. These critics of economic orthodoxy place their theorizing about the distribution of income in a social setting of class organization, collective standards of economic behavior, and group conflict. This social approach to the problem of income distribution is particularly appropriate to an analysis of the functioning of an economy which is dominated by collective action. It prepares the way for an interpretation of income distribution which draws attention to the lack of harmony of interests among the groups which are striving to enlarge their share of the nation's real income in the face of vigorous opposition.

In making this shift from an individualistic or subjectivistic approach to a more social or collective approach to the problem of income distribution, the latter-day holistic economists accept Veblen's dichotomy between serviceable goods-making and disserviceable money-making as the point of departure for their theorizing about the distribution of income. They do not, however, make as rigorous a use of the distinction between goods- and money-making as Veblen did. Unlike Veblen, these economists assume risk-taking to be an economic function which requires some reward if it is to continue to be forthcoming. They adopt the position that without the payment of returns for taking risks with one's savings or labor the private enterprise system could not continue in operation. Since the heterodox economists other than Veblen consider that a continuation of the private enterprise system is possible, they quite logically add risk-taking to laboring as a functional activity which requires a recompense. They would say that the saving of money is not in itself an activity that requires a return; a return is necessary, however, to induce individuals to invest their savings in risky enterprises. Savings will not be invested in risky ventures unless there is some prospect that gains will more than offset possible losses. As long as the ideological and institutional framework of the existing American economic system is maintained, the payment of returns for private risk-taking will continue to be a necessary payment.

The distribution theory of Mitchell, Clark, Commons, Tugwell, and Means revolves around the main proposition that there are only two important functions in the modern economic world which require remuneration, working and risk-taking. Although these latter-day holistic economists differ from Veblen by including risk-taking among the functions which contribute to a nation's annual real income, it does not appear on closer analysis that they disagree substantially with Veblen's explanation of the distribution of income. If the national planning programs of these economists were put into operation, they would cut down the importance of private risk-taking in modern economic life. It would be one of the aims of these planning programs to reduce monopolistic controls wherever possible in order to stimulate private, competitive risk-taking. But at the same time it would also be one of the major purposes of these planning proposals to regularize and stabilize economic activity in the inner monopolistic core of the economic system. In so far as this general aim of economic stabilization was achieved, the risks associated with private business enterprise would be greatly reduced. As these business risks were lessened, the necessity of making payments for risk-taking would likewise be curtailed. This would be especially true with respect to the large established key industries of the inner core of the economy which had reached a level of development in which the risk factor was no longer of great importance. The successful carrying out of the holistic economists' planning pro-

grams would tend to give the function of laboring a new significance.   Recompense for work done would tend to take precedence
over recompense for risk undertaken, with the result that the only
important class of claimants to national income would then be those
who labored.

Marginalism vs. Holistic Economics

It should be pointed out that the marginalism of Alfred Marshall
and John Bates Clark, which has been subjected to severe criticism
by Veblen and later heterodox economists, has not remained unchanged since the turn of the century.   The body of marginalist
economic thought has in recent decades been substantially altered
by economists who have been sensitive to the criticisms levelled
against the original formulations of this type of economic thought.
Among the economists in the United States who sought to revise
marginalism were Herbert J. Davenport and Frank A. Fetter, who
expressed a strong dissatisfaction with the hedonistic approach of
the earlier marginalists.   Davenport saw no need to plumb the
depths of subjective real-cost analysis, or to inquire into the ultimate nature of marginal utility.   "Purely as economists," he
wrote, "we are fortunately free from the necessity of investigating
the origin of choices or any of the psychological difficulties surrounding the question.   It is sufficient for us that these choices take place
as human nature presents itself." [39]   Davenport believed that by
taking things as they found them in the market place, and by not
going beyond supply and demand, economists could avoid all the
psychological difficulties in the work of the earlier marginalists.   He
was prepared to remove the objectionable psychological elements
from marginalism by the simple device of limiting the scope of economics to the point where all psychological problems would by
definition be no concern of the economist.   Economics would then
be no more than a "science of prices."

Frank A. Fetter raised the question of the desirability of abandoning the concept of marginal utility.   In the 1915 edition of his *Economics* he proposed to eliminate "the old utilitarianism and hedonism" of the marginalist school's economics by substituting the
concept of "choice" for that of "marginal utility."   According to

[39] Davenport, Herbert J., *The Economics of Enterprise,* page 60.   New York:
The Macmillan Company, 1913.

Fetter's volitional psychology men seek goods not because they calculate their utility, but because basic urges or impulses cause them to choose some goods over others.   The fundamental economic act of choosing is at bottom more impulsive or instinctive than rational. By making the basis of value "the simple act of choice and not a calculation of utility," Fetter was instrumental in making a theory of choice rather than calculation the central doctrine of marginalist theorizing.[40]   After 1915 marginalistic economists were much more concerned with developing the doctrine of "opportunity costs" and other theoretical refinements which dealt with the disposal of scarce means among alternative uses.   This emphasis on the theory of choice as the central interest of economic theorizing has reached its fullest expression in the work of Lionel Robbins, who states that economic "behaviour necessarily assumes the form of choice.   Every act which involves time and scarce means for the achievement of one end involves the relinquishment of their use for the achievement of another.   It has an economic aspect. . . .   Here, then, is the unity of subject of Economic Science, the forms assumed by human behaviour in disposing of scarce means." [41]   By centering his attention on how human ends or goals are chosen rather than upon the nature of these ends themselves, which he takes as "given data," Robbins endeavors to dispense with the introspective analysis of his marginalist predecessors.   But like Davenport and Fetter, he achieves this goal only by arbitrarily limiting the content of economic theory to those matters which exclude inquiries into the nature of changing human wants.

At the same time that Davenport and Fetter were attempting to improve the psychological foundations of marginalist economics, certain European economists were proceeding with a more fundamental revision of marginalism.   These economists thought that the marginalism of both Marshall and Clark was weakened by its close association in the minds of many people with an approval of a laissez-faire economy; and the reformist interests of both Marshall and Clark did nothing to weaken this view that marginalist economics lent support to *laissez faire* as a guiding principle in the arrangement of human affairs.   This close connection between the utilitarian philosophy of the neo-classicists, their marginal analysis, and

[40] Fetter, Frank A., *Economics*, page ix.   New York: The Century Co., 1915-16.
[41] *An Essay on the Nature and Significance of Economic Science*, pages 14-15.

the principle of *laissez faire* did not long remain undisturbed. At the turn of the century there developed in England, Germany, and other European countries a strong movement to rid marginalist economics of its connection with "normative" or ethical problems. The general aim of the European revisionists was to make marginalism much more "neutral" than it appeared to be at the time that Marshall published the first edition of his *Principles* (1890). These revisionists drew much of their inspiration from the late nineteenth-century development in German philosophical thought which found a fundamental distinction between science and history. According to the epistemological theories of Wilhelm Windelband (1848-1915) and Heinrich Rickert (1863-1936), historical research was essentially different from scientific research since it could not give rise to a body of abstract generalizations. History was the "discipline of the particular," whereas science was the discipline of the abstract and the general. Science consisted of a body of abstractions which only indirectly related to the world of historical experience. The aim of science was to simplify reality as far as possible in order to establish a system of general concepts or abstractions. Windelband and Rickert asserted that progress in science was a matter of moving from the concrete to the abstract, from the empirical to the ideal, or from the individual to the general. The more abstract a science became, the more "pure" or "neutral" it was; and the most satisfactory method of purifying or neutralizing a science was to give it a mathematical formulation. When a science was given this mathematico-logical formulation, it was free from all introspective, normative, and cultural connections; and it then reached the highest possible level of intellectual purity and neutrality.[42]

Working with these neo-Kantian views of Windelband and Rickert on the nature of truly scientific thought, the European revisionists running from Vilfredo Pareto to Lionel Robbins have sought to reduce marginalist economics to a system of universal, abstract generalizations. These economists have increasingly come to identify economic science with the schemata of formal logic. As one recent exponent of this formalistic view of marginalist economics has explained, economic theory "consists of a body of general principles

---

[42] For an analysis of Windelband's and Rickert's dichotomy between scientific and historical research, see De Ruggiero, Guido, *Modern Philosophy*, 1921, translated by A. H. Hannay and R. G. Collingwood, pages 73-85.

and a discipline of logic which may be applied to the interpretation of all economic problems, past or present . . . it rests on a broad foundation of the study of human nature, and its most fundamental propositions can be applied to all conditions of mankind." [43]

In reducing marginalism to a body of formal, universal economic doctrines, these revisionists have made economics little more than an analysis of the mechanics of resource disposal or allocation. One recent American exponent of this twentieth-century version of marginalism has summarized the position of the revisionists by defining economics as "the study of the principles governing the allocation of scarce means among competing ends when the objective of the allocation is to maximize the attainment of ends." [44] The abstractions of this economics of resource allocation are of only limited use in explaining the functioning of the mature American economy. They have little to say about the pricing process in those numerous circumstances of a mature economy where individuals are not "free," that is to say, where they are subject to the influence of many collective, coercive forces. Nor does this twentieth-century version of marginalism have much to say about the distribution of income in a mature capitalistic economy, since it is alleged by the marginalists that there is no necessary connection between problems of resource allocation and those of income distribution. Marginalist economics, when reduced to "pure economic analysis," is concerned with the allocation of resources but not with the problem of how incomes are distributed, because the principles governing the proper disposal of scarce means so as to maximize the attainment of given ends have nothing to say about who is entitled to income. Contemporary marginal analysis explains how factors of production are combined in order to minimize costs of production, but it does not purport to explain the incomes going to the owners of the factors of production. This latter problem, which is not amenable to the mathematico-logical procedures of the new version of marginalism, is pushed beyond the pale of economic analysis by twentieth-century marginalists on the ground that it is a "normative" or ethical, but not a scientific, problem.

Twentieth-century marginalists have succeeded in emancipating

---

[43] Boulding, Kenneth E., *Economic Analysis,* page 8. New York: Harper and Brothers, 1941.

[44] Stigler, George J., *The Theory of Competitive Price,* page 12.

economic science from the utilitarianism and hedonism which survived, even though in attenuated form, in the marginalism of Alfred Marshall and other late nineteenth-century orthodox economists, but only at the price of greatly reducing the relevancy of economic theory to concrete economic problems. Problems of disposing of scarce means in those circumstances where individuals are not free from the influence of collective, coercive forces, and problems of income distribution in a mature capitalistic economy are real, historico-cultural problems calling for investigation. These problems cannot be met by retreating from reality, or by making economic science pure, neutral, and universal. The ultimate purpose of scientists is not to build systems of abstraction but to explain the realities around us. If inherited economics does not prove to be a satisfactory instrument for explaining the working of the advanced capitalistic economy, the solution appears to lie in altering the science of economics so that it may be better prepared to interpret the complex economic realities of the twentieth century. Certainly the solution does not lie in pushing economics to higher and higher levels of abstraction where reality disappears in the thin air of uninhibited formalism.

In keeping their version of economics close to historico-cultural realities the holistic economists have no intention of making economics a "normative" science, or of attempting to mix scientific and ethical analyses. Their purpose is to explain the concrete economic issues which face the various groups at work in the twentieth-century American economy. These groups have diverse schemes of economic and social values or ends. Some groups see a special value in goods-making, while others pay more attention to money-making. Some groups assert that they are the victims of economic exploitation, while others feel no compunction in taking surplus or unearned incomes. The holistic economist takes the existing value schemes of individuals and groups as so much economico-cultural data, the significance of which is to be explained rather than taken for granted or ignored. He does not set up his own ethical standards or value schemes when explaining twentieth-century economic behavior; instead he takes the value schemes which he finds already established in the capitalistic economy, and attempts to show how they influence the flow of economic activity. The conflicts which grow out of the clash between the goals of different economic groups are real problems which no economist intent upon providing a rounded interpretation of American economic activity can properly ignore. When the holistic economist broadens the scope of economic investigation to include a study of conflicting aims with respect to income distribution, he investigates this problem with the intention of offering scientific explanations and not of passing upon the desirability of particular economic goals. Explaining the real issues at stake in the maturing American economy does not involve moving from the realm of the scientific to that of the ethical. It does involve, however, taking account of much more economico-cultural data than contemporary marginalists are willing to consider as proper material for those whose primary interest is in economic analysis.

Veblen and other heterodox economists are greatly concerned with the price-determining and income-distributing activities of the economic system, but they do not analyze these activities *in vacuo*. They never lose sight of the fact that they are explaining a total pattern of economic organization known as the twentieth-century American economy. Since these price-determining and income-distributing activities occupy a central place in the modern "money economy," they necessarily reflect all the influences of the forces which change the ways in which the American people provide for their material needs. The changes which have occurred in the American economy as it has passed through the era of free competition into what has variously been described as "monopoly," "corporate," or "finance" capitalism have left their marks on the economy's market mechanism. The market mechanism of 1945 is in many important ways quite different from that of 1845, and in the future it will continue to respond to changes in industrial technology, business organization, and the wants of the American people.

In order to explain the changing nature of the market mechanism and its relations to the whole complex of economic arrangements which constitute the American economy, the holistic economists find it essential to take note of the technological basis of economic activity. This is not to say that they are interested in technology per se. These economists are not concerned with the engineering problems which are raised by discussing the most efficient ways of using given resources to achieve a fixed end. These engineering or technological problems fall outside the boundaries of social science. As the history of economic science shows, no reputable economist has ever proposed to widen the scope of economics to include the problems of engineering; but this does not mean that economists should have no interest in the technological basis of modern industry. Technology is an especially important factor in the economic sphere of human culture, because the structure and functioning of the economic system reflect all the basic changes which occur in the ways in which men produce and distribute goods and services. Even the most orthodox of economists consider it important to pay attention to what Veblen called "the state of the industrial arts." Lionel Robbins states that economists are interested in technology as one of the influences determining the relative scarcity of commodities. In any given economic situation the relative scarcity of a good will be influenced by whether or not there exists a fruitful means of producing it. Robbins explains that in this way the conditions of technique "show" themselves in the existing production arrangements of a community.[45] But this is as far as Robbins is willing to push his inquiry into the influence of technology upon economic activity. He argues that it is not the duty of the economist to explain how technology alters the structure and functioning of the market mechanism, or of the entire economy itself. Such matters are alleged to fall outside the proper scope of economic science, and to relate to what Robbins describes as the "sociological penumbra." Just as Alfred Marshall had his convenient disposal cage or pound for intractable economic data in the form of a *ceteris paribus,* so also Robbins, a generation later, creates an equally convenient "sociological penumbra" to which he relegates all data that do not fit in with his static, analytical treatment of economic problems.

The holistic economists are unable to accept Robbins's orthodox position with respect to the extent to which economists should concern themselves with industrial technology as a factor shaping the flow of economic activity. They would assert that Robbins's method of handling the technological aspect of economic activity is much too limited. What about the influence of changes in technology on economic activity over those periods of time in which the structure and functioning of the whole economic system are significantly altered? Is this not a matter that properly falls within the scope of

[45] *An Essay on the Nature and Significance of Economic Science,* page 38.

the economist's interest? The changing industrial technology of the past three quarters of a century has altered the competitive economy in many important ways. The new large-scale technology has opened the doors to an extensive monopolization of economic life, and has fostered the growth of corporate enterprise. It has prepared the way for the development of price inflexibilities of many sorts, and has in addition led to the substitution of collective for individual bargaining in many types of markets. More than this, the new industrial technology of recent decades has shifted the interest of consumers from non-durable to durable consumer goods with many important consequences for the general functioning of the modern economy. The final outcome has been a change in the structure and functioning not only of many subsidiary economic institutions but also of the whole economy itself.

There are three ways in which economists may examine the economic system.[46] They may investigate this system as they find it at a particular point in historical time. To examine the economy as it exists is to exclude the time factor, in the sense of historical time, and to concentrate attention on "things as they are." This type of analysis necessarily pays no attention to the effects of a changing technology upon economic life, because it is primarily a cross-sectional way of looking at the flow of economic activity. This is not to say that all cross-sectional economic analysis ignores the time factor completely. But when the element of time is introduced into cross-sectional analysis, as in the case of Marshall's "long run" time analysis, it is "theoretical" rather than "historical" time that is brought under investigation. Theoretical time is the kind of time from which the historical elements have been largely eliminated; it is a matter of hypothetical rather than actual historical duration. The second way of inquiring into the operations of the economic system is to examine the functioning of the economy over a period of time, but over a period which is not long enough to involve any basic changes in the technology or structure of the economic order. The economist may inquire into the course of economic life over

[46] Frank H. Knight makes a similar three-fold division of the field of economic science, but he is somewhat more skeptical than are the holistic economists about the possibility of making worth-while scientific generalizations in the second and third divisions of the field. For a further discussion of this matter see Knight's essay entitled "The Limitations of Scientific Method in Economics," *The Trend of Economics*, 1924, pages 263-264.

seasons or over phases of the business cycle during which basic economic changes do not reveal themselves.   In this second type of analysis the economist's primary interest is in those economic adjustments which are made in relatively short periods of time for the purpose of coping with the effects of disturbing influences and re-establishing some previously existing condition of balance or equilibrium.

Thirdly, the economist may examine the functioning of the economic system over a period of time which reveals how a changing technology alters the structure and functioning of the total complex of economic institutions.   In the real economic world things are always undergoing change.   While it may be helpful at times to ignore the facts of economic change, as in the case of the orthodox economists' static analysis, in order to comprehend fully what exists at any one point in time one has to consider both what has gone on before and what is about to emerge.   The economic world, as it is seen today, inherits much from the past and reveals much of the future.   Just as an "event" in the natural world is taken by Alfred N. Whitehead to be something which incorporates the past, present, and future, so likewise economic activity is investigated by the holistic economists from a similar three-dimensional viewpoint. When these economists look at the existing market mechanism, or the whole economy of which this mechanism is a vital part, they see economic institutions which have come from the past, which now exist, and which are in the process of developing new configurations.   As Gardiner C. Means has expressed it, they see "the modern economy in action." [47]   In order to interpret the functioning of this economic system in action, Veblen, Commons, Mitchell and economists of a similar bent combine the three aforementioned ways of inquiring into the nature of economic activity. Since their primary interest is in explaining the whole developing American economy, and not just a cross-section of this economico-cultural continuum, these economists see a need for going far beyond

---

[47] In Wesley C. Mitchell's words, "A man who realizes that he is studying an institution keeps his work in historical perspective, even when he confines himself to analyzing the form that the institution has assumed at a particular stage of its evolution.   By so doing he opens vistas enticing to future exploration, instead of suggesting a closed system of knowledge." See Mitchell's essay on "Wieser's Theory of Social Economics," *The Backward Art of Spending Money,* 1937, page 256.

the limited approach of the equilibrium economists. In effect they discover that it is necessary for their purpose to broaden the scope of economic inquiry to include much of what Robbins and other latter-day disciples of economic orthodoxy place in the dark realm of the "sociological penumbra."

Besides being greatly concerned with the technological basis of the American economy, the holistic economists are also very much interested in the private and public goals which direct the course of economic activity. They do not take the goals of those who participate in the affairs of the mature American economy as "given" data which are then placed outside the scope of the economist's analysis. These economists insist upon studying the ends of economic activity, because they observe that these ends have a very important influence on the flow of economic life. There is in their economic analysis no arbitrary separation of means and ends. The ways in which people dispose of their scarce means affect the nature of their ends; and vice versa, what people take as their goals has much influence on the ways in which they dispose of economic resources. For some purposes, as in highly refined, static economic analysis, it is possible to ignore for the time being the ways in which private and public goals shape the flow of economic life. But where economic analysis is pushed beyond the limited abstractions of deductive economics, as in the work of the holistic economists, it becomes important to show how the existing scale of human ends favors or impedes the free flow of economic activity.

The two primary ends which the American economic system serves are goods- and money-making. It is not enough to say that the economic system operates to provide the goods and services which people want; in addition, the private enterprise economy operates to meet the needs of those who wish to accumulate pecuniary assets. For many of the individuals who occupy strategic positions in the modern economy the making of money is a major goal. Money or pecuniary assets are sought because those who possess these assets in significant amounts also possess the power to influence the flow of economic activity.[48] In explaining the working of the American economy the holistic economists discover that it is very

<hr/>

[48] For a recent discussion of this matter by an economist who pays tribute to the influence of Wesley C. Mitchell, see Brady, Robert A., *Business as a System of Power*. New York: Columbia University Press, 1943.

important to distinguish between the two goals of goods- and money-making, and to indicate their different effects upon the flow of economic activity. The individuals who make the accumulation of pecuniary assets their primary goal frequently interfere with the efforts of the majority of the population to obtain satisfactory supplies of goods and services. The underlying population reacts to this distressing situation by seeking to achieve such goals as full employment, parity incomes, or the guaranteed annual wage. The failures of small businessmen to enjoy "free competition," of farmers to get "parity income," and of workers to secure "full em- ployment" result in the setting up by the government of national or communal programs which meet the needs of depressed or exploited economic classes. Through these programs the government endeavors to supplement the coordination of economic life which is provided by the private market mechanism. In these circumstances the goals of laissez-faire capitalism are slowly transformed into the goals of a "security capitalism," which elevate security for the masses of the population above profits for the venturesome capital owner.

The holistic economists' views on the proper scope of economic science may be summarized by pointing out that their economic analysis includes a study of the interrelations among industrial technology, scarce means, and the ends toward which economic activity is directed. In the work of these economists technology, scarce means, and human ends are intimately associated with one another. Industrial technology influences both economic activity and the human ends toward which that activity is directed. In turn, the flow of economic activity and the scheme of human values have considerable influence on the state of the industrial arts. A theory of the mature American economy should not stop with an explanation of how the satisfaction of human wants is achieved through the disposal of scarce means. This theory of total economic organization should also inquire into the factors which in the long run condition the disposal of scarce resources. These factors include the state of the industrial arts and the scheme of private and public goals, both of which have very much to do with a nation's general level of economic activity. An analysis of these factors necessarily broadens the economist's understanding of the functioning of the total economy.

The Contributions of the Holistic Economists

What is it that the American exponents of economic heterodoxy have contributed to the science of economics? Is it true that these economists have done no more than gather a "certain amount of interesting statistical material," that they have not gotten beyond some "useful monographs on particular historical situations," and that no "economic laws" have come out of their theorizing? [49] These criticisms of holistic economics are of long standing. At the 1918 round-table conference on economic theory, at which Walton H. Hamilton delivered his paper on "The Institutional Approach to Economic Theory," Lewis H. Haney raised the objection that the new approach to economic theory would "merely lead to an ever changing description of an ever changing environment." It was Haney's opinion that Hamilton and other heterodox economists had nothing out of which to develop economic laws, or on which to build a science of economics.[50] A few years later Allyn A. Young, in his critical review of the contributions in the volume entitled *The Trend of Economics* (1924), concluded that those who followed Thorstein Veblen could not be classed as scientists, since Veblen was not himself a scientist. Young refers to Veblen as "a man of genius," but he goes on to say that "the term scientist does not fit him. He is something that may be as good or better: an artist, an impressionist, painting the picture of the world as he sees it. No one else would see it in just the same way, except through his eyes." [51]

[49] Robbins, Lionel, *An Essay on the Nature and Significance of Economic Science,* page 114. See also Normano, J. F., *The Spirit of American Economics,* 1943, page 186. Normano erroneously states that "The main aim of the institutionalists is not a logical system but knowledge of facts of economic life, and the distinction between them and the German younger historical school is [only] in the working conditions of economists in the last quarter of the nineteenth century and the second quarter of the twentieth: a distinction between the old and the new material and the old and new techniques."

[50] See Haney's discussion of Hamilton's paper on institutional economics in *The American Economic Review,* Vol. IX, March, 1919, Supp., pages 320-321. For an expression of similar views at a later date, see Haney's chapter on "Veblen and Institutionalism" in his *History of Economic Thought,* 1936, Third Edition, pages 740-753, and his *Value and Distribution,* 1939, pages 5, 35.

[51] Young, A. A., "The Trend of Economics, as Seen by Some American Economists," *The Quarterly Journal of Economics,* Feb., 1925, Vol. XXXIX, page 183. Paul T. Homan reiterates this criticism of Veblen at a later date in his *Contemporary Economic Thought,* 1928, pages 180-181.

It was Young's opinion that the new economics was very much of a subjective matter, which reflected the individual responses of economists to various economic problems, but which provided no common ground with sufficient objectivity to serve as the basis for a science of economics. If, as Young and other critics allege, holistic economics is a matter of mere description, and if what the holistic economists describe is a matter of their own capricious choosing, then their work can never achieve the status of a science. But these are charges against holistic economic thought which do not stand up under careful scrutiny.

The real reason why its critics deny that holistic economics can ever lay any valid claim to be a science is because this type of economic thought fails to conform with these critics' preconceived ideas of what economics as a science should be. Haney, Young, Homan, and Robbins accept the view that economic science is a body of abstract, universal principles. These critics of holistic economics describe the highly refined uniformities of behavior worked out by the equilibrium economists as "economic laws"; and they describe the totality of such laws or principles as "economic theory." Even though these so-called laws of equilibrium economics are more conspicuous for their logical neatness than for their conformity to fact, no economist would deny that they throw some light on the nature of economic activity. The only question is, should we be satisfied with what little light these analytical propositions or economic laws throw on the nature of twentieth-century capitalistic enterprise? Should we be satisfied with this narrow version of economic science, or should we broaden it with the aim of enlarging our interpretation of the contemporary economic order? If it is true, as Frank H. Knight asserts, that the final product of orthodox economic theorizing is "an exact science of the general form of [economic] relations" which "can tell us little in the concrete," and whose "chief function is negative—to offset as far as possible the stupid theorizing of the man in the street," then there is much need for getting beyond the narrow systematization of economic data provided by the orthodox economists.[52] The exponents of economic orthodoxy, however, deny this scientific need to broaden the scope of economics. They say, furthermore, that their type of abstract,

[52] "The Limitations of Scientific Method in Economics," page 267.

analytical proposition is the only really scientific type of economic generalization, and that their body of economic laws comprises the basic core of economic science.

The holistic economists deny that the equilibrium economics of the past and present centuries exhausts the field of economic theory, and that scientific generalizations in this field should be limited to the abstract propositions of formalistic economics. From their viewpoint a science is defined as accumulated knowledge which is systematized with the aim of discovering generalizations that relate to a body of given data. Any way of systematizing knowledge which is more than a matter of fact-gathering can properly claim to be "scientific"; and the generalizations which arise from any such scheme of data systematization can be properly labelled "scientific." The kind of scientific generalizations that economists discover depends upon the ways in which they go about systematizing their knowledge of the economic world. These ways may vary from the logically neat, but unrealistic, schemes of data systematization of certain mathematical or pure economists at the one extreme to those ways of ordering economic knowledge at the other extreme, which come close to being no more than simple description or fact gathering. An economist is free to choose the mode of data systematization which he finds most useful for his scientific purposes, but there is no valid reason for calling his special way of ordering data "scientific" to the exclusion of all other ways of systematizing data. It is the aim of the holistic economists to avoid the dangers of those modes of data systematization which lean too heavily upon either logical neatness or simple description. They seek to avoid the extremes of both excessive formalism and rank empiricism. Frederick C. Mills explains their position when he observes that "The instrument of logical deduction may yield an orderly theoretical structure, the counterpart of which it is difficult to find in reality, while a frontal attack on reality may reveal nothing but disorderly and disconnected phenomena. In steering between these two extremes economists must lean heavily upon their scientific inheritance. But, precious as this is, something more is required. Probably no economist would deny today the need of a mode of attack better adapted to the study of contemporary conditions than is that provided by the body of theory which had its origin in the conditions and problems of the nineteenth century and in the preconceptions of nineteenth-century thinking." [53]

The holistic economists point out that their mode of attack or way of systematizing economic knowledge is different from that of the analytical economists but is no less scientific. The analytical economists start off with a static, mechanistic framework of interpretation and end with logically precise but unrealistic generalizations. The exponents of holistic economic thought have as their point of departure a dynamic, systemic framework of interpretation which enables them to uncover generalizations which are much more realistic or empirical than those of the analytical economists. The fact that the economic generalizations worked out by the holistic economists are more empirical than the generalizations of the analytical economists does not make the generalizations of the former economists any less scientific than those of the latter economists. The scientificalness of a generalization about the economic world is not determined by the degree of abstraction or empiricism which it exhibits. All scientific generalizations are both abstract and empirical. The extent to which they are abstract or empirical is dependent upon the kind of problems with which the investigator is concerned, and not upon any fixed rule of logic or other analytical principle. It is because Veblen and other heterodox economists are interested in problems not contemplated by the equilibrium economists of the past and present that their economic generalizations are more empirical than those of the latter school of economists.

The body of holistic economic thought is far from being an amorphous *omnium gatherum*. It is much more than a series of monographs on unrelated economic topics or a medley of unconnected economic generalizations. The body of holistic economic thought, which is called to mind by "a theory of the economic order," is an organized intellectual schema or theoretical system which is designed to provide an interpretation of the functioning of the economic sphere of contemporary American culture. In their economic analyses the holistic economists go far beyond a simple description of the modern economy to create a systematic, orderly interpretation of the whole economic system. Their economic

[53] Mills, Frederick C., "On the Changing Structure of Economic Life," *Economic Essays in Honor of Wesley Clair Mitchell*, 1935, page 358.

interpretation has little resemblance to the logically precise, theoretical system of the neo-classical economists. Since the modern economy reveals little of the neatness and symmetry of the "solar system of counterpoise and balance" to which Alfred Marshall's body of economic theory has been likened, it is not to be expected that an interpretation of the modern economy which keeps close to its disorder and untidiness would bear much resemblance to the mathematico-logical thought structure of the formalistic equilibrium economists.[54] This was understood by the holistic economists at an early date in the development of their thought. At the round-table conference on economic theory, held in 1918, Walton H. Hamilton drew attention to the fact that it could be anticipated that his new economics would "lack the clear-cut, definite, and articulate character of neo-classical theory. Its concern with reality, its inability to ground a scheme of thought upon a few premises, its necessity of reflecting a changing economic life, alike make its development slow and prevent it from becoming a formal system of laws and principles. It must find in relevancy and truth a substitute for formal precision in statement."[55] At no point in his discussion did Hamilton assert or imply that the body of holistic economic thought is other than a systematized body of economic knowledge. As he pointed out at this early date, and as other heterodox economists have continued to explain, their body of economic theory is systematized with the primary aim of interpreting the realities of the twentieth-century economic world. In spite of its lack of formalistic or analytical traits the body of holistic economic thought remains a systematized body of economic knowledge which incorporates many significant scientific generalizations about the contemporary American economic system.

The theory of the American economic order developed by Veblen, Commons, Mitchell, and others pays special attention to the working of the inner monopolistic core of the American economy, and to its influence upon other segments of the economy. This

[54] Homan, Paul T., *Contemporary Economic Thought,* page 221.

[55] Hamilton, Walton H., "The Institutional Approach to Economic Theory," *The American Economic Review,* March, 1919, Vol. IX, Supp., page 318. At a later date Hamilton expressed a strong dissatisfaction with the "trim categories" and the "stark mechanics" of conventional economic theory. See his contribution to the volume entitled *Price and Price Policy,* 1938, pages 1-22, and *The Pattern of Competition,* 1940, page 93.

central monopolistic segment of the modern economy is an area of economic activity about which orthodox economists have little to say, since their equilibrium analysis has little application to a situation in which a small number of highly monopolistic or oligopolistic firms operate. Students of monopolistic enterprise such as Joan Robinson and Edward Chamberlin have been able to make use of the technique of equilibrium analysis only by confining their attention to the periphery of the central monopolistic core of the modern capitalistic nations, where there are industries which are neither highly competitive nor largely monopolistic. By making the assumption "that there is no collusion" or other form of collective behavior among the competing monopolists on the periphery of the inner monopolistic core of the total economy, Robinson and Chamberlin have worked out analytical propositions whose abstraction, however, is, as Robinson explains, "distressingly high." [56] These students of monopolistic or imperfect competition have been unable to create similar analytical propositions or "economic laws" which would be applicable to the inner core of highly monopolistic or oligopolistic enterprise, because their assumption "that there is no collusion among the monopolists" no longer has even a limited applicability to the central monopolistic area of the economy. The assumption that the monopolist "operates in a non-monopolistic framework," that is to say, that he behaves like a competitive businessman, is quite unrealistic when applied to the focal area of the American economy where there are large overhead costs, inflexible prices, and "conscious manipulation" of markets.[57] Since the technique of equilibrium analysis is found to be of very limited value in analyzing the operations of the central monopolistic area of the modern economy, the only course of action that remains is to work with the more realistic assumption that collective or collusive action is the typical behavior of oligopolistic or highly monopolistic enterprises. The economist must then be satisfied with whatever generalizations are revealed by ways of systematizing data other than the way employed by the equilibrium economists. This is pre-

[56] Robinson, Joan, *The Economics of Imperfect Competition*, pages 326-327. See also Chamberlin, Edward, *The Theory of Monopolistic Competition*, 1938, page 90.

[57] Wootton, Barbara, *Lament for Economics*, page 86. New York: Farrar and Rinehart, Inc., 1938. Reprinted by permission of Rinehart and Company, Inc., New York.

cisely what the holistic economists have done. Although they find that the price and production policies of highly monopolistic firms are largely indeterminate when the assumptions of the equilibrium economists are abandoned, the holistic economists nevertheless find it possible to make worth-while generalizations about these price and production policies in the various phases of the business cycle and in the longer secular movements of the business system, and also about the interrelations of the monopolistic and competitive segments of the total'economy.

When the holistic economists turn to their interpretation of the working of the total American economy, they find equilibrium economics of little help except when they are discussing the competitive areas of the economy. When they investigate the inner core of the mature American economy, these heterodox economists find themselves unable to create anything comparable to the precise, abstract "economic laws" developed by the equilibrium economists. This is not to say that the holistic economists can make no scientific generalizations about the internal functioning of the inner monopolistic core or about its interrelations with other segments of that economy. On the contrary, they have much to say about the interrelations between the monopolistic and the competitive areas of the hybrid economic system, and about the influence of monopolistic activity upon the general functioning of the total economy. What they have to say about these matters, however, does not fall into the form of the "economic laws" of the equilibrium economists. This is so because the economic data with which the holistic economists concern themselves do not permit the formulation of such analytical or formal propositions. It is for this reason that these economists state that the functioning of the hybrid American economy, with its many shades of economic enterprise ranging from the highly competitive to the highly monopolistic, cannot be satisfactorily reduced to a series of formal economic generalizations of the type which interested the orthodox economists of the nineteenth century.

The body of economic thought created by the holistic economists is not entirely different from the explanations of the organization of economic life found in the work of the orthodox or equilibrium economists.[58] In the early years of the movement to reconstruct

[58] For contrary views see Spann, Othmar, *The History of Economics,* 1930, page 277, and Homan, Paul T., "The Institutional School," *Encyclopædia of the Social Sciences,* Vol. V, page 392.

economics Walton H. Hamilton explained that "Here and there is much that can be fitted into a theory of the institutional organization of industrial society. Smith, Mill, Whately, and other classicists have given us much which with restatement can be used. The writings of the neo-classicists, even those of Clark and von Wieser, are not without pertinent material. The English classicists, Marshall, Pigou, Chapman, have materials for us; for in England the older economics has never lost the general concern which the Austrian and the American utility theorists have taken from it."[59]   John R. Commons was likewise careful to point out that the aim of his collective economics was to round out the contributions of economists from Smith to Marshall, and that he had no intention of offering a substitute for all their work.   Similarly, Wesley C. Mitchell has explained in no uncertain terms in his essay on "The Prospects of Economics" that "While fresh fields will thus be brought into the economist's demesne, he will find that his old fields of work gain new fertility from his new way of thinking. . . .   The better orientation we are getting will not lead economists to neglect pecuniary logic as a sterile or an exhausted field.   On the contrary not only will it make clear the limitations of the older work but it will also show how the old inquiries may be carried further, and how they may be fitted into a comprehensive study of economic behavior."[60] It is the extension or the rounding out of economic science, and not its reduction to the level of simple fact gathering, that is the primary theoretical aim of the holistic economists.   They want a broad version of economics which will spread its interpretative net over a larger realm of economic data than that encompassed by the theoretical system of the equilibrium economists of the past and present centuries.

The Significance of Holistic Economic Thought

The development of holistic economic thought has been marked by a paucity of general works which have as their aim a broad interpretation of the working of the modern American economy. There is a number of reasons for this scarcity of general works. Some members of the holistic school think that the reconstruction

---

[59] Hamilton, Walton H., "The Institutional Approach to Economic Theory," pages 317-318.

[60] The Trend of Economics, page 24.

of economics has not yet made sufficient progress to justify the writing of any generalized statements of the functioning of the modern hybrid economy.   A more important reason is that the holistic economists have been engaged in types of scientific work which have not emphasized the need for statements of precisely what it is that is encompassed by the general scheme of holistic economic thought.   Veblen, Commons, Mitchell, and their followers have not matched their specialized research work with similar endeavors in the fields of classroom instruction and popular education.   They have made few attempts to invade the fields of elementary instruction where they would have to compete with the writers of orthodox economics textbooks.[61]   Had they done otherwise, these heterodox economists would have felt the need to move from the realm of specialized research to that of general or synthetical analysis.   No one who understands the new movement in American economic thought would think in terms of an holistic economist writing an economics textbook that would closely resemble the products of economic orthodoxy.   But this does not mean that the holistic school is justified in ignoring the need to turn out general treatises which cover the essentials of their economic thought.   If these economists are to make the most of their position in the evolution of American economic thought, they must necessarily get beyond the writing of occasional papers and highly specialized research monographs.   They should at times pause to take stock of their contribu-

[61] In 1931 Willard E. Atkins and other members of the Department of Economics of New York University brought forth an elementary economics textbook, entitled *Economic Behavior,* which was presented as "an attempt to work out an institutional approach to the study of economics."   The authors explained that their treatise was designed for a "descriptive" course in elementary economics. In this general treatise on institutional economics far too much emphasis was placed upon description, and too little upon developing a theory of the maturing American economy.   One could go so far as to say that no such theory of the economic order was presented even in general outline.   The authors explain in the second (1939) edition of their textbook that their volume "attempts an institutional description of the behavior of the people of the United States at the present time."   By emphasizing "description" as opposed to "theory" the authors of this elementary textbook would appear to have done the movement to reconstruct economics a great disservice.   Although they have absorbed some of the terminology of the institutional economists, and have borrowed some of the latter's assumptions and scientific categories, the authors of *Economic Behavior* cannot be said to have provided anything like a general statement of the content of holistic economics as it has been developed by Veblen, Commons, Mitchell, Clark, Tugwell, Means, and others.

tions to the reconstruction of American economics, and then incorporate these contributions in general statements on the nature and scope of their version of economics.

In developing their economic thought the holistic economists have followed a method of investigation which has been described by Walton H. Hamilton as the method of "organic particularism." [62] In pursuing this method of investigation the economist selects some special economic problem for analysis, then develops the interconnections between the special problem and the working of the total economy, and finally turns to the more general scientific problem of constructing a theory of the total economic order. When this method of studying the economic system was adopted by Commons, Mitchell, Hoxie, Hamilton, and other heterodox economists in the early years of this century, there was much to recommend it. In 1904 Veblen had sketched the outlines of a theory of the American capitalistic system, but before this theory could be further developed it was necessary to provide it with a more solid inductive foundation. This need for a more inductive basis for economic theorizing came at a time when the current scientific outlook favored coming to closer grips with the hard and fast facts of concrete economic experience. Economists were thinking in terms of case studies, statistical investigations, comparative and historical analyses, and in general of bringing a better balance between theory and fact. It is not surprising, therefore, that after 1900 Commons and Hoxie should turn to an investigation of industrial strife, Mitchell to the study of the business cycle, John M. Clark to an analysis of industries with large overhead costs, Hamilton to the study of "sick" industries and the problem of preserving competitive enterprise, and Tugwell and Means at a later date to an inquiry into the problems of national economic planning. These economists were moved by

[62] Hamilton, Walton H., "The Development of Hoxie's Economics," *The Journal of Political Economy*, Nov., 1916, Vol. XXIV, page 871 fn. Hamilton explains that the way of studying the economic system described as "organic particularism" is "in contradistinction to the mechanistic particularism which characterized intellectual activity in the last half of the nineteenth century. The latter studies its object in isolation, the former the situation as a whole from the standpoint of its object; the latter looks for structural characteristics, the former for functional activities; the latter finds the reality of an object in itself, the former in its relationships, past and present, to other objects which make up its environment."

what they took to be the pressing scientific needs of the time. They took the reconstruction of economic science to mean that the new framework of interpretation, which had been only broadly outlined by Richard T. Ely's "new school of economists" and which had been somewhat improved upon at a later date by Thorstein Veblen, was to be given greater definiteness with the aid of many special studies. If the new theory of the American capitalistic order was to be more than a body of high-level abstractions, it had to have a firm foundation in studies of the concrete issues of the first half of the twentieth century. There was a need for considerable free play between broad economic generalizations relating to the functioning of the maturing capitalistic order and a long series of highly inductive investigations. Historical and statistical facts were to nourish general theories; while theory was in turn to integrate the many inductive studies, and to point the way to further worth-while investigations. It was clearly never the purpose of the holistic economists, however, to convert the reconstruction of economic science into a pointless accumulation of factual studies. This was a danger of which these economists were always well aware.

It is true that the work of the holistic economists has not always measured up to their original intentions. This has been due in part to the fact that their method of "organic particularism" has revealed a fundamental difficulty. Where the economist proposes to develop a theory of the total economic order by turning first to some specialized economic problem, and then moving on at a later date to a study of the total order, there is the possibility that his interest in the special economic problem will prove to be so absorbing as to cause the larger problem of interpreting the structure and functioning of the total economic order to be neglected. There is a very great danger that the economist will lose sight of the ultimate problem of creating a satisfactory theory of the total economic system, or that he will tend to find refuge in passing on the larger task to later generations of economists. This procedure can be adopted by a few members of a new school of economic thought without much harm being done, but when a majority of the members follow the same pattern of behavior the outcome is far from being satisfactory. This criticism can be levelled with fairness against most members of the holistic school. They have written about reconstructing the economist's framework of interpretation, and about developing what Wesley C. Mitchell once described as a theory of the "capitalistic organization of enterprise." But then these economists have plunged into the complexities of special economic investigations which have for the most part overshadowed the broader and more ultimate purpose of constructing a theory of the maturing American economic order. The result has been that all too frequently Veblen and other heterodox economists have failed to integrate their specialized economic investigations with a larger study of the working of the total economy.

The heterodox economists whose work has been the object of interest in preceding chapters have shown a certain reluctance to round out their economic thought and to push it to its logical limits. A full explanation of this intellectual phenomenon would require excursions into the realm of the sociology of knowledge, which would carry this study far afield. It can be pointed out, however, that holistic economic thought is of an exploratory, and hence innovative nature. Being much concerned with economic change and its consequences for both private and public welfare, this type of economic thought is by its very nature a source of discomfort to those individuals who have a stake in maintaining the *status quo*, or in preserving the myth that the *status quo* can possibly be maintained. The economists who seek to reconstruct economic science along the lines discussed in preceding chapters of this study are of necessity innovators. The logic of their theorizing necessarily places them in this category. But as Sumner H. Slichter explained in 1924, when he was one of the enterprising young authors of *The Trend of Economics* who were greatly interested in the "renaissance of economic thought" in the United States, there is a "stigma placed upon the inventive mind when applied to social rather than to natural phenomena." [63] Wesley C. Mitchell has also dwelt upon the obstacles that lie in the path of those economists who may be classed with the "social innovators." [64] These obstacles, including the stigma attached to the work of the social innovator, seem to have had considerable influence in delaying the crystallization of holistic

[63] Slichter, Sumner H., "The Organization and Control of Economic Activity," *The Trend of Economics,* page 354.

[64] Mitchell, Wesley C., "The Social Sciences and National Planning," *The Backward Art of Spending Money,* 1937, pages 96-98.

economic thought in the United States, where socio-economic innovation was scarcely respectable prior to 1929.

The orthodox economics of the nineteenth-century classicists and neo-classicists won the support of businessmen, who were the only powerful, organized economic group in the community. Although there was some opposition to it from landed and protectionist interests, the economics of Smith, Ricardo, Mill, and Marshall in general met the needs of the rapidly rising manufacturing and commercial classes of the nineteenth century. No such coincidence has occurred in the case of holistic economics. This heterodox economics of the twentieth century draws its support from the rapidly emerging economic groups which seek to bridle the business classes in the interest of a wider prosperity for all members of the community. Holistic economic thought appeals to middle-class representatives, government workers, labor officials, and leaders of consumers' organizations. It draws its support from the economic classes which seek to alter the orientation of private business enterprise. As this reorientation of private enterprise will probably not be accomplished without a great deal of strife, it should not be surprising if the opposition of the vested interests, which would like to maintain an unregulated, private enterprise economy, should be registered not only against the new power-seeking economic classes but also against those social scientists who lend them scientific support. That such a prospect has had some influence in retarding the development of holistic economic thought is a matter which can hardly be denied.

In spite of its deficiencies holistic economics is an intellectual development which has done much to further the reconstruction of American economics. One of the most important effects of the growth of this new economics has been the broadening of the scope of economic theorizing. Economics has become less "microcosmic" and more "macrocosmic" as attention has been shifted away from the behavior of the individual in the private market place and directed toward the general functioning of the total economy. The exponents of economic heterodoxy have gone beyond supply and demand conditions to inquire into the extra-market operations, which, together with market operations, comprise the total functioning of the economy. These heterodox economists have been willing to push their inquiries into any body of facts that throws light upon the creation and disposal of national income. They have realized that the price system of the modern economy has a cultural setting which conditions or influences it in many important ways. These economists have come to understand that one cannot fully understand the working of the modern hybrid price system by divorcing it from its cultural setting any more than one can fully comprehend individual behavior by isolating the individual from his cultural milieu. In the light of their understanding of the systemic or holistic nature of economic activity, Veblen, Commons, Mitchell and other economists of a similar stamp have broadened economic analysis until they have reached their goal of a theory of the total economic order. What is important to note is that these economists have worked toward this goal not by ignoring the conventional fields of economic inquiry but by going far beyond them.

A second very important consequence of the development of holistic economic thought has been the fostering of closer relations between economics and other social sciences. This is especially true of the relations among economics, psychology, and sociology. Orthodox economics has tended to pay little attention to the progress made in the fields of social psychology and sociology since 1875. The exponents of economic orthodoxy have usually clung to the psychological theories used by their eighteenth- and nineteenth-century predecessors. Even the psychology of the marginal utility school which flourished after 1870 was an individualistic rather than a social psychology. The situation is the same with respect to progress made in theorizing about the nature of cultural organization. Orthodox economists, not finding a need to alter the theory of social or cultural organization which underlies their inherited economics, have shown little interest in making use of whatever advances the cultural anthropologists and sociologists have made in recent decades in explaining the structure and functioning of the various spheres of human culture. As a result of this lack of interest on the part of orthodox economists in the recent contributions of social psychologists, sociologists, and other social scientists, orthodox economics has remained quite impervious to whatever progress has been made in related social sciences.

The situation is very different with the holistic economists. They have not only made good use of the recent contributions of other social scientists, but they also look forward to a further intermingling of the social sciences.[65]   These heterodox economists have taken a great deal from the work of the social psychologists and the sociologists.   They have accepted the dictum of John Dewey that all psychology is "social" psychology.   Radhakamal Mukerjee has explained in his study of modern economic theory that "Since the individual is not a discrete and separate atom, as the social sciences taking their cue from the older psychology and biology would have it, but rather like the atom of the new physics, dependent on the cosmos and at the same time a cosmos in itself, economics must adopt a different method of analysis.   Economics must base itself on a kind of social psychology which reveals the vital unity of the individual and the society, a unity which is more fully revealed in the individual's conduct and in social institutions than in his set instincts and overt desires." [66]   In working out the full significance of this statement the holistic economists have drawn attention to the influence of the cultural setting upon human conduct, to the collective nature of much economic behavior, and to the importance of habit as a factor controlling this behavior.   All these matters are of special interest for these economists when they come to fashion their theory of the economic order.

The cultural theory underlying the holistic economists' theory of the economic order has served as a common bond between their work and that of the sociologists.   The sociologists, along with the cultural anthropologists, have done much in the past three quarters of a century to explain the structure and functioning of human culture.   They have provided social scientists with a theory of institutions or of human culture which marks a great advance over the theory of human culture which was accepted at the time that Adam Smith, David Ricardo, and John Stuart Mill established their eco-

---

[65] The position of the holistic economists on this point has been well explained by A. B. Wolfe, who states that "The point to be emphasized is that just as economic institutions of a given time must be treated in close correlation with the other contemporary aspects of culture, so the stream of economic change is a substream of the total cultural movement and is constantly influencing, and being influenced by, its other elements.   Each cultural stream may be investigated by its own specialists, but not adequately unless they have reasonably wide and fresh knowledge of the main features of the collateral culture movements."   See Wolfe, A. B., "Sociology and Economics," *The Social Sciences and Their Interrelations,* edited by Ogburn, W. F. and Goldenweiser, A., page 308.   New York: Houghton Mifflin Company, 1927.

[66] *The Institutional Theory of Economics,* page 5.

nomics. While the equilibrium economists of recent decades have shown no tendency to make use of the contributions of the sociologists dealing with the nature of the society of which the economic system is but one part, Veblen, Commons, Mitchell and other heterodox economists have found it worth while to become acquainted with these sociological contributions. There has emerged from these contributions a theory of human culture which the holistic economists have found to be a very useful framework of interpretation within which to construct their theory of twentieth-century capitalistic economic organization. These economists have welcomed the progress made by students of human culture, since they agree that one of the greatest obstacles to the further progress of economic science is the tendency of economists to cling to outmoded theories of human culture or to oversimplify these theories in the interests of a highly formalized version of economic science. The holistic economists have succeeded in overcoming this obstacle by taking note of the contributions of other social scientists toward a more realistic interpretation of the structure and functioning of the human culture of which the sphere of economic relations forms but one segment.

A third significant result of the development of holistic economics has been the closing of the gap between economic theory and practice. Since the underlying assumptions of the new economics have a firm inductive basis, holistic economic theory is relevant to the economic problems with which the American people are currently burdened. This relevancy arises from the fact that the logic of capitalistic development, which is the main colligating principle of the holistic economists' theory of the economic order, is tied up with a logic of reform. The same factors or circumstances which canalize the development of the American economy, also indicate the general direction which workable schemes of economic reform should take. The logic of economic development shows that modern industrial technology is throwing economic activity into a mold which is becoming increasingly collective in nature. This technology, if not interrupted in its development, will continue its work of transforming the competitive economy into a system in which collective economic action is of major importance. The logic of this economic development necessarily leads to some form of intervention by forces which operate outside the private markets, since the modern economy cannot function smoothly and efficiently under the direction of private enterprise alone.[67]   The new hybrid economy of the twentieth century has what A. B. Wolfe describes as its own special "inner logic." This inner logic is a way of functioning which must not only be understood by the leaders of all major economic classes, but must also be accepted by them as the basis of their economic policy making, if we are to have a well-run economic system.[68]

Although Veblen and other heterodox economists think in terms of the same logic of reform, there is much disagreement among them when they discuss the specific form that economic intervention should take.   The laissez-faire economists of the nineteenth century and their twentieth-century followers show a certain unanimity of opinion about national economic policy, because there is only one way of following a negative national economic policy or of doing nothing to interfere with the working of the economic system.[69]   But there are many different ways of being positive in national economic policy making or of actively engaging in economic intervention.   It is not surprising, therefore, that while the holistic economists all agree on doing something about the poor functioning of the American economic system, they do not agree on the particular form that economic intervention should take.   Veblen called for a planned socialistic economy, while Commons thought in terms of piecemeal planning.   Working from a different viewpoint, Mitchell and other members of the holistic school think in terms of various forms of over-all or general economic planning within the framework of existing economic institutions.   Although these proposals

[67] For a similar view see Mannheim, Karl, *Man and Society in an Age of Reconstruction,* 1940, page 4, and *Diagnosis of Our Time,* 1944, pages 3-14.

[68] "Economy and Democracy," page 13. In Wolfe's opinion the logic of the hybrid American economy looks in the direction of a more centrally regulated economy than we now have.   As he expresses it, "Private enterprise lacks within its own organization the central authority which alone can secure inter-industry balance.   Here, if anywhere, is necessary that central government control to which business so vociferously objects, and which many competent economists view with misgivings. . . . Call it what you please, view it with caution as you will, I see no escape from centralized regulation of conditions which affect the whole nation."

[69] In other words, these exponents of economic orthodoxy are uniformly opposed to over-all economic planning.   For expressions of this orthodox, antiplanning view, see Hayek, F. A., *The Road to Serfdom,* 1944, Von Mises, Ludwig, *Bureaucracy,* 1944, and Robbins, Lionel, *The Great Depression,* 1934.

for economic intervention reveal a wide diversity of opinion on some major points, nevertheless they all have the common feature of looking to some form of collective economic management as a substitute for the laissez-faire operation of economic society. The fact that the planning proposals of Veblen and other critics of economic orthodoxy do not all follow the same detailed pattern does not, therefore, vitiate the assertion that these economists think in terms of the same basic logic of economic reform.

Holistic economics made its appearance in the United States at the turn of the century as a protest against the inability of academic economics to explain the real economic world and to show the way to a better economic system. Veblen played the leading role among the American economists who were originally interested in the reconstruction of economics. It was he who provided the philosophical foundation for the new version of economics, and who gave the dissenting economists a fresh framework of interpretation. But Veblen was in many ways not typical of the academic world of the United States, which in the closing decades of the nineteenth century, as even now, was basically an expression of middle-class American sentiment. Veblen was radical, and to some extent iconoclastic. In his ways of living and thinking he did not represent the strong tides of middle-class influence which swept over the United States during the era of critical realism which began around 1870.[70] Other economists, who made fewer contributions to the early reconstruction of economic science than did Veblen, possessed social philosophies which were more in line with the intellectual orientation of the majority of the thinking members of the middle classes. There was Richard T. Ely with his Christian Socialism, John R. Commons with his Populism, and Simon Nelson Patten with his broad social-welfare outlook. As time went by the gradualism of Ely, Commons, and Patten came to dominate the new movement in American economic thought to the exclusion of Veblen's radicalism. Furthermore, gradualism found strong philosophic support in the pragmatism of William James and John Dewey. By 1914 the

[70] For a discussion of the intellectual history of the United States in this period see Parrington, V. L., *The Beginnings of Critical Realism in America, 1860-1920*, 1930; Curti, M. E., *The Growth of American Thought*, 1943; and Hofstadter, R., *Social Darwinism in American Thought, 1860-1915*, 1944.

gradualistic social philosophy of Ely, Commons, and Patten, supported by similar views from the pen of the eminent American sociologist, Charles Horton Cooley, had supplanted the radical social philosophy of Veblen, and had won over all the younger disciples of economic heterodoxy such as Wesley C. Mitchell, Robert F. Hoxie, Walton H. Hamilton, and John M. Clark.

The holistic movement in American economic thought is today, like the pragmatism of John Dewey, an expression of middle-class thought and aspirations. The liberal leaders of the middle classes accept the pragmatic philosophy of adjustment, because they think in terms of making gradual adjustments to the changing economic environment. They do not think in terms of extensive revolutionary changes which would result in a complete overhauling of the cultural superstructure of modern society. The kind of economic thought which appeals to those members of the middle classes who are genuinely interested in economic reform is the kind which calls for gradual change through many small or limited adjustments. This is the economic thought of Commons, Mitchell, Clark, Tugwell, Means, and Hamilton, all of whom propose to domesticate the maturing American capitalistic system through a process of gradual adjustment and not through a revolutionary overturn of the existing social system. As Gardiner C. Means has phrased it, the problem is to "achieve a successful adjustment through gradual means." In sponsoring a program of economic gradualism the holistic economists speak for no special economic interest such as labor or capital. They are solidarists who believe that it is possible to harmonize the interests of all groups and classes in the community with the aid of a thoroughly representative and impartial government. These economists believe that it is the role of middle-class intellectuals to provide that impartiality of thought and action which is so necessary for a successful prosecution of the solidaristic program of gradual reform. They would agree with John M. Clark when he states that "I also have hopes that the stage may be set, as I have elsewhere suggested, for a revival of objectivity and impartiality, at least among economists not definitely attached to some special interest group. . . . Whether this comes about or not, and whether or not economists live up to their responsibilities as teachers or formulators of teachable doctrine, there has never been a time when the profession bore a greater responsibility for realism, for objectivity, and for relevance to issues of policy which will be vital in the coming decades." [71]

The holistic economists espouse a twentieth-century rather than a nineteenth-century liberalism. The liberalism of this century differs from that of the last century, because unlike the nineteenth-century liberals who relied upon competition and individual economic action to provide freedom and abundance, the modern liberals look to collective action as a guarantee of economic liberty, security, and abundance. With the closing of the geographical frontier and the relative decline of small-scale business enterprise, the monopolization of economic life has become a serious threat to the continued improvement of the country's standard of living. In the opinion of Commons, Mitchell, and the younger holistic economists the solution of this problem lies in a program of collective economic management within the existing institutional framework. Wesley C. Mitchell observes that present-day expressions of nineteenth-century liberalism may be clothed with "nostalgic charm," but they are unsuitable for the purpose of building a "community of higher purpose between different classes" because these expressions of the older liberalism ignore the collectivizing influence of the machine process.[72] The new twentieth-century liberalism emphasizes the point that the successful handling of the modern economy's problems "will depend on deliberate collaboration in the adjustment of mutual interests." [73]

When Commons, Mitchell, and the younger planners recommend putting their proposals for collective economic management into practice, while at the same time preserving the existing institutional structure, they raise the question of how far collective management can be applied to the American economic system without destroying its private enterprise nature. Rexford G. Tugwell quite flatly declares that "If we accept the principle of planning we must accept its implied destruction of a laissez-faire industry. . . . It is, in other words, a logical impossibility to have a planned economy and to have business operating its industries." In his planning proposals

[71] "Educational Functions of Economics After the War," page 67.

[72] See Mitchell's discussion of Herbert von Beckerath's paper on "Interrelations Between Moral and Economic Factors in the Postwar World," pages 48-50.

[73] Clark, J. M., "Economic Adjustments After Wars," The American Economic Review, March, 1942, Vol. XXXII, Supp., page 7.

Tugwell recommends that the price-making and capital-investing functions of the key industries be taken out of private hands and placed under the control of a national planning agency. The question then arises, would there be any justification for the preservation of the institution of private property in the key industries? Could private property survive in a situation in which the national planning agency would make the key decisions, and at the same time would accept responsibility for the risks associated with these decisions? These are problems about which Tugwell and other exponents of national planning have not had very much to say, since they feel that these problems can be solved only when they are met in the actual process of trying to create a planned economy. In their opinion the problem of private ownership of industrial capital is not an either-or problem; it is not a matter of merely choosing between private and public ownership. In some parts of the economy private property may in the future suffer few limitations; while in other parts public ownership may be the order of the day. In still other segments of the economy ownership of industrial wealth may remain in private hands, but its control may be shared in a variety of ways with the central government. How far the government may have to go in whittling down the extent to which owners actually manage or control their property is a matter which can be settled only pragmatically by the method of trial and error.[74] That there will be profound changes in the institutional structure and functioning of economic society is something for which the holistic economists as twentieth-century liberals are well prepared.[75]

[74] It appears that the holistic economists do not regard private property as an end to be preserved at any cost. They would preserve private property only as long as it contributed to general economic welfare. For a forthright statement with respect to this issue see Beveridge, William H., *Full Employment in a Free Society*, pages 23, 205-207. New York: W. W. Norton and Company, Inc., 1945. "The list of essential liberties . . . does not include liberty of a private citizen to own means of production and to employ other citizens in operating them at a wage. Whether private ownership of means of production to be operated by others [than the state] is a good economic device or not, it must be judged as a device. . . . In the view taken in this Report, full employment is in fact attainable while leaving the conduct of industry in the main to private enterprise. . . . But if, contrary to this view, it should be shown by experience or by argument that abolition of private property in the means of production was necessary for full employment, this abolition would have to be undertaken."

[75] See J. M. Clark's discussion at the 1932 round-table conference on "Institutional Economics," *The American Economic Review*, March, 1932, Vol. XXII, Supp., page 104.

Because of their pragmatic interests, Commons, Mitchell, and the younger holistic economists are not especially concerned with the origins and evolution of capitalism over the centuries as were Marx, Weber, and Sombart. Instead, they are primarily interested in the recent period in the growth of capitalistic enterprise which starts with the breakdown of competitive capitalism shortly after the Civil War. What they present is a theory of economic enterprise which applies primarily to mature capitalistic economies like those of the United States and Great Britain. They offer what Wesley C. Mitchell has described as a "theory of the current economic regime." Such a theory necessarily pays attention to the prior conditions out of which the contemporary economy has emerged, but it does not inquire into economic developments over very long periods of time. It is a theory which is designed to provide some help in meeting the immediate and pressing problem of shifting from one era of capitalistic enterprise to the next phase in its evolution. This is not to say that the holistic economists believe that economists in general should not be interested in the earlier phases of economic evolution. It means only that for their particular purposes Commons, Mitchell, and their followers have not found it necessary to push their theory of the American economic order very far into the historical past.

This theory of the American economic order is the end product of the reactions of Veblen and later critics of economic orthodoxy to the large-scale economic problems which made their appearance in the United States after 1875. These heterodox economists found themselves concerned with economic matters which failed to provoke much interest on the part of economists who worked in the orthodox tradition. They became very much interested in technological change, the restructuring of American economic life, the expansion of unearned income, the increasing monopolization of economic activity, and the growing failure of competitive forces to provide automatically for a full, balanced, and efficient use of economic resources. In seeking to provide ways of coping with these late nineteenth-century and early twentieth-century problems the holistic economists found it necessary to reconstruct the inherited body of neo-classical economics. This reconstruction was carried out by importing into the field of economic thought a new intellectual orientation out of which has sprung a novel way of comprehending the maturing American economy. This new way of looking at the modern hybrid economy takes it to be an historico-cultural product in the form of an evolving going concern. It substitutes for the orthodox economists' static, mechanistic way of grasping economic reality an evolutionary, holistic way of comprehending reality. It was in working out the full implications of this novel way of comprehending twentieth-century economic enterprise that Veblen and later exponents of economic heterodoxy converted economics from a deductive to a cultural type of social science.

When the question is raised as to what it is that distinguishes the holistic economist from other types of economists, the answer is his evolutionary, holistic view of the modern economy. All holistic economists have the same dynamic, emergent view of the economic world underlying their general approach to economic studies. They may use different techniques of scientific analysis, such as the historical, comparative, statistical, and case techniques, in their interpretation of the American economy as an emergent going concern, but their goal is always the same, to provide a realistic theory of the evolving economic order. In fashioning this theory of the economic order the holistic economists draw their intellectual inspiration from a post-Darwinian view of economic reality which is their common philosophical possession. The theorizing of the orthodox school of equilibrium economists centers in an eighteenth-century, static way of comprehending the economic world, while the heterodox school of holistic economists builds its theoretical system around a twentieth-century, dynamic view of the economic system. These two different ways of conceiving the economic system stem from different intellectual orientations. This is not to say, however, that these two ways of comprehending the maturing American economy cannot exist side by side in the world of scientific inquiry. We shall undoubtedly continue to have economists make use of both ways of comprehending the hard and fast facts of economic experience. But it should be pointed out that every economist must accept one or the other way of looking at the modern economy as the primary colligating principle of his life's work. If the dynamic way of conceiving the economic system which developed out of the thinking of Hegel, Marx, Darwin, and Peirce should prove to be more useful in the future than the static world outlook fashioned by Plato, Descartes, Newton and the eighteenth-century rationalistic philosophers, then we may have a further development and a wider acceptance of holistic economic thought. This would not mean that we could write finis to equilibrium economics, or that there would be less economic thinking of this type in the future, but it does mean that there would be more economic theorizing of the holistic or cultural type than we have had up to the present.

In the long run it is the flow of events, and the kinds of human problems which develop out of this historical flow, which are of major importance in determining the way of comprehending the economic system which economists come to accept, and in the light of which they do their scientific work. The holistic economists are convinced that impending events will favor a wider acceptance of their manner of interpreting the realities of the twentieth-century American economic world. They understand that the future of economics is more than a matter of argument between different schools of economists, and that the type of economic thought which becomes dominant in the long run is the type which mankind finds most useful for coping with its many economic problems. These heterodox economists would agree with the acute Simon Nelson Patten, who observed in the early years of the reconstruction of American economics that "The road of the economist becomes the road of the people, and the differences of economists are settled, not by their logic, but by the success or failure of the policy which each theory calls for." Since they are thoroughly convinced that their thought is quite relevant to the economic problems of this troubled century, the holistic economists look forward to a wider acceptance of their cultural version of economic science.

Bibliography
and
Index

Bibliography

CHAPTER 1

AYRES, C. E., *The Theory of Economic Progress.* Chapel Hill: University of North Carolina Press, 1944.

BEARD, C. A., "Written History as an Act of Faith," *The American Historical Review,* January, 1934, Vol. XXXIX.

CASSIRER, E., *Substance and Function, and Einstein's Theory of Relativity.* Chicago: The Open Court Publishing Company, 1923.

CHAMBERLIN, E. H., *The Theory of Monopolistic Competition,* Third Edition. Cambridge: Harvard University Press, 1938.

CLARK, J. B., "Patten's Dynamic Economics," *The Annals of the American Academy of Political and Social Science,* July, 1892, Vol. 3.

EDDINGTON, A. S., *The Nature of the Physical World.* New York: The Macmillan Company, 1928.

ELY, R. T., "The Past and the Present of Political Economy," *Johns Hopkins University Studies in Historical and Political Science,* Second Series, III, 1884.

GARVER, F. B., and HANSEN, A. H., *Principles of Economics,* Revised Edition. New York: Ginn and Company, 1937.

HAMILTON, W. H., "The Development of Hoxie's Economics," *The Journal of Political Economy,* November, 1916, Vol. XXIV.

———, "The Place of Value Theory in Economics," *The Journal of Political Economy,* March, 1918, Vol. XXVI.

———, "The Institutional Approach to Economic Theory," *The American Economic Review,* March, 1919, Vol. IX.

HOXIE, R. F., "Sociology and the Other Social Sciences: a Rejoinder," *The American Journal of Sociology,* 1907, Vol. XII.

JAMES, E. J., "The State as an Economic Factor," *Science-Economic Discussion.* New York, 1886.

JEVONS, W. S., *The Principles of Science,* Second Edition. London: Macmillan and Co., Ltd., 1924.

LÖWE, A., *Economics and Sociology.* London: G. Allen and Unwin, Ltd., 1935.

MUIRHEAD, J. H., "Peirce's Place in American Philosophy," *The Philosophical Review,* September, 1928, Vol. XXXVII.

NORMANO, J. F., *The Spirit of American Economics.* New York: The John Day Company, 1943.

PARKER, C. H., "Motives in Economic Life," *The American Economic Review,* March, 1918, Vol. VIII.

PARSONS, T., "Economics and Sociology: Marshall in Relation to the Thought of His Time," *The Quarterly Journal of Economics,* February, 1932, Vol. XLVI.

———, *The Structure of Social Action.* New York: McGraw-Hill Book Company, Inc., 1937.

PATTEN, S. N., "The Phenomena of Economic Dynamics," *Publications of the American Economic Association,* Third Series, 1910, Vol. XI.

PEIRCE, C. S., *Chance, Love and Logic.* New York: Harcourt, Brace and Company, Inc., 1923.

———, "The Origin of the Universe," *Collected Papers of Charles Sanders Peirce,* Vol. IV. Cambridge: Harvard University Press, 1935.

PERRY, A. L., *Elements of Political Economy,* Second Edition. New York: Charles Scribner and Company, 1867.

PLÒTNIK, M. J., *Werner Sombart and His Type of Economics.* New York: Eco Press, 1937.

RILEY, W., *American Thought from Puritanism to Pragmatism.* New York: Henry Holt and Company, 1915.

ROBBINS, L., *An Essay on the Nature and Significance of Economic Science,* Second Edition. London: Macmillan and Co., Ltd., 1935.

SELIGMAN, E. R. A., "Continuity of Economic Thought," *Science-Economic Discussion.* New York, 1886.

SMUTS, J. C., *Holism and Evolution.* New York: The Macmillan Company, 1926.

SOMBART, W., "Economic Theory and Economic History," *The Economic History Review,* January, 1929, Vol. II.

———, *Weltanschauung, Science and Economy.* New York: Veritas Press, 1939.

———, "Capitalism," *Encyclopaedia of the Social Sciences,* Vol. III.

TAUSSIG, F. W., *Principles of Economics,* Fourth Edition, Vol. I. New York: The Macmillan Company, 1939.

THORNDIKE, E. L., *Human Nature and the Social Order*. New York: The Macmillan Company, 1940.

TOWNSEND, H. G., *Philosophical Ideas in the United States*. New York: American Book Company, 1934.

WHITEHEAD, A. N., *Science and the Modern World*. New York: The Macmillan Company, 1925.

WOLFE, A. B., "Institutional Reasonableness and Value," *The Philosophical Review*, March, 1936, Vol. XLV.

YOUNG, A. A., "Economics as a Field of Research," *The Quarterly Journal of Economics*, November, 1927, Vol. XLII.

———, "English Political Economy," *Economica*, March, 1928, Vol. VIII.

———, "Economics," *Research in the Social Sciences*, edited by Wilson Gee. New York: The Macmillan Company, 1929.

ZUCKER, M., *The Philosophy of American History*, Vol. I, "The Historical Field Theory." New York: The Arnold-Howard Publishing Co., Inc., 1945.

CHAPTER 2

ANDERSON, K. L., "The Unity of Veblen's Theoretical System," *The Quarterly Journal of Economics*, August, 1933, Vol. XLVII.

BECK, L. W., "The Synoptic Method," *The Journal of Philosophy*, June 22, 1939, Vol. XXXVI, No. 13.

BERNARD, L. L., *Instinct, A Study in Social Psychology*. New York: Henry Holt and Company, 1924.

DEWEY, J., *Human Nature and Conduct*. New York: Henry Holt and Company, 1922.

DORFMAN, J., *Thorstein Veblen and His America*. New York: The Viking Press, 1934.

ELY, R. T., *Monopolies and Trusts*. New York: Grosset and Dunlap, 1900.

FREEMAN, E., *The Categories of Charles Peirce*. Chicago: The Open Court Publishing Company, 1934.

GOLDENWEISER, A., "Cultural Anthropology," *The History and Prospects of the Social Sciences*, edited by H. E. Barnes. New York: Alfred A. Knopf, 1925.

———, "Anthropology and Psychology," *The Social Sciences and Their Interrelations*. Boston: Houghton Mifflin Company, 1927.

GROSSMAN, H., "Evolutionist Revolt Against Classical Economics," *The Journal of Political Economy*, October-December, 1943, Vol. LI.

HARRIS, A., "Types of Institutionalism," *The Journal of Political Economy*, December, 1932, Vol. XL.

HOBSON, J. A., *Veblen*. New York: John Wiley and Sons, Inc., 1937.

HOMAN, P. T., "Thorstein Veblen," *Contemporary Economic Thought*. New York: Harper and Brothers, 1928.

JAMES, W., *The Principles of Psychology*, First Edition, Vol. II. New York: Henry Holt and Company, 1890.

KARPF, F. B., *American Social Psychology*, First Edition. New York: McGraw-Hill Book Company, 1932.

KEYNES, J. M., *The General Theory of Employment, Interest and Money*. New York: Harcourt, Brace and Company, 1936.

KEYNES, J. N., *Studies and Exercises in Formal Logic*, Fourth Edition. New York: The Macmillan Company, 1906.

———, *The Scope and Method of Political Economy*, Fourth Edition. London: Macmillan and Co., Ltd., 1930.

KÖHLER, W., *Gestalt Psychology*. New York: H. Liveright, 1929.

MACIVER, R. M., *Society, a Textbook of Sociology*. New York: Farrar and Rinehart, Inc., 1937.

MANNHEIM, K., *Ideology and Utopia*. New York: Harcourt, Brace and Company, 1936.

———, *Man and Society in an Age of Reconstruction*. New York: Harcourt, Brace and Company, 1940.

MARSHALL, A., *Industry and Trade*. London: Macmillan and Co., Ltd., 1919.

———, *Principles of Economics*, Eighth Edition. London: Macmillan and Co., Ltd., 1920.

———, *Money, Credit and Commerce*. London: Macmillan and Co., Ltd., 1923.

———, *Memorials of Alfred Marshall*, edited by A. C. Pigou. London: Macmillan and Co., Ltd., 1925.

MARSHALL, A. and M. P., *The Economics of Industry*, Second Edition. London: Macmillan and Co., Ltd., 1881.

MARX, K., *Capital*, Vol. I. Chicago: Charles H. Kerr and Company, 1906.

MITCHELL, W. C., "Thorstein Veblen," *The Backward Art of Spend-*

ing Money. New York: McGraw-Hill Book Company, Inc., 1937.

PARRINGTON, V. L., *The Beginnings of Critical Realism in America, 1860-1920,* Vol. III, "Main Currents in American Thought." New York: Harcourt, Brace and Company, 1930.

ROBINSON, J., *An Essay on Marxian Economics.* London: Macmillan and Co., Ltd., 1942.

SHERIF, M., *The Psychology of Social Norms.* New York: Harper and Brothers, 1936.

SUMNER, W. G., *Essays of William Graham Sumner,* Vol. I. New Haven: Yale University Press, 1934.

TEGGART, R. V., "Thorstein Veblen, A Chapter in American Economic Thought," *Publications in Economics,* Vol. II, No. 1. Berkeley: University of California Press, 1932.

VEBLEN, T., *The Theory of Business Enterprise.* New York: Charles Scribner's Sons, 1904.

————, *The Theory of the Leisure Class.* New York: The Macmillan Company, 1912.

————, *The Instinct of Workmanship and the State of the Industrial Arts.* New York: The Macmillan Company, 1914.

————, *An Inquiry into the Nature of Peace and the Terms of Its Perpetuation.* New York: The Macmillan Company, 1917.

————, *The Place of Science in Modern Civilisation.* New York: B. W. Huebsch, Inc., 1919.

————, *The Vested Interests and the State of the Industrial Arts.* New York: B. W. Huebsch, Inc., 1919.

————, *The Engineers and the Price System.* New York: B. W. Huebsch, Inc., 1921.

————, *Absentee Ownership and Business Enterprise in Recent Times.* New York: B. W. Huebsch, Inc., 1923.

————, *Essays in Our Changing Order.* New York: The Viking Press, 1934.

————, *Imperial Germany and the Industrial Revolution.* New York: The Viking Press, 1939.

WUNDT, W., *Elements of Folk Psychology.* New York: The Macmillan Company, 1916.

CHAPTER 3

ANDREWS, J. B., *Administrative Labor Legislation.* New York: Harper and Brothers, 1936.

————, *Labor Laws in Action.* New York: Harper and Brothers, 1938.

BOURGEOIS, L., *Solidarité,* 3. éd. Paris: A. Colin, 1902.

————, *Essai d'une philosophie de la solidarité,* 2. éd. Paris: F. Alcan, 1907.

————, "International Organization of Social Policies," *The American Labor Legislation Review,* March, 1914, Vol. IV.

CARLETON, F. T., review of *History of Labour in the United States,* Vols. I and II, *The Journal of Political Economy,* 1918, Vol. XXVI.

CLARK, L. D., review of J. R. Commons' and J. B. Andrews' *Principles of Labor Legislation, The Journal of Political Economy,* 1916, Vol. XXIV.

COMMONS, J. R., *The Distribution of Wealth.* New York: The Macmillan Company, 1893.

————, *Social Reform and the Church.* New York: T. Y. Crowell and Company, 1894.

————, *Proportional Representation,* Second Edition. New York: The Macmillan Company, 1907.

————, *Races and Immigrants in America.* New York: The Macmillan Company, 1907.

————, *Labor and Administration.* New York: The Macmillan Company, 1913.

————, *Industrial Goodwill.* New York: McGraw-Hill Book Company, Inc., 1919.

————, *Legal Foundations of Capitalism.* New York: The Macmillan Company, 1924.

————, *Institutional Economics.* New York: The Macmillan Company, 1934.

————, *Myself.* New York: The Macmillan Company, 1934.

————, and others, *Trade Unionism and Labor Problems.* New York: Ginn and Company, 1905.
and Company, 1905.

————, and others, *A Documentary History of American Industrial Society.* Cleveland: Arthur H. Clark Company, 1910.

————, and others, *History of Labour in the United States,* Vol. I. New York: The Macmillan Company, 1918.

————, and others, *Industrial Government.* New York: The Macmillan Company, 1921.

————, and ANDREWS, J. B., *Principles of Labor Legislation,* Fourth Edition. New York: Harper and Brothers, 1936.

————, "Proportional Representation," *The Annals of the American Academy of Political and Social Science,* March, 1892, Vol. 22.

————, "A Sociological View of Sovereignty," *The American Journal of Sociology,* 1899-1900, Vol. V.

————, "Immigration and Its Economic Effects," *Reports of the Industrial Commission on Immigration and on Education,* Vol. XV, Part III. Washington, 1901.

————, "A New Way of Settling Labor Disputes," *The American Monthly Review of Reviews,* March, 1901, Vol. XXIII.

————, "Some Taxation Problems and Reforms," *The American Monthly Review of Reviews,* February, 1903, Vol. XXVII.

————, "The New York Building Trades," *The Quarterly Journal of Economics,* 1903-04, Vol. XVIII.

————, "Types of American Labor Organization—The Teamsters of Chicago," *The Quarterly Journal of Economics,* 1904-05, Vol. XIX.

————, "Types of American Labor Unions: the Longshoremen of the Great Lakes," *The Quarterly Journal of Economics,* 1905-06, Vol. XX.

————, "Types of American Labor Unions: the Musicians of St. Louis," *The Quarterly Journal of Economics,* 1905-06, Vol. XX.

————, "The Wisconsin Public Utilities Law," *The American Monthly Review of Reviews,* July-December, 1907, Vol. XXXVI.

————, "Robert Marion LaFollette," *The North American Review,* May, 1908, Vol. CLXXXVII.

————, "Horace Greeley and the Working Class Origins of the Republican Party," *Political Science Quarterly,* September, 1909. Vol. XXIV.

————, "American Shoemakers, 1648-1895, A Sketch of Industrial Evolution," *The Quarterly Journal of Economics,* 1909-10, Vol. XXIV.

————, "How Wisconsin Regulates Her Public Utilities," *The American Monthly Review of Reviews,* July-December, 1910, Vol. XLII.

————, "Organized Labor's Attitude Toward Industrial Efficiency," *The American Economic Review,* Fourth Series, September, 1911, Vol. I.

——, "The Industrial Commission of Wisconsin," *The American Labor Legislation Review*, December, 1911, Vol. I.

——, "How the Wisconsin Industrial Commission Works," *The American Labor Legislation Review*, February, 1913, Vol. III.

——, "Unemployment Prevention," *The American Labor Legislation Review*, March, 1922, Vol. XII.

——, "Tendencies in Trade Union Development in the United States," *International Labour Review*, June, 1922, Vol. V.

——, "The True Scope of Unemployment Insurance," *The American Labor Legislation Review*, March, 1925, Vol. XV.

——, "Representative Advisory Committees in Labor Law Administration," *The American Labor Legislation Review*, December, 1929, Vol. XIX.

——, "Evaluating Institutions as a Factor in Economic Change," *Special Lectures on Economics*. Washington: U. S. Department of Agriculture, February-March, 1930.

——, "Twentieth Century Economics," *Journal of Social Philosophy*, 1939, Vol. V.

——, "American Federation of Labor," (Vol. II), "Bargaining Power," (Vol. II), "Fair Return," (Vol. VI), "Labor Movement," (Vol. VIII), and "Price Stabilization," (Vol. XII), *Encyclopaedia of the Social Sciences*.

——, testimony in the *Report of the Industrial Commission on the Relations and Conditions of Capital and Labor*, Vol. XIV. Washington, 1901.

——, testimony in *Stabilization Hearings, House Committee on Banking and Currency*, H. R. 7895. Washington, 1927.

——, review of R. F. Hoxie's *Trade Unionism in the United States, The Quarterly Journal of Economics*, 1917-1918, Vol. XXXII.

——, review of R. H. Tawney's *Religion and the Rise of Capitalism, The American Economic Review*, March, 1927, Vol. XVII.

——, review of W. Sombart's *Der moderne Kapitalismus, The American Economic Review*, March, 1929, Vol. XIX.

——, review of C. B. Swisher's *Stephen J. Field: Craftsman of the Law, The Journal of Political Economy*, December, 1931, Vol. XXXIX.

COPELAND, M. A., "Commons's Institutionalism in Relation to Problems of Social Evolution and Economic Planning," *The Quarterly Journal of Economics,* February, 1936, Vol. L.

CORWIN, E. S., *The Twilight of the Supreme Court.* New Haven: Yale University Press, 1934.

DEWEY, J., *Reconstruction in Philosophy.* New York: Henry Holt and Company, 1920.

DIEHL, C., "The Life and Work of Max Weber," *The Quarterly Journal of Economics,* November, 1923, Vol. XXXVIII.

DOUGLAS, P. H., review of J. R. Commons' *Industrial Government, The Journal of Political Economy,* 1921, Vol. XX.

ELY, R. T., *The Labor Movement in America.* New York: T. Y. Crowell and Company, 1886.

———, *Ground Under Our Feet.* New York: The Macmillan Company, 1938.

FREUND, E., "Administrative Law," *Encyclopaedia of the Social Sciences,* Vol. I.

GOODNOW, F. J., *Comparative Administrative Law.* New York: G. P. Putnam's Sons, 1893.

———, *The Principles of the Administrative Law of the United States.* New York: G. P. Putnam's Sons, 1905.

HOBSON, J. A., *Confessions of an Economic Heretic.* London: G. Allen and Unwin, Ltd., 1938.

HOOK, S., *John Dewey, An Intellectual Portrait.* New York: The John Day Company, 1939.

HOXIE, R. F., *Trade Unionism in the United States,* Second Edition. New York: D. Appleton and Company, 1923.

JOAD, C. E. M., *Introduction to Modern Philosophy.* London: Oxford University Press, 1924.

LANDIS, J. M., *The Administrative Process.* New Haven: Yale University Press, 1938.

LESCOHIER, D. D., and BRANDEIS, E., *History of Labor in the United States, 1896-1932,* Vol. III. New York: The Macmillan Company, 1935.

MITCHELL, W. C., "Commons on the Legal Foundations of Capitalism," *The American Economic Review,* June, 1924, Vol. XIV.

———, review of J. R. Commons' *Legal Foundations of Capitalism, The American Economic Review,* June, 1924, Vol. XIV.

PARKER, C. H., *The Casual Laborer and Other Essays.* New York: Harcourt, Brace and Company, 1920.

PARSONS, K. H., "John R. Commons' Point of View," *The Journal of Land and Public Utility Economics,* August, 1942, Vol. XVIII.

PERLMAN, S., *A Theory of the Labor Movement.* New York: The Macmillan Company, 1928.

——, "John Rogers Commons, 1862-1945," *The American Economic Review,* September, 1945, Vol. XXV.

RUSSELL, B., *Power, A New Social Analysis.* New York: W. W. Norton and Company, Inc., 1938.

SHARFMAN, I. L., "Commons' Legal Foundations of Capitalism," *The Quarterly Journal of Economics,* February, 1925, Vol. XXXIX.

TAYLOR, F. W., *The Principles of Scientific Management.* New York: Harper and Brothers, 1911.

WHITE, L., "Administration," *Encyclopaedia of the Social Sciences,* Vol. I.

CHAPTER 4

ADAMS, A. B., *Economics of Business Cycles.* New York: McGraw-Hill Book Company, Inc., 1925.

CLARK, J. M., "Wesley C. Mitchell's Contribution to the Theory of Business Cycles," *Methods in Social Science,* edited by S. A. Rice. Chicago: University of Chicago Press, 1931.

COOLEY, C. H., "The Progress of Pecuniary Valuation," *The Quarterly Journal of Economics,* November, 1915, Vol. XXX.

DAVENPORT, H. J., *The Economics of Enterprise.* New York: The Macmillan Company, 1913.

EDMAN, I., *Four Ways of Philosophy.* New York: Henry Holt and Company, 1937.

HARAP, H., *The Education of the Consumer.* New York: The Macmillan Company, 1924.

HOMAN, P. T., "Wesley C. Mitchell," *Contemporary Economic Thought.* New York: Harper and Brothers, 1928.

KYRK, H., *A Theory of Consumption.* Boston: Houghton Mifflin Company, 1923.

MILLS, F. C., "On the Changing Structure of Economic Life," *Economic Essays in Honor of Wesley Clair Mitchell.* New York: Columbia University Press, 1935.

MITCHELL, W. C., *A History of the Greenbacks.* Chicago: University of Chicago Press, 1903.

————, *Gold, Prices, and Wages under the Greenback Standard.* Berkeley: University of California Press, 1908.

————, *Business Cycles.* Berkeley: University of California Press, 1913.

————, *History of Prices during the War.* Washington: U. S. War Industries Board, 1919.

————, *Business Cycles, The Problem and Its Setting.* New York: National Bureau of Economic Research, Inc., 1927.

————, *Lectures on Types of Economic Theory* (mimeographed). New York: Columbia University, 1931.

————, *The Backward Art of Spending Money.* New York: McGraw-Hill Book Company, Inc., 1937.

———— and BURNS, A. F., *Measuring Business Cycles.* New York: National Bureau of Economic Research, Inc., 1946.

————, "The Rationality of Economic Activity," *The Journal of Political Economy*, February, 1910, Vol. XVIII.

————, "The Backward Art of Spending Money," *The American Economic Review*, June, 1912, Vol. II.

————, "Human Behavior and Economics," *The Quarterly Journal of Economics*, November, 1914, Vol. XXIX.

————. "The Role of Money in Economic Theory," *The American Economic Review*, March, 1916, Vol. VI.

————, "Wieser's Theory of Social Economics," *Political Science Quarterly*, March, 1917, Vol. XXXII.

————, "Prices and Reconstruction," *The American Economic Review*, March, 1920, Vol. X.

————, "The Crisis of 1920 and the Problem of Controlling Business Cycles," *The American Economic Review*, March, 1921, Vol. XII.

————, "Accountants and Economics with Reference to the Business Cycle," *The Journal of Accountancy*, March, 1923, Vol. XXXV.

————, "The Prospects of Economics," *The Trend of Economics*, edited by R. G. Tugwell. New York: Alfred A. Knopf, 1924.

————, "Quantitative Analysis in Economic Theory," *The American Economic Review*, March, 1925, Vol. XV.

———, "A Review," *Recent Economic Changes in the United States.* New York: McGraw-Hill Book Company, Inc., 1929.

———, "Sombart's Hochkapitalismus," *The Quarterly Journal of Economics,* February, 1929, Vol. XLIII.

———, "Thorstein Veblen, 1857-1929," *The New Republic,* September 4, 1929.

———, "Engineering, Economics, and the Problem of Social Well-Being," *Mechanical Engineering,* February, 1931, Vol. 53.

———, "Economics, 1904-1929," *A Quarter Century of Learning.* New York: Columbia University Press, 1931.

———, "Mr. Hoover's 'The Challenge to Liberty,'" *Political Science Quarterly,* Vol. XLIX, December, 1934.

———, "The Social Sciences and National Planning," *Science,* January 18, 1935, Vol. LXXXI.

———, "Commons on Institutional Economics," *The American Economic Review,* December, 1935, Vol. XXV.

———, "Intelligence and the Guidance of Economic Evolution," *Scientific Monthly,* November, 1936, Vol. XLIII.

———, "Introduction," *What Veblen Taught.* New York: The Viking Press, 1936.

———, "Science and the State of Mind," *Science,* January 6, 1939, Vol. LXXXIX.

———, "The Public Relations of Science," *Science,* December 29, 1939, Vol. XC.

———, "The National Bureau's Social Function," *Twentieth Annual Report of the Director of Research.* New York: National Bureau of Economic Research, Inc., March, 1940.

———, "Economic Resources in Economic Theory," *Studies in Economics and Industrial Relations.* Philadelphia: University of Pennsylvania Press, 1941.

———, "J. Laurence Laughlin," *The Journal of Political Economy,* December, 1941, Vol. XL.

———, "National Unity and Individual Liberties," *School and Society,* June 13, 1942, Vol. 55.

———, "Economics in a Unified World," *Social Research,* February, 1944, Vol. XI.

———, "Business Cycles," *Encyclopaedia of the Social Sciences,* Vol. III.

SCHUMPETER, J., "Mitchell's Business Cycles," *The Quarterly Journal of Economics,* November, 1930, Vol. XLIV.

TAYLOR, H., "On the Current Skepticism toward Systematic Economics," *Economic Essays in Honor of Wesley Clair Mitchell.* New York: Columbia University Press, 1935.

THORNDYKE, E. L., "The Original Nature of Man," *Educational Psychology,* Vol. I. New York: Teachers College, Columbia University, 1918.

WATSON, J. B., *Behaviorism, An Introduction to Comparative Psychology.* New York: Henry Holt and Company, 1914.

WOLF, A., *Essentials of Scientific Method,* Second Edition. London: G. Allen and Unwin, Ltd., 1928.

WOLFE, A. B., "Thoughts on Perusal of Wesley Mitchell's Collected Essays," *The Journal of Political Economy,* February, 1939, Vol. XLVII.

CHAPTER 5

ANDERSON, B. M., "Static Economics and Business Forecasting," *Economic Essays Contributed in Honor of John Bates Clark,* edited by Jacob H. Hollander. New York: The Macmillan Company, 1927.

CLARK, J. B., *The Philosophy of Wealth,* Second Edition. Boston: Ginn and Company, 1894.

———, *The Distribution of Wealth.* New York: The Macmillan Company, 1899.

———, *The Problem of Monopoly.* New York: Columbia University Press, 1904.

———, *Social Justice without Socialism.* Boston: Houghton Mifflin Company, 1914.

———, and CLARK, J. M., *The Control of Trusts,* Revised. New York: The Macmillan Company, 1912.

CLARK, J. M., *Standards of Reasonableness in Local Freight Discriminations.* New York: Columbia University Press, 1910.

———, editor, *Readings in the Economics of War.* Chicago: University of Chicago Press, 1918.

———, *Studies in the Economics of Overhead Costs.* Chicago: University of Chicago Press, 1923.

———, *Strategic Factors in Business Cycles.* New York: The National Bureau of Economic Research, Inc., 1934.

————, *Economics of Planning Public Works.* Washington: National Planning Board, 1935.

————, *Preface to Social Economics,* New York: Farrar and Rinehart, Inc., 1936.

————, *John Bates Clark, A Memorial.* New York: (privately printed), 1938.

————, *Social Control of Business,* Second Edition. New York: McGraw-Hill Book Company, 1939.

————, *How to Check Inflation.* New York: Public Affairs Committee, Inc., 1942.

————, "A Contribution to the Theory of Competitive Price," *The Quarterly Journal of Economics,* August, 1914, Vol. XXVIII.

————, "Business Acceleration and the Law of Demand: a Technical Factor in Economic Cycles," *The Journal of Political Economy,* March, 1917, Vol. XXV.

————, "The Basis of War-Time Collectivism," *The American Economic Review,* December, 1917, Vol. VII.

————, "Economics and Modern Psychology," *The Journal of Political Economy,* 1918, Vol. XXVI.

————, "Economic Theory in an Era of Social Readjustment," *The American Economic Review,* March, 1919, Vol. IX.

————, "Soundings in Non-Euclidean Economics," *The American Economic Review,* March, 1921, Vol. XI.

————, "The Empire of Machines," *The Yale Review,* October, 1922, Vol. XII.

————, "Overhead Costs in Modern Industry," *The Journal of Political Economy,* February, April, and October, 1923, Vol. XXXI.

————, "Some Social Aspects of Overhead Costs," *The American Economic Review,* March, 1923, Vol. XIII.

————, "The Socializing of Theoretical Economics," *The Trend of Economics,* edited by Rexford G. Tugwell. New York: Alfred A. Knopf, 1924.

————, "Recent Developments in Economics," *Recent Developments in the Social Sciences,* edited by E. C. Hayes. Philadelphia: J. B. Lippincott Company, 1927.

————, "The Relation between Statics and Dynamics," *Economic Essays Contributed in Honor of John Bates Clark,* edited by Jacob H. Hollander. New York: The Macmillan Company, 1927.

———, "Thorstein Bundy Veblen, 1857-1929," *The American Economic Review,* December, 1929, Vol. XIX.

———, "Sombart's Die drei Nationalökonomien," *The Quarterly Journal of Economics,* May, 1931, Vol. XLV.

———, "Capital Production and Consumer-Taking," *The Journal of Political Economy,* December, 1931, Vol. XXXIX, and October, 1932, Vol. XL.

———, "The Contribution of Economics to Method in Social Science," *Essays on Research in the Social Sciences.* Washington: The Brookings Institution, 1931.

———, "Long-Range Planning for the Regularization of Industry," *The New Republic,* January 13, 1932, Part 2.

———, round-table conference on "Institutional Economics," *The American Economic Review,* March, 1932, Vol. XXII.

———, "Convulsion in the Price Structure," *The Yale Review,* March, 1933, Vol. XXII.

———, "Economics and the National Recovery Administration," *The American Economic Review,* March, 1934, Vol. XXIV.

———, "Productive Capacity and Effective Demand," *Economic Reconstruction, Report of the Columbia University Commission.* New York: Columbia University Press, 1934.

———, "Adam Smith and the Currents of History," *Preface to Social Economics.* New York: Farrar and Rinehart, Inc., 1936.

———, "Past Accomplishments and Present Prospects of American Economics," *The American Economic Review,* March, 1936, Vol. XXVI.

———, "Toward a Concept of Social Value," *Preface to Social Economics.* New York: Farrar and Rinehart, Inc., 1936.

———, "Toward a Concept of Workable Competition," *The American Economic Review,* June, 1940, Vol. XXX.

———, "Investment in Relation to Business Activity and Employment," *Studies in Economics and Industrial Relations,* Philadelphia: University of Pennsylvania Press, 1941.

———, "The Relation of Government to the Economy of the Future," *The Journal of Political Economy,* December, 1941, Vol. XLIX.

———, "Forms of Economic Liberty and What Makes Them Important," *Freedom, Its Meaning,* edited by R. N. Anshen. New York: Harcourt, Brace and Company, 1940.

————, "Economic Adjustments after Wars," *The American Economic Review,* March, 1942, Vol. XXXII.

————, "The Theoretical Issues," *The American Economic Review,* March, 1942, Vol. XXXII.

————, "Our Economic Freedom," *The Annals of the American Academy of Political and Social Science,* March, 1942, Vol. 220.

————, "The Democratic Concept in the Economic Realm," *Science, Philosophy and Religion, Third Symposium.* New York: Conference on Science, Philosophy and Religion in their Relation to the Democratic Way of Life, Inc., 1943.

————, "Financing High-Level Employment," *Financing American Prosperity.* New York: The Twentieth Century Fund, 1945.

————, "General Aspects of Price Control and Rationing in the Transition Period," *The American Economic Review,* May, 1945, Vol. XXXV.

————, testimony in *Hearings Before a Subcommittee of the Committee on Manufactures,* 71st Congress, S. 6215, October 22, December, 1931.

————, "Educational Functions of Economics after the War," *The American Economic Review,* March, 1944, Vol. XXXIV.

————, "How Not to Reconvert," *Political Science Quarterly,* June, 1944, Vol. LIX.

————, "Diminishing Returns" and "Distribution," (Vol. V), "Government Regulation of Industry" and "Increasing Returns" (Vol. VII), "Monopoly" (Vol. X), "Overhead Costs" (Vol. XI), and "Statics and Dynamics" (Vol. XIV). *Encyclopaedia of the Social Sciences.*

Cooley, C. H., *Human Nature and the Social Order.* New York: Charles Scribner's Sons, 1902.

————, "The Institutional Character of Pecuniary Valuation," *The American Journal of Sociology,* January, 1913, Vol. XVIII.

————, "The Sphere of Pecuniary Valuation," *The American Journal of Sociology,* September, 1913, Vol. XIX.

————, "Political Economy and Social Process," *The Journal of Political Economy,* April, 1918, Vol. XXVI.

————, "Now and Then," *Sociological Theory and Social Research,* New York: Henry Holt and Company, 1930.

Dewey, J., *Liberalism and Social Action.* New York: G. P. Putnam's Sons, 1935.

EZEKIEL, M., *Jobs for All through Industrial Expansion.* New York: Alfred A. Knopf, 1939.

GRUCHY, A. G., "The Concept of National Planning in Institutional Economics," *The Southern Economic Journal,* October, 1939, Vol. VI.

CHAPTER 6

ARNOLD, T. W., *The Bottlenecks of Business.* New York: Reynal and Hitchcock, 1940.

———, *Democracy and Free Enterprise.* Norman: University of Oklahoma Press, 1942.

COLE, G. D. H., *Guild Socialism.* New York: Frederick A. Stokes Company, 1921.

HANSEN, A. H., *Fiscal Policy and Business Cycles.* New York: W. W. Norton and Company, Inc., 1941.

LERNER, M., *Ideas Are Weapons.* New York: The Viking Press, 1939.

LYND, R. S., *Knowledge for What?* Princeton: Princeton University Press, 1939.

PATTEN, S. N., *The New Basis of Civilization.* New York: The Macmillan Company, 1912.

———, "The Political Significance of Recent Economic Theories," *Essays in Economic Theory,* edited by R. G. Tugwell. New York: Alfred A. Knopf, 1924.

———, "Pragmatism and Social Science," *Essays in Economic Theory.*

———, "The Reconstruction of Economic Theory," *Essays in Economic Theory.*

———, "The Theory of Dynamic Economics," *Essays in Economic Theory.*

TUGWELL, R. G., *The Economic Basis of Public Interest.* Menasha: George Banta Publishing Company, 1922.

———, MUNRO, T., and STRYKER, R. E., *American Economic Life and the Means of Its Improvement.* New York: Harcourt, Brace and Company, 1925.

———, *Industry's Coming of Age.* New York: Harcourt, Brace and Company, 1927.

———, *Soviet Russia in the Second Decade.* New York: The John Day Company, 1928.

———, *Mr. Hoover's Economic Policy.* New York: The John Day Company, 1932.

———, *The Industrial Discipline and the Governmental Arts.* New York: Columbia University Press, 1933.

———, *Agriculture and the Consumer.* Washington: U. S. Department of Agriculture, 1934.

———, and HILL, H. C., *Our Economic Society and Its Problems.* New York: Harcourt, Brace and Company, 1934.

———, *The Battle for Democracy.* New York: Columbia University Press, 1935.

———, *Puerto Rican Public Papers of R. G. Tugwell, Governor.* San Juan: Office of Information of Puerto Rico, 1945.

———, *The Stricken Land.* New York: Doubleday and Company, Inc., 1947.

———, and KEYSERLING, L. H., *Redirecting Education.* Vol. 1. New York: Columbia University Press, 1934.

———, "Casual of the Woods," *Survey,* July 3, 1920, Vol. XLIV.

———, "The Gipsy Strain," *The Pacific Review,* September, 1921, Vol. II.

———, "Economic Basis for Business Regulation," *The American Economic Review,* December, 1921, Vol. XI.

———, "Human Nature in Economic Theory," *The Journal of Political Economy,* June, 1922, Vol. XXX.

———, "Economic Theory and Practice," *The American Economic Review* March, 1923, Vol. XIII.

———, "Some Formative Influences in the Life of Simon Nelson Patten," *The American Economic Review,* March, 1923, Vol. XIII.

———, "Notes on the Life and Work of Simon Nelson Patten," *The Journal of Political Economy,* April, 1923, Vol. XXXI.

———, "The Dr. Simon Nelson Patten Memorial," *The Annals of the American Academy of Political and Social Science,* May, 1923, No. 196, Vol. CVII.

———, "Experimental Economics," *The Trend of Economics.* New York: Alfred A. Knopf, 1924.

———, "The Problem of Agriculture," *Political Science Quarterly,* December, 1924, Vol. XXXIX.

———, "America's War-Time Socialism," *The Nation,* April 6, 1927, Vol. CXXIV.

————, "The Paradox of Peace," *The New Republic,* April 18, 1928, Vol. LIV.

————, "Experimental Control in Russian Industry," *Political Science Quarterly,* June, 1928, Vol. XLIII.

————, "Farm Relief and a Permanent Agriculture," *The Annals of the American Academy of Political and Social Science,* March, 1929, Vol. 142.

————, "The Agricultural Policy of France," *Political Science Quarterly,* June, 1930, Vol. XLV.

————, "Human Nature and Social Economy," *The Journal of Philosophy,* August 14, 1930, Vol. XXVII.

————, "The Theory of Occupational Obsolescence," *Political Science Quarterly,* June, 1931, Vol. XLVI.

————, "The Principle of Planning and the Institution of Laissez-Faire," *The American Economic Review,* March, 1932, Vol. XXII.

————, "Where the New Deal Succeeds," *New York Times,* April 22, 1934.

————, "The Responsibilities of Partnership," address delivered before the Iowa Bankers Association, June 27, 1934 (mimeographed).

————, "The Progressive Tradition," *The Atlantic Monthly,* January-June, 1935, Vol. CLV.

————, "The Future of National Planning," *The New Republic,* December 9, 1936, Vol. LXXXVI.

————, "Economics," *Roads to Knowledge,* edited by W. A. Neilson. New York: W. W. Norton and Company, Inc., 1937.

————, "Wesley Mitchell: An Evaluation," *The New Republic,* October 6, 1937, Vol. LXXXXVII.

————, "Veblen and 'Business Enterprise,'" *The New Republic,* March 22, 1939, Vol. LXXXXIX.

————, "The Fourth Power," *Planning and Civic Comment,* April-June, 1939, Part II.

————, "After the New Deal," *The New Republic,* July 26, 1939, Vol. LXXXXIX.

————, "Implementing the General Interest," *Public Administration Review,* Autumn, 1940, Vol. I.

————, "The Directive," *Journal of Social Philosophy and Jurisprudence,* October, 1941, Vol. 7.

————, review of G. D. H. Cole's *Guild Socialism and the Indus-*

trial Future, The International Journal of Ethics, April, 1922, Vol. XXXII.

CHAPTER 7

BACKMAN, J., "Price Inflexibility and Changes in Production," *The American Economic Review,* September, 1939, Vol. XXIX.

BERLE, A. A., JR., and MEANS, G. C., *The Modern Corporation and Private Property.* New York: The Macmillan Company, 1933.

———, and ———, "Corporations and the Public Investor," *The American Economic Review,* March, 1930, Vol. XX.

———, and ———, "Corporation," *Encyclopaedia of the Social Sciences,* Vol. IV.

BONBRIGHT, J. C., and MEANS, G. C., *The Holding Company, Its Public Significance and Its Regulation.* New York: McGraw-Hill Book Company, 1932.

———, and ———, "Holding Companies," *Encyclopaedia of the Social Sciences,* Vol. VII.

CARPENTER, W. S., *Democracy and Representation.* Princeton: Princeton University Press, 1925.

GRUCHY, A. G., "The Economics of the National Resources Committee," *The American Economic Review,* March, 1938, Vol. XXIX.

HAMILTON, W., and others, *Price and Price Policies.* New York: McGraw-Hill Book Company, Inc., 1938.

HANSEN, A. H., "Price Flexibility and Full Employment of Resources," *The Structure of the American Economy,* Part II. Washington: National Resources Planning Board, June, 1940.

HENDERSON, L., testimony in "Economic Prologue," *Hearings before the Temporary National Economic Committee,* P. R. No. 113, Part I, December, 1938.

HUMPHREY, D. D., "The Nature and Meaning of Rigid Prices," *The Journal of Political Economy,* October, 1937, Vol. XLV.

LUBIN, I., testimony in "Economic Prologue," *Hearings before the Temporary National Economic Committee,* P. R. No. 113, Part I, December, 1938.

MEANS, G. C., "The Diffusion of Stock Ownership in the United States," *The Quarterly Journal of Economics,* August, 1930, Vol. XLIV.

——, "The Growth in the Relative Importance of the Large Corporation in American Economic Life," *The American Economic Review*, March, 1931, Vol. XXI.

——, "Stock Dividends, Large Scale Business, and Corporate Savings," *The Quarterly Journal of Economics*, May, 1931, Vol. XLV.

——, "The Separation of Ownership and Control in American Industry," *The Quarterly Journal of Economics*, November, 1931, Vol. XLVI.

——, "The Corporate Revolution," *Summaries of Theses Accepted in Partial Fulfillment of the Requirements for the Degree of Doctor of Philosophy, 1933*. Cambridge: Harvard University Press, 1933.

——, "The Consumer and the New Deal," *The Annals of the American Academy of Political and Social Science*, May, 1934, Vol. 173.

——, *Industrial Prices and Their Relative Inflexibility*, Senate Document 13, 74th Congress, First Session, January 17, 1935.

——, "The Distribution of Control and Responsibility in a Modern Economy," *The Political Science Quarterly*, May, 1935, Vol. L.

——, "Notes on Inflexible Prices," *The American Economic Review*, March, 1936, Vol. XXVI.

——, "Business Combinations and Agriculture," *The Journal of Farm Economics*, February, 1938, Vol. XX.

——, "The Location of Economic Control of American Industry," *The American Economic Review*, March, 1939, Vol. XXIX.

——, "Democracy and Business," *The Virginia Quarterly Review*, Autumn, 1941, Vol. XVII.

——, "Economic Institutions," *The American Journal of Sociology*, May, 1942, Vol. XLVII.

NATIONAL PLANNING BOARD, *Final Report, 1933-34*. Washington, 1934.

NATIONAL RESOURCES COMMITTEE, *Progress Report, 1937*. Washington, 1937.

——, *Technological Trends and National Policy*, Washington, 1937.

——, *Consumer Incomes in the United States, Their Distribution in 1935-36*. Washington, 1938.

——, *Patterns of Resource Use*. Washington, 1938.

——, *The Problems of a Changing Population.* Washington, 1938.

——, *Consumer Expenditures in the United States, Estimates for 1935-36.* Washington, 1939.

——, *Progress Report, 1938.* Washington, 1939.

——, *The Structure of the American Economy,* Part I. Washington, 1939.

NATIONAL RESOURCES PLANNING BOARD, *The Structure of the American Economy,* Part II. Washington, 1940.

——, *Capital Requirements, A Study in Methods as Applied to the Iron and Steel Industry.* Washington, 1940.

ROBBINS, L., *The Great Depression.* London: Macmillan and Co., Ltd., 1934.

TUCKER, R. S., "The Reasons for Price Rigidity," *The American Economic Review,* March, 1938, Vol. XXVIII.

WARE, C. F., and MEANS, G. C., *The Modern Economy in Action.* New York: Harcourt, Brace and Company, 1936.

CHAPTER 8

ATKINS, W. E., and others, *Economic Behavior, An Institutional Approach.* Boston: Houghton Mifflin Company, 1931.

BEVERIDGE, W. H., *Full Employment in a Free Society.* New York: W. W. Norton and Co., Inc., 1945.

BOULDING, K. E., *Economic Analysis.* New York: Harper and Brothers, 1941.

BRADY, R. A., *Business as a System of Power.* New York: Columbia University Press, 1943.

CLARK, J. B., *Essentials of Economic Theory.* New York: The Macmillan Company, 1907.

COPELAND, M. A., "Economic Theory and the Natural Science Point of View," *The American Economic Review,* March, 1931, Vol. XXI.

CURTI, M. E., *The Growth of American Thought.* New York: Harper and Brothers, 1943.

DICKINSON, H. D., "Price Formation in a Socialist Community," *The Economic Journal,* June, 1933, Vol. XLIII.

FETTER, F. A., *Economic Principles,* Vol. I. New York: The Century Co., 1915.

GRUCHY, A. G., "Facts and Reality in the Social Sciences," *Ethics,* April, 1944, Vol. LIV.

HAMILTON, W. H., *The Pattern of Competition.* New York: Columbia University Press, 1940.

HANEY, L. H., *Value and Distribution.* New York: D. Appleton-Century Company, Inc., 1939.

———, "Veblen and Institutionalism," *History of Economic Thought,* Third Edition. New York: The Macmillan Company, 1936.

———, round-table conference on "Economic Theory," *The American Economic Review,* March, 1919, Vol. IX.

HANSEN, A. H., *Full Recovery or Stagnation?* New York: W. W. Norton and Co., Inc., 1938.

HAYEK, F. A., *The Road to Serfdom.* Chicago: University of Chicago Press, 1944.

HEIMANN, E., "Industrial Society and Democracy," *Social Research,* February, 1945, Vol. XII.

HOFSTADTER, R., *Social Darwinism in American Thought, 1860-1915.* Philadelphia: University of Pennsylvania Press, 1944.

HOMAN, P. T., *Contemporary Economic Thought.* New York: Harper and Brothers, 1928.

———, "The Institutional School," *Encyclopaedia of the Social Sciences,* Vol. V.

HUTCHINSON, T. W., *The Significance and Basic Postulates of Economic Theory.* London: Macmillan and Co., Ltd., 1938.

KLUCKHOHN, C., and KELLY, W. H., "The Concept of Culture," *The Science of Man in the World Crisis,* edited by Ralph Linton. New York: Columbia University Press, 1945.

KNIGHT, F. H., "The Limitations of Scientific Method in Economics," *The Trend of Economics.* New York: Alfred A. Knopf, 1924.

———, "The Place of Marginal Economics in a Collectivist System," *The American Economic Review,* March, 1936, Vol. XXVI.

———, "What Is Truth in Economic Science?" *The Journal of Political Economy,* February, 1940, Vol. XLVIII.

KUZNETS, S., "Equilibrium Economics and Business-Cycle Theory," *The Quarterly Journal of Economics,* May, 1930, Vol. XLIV.

———, "Static and Dynamic Economics," *The American Economic Review,* September, 1930, Vol. XX.

LERNER, A. P., "Economic Theory and Socialist Economy," *Review of Economic Studies,* October, 1934, Vol. II.

MANNHEIM, K., *Diagnosis of Our Time.* New York: Oxford University Press, 1944.

MILLS, F. C., round-table conference on "The Theory of Economic Dynamics as Related to Industrial Stability," *The American Economic Review,* March, 1930, Vol. XX.

MITCHELL, W. C., "Interrelations between Moral and Economic Factors in the Postwar World," *The American Economic Review,* March, 1944, Vol. XXXIV.

MUKERJEE, R., *The Institutional Theory of Economics.* London: Macmillan and Co., Ltd., 1942.

ROBINSON, J., *The Economics of Imperfect Competition.* London: Macmillan and Co., Ltd., 1933.

RUGGIERO, G. DE, *Modern Philosophy.* New York: The Macmillan Company, 1921.

SLICHTER, S. H., "The Organization and Control of Economic Activity," *The Trend of Economics.* New York: Alfred A. Knopf, 1924.

SPANN, O., *The History of Economics.* New York: W. W. Norton and Co., Inc., 1930.

STIGLER, G. J., *The Theory of Competitive Price.* New York: The Macmillan Company, 1942.

TAYLOR, O. H., round-table conference on "Institutionalism," *The American Economic Review,* March, 1931, Vol. XXI.

THORP, W. L., testimony in "Economic Prologue," *Hearings before the Temporary National Economic Committee,* 75th Congress, P.R. No. 113, Part I, December, 1938.

TRIFFIN, R., *Monopolistic Competition and General Equilibrium Theory.* Cambridge: Harvard University Press, 1940.

VEBLEN, T., "The Limitations of Marginal Utility," *The Journal of Political Economy,* November, 1909, Vol. XVII.

VON MISES, L., *Bureaucracy.* New Haven: Yale University Press, 1944.

WATKINS, M., "Trustification and Economic Theory," *The American Economic Review,* March, 1931, Vol. XXI.

WOLFE, A. B., "Sociology and Economics," *The Social Sciences and Their Interrelations,* edited by W. F. Ogburn and A. Goldenweiser. Boston: Houghton Mifflin Company, 1927.

―――, "Economy and Democracy," *The American Economic Review,* March, 1944, Vol. XXXIV.

WOOTTON, B., *Lament for Economics.* New York: Farrar and Rinehart, Inc., 1938.

YOUNG, A. A., "The Trend of Economics, as Seen by Some American Economists," *The Quarterly Journal of Economics,* February, 1925, Vol. XXXIX.

Index

A

Absentee owners and the underlying population, 100
Absentee ownership:
corporations and, 94, 491
defined, 82
di:.;ilowance of, 101
institution of, 68
investment bankers and, 88
Accounting:
private, 368
social, 316, 368 f.
Adams, Henry C., 12 n.
Administered prices:
depressions and, 488
government-operated enterprises and, 486
Administrative economics:
nature of, 527
new assumptions of, 530
principles of, 479
scope of, 532 f.
significance of, 537 f.
Administrative enterprise, 518
Administrative government:
industrial commissions and, 177 f.
judicial sovereignty and, 205
Agricultural Adjustment Administration, 444, 524
Agricultural planning, 442 f.
Agriculture, U. S. Department of, 407, 446, 447
American economy:
centralization of the, 568 f.
functioning of, 567 ff.
polarity of, 571
structure of, 565 f.
American Federation of Labor:
banker capitalism and, 189
economic power and, 98
labor movement and, 96, 168
union policy and, 92

A

Analytical description, 266, 291, 293
Analytical economics, 229, 273, 541, 548
Angell, J. R., 353
Anthropology, cultural, and Veblen 71 f.
Applied economics, 547
Atkins, Willard E., 613 n.

B

Baldwin, James M., 60
Banker capitalism:
Great Depression and, 151
judicial sovereignty and, 199
proprietary economy and, 196
reasonable capitalism and, 212
stabilized scarcity and, 192
theory of, 189 ff.
Banks (see Private banks)
Bargaining power, 238, 591
Beard, C. A., 10 n.
Bentham, Jeremy, 224
Berle, Adolf A., Jr., 473, 475, 481, 484
Biological organism, concept of, 357
Bonbright, James C., 475, 534
Boulding, Kenneth E., 13, 596
Bourgeois, Léon, and solidarism, 173
Bowen, F., 11
Bücher, Karl, 190
Business:
new order of, 89
pecuniary values and, 110
Business cycles:
definition of, 296
Federal Reserve System and, 363
long-range planning and, 304
pioneer students of, 291
recovery phase of, 297
self-generation and, 299
strategic factors in, 376
theory of, 290, 377
typical cycles and, 293

C

Cairnes, J. E., 22
Capital:
  allocation of, 441
  futurity and, 226
  immobility of, 358
  saving process and, 499
  two aspects of, 110
Capital expansion, 379
Capitalism:
  banker (see Banker capitalism)
  commercial, 259
  competitive, 555, 577
  corporate, 192, 194
  development of, 104
  employer, 191
  industrial stalemate and, 99
  logic of, 104
  mature, 8, 98, 428, 555, 575
  merchant, 190
  monopoly, 555
  new industrial hierarchy and, 90
  reasonable (see Reasonable capital-
    ism)
  regulated, 311, 519
  theory of, 67, 80, 127
  voluntary, 210
Capitalistic culture, 120
Carlton, Frank T., 181
Cartelization of the economy, 193
Causation, theory of, 292
Central monetary authority, 498
Centripetancy of the American economy, 571
Chamberlin, Edward H., 13, 578, 610
Clark, John B., 12, 18, 72, 320, 338, 344,
  352, 546, 548, 593
Clark, John M.:
  business cycle theory and, 377
  Charles H. Cooley and, 346
  dynamic economics and, 341
  intellectual background of, 340 ff.
  marginal utility and, 351
  overhead costs and, 357 ff.
  pragmatic psychology of, 349 ff.
  social control of business and, 375
  social economics of, 393
  social-liberal planning program of,
    384
  theory of social organization, 370
  theory of social values, 366 ff.

Class conflict:
  administrative government and, 205
  concept of, 78, 412
  era of free competition and, 85
  modern corporation and, 96
  role of the state and, 166 f.
  Veblen's analysis of, 75
Class organization, theory of:
  industrial classes and, 77
  leisure class and, 76
  Veblen's analysis of, 74
Classical economics, assumptions of,
  339, 409
Classless democracy, 412
Coercion:
  private property and, 97, 219
  public, 166
Cole, G. D. H., 526
Collective action:
  going concern and, 193
  individual action and, 221
  individual freedom and, 321
  inflexibilities and, 572
  self-interest and, 162
  vested interests and, 96
Collective bargaining:
  extensive developments of, 180
  intensive developments of, 182
  nation-wide, 185
Collective economics:
  definition of, 237
  nature of, 233
  principles of, 236
  traditional economics and, 230
Collective management, 14, 470, 494,
  624
Collective psychology, 79
Collusive action, 97, 610
Committee for Economic Development, 475
Common law, 434
Commons, John R.:
  background influences of, 138 ff.
  concept of economic conflict and,
    164
  concept of economic power and, 219
  definition of economics, 237
  framework of interpretation, 214 ff.
  labor economics and, 147 ff.
  nature of economics and, 233 ff.
  pragmatic approach and, 155 ff.
  principles of explanation of, 221

Commons, John R. (*Cont.*):
 public utility economics and, 145 *ff.*
 psychological theory of, 159
 scientific methodology of, 157
 theory of capitalism, 189 *ff.*
 theory of the labor movement, 168 *ff.*
 Veblen and, 154
Communism, 311, 314
Competition:
 cutthroat, 87, 360
 disposal of national income and, 543
 era of free, 84 *f.*, 94
 imperfect, 271
 income-equalizing powers of, 543, 572
 intra-industry, 91
 monopolistic, 13, 527, 584
 pecuniary values and, 109
 price, 486
 workable, 567
Concentration:
 American economy, in the, 486
 corporate, 479
 economic, 488
 wealth, of, 543
Conceptual scheme:
 Commons', 218
 neo-classicists', 218
Conceptualism, 142, 422
Consumer movement, 260
Consumers:
 national planning and, 524
 unorganized, 506
 unsaddled, 8
Consumption:
 conspicuous, 260
 patterns of, 490
Control:
 administrative, 512
 economic, 391
 market, 477
Cooley, Charles H., 34, 60, 342, 346, 372
Cooperation:
 mankind's bent for, 562
 new age of, 451
Cooperatives, 505
Coordination:
 administrative, 487
 consumer and, 490
 market, 431, 487
 over-all, 487

Copeland, Morris A., 7, 567 *n.*
Corporate absolutism, 491
Corporate concentration, 479
Corporate credit, 95
Corporate economics, 476
Corporate enterprise:
 changes in concept of, 483
 price policy and, 488
Corporate norm, 529
Corporate revolution:
 industrial stalemate and, 99
 Means, G. C., and, 479 *ff.*
 Veblen's analysis of, 93
Corporations:
 absentee ownership and, 94
 centrifugal forces and, 482
 concentration of, 479
 defined by J. R. Commons, 227
 economic power and, 97
 liquid reserves and, 433, 441
 risk-taking and, 114 *f.*
 strategic importance of, 480
Costs:
 cost accounting and, 359
 determinateness of, 531
 marginal, 368
 overhead (*see* Overhead costs)
 real, 588, 591
 social, 369
 unpaid, 369
 variable, 358
Crisis, theory of, 454
Cultural anthropology and Veblen, 71 *f.*
Cultural cumulation, theory of, 299
Cultural development, theory of, 25, 374, 454
Cultural economics:
 principle of relatedness and, 24
 versus formal economics, 21
Cultural emergence, 415
Cultural equilibrium, 454, 426
Cultural lag, 42, 78, 182, 415, 556, 576
Cultural science, economics as, 118
Cultural unbalance, 454
Currie, Laughlin, 309
Customary behavior, principle of, 224

D

Darwin, Charles, 15, 44, 54, 216, 254, 542
Davenport, Herbert J., 248, 253, 594

Deductive analysis, 250
Deductive economics, 356
Deflation and chronic stagnation, 579
Demand:
consumer, 380
derived, 382
Democracy:
battle for, 452
classless, 412
effective, 507
representative, 437
Democratic gradualism, 391
Democratization of industry, 507
Depression: (see also Great Depression
of 1929)
administered prices and, 488
business consolidation and, 88
chronic, 87
defined by G. C. Means, 488
key industries and, 90
Description:
analytical, 266, 291, 293
ordinary, 266
Dewey, John, 15, 79, 155, 159, 163, 247,
249, 317, 322, 406
Dichotomy, Veblen's concept of, 120 f.
Dictatorship, American brand of, 199
Directive branch of government, 437
Distribution of income, 115, 282, 413,
504, 508
Distribution theory:
heterodox, 593
Marshall's, 588
Dorfman, Joseph, 32 n.
Durable-goods industries and business
cycles, 297
Dynamic economics, 339, 342, 409, 546

E

Economic absolutism, 491
Economic activity:
influence of technology and, 600
public goals and, 602
Economic behavior, logical character
of, 233
Economic concentration, 488
Economic conflict:
Commons' view of, 167
economic trends and, 121
habitual behavior and, 164
Marxian view of, 167
Economic control, tactics of, 391

Economic determinism:
Commons' analysis, in, 181
institutional development and, 70
social voluntarism and, 164, 374
Tugwell's voluntarism and, 427
Economic development:
laws of, 556
logic of (see Logic of economic development)
mechanistic framework of interpretation and, 14
new industrial order and, 89
theory of, 51, 345, 425, 555
Economic disequilibrium:
corporate revolution and, 171
suggestions for reduction of, 495
Economic disharmony, theory of, 66
Economic enterprise:
logic of, 433, 436
reorientation of, 477
Economic field:
concept of, 25, 55
cultural economics and, 25
definition of holistic economics and,
550
Economic freedom, 321, 439
Economic guidance:
consumers and, 287
Mitchell's theory of, 282
national policy for, 439
orthodox economists' theory of, 285
role of government and, 288
Economic heterodoxy:
common goal of, 542
criticisms of orthodox economics and,
401
growth of, 2
philosophical foundations of, 15
theory of economic control and, 8
Economic holism, 558
Economic instability, 493, 501
Economic interests, conflict of, 559
Economic motivation, 484
Economic order, theory of, 555, 557,
565 ff.
Economic orthodoxy:
philosophical basis of, 10
static orientation and, 11
Economic power:
concept of, 219
corporate enterprise and, 97
labor unions and, 98

Economic power (*Cont.*):
  relocation of, 449
Economic progress, idea of, 318
Economic reconstruction, 399
Economic reform, 301
Economic resources:
  efficient use of, 514
  full use of, 388, 499, 513
  optimum use of, 514, 572
  price system and, 573
Economic science:
  functional view of, 263
  ultimate nature of, 547
Economic security and national planning, 320
Economic statesmanship, 446, 521
Economic system:
  definition of, 117
  logic of, 435
Economic theory:
  defined, 453
  growth of monopoly and, 543 *ff.*
  pure theory, as, 262, 469
  reconstruction of, 416
Economic value: (*see also* Value, economic)
  handicraft era and, 81
  risk-taking and, 114
  serviceability and, 107 *ff.*
  theory of, 105
Economic welfare:
  content of, 272, 317 *ff.*, 447
  freedom and, 321
  national planning and, 314
  Tugwell's views on, 447
Economico-cultural patterns, 27
Economico-psychological adjustments, 562
Economics:
  administrative (*see* Administrative economics)
  analytical (*see* Analytical economics)
  applied, 547
  boundaries of, 397
  classical, 339, 409
  collective (*see* Collective economics)
  collective action, of, 147
  control, of, 519
  corporate, 476
  cultural (*see* Cultural economics)
  cultural science, as a, 118 *f.*, 214, 414, 468

Economics (*Cont.*):
  deductive science, as a, 214, 356
  defined, 13, 27, 118, 237, 396
  engineering, 222
  equilibrium (*see* Equilibrium economics)
  evolutionary (*see* Evolutionary economics)
  experimental (*see* Experimental economics)
  formalistic (*see* Formalistic economics)
  functional, 416
  functional nature of, 126, 138, 155, 469
  genetic, 281, 331
  holistic (*see* Holistic economics)
  instrumentalism and, 406
  law and, 533
  Marshallian, 531
  mathematical, 271
  mathematical approach and, 43
  nature and scope of, 116, 275
  neo-classical (*see* Neo-classical economics)
  normative, 281, 598
  orthodox (*see* Orthodox economics)
  political science and, 525
  pragmatic, 323
  proprietary, 222, 226
  psychology and, 34, 59, 326
  quantitative, 3, 281
  social, 3, 349, 394 *ff.*
  sociology and, 316
  static, 338, 344, 545
  systematic, 36, 53, 276
  traditional (*see* Traditional economics)
  transactional, 221
  volitional, 160
Economy:
  American (*see* American economy)
  cartelization of, 193·
  hybrid (*see* Hybrid economy)
  mature, 150
  mixed, 533
  money, 259, 303
  mongrel, 431, 457
  proprietary, 196, 223, 226
  scarcity, of, 385
  self-reinforcing forces, of, 494
  socialistic, 115

Economy (Cont.):
  technological, 194
  tripartite, 566
Efficiency:
  business, 366
  collective, 366, 397
  commercial, 365
  distribution, in, 319
  pecuniary, 111
  principle of, 222
  social, 289, 366, 389
  technological, 107, 366
Ely, Richard T., 1, 12, 135, 138, 143,
  168, 243
Emergence, concept of, 35, 53, 80, 415,
  417
Employment:
  banker capitalism and, 198
  full (see Full employment)
  industrial, 251, 411
  partial, 6, 92
  pecuniary, 251, 411
  stabilization of, 198
Equilibrium:
  analysis, 12, 23, 31
  automatic, 330
  competitive, 218
  concept of, 37, 48, 51
  cultural (see Cultural equilibrium)
  economics, 39, 42, 274, 343, 364
  economists, 220
  managed, 330, 509, 516
Ethico-economic analysis, 318, 455 ff.,
  458
Evolutionary economics, 2, 39, 58, 118
Evolutionary method, 55, 126 f.
Evolutionary outlook, 15
Experimental attitude, 421
Experimental economics:
  boundaries of, 458
  defined, 454
  Tugwell's version, 3, 452 ff.
Experimental psychology, 255
Experimentalism, 422 f., 462
Exploitation:
  hybrid price system and, 575
  price fluctuations and, 207, 209
Ezekiel, Mordecai, 309, 386, 520

          F

Fascism, 311, 314, 450
Federal incorporation, 442

Federal Reserve System, 89, 150, 207,
  304, 305, 363, 497
Fetter, Frank A., 12, 594
Fisher, Irving, 12
Folk psychology, 59
Formalism in economics, 122
Formalistic economics, 13, 21, 23, 233
Framework of interpretation:
  dynamic, 17, 24
  holistic, 17
  Means, G. C., of, 475
  Mitchell, Wesley C., of, 281, 282
  organismal, 20
  post-Darwinian, 20
  static, 11
  Tugwell, R. G., of, 456
Full employment, 92, 271, 513, 515,
  574, 604
Functional economics, 416
Futurity:
  institutionalism and, 231
  principle of, 146, 225
  sovereignty and, 228
  transactions and, 226

          G

Genetic economics, 281, 331
Gestalt psychology, 59, 416
Going concern:
  administrative economics, in, 536
  class conflict and, 171
  Commons' analysis, in, 219
  defined, 193
  economy as, 456, 557
  going business and, 193 f.
  going plant and, 194 f.
  Veblen's concept of, 52 ff.
Going concern values, 145
Goldenweiser, Alexander, 34, 59
Gompers, Samuel, 168
Goodwill:
  business, 94
  capitalization of, 115
  industrial, 174
Goods-making, 82, 278, 283
Government:
  administrative (see Administrative
    government)
  business and, 436, 525
  control, 505
  ownership, 505
  policeman doctrine of, 436

Government (Cont.):
political centralism and, 527
spending, 303
Great Depression of 1929, 5, 407, 478

H

Hamilton, Walton H., 2, 7, 529 n., 585, 605, 609, 614
Handicraft era:
economic values and, 109
Veblen's analysis of, 81 ff.
Handman, Max S., 2 n.
Haney, Lewis H., 605
Hansen, Alvin H., 8, 13, 576
Hedonistic economists, 235
Hegel, Georg, 15, 54
Hegelian metaphysics, 275
Henderson, Leon, 309, 533
Historical economists, 156, 233, 265, 347, 394, 408
History, interpretation of (see Interpretation of history)
Hobson, John A., 32, 280, 316, 458
Holistic economics:
basic assumptions of, 553 ff.
cultural science, as, 23
definition of, 26, 550
equilibrium economics and, 611, 612 ff.
field concept and, 25
marginalism and, 594 ff.
origin of term, 4
pragmatic bias of, 27
school of, 17, 18, 20
scope of, 552 ff., 604
significance of, 612 ff.
theory of development and, 25
unity of, 19, 541
Holistic economists:
academic economics and, 545
contributions of, 542, 605
distribution theory of, 588 ff.
economic planning and, 580 f.
price theory of, 581 ff.
psychological theory of, 560 ff.
role of technology and, 600
theory of economic development and, 555
theory of American economic order and, 565 ff.
Holistic method, 57, 80

Holistic movement and middle-class aspirations, 623
Holistic outlook, 542
Holistic school, 541, 542
Hoxie, Robert F., 2, 7, 142, 182, 248, 614
Hybrid economy, 92 f., 434, 530, 572
Hybrid price system, 572
Human behavior:
economic change and, 164
science of, 116
social product, as a, 163
tropismatic action and, 60
Human culture:
class organization and, 77
concept of status and, 74
cultural lags and, 78
stone age and, 75
theory of, 454
Hutchison, T. W., 549

I

Imperfect markets, 566
Income:
distribution of, 115, 413, 504, 508
earned, 81, 589
free, 81, 86
inequality of, 578
scarcity, 545
surplus, 83, 575
unearned, 544, 575, 576
Inductive method, 138, 143, 269
Industrial commission, 176, 177
Industrial council, 505, 520
Industrial employment (see Employment, industrial)
Industrial goodwill, 175
Industrial government, 186
Industrial price policy:
central planning and, 442
control of, 504 ff.
depressions and, 488
maldistribution of income and, 504
restriction of output and, 503
Industrial technology:
community ownership and, 94
cultural lags and, 556
regime of workmanship and, 102
surplus product and, 112
values and, 106
Veblen and, 69

Industrialism, new (see New industrialism)
Industry, democratization of, 507
Instinct:
 idle curiosity, of, 65 ff.
 parental, 64 ff., 120
 self-regarding, 64, 82, 120
 workmanship, of:
  competition and, 84
  handicraft era and, 82
  industrial arts and, 112
  self-aggrandizement and, 64
  social frustration and, 521
  socialized economy and, 101
Instinct psychology, 61, 128 f.
Institutional economics:
 conflict of interests and, 147
 defined, 118, 275
 described by Mitchell, 274
 Marx, the originator of, 275
 origin of term, 2
 significance of, 123 ff.
 Veblen's, 116 ff.
Institutionalism, 137, 395, 462, 464, 478
Institutions:
 absentee ownership and, 82
 class conflict and, 79
 cultural lags and, 78
 defined by Commons, 221
 definition of, 68
 disserviceable, 121
 imbecile, 69, 124
 Mitchell's analysis, in, 257
 orthodox economics and, 72
 predatory, 411
 serviceable, 121
 technology and, 69
 theory of, 68
Instrumentalism, 399, 406, 464, 470
Interest rates, flexible, 499
Interpretation of history:
 materialist, 428
 S. N. Patten's, 415
 technological, 427, 454
 Veblen's, 69

J

James, E. E., 12 n.
James, William, 15, 64, 250, 254
Jevons, William S., 22, 43, 232, 343
Judicial sovereignty, 199, 200, 205

K

Key industries, 90, 491, 576
Keynes, J. N., 22, 44
Keynes, John M., 71 n.
Keyserling, Leon H., 439 n.
Knight, Frank H., 606
Köhler, Wolfgang, 59 n.
Kuznets, Simon, 549 n.

L

Labor:
 economics, 168
 key industries and, 576
 public-utility theory of, 172 f., 188
Labor legislation, 175
Labor movement:
 centripetal tendencies of, 180
 public utility principle and, 188
Labor unions (see also American Federation of Labor and Unionism), 398, 505, 506, 524, 576
La Follette, Robert M., 147
Laissez faire:
 economic balance and, 308
 institutional basis of, 258
 man's rationality and, 309
 principles of, 309, 479
Laski, Harold J., 526
Laughlin, J. Lawrence, 247
Law courts:
 problem of income inequality and, 578
 reasonable practices and, 201
 reasonable values and, 203
Liberalism, twentieth-century, 624
Liquid savings, 500
Locke, John, 11, 16, 159, 161, 232
Logic of:
 economic development, 556, 559, 570, 620
 economic enterprise, 433, 436
 economic system, 435
 events, 559
 experimentation, 460, 461
 private property, 482
 reform, 621
 science, 32
 technology, 121, 432
Löwe, Adolf A., 24
Lubin, Isador, 309, 533
Lynd, Robert S., 455

M

Management:
    collective (*see* Collective management)
    scientific (*see* Scientific management)
    social (*see* Social management)
Marginal analysis, technique of, 555, 571
Marginalism:
    J. B. Clark, of, 593
    holistic economics and, 594
    laissez faire and, 595
    principles of, 555
    twentieth-century, 597
Market:
    administered, 486, 530
    closed, 91
    free, 411, 485
    imperfect, 566
    open, 93
    trading, 530
Marshall, Alfred, 18, 250, 480, 515, 528, 561, 572, 588, 609
Marshall, Alfred:
    basic assumptions of, 35
    concept of equilibrium, 48
    concept of normality, 40
    cultural lag and, 42
    philosophical orientation of, 40
    psychological theory of, 47
    scientific methodology of, 45
Marshallian economics, 531
Mathematical economics, 271
Mature economy, 150
Marx, Karl, 15, 51, 67, 77, 79, 98, 104, 112, 120, 166, 182, 275
Mechanism, concept of, 215, 216
Means, Gardiner C.:
    administered prices and, 488
    administrative economics of, 527 ff.
    corporate revolution and, 479 ff.
    planning program of, 516
    price policy and, 504 ff.
    problem of economic instability and, 493
    Veblen and, 491
Means-end problem, 119, 398
Mechanism:
    adjustment, 509
    concept of, 417
    market, 490, 511

Menger, Carl, 343
Merriam, Charles E., 308
Metaphysics, twentieth-century, 418
Method of analysis:
    additive, 45 ff.
    case, 143
    evolutionary, 55, 126 f.
    introspective, 256
    quantitative, 264
    synoptic, 56
Method of organic particularism, 614
Meyers, Albert L., 13
Mill, James, 11
Mill, John Stuart, 247, 268, 275, 358, 394, 409, 544
Mills, Frederick C., 330, 607
Mitchell, Wesley C.:
    business cycle theory of, 290
    Commons, John R., and, 277
    deductive analysis and, 250
    definition of economics and, 26, 27
    Dewey, John, and, 248 f.
    economic welfare and, 314
    functional economics and, 263
    Laughlin's influence on, 251
    national planning and, 301
    pragmatic economics of, 323
    pragmatic psychology of, 253 ff.
    quantitative method of analysis and, 265 ff.
    scope of economics and, 273 ff.
    Veblen's influence on, 252
Money:
    institution of, 280, 294
    redundant, 509
    right amount of, 495
    role of, 280
    supply of and demand for, 498
Money economy, 259, 303
Money making, 82, 278, 283, 589
Money problem, 495, 496 f.
Mongrel economy, 431, 457
Monopoly:
    corporate enterprise and, 97
    full employment and, 574
    income distribution and, 578
    key industries and, 566
    partial, 110
    pecuniary values and, 109
    secular stagnation and, 575
    Veblen's analysis, in, 93
Monopolistic competition, 13, 527, 584

Monopolistic enterprise:
heartland of, 565, 566
secular stagnation and, 575
Motivation:
economic, 449, 484
theory of, 256
Mukerjee, Radhakamal, 455 n. 553, 619

N

National Bureau of Economic Research, 305, 375, 493 n.
National Civic Federation, 141 f., 145
National economic council, 388, 441, 442
National economic policy, 510
National income, distribution of (see Income, distribution of)
National land program, 443
National Monetary Association, 150
National planning:
allocation of capital and, 441
balance between industry and agriculture and, 442
Commons' views on, 209 f.
control of prices and, 441
economic welfare and, 314
economic security and, 320
Federal Reserve System and, 305
future of, 314
holistic economists and, 580
Mitchell's views on, 301
new role of government and, 310
over-all, 516
price theory and, 586
regimentation and, 439
requirements of, 313
National Planning Board, 308
National Recovery Administration, 416, 475, 505, 523
National Resources Committee, 475
National Resources Planning Board, 315, 519, 523
National scale of values, 314
Natural resources, preservation of, 517
Neo-classical economics:
one-dimensional approach and, 118
rationalist psychology and, 77
revision of, 13
revival of, 12
Neo-classicists:
closed system of, 234
conceptual scheme of, 218

Neo-classicists (Cont.):
distribution theory of, 589
methodology of, 19
psychological theory of, 18, 254
unearned income and, 544
unity of, 19
New Deal, 405, 407, 474, 523
New industrialism, 374, 411, 413, 426
New political economy, 1, 12, 139, 525, 536, 543
New theory of the economic order, 555
New York City Planning Commission, 408
Newton, Sir Isaac, 11, 16, 231
Non-differentiated products, 489
Normality:
Alfred Marshall's concept of, 40 f.
preconception of, 40, 47, 50
Normative economics, 281, 598

O

Occupational obsolescence, 434
Oligopolistic enterprise, 6, 528, 579, 610
Organic particularism, method of, 614
Organism, concept of, 215, 216
Orthodox economics:
cross-sectional approach of, 118
deficiencies of, 545
methodology of, 269
W. Nassau Senior and, 22
unity of, 19
Overhead costs:
disequilibrium and, 365
economics of, 357 ff.
labor as, 360
raw materials as, 361
Ownership:
function of, 113
futurity and, 232
multiple, 477

P

Pareto, Vilfredo, 596
Parker, Carleton H., 182, 419
Parrington, V. L., 32
Parsons, Talcott, 19 n.
Patten, Simon N., 406, 408 ff., 412
Patterns of behavior, 117
Pecuniary employment (see Employment, pecuniary)
Pecuniary logic, 264

Pecuniary value, 84, 108 ff., 113
Peirce, Charles S., 15, 16, 32, 250
Perry, A. L., 11
Personnel departments, 183
Philosophic and scientific thought:
　new era of, 542
　post-Darwinian, 542
Pigou, A. C., 316
Planning:
　agricultural, 442 f.
　business, 311 f., 521
　comprehensive, 384
　compulsory, 393
　emergency, 311
　general, 522
　limited, 384, 521
　long-range, 304, 312, 314
　national (see National planning)
　national budget and, 387
　piecemeal, 311
　private enterprise and, 389
　regional, 521
　social-liberal, 384
　socialist, 385
　totalitarian, 389
Polarization of technology and business, 569
Policeman doctrine of government, 436
Political economy, new version of, 1, 12, 139, 525, 536, 543
Political theory, 437
Power, economic (see Economic power)
Pragmatic economics, 323
Pragmatic psychology, 253 ff., 349 ff., 562
Pragmatism:
　class conflict and, 167
　C. S. Peirce, of, 17
　philosophy of, 333
　psychological theory and, 160, 253
　scientific methodology and, 268
　scientific truth and, 158
Preconception:
　normality, of, 40, 47, 50
　process, of, 50
Pressure groups, 457
Price-cost disparities, 523
Price-cost harmonies, 489
Price fluctuations:
　economic exploitation and, 207
　national planning and, 209

Price policy (see Industrial price policy)
Price system, 284, 572
Price theory, 578, 579
Prices:
　administered, 477, 486, 488, 504
　business policy and, 110
　control of, 441, 581
　depression sensitivity of, 512
　free, 93
　inflexibility of, 486, 496, 511, 530
　restriction of output and, 91
　secular sensitivity of, 512
　security of, 500
　short-run sensitivity of, 383, 511
　sticky, 383, 580
Private banks:
　profit policies of, 497
　reorganization of, 303
Private enterprise:
　economic disequilibrium and, 308
　national planning and, 389
Private property:
　coercion and, 165
　corporate revolution and, 482
　economic power and, 219
　logic of, 482
　role of, 449
　technology and, 95
　theory of sovereignty and, 140
Process:
　biological, 53, 215
　concept of, 15, 16, 34, 35, 50, 51, 53, 80, 345
　historical, 217
　machine, 373
　preconception of, 50
　saving, 500
　social, 216, 557
　Veblen's concept of, 53
Producer-goods industries, 380 f., 499
Product:
　distribution of, 115
　net, 110, 113
　surplus, 92, 110, 113, 115
Production-consumption patterns, 522
Production, theory of, 354
Profits:
　efficiency, 197
　logic of, 484
　scarcity, 197
　stabilization of, 197

Profits (*Cont.*):
  undistributed, 442
Proprietary economics, 222, 226
Psychology:
  collective, 79
  empirical, 159 *f.*
  experimental, 255
  folk, 59
  gestalt (*see* Gestalt psychology)
  instinct, 61, 128 *f.*
  pragmatic (*see* Pragmatic psychology)
  social, 34, 80, 343
  subjectivistic, 59, 160
  volitional, 160
Psychological theory of:
  Alfred Marshall, 47
  Karl Marx, 77
  Thorstein Veblen, 58
Public utilities, economics of, 145
Pump-priming, 510

Q

Quantitative analysis, 260, 304, 355, 424
Quantitative economics, 3, 281
Quasi-rent, 589

R

Reasonable capitalism:
  class collaboration and, 189
  judicial sovereignty and, 199
  price fluctuations and, 209
  solidarism and, 189
Reasonable practice, 201
Reasonableness:
  as seen by courts, 199
  concept of, 146
  defined, 201
  "rule of reason" and, 200
Recent price theory, 583
Reconstruction of economics, 3, 20, 116, 416, 457, 466, 492, 546, 617
Regimentation, economic, 437, 520
Representative firm, 480, 531
Representation:
  functional, 526 *f.*
  geographical, 526
Research Committee on Social Trends, 306
Revolution:
  corporate, 479

Revolution (*Cont.*):
  economic, 411
  technological, 481
Ricardo, David, 11, 250, 409, 544
Rickert, Heinrich, 596
Ripley, W. Z., 475
Risk-taking, 114, 282, 593
Robbins, Lionel, 546, 547, 595, 600
Robinson, Joan, 548, 581, 610
Rogers, Thorold, 415
Role of reason, 70, 71
Ross, E. A., 135, 139

S

Saving:
  balanced with capital creation, 502
  capital creation and, 499
  liquid, 500
  process, 500
  speculation and, 500
Scarcity:
  defined, 222
  economy of (*see* Economy of scarcity)
  principle of, 222 *f.*
Schmoller, Gustav, 156, 265
School of economists:
  bargaining, 209
  managerial, 209
Science:
  logic of, 32
  nature of, 596
  pure, 596
Scientific generalizations:
  holistic economics and, 608
  nature of, 607
Scientific management, 173, 206, 384, 450
Scope of economics, 116, 273 *ff.*, 275, 547
Secular stagnation, 575, 579
Self-generation, theory of, 299 *ff.*
Self-limiting forces, theory of, 6, 299, 494, 501
Seligman, E. R. A., 12
Senior, W. Nassau, 22, 72, 358
Serviceability, 96, 97, 278
Sherif, Muzafer, 74
Shop committees, 183, 186
Slichter, Sumner H., 7, 616
Smith, Adam, 272, 275, 309, 399, 402, 544, 546
Smuts, J. C., 4

Social budget, 387
Social control:
  business, of, 370, 375
  business cycles, of, 303
  modern technology and, 372
Social Darwinism, 16
Social economics, 3, 349, 394 ff.
Social engineering, 314, 315, 399
Social ethics, 316, 318
Social management, 406, 436, 439, 450, 457
Social organization, theory of, 166, 370
Social sciences:
  cooperation among, 322, 525, 618
  progress of, 322
Social Security Board, 437
Socialism, 101, 115, 450, 522
Sociology and economics, 316
Solidarism, 173, 189, 623
Sombart, Werner, 26, 190, 267, 276, 554
Sovereignty:
  defined, 229
  judicial, 199
  principle of, 228 ff.
Spann, Othmar, 612 n.
Stabilization of:
  dollar, 303
  employment, 198
  profits, 197
Static economics, 338, 344, 545
Statistical analysis, 254, 273, 320, 424
Status:
  concept of, 74
  pecuniary, 96
  serviceability, 96, 97, 278
  types of, 76
Stewart, Walter W., 305
Stigler, George J., 597
Strasser, Adolph, 168
Sumner, William G., 34
Synoptic method, 56
Synthetical-emergent approach, 414, 416
Systematic economics, 36, 53, 276

T

Taussig, F. W., 12, 15
Tawney, R. H., 280
Taylor, Horace, 9

Taylor, O. H., 553
Technology:
  logic of, 121, 432
  role of habits and, 125
Technological change:
  class conflict and, 79
  competition and, 84
  development of corporations and, 93
  logic of development and, 104
  national planning and, 310
  new industrial order and, 90
  Veblen and, 70
Technological interpretation of history, 427, 428, 457
Technological progress, 488, 569
Technological unemployment, 320
Teggart, R. V., 32
Temporary National Economic Committee, 442 n., 569
Thorndike, E. L., 10 n., 73, 256
Thorp, Willard L., 569
Trade agreement and union-management cooperation, 168
Trade unionism, 170
Transactions:
  bargaining, 116, 190
  customary, 224
  defined, 220
  futurity and, 226
  managerial, 222
  rationing, 229
  types of, 221
Traditional economics, 342, 406, 487, 531
Transactional economics, 221
Triffin, Robert, 585
Tripartite economy, 566
Tropismatic action, 60
Tugwell, Rexford G.:
  contributions of, 467 f.
  economic welfare and, 447 f.
  experimental economics, and his, 452 ff.
  gestalt approach and, 416
  Mitchell and, 464
  Patten, S. N., and, 408 ff.
  psychological views of, 416 ff.
  social management program, 436 ff.
  theory of economic development of, 425 ff.
  Veblen and, 462
  views on scientific methodology, 421

U

Unemployment:
  cumulative, 494
  cyclical, 320
  involuntary, 361
  mass, 579
  technological, 300
Unionism:
  business, 142, 169
  revolutionary, 142, 168
  trade, 170, 410
United States Department of Agriculture, 407, 446, 447
Utilitarianism, philosophy of, 310
Utility:
  individual, 352
  marginal, 343, 351, 594
  prestige values and, 110
  social, 107, 352
  substantial, 106

V

Validity of economic doctrine, 421
Value:
  economic, 82 f., 108, 114, 397
  going concern, 145
  national scale of, 314
  pecuniary, 84, 108, 192
  prestige, 110, 567
  public, 146
  reasonable, 146, 152, 199, 202 f.
  service, 570
  social, 320, 366 ff.
  use, 191, 195, 223
  Veblen's theory of, 105
  volitional theory of, 236
Veblen, Thorstein:
  absentee ownership and, 82
  class organization and, 74
  concept of process and, 50
  criticism of Marshall, 35
  deficiencies of, 126 ff.
  definition of economics of, 26, 118
  economic reform and, 124
  evolutionary method and, 56
  field concept and, 54

  Hegel and, 34
  instincts and, 61 ff.
  Marx and, 33, 34, 79
  new industrial order and, 90
  Peirce and, 32
  role of reason and, 73
  scope of economics and, 116
  social psychology and, 58
  socialized economy and, 101
  theory of institutions and, 68 ff.
  value theory of, 105
Vested interests:
  absentee ownership and, 82
  big business and, 89
  corporate credit and, 95
  partial employment and, 92
Vethake, Henry, 11
Volitional economics, 160
Voluntarism, 427

W

Wage rates, sticky, 580
Wallas, Graham, 263
Ware, Caroline F., 477, 495 n.
Watkins, Myron W., 569 n.
Watson, John B., 255
Wayland, Francis, 11
Wealth:
  corporate, 94
  distribution of, 79
  double meaning of, 223
  proprietary economics and, 222
Weber, Max, 26
Whitehead, Alfred N., 24 n., 602
Willingness, principle of, 164, 230 f.
Windelband, Wilhelm, 596
Wolfe, A. B., 2 n., 7, 576, 587, 621
Wootton, Barbara, 610 n.
Workmanship:
  instinct of, 64
  regime of, 101
  technology and, 112
Wundt, Wilhelm, 59

Y

Young, Allyn A., 10, 14, 475, 605
Youngman, Anna, 301